Triumph Triples & Fours
Service and Repair Manual

Penny Cox and Matthew Coombs

(2162-272-6Y3)

Models covered

750 Trident. 748cc. 1991 to 1998
750 Daytona. 748cc. 1991 to 1993
750 Speed Triple. 748cc. 1996
900 Trident. 885cc. 1991 to 1998
900 Trophy. 885cc. 1991 to 1999
900 Daytona. 885cc. 1992 to 1996
900 Daytona Super III. 885cc. 1994 to 1996
900 (Trident) Sprint. 885cc. 1993 to 1998
900 Sprint Sport. 885cc. 1996 to 1998
900 Sprint Executive. 885cc. 1998
900 Speed Triple. 885cc. 1994 to 1996
900 Thunderbird. 885cc. 1995 to 1999
900 Thunderbird Sport. 885cc. 1998 to 1999
900 Adventurer. 885cc. 1996 to 1999
900 Legend TT. 885cc. 1998 to 1999
900 Tiger. 885cc. 1993 to 1998
1000 Daytona. 998cc. 1991 to 1993
1200 Trophy. 1180cc. 1991 to 1999
1200 Daytona. 1180cc. 1993 to 1998

Note: The fuel injected 1997-on T509/955i Speed Triple, 1998-on 955i Sprint ST, 1997-on T595/955i Daytona and 1999 Tiger models are not covered by this manual.

ABCDE
FGH

A book in the **Haynes Service and Repair Manual Series**

ISBN **1 85960 564 8**

British Library Cataloguing in Publication Data
A catalogue record for this book is available from the British Library

Library of Congress Catalog Card Number **99-73679**

Printed in the USA

Haynes Publishing
Sparkford, Yeovil, Somerset BA22 7JJ, England

Haynes North America, Inc
861 Lawrence Drive, Newbury Park, California 91320, USA

Editions Haynes
4, Rue de l'Abreuvoir
92415 COURBEVOIE CEDEX, France

Haynes Publishing Nordiska AB
Box 1504, 751 45 UPPSALA, Sweden

Contents

LIVING WITH YOUR TRIUMPH

Introduction

Daily (pre-ride) Checks

MAINTENANCE

Routine maintenance and Servicing

Contents

A Phoenix from the ashes

by Julian Ryder

Where is the most modern motorcycle factory in the World? Tokyo? Berlin? Turin, maybe? No, it's in Hinckley, Leicestershire. Improbable as it may seem, the Triumph factory in the Midlands of England is a more advanced production facility than anything the mighty Japanese industry, German efficiency or Italian flair can boast. Still more amazingly, the first motorcycle rolled off the brand new production line in July 1991, nine years after the last of the old Triumphs had trickled out of the old Meriden factory.

It's important to realise that the new Triumph company has very little to do with the company that was a giant on the world stage in the post-war years when British motorcycle makers dominated the global markets. It is true that new owner John Bloor bought the patents, manufacturing rights and, most importantly, trademarks when the old factory's assets were sold in 1983, but the products of the old and new companies bear no relation at all to one another. Apart, of course, from the name on the tanks. Bloor's research-and-development team started work in Collier Street, Coventry and in 1985 work started on the ten-acre green-field factory site which was occupied for the first time the following year.

The original 1200 Trophy

The reborn Triumphs

The R & D team soon dispensed with the old Meriden factory's project for a modern DOHC, eight-valve twin known within the factory as the Diana project (after Princess Di) but shown at the NEC International Bike Show in 1982 as the Phoenix. The world got to see the new Triumphs for the first time at the Cologne Show in late 1990. The company was obviously anxious to distance itself from the old, leaky, unreliable image of the traditional British motorcycle, but it was equally anxious not to engage in a head-on technology war with the big four Japanese factories. The new motto was 'proven technology', the new engines were in-line threes and fours with double overhead camshafts and four valves per cylinder. They were all housed in a universal steel chassis with a large-diameter tubular backbone, and interestingly the new bikes would all carry famous model names from Triumph's past.

If you were looking to compare the technology level with an established machine, you'd have to point to the Kawasaki GPZ900R launched back in '84. Do not take this as a suggestion, current in '91, that the new Triumphs were in some way Kawasakis in disguise because the cam chain was sited on the right side of the motor rather than between the middle cylinders. Yes, of course Triumph had looked at the technology and manufacturing of the Japanese companies and naturally found that an in-line multi-cylinder motor was the most economical way to go. It's just the same in the car world, the straight four is cheaper than the V6 because it uses fewer, simpler parts. In fact the layout of the new motor would seem to indicate that designers from the car world had been brought in by John Bloor. If anyone still harbours the belief that Triumph copied or co-operated with Kawasaki, try and find a contemporary Kawasaki that uses wet liners (cylinder liners in direct contact with coolant as opposed to sleeves fitted into the barrels).

But if Triumph's technology wasn't exactly path-breaking it was certainly very clever. The key concept was the modular design of the motor based around long and short-throw crankshafts in three and four-cylinder configurations. Every engine used the common 76 mm bore with either 55 or 65 mm throw cranks so that the short-stroke engine would be 750 cc in three-cylinder form and 1000 cc as a four. Put the long-stroke crank in and you get a 900 cc triple and a 1200 cc four. The first, six-bike range consisted of two 750-3s, two 900-3s, a 1000-4 and a 1200-4. The first bike to hit the shops was the 1200 Trophy, a four-cylinder sports tourer which was immediately competitive in a very strong class. There was also a 900 cc, three-cylinder Trophy. The 750 and 1000 Daytonas used the short-stroke motor in three and four-cylinder forms in what were intended to be the sportsters of the range. The other two models, 750 and 900 cc three-cylinder Tridents, cashed in on the early-'90s fad for naked retro bikes that followed the world-wide success of the Kawasaki Zephyr.

The 1996-on 1200 Trophy

Even though it was lumbered with the retro label, the Trident was in no way harking back to the good old days. Retro bikes were supposed to look like they'd stepped out of a 1970s time warp with wire wheels, twin shock absorbers and a sit-up-and-beg riding position, but the first Trident was clearly a modern bike that simply didn't have a fairing. It was fairly obviously a Trophy with some body panels removed.

The reborn Triumphs were received with acclaim from the motorcycle press – tinged with not a little surprise. They really were very good motorcycles, the big Trophy was a match for the Japanese opposition in a class full of very accomplished machinery. The fact it could live with a modern day classic like the Yamaha FJ1200 straight off the drawing board was a tribute to John Bloor's designers and production engineers. The bike was big, fast, heavy and quite high, but it worked and worked well. And it didn't leak oil or break down, it was obvious that whatever else people were going to say about Triumphs they weren't going to able to resurrect the old jokes about British bangers leaving puddles of lubricant under them.

Six months into production, I surveyed a group of 1200 Trophy owners and found the only problem had been rust attacking a welded seam between the exhaust pipe and the hanger bracket that attached it to the chassis. For a brand new design to be so reliable was quite outstanding and gave the lie to the impression current in several countries that British industry could no longer produce a top-quality engineered product. John Bloor does not give interviews, but it is thought that his major motivation in spending a large chunk of his considerable personal fortune in setting up the Triumph factory was simply to prove that a British factory could still turn out high-tech products that could succeed in world markets. He succeeded.

As the rest of the range arrived and tests of them got into print, the original impression was underlined and the star of the show emerged; it was the long-stroke, three-cylinder, 900 cc motor. It didn't matter how it was dressed up, the big triple had that indefinable quality – character. It was the motor the Japanese would never have made, very torquey but with a hint of vibration that endears rather than annoys. Somewhere among the modern, water-cooled, multi-valve technology, the 900-triple had the genes of the old air-cooled, OHV Triumph Tridents that appeared in 1969 and stayed in production until '75. If there was an under-achiever in the range it was the Daytona. With hindsight it is

The 1200 Daytona

The 900 Trident

The Sprint

The Speed Triple

easy to see that taking on the Japanese on their own territory – something Triumph said they never intended to do – was not a good idea, up against the cutting edge race-replicas of the day the Daytonas couldn't live up to their billing as sportsters.

Model development

The range stayed basically unchanged for two years, until the Cologne Show of '92. Looking back at the first range it is now easy to see – hindsight again – that the identity of all the models were far too close. The sports tourer Trophy models were reckoned to be a little too sporting, the basic Tridents still had the handlebar and footrest positions of faired bikes. Triumph management later agreed that the first range evinced a certain lack of confidence, that was certainly not the case of the revamped 1993 range.

Visitors to the Cologne Show in September '92 agreed that the Triumphs were the stars, any lack of confidence there may have been two years before was completely gone. The only short-stroke motor left in the range was in the 750 Trident which, like its 900 cc big brother, got a total cosmetic revamp. Any shyness the management may have felt about the Triumph name's past was shaken off as the new Tridents went retro style. Footrests were lowered and bars raised, the engine's cosmetics were tidied up and the motor and exhausts got a black finish. The engine styling was important as the original Tridents looked very much like faired bikes with the bodywork off, such was the plumber's nightmare of hoses and cables open to view. But most strikingly, these new Tridents unashamedly drew on the old Triumph heritage in their colour schemes with two-tone tanks featuring gold pinstriping – and all in very classic colours.

The original Trident wasn't totally abandoned though, it metamorphosed into the Trident Sprint, a 900 Trident with the addition of a striking twin-headlight half-fairing but retaining the sporty riding position of the first models. The two Daytona models quietly changed into one, this time with the 900 triple motor rather than the short-stroke three or four-cylinder motors. A slightly lower screen, new side panels and upswept silencers gave the bike a much sportier look; the lines were good enough to win a British Design Council Award for the bike's styling. The sports tourer identity of the Trophy models was emphasised by a more relaxed riding position with higher bars and lower footrests for both rider and pillion. The only real criticism of the 1200 Trophy – that it could do with more braking power – was answered with new four-piston calipers on the front discs. Its long distance credentials were underlined with better mirrors, a higher screen option and a clock.

Overall, the identities of the original bikes became more individual and more obviously separated; the Trophy models became more touring oriented, the Daytona more sporty looking and the Trident models more traditional. The factory even had the confidence to put small Union Flag emblems on the side panels of each model, no more apologising for the imagined shortcomings of British engineering.

Despite this spreading of the range's appeal, all these bikes were still built on the original modular concept. All the 900 triples made 100 PS (74 kW), the 750 Trident 97 PS (71 kW) and the 1200 Trophy 110 PS (80 kW). Note that the smaller Trident made nearly as much peak power as the 900, but the bigger motor made over 25% more torque for astounding mid-range punch. There was, however, an exception to this rule of uniformity in the shape of a brand new bike, the Tiger 900. This model was in the enduro/desert-racer style much favoured on Continental Europe but not at all popular at home in the UK. Here was a Triumph with a 19-inch front tyre, wire wheels and a lower power output than the other 900s, 85 PS (63 kW). Both the chassis and engine parts were slightly different from the rest of the range, the Tiger got a higher seat and longer wheelbase and a retuned – the factory would not like the word detuned – motor with a massive spread of power and torque traded off against a loss of top-end power and speed, not the most important requirements on a bike of this type. This retuning was accomplished by internal changes to such things as camshaft lift and timing and set the precedent for what was to come. Lack of ultimate performance

The 900 Daytona Super III

The Tiger

compared to some of the opposition hadn't handicapped the first Triumphs and it hasn't held the Tiger back, especially in the important German market where it is a top seller.

Judging their market as cleverly as ever, the factory held back another new model for the International Bike Show at the Birmingham NEC. This was the Daytona 1200, an out and out speed machine with a hidden political agenda. Its high-compression, 147 PS engine gave it brutal straight-line performance in much the same way as the big Kawasakis of the mid-'80s, and like them it wasn't too clever in the corners because of its weight and length. The bike was built as much to show that Triumph could do it as to sell in big numbers, it also had the secondary function of thumbing the corporate nose at the UK importers' gentlemen's agreement not to bring in bikes of over 125 PS.

Next year's NEC show saw two more new Triumphs, both reworkings of what was now regarded as a modern classic, the 900 triple. The Speed Triple was a clever reincarnation of the British cafe, racer style, complete with clip-on handlebars and rear-set footrests. The big three-cylinder engine in standard tune got an all-black finish with black chrome pipes and silencers for the appropriately mean look. Black wheel rims and new bodywork completed a superbly styled bike available with black or yellow bodywork, the Speed Triple was the star of the show, a bike with an attitude. A one-make race series with generous prize money helped give the factory's products some race-track credibility that would otherwise have been impossible to come by.

The other newcomer was a more radical project, the Daytona Super III. Externally the motor looked like the usual 900 cc three, but a lot of work by Cosworth Engineering was hidden under the cases, notably reworked heads, ports and cam profiles. The result was 115 PS as opposed to the standard 900 Daytona's 98. New six-piston calipers built and designed by Triumph, not bought in, stopped the plot which was a couple of kilos lighter thanks to judicious use of lightweight carbon-fibre materials.

But the new Triumphs aren't really about out-and-out performance, as Rolls Royce like to say power is 'adequate' and quite enough for real world motorcycling as evidenced by commercial success in demanding markets like Germany where Triumph's strict quality control and top-quality finish are paying dividends. One German magazine, MO, ran an early Trident for 100,000 km with hardly a problem. When it was stripped for inspection at the Hinckley factory the engine was found to be as good as new, a tribute to the original design and production engineering.

Triumphs in America

Triumph's next big step was into the US market, where the old company was so strong in the post-war years when the only competition was Harley-Davidson and where there is considerable affection for the marque. The name Triumph chose to spearhead this new challenge is Thunderbird, a trademark sourced in Native American mythology. This time the famous name adorns yet another version of the 900 triple but this time heavily restyled and in a retro package. This is the first of the new-generation Triumph motors designed to be looked at without a fairing covering most of it. Dummy cooling fins give it the look of an air-cooled motor, the logo was cast into the clutch cover, and there were soft

The Thunderbird

The Adventurer

edges and large expanses of polished alloy. Inside those restyled cases, the motor was retuned even more than the Tiger's to give 70 PS for a very user friendly dose of low-down punch and mid-range power – maximum torque is at just 4800 rpm as opposed to the 900 Trident's 6500 rpm. The cycle parts were given an equally radical redesign, although the retro style stopped short of giving the Thunderbird twin rear shock absorbers. But everything else, the shape of the tank, the chrome headlight and countless other details, harks back to the original Thunderbird and nothing does so as shamelessly as the 'mouth-organ' tank badge, a classic icon if ever there was one.

But the Thunderbird was more than just another new model, it was the start of a whole new marketing game. With one eye on Harley-Davidson's success, Triumph designed a range of bolt-on accessories for the Thunderbird and a family of Thunderbird derivatives. The first bolt-on goodies offered extra chrome, leather panniers, a windshield, and two-tone front mudguards for the bike, with boots, leathers, jackets and helmet options for the rider. Sounds familiar? It looks very like the formula that Harley-Davidson used to such effect in their comeback from the commercial grave.

The first Thunderbird derivative, the Adventurer, appeared for 1996 with a different rear subframe and rear-end styling including a sissy bar and single seat. Frankly, it looked like a naff '70s custom Harley and sold like one. That same year, the short-stroke 750 cc motor bowed out of the range, but it went with a bang not a whimper not in a final batch of Tridents but in a limited-edition (limited to the number of spares they had on the shelves) run of 750 Speed Triples. Another very clever piece of marketing, as was putting the original, bigger Speed Triple's motor in the Sprint and calling it the Sprint Sport. The 750 Speed Triple only stayed in the range for one year, 1996, while the Sprint Sport hung on for an extra two years. The reason for using up all those motors was the advent of the new range of fuel-injected and heavily revised three-cylinder engines that first powered the T509 Speed Triple and T595 Daytona of 1997.

Not that development of the carburetted bikes was neglected. Triumph got a Thunderbird derivative right in '98 with the Thunderbird Sport. If there was a criticism of the original T'bird it was that it was a trifle soft and underbraked. That was cured with the Speed Triple's forks and twin front disc brakes, 17-inch wheels front and rear, and the styling was cleverly reminiscent of the old Hurricane version of the first Triumph triples. The Legend TT is the same bike with a different exhaust system and graphics. For the rider who didn't want the hard-edge of the Daytonas or the custom style of the Thunderbird it was the perfect compromise and looked as good as the Adventurer looked wrong.

The long-serving Trophy 900 and 1200 models weren't neglected, in 1996 they received total restyles complete with fox-eye headlights, a new fairing and integrated panniers. The carburettors were changed on the 900 and the gearing lengthened on the 1200 to try and get better fuel consumption. The Trophy models were still big, heavy bikes but the new bodywork vastly improved the way in which they performed their chosen task.

From '97 on, the cutting-edge sports bikes in the range were all using the new fuel-injected motor but Triumph had one last hurrah with their biggest carburretted engine. The company had never tried to build four-cylinder engines to compete with the Japanese race-replicas despite the 147 PS Daytona 1200 of 1992, instead concentrating on developing the three-cylinder bikes that are Triumph's hallmark. Nevertheless, in 1999 the final batch of 250 1200 Daytonas were released as the 1200SE (for Special Edition). In yet another clever little marketing ploy, the SE got six-piston calipers, a pillion seat cover and black paintwork with gold detailing. There is also a little numbered plaque telling which of the 250 examples it is. The colour scheme manages to make the Daytona look a lot older than it is. It's yet another example of how Triumph use a comparatively limited kit of parts to produce the maximum number of models but manage to make them all not just distinctive but different to ride as well.

The Legend TT

Photograph courtesy of Kel Edge

The Speed Triple Challenge went international in 1995 – riders from all over the world met at the Bol d'Or

Acknowledgements

Our thanks are due to Riders of Bridgwater, Bridge of Exeter and Fowlers of Bristol who supplied the machines featured in the photographs throughout this manual. Mel Rawlings A.I.R.T.E. of MHR Engineering carried out some of the mechanical work.

Thanks are also due to Julian Ryder for providing the introductory copy (A Phoenix from the ashes), to Kel Edge for the Speed Triple racing photographs, and to Kyoichi Nakamura for the rear cover action photograph. We would also like to extend thanks to Triumph Motorcycles, Hinckley, for permission to use pictures of the Triumph models. Triumph Motorcycles Limited bears no responsibility for the content of this book, having had no part in its origination or preparation.

NGK Spark Plugs (UK) Ltd supplied the colour spark plug condition photos and the Avon Rubber Company supplied information on tyre fitting.

About this manual

The aim of this manual is to help you get the best value from your motorcycle. It can do so in several ways. It can help you decide what work must be done, even if you choose to have it done by a dealer; it provides information and procedures for routine maintenance and servicing; and it offers diagnostic and repair procedures to follow when trouble occurs.

We hope you use the manual to tackle the work yourself. For many simpler jobs, doing it yourself may be quicker than arranging an appointment to get the motorcycle into a dealer and making the trips to leave it and pick it up. More importantly, a lot of money can be saved by avoiding the expense the shop must pass on to you to cover its labour and overhead costs. An added benefit is the sense of satisfaction and accomplishment that you feel after doing the job yourself.

References to the left or right side of the motorcycle assume you are sitting on the seat, facing forward.

We take great pride in the accuracy of information given in this manual, but motorcycle manufacturers make alterations and design changes during the production run of a particular motorcycle of which they do not inform us. No liability can be accepted by the authors or publishers for loss, damage or injury caused by any errors in, or omissions from, the information given.

Professional mechanics are trained in safe working procedures. However enthusiastic you may be about getting on with the job at hand, take the time to ensure that your safety is not put at risk. A moment's lack of attention can result in an accident, as can failure to observe simple precautions.

There will always be new ways of having accidents, and the following is not a comprehensive list of all dangers; it is intended rather to make you aware of the risks and to encourage a safe approach to all work you carry out on your bike.

Asbestos

● Certain friction, insulating, sealing and other products - such as brake pads, clutch linings, gaskets, etc. - contain asbestos. Extreme care must be taken to avoid inhalation of dust from such products since it is hazardous to health. If in doubt, assume that they do contain asbestos.

Fire

● Remember at all times that petrol is highly flammable. Never smoke or have any kind of naked flame around, when working on the vehicle. But the risk does not end there - a spark caused by an electrical short-circuit, by two metal surfaces contacting each other, by careless use of tools, or even by static electricity built up in your body under certain conditions, can ignite petrol vapour, which in a confined space is highly explosive. Never use petrol as a cleaning solvent. Use an approved safety solvent.

● Always disconnect the battery earth terminal before working on any part of the fuel or electrical system, and never risk spilling fuel on to a hot engine or exhaust.

● It is recommended that a fire extinguisher of a type suitable for fuel and electrical fires is kept handy in the garage or workplace at all times. Never try to extinguish a fuel or electrical fire with water.

Fumes

● Certain fumes are highly toxic and can quickly cause unconsciousness and even death if inhaled to any extent. Petrol vapour comes into this category, as do the vapours from certain solvents such as trichloroethylene. Any draining or pouring of such volatile fluids should be done in a well ventilated area.

● When using cleaning fluids and solvents, read the instructions carefully. Never use materials from unmarked containers - they may give off poisonous vapours.

● Never run the engine of a motor vehicle in an enclosed space such as a garage. Exhaust fumes contain carbon monoxide which is extremely poisonous; if you need to run the engine, always do so in the open air or at least have the rear of the vehicle outside the workplace.

The battery

● Never cause a spark, or allow a naked light near the vehicle's battery. It will normally be giving off a certain amount of hydrogen gas, which is highly explosive.

● Always disconnect the battery ground (earth) terminal before working on the fuel or electrical systems (except where noted).

● If possible, loosen the filler plugs or cover when charging the battery from an external source. Do not charge at an excessive rate or the battery may burst.

● Take care when topping up, cleaning or carrying the battery. The acid electrolyte, evenwhen diluted, is very corrosive and should not be allowed to contact the eyes or skin. Always wear rubber gloves and goggles or a face shield. If you ever need to prepare electrolyte yourself, always add the acid slowly to the water; never add the water to the acid.

Electricity

● When using an electric power tool, inspection light etc., always ensure that the appliance is correctly connected to its plug and that, where necessary, it is properly grounded (earthed). Do not use such appliances in damp conditions and, again, beware of creating a spark or applying excessive heat in the vicinity of fuel or fuel vapour. Also ensure that the appliances meet national safety standards.

● A severe electric shock can result from touching certain parts of the electrical system, such as the spark plug wires (HT leads), when the engine is running or being cranked, particularly if components are damp or the insulation is defective. Where an electronic ignition system is used, the secondary (HT) voltage is much higher and could prove fatal.

Remember...

✗ **Don't** start the engine without first ascertaining that the transmission is in neutral.

✗ **Don't** suddenly remove the pressure cap from a hot cooling system - cover it with a cloth and release the pressure gradually first, or you may get scalded by escaping coolant.

✗ **Don't** attempt to drain oil until you are sure it has cooled sufficiently to avoid scalding you.

✗ **Don't** grasp any part of the engine or exhaust system without first ascertaining that it is cool enough not to burn you.

✗ **Don't** allow brake fluid or antifreeze to contact the machine's paintwork or plastic components.

✗ **Don't** siphon toxic liquids such as fuel, hydraulic fluid or antifreeze by mouth, or allow them to remain on your skin.

✗ **Don't** inhale dust - it may be injurious to health (see Asbestos heading).

✗ **Don't** allow any spilled oil or grease to remain on the floor - wipe it up right away, before someone slips on it.

✗ **Don't** use ill-fitting spanners or other tools which may slip and cause injury.

✗ **Don't** lift a heavy component which may be beyond your capability - get assistance.

✗ **Don't** rush to finish a job or take unverified short cuts.

✗ **Don't** allow children or animals in or around an unattended vehicle.

✗ **Don't** inflate a tyre above the recommended pressure. Apart from overstressing the carcass, in extreme cases the tyre may blow off forcibly.

✓ **Do** ensure that the machine is supported securely at all times. This is especially important when the machine is blocked up to aid wheel or fork removal.

✓ **Do** take care when attempting to loosen a stubborn nut or bolt. It is generally better to pull on a spanner, rather than push, so that if you slip, you fall away from the machine rather than onto it.

✓ **Do** wear eye protection when using power tools such as drill, sander, bench grinder etc.

✓ **Do** use a barrier cream on your hands prior to undertaking dirty jobs - it will protect your skin from infection as well as making the dirt easier to remove afterwards; but make sure your hands aren't left slippery. Note that long-term contact with used engine oil can be a health hazard.

✓ **Do** keep loose clothing (cuffs, ties etc. and long hair) well out of the way of moving mechanical parts.

✓ **Do** remove rings, wristwatch etc., before working on the vehicle - especially the electrical system.

✓ **Do** keep your work area tidy - it is only too easy to fall over articles left lying around.

✓ **Do** exercise caution when compressing springs for removal or installation. Ensure that the tension is applied and released in a controlled manner, using suitable tools which preclude the possibility of the spring escaping violently.

✓ **Do** ensure that any lifting tackle used has a safe working load rating adequate for the job.

✓ **Do** get someone to check periodically that all is well, when working alone on the vehicle.

✓ **Do** carry out work in a logical sequence and check that everything is correctly assembled and tightened afterwards.

✓ **Do** remember that your vehicle's safety affects that of yourself and others. If in doubt on any point, get professional advice.

● If in spite of following these precautions, you are unfortunate enough to injure yourself, seek medical attention as soon as possible.

VIN (Vehicle Identification Number)

The frame VIN is stamped into the right side of the steering head. It is duplicated on a plate attached to the frame under the seat (UK models) or attached to the steering head (US models). The engine VIN is stamped into the right upper side of the crankcase, directly above the clutch cover. Both of these numbers should be recorded and kept in a safe place so they can be furnished to law enforcement officials in the event of a theft.

The frame and engine VINs should also be kept in a handy place (such as with your driving licence) so they are always available when purchasing or ordering parts for your machine.

Models are identified in the manual by their engine size and model name (eg 1200 Trophy). Where a modification necessitates a different working method, the engine or frame VIN may be used to indicate early and later models. Owners of the 900 Daytona Super III should refer to information for the 900 Daytona unless specific mention is made of the Super III model. Likewise owners of the Sprint Sport and Sprint Executive should refer to information for the Sprint unless specific mention is made of them.

Buying spare parts

Always provide the model name, engine size and engine or frame VIN (Vehicle Identification Number) when ordering parts. Providing the VIN will ensure that you obtain the correct part if a modification has been introduced.

Whenever possible, take the worn part to the dealer so direct comparison with the new component can be made. Along the trail from the manufacturer to the parts shelf, there are numerous places that the part can end up with the wrong number or be listed incorrectly.

A Triumph dealer will be able to obtain all parts for your machine, although a motor accessory store is a good source for lubricants, spark plugs etc.

Used parts can be obtained for roughly half the price of new ones, but you can't always be sure of what you're getting. Once again, take your worn part to the breaker for direct comparison.

The engine VIN is located on the upper crankcase

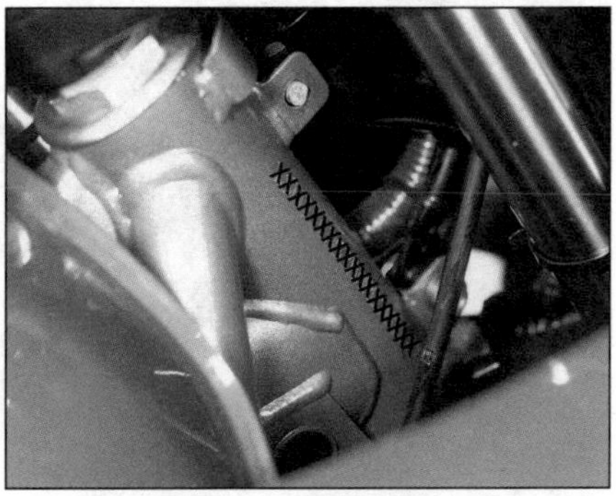

Frame VIN is stamped into right side of steering head

On UK models the frame VIN is also on a plate riveted to the frame under the seat

Note: *The daily (pre-ride) checks outlined in the owner's manual covers those items which should be inspected on a daily basis.*

1 Engine/transmission oil level check

Before you start:

✔ Place the bike on its centrestand. Where no centrestand is fitted hold the bike upright – do not check the level with the bike on its sidestand. The bike should be on level ground when checking the oil level.

✔ The oil level should be checked when the engine is cold. If the engine has just been run, allow it to cool down for ten minutes before checking the oil level.

Bike care:

● If you have to add oil frequently, you should check whether you have any oil leaks. If there is no sign of oil leakage from the joints and gaskets the engine could be burning oil (see *Fault Finding*).

The correct oil

● Modern, high-revving engines place great demands on their oil. It is very important that the correct oil for your bike is used

● Always top up with a good quality oil of the specified type and viscosity and do not overfill the engine.

Oil standard	API grade SG (minimum)
Oil type 900 Daytona Super III and 1200 Daytona	Fully synthetic 5W/40 motorcycle oil
All other models	Fully synthetic 5W/40 or semi-synthetic 10W/40 motorcycle oil
Triumph recommendation – all models	Mobil 1 Racing 4T 15W/50 (conforms to JASO MA and API SH grade)

Trident, Sprint, 900 Trophy, 1200 Trophy (grey engine), Speed Triple, Daytona, Tiger

1 The dipstick is integral with the filler cap and is located in the engine sprocket cover. Unscrew it to check the engine oil level.

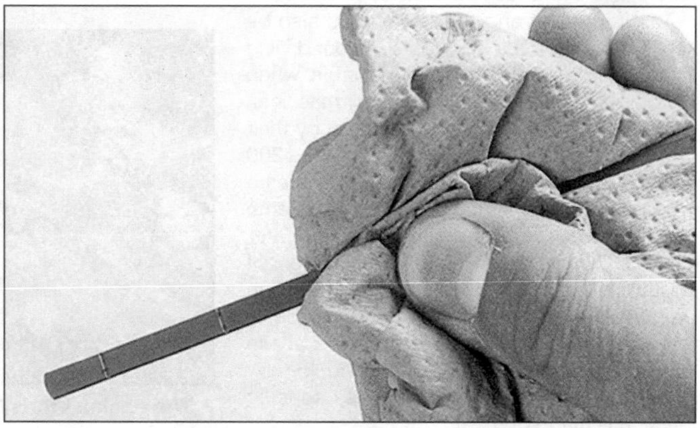

2 Using a clean rag or paper towel remove all oil from the dipstick. Insert the clean dipstick back into the sprocket cover and screw it fully in.

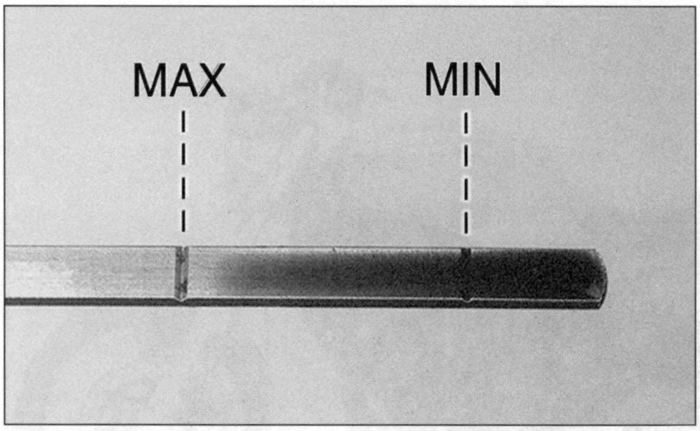

3 Unscrew the dipstick. The oil level should be between the MAX and MIN marks on the end of the dipstick. On early models, the dipsticks are marked 3 and 4 in relation to the number of cylinders; on later models the markings are the same for all engines

4 If the level is below the lower (minimum) dipstick mark, top up with oil of the recommended grade and type, to bring the level up to the upper (maximum) mark.

Thunderbird, Thunderbird Sport, Adventurer, Legend TT, 1200 Trophy (black engine) models

1 On Thunderbird, Thunderbird Sport, Adventurer and Legend TT models, the oil level sightglass is set beneath the crankshaft right cover. The oil level is correct if it lies midway up the sightglass, when the motorcycle is held upright.

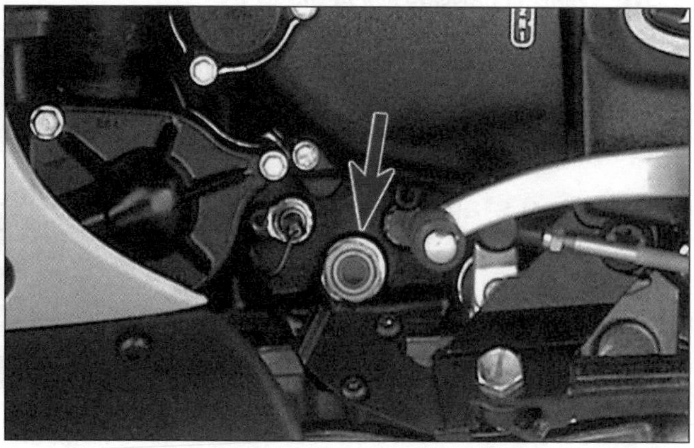

2 On 1200 Trophy models (with black engine), the oil level sightglass is set in the left side of the crankcase, below the sprocket cover. With the motorcycle on its centrestand the oil level should be midway up the sightglass.

3 If topping up is required, use a large flat-bladed screwdriver to unscrew the filler cap from the clutch cover. The cap will be tight so make sure the screwdriver is a good fit to prevent damaging the slot.

4 Top up the oil level using a funnel to prevent spillage. When the level is correct, check the condition of the filler cap seal, then tighten the cap securely.

2 Coolant level check

> ***Warning: DO NOT remove the radiator pressure cap to add coolant. Topping up is done via the coolant reservoir tank filler. DO NOT leave open containers of coolant about, as it is poisonous.***

Before you start:

✔ Make sure you have a supply of coolant available (a mixture of 50% distilled water and 50% corrosion inhibited ethylene glycol antifreeze is needed).

✔ Place the motorcycle on its centre stand, or hold it upright, whilst checking the level. Make sure the motorcycle is on level ground.

✔ Always check the coolant level when the engine is cold – a false reading will otherwise result.

Bike care:

- Use only the specified coolant mixture . It is important that antifreeze is used in the cooling system all year round, not just during the winter months. Don't top-up with water alone, as the antifreeze will become too diluted.
- Do not overfill the reservoir tank. If the coolant is significantly above the MAX line at any time, the surplus coolant should be siphoned off to prevent it from being expelled out of the overflow hose when the engine is running.
- If the coolant level falls steadily, check the system for leaks as described in Chapter 1. If no leaks are found and the level still continues to fall, it is recommended that the machine be taken to a Triumph dealer who will pressure test the system.

Trident, Sprint, Trophy, Speed Triple, Daytona and Tiger models

1 The coolant reservoir is located underneath the seat. The coolant level markings are moulded into the right side of the reservoir.

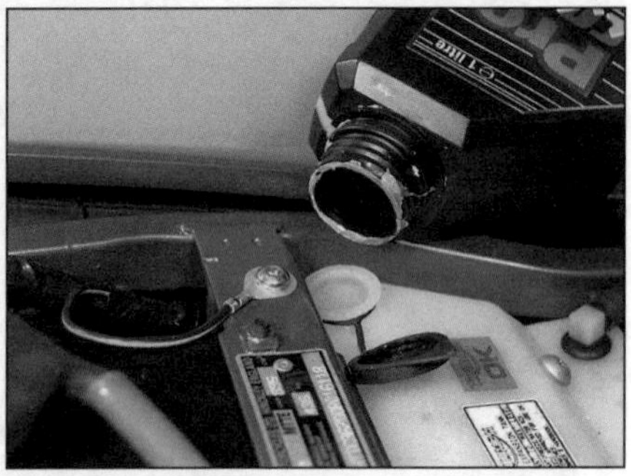

2 If the coolant level does not lie between the MAX and MIN markings, pull off the filler cap and top up with coolant.

Thunderbird, Thunderbird Sport, Adventurer and Legend TT models

3 The coolant reservoir is located under the fuel tank. It is possible to view the level markings via the front right side of the fuel tank.

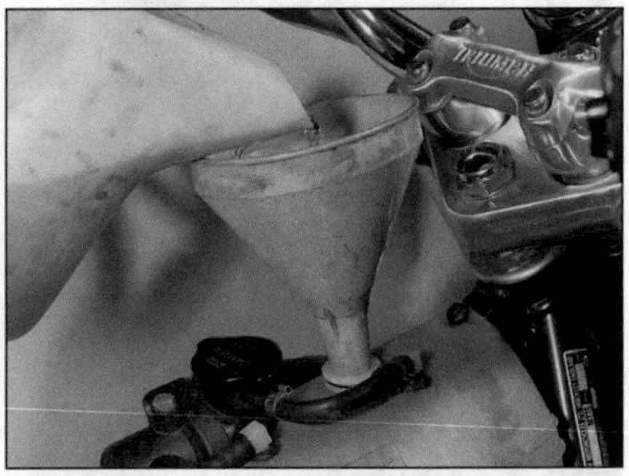

4 If the coolant level does not lie between the MAX and MIN markings, remove the fuel tank (see Chapter 4), pull off the filler cap and top up with coolant.

3 Suspension, steering and drive chain checks

Drive chain

- Check that drive chain slack isn't excessive, and adjust if necessary (see Chapter 1).
- If the chain looks dry, lubricate it (see Chapter 1).

Suspension and Steering

- Check that the front and rear suspension operates smoothly without binding.
- Check that the suspension adjustment settings are as required.
- Check that the steering moves smoothly from lock-to-lock.

4 Brake and clutch fluid level checks

Before you start:

✔ Hold the motorcycle upright and turn the handlebars until the top of the master cylinder is as level as possible.

✔ Make sure you have the correct hydraulic fluid – DOT 4 is recommended.

Bike care:

● The fluid in the front and rear brake master cylinder reservoirs will drop slightly as the brake pads wear down.

● If any fluid reservoir requires repeated topping-up this is an indication of an hydraulic leak somewhere in the system, which should be investigated immediately.

● Check for signs of fluid leakage from the hydraulic hoses and components – if found, rectify immediately.

● Check the operation of both brakes and the clutch before taking the machine on the road; if there is evidence of air in the system (spongy feel to lever or pedal), it must be bled as described in Chapter 7 (brake) or Chapter 2 (clutch).

Warning: Brake and clutch hydraulic fluid can harm your eyes and damage painted surfaces, so use extreme caution when handling and pouring it. Do not use fluid that has been standing open for some time, as it absorbs moisture from the air which can cause a dangerous loss of braking and clutch effectiveness.

1 On the front brake and clutch reservoirs, make sure that the fluid level, visible through the sightglass, is above the LOWER level line

2 To top up the front brake and clutch reservoirs, remove the two screws retaining the reservoir cover. Lift off the cover with the diaphragm.

3 After topping up ensure that the diaphragm is correctly folded and install the cap.

4 Remove the right side cover (see Chapter 8) and pull off the air intake tube for improved access to the rear reservoir.

5 To top up the rear brake reservoir, unscrew its cap and remove the diaphragm.

6 Top up the reservoir with the specified fluid. The fluid level must lie between the UPPER and LOWER lines.

7 After topping up, install the diaphragm, plastic ring and cap.

8 Set the lever span adjuster to suit the rider. Note that the number on the span adjuster wheel must align exactly with the triangular mark on the lever bracket (circled).

5 Tyres

The correct pressures

- The tyres must be checked when **cold**, not immediately after riding. Note that low tyre pressures may cause the tyre to slip on the rim or come off. High tyre pressures will cause abnormal tread wear and unsafe handling.
- Use an accurate pressure gauge.
- Proper air pressure will increase tyre life and ensure stability and ride comfort.

Tyre care

- Check the tyres carefully for cuts, tears, embedded nails or other sharp objects and excessive wear. Operation of the motorcycle with excessively worn tyres is extremely hazardous, as traction and handling are directly affected.
- Check the condition of the tyre valve and ensure the dust cap is in place.
- Pick out any stones or nails which may have become embedded in the tyre tread. If left, they will eventually penetrate through the casing and cause a puncture.
- If tyre damage is apparent, or unexplained loss of pressure is experienced, seek the advice of a tyre fitting specialist without delay.

Model	Front tyre	Rear tyre
750 and 1000 Daytona	36 psi (2.5 Bar)	36 psi (2.5 Bar)
Trident, Sprint, Trophy, Speed Triple, 900/1200 Daytona, Thunderbird, Thunderbird Sport, Adventurer, Legend TT	36 psi (2.5 Bar)	41 psi (2.9 Bar)
Tiger	30 psi (2.1 Bar)	33 psi (2.3 Bar)

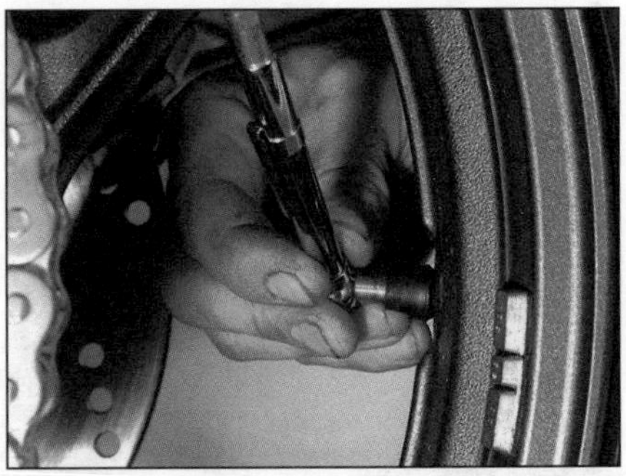

1 Check the tyre pressures when the tyres are **cold** and keep them properly inflated.

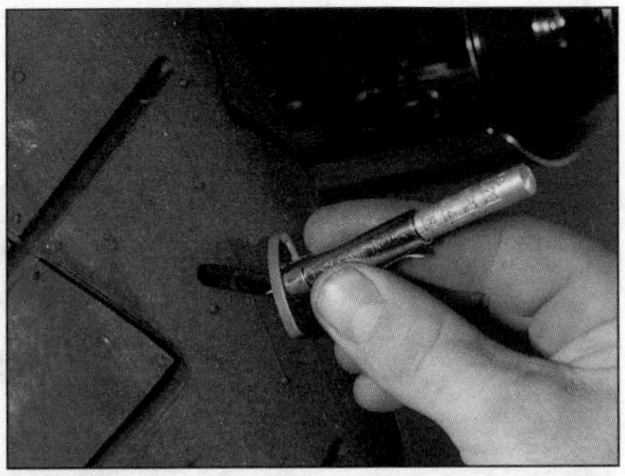

2 Measure the tread depth at the centre of the tyre using a tread depth gauge. The tyre must be renewed when the depth is less than specified.

3 Many tyres incorporate wear indicators (arrowed). Renew the tyre when the tread has worn down to the indicator bar.

Tyre tread depth

- At the time of writing UK law requires that tread depth must be at least 1 mm over 3/4 of the tread breadth all the way around the tyre, with no bald patches.
- Readers are advised to adhere to the maker's minimum tread depth (see table).

Front tyre	2 mm minimum
Rear tyre	
At speeds under 80 mph (130 kph)	2 mm minimum
At speeds above 80 mph (130 kph)	3 mm minimum

6 Legal and safety checks

Lighting and signalling

- Take a minute to check that the headlight(s), tail light, brake light, turn signals all work correctly.
- Check that the horn sounds when the switch is operated.
- A working speedometer, graduated in mph, is a statutory requirement in the UK.

Safety

- Check that the throttle grip rotates smoothly and snaps shut when released.
- Check that the engine shuts off when the kill switch is operated.
- Check that sidestand return spring holds the stand securely up when retracted. The same applies to the centre stand (where fitted).

Fuel

- This may seem obvious, but check that you have enough fuel to complete your journey. If you notice signs of fuel leakage – rectify the cause immediately.
- Ensure you use the correct grade unleaded fuel – see Chapter 4 Specifications.

Chapter 1
Routine maintenance and servicing

Contents

Degrees of difficulty

Easy, suitable for novice with little experience	**Fairly easy,** suitable for beginner with some experience	**Fairly difficult,** suitable for competent DIY mechanic	**Difficult,** suitable for experienced DIY mechanic	**Very difficult,** suitable for expert DIY or professional

Engine

Spark plugs	
Type	NGK DPR9EA-9
Electrode gap	0.8 to 0.9 mm
Valve clearances (COLD engine)	
Inlet	0.10 to 0.15 mm
Exhaust	0.15 to 0.20 mm
Engine idle speed	1000 ± 50 rpm
Carburettor synchronisation vacuum range	127 to 152 mm Hg
Cylinder numbering (from left side to right side of the bike)	1-2-3 (3 cylinder), 1-2-3-4 (4 cylinder)
Firing order	1-2-3 (3 cylinder), 1-2-4-3 (4 cylinder)

Cycle parts

Brake pad minimum thickness	1.5 mm
Drive chain 20-link length service limit	319 mm
Freeplay adjustments	
Throttle grip	2 to 3 mm
Choke shaft	2 to 3 mm
Drive chain	
Trident, Sprint, Trophy, Speed Triple, Daytona and Tiger models	35 to 40 mm
Thunderbird, Thunderbird Sport, Adventurer, Legend TT models	25 to 30 mm
Tyre pressures and tread depth	see *Daily (pre-ride) checks*

Torque settings

Spark plugs	18 Nm
Oil drain plug	
M22 thread size	48 Nm
M14 thread size	28 Nm
Oil filter centre bolt	18 Nm
Valve cover bolts	10 Nm
Coolant drain plugs	13 Nm
Steering stem nut	65 Nm
Steering head bearing adjuster ring pinch bolt (early models)	7 Nm
Steering head bearing adjuster locknut (later models)	40 Nm
Front brake and clutch master cylinder clamp bolts	15 Nm
Top yoke fork clamp bolts	
Tiger	18 Nm
All other models	20 Nm
Handlebar clamp bolts	
Tiger	18 Nm
Thunderbird Sport	20 Nm
All other models	22 Nm
Rear wheel axle bolt/nut	85 Nm
Drive chain adjuster clamp bolts (Trident, Sprint, Trophy, Speed Triple, Daytona, Thunderbird (to VIN 29155), Tiger)	35 Nm

Recommended lubricants and fluids

Engine/transmission oil type	API grade SG minimum
Engine/transmission oil viscosity	
900 Daytona Super III, 1200 Daytona	Fully synthetic 5W/40 motorcycle oil
All other models	Fully synthetic 5W/40 or semi-synthetic 10W/40 motorcycle oil
Engine/transmission oil capacity	
Trident, Sprint, 900 Trophy, Speed Triple, 900 Daytona, Tiger, Thunderbird, Thunderbird Sport, Adventurer, Legend TT models	4.0 litres
1000 Daytona	3.5 litres
750 Daytona, 1200 Trophy, 1200 Daytona	3.75 litres
Coolant	
Mixture type	50% distilled water, 50% corrosion inhibited ethylene glycol antifreeze
Coolant capacity	
3 cylinder engine	2.8 litres
4 cylinder engine	3.0 litres
Front fork oil type and level	see Chapter 6 Specifications
Brake and clutch fluid	DOT 4
Drive chain	Aerosol chain lubricant, marked as being suitable for O-ring type chains, or EP80 gear oil
Wheel bearings	High-melting-point grease
Rear suspension bearings	Molybdenum disulphide grease
Cables, lever and stand pivot points	Motor oil
Throttle grip	Multi-purpose grease or dry film lubricant

Note: *Always perform the pre-ride inspection at every maintenance interval (in addition to the procedures listed). The intervals listed below are the intervals recommended by the manufacturer for each particular operation during the model years covered in this manual. Your owner's manual may have different intervals for your model.*

Daily (pre-ride)

- ☐ See '*Daily (pre-ride) checks*' at the beginning of this manual.

After the initial 500 miles (800 km)

Note: *A one-off check is usually performed by a Triumph dealer after the first 500 miles (800 km) from new. Thereafter, maintenance is carried out according to the following intervals of the schedule.*

Every 200 miles (300 km)

- ☐ Lubricate the drive chain (Section 1).

Every 500 miles (800 km)

- ☐ Check and adjust drive chain freeplay (Section 2).

Every 3000 miles (5000 km)

Carry out all items in the Daily (pre-ride) checks, plus the following:

- ☐ Check and adjust the idle speed (Section 3).
- ☐ Drain the airbox (Section 4).
- ☐ Check the steering head bearing freeplay (Section 5).
- ☐ Check the front and rear suspension (Section 6).
- ☐ Check the drive chain for wear or stretch (Section 7).
- ☐ Check the brake light switches (Section 8).
- ☐ Check the brake pads (Section 9).
- ☐ Check the tyre and wheel condition, and the tyre tread depth (Section 10).
- ☐ Check the battery electrolyte level (or every month) – not maintenance-free batteries (Section 11).

Every 6000 miles (10,000 km)

Carry out all items in the 3000 mile (5000 km) check, plus the following:

- ☐ Change the engine oil and filter (Section 12).
- ☐ Check the valve clearances (Section 13).
- ☐ Check the condition of the cooling system hoses and connections (Section 14).
- ☐ Check throttle/choke cable operation and freeplay (Section 15).
- ☐ Check carburettor synchronisation (Section 16).
- ☐ Check the fuel system components (Section 17).
- ☐ Check the condition of the evaporative loss system hoses (California only) (Section 18).
- ☐ Check the spark plug gaps (Section 19).
- ☐ Check the tightness of all nuts and bolts (Section 20).
- ☐ Lubricate all stand and lever pivot points and cables (Section 21).

Every 12,000 miles (20,000 km)

Carry out all items in 6000 mile (10,000 km) check, plus the following:

- ☐ Change the clutch fluid (or every 2 years, whichever comes first) (Section 22).
- ☐ Renew the spark plugs (Section 23).
- ☐ Change the front fork oil (Section 24).
- ☐ Re-grease the steering head bearings (or every 2 years, whichever comes first) (Section 25).
- ☐ Change the brake fluid (or every 2 years, whichever comes first) (Section 26).

Every 18,000 miles (30,000 km)

Carry out all items in 6000 mile (10,000 km) check, plus the following:

- ☐ Change the coolant (or every 2 years, whichever comes first) (Section 27).

Every 24,000 miles (40,000 km)

- ☐ Renew the airbox (Section 28).
- ☐ Lubricate rear suspension linkage bearings (or every 3 years, whichever comes first) (Section 29).
- ☐ Lubricate the swingarm bearings (or every 3 years, whichever comes first) (Section 30).
- ☐ Renew the drive chain slider block – Tiger models (or every 2 years, whichever comes first) (Section 31).

Every 2 years

- ☐ Change the clutch fluid (or every 12,000 miles (20,000 km), whichever comes first) (Section 22).
- ☐ Renew the clutch master cylinder and release cylinder seals (Section 32).
- ☐ Change the coolant (or every 18,000 miles (30,000 km), whichever comes first) (Section 27).
- ☐ Re-grease the steering head bearings (or every 12,000 miles (20,000 km), whichever comes first) (Section 25).
- ☐ Renew drive chain slider block – Tiger models (or every 24,000 miles (40,000 km), whichever comes first) (Section 31).
- ☐ Change the brake fluid (or every 12,000 miles (20,000 km), whichever comes first) (Section 26).
- ☐ Renew the brake master cylinder and caliper seals (Section 33).

Every 3 years

- ☐ Lubricate the rear suspension linkage bearings (or every 24,000 miles (40,000 km) whichever comes first) (Section 29).
- ☐ Lubricate swingarm bearings (or every 24,000 miles (40,000 km) whichever comes first) (Section 30).

Every 4 years

- ☐ Renew the clutch hose (Section 34).
- ☐ Renew the fuel hose (Section 35).
- ☐ Renew the brake hoses (Section 36).

Component locations on right side (applies to Trident, Sprint, Trophy, Speed Triple, Daytona and Tiger models)

1 Coolant reservoir
2 Battery
3 Airbox
4 Rear brake master cylinder fluid reservoir
5 Steering head bearings
6 Front master cylinder
7 Throttle cable upper adjuster
8 Fork seals
9 Brake pads
10 Rear suspension linkage

Component locations on left side (applies to Trident, Sprint, Trophy, Speed Triple, Daytona and Tiger models)

1 Idle speed knob
*2 Oil filler/dipstick**
3 Oil filter
4 Oil drain plug
5 Radiator pressure cap
6 Coolant drain plugs
7 Choke cable adjuster
8 Drive chain
9 Clutch release cylinder

*Oil filler cap is on opposite side on later 1200 Trophy model with black engine

Component locations on right side (applies to Thunderbird, Thunderbird Sport, Adventurer and Legend TT models)

1 Coolant reservoir
2 Battery
3 Airbox
4 Rear brake master cylinder fluid reservoir
5 Steering head bearings
6 Front master cylinder
7 Throttle cable upper adjuster
8 Fork seals
9 Brake pads
10 Rear suspension linkage
11 Oil level sightglass
12 Oil filler

Component locations on left side (applies to Thunderbird, Thunderbird Sport, Adventurer and Legend TT models)

1 Idle speed knob
2 Oil filter
3 Oil drain plug
4 Radiator pressure cap
5 Coolant drain plugs
6 Choke cable adjuster
7 Drive chain
8 Clutch release cylinder

1 This Chapter is designed to help the home mechanic maintain his/her motorcycle for safety, economy, long life and peak performance.
2 Deciding where to start or plug into the routine maintenance schedule depends on several factors. If the warranty period on your motorcycle has just expired, and if it has been maintained according to the warranty standards, you may want to pick up routine maintenance as it coincides with the next mileage or calendar interval. If you have owned the machine for some time but have never performed any maintenance on it, then you may want to start at the nearest interval and include some additional procedures to ensure that nothing important is overlooked. If you have just had a major engine overhaul, then you may want to start the maintenance routine from the beginning. If you have a used machine and have no knowledge of its history or maintenance record, you may desire to combine all the checks into one large service initially and then settle into the maintenance schedule prescribed.
3 Before beginning any maintenance or repair, the machine should be cleaned thoroughly, especially around the oil filter, spark plugs, valve cover, sidepanels, carburettors, etc. Cleaning will help ensure that dirt does not contaminate the engine and will allow you to detect wear and damage that could otherwise easily go unnoticed.
4 Certain maintenance information is sometimes printed on decals attached to the motorcycle. If the information on the decals differs from that included here, use the information on the decal.

Every 200 miles (300 km)

1 Drive chain and sprockets – lubrication

Note: *If the chain is extremely dirty, it should be removed and cleaned before it is lubricated (see Chapter 6).*
1 For routine lubrication, the best time to lubricate the chain is after the motorcycle has been ridden. When the chain is warm, the lubricant will penetrate the joints between the side plates better than when cold.
2 Apply the lubricant to the area where the side plates overlap – not the middle of the rollers **(see illustration)**. After applying the lubricant, let it soak in a few minutes before wiping off any excess.

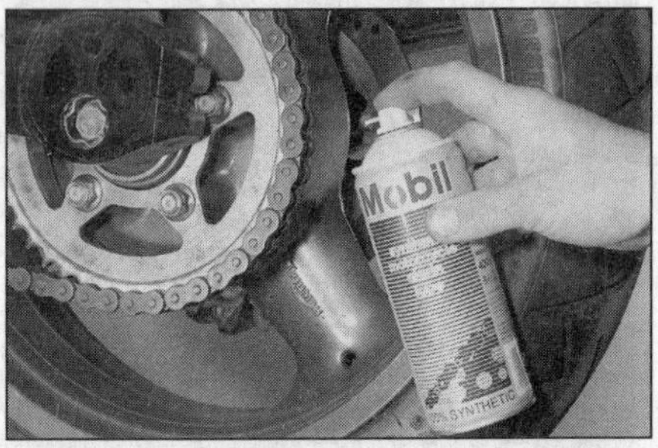

1.2 Aerosol chain lubricant being applied

Every 500 miles (800 km)

2 Drive chain – freeplay check and adjustment

Check

1 A neglected drive chain won't last long and can quickly damage the sprockets. Routine chain adjustment will ensure maximum chain and sprocket life.
2 To check the chain, shift the transmission into neutral and make sure the ignition switch is OFF. Position the bike on its centrestand; where no centrestand is fitted the sidestand can be used, or preferably an auxiliary stand so the that rear wheel can be raised off the ground and rotated easily.
3 Measure freeplay on the chain's bottom run, at a point midway between the two sprockets, then compare your measurement to the value listed in this Chapter's Specifications **(see illustration)**. Since the chain will rarely wear evenly, rotate the rear wheel so that another section of chain can be checked; do this several times to check the entire length of chain. In some cases where lubrication has been neglected, corrosion and galling may cause the links to bind and kink, which effectively shortens the chain's length. If the chain is tight between the sprockets, rusty or kinked, it's time to renew it. If you find a tight area, mark it with felt pen or paint, and repeat the measurement after the bike has been ridden. If the chain's still tight in the same area, it may be damaged or worn. Because a tight or kinked chain can damage the transmission countershaft bearing, it's a good idea to renew it.

Adjustment – Trident, Sprint, Trophy, Speed Triple, Daytona, Thunderbird (to VIN 29155) and Tiger models

4 Rotate the rear wheel until the chain is positioned with the tightest point at the centre of its bottom run.
5 Slacken the chain adjuster clamp bolt on each side of the swingarm **(see illustration)**.
6 Insert a 12 mm Allen key (as supplied in the tool kit) in the hexagon socket of the chain adjuster on each side of the swingarm, and operating both keys simultaneously, rotate the chain adjusters until the specified chain freeplay is reached **(see illustration)**. Tighten the chain adjuster clamp bolts to the specified torque setting.
7 Following chain adjustment, check the markings on each chain adjuster in relation to

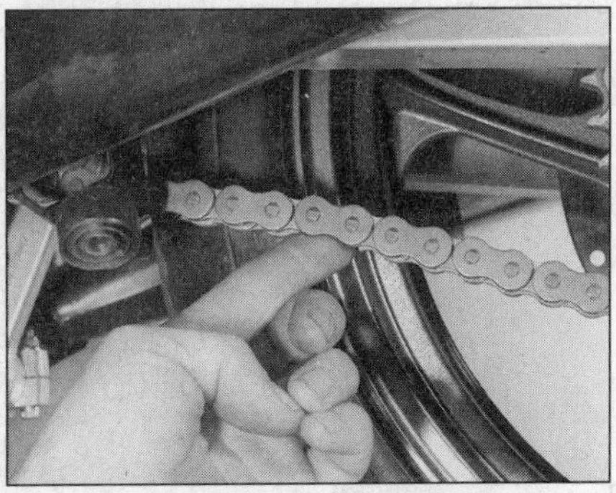
2.3 Measuring drive chain freeplay

2.5 Slacken the chain adjuster clamp bolts on each side . . .

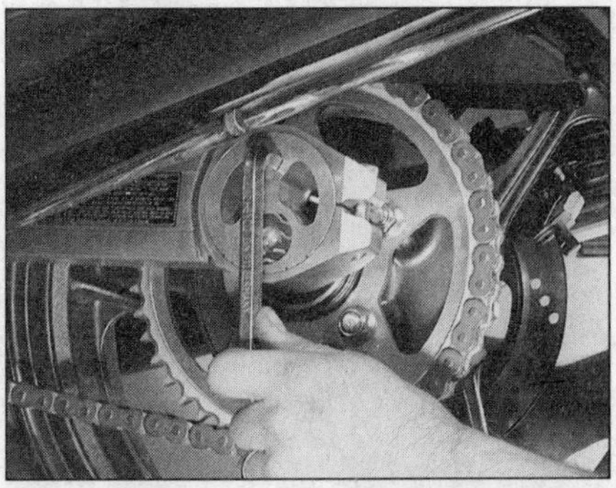
2.6 . . . and rotate the adjusters using the 12 mm Allen key supplied in the tool kit

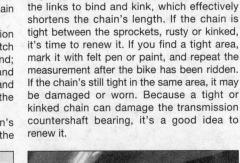

2.7 Wheel alignment can be checked via the alignment marks on the adjusters and swingarm (arrowed)

2.8a Wheel alignment can be adjusted after removing the spring clip from each side of the wheel axle . . .

2.8b . . . and slackening the axle bolt from the right side

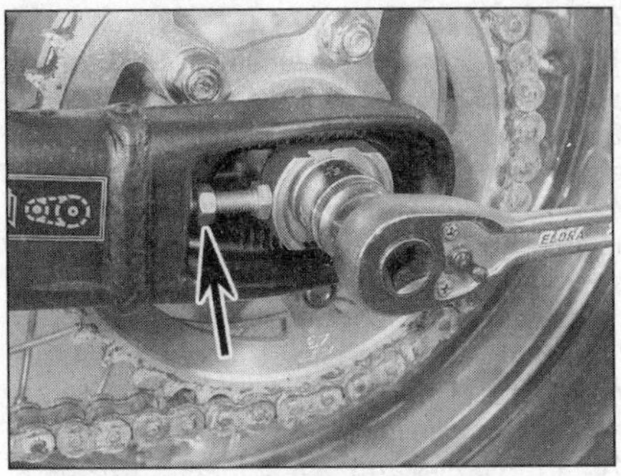

2.11 Back off the adjuster bolt nut (arrowed) and the axle nut

2.12a Adjusting the chain tension

2.12b Adjuster collar alignment groove (arrowed) and alignment marks on swingarm

the notch on the swingarm **(see illustration)**. It is important that the same mark on each adjuster aligns with the notch; if not, the rear wheel will be out of alignment with the front.

8 If there is a discrepancy in the chain adjuster positions, pick out the spring clip from each side of the wheel axle and slacken the axle bolt from the wheel right side **(see illustrations)**. Slacken the chain adjuster clamp bolt on each side of the swingarm **(see illustration 2.5)**. Using the 12 mm Allen key in the hexagon socket of the chain adjuster, rotate one of the chain adjusters so that its position is exactly the same as the other. Check the chain freeplay and readjust if necessary.

9 Tighten the axle bolt and chain adjuster clamp bolts to the specified torque settings. Secure the wheel axle with new spring clips, making sure they seat correctly.

Adjustment – Thunderbird (from VIN 29156), Thunderbird Sport, Adventurer and Legend TT models

10 Rotate the rear wheel until the chain is positioned with the tightest point at the centre of its bottom run.

11 Slacken the rear wheel axle nut off a few turns and slacken the chain adjuster bolt locknuts off a few turns on each side **(see illustration)**.

12 To tension the chain turn each adjuster bolt out **(see illustration)**. To slacken the chain turn the adjuster bolts inwards. Check that the rear wheel is pushed fully forwards, then check that the amount of chain slack is correct. It is important that each adjuster bolt is turned by the same amount to preserve correct wheel alignment. The swingarm has alignment marks scribed on each side and the groove in the top of each adjuster collar should align with the same mark on each side of the swingarm **(see illustration)**; if not, use the adjuster bolts to correct it.

HAYNES HiNT ***If you are in doubt about the wheel alignment, refer to Chapter 7 and check it using a gauge.***

13 When chain slack and wheel alignment are correct, tighten the adjuster bolt locknuts. Tighten the wheel axle nut to the specified torque setting.

1

Every 3000 miles (5000 km)

3 Idle speed – check

1 The idle speed should be checked and adjusted before and after the carburettors are synchronised, or if it is obviously too high or too low. Before adjusting the idle speed, make sure the valve clearances and spark plug gaps are correct. Also, turn the handlebars back-and-forth and see if the idle speed changes as this is done. If it does, the throttle cable may not be adjusted correctly, or may be worn out. This is a dangerous condition that can cause loss of control of the bike. Be sure to correct this problem before proceeding.

2 The engine should be at normal operating temperature, which is usually reached after 10 to 15 minutes of stop and go riding. Place the motorcycle on its stand and make sure the transmission is in neutral.

3 Turn the idle speed knob, which is located in a wire guide which extends from the left side of the carburettor assembly, until the idle speed listed in this Chapter's Specifications is obtained **(see illustration)**.

3.3 Idle speed screw is located on left side of carburettor assembly

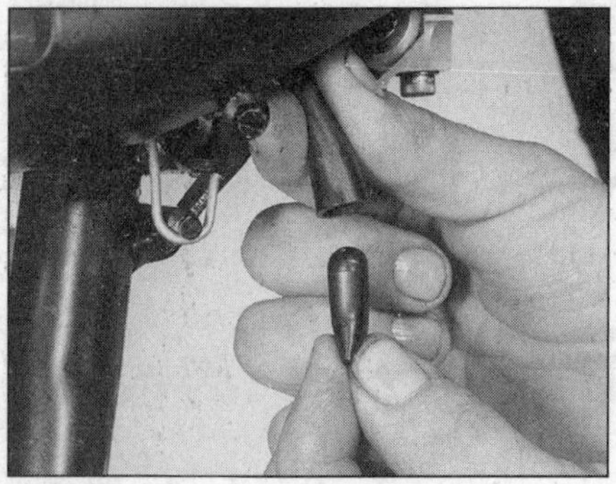

4.1 Remove plug to drain airbox

4 Snap the throttle open and shut a few times, then recheck the idle speed. If necessary, repeat the adjustment procedure.
5 If a smooth, steady idle can't be achieved, the fuel/air mixture may be incorrect. Refer to Chapter 4 for additional carburettor information.

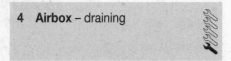

4 Airbox – draining

1 Trace the drain hose from the base of the airbox and remove the plug from its end **(see illustration)**. Allow any fluid to drain into a container. Install the plug when draining is complete.

5 Steering head bearings – freeplay check and adjustment

1 The steering head bearings can become dented, rough or loose during normal use of the machine. In extreme cases, worn or loose steering head bearings can cause steering wobble, which is potentially dangerous.

Check

2 Place the motorcycle on its centre stand. Where only a sidestand is fitted, an auxiliary stand will be needed to hold the motorcycle securely upright and allow the front wheel to be raised off the ground.

5.4 Checking for looseness in the steering head bearings

3 Point the front wheel straight-ahead and slowly move the handlebars from side-to-side; imperfections in the bearing races will be felt and the bars will not move smoothly.
4 Next, grasp the fork sliders and try to move them forward and backward **(see illustration)**. Any looseness in the steering head bearings will be felt as front-to-rear movement of the forks. If play is felt in the bearings, adjust the steering head as follows.

> **HAYNES HiNT** *Freeplay in the fork due to worn fork bushes can be misinterpreted for steering head bearing play – do not confuse the two*

Adjustment

Early Trident, Trophy and Daytona models

Note: *On early models, the bearing adjuster incorporates a pinch bolt to clamp it in place. This design was superseded by a separate adjuster nut and locknut on all later machines. It is possible to replace the early type adjuster with the two-piece arrangement used on later models.*
5 Position the bike as described in Step 2.
6 Slacken the fork clamp bolts in the top yoke **(see illustration 5.14)**. Access to these bolts may be restricted by the front brake and clutch master cylinders on certain models; if so, slacken off the master cylinder clamp bolts and rotate the cylinder slightly about the handlebar to provide access. On Daytona models also slacken the handlebar clamp bolts.
7 Slacken off the steering stem nut **(see illustration 5.15)** and bearing adjuster ring pinch bolt.
8 Rotate the adjuster ring clockwise to take up bearing freeplay and preload the bearings, vice versa to reduce preload **(see illustration)**. The object is to set the adjuster ring so that the bearings are under a very light loading, just enough to remove any freeplay.

Caution: Take great care not to apply excessive pressure because this will cause premature failure of the bearings.

9 When the setting is correct, tighten the pinch bolt to the specified torque setting to lock the adjuster ring's position. Tighten the fork clamp bolts and steering stem nut to their specified torque settings. On Daytona models, make sure the handlebar abuts the lug on the underside of the top yoke and tighten the handlebar clamp bolts to the specified torque setting.
10 If the brake and clutch master cylinders were disturbed, align the joining line of their clamps with the dot on the handlebars **(see illustration 5.19)**. Tighten the clamp top bolt first, then the lower, to the specified torque setting.
11 Re-check the head bearing adjustment as described in Steps 3 and 4.

All other models

Note: *Adjustment of the bearings with the top yoke in place requires the use of two very slim open-end spanners – these can be obtained under Pt. No. 3880140.*
12 Position the motorcycle as described in Step 2.
13 Remove the fuel tank for easier access to the adjuster nuts (see Chapter 4). On Trophy models from VIN 29156, remove the top yoke cover (it is retained by two press studs at the front and a single stud on the inside **(see illustrations)**), then slacken off each

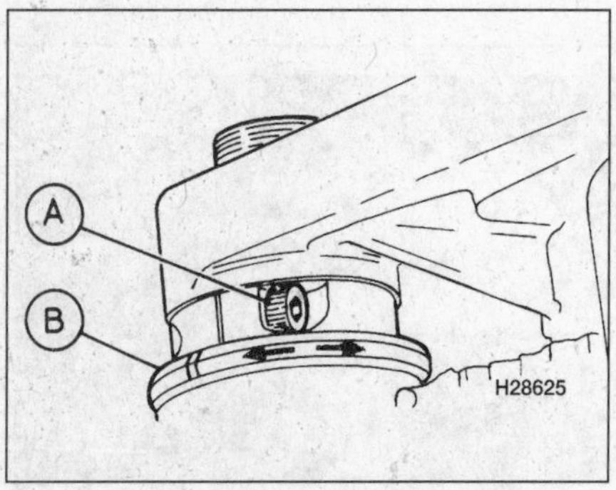

5.8 Bearing adjuster pinch bolt (A) and adjuster ring (B) – early models

5.13a Prise out the two press studs . . .

5.13b . . . and prise the inner stud (arrowed) out of the top yoke

5.13c Slacken the handlebar pinch bolt

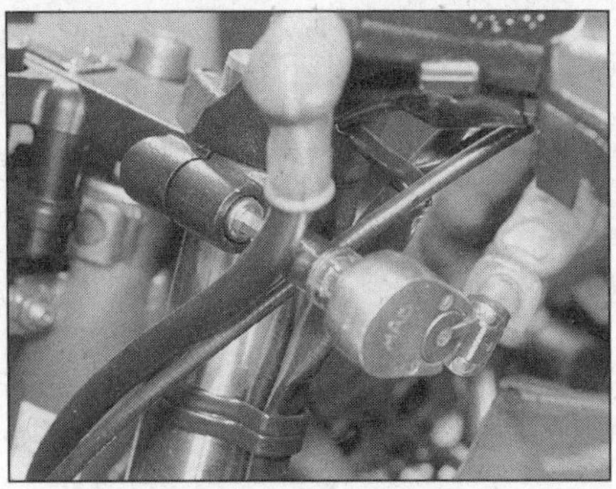

5.14 Slacken the fork top yoke clamp bolts

5.15 Slacken the steering stem nut

handlebar pinch bolt **(see illustration)**; there is no need to remove the handlebars.

14 Slacken the fork clamp bolts in the top yoke **(see illustration)**. Access to these bolts may be restricted by the front brake and clutch master cylinders on certain models; if so, slacken off the master cylinder clamp bolts and rotate the cylinder slightly about the handlebar to provide access. On Daytona and Speed Triple models, also slacken the handlebar clamp bolts.

15 Slacken off the steering stem nut **(see illustration)**. Unclamp the handlebars from the top yoke on Thunderbird, Thunderbird Sport, Adventurer, Legend TT and Tiger models to improve access to the steering stem nut.

16 Slacken off the bearing adjuster locknut, then rotate the adjuster nut beneath it to adjust bearing freeplay **(see illustration)**. Turn the adjuster nut clockwise to take up bearing freeplay and preload the bearings, vice versa to reduce preload. The object is to set the adjuster nut so that the bearings are under a very light loading, just enough to remove any freeplay.

Caution: Take great care not to apply excessive pressure because this will cause premature failure of the bearings.

17 When the setting is correct, hold the adjuster nut with one spanner and tighten the locknut against it with another spanner. **Note:** *The torque setting for the locknut can be applied if using the service tool specified in the* ***Note*** *above; the torque wrench locates in the square machined in the tool* ***(see illustrations).***

18 Tighten the fork clamp bolts (and the handlebar pinch bolts on later Trophy models) and steering stem nut to their specified torque settings. On Daytona and Speed Triple models, make sure the handlebar abuts the lug on the underside of the top yoke and tighten the handlebar clamp bolts to the specified torque setting. On Thunderbird, Thunderbird Sport, Adventurer, Legend TT and Tiger models, align the punch mark(s) on the handlebar with the mating surfaces of the handlebar clamps and tighten the clamp bolts to the specified torque.

19 If the brake and clutch master cylinders were disturbed, align the joining line of their clamps with the dot on the handlebars **(see illustration)**. Tighten the clamp top bolt first, then the lower, to the specified torque setting.

20 Re-check the head bearing adjustment as described in Steps 3 and 4.

21 Install the fuel tank (see Chapter 4).

6 Suspension – checks

1 The suspension components must be maintained in top condition to ensure rider safety. Loose, worn or damaged suspension parts decrease the bike's stability and control.

Front suspension

2 Carefully inspect the area around the fork seals for any signs of fork oil leakage **(see illustration)**. If leakage is evident, the seals

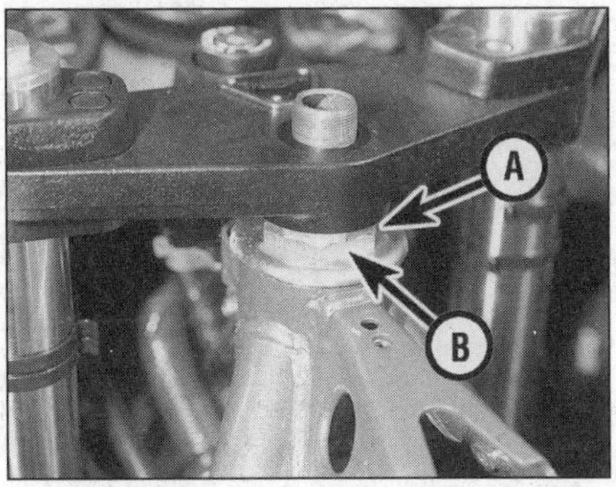

5.16 Back off the locknut (A) and adjust freeplay with the adjuster nut (B)

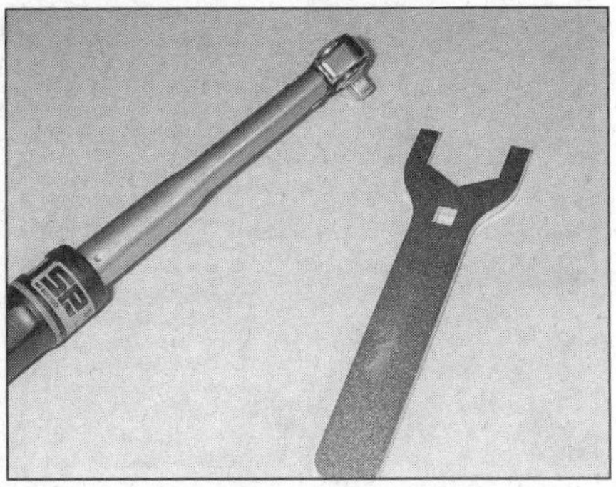

5.17a If the Triumph tool is available (right of photo) . . .

5.17b . . . the locknut can be secured to the specified torque

5.19 If the master cylinders were disturbed, align their clamp top joint with the dot (arrowed) on the handlebar

6.2 Inspect the area above the fork oil seal for oil leakage

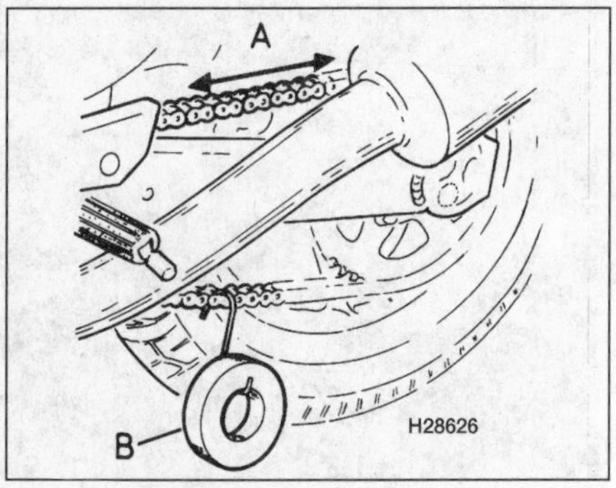

7.2a Drive chain stretch check
A 20-link length B Weight

must be renewed as described in Chapter 6. On Tiger models, slacken the gaiter clamp and pull the gaiter up off the fork slider to examine the seals.

Rear suspension

3 Inspect the rear shock for fluid leakage and tightness of its mountings. If leakage is found, the shock should be renewed.

4 Position the motorcycle on its centre stand; where only a sidestand is fitted, position the motorcycle on an auxiliary stand so that the rear wheel is off the ground. Grab the swingarm on each side, just ahead of the axle. Rock the swingarm from side to side – there should be no discernible movement at the rear. If there's a little movement or a slight clicking can be heard, make sure the swingarm pivot bolt is tight. If movement is still noticeable, the swingarm bearings or suspension linkage bearings require attention (see Chapter 6).

7 Drive chain – wear and stretch check

1 Check the entire length of the chain for damaged rollers, loose links and pins and renew the chain (and both sprockets) if damage is found.

2 If the chain has reached the end of its adjustment, it must be renewed. The amount of chain stretch can be measured by hanging a 10 to 20 kg weight midway between the sprockets on the chain's bottom run **(see illustration)**. Remove the chainguard for access to the top run of the chain. With the weight applied, measure along the top run the length of 20-links (from the centre of the 1st pin to the centre of the 21st pin) and compare with the service limit **(see illustration)**. Rotate the rear wheel so that several sections of the chain are measured, then calculate the average. If the chain exceeds the service limit it must be renewed (see Chapter 6). **Note:** *It is good practice to renew the chain and sprockets as a set.*

3 Remove the engine sprocket cover (see Chapter 6). Check the teeth on the engine sprocket and the rear wheel sprocket for wear **(see illustration)**.

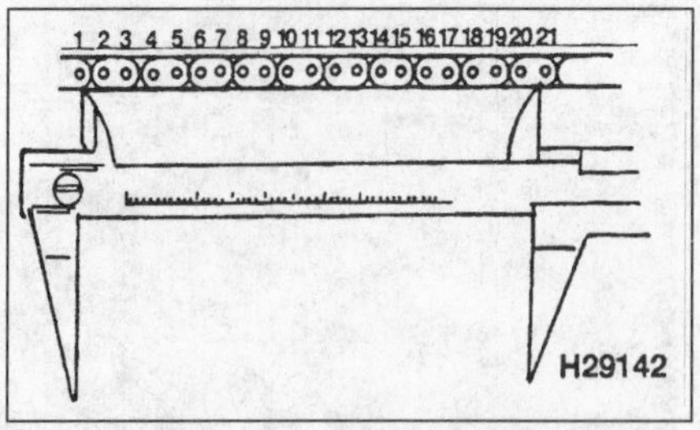

7.2b Measure the distance between the 1st and 21st pins to determine drive chain stretch

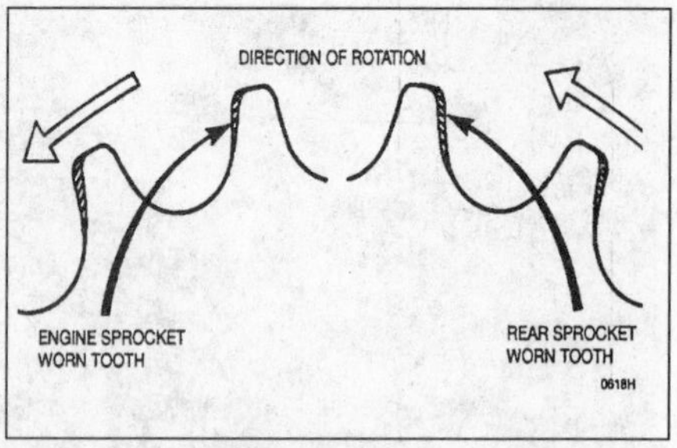

7.3 Check the engine and rear wheel sprockets for wear

4 Inspect the drive chain slider on the swingarm for excessive wear and renew it if necessary (see Chapter 6). On Tiger models check the condition of the chain slider block mounted to the frame; if the chain slider block is renewed, repeat the chain freeplay check described in Section 2.

8 Brake light switches – check

1 Make sure the brake light comes on when the front brake lever is operated, then check with the rear brake pedal depressed. Neither brake light switch is adjustable; if it fails to operate properly, and the fault cannot be traced to the bulbs or wiring, renew the switch (see Chapter 9).

9 Brake pads – wear check

1 It is possible on certain caliper types to view the pads with the caliper installed on the disc. However, it is advised that the caliper be removed to enable the pads to be viewed properly. Remove the two caliper mounting bolts and slide the caliper off the disc.

2 If the friction material has worn down so that the three grooves are no longer visible, ie so that friction material remaining is level with the base of the grooves, both pads must be renewed immediately **(see illustrations)**. **Note:** *If the front brake pads require renewal, note that the pads in both calipers must be renewed at the same time (models with twin discs).* The amount of friction material can be

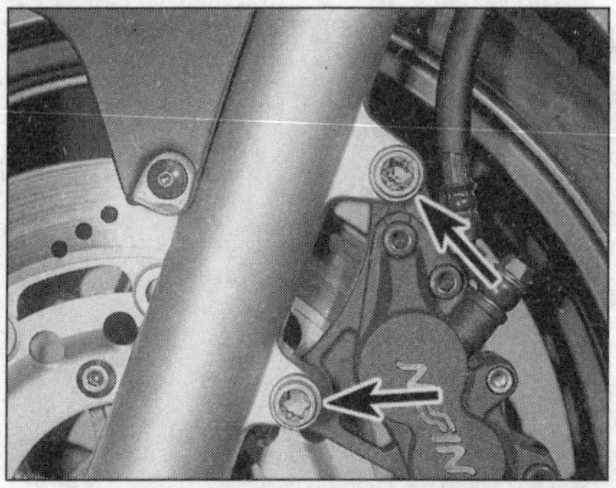

9.2a Remove the two mounting bolts (arrowed) to free the front brake caliper – type A caliper shown

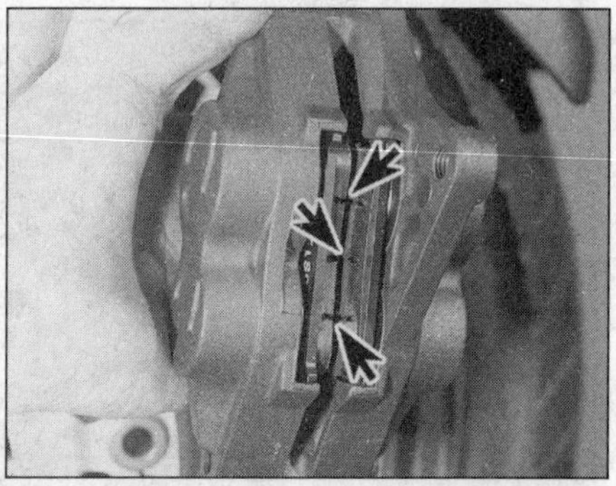

9.2b View pad friction material thickness via caliper mouth. Renew pads if wear grooves (arrowed) are no longer visible

9.2c Remove the two mounting bolts (arrowed) to free the rear brake caliper – type B caliper shown

9.2d Inspect the rear caliper pad condition via caliper mouth

measured to determine whether renewal is required (see the Specifications section of this Chapter). Tighten the caliper bolts to the specified torque (see Chapter 7 Specifications).

3 Refer to Chapter 7 for pad renewal.

10 Wheels and tyres – checks

Tyres

1 Check the tyre condition and tread depth thoroughly – see *'Daily (pre-ride) checks'*.

Wheels

2 The cast wheels used on Trident, Sprint, Trophy, Speed Triple and Daytona models are virtually maintenance free, but they should be kept clean and checked periodically for cracks and other damage. Never attempt to repair damaged cast wheels; they must be renewed. Check the valve rubber for signs of damage or deterioration and have it renewed if necessary. Also, make sure the valve stem cap is in place and tight.

3 On Thunderbird, Thunderbird Sport, Adventurer, Legend TT and Tiger models, visually check the spokes for damage, breakage or corrosion. A broken or bent spoke must be renewed immediately because the load taken by it will be transferred to adjacent spokes which may in turn fail.

4 If you suspect that any of the spokes are incorrectly tensioned, tap each one lightly with a screwdriver and note the sound produced. Properly tensioned spokes will make a sharp pinging sound, loose ones will produce a lower pitch and overtightened ones will be higher pitched. Unevenly tensioned spokes will promote rim misalignment – seek the help of a wheel building expert if this is suspected.

5 Support the motorcycle upright using an auxiliary stand. Check for any play in the bearings by pushing and pulling the wheel against the hub. Also rotate the wheel and check that it rotates smoothly. If any play is detectable in the hub, or if the wheel does not rotate smoothly (and this is not due to brake or transmission drag), the wheel bearings must be removed and inspected for wear or damage (see Chapter 7).

11 Battery – checks

Warning: Be extremely careful when handling or working around the battery. The electrolyte is very caustic and an explosive gas (hydrogen) is given off when the battery is charging.

Note: *This section does not apply to maintenance-free batteries, as fitted to the Trophy from VIN 71699.*

1 Remove the seat; on Thunderbird, Thunderbird Sport, Adventurer and Legend TT models also remove the right side panel (see Chapter 8).

2 Unhook the battery retaining strap and free the plastic tray. Remove the screws securing the battery cables to the battery terminals; remove the negative cable first, positive cable last **(see illustration)**.

3 On Trident, Sprint, Trophy, Speed Triple, Daytona and Tiger models, lift the battery upwards out of its holder **(see illustration)**. On Thunderbird, Thunderbird Sport, Adventurer and Legend TT models, remove the screw and unclip the side of the battery holder, being careful not to strain the fusebox and turn signal relay wiring **(see illustrations)**. Pull the vent hose off the battery and slide the battery out of its holder.

4 The electrolyte level is visible through the translucent battery case – it should be between the UPPER and LOWER level marks **(see illustration)**.

5 If the electrolyte is low, remove the cell caps and fill each cell to the upper level mark with distilled water. Do not use tap water (except in an emergency), and do not overfill. The cell holes are quite small, so it may help to use a clean plastic squeeze bottle with a small spout to add the water. Install the battery cell caps, tightening them securely.

6 Install the battery in a reverse of the removal sequence, making sure that its vent tube is properly connected and routed **(see illustration)**.

11.2 Remove the battery negative lead (A) first, then the positive lead (B)

11.3a On Trident, Sprint, Trophy, Speed Triple, Daytona and Tiger models, lift the battery out of its holder

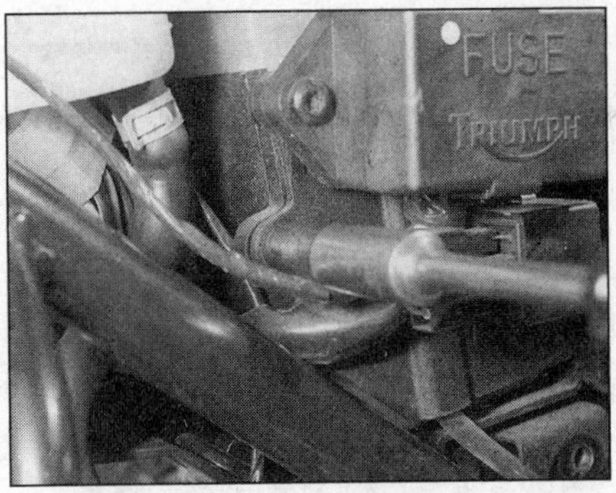

11.3b On Thunderbird, Thunderbird Sport, Adventurer and Legend TT models, remove the screw . . .

11.3c . . . and unclip the side of the battery holder

11.4 Electrolyte level must be between UPPER and LOWER marks on battery case

11.6 Battery vent tube is routed through hole in base of battery holder (arrowed)

Warning: It is important that the vent tube is not pinched or trapped at any point, because the battery may build up enough internal pressure during normal charging to explode – always refer to the routing label.

7 Reconnect the cables to the battery, attaching the positive cable first and the negative cable last. Make sure to install the insulating boot over both terminals. Install the plastic tray and battery strap.

8 If the machine is not in regular use, disconnect the battery and give it a refresher charge every month to six weeks, as described in Chapter 9.

HAYNES HiNT ***Battery corrosion can be minimised by applying a layer of petroleum jelly to the terminals after the cables have been connected.***

Every 6000 miles (10,000 km)

12 Engine – oil and filter change

1 Consistent routine oil and filter changes are the single most important maintenance procedure you can perform on a motorcycle. The oil not only lubricates the internal parts of the engine, transmission and clutch, but it also acts as a coolant, a cleaner, a sealant, and a protectant. Because of these demands, the oil takes a terrific amount of abuse and should be changed often with new oil of the recommended grade and type. Saving a little money on the difference in cost between a good oil and a cheap oil won't pay off if the engine is damaged.

12.4 Engine oil drain plug is located in sump

2 Before changing the oil and filter, warm up the engine so the oil will drain easily. Be careful when draining the oil, as the exhaust pipes, the engine, and the oil itself can cause severe burns.

3 Put the motorcycle on its centre stand; where no centre stand is fitted position the motorcycle on an auxiliary stand, or have an assistant hold it upright during the procedure to ensure that the oil drains fully. Position a clean drain tray below the engine. Unscrew the oil filler cap to vent the crankcase to act as a reminder that there is no oil in the engine.

4 Next, remove the drain plug from the sump and allow the oil to flow into the drain tray **(see illustration)**. Discard the sealing washer on the drain plug; it should be renewed whenever the plug is removed.

5 Unscrew the oil filter centre bolt and withdraw the filter assembly from the sump **(see illustration)**. Discard the filter element, but retain all other filter components.

6 Slip a new sealing washer over the drain plug. Fit the plug to the sump and tighten it to the specified torque setting. Avoid overtightening, as damage to the sump will result.

7 Install new O-rings on the centre bolt and cover **(see illustrations)**. Install the centre bolt through the cover, then install the coil spring and washer **(see illustration)**. Work the new oil filter on the centre bolt, having lubricated the filter seals with engine oil, then install the washer **(see illustrations)**. Install the oil filter assembly on the sump and tighten

12.5 Unscrew the oil filter centre bolt to free the filter assembly

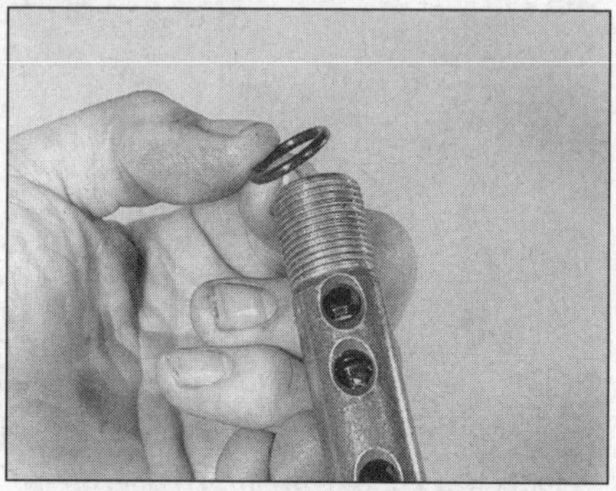

12.7a Install a new O-ring on the centre bolt . . .

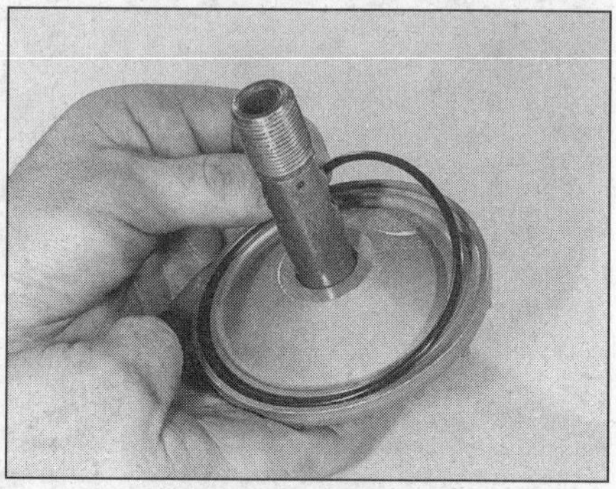

12.7b . . . and cover

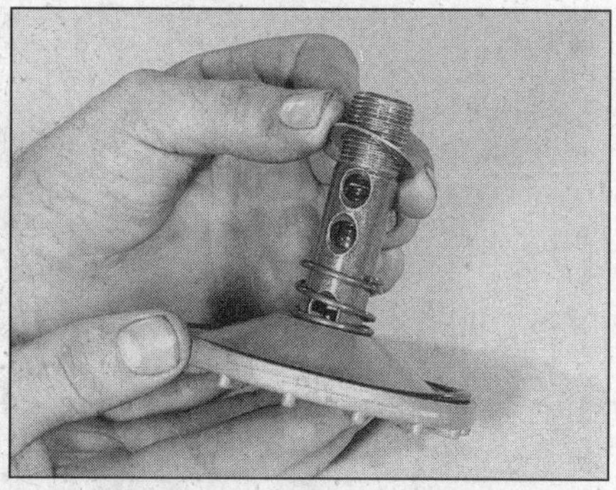

12.7c Install the coil spring and washer on the centre bolt . . .

12.7d . . . followed by the new filter . . .

12.7e . . . and washer

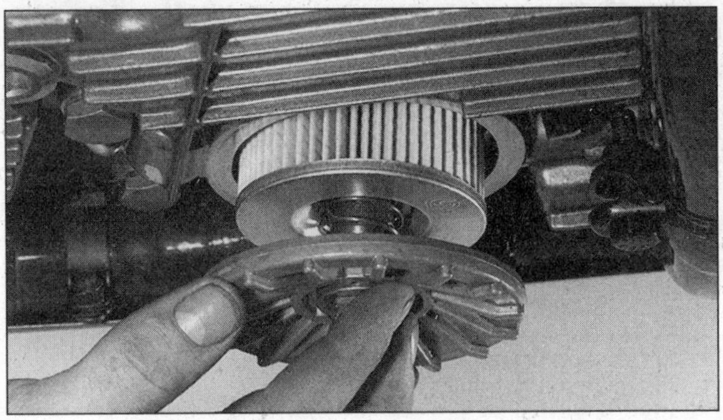

12.7f Install the filter assembly in the sump

13.3 Engine can be rotated with a ring spanner on the hexagon – rotate clockwise

the centre bolt to the specified torque **(see illustration)**.

8 Refill the crankcase to the proper level with the recommended type and amount of oil and install the filler cap. Start the engine and let it run for two or three minutes (make sure that the oil pressure light extinguishes after a few seconds). Shut it off, wait a few minutes, then check the oil level. If necessary, add more oil to bring the level up to the upper mark (see *'Daily (pre-ride) checks'*). Check around the drain plug and filter for leaks.

9 The old oil drained from the engine cannot be re-used and should be disposed of properly. Check with your local refuse disposal company, disposal facility or environmental agency to see whether they will accept the used oil for recycling. Don't pour used oil into drains or onto the ground.

HAYNES HiNT ***Check the old oil carefully – if it is very metallic coloured, then the engine is experiencing wear from break-in (new engine) or from insufficient lubrication. If there are flakes or chips of metal in the oil, then something is drastically wrong internally and the engine will have to be disassembled for inspection and repair. If there are pieces of fibre-like material in the oil, the clutch is wearing excessively and should be checked.***

OIL CARE – FOLLOW THE CODE
OIL BANK LINE
0800 66 33 66

Note: It is antisocial and illegal to dump oil down the drain. To find the location of your local oil recycling bank, call this number free.

In the USA, note that any oil supplier must accept used oil for recycling.

13 Valve clearances – check

1 The engine must be completely cool for this maintenance procedure, so let the machine sit overnight before beginning.

2 Remove the valve cover (see Chapter 2). Unscrew the spark plugs to allow the engine to be turned over easier.

3 The engine can be turned over by placing the motorcycle on its centre stand (or an auxiliary stand), selecting a high gear and rotating the rear wheel by hand. Alternatively, remove the crankshaft right cover; have a drain tray ready in case of oil loss. Rotate the crankshaft using a ring spanner on the large engine turning hexagon **(see illustration)**. If the latter approach is adopted, the fairing right lower panel must be removed on Trophy and Daytona models (see Chapter 8).

4 Make a chart or sketch of all twelve (3 cylinder) or sixteen (4 cylinder) valve positions so that all four valves for each cylinder can be identified.

5 Starting with cylinder No 1, rotate the engine until one pair of valves is completely closed, ie with their lobes pointing diametrically opposite the valve. At this point insert a feeler blade of the correct thickness (see Specifications) between each cam base and shim and check that it is a firm sliding fit **(see illustration)**. If it is not, use the feeler blades to obtain the exact clearance. Record the measured clearance on the chart.

6 Proceed to check all other clearances in the same way, noting that the specification differs for inlet and exhaust valves.

7 When all clearances have been measured and charted, identify whether the clearance on any valve falls outside of that specified. If it does, the shim between the tappet and camshaft must be changed for one of a different thickness.

8 Remove the camshafts to access the shims (see Chapter 2).

9 The shim size (eg 2.60) should be stamped on its face, however, it is recommended that the shim is measured to check that it has not worn **(see illustrations)**. Shims are available in 0.05 mm increments from 2.00 to 3.20 mm.

10 Use the shim selection chart, find where the measured valve clearance and existing

13.5 Measuring a valve clearance. Lobe must point diametrically opposite valve

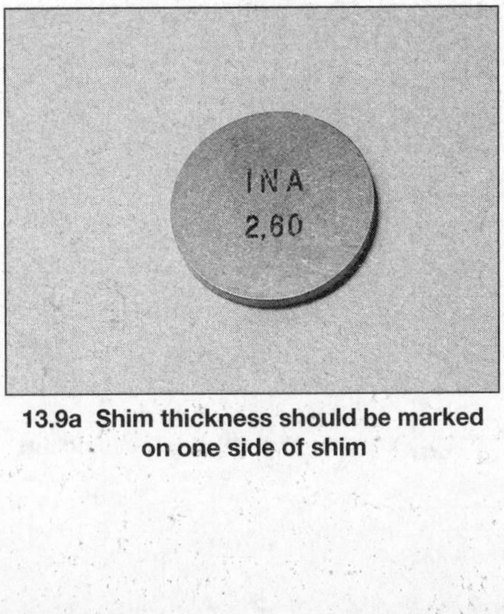

13.9a Shim thickness should be marked on one side of shim

13.9b Shim can be sized by direct measurement

MEASURED INTAKE VALVE CLEARANCE	MEASURED THICKNESS OF FITTED SHIM																								
	2.00	2.05	2.10	2.15	2.20	2.25	2.30	2.35	2.40	2.45	2.50	2.55	2.60	2.65	2.70	2.75	2.80	2.85	2.90	2.95	3.00	3.05	3.10	3.15	3.20
0.00-0.04			2.00	2.05	2.10	2.15	2.20	2.25	2.30	2.35	2.40	2.45	2.50	2.55	2.60	2.65	2.70	2.75	2.80	2.85	2.90	2.95	3.00	3.05	3.10
0.05-0.09		2.00	2.05	2.10	2.15	2.20	2.25	2.30	2.35	2.40	2.45	2.50	2.55	2.60	2.65	2.70	2.75	2.80	2.85	2.90	2.95	3.00	3.05	3.10	3.15
0.10-0.15	CORRECT CLEARANCE. NO CHANGE OF SHIM REQUIRED																								
0.16-0.20	2.05	2.10	2.15	2.20	2.25	2.30	2.35	2.40	2.45	2.50	2.55	2.60	2.65	2.70	2.75	2.80	2.85	2.90	2.95	3.00	3.05	3.10	3.15	3.20	
0.21-0.25	2.10	2.15	2.20	2.25	2.30	2.35	2.40	2.45	2.50	2.55	2.60	2.65	2.70	2.75	2.80	2.85	2.90	2.95	3.00	3.05	3.10	3.15	3.20		
0.26-0.30	2.15	2.20	2.25	2.30	2.35	2.40	2.45	2.50	2.55	2.60	2.65	2.70	2.75	2.80	2.85	2.90	2.95	3.00	3.05	3.10	3.15	3.20			
0.31-0.35	2.20	2.25	2.30	2.35	2.40	2.45	2.50	2.55	2.60	2.65	2.70	2.75	2.80	2.85	2.90	2.95	3.00	3.05	3.10	3.15	3.20				
0.36-0.40	2.25	2.30	2.35	2.40	2.45	2.50	2.55	2.60	2.65	2.70	2.75	2.80	2.85	2.90	2.95	3.00	3.05	3.10	3.15	3.20					
0.41-0.45	2.30	2.35	2.40	2.45	2.50	2.55	2.60	2.65	2.70	2.75	2.80	2.85	2.90	2.95	3.00	3.05	3.10	3.15	3.20						
0.46-0.50	2.35	2.40	2.45	2.50	2.55	2.60	2.65	2.70	2.75	2.80	2.85	2.90	2.95	3.00	3.05	3.10	3.15	3.20							
0.51-0.55	2.40	2.45	2.50	2.55	2.60	2.65	2.70	2.75	2.80	2.85	2.90	2.95	3.00	3.05	3.10	3.15	3.20								
0.56-0.60	2.45	2.50	2.55	2.60	2.65	2.70	2.75	2.80	2.85	2.90	2.95	3.00	3.05	3.10	3.15	3.20									
0.61-0.65	2.50	2.55	2.60	2.65	2.70	2.75	2.80	2.85	2.90	2.95	3.00	3.05	3.10	3.15	3.20										
0.66-0.70	2.55	2.60	2.65	2.70	2.75	2.80	2.85	2.90	2.95	3.00	3.05	3.10	3.15	3.20											
0.71-0.75	2.60	2.65	2.70	2.75	2.80	2.85	2.90	2.95	3.00	3.05	3.10	3.15	3.20												
0.76-0.80	2.65	2.70	2.75	2.80	2.85	2.90	2.95	3.00	3.05	3.10	3.15	3.20													
0.81-0.85	2.70	2.75	2.80	2.85	2.90	2.95	3.00	3.05	3.10	3.15	3.20														
0.86-0.90	2.75	2.80	2.85	2.90	2.95	3.00	3.05	3.10	3.15	3.20															
0.91-0.95	2.80	2.85	2.90	2.95	3.00	3.05	3.10	3.15	3.20																
0.96-1.00	2.85	2.90	2.95	3.00	3.05	3.10	3.15	3.20																	
1.01-1.05	2.90	2.95	3.00	3.05	3.10	3.15	3.20																		
1.06-1.10	2.95	3.00	3.05	3.10	3.15	3.20																			
1.11-1.15	3.00	3.05	3.10	3.15	3.20																				
1.16-1.20	3.05	3.10	3.15	3.20																					
1.21-1.25	3.10	3.15	3.20																						
1.26-1.30	3.15	3.20																							
1.31-1.35	3.20																								

H28659

13.10a Inlet valve shim selection chart

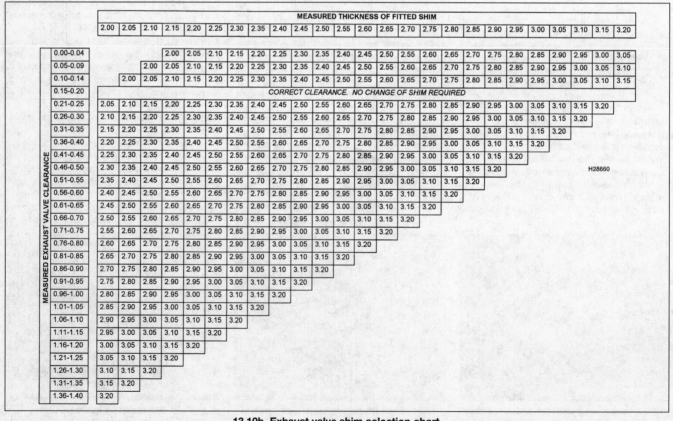

MEASURED EXHAUST VALVE CLEARANCE	MEASURED THICKNESS OF FITTED SHIM																								
	2.00	2.05	2.10	2.15	2.20	2.25	2.30	2.35	2.40	2.45	2.50	2.55	2.60	2.65	2.70	2.75	2.80	2.85	2.90	2.95	3.00	3.05	3.10	3.15	3.20
0.00-0.04				2.00	2.05	2.10	2.15	2.20	2.25	2.30	2.35	2.40	2.45	2.50	2.55	2.60	2.65	2.70	2.75	2.80	2.85	2.90	2.95	3.00	3.05
0.05-0.09			2.00	2.05	2.10	2.15	2.20	2.25	2.30	2.35	2.40	2.45	2.50	2.55	2.60	2.65	2.70	2.75	2.80	2.85	2.90	2.95	3.00	3.05	3.10
0.10-0.14		2.00	2.05	2.10	2.15	2.20	2.25	2.30	2.35	2.40	2.45	2.50	2.55	2.60	2.65	2.70	2.75	2.80	2.85	2.90	2.95	3.00	3.05	3.10	3.15
0.15-0.20	CORRECT CLEARANCE. NO CHANGE OF SHIM REQUIRED																								
0.21-0.25	2.05	2.10	2.15	2.20	2.25	2.30	2.35	2.40	2.45	2.50	2.55	2.60	2.65	2.70	2.75	2.80	2.85	2.90	2.95	3.00	3.05	3.10	3.15	3.20	
0.26-0.30	2.10	2.15	2.20	2.25	2.30	2.35	2.40	2.45	2.50	2.55	2.60	2.65	2.70	2.75	2.80	2.85	2.90	2.95	3.00	3.05	3.10	3.15	3.20		
0.31-0.35	2.15	2.20	2.25	2.30	2.35	2.40	2.45	2.50	2.55	2.60	2.65	2.70	2.75	2.80	2.85	2.90	2.95	3.00	3.05	3.10	3.15	3.20			
0.36-0.40	2.20	2.25	2.30	2.35	2.40	2.45	2.50	2.55	2.60	2.65	2.70	2.75	2.80	2.85	2.90	2.95	3.00	3.05	3.10	3.15	3.20				
0.41-0.45	2.25	2.30	2.35	2.40	2.45	2.50	2.55	2.60	2.65	2.70	2.75	2.80	2.85	2.90	2.95	3.00	3.05	3.10	3.15	3.20					
0.46-0.50	2.30	2.35	2.40	2.45	2.50	2.55	2.60	2.65	2.70	2.75	2.80	2.85	2.90	2.95	3.00	3.05	3.10	3.15	3.20						
0.51-0.55	2.35	2.40	2.45	2.50	2.55	2.60	2.65	2.70	2.75	2.80	2.85	2.90	2.95	3.00	3.05	3.10	3.15	3.20							
0.56-0.60	2.40	2.45	2.50	2.55	2.60	2.65	2.70	2.75	2.80	2.85	2.90	2.95	3.00	3.05	3.10	3.15	3.20								
0.61-0.65	2.45	2.50	2.55	2.60	2.65	2.70	2.75	2.80	2.85	2.90	2.95	3.00	3.05	3.10	3.15	3.20									
0.66-0.70	2.50	2.55	2.60	2.65	2.70	2.75	2.80	2.85	2.90	2.95	3.00	3.05	3.10	3.15	3.20										
0.71-0.75	2.55	2.60	2.65	2.70	2.75	2.80	2.85	2.90	2.95	3.00	3.05	3.10	3.15	3.20											
0.76-0.80	2.60	2.65	2.70	2.75	2.80	2.85	2.90	2.95	3.00	3.05	3.10	3.15	3.20												
0.81-0.85	2.65	2.70	2.75	2.80	2.85	2.90	2.95	3.00	3.05	3.10	3.15	3.20													
0.86-0.90	2.70	2.75	2.80	2.85	2.90	2.95	3.00	3.05	3.10	3.15	3.20														
0.91-0.95	2.75	2.80	2.85	2.90	2.95	3.00	3.05	3.10	3.15	3.20															
0.96-1.00	2.80	2.85	2.90	2.95	3.00	3.05	3.10	3.15	3.20																
1.01-1.05	2.85	2.90	2.95	3.00	3.05	3.10	3.15	3.20																	
1.06-1.10	2.90	2.95	3.00	3.05	3.10	3.15	3.20																		
1.11-1.15	2.95	3.00	3.05	3.10	3.15	3.20																			
1.16-1.20	3.00	3.05	3.10	3.15	3.20																				
1.21-1.25	3.05	3.10	3.15	3.20																					
1.26-1.30	3.10	3.15	3.20																						
1.31-1.35	3.15	3.20																							
1.36-1.40	3.20																								

H28660

13.10b Exhaust valve shim selection chart

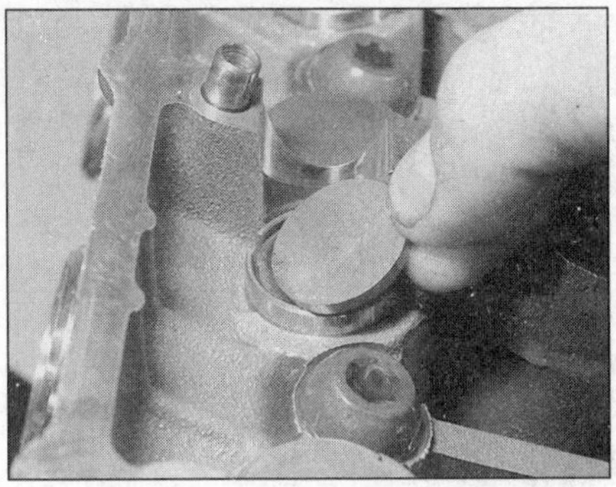

13.10c Install shim with its size marking downwards, towards the valve

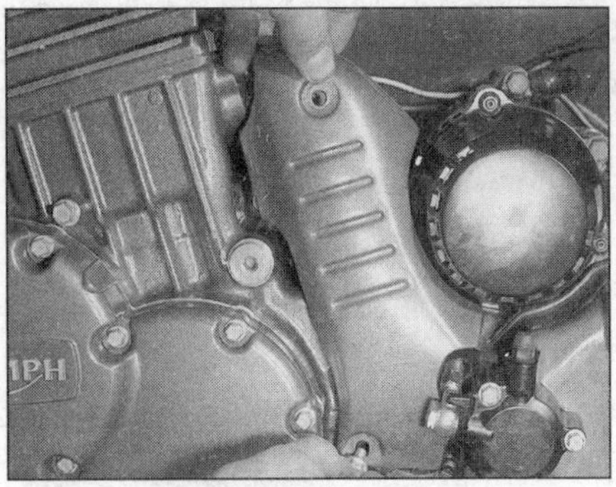

14.3a On later models, release the trim cover . . .

14.3b . . . for access to water pump coolant hose

shim thickness values intersect and read off the shim size required **(see illustrations)**. Note that the charts differ for inlet and exhaust valves so make sure you are using the correct one. Obtain and install the new shim, noting that its size marking should be installed downwards and that the shim should be lubricated with engine oil **(see illustration)**.

11 Install the camshafts as described in Chapter 2.

12 Check that the valve clearance is correct (see Step 5).

13 Install all disturbed components in a reverse of the removal sequence.

14 Cooling system – checks

Warning: The engine must be cool before beginning this procedure.

1 Check the coolant level as described in *'Daily (pre-ride) checks'*.

2 On Trophy and Daytona models, remove the lower fairing panels as described in Chapter 8. On Thunderbird, Thunderbird Sport, Adventurer and Legend TT models, remove the fuel tank (see Chapter 4).

3 A trim cover is fitted over the water pump-to-cylinder block hose on later models; release the cover by removing its two retaining screws **(see illustrations)**. On Speed Triple and later Trident models, the radiator top hose cover screw can be accessed after removing the side cover from the radiator; peel off the reflector and remove the two screws to free the radiator side cover.

4 The entire cooling system should be checked for evidence of leakage. Examine each rubber coolant hose looking for cracks, abrasions and other damage **(see illustration)**. Squeeze each hose at various points. They should feel firm, yet pliable, and return to their original shape when released. If they are dried out or hard, renew them.

5 Check for evidence of leaks at each cooling system joint. Tighten the hose clips carefully to prevent future leaks.

6 Check the radiator for leaks and other damage. Leaks in the radiator leave telltale scale deposits or coolant stains on the outside of the core below the leak. If leaks are noted, remove the radiator, detach the grille (see Chapter 3) and have it repaired or renew it.

Caution: Do not use a liquid leak-stopping compound to try to repair leaks.

7 Check the radiator fins for mud, dirt and insects, which may impede the flow of air through the radiator. If the fins are dirty, force water or low pressure compressed air through the fins from the rear of the radiator. If the fins are bent or distorted, straighten them carefully with a screwdriver.

8 The pressure cap is located in the top left side of the radiator on Trident, Sprint, Trophy, Speed Triple, Daytona and Tiger models. On Thunderbird, Thunderbird Sport, Adventurer and Legend TT models it is located in the radiator filler neck/thermostat housing **(see illustrations)**. On models with fairings, either reach up underneath the front of the fairing for access or remove the detachable inner panel; on Trophy models from VIN 29156 remove the left lower fairing panel (see Chapter 8). Remove the pressure cap by turning it anti-clockwise until it reaches a stop. If you hear a hissing sound (indicating there is still pressure in the system), wait until it stops. Now press down on the cap and continue turning the cap until it can be removed. Check the condition of the coolant in the system. If it is rust-coloured or if accumulations of scale are visible, drain, flush and refill the system with new coolant (see Section 27). Check the cap seal for cracks and other damage. If in doubt about the pressure cap's condition, have it tested by a Triumph dealer or renew it. Install the cap by turning it clockwise until it reaches the first stop, then push down on the cap and continue turning until it can turn no further.

9 Check the antifreeze content of the coolant with an antifreeze hydrometer. Sometimes coolant looks like it's in good condition, but might be too weak to offer adequate protection. If the hydrometer indicates a weak mixture, drain, flush and refill the system (see Section 27).

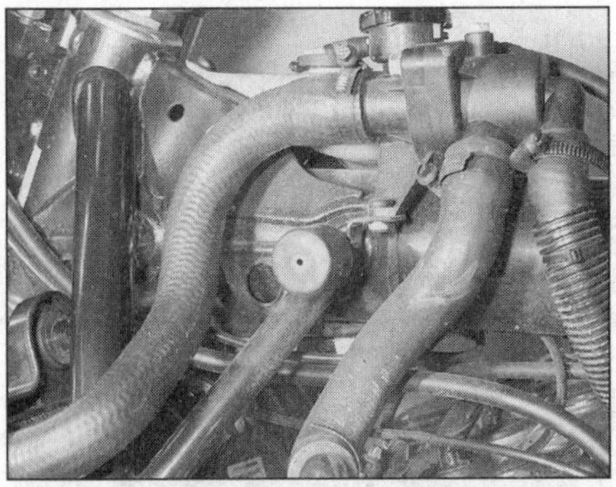

14.4 On Thunderbird, Thunderbird Sport, Adventurer and Legend TT models, fuel tank must be removed to check coolant hoses

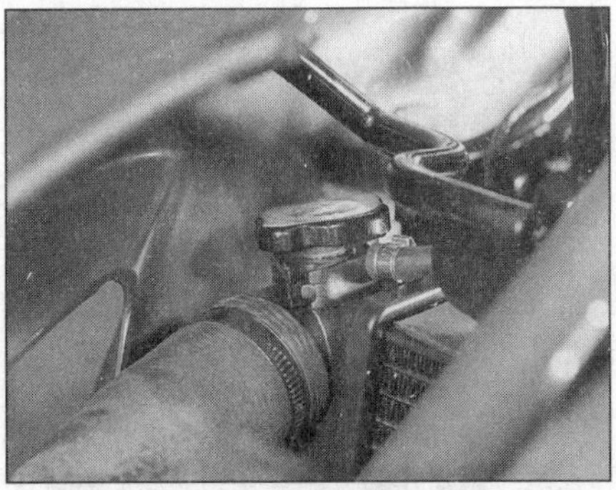

14.8a Pressure cap is located at top left corner of radiator . . .

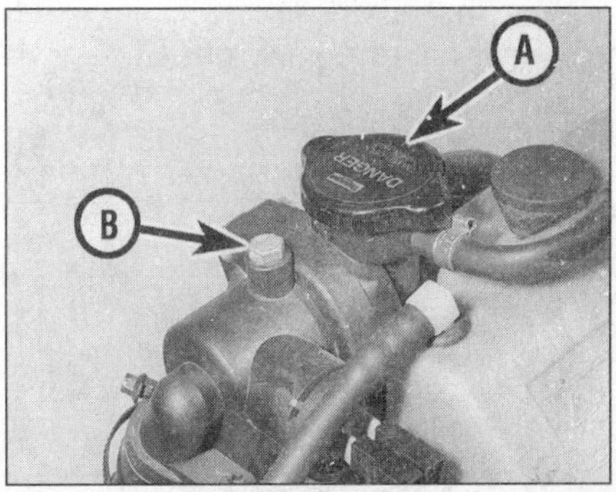

14.8b . . . or on the thermostat housing (A). Note coolant bleed screw (B)

HAYNES HiNT

Periodically, check the drainage hole on the underside of the water pump – leakage from this hole indicates failure of the pump's mechanical seal

10 Start the engine and let it reach normal operating temperature, then check for leaks again. As the coolant temperature increases, the fan should come on automatically and the temperature should begin to drop. If it does not, refer to Chapter 3 and check the fan and fan circuit carefully.

11 If the coolant level is consistently low, and no evidence of leaks can be found, have the entire system pressure checked by a Triumph dealer.

15 Throttle and choke cable – checks

Throttle cable

1 Make sure the throttle grip rotates easily from fully closed to fully open with the front wheel turned at various angles. The grip should return automatically from fully open to fully closed when released.

2 If the throttle sticks, this is probably due to a cable fault. Remove the cable as described in Chapter 4 and lubricate it as described in Section 21. Install the cable, routing it so that it takes the smoothest route possible. If this fails to improve the operation of the throttle, the cable must be renewed. Note that in very rare cases the fault could lie in the carburettors rather than the cable, necessitating the removal of the carburettors and inspection of the throttle linkage (see Chapter 4).

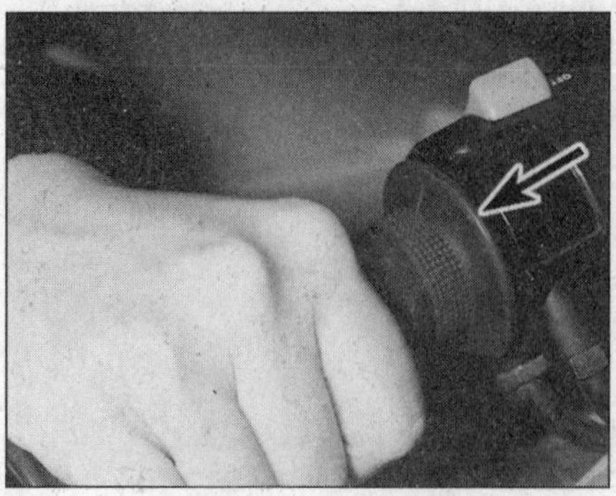

15.3 Throttle cable freeplay is measured in terms of twistgrip rotation at the grip flange (arrowed)

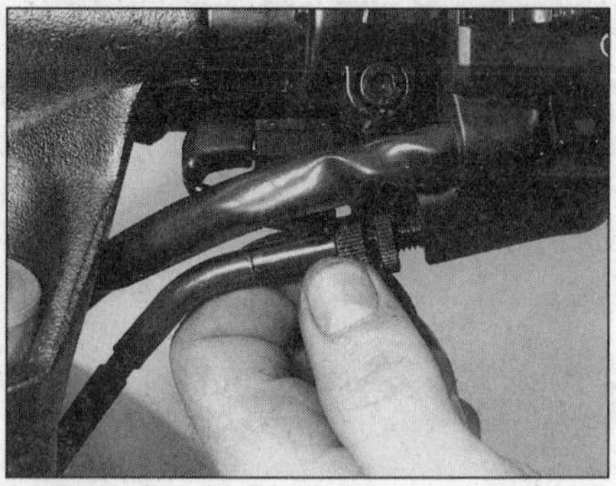

15.4a Small adjustments can be made using the throttle cable upper adjuster

3 With the throttle operating smoothly, check for a small amount of freeplay at the grip **(see illustration)**. The amount of freeplay in the throttle cable, measured in terms of twistgrip rotation, should be as given in this Chapter's Specifications. If adjustment is necessary, adjust idle speed first (see Section 3).

4 Slacken the lockwheel on the cable upper adjuster and rotate the adjuster until the correct amount of freeplay is obtained, then tighten the lockwheel against the adjuster **(see illustration)**. If it is not possible to obtain the correct freeplay with the upper adjuster, it will also be necessary to make adjustment at the lower adjuster, situated on the carburettors **(see illustration)**.

5 To gain access to the lower adjuster remove the fuel tank (see Chapter 4). Prior to making adjustment at the carburettor end of the cable, fully back off the lockwheel on the upper adjuster and screw the adjuster into the throttle housing; this will create more slack in the cable and allow for future cable adjustment to be taken up with the upper adjuster.

6 Where fitted, free the spring clip from the cable adjuster locknut on the lower adjuster. Slacken the adjuster locknut and rotate the adjuster until the correct freeplay is obtained at the throttle grip (see Step 3). When the freeplay is correct, tighten the lower adjuster locknut and where fitted, secure it with the spring clip. Tighten the upper adjuster lockwheel. Install the fuel tank (Chapter 4). **Note:** *Access to the lower adjuster is limited with the carburettors in situ – it is advised that they are detached from the inlet manifolds.*

7 Check that the throttle twistgrip operates smoothly and snaps shut quickly when released.

Caution: Turn the handlebars all the way through their travel with the engine idling. Idle speed should not change. If it does, the cable may be routed incorrectly. Correct this condition before riding the bike (see Chapter 4).

Choke cable

8 Operate the choke lever whilst observing the movement of the carburettor choke shaft on the left side of the carburettor assembly. There should be a small amount of freeplay (see Specifications) before the choke shaft contacts the choke plunger **(see illustration)**. To make adjustment, remove the fuel tank (see Chapter 4) and locate the in-line adjuster in the choke cable **(see illustration)**. Slacken its locknut and rotate the adjuster body as required; tighten the locknut.

9 If the choke does not operate smoothly this is probably due to a cable fault. Remove the cable as described in Chapter 4 and lubricate it as described in Section 21. Install the cable, routing it so it takes the smoothest route

15.4b Lower adjuster is situated on carburettor (arrowed)

15.8a Check for freeplay between the choke shaft and plunger tip (arrowed)

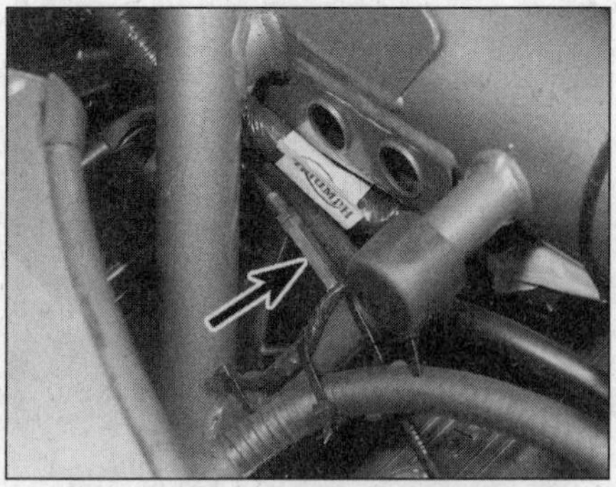

15.8b Choke cable adjustment is made using the in-line adjuster (arrowed)

possible. If this fails to improve the operation of the choke, the cable must be renewed. Note that in very rare cases the fault could lie in the carburettors rather than the cable, necessitating the removal of the carburettors and inspection of the choke plungers and choke shaft as described in Chapter 4.

16 Carburettors – synchronisation

Warning: Petrol is extremely flammable, so take extra precautions when you work on any part of the fuel system. Don't smoke or allow open flames or bare light bulbs near the work area, and don't work in a garage where a natural gas-type appliance is present. If you spill any fuel on your skin, rinse it off with soap and water. When you perform any work on the fuel system, wear safety glasses and have a fire extinguisher suitable for a Class B type fire (flammable liquids) on hand.

Warning: Take great care not to burn your hand on the hot engine when accessing the gauge take-off points on the inlet manifolds. Do not allow exhaust gases to build up in the work area; either perform the check outside or use an exhaust gas extraction system.

1 Carburettor synchronisation is simply the process of adjusting the carburettors so they pass the same amount of fuel/air mixture to each cylinder. This is done by measuring the vacuum produced in each cylinder. Carburettors that are out of synchronisation will result in decreased fuel mileage, increased engine temperature, less than ideal throttle response and higher vibration levels.

2 To properly synchronise the carburettors, you will need a set or three or four (according to the number of cylinders) vacuum gauges or a manometer (see the 'Specialist Tools' section of *Tools and Workshop Tips* in the Reference section at the end of this Manual). If you don't have access to either of these test instruments, leave the task to a Triumph dealer.

3 Position the bike on its centrestand; where only a sidestand is fitted, support the bike using an auxiliary stand. Start the engine and let it run until it reaches normal operating temperature, then shut it off.

16.7 Position the vacuum gauges where they can be easily seen

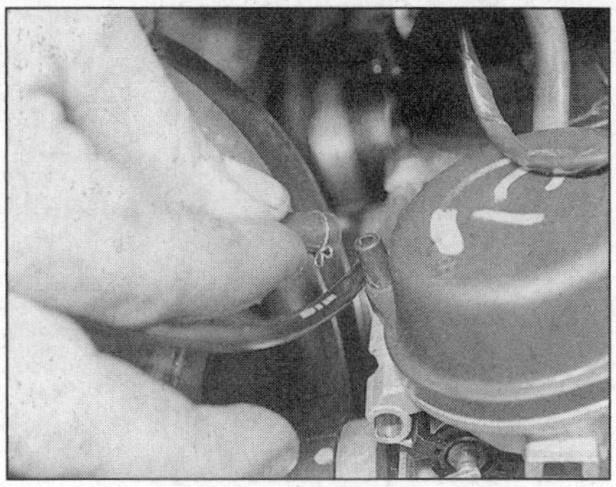

16.5 Disconnect the fuel tap vacuum pipe from No. 3 carburettor (Mikuni carburettor shown)

4 Remove the fuel tank (see Chapter 4).

5 Disconnect the fuel tap vacuum hose from the vacuum take-off stub of No. 3 carburettor **(see illustration)**. **Note:** *This does not apply to Thunderbird, Thunderbird Sport, Adventurer, Legend TT or Tiger models which have a gravity-fed fuel tap.*

6 On California models, disconnect the evaporative loss system hoses from the vacuum take-off stubs, having labelled them for easy reconnection. On all other models, remove the blanking caps from the vacuum take-off stubs **(see illustration)**.

7 Connect the gauge hoses to the take-off stubs. Make sure there are no air leaks as false readings will result. Position the vacuum gauges across the instruments or steering head so that they are horizontal **(see illustration)**. The manometer usually has a strap which enables it to be hung from the handlebar.

8 Arrange a temporary fuel supply, either by using a small temporary tank or by using extra long fuel pipes to the now remote fuel tank on a nearby bench. Turn the fuel tap to the PRI position (the ON position on Thunderbird, Thunderbird Sport, Adventurer, Legend TT and Tiger models).

9 Start the engine and make sure the idle speed is correct. If it isn't, adjust it (see Section 3). If the gauges are fitted with damping adjustment, set this so that the needle flutter is just eliminated but so that they can still respond to small changes in pressure.

16.11 Synchronising screw locations on 3 cylinder engine (arrowed)

16.6 Disconnect the caps from vacuum take-off points on the other carburettors (Keihin carburettor shown)

10 The vacuum readings for all of the cylinders should be the same, or at least within the tolerance listed in this Chapter's Specifications. If the vacuum readings vary, adjust as necessary. Cylinder No. 2 is the base carburettor on 3 cylinder engines, and cylinder No. 3 on 4 cylinder engines. Set the base carburettor using the idle adjuster screw, then balance all other carburettors to its setting as follows using the synchronisation screws.

11 The carburettors are adjusted by the two (3 cylinder engines) or three (4 cylinder engines) screws situated in-between each carburettor, in the throttle linkage **(see illustration)**. **Note:** *Do not press down on the screws whilst adjusting them, otherwise a false reading will be obtained.* When all the carburettors are synchronised, open and close the throttle quickly to settle the linkage, and recheck the gauge readings, readjusting if necessary.

12 When the adjustment is complete, recheck the vacuum readings and idle speed, then stop the engine. Remove the vacuum gauge or manometer. Install the blanking caps, fuel tap vacuum hose and evaporative loss hoses (as applicable).

13 Detach the temporary fuel supply and install the fuel tank (see Chapter 4).

17 Fuel system – checks

Warning: Petrol is extremely flammable, so take extra precautions when you work on any part of the fuel system. Don't smoke or allow open flames or bare light bulbs near the work area, and don't work in a garage where a natural gas-type appliance is present. If you spill any fuel on your skin, rinse it off with soap and water. When you perform any work on the fuel system, wear safety glasses and have a fire extinguisher suitable for a Class B type fire (flammable liquids) on hand.

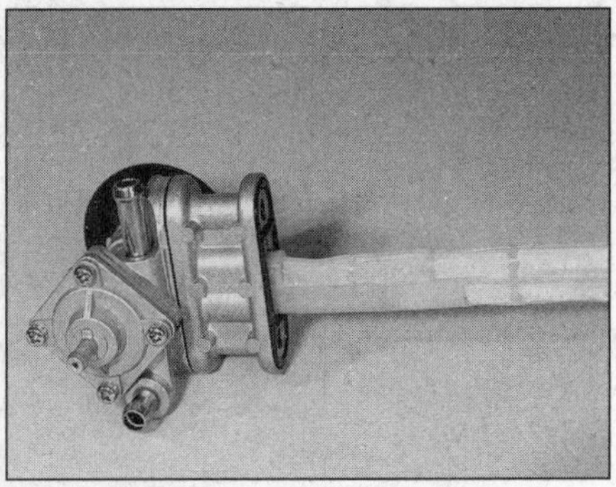

17.3 Fuel tap incorporates a gauze filter – vacuum tap shown

17.4a Release its clip and pull the fuel hose off the carburettor union

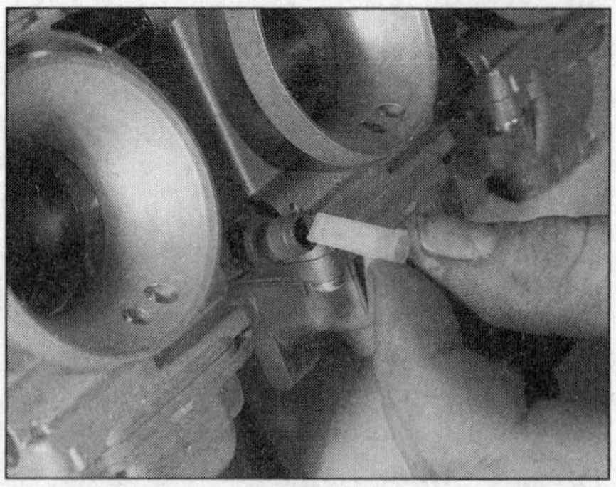

17.4b Slip the fuel filter out of the union

Check

1 Remove the fuel tank (see Chapter 4) and check the fuel hose(s), vacuum hose (where fitted) and breather hose for signs of damage; in particular check that there is no leakage from the fuel hose(s). Renew any hoses which are cracked or deteriorated.

Filter cleaning

2 Although not part of the maintenance schedule, cleaning of the fuel filters is advised after a particularly high mileage has been covered. It is also necessary if fuel starvation is suspected.

3 The fuel tap incorporates a gauze type filter inside the fuel tank **(see illustration)**. Remove the fuel tap as described in Chapter 4 and clean the filter being careful not to tear the gauze.

4 A gauze filter is fitted in the fuel delivery hose T-piece(s) on the carburettors. Remove the fuel tank (see Chapter 4) and disconnect the fuel hose where it joins the T-piece union on the carburettors; note that the Thunderbird, Thunderbird Sport, Adventurer, Legend TT and Tiger have a single fuel delivery hose, and all other models have two **(see illustration)**. Remove the gauze filter from the union and clean it **(see illustration)**. Install the filter and secure the hose with its clip. Install the fuel tank (see Chapter 4) and check that there is no leakage from the fuel hose(s).

18 Evaporative loss system – check (California only)

1 This system is installed on California models to conform to stringent state emission control standards. It is explained in greater detail in Chapter 4.

2 To begin the inspection of the system, remove the seat and fuel tank (see Chapters 8 and 4). Refer to the vacuum hose routing diagram on the frame, and trace the hoses between the system components, looking for signs of cracking, perishing or other damage. Any such hoses must be renewed.

3 Check the charcoal canister for damage or fuel leakage. The canister is mounted beneath the rear mudguard on Trident, Sprint, Trophy, Speed Triple, Daytona and Tiger models and inside the auxiliary air chamber on Thunderbird, Thunderbird Sport, Adventurer and Legend TT models.

19 Spark plugs – gap check

1 This motorcycle is equipped with spark plugs that have 12 mm threads and an 18 mm wrench hex. Make sure your spark plug socket is the correct size before attempting to remove the plugs, a suitable one is supplied in the motorcycle's tool kit and is operated by the 12 mm Allen key also contained in the tool kit.

2 Remove the seat and disconnect the battery negative lead.

3 Remove the fuel tank (see Chapter 4).

4 Remove the valve cover cowls on Trident, Sprint, Trophy, Speed Triple, Daytona and Tiger models; they are secured by two screws **(see illustration)**.

5 Clean the area around the valve cover and plug caps to prevent any dirt falling into the spark plug channels.

6 Pull the spark plug caps off the spark plugs, having checked that the cylinder location is marked on each lead, and using a deep socket type wrench, unscrew them from the cylinder head **(see illustrations)**. Lay the plugs out in relation to their cylinder number; if any plug shows up a problem it will then be easy to identify the troublesome cylinder.

7 Inspect the electrodes for wear. Both the centre and side electrodes should have square edges and the side electrode should be of uniform thickness. Look for excessive deposits and evidence of a cracked or chipped insulator around the centre electrode. Compare your spark plugs to the colour spark plug reading chart on the inside rear cover.

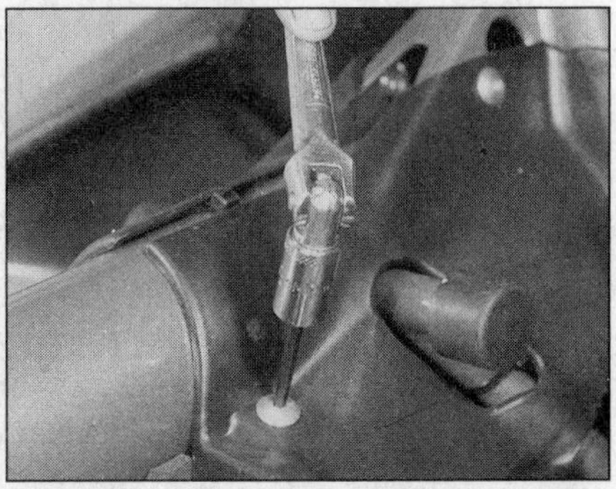

19.4 Valve cover cowls are secured by two screws

19.6a Pull the spark plug caps out of the valve cover

19.6b Use the 12 mm Allen key supplied in the tool kit together with the plug spanner to unscrew the spark plugs

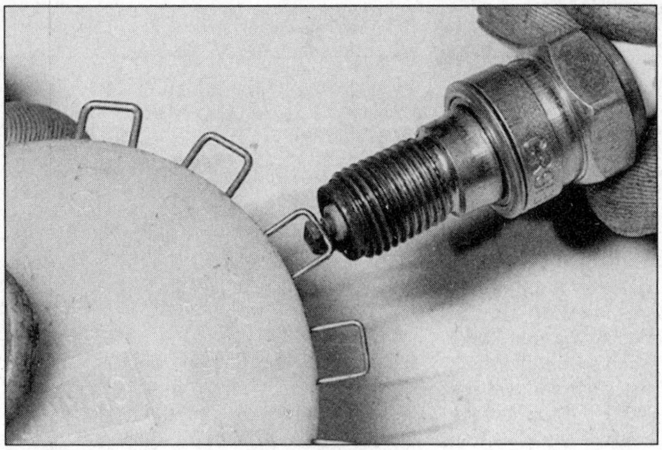

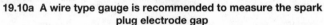

19.10a A wire type gauge is recommended to measure the spark plug electrode gap

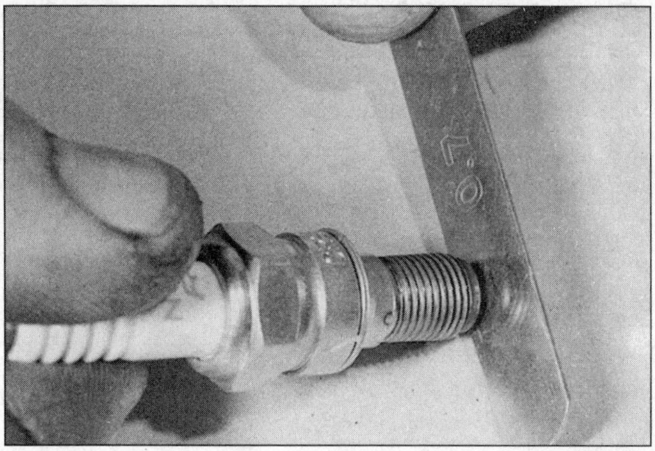

19.10b Using a feeler blade to measure spark plug electrode gap

Check the threads, the washer and the ceramic insulator body for cracks and other damage.

8 If the electrodes are not excessively worn, and if the deposits can be easily removed with a wire brush, the plugs can be regapped and re-used (if no cracks or chips are visible in the insulator). If in doubt concerning the condition of the plugs, renew them, as the expense is minimal.

9 Cleaning spark plugs by sandblasting is permitted, provided you clean the plugs with a high flash-point solvent afterwards.

10 Before installing new plugs, make sure they are the correct type and heat range. Check the gap between the electrodes, as they are not preset. For best results, use a wire-type gauge rather than a flat (feeler) gauge to check the gap. If the gap must be adjusted, bend the side electrode only and be very careful not to chip or crack the insulator nose **(see illustrations)**. Make sure the washer is in place before installing each plug.

11 Since the cylinder head is made of aluminium, which is soft and easily damaged, thread the plugs into the heads by hand. Once the plugs are finger-tight, the job can be finished with a socket (see ***Haynes Hint***). Tighten the spark plugs to the specified torque listed in this Chapter's Specifications; do not over-tighten them.

12 Reconnect the spark plug caps and reinstall all disturbed components.

HAYNES HiNT

Since the plugs are deeply recessed, slip a short length of hose over the end of the plug to use as a tool to thread it into place. The hose will grip the plug well enough to turn it, but will start to slip if the plug begins to cross-thread in the hole – this wili prevent damaged threads and the resultant repair costs.

20 Nuts and bolts – tightness check

1 Since vibration of the machine tends to loosen fasteners, all nuts, bolts, screws, etc. should be periodically checked for proper tightness.

2 Pay particular attention to the following:

Spark plugs
Engine oil drain plug
Gearchange pedal bolt
Footrest and stand bolts
Engine mounting bolts
Shock absorber mounting bolts
Handlebar and yoke bolts
Rear suspension linkage bolts
Front axle and clamp bolts
Rear axle bolt
Exhaust system bolts/nuts

3 If a torque wrench is available, use it along with the torque specifications at the beginning of this, or other Chapters.

21 Stand, lever pivots and cables – lubrication

1 Since the controls, cables and other components of a motorcycle are exposed to the elements, they should be lubricated periodically to ensure safe and trouble-free operation.

2 The footrests, clutch and brake levers, brake pedal, gearchange lever linkage (where applicable) and stand pivots should be lubricated frequently. In order for the lubricant to be applied where it will do the most good, the component should be disassembled. However, if and aerosol cable lubricant is being used, it can be applied to the pivot joint gaps and will usually work its way into the areas where friction occurs. If motor oil or light grease is being used, apply it sparingly as it may attract dirt (which could cause the controls

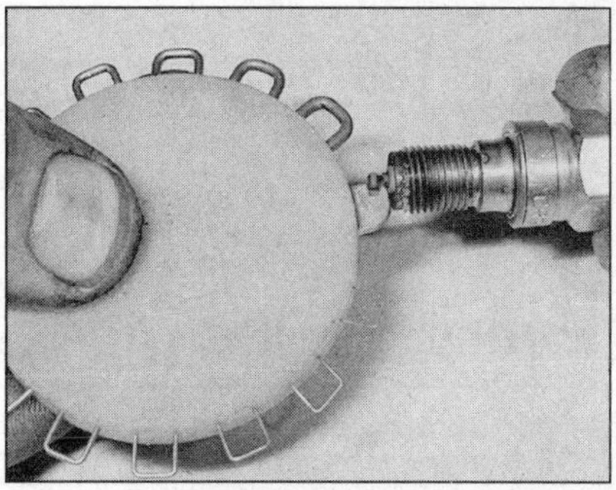

19.10c Electrode gap is adjusted by bending the side electrode

to bind or wear at an accelerated rate). **Note:** *One of the best lubricants for the control lever pivots is a dry-film lubricant (available from many sources by different names).*

3 To lubricate the cables, disconnect the relevant cable at its upper end, then lubricate the cable with a cable luber clamp **(see illustration)**. See Chapter 4 for the choke and throttle cable removal procedures.

4 The speedometer cable should be removed from its housing and lubricated with motor oil or cable lubricant. Do not lubricate the upper few inches of the cable as the lubricant may travel up into the speedometer head.

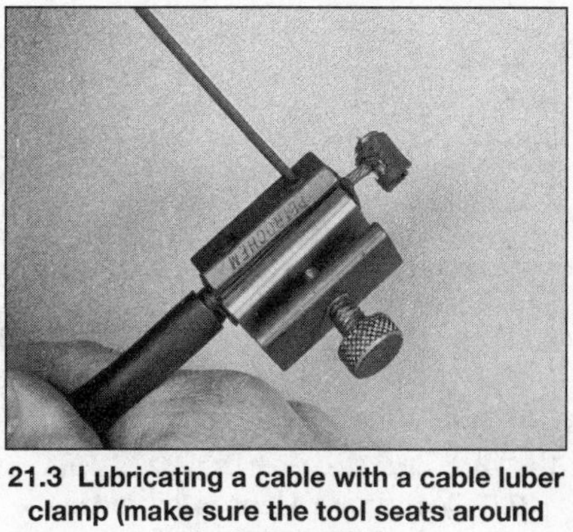

21.3 Lubricating a cable with a cable luber clamp (make sure the tool seats around the inner cable)

1

Every 12,000 miles (20,000 km)

22 Clutch fluid – change

Or every two years

1 Refer to the clutch bleeding section in Chapter 2, noting that all old fluid must be pumped from the fluid reservoir and hydraulic line before filling with new fluid.

23 Spark plugs – renewal

See *'Spark plug gap check'* under the 6000 mile (10,000 km) heading for details.

24 Front forks – oil change

1 Since oil drain plugs are not fitted, the forks must be removed from the yokes (see Chapter 6, Section 6) and the top bolt, spacer (where applicable), spring seat and spring removed; follow the procedure in Chapter 6, Section 7 to remove these components, noting that there is no need to slacken the damper rod bolt.

2 Invert the fork and slowly pump the fork tube and slider to expel as much of the damping oil as possible. Refer to the reassembly part of Chapter 6, Section 7 and add the new fork oil, check its level then refit the spring, spring seat, spacer (where fitted) and top bolt as described. Details of the oil type, quantity and level are given in the Specifications at the beginning of Chapter 6.

25 Steering head bearings – greasing

Or every two years

1 Disassemble the steering head for re-greasing of the bearings. Refer to Chapter 6 for details.

26 Brake fluid – change

Or every two years

1 Refer to the brake bleeding section in Chapter 7, noting that all old fluid must be pumped from the fluid reservoir and hydraulic line before filling with new fluid.

HAYNES HiNT ***Old brake fluid is invariably much darker in colour than new fluid, making it easy to see when all old fluid has been expelled from the system.***

Every 18,000 miles (30,000 km)

27 Coolant – change

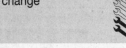

Or every two years

Warning: Let the engine cool completely before starting. Also, don't allow antifreeze to come into contact with your skin or the painted surfaces of the motorcycle. Rinse off spills immediately with plenty of water. Antifreeze is highly toxic if ingested. Never leave antifreeze lying around in an open container or in puddles on the floor; children and pets are attracted by its sweet smell and may drink it. Check with local authorities about disposing of antifreeze. Many communities have collection centres which will see that antifreeze is disposed of safely. Antifreeze is also combustible, so don't store it near open flames.

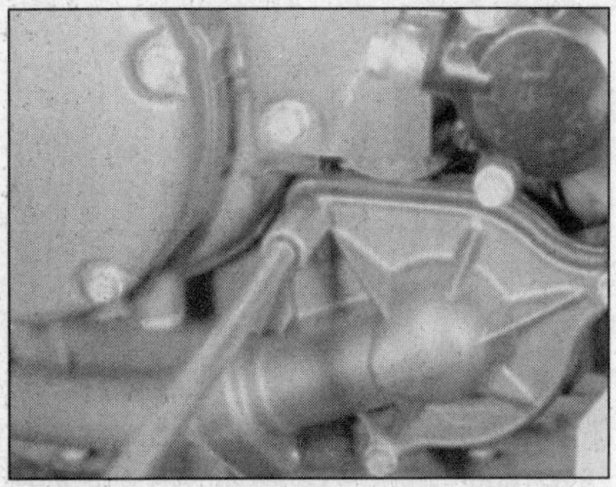

27.2 Coolant drain plug is located in the water pump

Draining

1 On Trophy, Daytona, Sprint and Tiger models, remove the fairing panels necessary to provide easy access to the radiator pressure cap (see Chapter 8). On Thunderbird, Thunderbird Sport, Adventurer and Legend TT models, remove the fuel tank (see Chapter 4).

2 Position a suitable container beneath the water pump, then remove the drain plug and sealing washer from the pump cover **(see illustration)**.

HAYNES HiNT

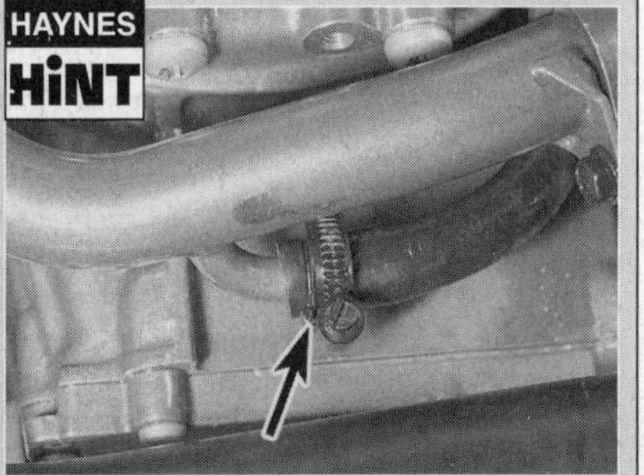

Slacken its clamp and pull the air bleed hose off the metal coolant pipe – this is the lowest point in the system, and will allow the coolant to drain fully

3 Remove the pressure cap by turning it anti-clockwise until it reaches a stop. If you hear a hissing sound (indicating there is still pressure in the system), wait until it stops. Now press down on the cap and continue turning the cap until it can be removed. As the cap is removed, the flow of coolant will increase – be prepared for this.

4 Have the container to hand, and remove the water jacket drain plug and sealing washer from the cylinder block **(see illustration)**.

5 Drain the coolant reservoir. Refer to Chapter 3 for reservoir removal procedure. Wash out the reservoir with fresh water and re-install it.

Flushing

6 Flush the system with clean tap water by inserting a garden hose in the radiator filler

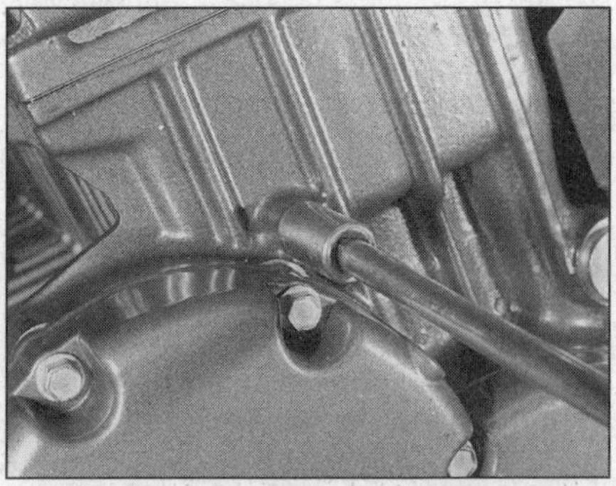

27.4 Remove drain plug from cylinder block to drain coolant from water jacket

neck. Allow the water to run through the system until it is clear and flows cleanly out of the drain holes.
7 Clean the drain holes, then install the drain plugs and sealing washers.
8 Fill the cooling system with clean water mixed with a flushing compound. Make sure the flushing compound is compatible with aluminium components, and follow the manufacturer's instructions carefully. Install the pressure cap on the radiator. On Thunderbird, Thunderbird Sport, Adventurer and Legend TT models, install the fuel tank, noting that it need only be connected temporarily at this stage.
9 Start the engine and allow it reach normal operating temperature. Let it run for about ten minutes.
10 Stop the engine. Let it cool for a while, then cover the pressure cap with a heavy cloth and turn it anti-clockwise to the first stop, releasing any pressure that may be present in the system. Once the hissing stops, push down on the cap and remove it.
11 Drain the system once again.
12 Fill the system with clean water and repeat the procedure in Steps 9 through 11.

Refilling

13 Fit a new sealing washer to both drain plugs and tighten them to the specified torque.
14 On Thunderbird, Thunderbird Sport, Adventurer and Legend TT models, slacken the bleed screw on the thermostat housing **(see illustration 14.8b)**.
15 Fill the system with the proper coolant mixture via the radiator filler neck (see this Chapter's Specifications). **Note:** *Pour the coolant in slowly to minimise the amount of air entering the system.*
16 When the system is full (all the way up to the top of the radiator filler neck), install the pressure cap. On Thunderbird, Thunderbird Sport, Adventurer and Legend TT models, tighten the bleed screw when coolant runs out of it and the system is full.
17 Top-up the coolant reservoir to the UPPER level mark. On Thunderbird, Thunderbird Sport, Adventurer and Legend TT models, reconnect the fuel tank, noting that it need only be connected temporarily at this stage.
18 Start the engine and allow it to idle for 2 to 3 minutes. Flick the throttle twistgrip part open 3 or 4 times, so that the engine speed rises to approximately 4000 – 5000 rpm, then stop the engine. Any air trapped in the system should now have been expelled.
19 Let the engine cool, then remove the pressure cap as described in Step 10. Check that the coolant level is still up to the radiator filler neck. If it's low, add the specified mixture until it reaches the top of the filler neck. Reinstall the pressure cap.
20 Check the coolant level in the reservoir and top-up if necessary.
21 Check that there are no leaks from the cooling system. If all is well, install the fairing panels on Trophy, Daytona, Sprint and Tiger models (see Chapter 8). On Thunderbird, Thunderbird Sport, Adventurer and Legend TT models, install the fuel tank (see Chapter 4).
22 Do not dispose of the old coolant by pouring it down the drain. Instead pour it into a heavy plastic container, cap it tightly and take it into an authorised disposal site or garage – see **Warning** at the beginning of this Section.

Every 24,000 miles (40,000 km)

28 Airbox – renewal

1 The air inlet system on these machines does not have a renewable filter element. At the specified interval, the airbox must be renewed. Refer to Chapter 4 for removal and installation procedures.

29 Rear suspension linkage bearings – lubrication

Or every three years
1 Identify the grease nipple locations on the suspension linkage pivots and wipe any dirt off them and remove their caps **(see illustrations)**. Using a grease gun and the specified grease, work lubricant into all pivots.

30 Swingarm bearings – lubrication

Or every three years
1 The swingarm is equipped with grease

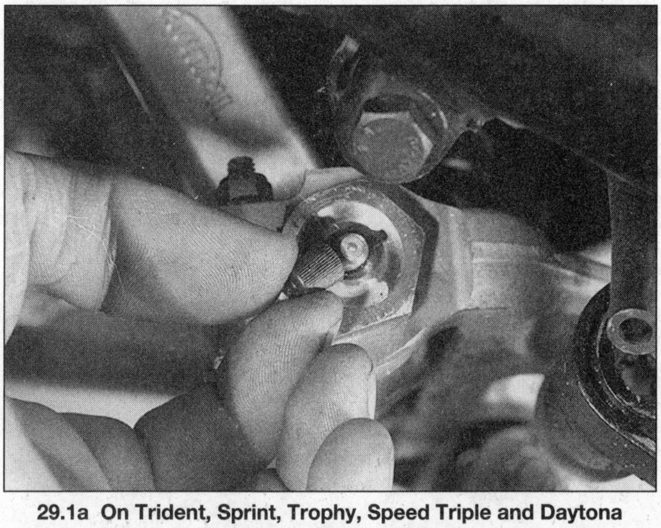

29.1a On Trident, Sprint, Trophy, Speed Triple and Daytona models, remove dust cap from grease nipples . . .

29.1b . . . and force grease into the linkage spindle ends . . .

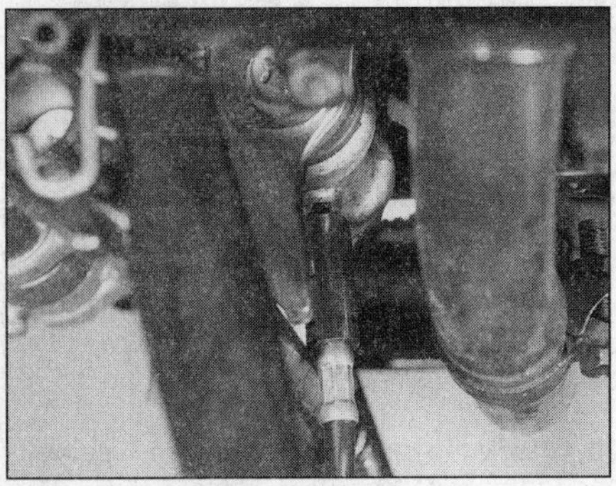

29.1c . . . linkage arm pivot . . .

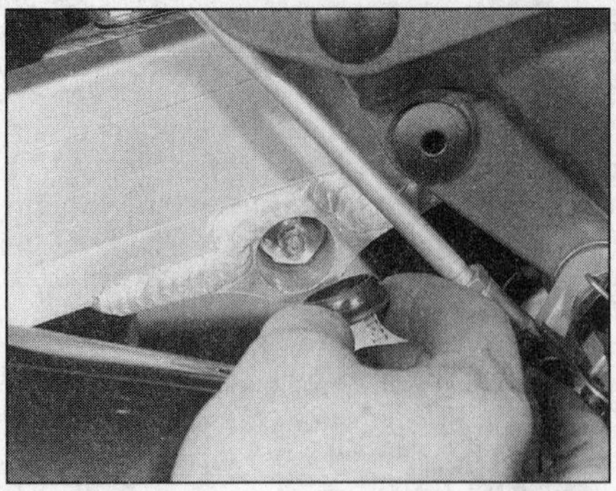

29.1d . . . and connecting rod-to-swingarm pivots

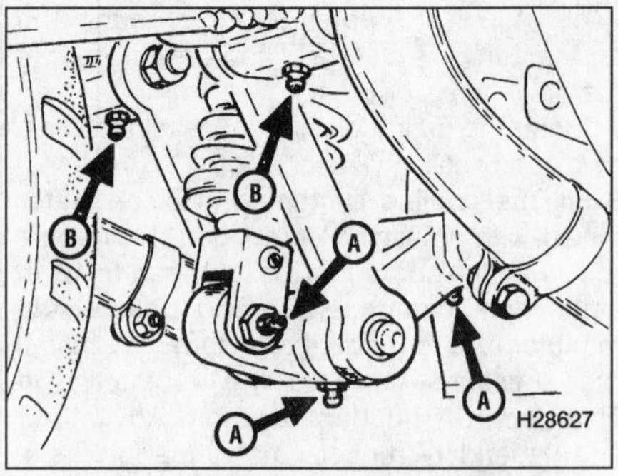

29.1e Suspension linkage (A) and swingarm (B) grease nipple locations on Thunderbird, Thunderbird Sport, Adventurer, Legend TT and Tiger models

nipples on the Tiger, Thunderbird, Thunderbird Sport, Adventurer and Legend TT models. Wipe any dirt off them and remove their caps **(see illustration 29.1e)**, then using a grease gun and the specified grease, work lubricant into both pivots.

2 Trident, Sprint, Trophy, Speed Triple and Daytona models are not equipped with grease nipples. The swingarm must be removed as described in Chapter 6 for greasing of the bearings.

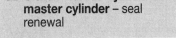

31 Drive chain slider – block renewal (Tiger model)

Or every two years

1 Unbolt the drive chain slider block from the frame and renew it. Don't forget the spacer when installing the new block and tighten the nut securely.

2 Always check the chain freeplay after installing a new slider block.

Every two years

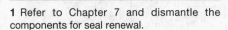

32 Clutch release cylinder and master cylinder – seal renewal

1 Refer to Chapter 2 and dismantle the components for seal renewal.

33 Brake caliper and master cylinder – seal renewal

1 Refer to Chapter 7 and dismantle the components for seal renewal.

Every four years

34 Clutch hose – renewal

1 Refer to Chapter 2 and disconnect the hydraulic hose from the clutch master cylinder and release cylinder. The hose should be renewed regardless of its condition. Always renew the banjo union sealing washers.

35 Fuel hose – renewal

1 The fuel hose (there will one or two fuel supply hoses from the tap to the carburettors depending on the model) should be renewed regardless of condition. Refer to Chapter 4 and remove the fuel tank. Disconnect the fuel hose from the carburettor and discard it. Make sure the new hose is properly secured and that the gauze filter in its union at the carburettors is clean (see Section 17).

36 Brake hoses – renewal

1 Refer to Chapter 7 and disconnect the brake hoses from the master cylinders and calipers. The hoses should be renewed regardless of their condition. Always renew the banjo union sealing washers.

Chapter 2
Engine, clutch and transmission

Contents

Degrees of difficulty

Easy, suitable for novice with little experience	**Fairly easy,** suitable for beginner with some experience	**Fairly difficult,** suitable for competent DIY mechanic	**Difficult,** suitable for experienced DIY mechanic	**Very difficult,** suitable for expert DIY or professional

Specifications

General

Capacity	
750 models	748 cc
900 models	885 cc
1000 model	998 cc
1200 models	1180 cc
Bore – all models	76 mm
Stroke	
750 and 1000 models	55 mm
900 and 1200 models	65 mm
Compression ratio	
Thunderbird	10.0 to 1
900/1200 Trophy, 900 Daytona, 900 Speed Triple, 900 Trident, Sprint, Tiger	10.6 to 1
750/1000 Daytona, 750 Trident, 750 Speed Triple	11.0 to 1
900 Daytona Super III, 1200 Daytona	12.0 to 1
Cylinder numbering (from left side to right side of the bike)	1-2-3 (3 cylinder), 1-2-3-4 (4 cylinder)
Firing order	1-2-3 (3 cylinder), 1-2-4-3 (4 cylinder)

Camshafts and tappets

Camshaft runout	0.05 mm maximum
Camshaft bearing oil clearance	0.12 mm maximum
Camshaft journal diameter – all journals except outrigger	22.90 to 22.93 mm
Camshaft journal diameter – outrigger journals (cam chain end)	22.923 to 22.936 mm
Camshaft bearing bore diameter	23.000 to 23.021 mm
Tappet OD*	
Blue marking	27.983 to 27.993 mm
Red marking	27.980 to 27.986 mm
White marking	27.974 to 27.979 mm
Tappet bore diameter	28.000 to 28.021 mm
Cam chain tensioned spring length	73.7 mm

**Replacement tappets are no longer size/colour graded*

Valves, guides and springs

Inlet valve stem diameter	
Standard	5.475 to 5.490 mm
Service limit	5.47 mm
Exhaust valve stem diameter	
Standard	5.455 to 5.470 mm
Service limit	5.45 mm
Valve guide bore diameter – inlet and exhaust	5.500 to 5.515 mm
Valve stem-to-guide clearance – inlet	
Standard	0.01 to 0.04 mm
Service limit	0.07 mm
Valve stem-to-guide clearance – exhaust	
Standard	0.03 to 0.06 mm
Service limit	0.09 mm
Valve face width	1.8 to 2.5 mm
Valve seat width	
Standard	0.9 to 1.1 mm
Service limit	1.5 mm

Clutch

Friction plate thickness	
Standard	3.80 + 0.8 mm
Service limit	3.60 mm
Plain plate maximum warpage	
Standard	0.15 mm
Service limit	0.20 mm
Master cylinder bore diameter	14.0 mm
Release cylinder bore diameter	33.6 mm

Lubrication system

Oil pressure @ 5000 rpm	40 psi (2.76 Bars) at 80°C
Oil pump rotor tip-to-outer rotor clearance	
Standard	0.15 mm
Service limit	0.20 mm

Lubrication system (continued)

Oil pump outer rotor-to-body clearance	
Standard	0.15 to 0.22 mm
Service limit	0.35 mm
Oil pump rotor endfloat	
Standard	0.02 to 0.07 mm
Service limit	0.10 mm

Cylinder liners

Cylinder bore ID	
Bore Nos. 1 and 3 (3 cylinder), Nos. 1, 3 and 4 (4 cylinder)	76.03 to 76.05 mm
Bore No. 2	76.04 to 76.05 mm
Service limit	76.1 mm

Pistons

Piston OD (measured 5 mm up from skirt, at 90° to piston pin axis)	
Bore Nos. 1 and 3 (3 cylinder), Nos. 1, 3 and 4 (4 cylinder)	75.96 to 75.98 mm
Bore No. 2	75.97 to 75.98 mm
Piston pin bore diameter in piston	19.002 to 19.008 mm
Piston pin diameter	18.995 to 19.000 mm
Connecting rod small-end diameter	19.016 to 19.034 mm

Piston rings

Ring-to-groove clearance (top and second rings)	0.02 to 0.06 mm
Groove width in piston	
Top and second rings	1.01 to 1.03 mm
Oil control ring	2.01 to 2.03 mm
End gap (installed)	
Top ring	0.20 to 0.41 mm
Second ring	0.35 to 0.56 mm
Oil control ring side rails	0.29 to 0.85 mm

Connecting rods and bearings

Connecting rod side clearance	0.5 mm
Connecting rod big-end bearing oil clearance	
Standard	0.036 to 0.066 mm
Service limit	0.1 mm
Connecting rod big-end journal diameter (Trident, Sprint, Thunderbird, Thunderbird Sport, Adventurer, Legend TT, Tiger, 750 Speed Triple)	40.946 to 40.960 mm
Connecting rod big-end journal diameter (Trophy, Daytona, 900 Speed Triple)	40.951 to 40.965 mm

Crankshaft and main bearings

Main bearing oil clearance	
Standard	0.020 to 0.044 mm
Service limit	0.1 mm
Main bearing journal diameter (Trident, Sprint, Thunderbird, Thunderbird Sport, Adventurer, Legend TT, Tiger, 750 Speed Triple)	37.960 to 37.976 mm
Main bearing journal diameter (Trophy, Daytona, 900 Speed Triple)	37.965 to 37.981 mm

Transmission

Gear ratios (No. of teeth)	
First gear	2.733 to 1 (41/15T)
Second gear	1.947 to 1 (37/19T)
Third gear	1.545 to 1 (34/22T)
Fourth gear	1.291 to 1 (31/24T)
Fifth gear	1.154 to 1 (30/26T)
Sixth gear (except early Speed Triple and early Thunderbird)	1.074 to 1 (29/27T)
Gearchange fork end width	
Standard	5.8 to 5.9 mm
Service limit	5.7 mm
Gearchange fork groove width in gears	
Standard	6.0 to 6.1 mm
Service limit	6.25 mm
Gearchange fork-to-groove clearance	0.55 mm maximum

Torque settings

Engine mounting bolts	95 Nm
Swingarm pivot shaft bolt	85 Nm
Sidestand bracket-to-frame bolt (Trident, Sprint, Trophy, Speed Triple, Daytona, Tiger)	22 Nm
Valve cover bolts	10 Nm
Cylinder head bolts	
Stage 1	20 Nm
Stage 2 (engines with alternator/starter clutch access cover)	35 Nm
Stage 2 (engines without alternator/starter clutch access cover)	27 Nm
Stage 3	Angle-tighten 90°
Cylinder head-to-cylinder block screws	12 Nm
External oil pipe banjo union bolts	
Upper bolt	20 Nm
Lower bolt	25 Nm
Camshaft sprocket bolts	15 Nm
Camshaft cap bolts	10 Nm
Cam chain upper guide screws	12 Nm
Cam chain tensioned body bolts	9 Nm
Cam chain tensioned body end bolt	23 Nm
Cam chain tensioned blade pivot bolt	18 Nm
Ignition pick-up coil screws	10 Nm
Ignition rotor bolt	27 Nm
Crankshaft end cover bolts	9 Nm
Clutch cover bolts	9 Nm
Clutch centre nut	105 Nm
Clutch pressure plate bolts	10 Nm
Clutch release cylinder bolts	9 Nm
Clutch hose banjo union bolts	25 Nm
Clutch master cylinder clamp bolts	15 Nm
Engine output sprocket nut	132 Nm
Crankcase 6 mm bolts (see text)	12 Nm
Crankcase 8 mm bolts (see text)	28 Nm
Connecting rod nuts	
Stage 1	14 Nm
Stage 2	32 Nm
Stage 3	36 Nm
Crankshaft breather disc screws (later 4 cylinder engines and 900 Trophy (from VIN 29156), Thunderbird, Thunderbird Sport, Adventurer, Legend TT)	8 Nm
Neutral switch	14 Nm
Balancer retaining plate bolts (3 cylinder engines)	9 Nm
Balancer clamp retaining screws (4 cylinder engines)	12 Nm
Balancer shaft pinch bolts (4 cylinder engines)	11 Nm
Alternator driveshaft shock absorber housing and drive gear bolts (up to VIN 56684)	35 Nm
Alternator driveshaft throughbolt nut (from VIN 56685)	40 Nm
Alternator driveshaft/starter clutch access cover bolts (early models only)	9 Nm
Starter clutch screws	11 Nm
Starter idler gear shaft retaining bolt	12 Nm
Gearchange drum ball bearing retaining screw	9 Nm
Gearchange detent arm nuts	9 Nm
Gearchange detent cam screw	9 Nm
Gearchange rod retaining plate screw	9 Nm
Gearchange shaft quadrant stopper bolt	28 Nm
Main oil gallery plug	25 Nm
Oil pump mounting screws	12 Nm
Oil pump intermediate gear screw	9 Nm
Oil pressure relief valve	15 Nm
Oil pressure switch	8 Nm
Sump bolts	12 Nm
Oil pipe (internal) banjo bolts	8 Nm
Oil strainer screws	11 Nm
Oil cooler pipe banjo union bolts	25 Nm

1 General information

The engine/transmission is of water-cooled three- or four-cylinder in-line design, fitted transversely across the frame. The twelve (3 cylinder) or sixteen (4 cylinder) valves are operated by double overhead camshafts, chain driven off the right end of the crankshaft. The pistons run in wet liners, surrounded by a water jacket.

The engine/transmission is constructed in aluminium alloy with the crankcase being divided horizontally. The crankcase incorporates a wet sump, pressure fed lubrication system, and houses a gear driven oil pump. An external oil feed pipe supplies oil to the cylinder head and cam components. A single balancer shaft is fitted on 3 cylinder models and is driven directly off a gear on the crankshaft left end. Two balancer shafts are located in the lower crankcase of 4 cylinder engines; drive is taken off the clutch outer drum.

The clutch is of the wet multi-plate type and is gear driven off the crankshaft. An auxiliary gear on the back of the clutch drives the oil pump (and thence the water pump) and the alternator driveshaft.

The transmission is of the six-speed constant mesh type, five-speed on early Speed Triple and early Thunderbird models. Final drive to the rear wheel is by chain and sprockets.

2 Operations possible with the engine in the frame

The components and assemblies listed below can be removed without having to remove the engine/transmission assembly from the frame. If however, a number of areas require attention at the same time, removal of the engine is recommended.

Valve cover
Cam chain tensioned
Camshafts and tappets
Cam chain and tensioner/guide blades
Cylinder head
Cylinder liners and pistons
Starter motor
Alternator
Water pump
Clutch
Gearchange detent cam and arms
Oil cooler (where fitted)
Sump and pressure relief valve
Alternator/starter clutch drive – early models
Balancer shaft (3 cylinder)
Balancer shafts (4 cylinder) – not advised due to poor access

3 Operations requiring engine removal

It is necessary to remove the engine/transmission assembly from the frame and separate the crankcase halves to gain access to the following components.

Transmission shafts
Crankshaft and bearings
Connecting rod assemblies and bearings
Oil pump
Gearchange mechanism (except detent cam and arms)
Balancer shafts (4 cylinder)
Alternator/starter clutch drive – later models

4 Major engine repair – general note

1 It is not always easy to determine when or if an engine should be completely overhauled, as a number of factors must be considered.

2 High mileage is not necessarily an indication that an overhaul is needed, while low mileage, on the other hand, does not preclude the need for an overhaul. Frequency of servicing is probably the single most important consideration. An engine that has regular and frequent oil and filter changes, as well as other required maintenance, will most likely give many miles of reliable service. Conversely, a neglected engine, or one which has not been run in properly, may require an overhaul very early in its life.

3 Exhaust smoke and excessive oil consumption are both indications that piston rings and/or valve guides are in need of attention, although make sure that the fault is not due to oil leakage.

4 If the engine is making obvious knocking or rumbling noises, the connecting rod and/or main bearings are probably at fault.

5 Loss of power, rough running, excessive valve train noise and high fuel consumption rates may also point to the need for an overhaul, especially if they are all present at the same time. If a complete tune-up does not remedy the situation, major mechanical work is the only solution.

6 An engine overhaul generally involves restoring the internal parts to the specifications of a new engine. The piston rings and main and connecting rod bearings are usually renewed during a major overhaul. Generally the valve seats are reground, since they are usually in less than perfect condition at this point. The end result should be a like new engine that will give as many trouble-free miles as the original.

7 Before beginning the engine overhaul, read through the related procedures to familiarise yourself with the scope and requirements of the job. Overhauling an engine is not all that difficult, but it is time consuming. Plan on the motorcycle being tied up for a minimum of two weeks. Check on the availability of parts and make sure that any necessary special tools, equipment and supplies are obtained in advance.

8 Most work can be done with typical workshop hand tools, although a number of precision measuring tools are required for inspecting parts to determine if they must be renewed. Often a dealer will handle the inspection of parts and offer advice concerning reconditioning and renewal. As a general rule, time is the primary cost of an overhaul so it does not pay to install worn or substandard parts.

9 As a final note, to ensure maximum life and minimum trouble from a rebuilt engine, everything must be assembled with care in a spotlessly clean environment.

5 Engine – removal and installation

Note: *Engine removal and installation should be carried out with the aid of at least one assistant; injury or damage could occur if the engine falls or is dropped. An hydraulic floor-type jack should be used to support and lower the engine to the floor if possible.*

Removal

1 Position the bike on its centre stand. If no centre stand is fitted, use an auxiliary bike stand to support the bike securely in an upright position. Work will be made easier by raising the machine to a suitable working height on an hydraulic ramp or a suitable platform.

2 If the engine is dirty, particularly around its mountings, wash it thoroughly before starting any major dismantling work. This will make work much easier and rule out the possibility of caked on lumps of dirt falling into some vital component.

3 Remove the seat and disconnect the battery negative lead.

4 Remove the fairing on Trophy, Daytona, Sprint and Tiger models (see Chapter 8). Where the fairing bolts to a mounting bracket on the cylinder head, it is advisable to detach the bracket from the head to prevent it becoming bent or damaged **(see illustration)**.

5.4 Unbolt fairing brackets from the cylinder head

5.9a Remove horn from cylinder head

5.9b Remove the pinch bolt (arrowed) and pull the gear pedal off its shaft

On Tiger models, also remove the sump guard and free the rear shock absorber reservoir from its bracket on the left of the cylinder head (see Chapter 8). Remove the panniers (where fitted) as described in Chapter 8.

5 Remove the fuel tank (see Chapter 4).

6 Drain the engine oil and coolant (see Chapter 1). Remove the radiator (see Chapter 3). On Thunderbird, Thunderbird Sport, Adventurer and Legend TT models, disconnect the coolant bypass hose and engine outlet hose from the thermostat housing (see Chapter 3).

7 On models with an oil cooler, disconnect the hoses from the sump and remove the oil cooler and its sub-frame (see Section 21).

8 On later Trophy models (from VIN 29156) and Sprint Executive models, remove the footrest carriers from each side (see Chapter 6). Disconnect the sidestand switch wiring connector, then remove the sidestand bracket bolt and the engine left rear lower bolt **(see illustrations 5.10b and c)**. Remove the sidestand with its bracket. Mark a line across the gearchange shaft end and shaft lever as an aid to installation, then remove the pinch bolt and withdraw the shaft lever **(see illustration 5.10d)**.

9 On Thunderbird, Thunderbird Sport, Adventurer and Legend TT models, disconnect the horn wires and remove it from the cylinder head **(see illustration)**. Also unscrew the sidestand switch from the stand bracket, then remove the three bolts to free the stand bracket from the engine. On Thunderbird, Adventurer and Legend TT models mark a line across the gearchange shaft end and gear pedal as an aid to installation, then remove the pinch bolt and withdraw the gear pedal **(see illustration)**. On the Thunderbird Sport, detach the link rod from the gearchange shaft lever by slackening its locknuts and rotating the rod via its knurled centre section so that it unscrews from the lever and pedal at the same time; mark a line across the gearchange shaft end and shaft lever as an aid to installation, then remove the pinch bolt and withdraw the shaft lever

10 On Trident, Sprint, early Trophy (up to VIN 29155), Speed Triple, Daytona and Tiger models, detach the link rod from the gearchange shaft lever by slackening its locknuts and rotating the rod via its knurled centre section so that it unscrews from the lever and pedal at the same time **(see illustration)**. Where a dog-leg link rod is fitted, slacken off the locknut and unscrew the threaded sleeve to separate the link rod from the shaft lever. Disconnect the sidestand switch wiring connector, then remove the sidestand bracket bolt and the engine left rear lower bolt **(see illustrations)**. Remove the sidestand with its bracket. Mark a line across the gearchange shaft end and shaft lever as an aid to installation, then remove the pinch bolt and withdraw the shaft lever **(see illustration)**.

11 Remove the exhaust system (Chapter 4).

12 Remove the airbox and carburettors (see Chapter 4). Plug the inlet manifold joints with clean rags to prevent engine contamination.

13 Remove the alternator and starter motor (see Chapter 9).

14 Pull the spark plug caps off the spark plugs. On Trident, Sprint, Trophy, Speed Triple, Daytona and Tiger models, remove the two plastic valve cover cowls to access the plug caps.

15 Unbolt the water pump hose cover from the left side of the engine (later models only) **(see illustration)**. Slacken the clamp at the bottom of the hose and the two bolts retaining the union at the top of hose and withdraw it from the engine.

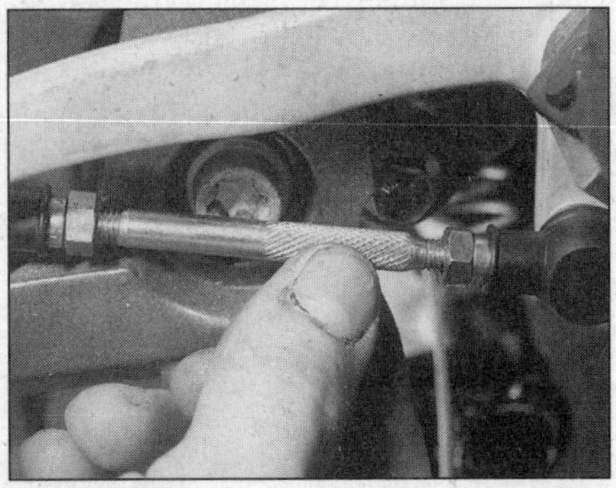
5.10a Rotate the link rod via its knurled section to unscrew it from the shaft lever and pedal

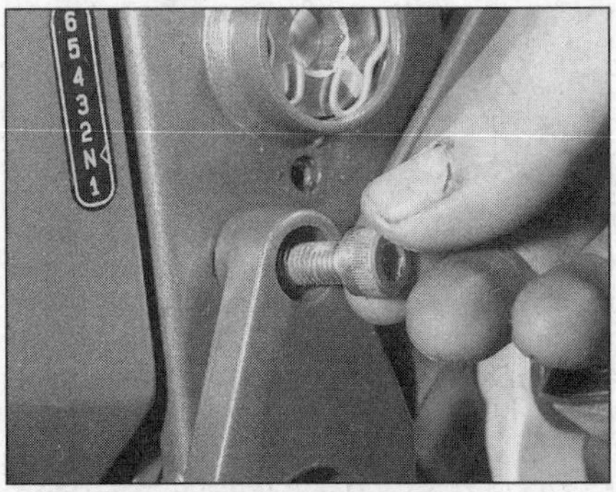

5.10b Remove the sidestand bracket retaining bolt . . .

5.10c . . . then remove left rear lower mounting bolt to free the sidestand bracket

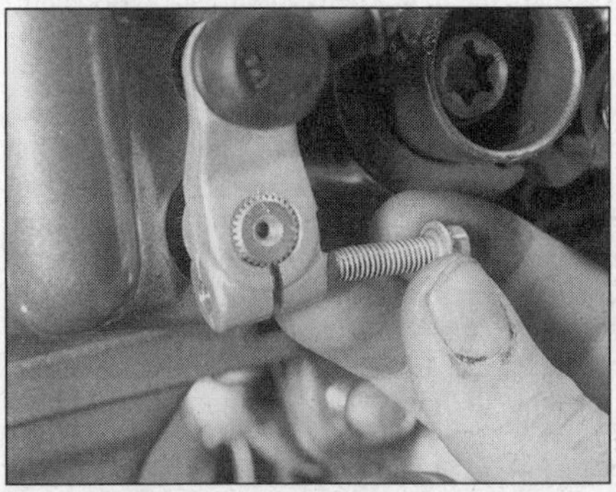
5.10d Remove the pinch bolt and pull the lever off the gearchange shaft

5.15 Remove its two bolts and free the water pump hose cover (later models)

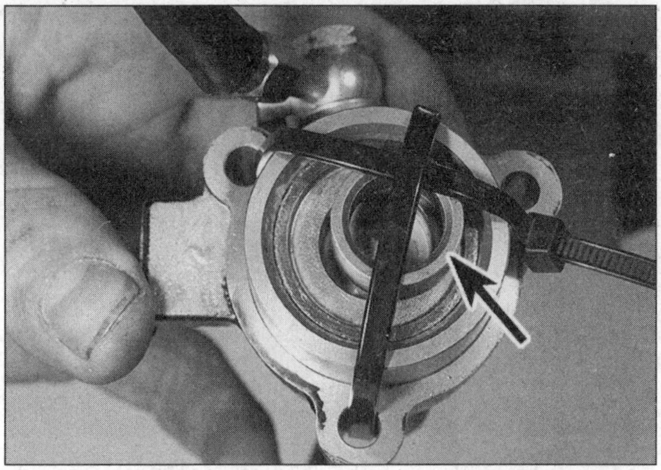

5.16 Note the use of plastic cable-ties and spacer (arrowed) to retain the piston in the clutch release cylinder

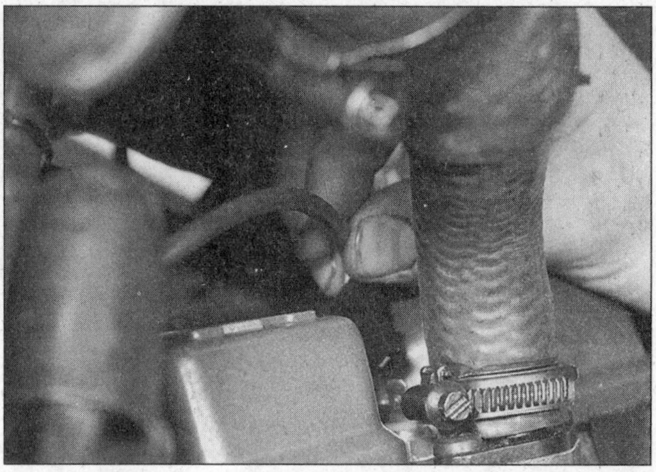

5.19 Pull the wire off the coolant temperature sender on the cylinder head

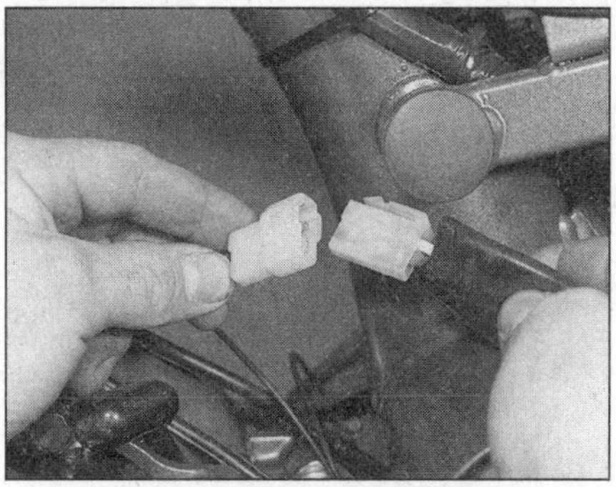

5.20a Trace the alternator wiring to the 2-pin connector and disconnect it

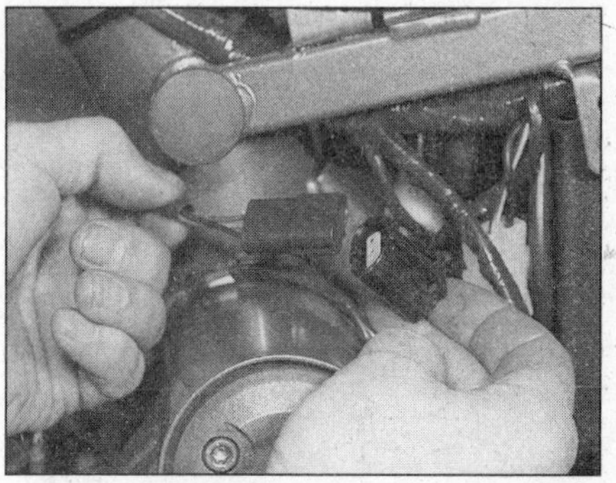

5.20b Sidestand switch wiring should be disconnected at the 3-pin connector

16 Remove the three clutch release cylinder bolts and lift off the release cylinder. Use plastic cable-ties to prevent the piston creeping out of the release cylinder body and loop the hose over the frame so it is clear of the engine **(see illustration)**.

17 Remove the sprocket cover and detach the final drive chain and sprocket from the engine (see Chapter 6).

18 On all except later Trophy models (from VIN 29156) and the Sprint Executive, unhook one end of the rear brake pedal return spring. Extract the split pin (or spring clip on later models) from the rear brake pedal-to-master cylinder pushrod clevis. Recover the washer and withdraw the clevis pin. Separate the pushrod from the pedal, allowing the pedal to drop away from the engine's lower rear mounting bolt.

19 Disconnect the wire from the temperature sender on the cylinder head **(see illustration)**.

20 Disconnect the wires from the alternator and sidestand switch at their block connectors **(see illustrations)**. It was found that the water pump had to be removed because the sidestand connector would not pass down behind the pump (see Chapter 3 for water pump removal details).

21 Disconnect the wires from the ignition pick-up coil at the block connector **(see illustration)**. Similarly, disconnect the wire connector which contains the wires from the neutral and oil pressure switch sub-harness. If desired, the sub-harness can be freed by disconnecting the wire from the neutral switch **(see illustration 5.29)** and oil pressure switch **(see illustration)**.

22 Remove the plug from the frame for access to the engine's rear lower mounting bolt. Remove the plug (early models) or end plate (later models) for access to the swingarm pivot; note that the Sprint Executive and later Trophy (from VIN 29156) are not fitted with the plug or end plate. Pry out the wire clips (where fitted) on both sides and slacken the swingarm pivot bolt on the right side of the frame **(see illustration)**.

23 At this point, position an hydraulic jack

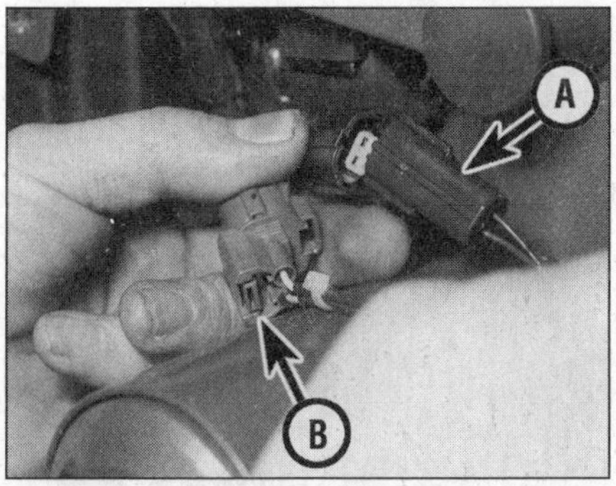

5.21a Disconnect the ignition pick-up coil (A) and neutral/oil pressure switch (B)

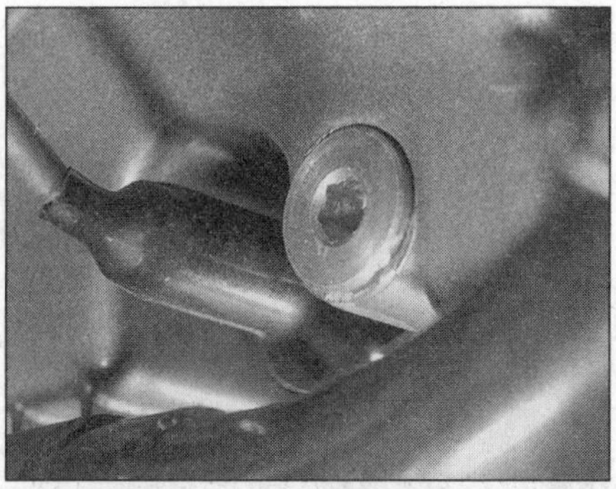

5.21b Oil pressure switch wire can also be disconnected at the switch (early model location shown)

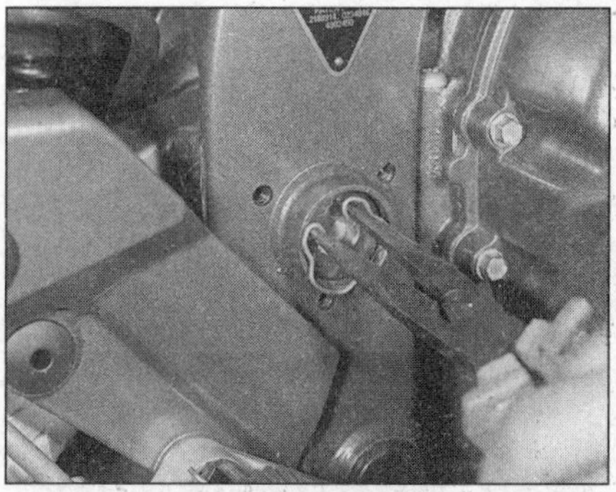

5.22 Remove the wire clip from each side of the swingarm

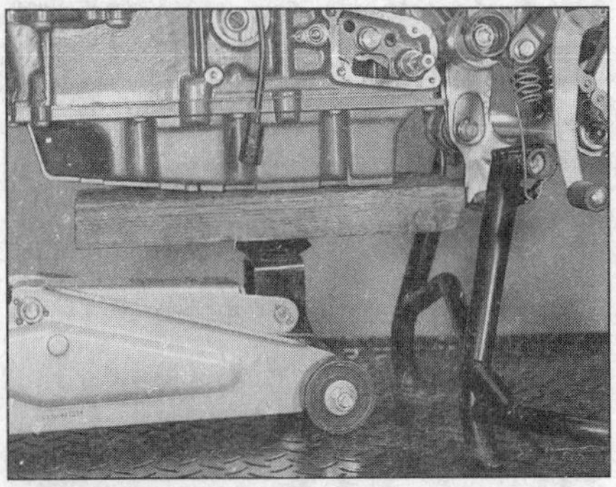

5.23 Support the engine on a jack prior to removing its mounting bolts

5.24a The engine rear upper mounting is formed by a bolt . . .

5.24b . . . and nut (arrowed) on each side of the crankcase lugs

under the engine with a block of wood between the jack head and sump **(see illustration)**. Take the weight of the engine on the jack. Also place a block of wood under the rear wheel to prevent it dropping when the engine mountings are withdrawn.

24 Slacken the engine mounting bolt nuts and withdraw the mounting bolts from all three locations on each side of the engine **(see illustrations)**. Retrieve all washers from the mountings and slip them back on the bolts for safekeeping. Early models may have a spacer fitted between each linkage carrier and rear upper mounting bolt nut.

25 Have an assistant steady the engine as it is lowered on the jack until it is clear of the frame lugs, then move it to one side. Lift the engine off the jack and onto the work surface.

Warning: The engine is heavy and may cause injury if it falls.

Installation

26 With the aid of an assistant place the engine on top of the jack and block of wood and carefully raise it into position in the frame. Check the alignment of the linkage carriers with the frame lugs and ensure that the rear wheel is supported.

27 Triumph advise the use of **new** engine mounting bolts. Install the washers on the mounting bolts then install them in the frame. Install any spacers previously fitted and the mounting bolt nuts. Don't forget to install the radiator mounting brackets on the front mountings. Counterhold the nuts and tighten each mounting bolt to the specified torque setting.

28 Tighten the swingarm pivot bolt to the specified torque setting and install the wire clips. Install the end plate or plug (as applicable) over the swingarm pivot. Install the plug in the engine's rear lower bolt location in the frame.

29 The remainder of the installation procedure is a direct reversal of the removal sequence, noting the following points.

a) Tighten all nuts and bolts to the specified torque settings (where given).
b) Align the previously made mark on the gearchange lever (or pedal) with that on the gearchange shaft end. Where a linkage rod is fitted adjust it to a comfortable riding position and secure with the locknuts.
c) Make sure all wiring is correctly routed. In particular, check that the oil pressure switch wire does not become trapped between the crankcase and frame, and remember to route the neutral and sidestand switch wiring behind the water pump ***(see illustration)****.*
d) Adjust the drive chain as described in Chapter 1.
e) Fill the engine oil and cooling systems as described in Chapter 1.

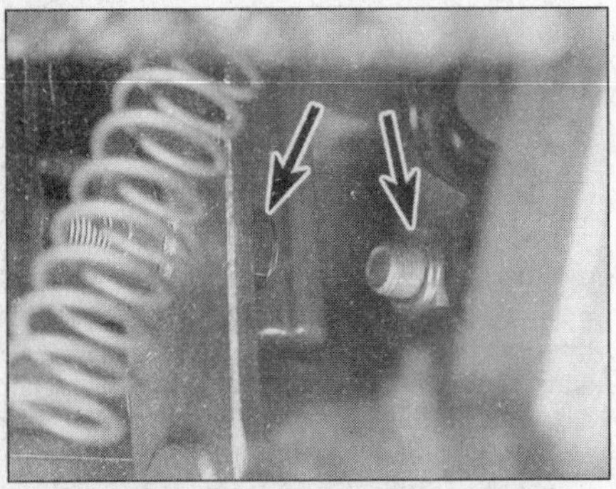

5.24c Engine rear lower mounting nuts (arrowed) are inside the linkage carriers

5.24d Right rear lower mounting bolt is accessed after removal of plastic plug

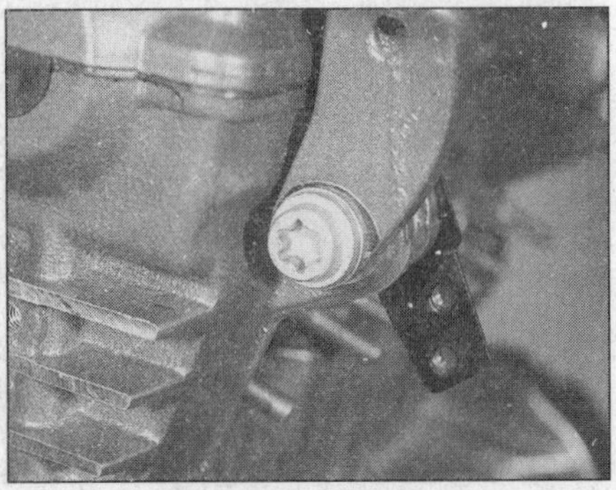

5.24e Remove engine-to-frame mounting bolt on the right . . .

5.24f . . . and left side

5.29 Sidestand and neutral switch wiring must be installed before the water pump

6 Engine disassembly and reassembly – general information

Disassembly

1 Before disassembling the engine, the external surfaces of the unit should be thoroughly cleaned and degreased. This will prevent contamination of the engine internals, and will also make working a lot easier and cleaner. A high flash-point solvent, such as paraffin can be used, or better still, a proprietary engine degreaser such as Gunk. Use old paintbrushes and toothbrushes to work the solvent into the various recesses of the engine casings. Take care to exclude solvent or water from the electrical components and inlet and exhaust ports.

Warning: The use of petrol as a cleaning agent should be avoided due to the risk of fire.

2 When clean and dry, arrange the unit on the workbench, leaving a suitable clear area for working. Gather a selection of small containers and plastic bags so that parts can be grouped together in an easily identifiable manner. Some paper and a pen should be on hand to permit notes to be made and labels attached where necessary. A supply of clean rag is also required.

3 Before commencing work, read through the appropriate section so that some idea of the necessary procedure can be gained. When removing various engine components it should be noted that great force is seldom required, unless specified. In many cases, a component's reluctance to be removed is indicative of an incorrect approach or removal method. If in any doubt, re-check with the text.

4 When disassembling the engine, keep 'mated' parts together (including gears, liners, pistons, valves, etc. that have been in contact with each other during engine operation). These 'mated' parts must be reused or renewed as an assembly.

5 Engine/transmission disassembly should be done in the following general order with reference to the appropriate Sections.

Remove the camshafts
Remove the cam chain/tensioned blade
Remove the cylinder head and cam chain guide blade
Remove the cylinder liners and pistons
Remove the clutch
Remove the alternator (see Chapter 9)
Remove the starter motor (see Chapter 9)
Remove the water pump (see Chapter 3)
Remove the sump
Remove the balancer(s)
Separate the crankcase halves
Remove the crankshaft/connecting rods
Remove the transmission shafts/gears
Remove the gearchange components
Remove the oil pump
Remove the alternator/starter drive

Reassembly

6 Reassembly is accomplished by reversing the general disassembly sequence.

7 Valve cover – removal and installation

Note: *The valve cover can be removed with the engine in the frame. If the engine has been removed, ignore the steps which do not apply.*

Removal

1 Remove the seat and disconnect the battery negative lead.

2 Remove the fuel tank (see Chapter 4).

3 Remove the valve cover cowls on Trident, Sprint, Trophy, Speed Triple, Daytona and Tiger models; they are secured by two screws.

4 Pull the plug caps off the spark plugs and remove the ignition HT coils (see Chapter 5).

5 Remove the eight (3 cylinder) or ten (4 cylinder) bolts, together with their seals, to free the valve cover from the cylinder head **(see illustration)**. Certain models will have plastic caps inserted in the bolt heads – pry these out.

6 Withdraw the valve cover from the right side of the frame and retrieve the main cover seal and the two (3 cylinder) or three (4 cylinder) separate plug hole seals.

7 Examine the seals for signs of damage or deterioration and renew them if necessary. Also check the cover bolt seals for signs of damage and renew if necessary.

Installation

8 Apply silicone sealant to the plug hole seals and stick them to the valve cover. Insert the main seal into the cover groove, using silicone sealant, particularly at the ends, to hold it in place **(see illustration)**.

9 Smear silicone sealant on the cylinder head gasket face in the camshaft end areas **(see illustrations)**.

10 Install the valve cover on the cylinder head, making sure the seals stay in place **(see illustration)**. Install the valve cover bolt seals

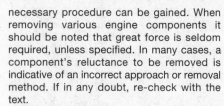

7.5 Valve cover is retained by eight bolts on the 3 cylinder engine

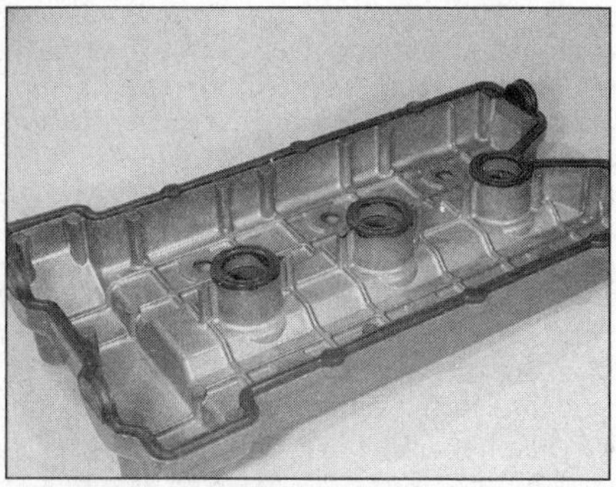

7.8 Ensure that the main valve cover seal and plug hole seals are stuck in place

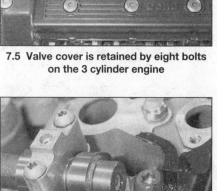

7.9a Apply sealant to the cylinder head surface . . .

7.9b . . . at each of the four corners

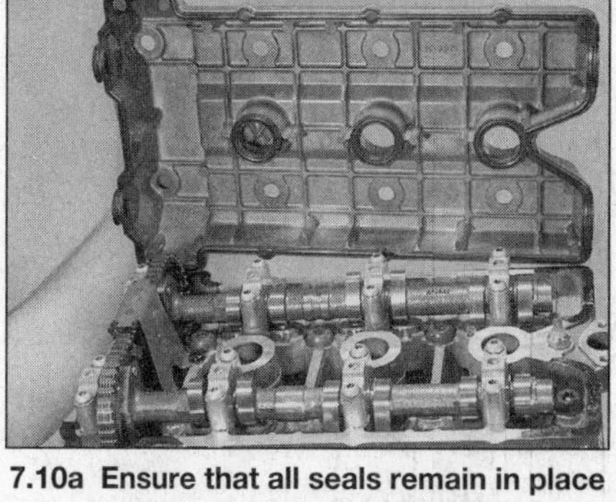

7.10a Ensure that all seals remain in place as the valve cover is installed

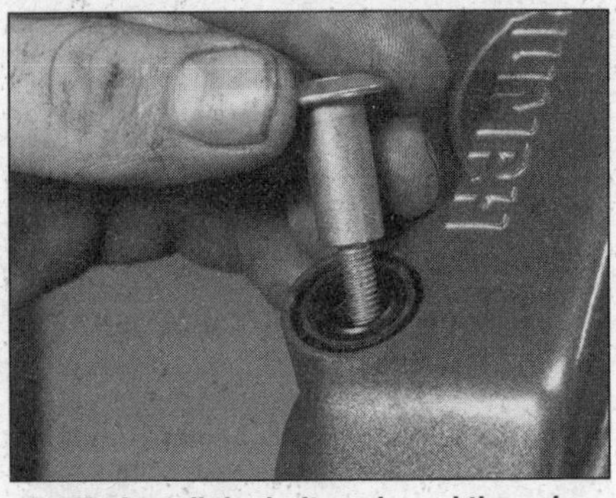

7.10b Install the bolt seals and the valve cover bolts . . .

7.10c . . . tightening them evenly to the specified torque setting

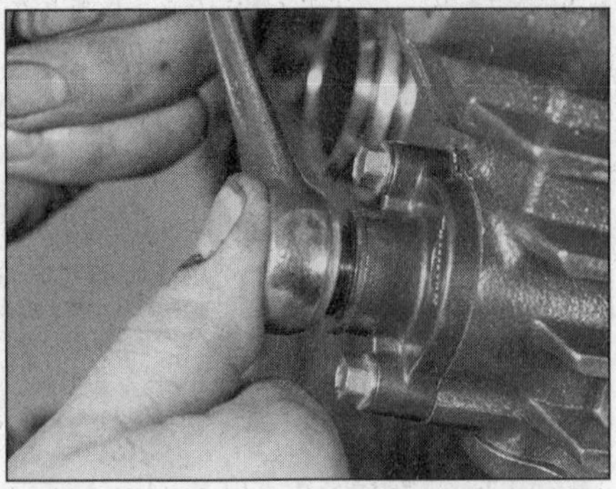

8.4 Be careful unscrewing the tensioner end cap – it will be under spring tension

and bolts; the two longer bolts are located at the cam chain end **(see illustration)**. Tighten the bolts evenly in a criss-cross pattern, starting at the centre and working outwards; tighten to the specified torque **(see illustration)**. Insert the plastic caps into the bolt heads (where applicable).

11 Install the ignition HT coils and plug caps (see Chapter 5).

12 Install the valve cover cowls and secure with the two screws (where applicable).

13 Install the fuel tank (see Chapter 4). Refit the battery negative lead and install the seat.

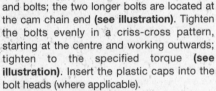

8 Cam chain tensioner – removal, inspection and installation

Removal

1 Remove the valve cover (see Section 7). Remove the fairing right lower panel on Trophy and Daytona models (see Chapter 8).

2 Remove the screws to free the crankshaft right end cover; be prepared for oil loss as the cover is removed. Discard the cover gasket, a new one must be used on installation. Using a ring spanner on the engine turning hexagon, rotate the crankshaft clockwise so that the T 1 mark (3 cylinder) or T 1.4 mark (4 cylinder) on the ignition rotor is aligned with the centre of the pick-up coil **(see illustrations 9.2a and 9.2b)**. In this position, the arrow marks on the cam sprockets should face inwards towards each other **(see illustration 9.2c)**.

3 When the tensioned is withdrawn from the cylinder block, the cam chain will be untensioned, and may jump a tooth on the inlet cam sprocket. To prevent this, Triumph recommend that a wood wedge be inserted between the tensioned blade and the crankcase (via the crankshaft end cover aperture) to hold the tensioned blade in firm contact with the cam chain whilst the tensioned is removed.

4 Undo the large end bolt from the tensioned and withdraw the spring, noting that it will be under tension **(see illustration)**.

5 Remove the two bolts and withdraw the tensioned. Recover its gasket.

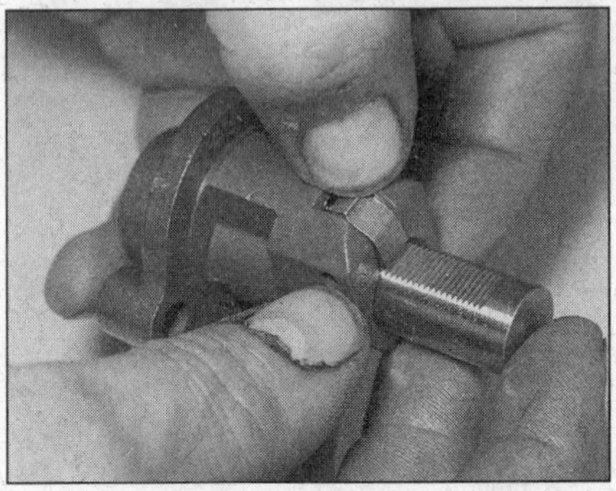

8.8a Hold back the catch and press the plunger inwards . . .

Inspection

6 Examine the tensioned components for signs of wear or damage. Check that the plunger moves smoothly in the tensioned body. **Note:** *Very early Trophy and Trident models had a cap over the tensioned plunger's tip. This was not fitted to all subsequent models, and Triumph advise that it be discarded where found on early machines.*

7 If the spring has sagged, the tensioned will not be able to take up chain play effectively. Measure the free length of the spring and compare to the specification. If the spring length has reduced significantly, the tensioned must be renewed.

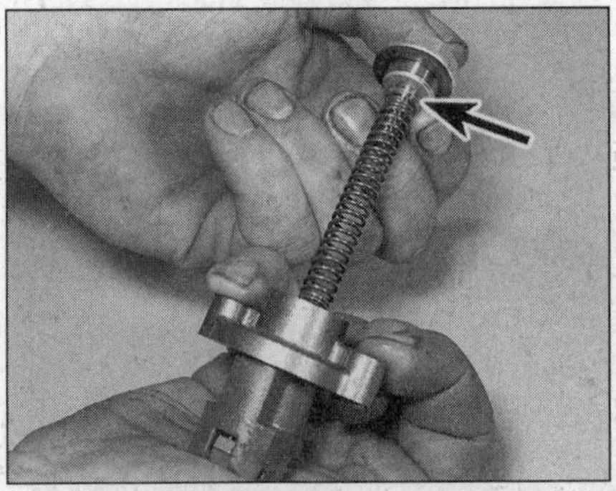

8.9a Hold the tensioner body as shown and compress the spring until the brass ring (arrowed) can be screwed into the body – note that it has a left-hand thread

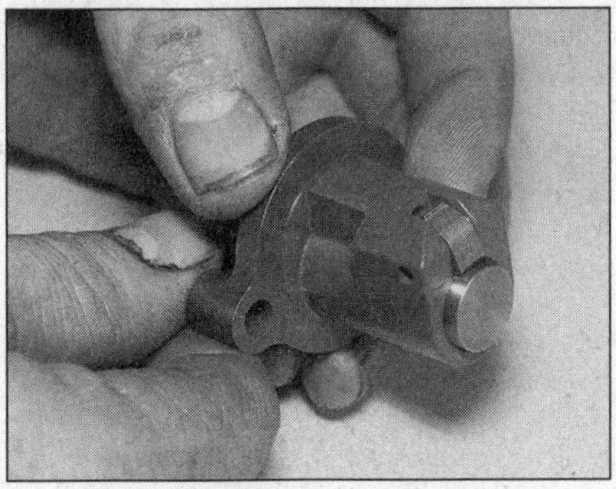

8.8b . . . so that it is fully retracted

Installation

Method A

8 Lift the catch on the tensioned body and push the plunger inwards **(see illustration)**. Release the catch to lock the tensioned in the retracted position **(see illustration)**.

9 Install the spring in the tensioned. Fit a new sealing washer to the end bolt and install the end bolt in the end of the spring **(see illustration)**. Hold the tensioned body against the palm of your hand and compress the spring into the body so that the brass threaded ring on the end bolt contacts the body surface; turn the end bolt anti-clockwise to thread the brass ring into the end of the body **(see illustration)**. This will hold the

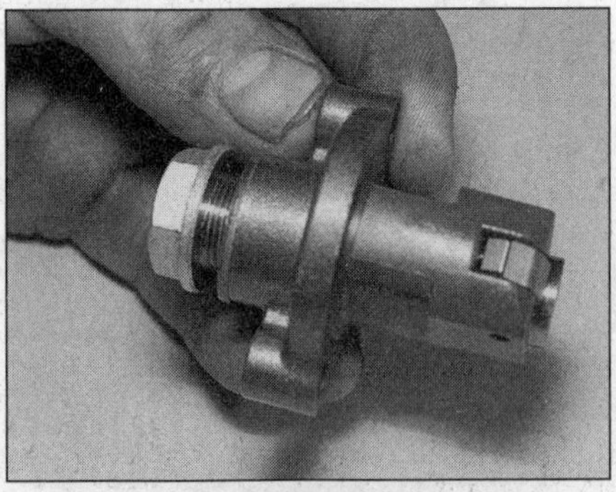

8.9b The tensioner is now held in the retracted position and ready for installation

8.10a Install the tensioner on the engine using a new gasket . . .

8.10b . . . and retain with the two bolts

spring compressed whilst the tensioned is installed in the engine. **Note:** *It may take several attempts to achieve this.*

10 Slip a new gasket over the tensioned body and install the tensioned in the cylinder block **(see illustration)**. Secure it with the two bolts, tightening them to the specified torque setting **(see illustration)**.

11 Remove the wood wedge from the tensioned blade. Screw the tensioned end bolt into the tensioned body; the tensioned ratchet will be heard to release and the plunger shoot out into contact with the tensioned blade as the brass ring releases the spring. Tighten the end bolt to the specified torque setting.

12 Check that the valve timing marks are correct (see Step 2). Rotate the engine several times and recheck the timing marks – if the cam chain has jumped whilst the tensioned was removed, reposition it as described in Section 9. Install the valve cover (see Section 7).

13 Install the crankshaft right end cover using a new gasket and tighten its bolts to the specified torque setting.

14 Check the engine oil level and top-up if necessary (see Chapter 1).

Method B

15 Lift the catch on the tensioned body and push the plunger fully inwards **(see illustration 8.8a)**. Release the catch to lock the plunger in the retracted position **(see illustration 8.8b)**.

16 Slip a new gasket over the tensioned body and install the tensioned on the cylinder block. Secure it with the two bolts, tightening them to the specified torque setting.

17 Remove the wood wedge from the tensioned blade. Using a slim rod inserted into the tensioned body, use finger pressure only to push the tensioned plunger into contact with the tensioned blade; the ratchet and catch will hold it in this position. Fit a new sealing washer to the end bolt and install the spring and end bolt into the tensioned body. Tighten the end bolt to the specified torque setting.

18 Check that the valve timing marks are correct (see Step 2). Rotate the engine several times and recheck the timing marks – if the cam chain has jumped whilst the tensioned was removed, reposition it as described in Section 9. Install the valve cover (see Section 7).

19 Install the crankshaft right end cover using a new gasket and tighten its bolts to the specified torque setting.

20 Check the engine oil level and top-up if necessary (see Chapter 1).

9 Camshafts and tappets – removal, inspection and installation

Note: *This procedure can be carried out with the engine in the frame.*

Removal

1 Remove the valve cover (see Section 7). Remove the fairing right lower panel on Trophy and Daytona models (see Chapter 8).

2 Remove its retaining screws to free the crankshaft right end cover; be prepared for oil loss as the cover is removed. Discard the cover gasket, a new one must be used on installation. Using a ring spanner on the engine turning hexagon, rotate the crankshaft so that the T 1 mark (3 cylinder) or T 1.4 mark (4 cylinder) on the ignition rotor is aligned with the centre of the pick-up coil **(see illustrations)**. In this position, the arrow marks on the cam sprockets should face inwards towards each other **(see illustration)**.

2

9.2a Using a ring spanner on the hexagon, rotate the crankshaft clockwise . . .

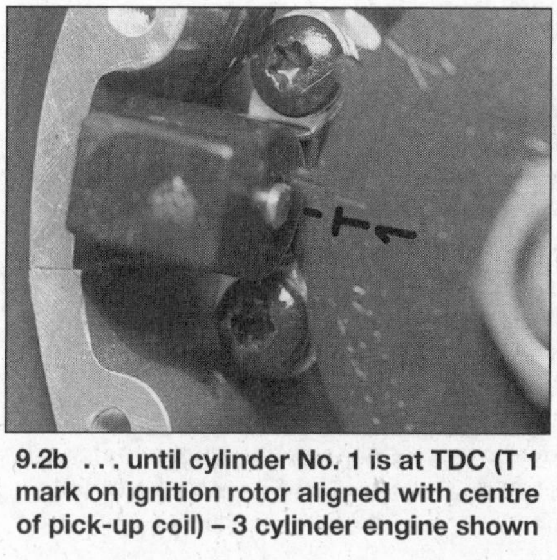

9.2b . . . until cylinder No. 1 is at TDC (T 1 mark on ignition rotor aligned with centre of pick-up coil) – 3 cylinder engine shown

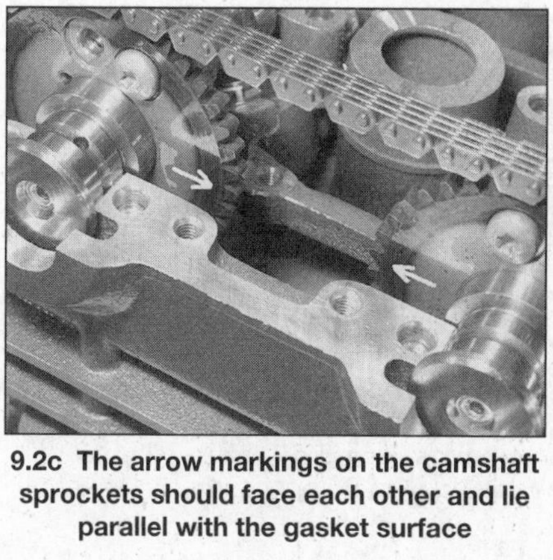

9.2c The arrow markings on the camshaft sprockets should face each other and lie parallel with the gasket surface

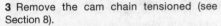

9.4 Cam chain upper guide is retained by four screws (arrowed)

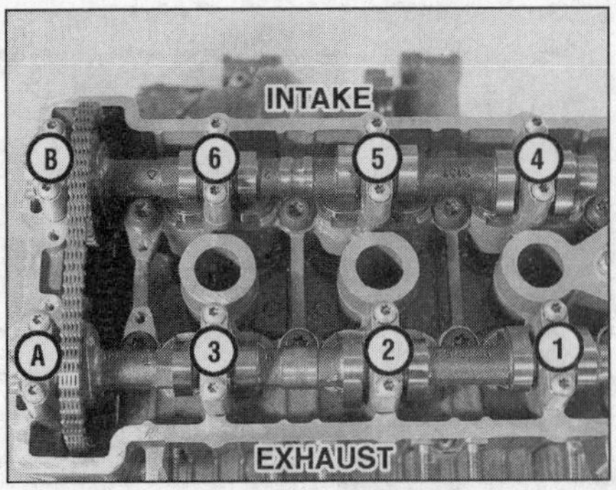

9.5a Camshaft cap markings – 3 cylinder engine

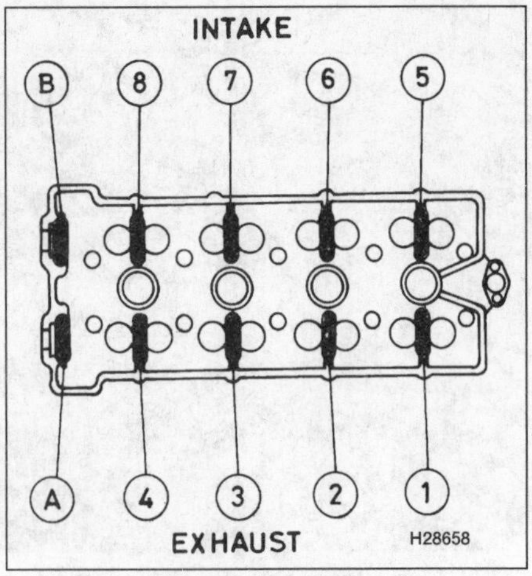

9.5b Camshaft cap markings – 4 cylinder engine

3 Remove the cam chain tensioned (see Section 8).

4 Remove its four screws and lift off the cam chain upper guide **(see illustration)**.

5 Before disturbing the camshaft caps, check for identification markings scribed on their top surfaces. These markings ensure that the caps can be matched up to their original journals on installation. The caps are numbered 1 to 6 on 3 cylinder engines, and 1 to 8 on 4 cylinder engines; the two outrigger caps on the cam chain end are denoted A and B **(see illustrations)**.

6 Working on one camshaft at a time, slacken all eight (3 cylinder) or ten (4 cylinder) cap bolts evenly in a criss-cross sequence, then remove the caps. Retrieve the dowels on each cap if they are loose.

7 Slip the cam chain off the sprocket and withdraw the camshaft.

8 Repeat the procedure for the other camshaft.

9 Obtain a container which is divided into twelve (3 cylinder) or sixteen (4 cylinder) compartments, and label each compartment with the number of its corresponding valve in the cylinder head. Pick each shim and tappet out of the cylinder head and store it in the corresponding compartment in the container.

Inspection

Note: *Before renewing the camshafts or the cylinder head and camshaft caps because of damage, check with local machine shops specialising in motorcycle engineering work. In the case of the camshafts, it may be possible for cam lobes to be welded, reground and hardened, at a cost far lower than that of a new camshaft. If the bearing surfaces in the cylinder head are damaged, it may be possible for them to be bored out to accept bearing inserts. Due to the cost of a new cylinder head, it is recommended that all options be explored.*

10 Inspect the cam bearing surfaces of the head and the caps. Look for score marks, deep scratches and evidence of spalling (a pitted appearance). Check the camshaft lobes for heat discoloration (blue appearance), score marks, chipped areas, flat spots and spalling **(see illustration)**.

11 Camshaft runout can be checked by supporting each end of the camshaft on V-blocks, and measuring any runout using a dial gauge. If the runout exceeds the specified limit the camshaft must be renewed.

12 The camshaft bearing oil clearance should then be checked using a product known as Plastigauge.

13 Clean the camshafts, the bearing surfaces in the cylinder head and the caps with a clean, lint-free cloth, then lay the camshafts in place in the cylinder head. The inlet camshaft can be identified by its grooved centre section and the exhaust by its plain section **(see illustration)**.

14 Cut strips of Plastigauge and lay one piece on each bearing journal, parallel with the camshaft centreline. Make sure the camshaft cap dowels are installed and fit the caps in their proper positions **(see illustration 9.5a or b)**. Ensuring that the camshafts are not rotated at all, tighten all eight (3 cylinder) or ten (4 cylinder) cap bolts evenly, a little at a time, in a criss-cross sequence, until the specified torque setting is reached. Repeat for the other camshaft.

15 Now unscrew the bolts evenly, a little at a time, in a criss-cross sequence and carefully lift off the caps, again making sure the camshaft is not rotated. Repeat on the other camshaft.

16 To determine the oil clearance, compare the crushed Plastigauge (at its widest point) on each journal to the scale printed on the Plastigauge container. Compare the results to this Chapter's Specifications. If the oil clearance is greater than specified, the camshaft and/or cylinder head and camshaft cap bearing surfaces are worn. Remove all traces of Plastigauge from the components when the check is complete. **Note:** *You can measure the camshaft journal diameter and the head/cap bearing inside diameter to determine which component is worn.*

17 Check the sprockets for wear, cracks and other damage, renewing them if necessary. If the sprockets are worn, the cam chain is also worn, and also the sprocket on the crankshaft. If wear this severe is apparent, the cam chain and all sprockets should be renewed (see Section 10).

18 The same design sprocket is used for each camshaft, but different hole positions are provided for fitting to the inlet or exhaust camshaft. When fitted to the inlet camshaft the holes next to the IN marking should be used, and those next to the EX marking for the exhaust camshaft. The sprocket bolts must have a drop of non-permanent thread locking compound applied to their threads and be tightened to the specified torque setting.

19 Inspect the outer surfaces of the tappets for evidence of scoring or other damage. If a

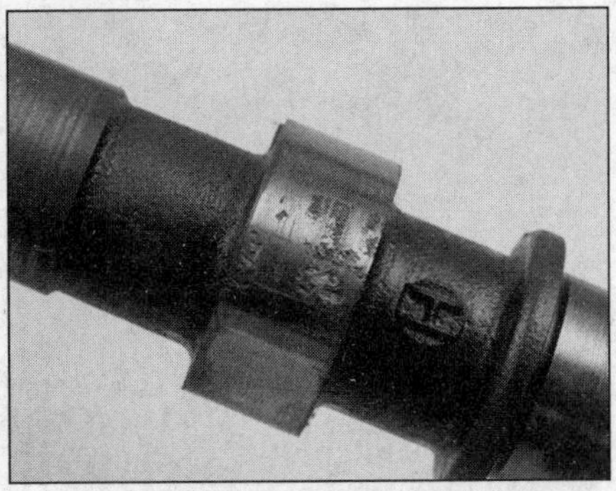

9.10 Check the cam lobes for wear – damage like this requires attention

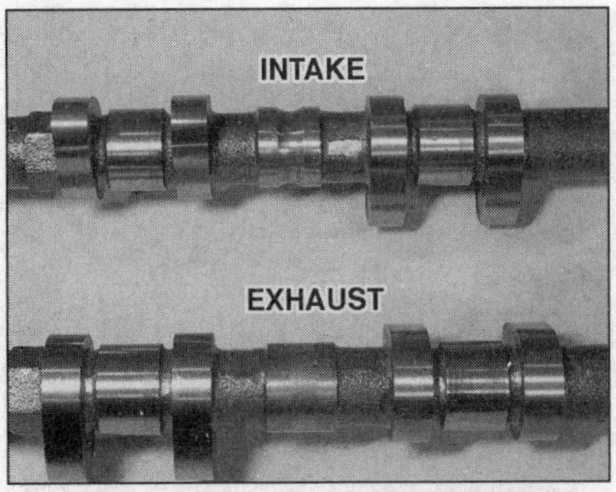

9.13 The camshafts can be identified by their grooved (inlet) or plain (exhaust) centre section

9.20a Lubricate each tappet with engine oil and install in the cylinder head

9.20b Insert the corresponding shim in the top of the tappet

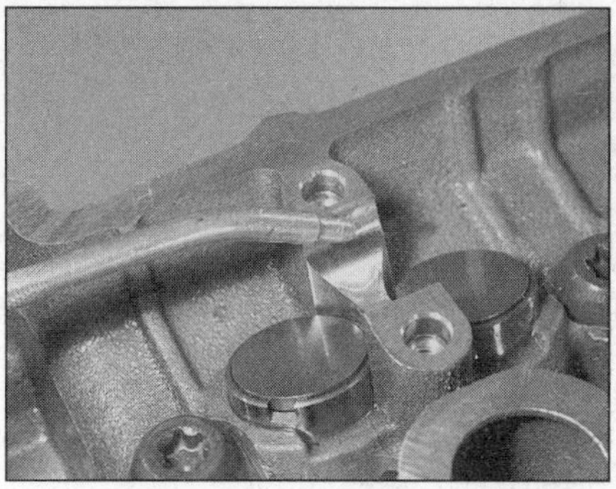

9.22 Apply engine oil to the camshaft bearing surfaces in the cylinder head

9.23 Keeping the front run of the chain taut, install the exhaust camshaft in the cylinder head . . .

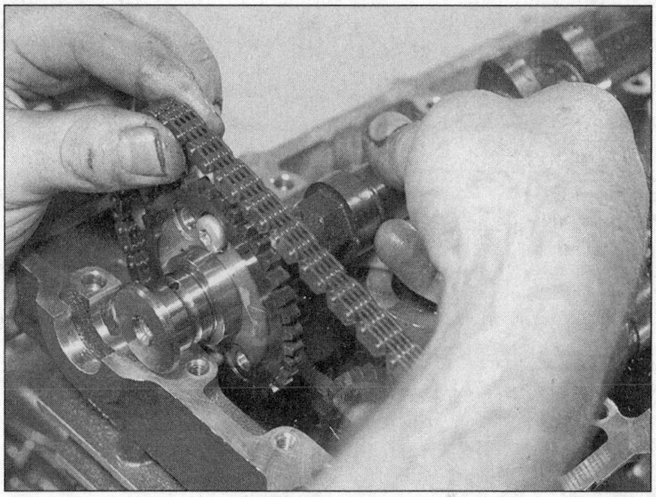

9.24 . . . then install the inlet camshaft

tappet is in poor condition, it is probable that the bore in which it works is also damaged. Check for clearance between the tappets and their bores. Whilst no specifications are given, if slack is excessive, renew the tappets. If the bores are seriously out-of-round or tapered, the cylinder head and the tappets must be renewed. Note that on early engines the tappets were size graded using a colour coding on the bottom edge of the tappet.

Installation

20 Lubricate each tappet with engine oil and install with its shim in the cylinder head **(see illustrations)**. **Note:** *It is most important that the tappets and shims are returned to their original valves otherwise the valve clearances will be inaccurate.*

21 Position the crankshaft as described in Step 2.

22 Apply a smear of clean engine oil to the cylinder head camshaft bearing surfaces **(see illustration)**.

23 Hook the cam chain up from its tunnel so that it is engaged around the lower sprocket teeth on the crankshaft. Check that the crankshaft is positioned as described in Step 2. Keeping the front run of the chain taut, lay the exhaust camshaft in position so that the arrow mark on its sprocket points rearwards, then engage the chain on the sprocket teeth **(see illustration)**.

24 Slip the inlet camshaft through the cam chain so that the arrow mark on its sprocket points forwards **(see illustration)**. Engage the chain fully on the sprocket teeth. Before proceeding, check that everything aligns as described in Step 2. If it doesn't, the valve timing is inaccurate, and the valve will contact the pistons when the engine is turned over.

25 Oil the camshaft journals **(see illustration)**. Ensure that the camshaft cap dowels are installed **(see illustration)** and fit the caps in their proper positions **(see illustration 9.5a or b)**. Oil the threads of the

9.25a Apply engine oil to the camshaft journals

9.25b Check that the two dowels are in place . . .

9.25c . . . and install the camshaft caps

cap bolts and tighten all eight (3 cylinder) or ten (4 cylinder) cap bolts evenly, a little at a time, in a criss-cross sequence, until the specified torque setting is reached **(see illustration)**. Repeat for the other camshaft. **Note:** *Be careful that the cam chain doesn't jump a tooth as the inlet camshaft is tightened down* (see ***Haynes Hint***).

26 With all caps tightened down, check that the valve timing marks still align (see Step 2). If the chain has jumped a tooth, the camshafts must be released and the chain repositioned. Check that each camshaft is not pinched by turning it a few degrees in each direction with a spanner on the camshafts' cast hexagon.

27 Install the cam chain upper guide and

9.30 Use a new gasket on the crankshaft right cover

HAYNES HiNT

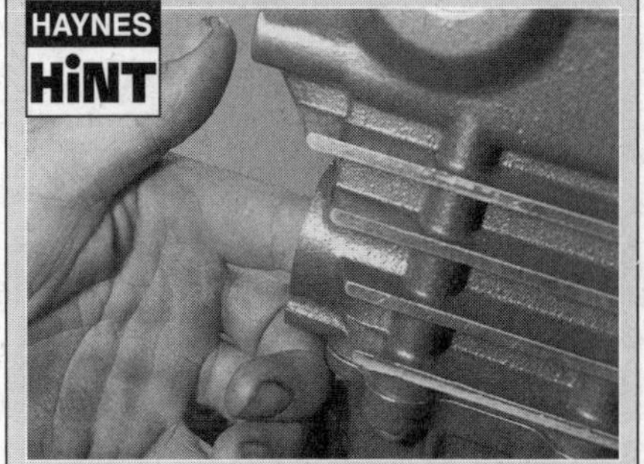

Apply pressure to the cam chain tensioner blade by pressing on it with a finger through the tensioner hole to prevent the chain jumping a tooth on the inlet sprocket

tighten its screws to the specified torque setting **(see illustration)**.

28 Install the cam chain tensioned (Section 8).

29 If any of the valve components have been renewed, check the valve clearances (see Chapter 1).

30 Install the crankshaft right end cover using a new gasket and tighten its bolts to the specified torque setting **(see illustration)**.

31 Install the valve cover (see Section 7).

32 Check the engine oil level and top-up if necessary (see Chapter 1).

10 Cam chain and tensioner/ guide blades – removal and installation

Note: *The cam chain and blades can be removed with the engine in the frame.*

Cam chain tensioner blade (rear)

Removal

1 Remove the inlet camshaft as described in Section 9.

2 Undo the tensioner blade pivot bolt from

9.27 Install the cam chain upper guide on the cylinder head

the crankcase right cover aperture **(see illustration)**. Retrieve the washer, collar and bolt and lift the blade out of the cam chain tunnel **(see illustration)**.

3 Check the tensioner blade for cracking and other damage, renewing it if necessary.

Installation

4 Install the tensioner blade down through the chain tunnel. Install the collar on the pivot bolt with its shoulder against the bolt flange, slip the bolt through the blade, then install the washer and thread the bolt into the crankcase. Tighten the bolt to the specified torque setting.

5 Install the inlet camshaft (see Section 9).

Cam chain guide blade (front)

6 The blade can only be accessed once the cylinder head has been removed. Refer to Section 11 for details.

Cam chain

Removal

7 Remove the camshafts (see Section 9).

8 Remove the tensioner blade pivot bolt and withdraw it from the engine **(see illustration 10.2a)**.

9 Counterhold the engine turning hexagon with a ring spanner and unscrew the Allen bolt from the end of the crankshaft **(see illustration)**. Withdraw the hexagon and

10.2a Remove the cam chain tensioner blade pivot bolt . . .

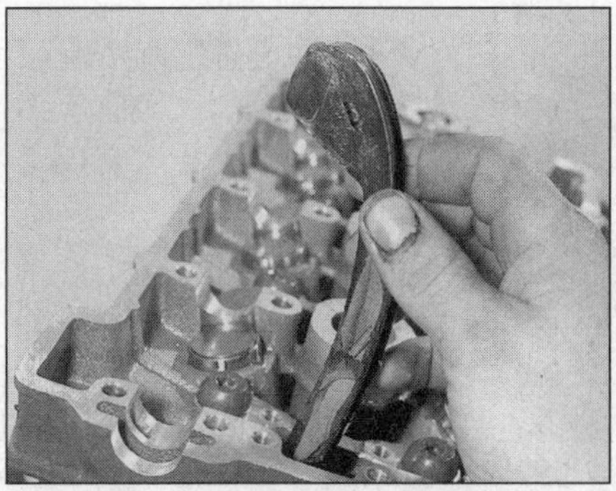

10.2b . . . and lift the blade out of the cylinder head

10.9a Counterhold the engine turning hexagon with a ring spanner and undo the bolt from the end of the crankshaft

10.9b Lift off the hexagon . . .

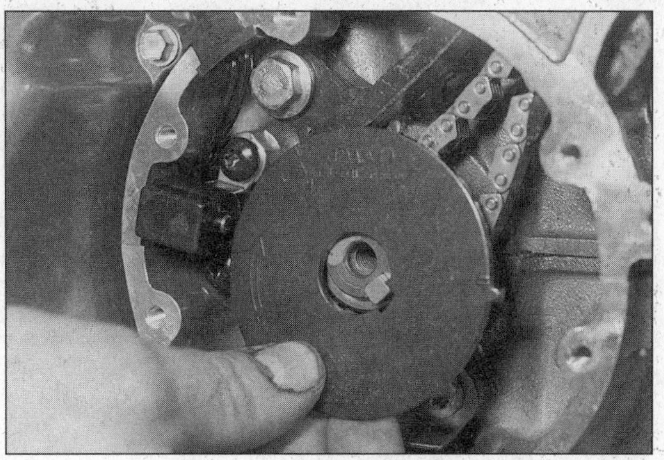

10.9c . . . and the ignition rotor

10.10a Loop the cam chain off the crankshaft sprocket . . .

10.10b . . . and out of the cam chain tunnel

ignition rotor from the crankshaft **(see illustrations)**. On later 1200 Trophy models (with black engine) remove the bolt from the centre of the right-hand side of the cylinder head.

10 Slip the chain off the crankshaft sprocket and lift it out of the head **(see illustrations)**.

11 The crankshaft sprocket can be slipped off the crankshaft; it is located by a square-section key.

Inspection

12 Check the cam chain for binding and obvious damage and renew it if necessary. Inspect the sprocket for chipped or missing teeth. If the chain and sprocket show signs of extensive wear renew them as a set (including the camshaft sprockets).

Installation

13 Installation is a reverse of the removal procedure, noting the following:

a) Locate the sprocket, ignition rotor and hexagon on the crankshaft with the square-section key.

b) Install the ignition rotor with its marked side facing outwards.

c) Apply a drop of non-permanent thread locking compound to the Allen bolt threads and tighten it to the specified torque setting.

11 Cylinder head – removal and installation

Caution: The engine must be completely cool before beginning this procedure or the cylinder head may become warped.

Note: *This procedure can be performed with the engine in the frame. If the engine has already been removed, ignore the preliminary steps which don't apply. It will be necessary to support the engine under the sump during this procedure, therefore position the bike on its centre stand or, where only a sidestand is fitted, support the bike using an auxiliary motorcycle stand.*

Removal

1 Remove the exhaust system as described in Chapter 4.

2 On Thunderbird, Thunderbird Sport, Adventurer and Legend TT models detach the two wires from the horn and remove its mounting nut to free the horn from the cylinder head.

3 On models so equipped, it is advisable to detach the fairing mounting brackets from the side of the cylinder head. If left in place they may become distorted when the cylinder head is being manoeuvred or valve service work is being carried out.

4 Remove the carburettors as described in Chapter 4.

5 Remove the valve cover (see Section 7).

6 Disconnect the wire from the coolant temperature sender unit. Drain the cooling system (see Chapter 1), then slacken its clamp and pull the coolant hose off the cylinder head top surface.

7 Remove the camshafts and tappets (see Section 9). On later 1200 Trophy models (with black engine) remove the bolt from the centre of the right-hand side of the cylinder head.

8 Remove the two banjo bolts which retain the external oil pipe to the cylinder head and

11.8a The external oil pipe is secured to the cylinder head . . .

11.8b . . . and crankcase by banjo union bolts

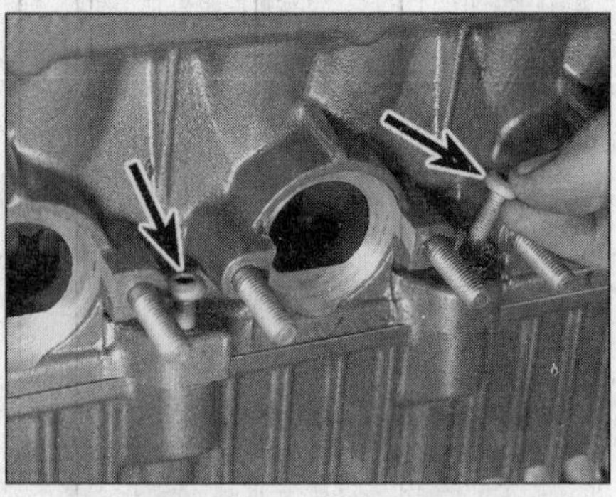

11.9a The cylinder head front edge is retained by two (3 cylinder) or three (4 cylinder) screws (arrowed)

crankcase **(see illustrations)**. Withdraw the oil pipe and discard the sealing washers – new washers must be fitted on installation.

9 Remove the two (3 cylinder) or three (4 cylinder) screws from the front of the cylinder head-to-crankcase joint and the three screws from the right side **(see illustrations)**. Note that on Thunderbird, Thunderbird Sport, Adventurer and Legend TT models, the three side screws are hidden inside the cam chain tunnel **(see illustration)**.

10 Make sure the wood block and jack are positioned under the sump, and remove the cylinder head-to-frame bolts on each side. As they are withdrawn, take the weight of the engine on the jack so that no additional strain is placed on the rear engine mountings.

11 Slacken the eight (3 cylinder) or ten (4 cylinder) head bolts by half a turn at a time in a **reverse** of the specified sequence **(see illustration 11.22b or 11.22c)**.

12 Tap around the joint faces of the cylinder head with a soft-faced mallet to free the head. Don't attempt to free the head by inserting a screwdriver between the head and cylinder block – you'll damage the sealing surfaces.

13 Lift the head off the block, and remove it from the engine. Remove the old gasket and the horseshoe-shaped pieces from the front of the gasket. Recover the two dowels if they are loose.

14 Lift the cam chain guide blade from the front of the cylinder block **(see illustration)**.

15 Whenever the cylinder head is disturbed the seal between the liners and crankcase will be broken. It is essential that this procedure is not overlooked, otherwise coolant from the cylinder block water jacket will seep into the crankcase. Refer to Section 14 for liner removal and installation details.

Installation

16 Fit and seal the liners in the cylinder block (see Section 14).

17 Install the cam chain guide blade into the cylinder block. Its lower end locates in a cast recess in the cam chain tunnel and the two lugs near its upper end locate in the cutouts in the cylinder head surface **(see illustrations)**.

18 Ensure both cylinder head and block mating surfaces are clean. Fit the dowels to the block (if removed). Check that the cylinder head bolt holes in the block are clean and dry.

19 Fit the new head gasket over the dowels **(see illustration)**.

11.9b Three screws retain the right side of the cylinder head . . .

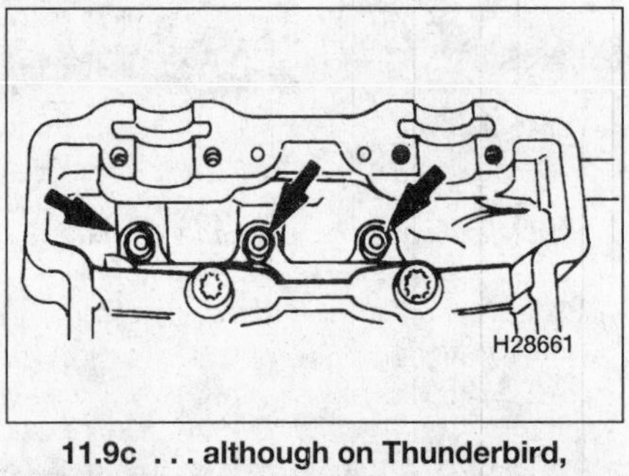

11.9c . . . although on Thunderbird, Thunderbird Sport, Adventurer and Legend TT models these are accessed from inside the cam chain tunnel (arrowed)

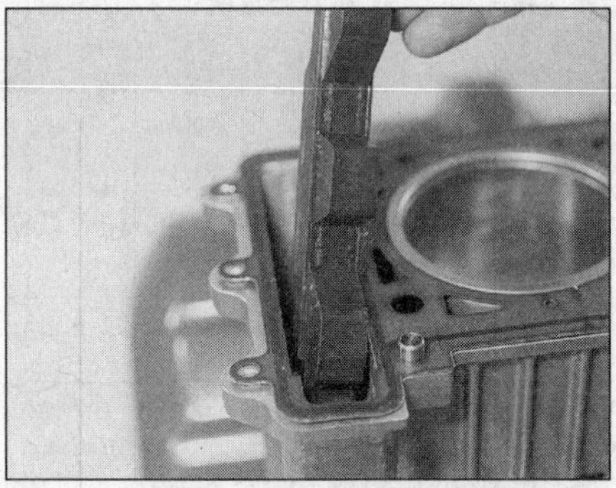

11.14 The cam chain guide blade can be removed once the cylinder head is off

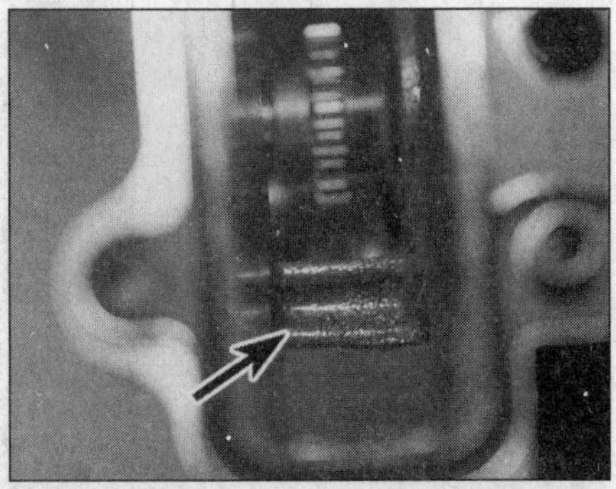

11.17a The cam chain guide blade lower end locates in the recess . . .

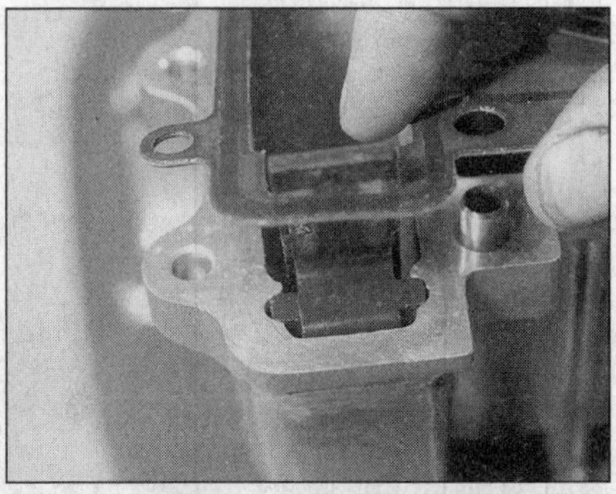

11.17b . . . and its upper end lugs locate in the cast slots

11.19 Always use a new cylinder head gasket

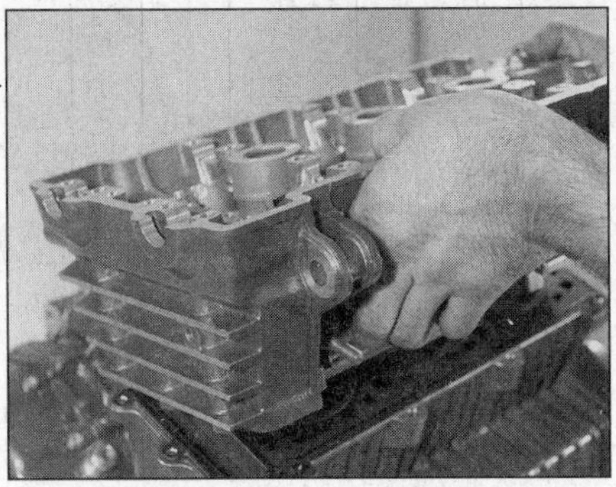

11.20a Install the cylinder head . . .

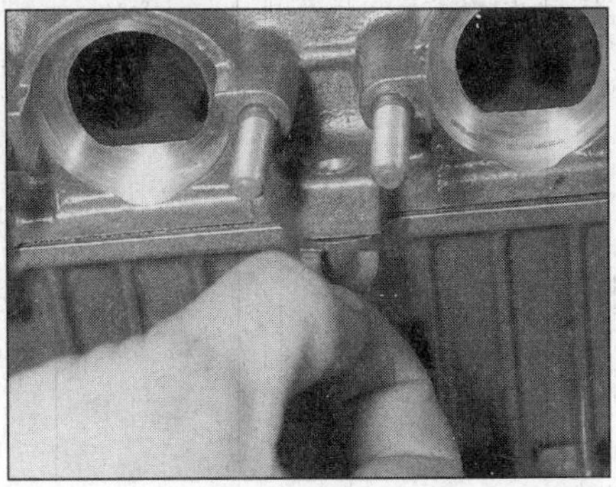

11.20b . . . then slip the horseshoe-shaped pieces in the front screw mountings

11.21 Ensure that the cylinder head bolt threads are clean and dry before inserting them in the head

11.22a Tighten the cylinder head bolts . . .

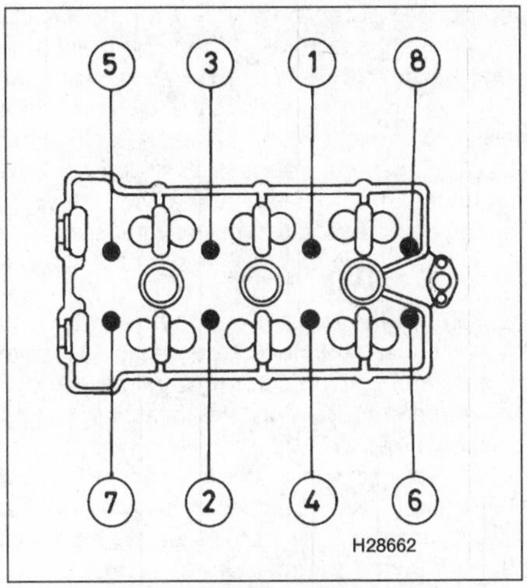

11.22b . . . in the correct sequence (3 cylinder engine) . . .

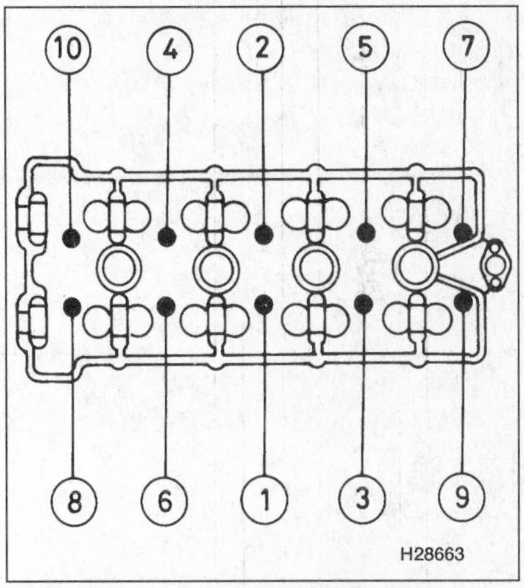

11.22c . . . (or 4 cylinder engine) . . .

20 Carefully lower the cylinder head onto the block **(see illustration)**. Slip the two (3 cylinder) or three (4 cylinder) horseshoe-shaped pieces between the head and block protrusions at the front of the engine **(see illustration);** these gaskets are not fitted on the later 1200 Trophy (with black engine). **Note:** *If was found that the new gaskets required cutting in half to create the required shape.* If the cam chain is still in the engine, pass it up through the tunnel and slip a piece of wire through the chain to prevent it falling back into the engine.

21 Install the cylinder head bolts and tighten only finger-tight at this stage **(see illustration).**

22 Tighten the cylinder head bolts in the correct sequence to the stage 1 torque setting **(see illustrations)**. Repeat to the stage 2 torque setting, noting that the torque differs on early and late models; the cylinder head bolts were modified at the same time as the detachable cover for alternator/starter clutch access was deleted from the upper crankcase top surface. Finally, attached a degree disc to the torque wrench and angle-tighten each bolt 90° following the sequence **(see illustration). Note:** *The cylinder head may not seat fully when placed on the block due to the liners being slightly proud – if it does not pull down during tightening, remove the head for investigation. If the head is detached, the liners must be resealed.*

23 Tighten the screws at the front and right side (inside on Thunderbird, Thunderbird Sport, Adventurer and Legend TT models) of the cylinder head to the specified torque setting.

24 Realign the engine mounting lugs with the frame, using pressure from the jack if necessary, and install the mounting bolts, washers and nuts, including the radiator mounting brackets. Tighten the bolts to the specified torque setting. Remove the jack.

25 Using new sealing washers on each side of the external oil pipe banjo unions, install the pipe on the engine and tighten the banjo union bolts to the specified torque setting **(see illustration)**.

26 Push the coolant pipe onto its union on the cylinder head, tightening the clamp securely. Reconnect the coolant temperature sensor wire.

27 Install the tappets and camshafts (see Section 9).

28 Install the valve cover (see Section 7).

29 Fill the cooling system (see Chapter 1).

11.22d . . . noting that final tightening is expressed in terms of degrees

11.25 Use new sealing washers on each side of the oil pipe banjo union

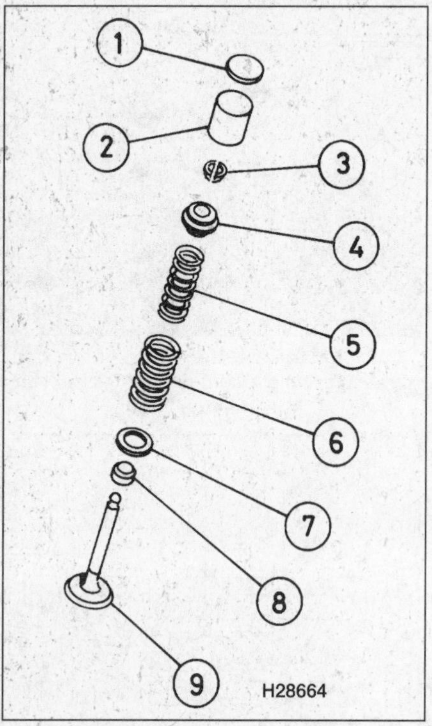

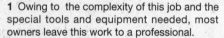

13.6a Valve components

1 Shim
2 Tappet
3 Collets
4 Spring retainer
5 Inner spring
6 Outer spring
7 Spring seat
8 Seal
9 Valve

12 Valves/valve seats/valve guides - overhaul

1 Owing to the complexity of this job and the special tools and equipment needed, most owners leave this work to a professional.

2 The home mechanic can, however, remove the valves from the cylinder head, check the components for wear and grind in the valves (Section 13). Tasks like valve seat recutting should be entrusted to a Triumph dealer.

3 After the valve overhaul has been performed, the head will be in like-new condition. When the head is returned, be sure to clean it again very thoroughly before installation on the engine to remove any metal particles or abrasive grit that may still be present from the valve service operations. Use compressed air, if available, to blow out all the holes and passages.

13 Cylinder head and valves - disassembly, inspection and reassembly

1 As mentioned in the previous section, valve seat recutting should be left to a Triumph dealer. However, disassembly, cleaning and inspection of the valves and related components can be done (if the necessary special tools are available) by the home mechanic. This way no expense is incurred if the inspection reveals that overhaul is not required at this time.

2 To disassemble the valve components without the risk of damaging them, a valve spring compressor is absolutely necessary.

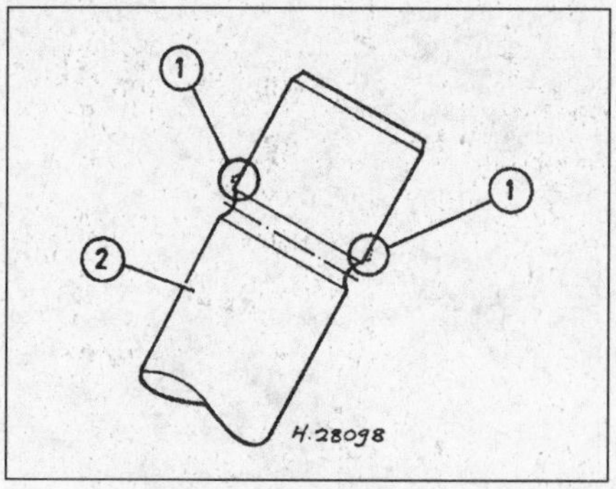

13.6b Remove burrs (1) if valve stem (2) won't pull through the guide

Disassembly

3 Remove the tappets and their shims if you haven't already done so (see Section 9). Store the components in such a way that they can be returned to their original locations without getting mixed up.

4 Carefully scrape all carbon deposits out of the combustion chamber area. A hand held wire brush or a piece of fine emery cloth can be used once the majority of deposits have been scraped away. Do not use a wire brush mounted in a drill motor, or one with extremely stiff bristles, as the head material is soft and may be eroded away or scratched by the wire brush.

5 Arrange to label and store the valves along with their related components so they can be kept separate and reinstalled in the same valve guides they are removed from (labelled plastic bags work well for this).

6 Compress the valve spring on the first valve with a spring compressor, then remove the collets and the retainer from the valve assembly. **Note:** *Take great care not to mark the tappet bore with the spring compressor.* Do not compress the springs any more than is necessary. Carefully release the valve spring compressor and remove the springs and the valve from the head **(see illustration)**. If the valve binds in the guide (won't pull through), push it back into the head and deburr the area around the collet groove with a very fine file or whetstone **(see illustration)**.

7 Repeat the procedure for the other valves. Keep the parts for each valve together so they can be reinstalled in the same location.

8 Once the valves have been removed and labelled, pull off the valve stem seals with pliers and discard them (the old seals should not be reused), then remove the spring seats.

9 Next, clean the cylinder head with solvent and dry it thoroughly. Compressed air will speed the drying process and ensure that all holes and recessed areas are clean.

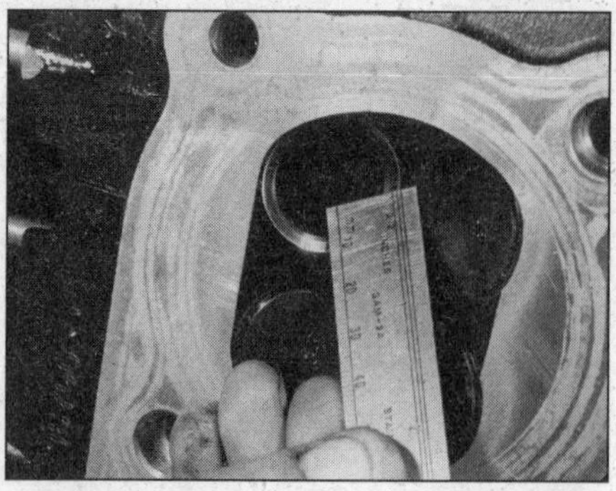

13.13 Measuring the valve seat width

10 Clean all of the valve springs, collets, retainers and spring seats with solvent and dry them thoroughly. Do the parts from one valve at a time so that no mixing of parts between valves occurs.

11 Scrape off any deposits that may have formed on the valve, then use a motorised wire brush to remove deposits from the valve heads and stems. Again, make sure the valves do not get mixed up.

Inspection

12 Inspect the head very carefully for cracks and other damage. If cracks are found, a new head will be required. Check the cam bearing surfaces for wear and evidence of seizure. Check the camshafts and tappets for wear as well (see Section 9).

13 Examine the valve seats in each of the combustion chambers. If they are pitted, cracked or burned, the head will require work beyond the scope of the home mechanic. Measure the valve seat width and compare it to the Specifications **(see illustration)**. If it exceeds the service limit, or if it varies around its circumference, valve overhaul is required.

14 Clean the valve guides to remove any carbon build-up, then measure the inside diameters of the guides (at both ends and the centre of the guide) with a small hole gauge and micrometer **(see illustrations)**. Record the measurements for future reference. These

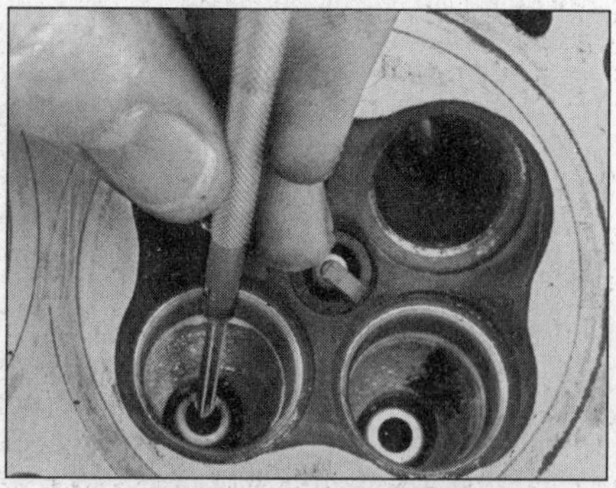

13.14a Insert a small hole gauge in the valve guide and expand it so there's a slight drag . . .

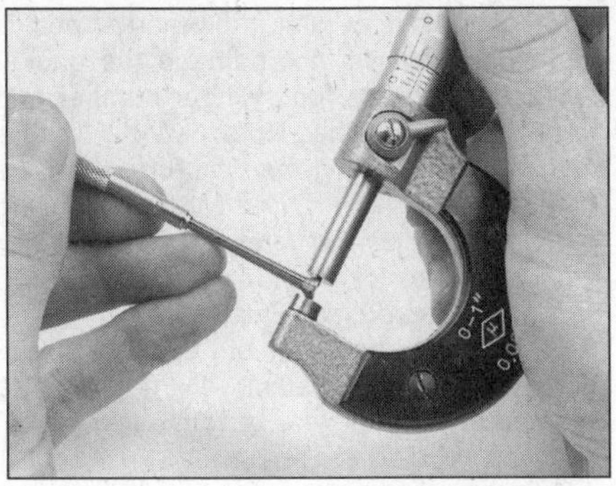

13.14b . . . then measure the small hole gauge with a micrometer

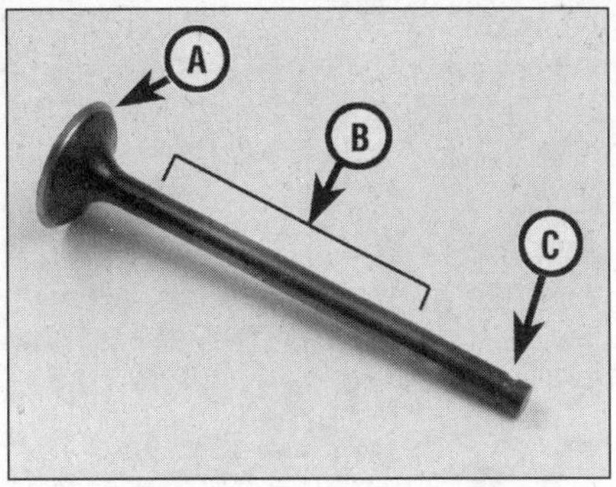

13.15 Check the valve face (A), stem (B) and collet groove (C) for signs of wear

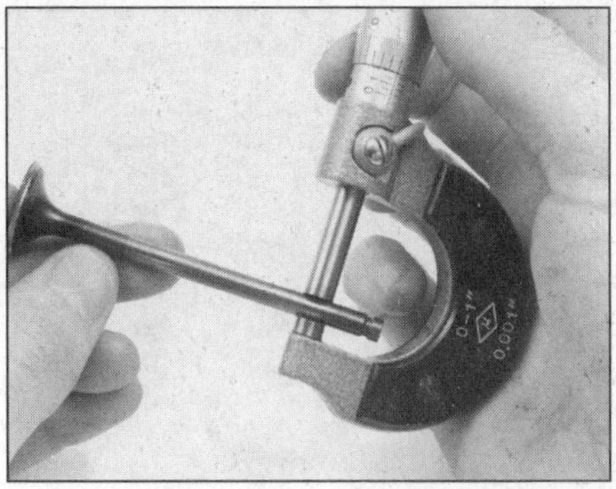

13.16 Measure the valve stem diameter with a micrometer

measurements, along with the valve stem diameter measurements, will enable you to compute the valve stem-to-guide clearance. This clearance, when compared to the Specifications, will be one factor that will determine the extent of the valve service work required. The guides are measured at the ends and at the centre to determine if they are worn in a bell-mouth pattern (more wear at the ends). If the guides are worn they must be renewed – check the availability of new guides with a Triumph dealer.

HAYNES HiNT ***Refer to 'Tools and Workshop Tips' in the Reference section for details of how to read the micrometer scale.***

15 Carefully inspect each valve face for cracks, pits and burned spots. Check the valve stem and the collet groove area for cracks **(see illustration)**. Rotate the valve and check for any obvious indication that it is bent. Check the end of the stem for pitting and excessive wear. Measure the valve seat width and compare to the Specifications. The presence of any of the above conditions indicates the need for valve overhaul.

16 Measure the valve stem diameter **(see illustration)**. By subtracting the stem diameter from the valve guide diameter, the valve stem-to-guide clearance is obtained. If any valve stem is worn the valve must be renewed.

17 Check the spring retainers and collets for obvious wear and cracks. Any questionable parts should not be reused, as extensive damage will occur in the event of failure during engine operation.

18 If the inspection indicates that no overhaul work is required, the valve components can be reinstalled in the head.

Reassembly

19 Before installing the valves in the head, they should be ground in to ensure a positive seal between the valves and seats. This procedure requires coarse and fine valve grinding compound and a valve grinding tool. If a grinding tool is not available, a piece of rubber or plastic hose can be slipped over the valve stem (after the valve has been installed in the guide) and used to turn the valve.

20 Apply a small amount of coarse grinding compound to the valve face, then slip the valve into the guide **(see illustration)**. **Note:** *Make sure the valve is installed in the correct guide and be careful not to get any grinding compound on the valve stem.*

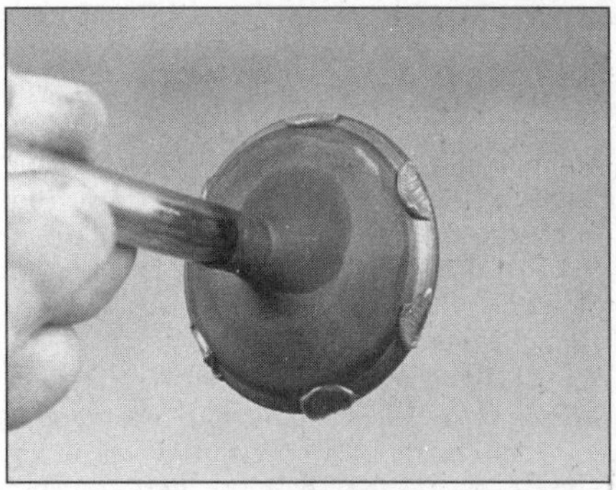

13.20 Apply grinding compound very sparingly, in small dabs to the valve face

21 Attach the grinding tool (or hose) to the valve and rotate the tool between the palms of your hands. Use a back-and-forth motion rather than a circular motion. Lift the valve off the seat and turn it at regular intervals to distribute the grinding compound properly. Continue grinding until the valve face and seat contact area is of uniform width and unbroken around the entire circumference of the valve face and seat **(see illustrations)**.

22 Carefully remove the valve from the guide and wipe off all traces of grinding compound. Use solvent to clean the valve. Wipe the seat area thoroughly with a solvent soaked cloth.

2

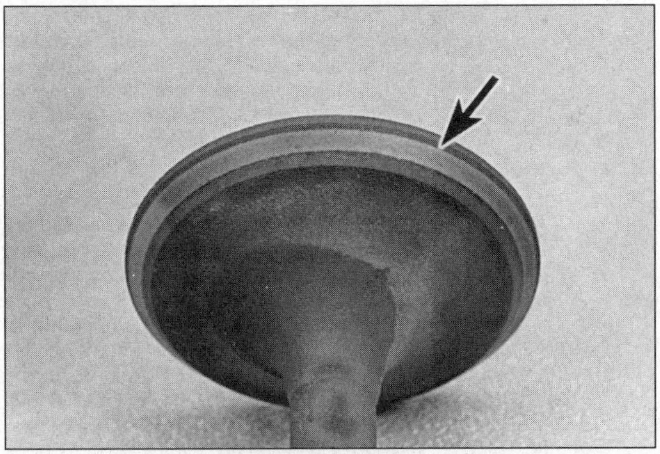

13.21a After grinding, the valve face should exhibit a uniform unbroken appearance . . .

13.21b . . . and the seat should be the specified width (arrowed) with a smooth unbroken appearance

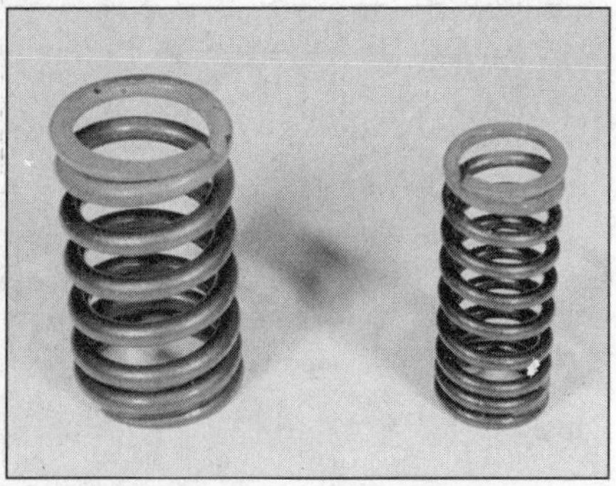

13.25a Install the valve springs with their closer-wound coils downwards, towards the valve head

23 Repeat the procedure with fine valve grinding compound, then repeat the entire procedure for the remaining valves.

24 Lay the spring seats in place in the cylinder head, then install new valve stem seals on each of the guides. Use a deep socket to push the seals over the end of the valve guide until they are felt to clip into place. Don't twist or cock them, or they will not seal properly against the valve stems. Also, don't remove them again or they will be damaged.

25 Coat the valve stems with clean engine oil, then install one of them into its guide. Next, install the springs and retainer, compress the springs and install the collets. **Note:** *Install the springs with the closely-wound coils at the bottom, towards the valve head* ***(see illustration).*** When compressing

14.2 Liner for cylinder No. 2 has a size marking (arrowed) on its top face

14.5 Prise the circlip from one side of the piston – make sure it's the inner side if working on either of the outer pistons

13.25b A small dab of grease will help hold the collets in place as they are installed

the springs with the valve spring compressor, depress them only as far as is absolutely necessary to slip the collets into place. Apply a small amount of grease to the collets to help hold them in place as the pressure is released from the springs **(see illustration)**. Make certain that the collets are securely locked in their retaining grooves.

26 Support the cylinder head on blocks so the valves can't contact the workbench top, then very gently tap each of the valve stems with a soft-faced hammer. This will help seat the collets in their grooves.

> **HAYNES HiNT** ***You can check for proper sealing of the valves by pouring a small amount of solvent into each of the valve ports. If the solvent leaks past any valve into the combustion chamber area the valve grinding operation on that valve should be repeated.***

14 Cylinder liners and pistons – removal, inspection and installation

Note: *This procedure can be performed with the engine in the frame.*

Removal

1 Remove the cylinder head (see Section 11).

2 Before removing the liners, mark the top edge of each liner with a felt marker pen or similar, which will not damage the gasket surfaces. Indicate the cylinder number and front face of each liner. **Note:** *Cylinder No. 2 is a selective fit during manufacture; it will be denoted by a green dot on early engines and by the letter 'B' on later engines – other markings are for manufacturing use and should be ignored* ***(see illustration).***

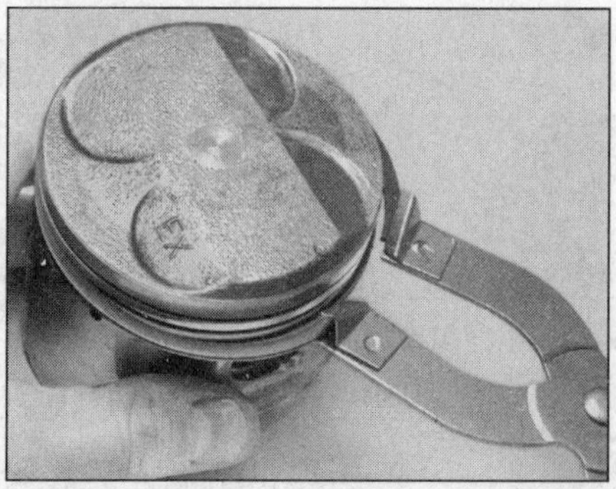

14.9 Compression rings can be removed with a ring removal and installation tool

3 Gently pull each liner out of the cylinder block using hand force only. Do not resort to the use of metal levers because the gasket surfaces will be damaged.

4 As each liner is removed, stuff the crankcase aperture with clean rag to cushion the piston and prevent anything falling into the crankcase.

5 Before removing the pistons, use a felt marker pen to write the cylinder number on the crown of each piston. Pry out the circlip on one side and push the piston pin out from the other side **(see illustration)**. On the outer pistons, the piston pins will have to be extracted inwards. Rotate the crankshaft so that the best access is obtained and remember the importance of the rag in preventing dropped circlips from falling into the crankcase.

> **HAYNES HiNT** ***If a piston pin is a tight fit in the piston bosses, soak a rag in boiling water then wring it out and wrap it around the piston – this will expand the alloy piston sufficiently to release its grip of the pin. Alternatively purchase (or make up) a piston pin drawbolt tool – see 'Tools and Workshop Tips' in the Reference section.***

Inspection

Liners

6 Check the cylinder walls carefully for scratches and score marks.

7 Using the appropriate precision measuring tools, check each bore's diameter. Measure near the top, centre and bottom of the bore, parallel to the crankshaft axis. Next, measure each bore's diameter at the same three locations across the crankshaft axis. Compare the results to this Chapter's Specifications. If any cylinder bore is tapered, out-of-round, worn beyond the service limit, or badly scuffed or scored, it should be renewed together with its piston.

Pistons

8 Before the inspection process can be carried out, the pistons must be cleaned and the old piston rings removed.

9 Using the thumbs or a piston ring removal and installation tool, carefully remove the rings from the pistons **(see illustration)**. Do not nick or gouge the pistons in the process.

10 Scrape all traces of carbon from the tops of the pistons. A hand-held wire brush or a piece of fine emery cloth can be used once most of the deposits have been scraped away. Do not, under any circumstances, use a wire brush mounted in a drill motor to remove deposits

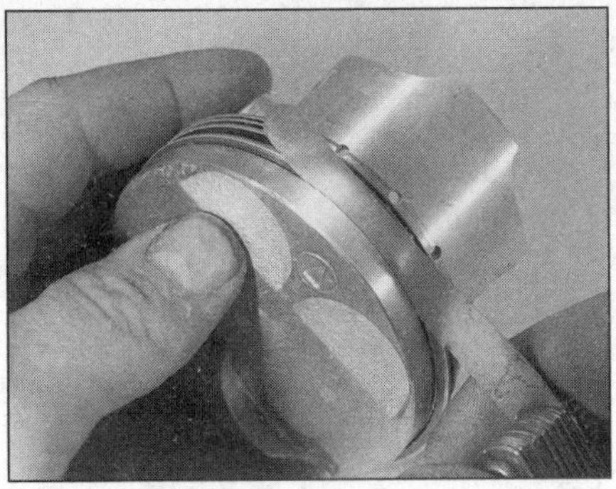

14.15 Measuring the ring-to-groove clearance

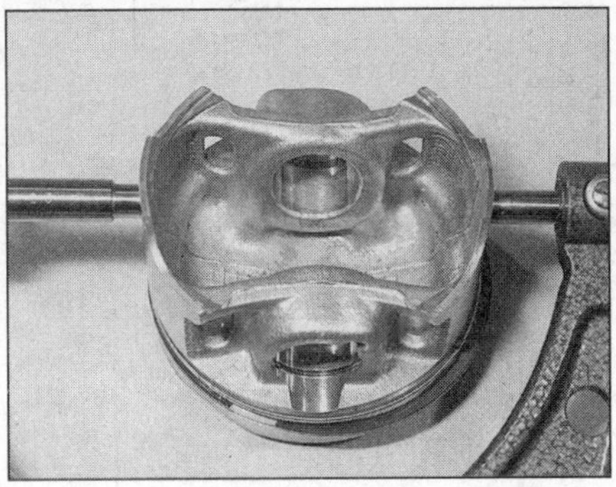

14.16 Measuring the piston diameter

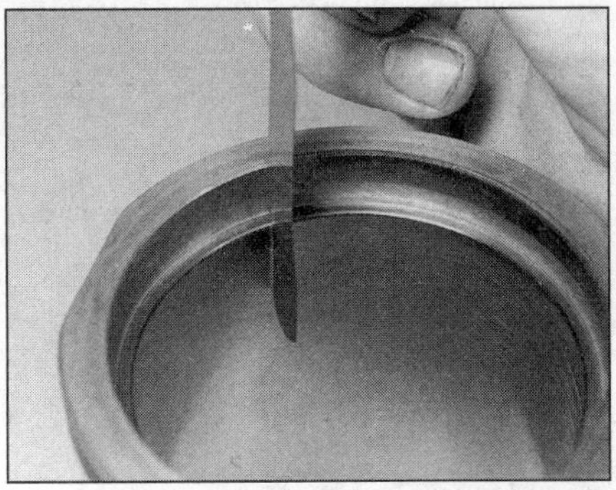

14.20 Measuring piston ring end gap

from the pistons; the piston material is soft and will be eroded away by the wire brush.

11 Use a piston ring groove cleaning tool to remove any carbon deposits from the ring grooves. If a tool is not available, a piece broken off an old ring will do the job. Be very careful to remove only the carbon deposits. Do not remove any metal and do not nick or gouge the sides of the ring grooves.

12 Once the deposits have been removed, clean the pistons with solvent and dry them thoroughly. Make sure the oil return holes below the oil ring groove are clear.

13 Carefully inspect each piston for cracks around the skirt, at the pin bosses and at the ring lands. Normal piston wear appears as even, vertical wear on the thrust surfaces of the piston and slight looseness of the top ring in its groove. If the skirt is scored or scuffed, the engine may have been suffering from overheating and/or abnormal combustion, which caused excessively high operating temperatures. The oil pump and cooling systems should be checked thoroughly.

14 A hole in the piston crown, an extreme to be sure, is an indication that abnormal combustion (pre-ignition) was occurring. Burned areas at the edge of the piston crown are usually evidence of spark knock (detonation). If any of the above problems exist, the causes must be corrected or the damage will occur again.

15 Measure the piston ring-to-groove clearance by laying a new piston ring in the ring groove and slipping a feeler blade in beside it **(see illustration)**. Check the clearance at three or four locations around the groove. If the clearance is greater than that specified, the piston is worn. Confirm this by measuring the piston ring groove width and comparing with the specification. **Note:** *Make sure you have the correct ring for the groove – the two compression rings can be identified by their profile* ***(see illustration 14.28a)***.

16 Measure the piston diameter 5 mm up from the bottom of the skirt and at 90° to the piston pin axis **(see illustration)**. If outside of the specified figure, the piston must be renewed.

17 If the necessary measuring equipment is available, measure the connecting rod small-end bore diameter, the piston pin outside diameter and the inside diameter of the piston bosses. Renew any component which is outside of the specification.

Piston rings

18 It is good practice to renew the piston rings when an engine is being overhauled. Before installing the new piston rings, the ring end gaps must be checked.

19 Lay out the pistons and the new ring sets so the rings will be matched with the same piston and cylinder during the end gap measurement procedure and engine assembly.

20 Insert the top ring into the top of the first liner and square it up with the cylinder walls by pushing it in with the top of the piston. The ring should be about 20 mm below the top edge of the liner. To measure the end gap, slip a feeler blade between the ends of the ring and compare the measurement to the Specification **(see illustration)**.

21 If the gap is larger or smaller than specified, double check to make sure that you have the correct rings before proceeding.

22 If the gap is too small, it must be enlarged or the ring ends may come in contact with each other during engine operation, which can cause serious damage. The end gap can be increased by filing the ring ends very carefully with a fine file. When performing this operation, file only from the outside in **(see illustration)**.

23 Excess end gap is not critical unless it is greater than 1 mm. Again, double check to make sure you have the correct rings for your engine and check that the bore is not worn.

24 Repeat the procedure for each ring that will be installed in the first cylinder and for each ring in the remaining cylinders. Remember to keep the rings, pistons and cylinders matched up.

25 Once the ring end gaps have been checked/corrected, the rings can be installed on the pistons.

26 The oil control ring (lowest on the piston) is installed first. It is composed of three separate components. Slip the expander into the groove, then install the upper side rail. Do not use a piston ring installation tool on the oil ring side rails as they may be damaged. Instead, place one end of the side rail into the groove between the expander and the ring land. Hold it firmly in place and slide a finger around the piston while pushing the rail into the groove. Next, install the lower side rail in the same manner **(see illustrations)**.

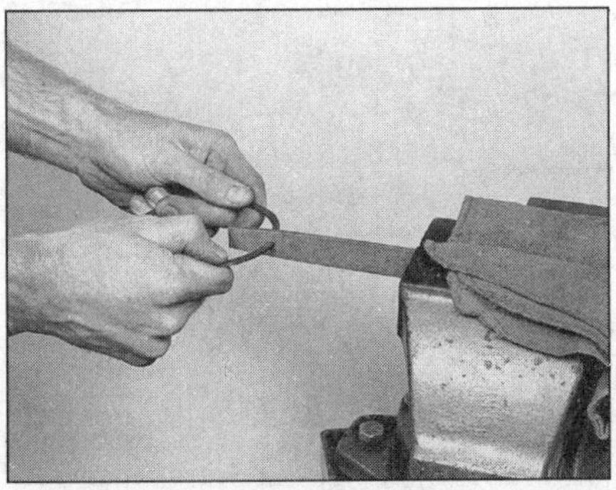

14.22 Ring end gap can be enlarged by clamping a file in a vice and filing

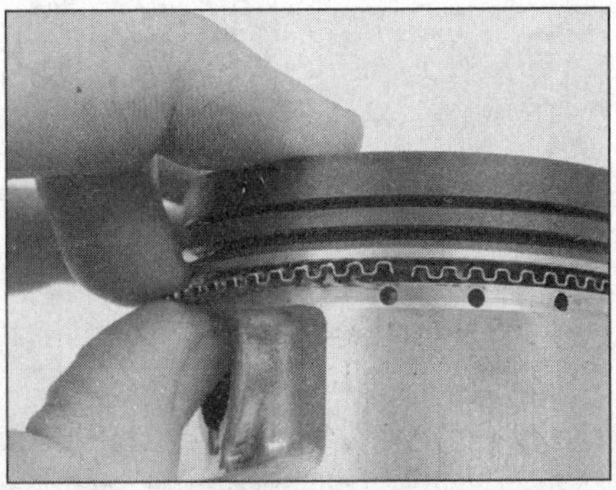

14.26a Install the oil ring expander in its groove . . .

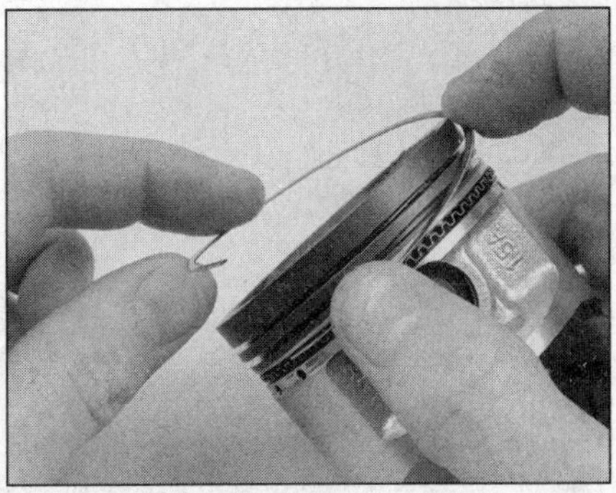

14.26b . . . and fit the side rails each side of it – the oil ring must be installed by hand

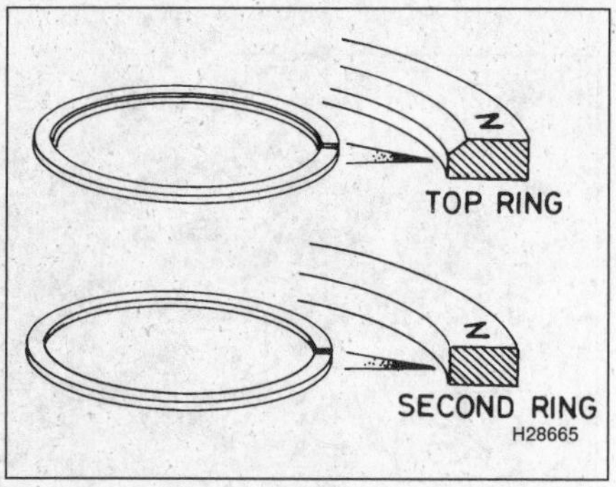

14.28a The compression rings differ in profile – the N mark indicates top surface

27 After the three oil ring components have been installed, check to make sure that both the upper and lower side rails can be turned smoothly in the ring groove.

28 Install the second (middle) ring next. **Note:** *The second ring and top rings are slightly different in profile.* Make sure that the letter N near the end gap is facing up **(see illustration)**. Fit the ring into the middle groove on the piston. Either use your thumbs to hold the ring ends apart when installing the ring over the piston, or slip sections of old feeler gauge blades between the ring and piston to guide it into its groove **(see**

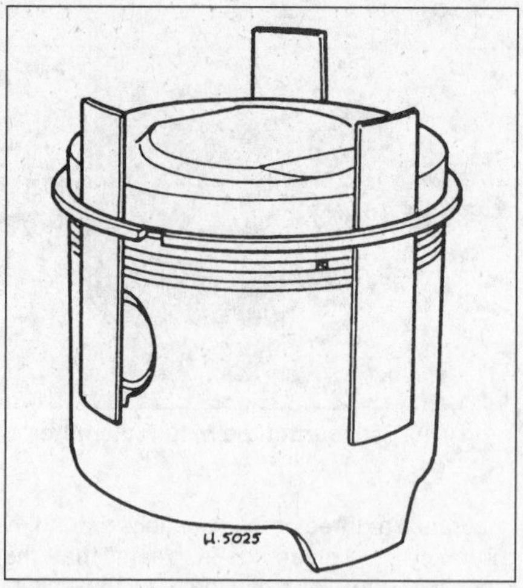

14.28b Old feeler gauge blades being used to guide the ring down over the piston and into its groove

illustration), or use a ring removal/installation tool **(see illustration 14.9)**.

Caution: Do not expand the ring any more than is necessary to slide it into place – the ring material is brittle and is easily broken if overstressed.

29 Finally, install the top ring in the same manner. The top ring can be distinguished

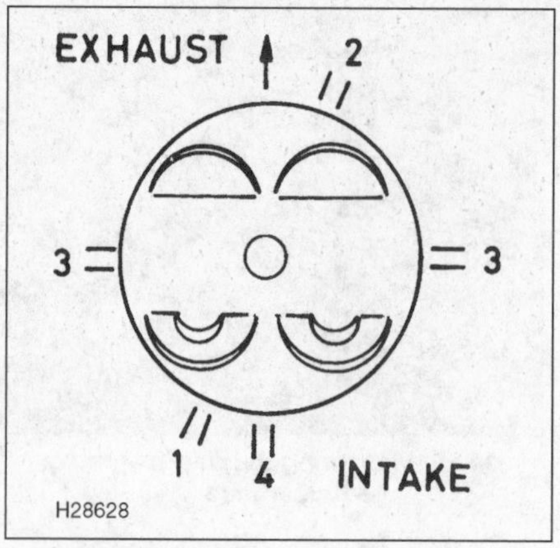

14.30 Position the ring end gaps correctly

1 Top ring end gap
2 Second (middle) ring end gap
3 Oil ring side rail end gaps
4 Oil ring expander end gap

from the second ring by its chamfer and chromed finish **(see illustration 14.28a)**. Make sure the letter N near the end gap is facing up.

30 Correct positioning of the ring end gaps is important **(see illustration)**.

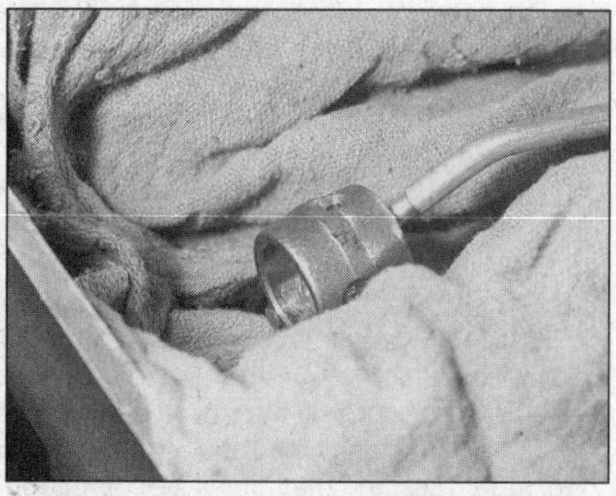

14.31 Lubricate the connecting rod small-end with engine oil

14.32a Install the piston so the arrow mark is opposite the con-rod oilway (arrowed)

Installation

31 Remove all traces of old sealant from around the cylinder liners and their sealing surface in the crankcase. Stuff clean rag into the crankcase mouth to prevent any dropped circlips falling in. Lubricate the small-end bore with engine oil **(see illustration)**.

32 Insert a new circlip in one side of the piston bore and install the piston on its rod so that the arrow marking on its crown is facing forwards, and opposite to the oilway in the connecting rod **(see illustration)**. Push the piston pin fully into the piston and secure with a second new circlip – make sure the circlip is fully seated in its groove **(see illustrations)**.

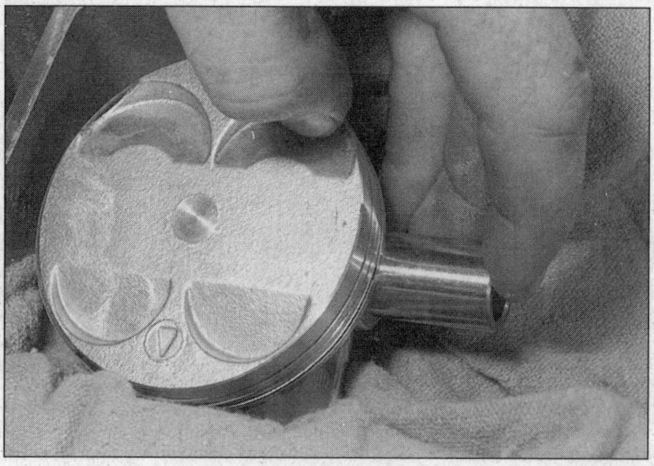

14.32b Install the piston pin . . .

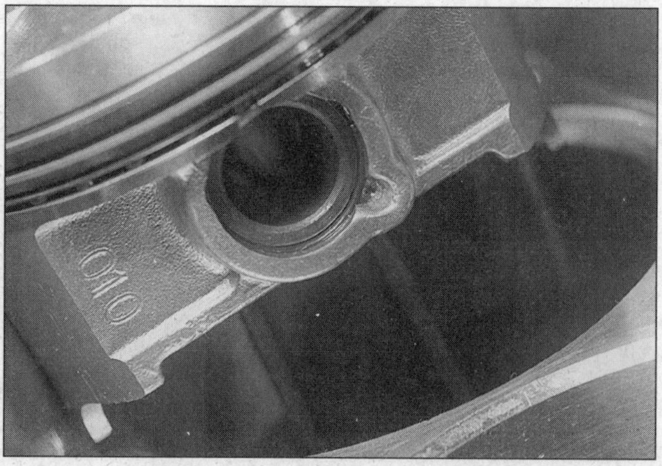

14.32c . . . and secure with a new circlip

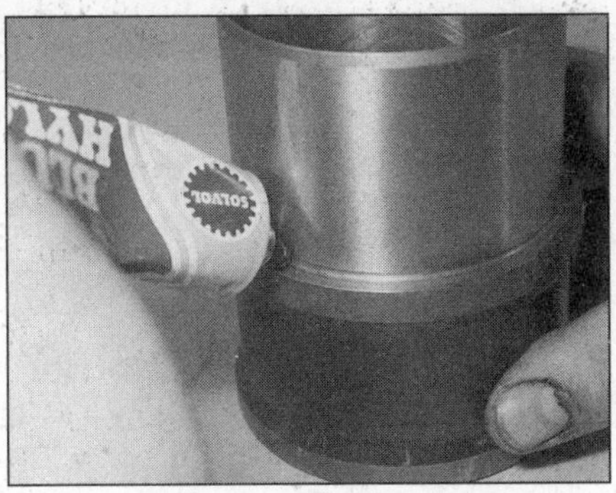

14.34a Apply a continuous bead of Blue Hylomar sealant to the liner seating . . .

14.34b . . . smooth it off and wait for it to cure

14.36 Install the cylinder liners in their original locations

33 Install the other pistons in the same way, rotating the crankshaft to gain the best access.

34 Remove any rag from the crankcase and make sure the liner seating area is clean, oil-free and dry. Do the same with the seating on the liners. Apply a continuous bead of Blue Hylomar sealant, 3 to 4 mm wide, to the liner seating **(see illustrations)**. Wait 15 minutes for the sealant to cure.

35 Check that the piston rings are correctly positioned in relation to the front of the engine **(see illustration 14.30)**.

36 Lubricate the bore surface of the liner with engine oil. Make sure that the piston is at TDC and slip the liner for that piston over the rings; make sure the liner is the correct way round **(see illustration)**. Compress each ring with your fingers as it enters the liner and use a gentle rocking motion as the liner is pushed downwards. The liner has a chamfered lead-in to enable the pistons to be installed without the use of ring compressors.

37 Install the other liners in the same way. As the piston is rotated to position the other pistons at TDC make sure that the installed liners do not lift off their seating. If this happens, the liners must be removed, cleaned and fresh sealant applied.

38 When all liners are in position with their top surfaces level with the cylinder block, install the cylinder head (see Section 11) **(see illustration)**.

15 Clutch – removal, inspection and installation

Note: *This procedure can be performed with the engine in the frame. If the engine has already been removed, ignore the preliminary steps which don't apply.*

Removal

1 On Trophy and Daytona models, remove the fairing right lower panel (see Chapter 8).

2 Drain the engine oil (Chapter 1).

3 On models where the crankcase breather hose comes off the clutch cover, detach the hose from its union **(see illustration)**.

4 Working in a criss-cross pattern, evenly slacken the clutch cover retaining bolts **(see illustration)**. Lift the cover away from the engine, being prepared to catch any residual oil which may be released as the cover is removed.

5 Remove the gasket and discard it. Note the two locating dowels fitted to the crankcase and remove these for safe-keeping if they are loose.

6 Remove the crankshaft right end cover with its gasket.

7 Working in a criss-cross pattern, gradually slacken the clutch spring retaining bolts until spring pressure is released **(see illustration)**. Remove the bolts, washers and springs, then lift out the clutch pressure plate complete with bearing and pushrod end piece. Withdraw the long pushrod.

14.38 Make sure the liner top surfaces are level with the cylinder block surface

8 Grasp the complete set of clutch plates and remove them as a pack. Unless the plates are being renewed, keep them in their original order.

9 The mainshaft must be locked to enable the clutch nut to be slackened. This can be done in several ways. If the engine is in the frame, engage 1st gear and have an assistant hold the rear brake on hard with the rear tyre in firm contact with the ground. Alternatively, the Triumph service tool (Pt. No. 3880025) can be located between the clutch centre and outer drum, and the engine positioned at TDC for cylinder No. 1 (T 1 mark aligned on 3 cylinder, T 1.4 mark aligned on 4 cylinder) and the transmission in gear as described above. If the engine is out of the frame, the tool shown in the reassembly sequence **(see illustration 15.27d)**, or in the 'Repair and overhaul tools' section of *Tools and Workshop Tips* at the end

15.3 Detach the breather hose from the clutch cover (arrowed)

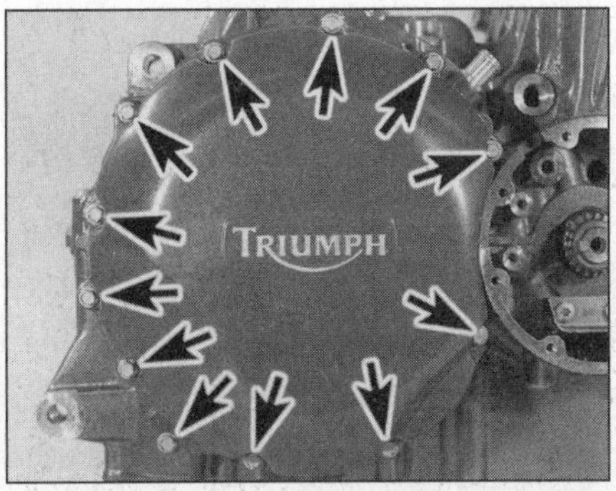

15.4 The clutch cover is retained by twelve bolts on 3 cylinder engines (arrowed)

15.7 Remove the five bolts to free the pressure plate

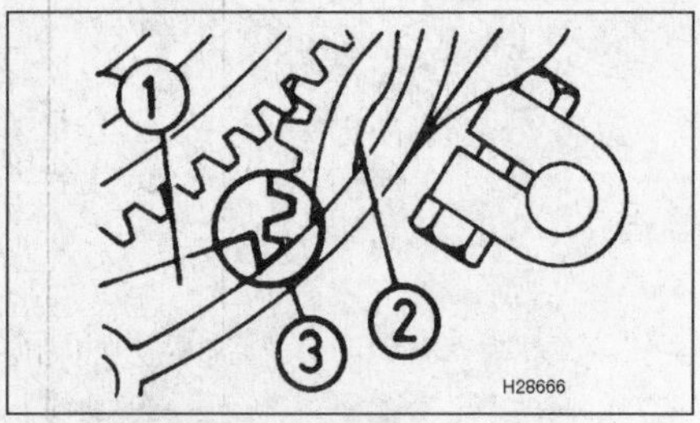

15.10 Balancer timing – 4 cylinder engine

1 Crankcase index mark
2 Balancer gear
3 Gear tooth and index mark alignment

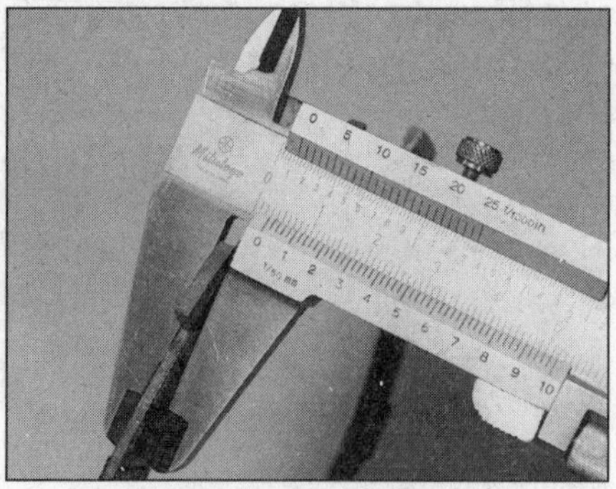

15.14 Measuring friction plate thickness

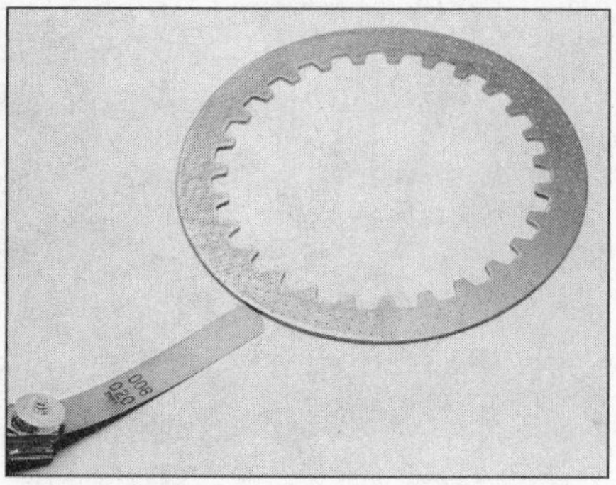

15.15 Measuring plain plate warpage

of this manual, can be used to grip the clutch centre whilst the nut is slackened. Unscrew the nut and washer from the mainshaft.

10 On 4 cylinder models, it is important to make a reference mark on the rear balancer drive gear at this stage. This will ensure correct timing of the balancers on reassembly. Position the engine at TDC for cylinders 1 and 4 (ie the T 1.4 mark on the ignition rotor in alignment with the centre of the pickup coil). Using white paint, or a permanent marker pen, mark the gear tooth of the balancer drive gear which is in alignment with the crankcase index mark in this position **(see illustration)**.

11 On all models, slide the clutch centre off the mainshaft, followed by the large thrustwasher and shim.

12 Pick the needle roller bearing and splined sleeve out of the middle of the clutch boss. Wiggle the outer drum gently back and forth to assist their removal. The outer drum can then be manoeuvred out of the crankcase.

13 Disengage the large auxiliary drive gear from the oil pump drive gear and alternator driveshaft gear. Slip the bush off the mainshaft.

Inspection

14 After an extended period of service the clutch friction plates will wear and promote clutch slip. Measure the thickness of each friction plate using a vernier caliper **(see illustration)**. If any plate has worn to or beyond the service limit given in the Specifications, the friction plates must be renewed as a set.

15 The plain plates should not show any signs of excess heating (bluing). Check for warpage using a flat surface and feeler blades **(see illustration)**. If any plate exceeds the maximum permissible amount of warpage, or shows signs of bluing, all plain plates must be renewed as a set. Check that there is no obvious sign of wear to the anti-judder plain plate in the middle of the clutch pack.

16 Inspect the clutch assembly for burrs and indentations on the edges of the protruding tangs of the friction plates and/or slots in the edge of the outer drum with which they engage. Similarly check for wear between the inner tongues of the plain plates and the slots in the clutch centre. Wear of this nature will cause clutch drag and slow disengagement during gear changes, as the plates will snag when the pressure plate is lifted. With care a small amount of wear can be corrected by dressing with a fine file, but if this is excessive the worn components should be renewed.

17 Inspect the mainshaft, bush and splined sleeve bearing surfaces for signs of wear and damage. Similarly, check the condition of the needle roller bearing.

18 Check the pressure plate bearing for wear. Ensure that the inner race of the bearing spins freely without any sign of notchiness. Push the bearing out of the pressure plate if renewal is required **(see illustration)**.

19 The clutch cover incorporates a noise damper on all models, and on certain models, also a breather. Where applicable, remove the retaining screws to free the breather plate, then remove the rubber seal **(see illustrations)**. Remove the retaining screws to free the noise damper plate, then lift out the damping foam pad **(see illustrations)**.

15.18 Bearing can be pressed out of pressure plate with hand pressure

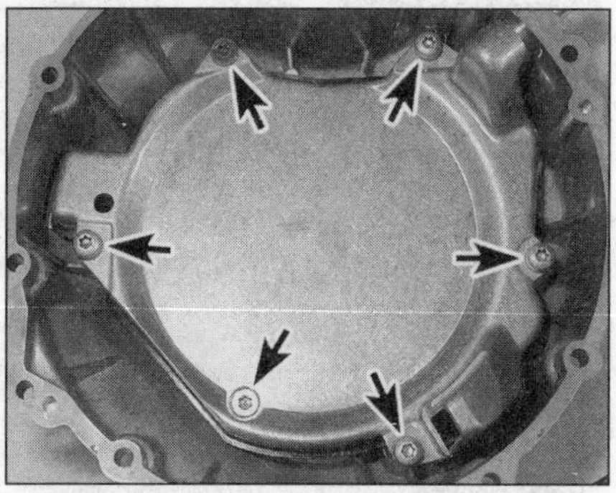

15.19a Where fitted, remove six screws (arrowed) to release breather plate

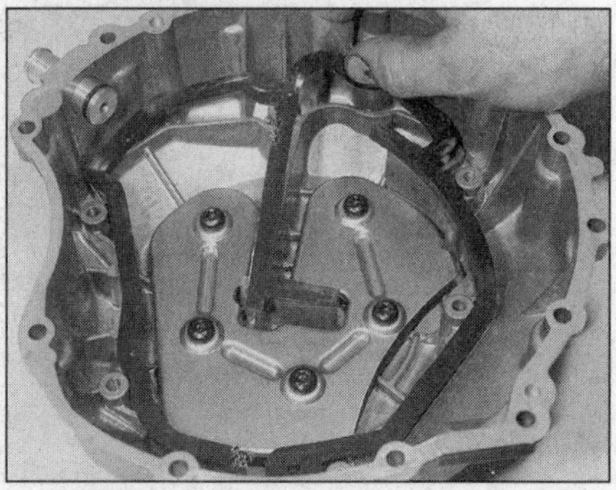

15.19b Seal resides between breather plate and clutch cover

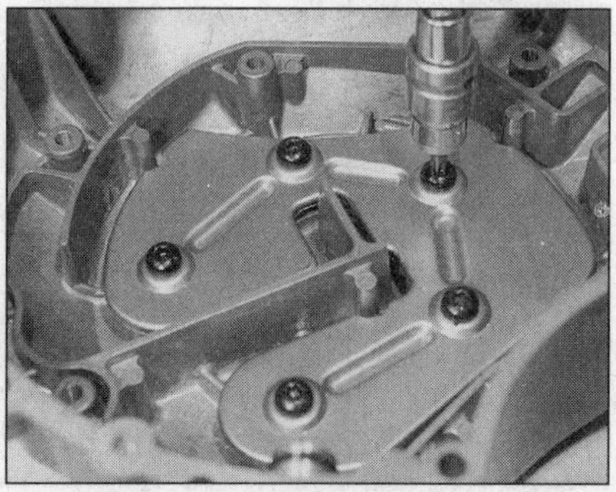

15.19c All models incorporate a noise damper in the clutch cover . . .

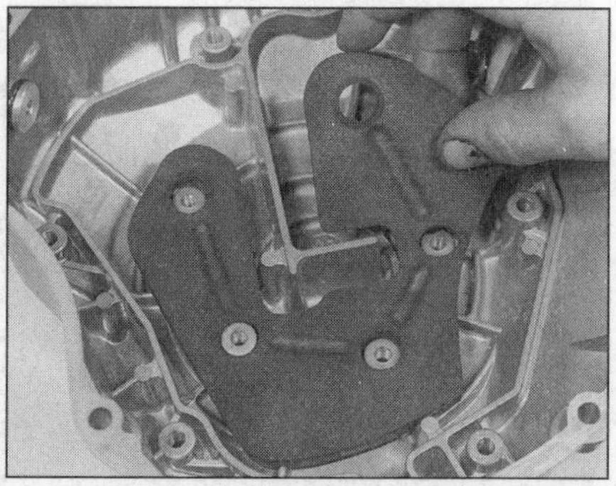

15.19d . . . which consists of a foam pad

15.21 Install bush on mainshaft – shouldered side faces the crankcase

15.22 Auxiliary gear meshes with alternator driveshaft gear at the top and oil pump drive gear at the bottom

Installation

20 Remove all traces of gasket from the crankcase and clutch cover surfaces.

21 Lubricate the bush with engine oil and slide it on the mainshaft so that its shouldered side faces the crankcase **(see illustration)**.

22 Install the auxiliary gear so that its dished side faces that the crankcase, meshing it with the oil pump drive gear and alternator driveshaft gear **(see illustration)**. **Note:** *If necessary, rotate the two-piece alternator driveshaft gear until its teeth align, permitting engagement with the auxiliary gear.* Make sure the auxiliary gear is central about the mainshaft.

23 On 3 cylinder engines, guide the outer drum over the mainshaft and into engagement with the primary drive gear on the crankshaft **(see illustration)**.

24 On 4 cylinder engines, check that the balancer shaft mark is aligned exactly with the index mark on the crankcase (see Step 10). Guide the outer drum over the mainshaft and into engagement with the primary drive gear on the crankshaft and the balancer drive gear – check that the marks still align.

25 On all models, hold the outer drum central to the mainshaft and insert the splined sleeve, ensuring that it passes through the auxiliary drive gear **(see illustrations)**. Lubricate the needle roller bearing and insert it between the sleeve and bush **(see illustration)**. Recheck the balancer shaft markings on 4 cylinder models.

26 Install the shim and large thrustwasher over the mainshaft **(see illustrations)**.

15.23 Manoeuvre clutch outer drum into the crankcase

15.25a Install the splined sleeve in the outer drum . . .

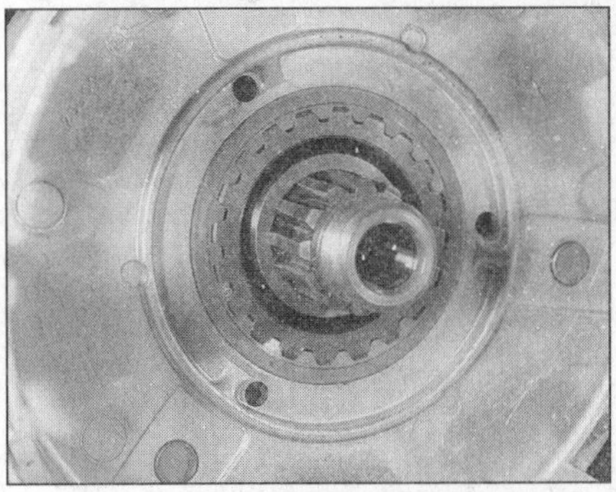

15.25b . . . and push it through into the auxiliary gear so that it lies flush with the outer drum boss

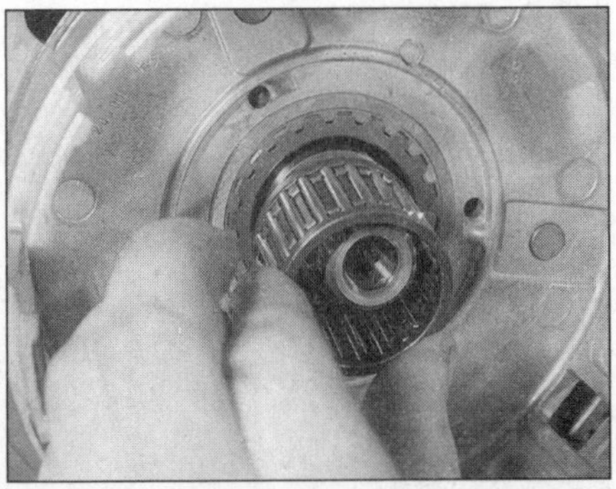

15.25c Slip the needle roller bearing between the outer drum and mainshaft bush

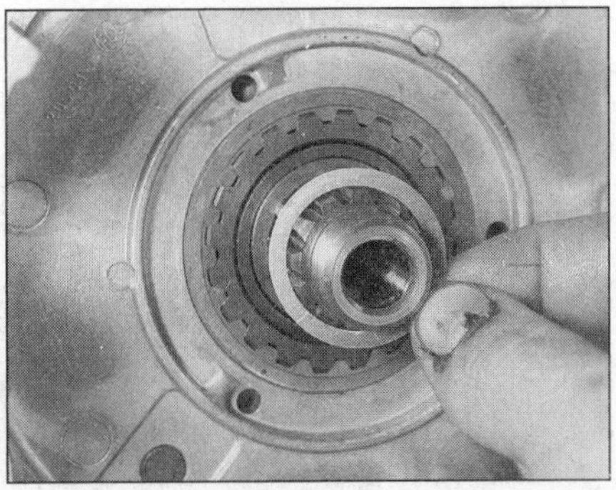

15.26a Install the shim on the mainshaft . . .

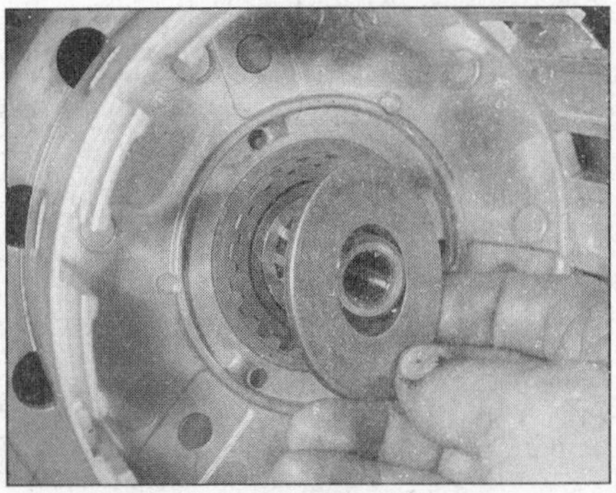

15.26b . . . followed by the large thrustwasher

15.27a Install the clutch centre over the mainshaft splines

15.27b OUT marked face of washer must face outwards

15.27c Install the clutch nut . . .

15.27d . . . and tighten to the specified torque, holding the clutch centre stationary

TOOL TIP

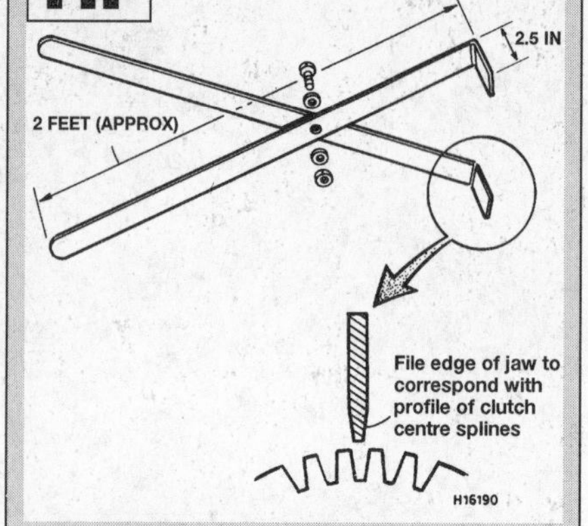

The clutch centre holding tool in illustration 15.27d can be made from steel strips

27 Insert the clutch centre over the mainshaft splines and install the washer, with its OUT marking facing outwards, followed by the clutch nut **(see illustrations)**. Using the method employed on dismantling to lock the mainshaft, secure the nut to the specified torque setting **(see illustration)**. **Note:** *Check that the clutch centre rotates freely after tightening.*

28 Build up the clutch plates in the outer drum, starting with a friction plate, then a plain plate and alternating friction and plain plates until all are installed **(see illustrations)**. The special plain plate (incorporating the anti-judder device) is installed in the middle of the clutch pack, as the 4th or 5th plain plate. **Note:** *If new plates are being fitted, coat their surfaces with engine oil to prevent seizure.*

29 Slip the pushrod into the mainshaft and install the end piece in the pressure plate bearing **(see illustrations)**.

30 Insert the pressure plate in the clutch, engaging the pushrod end piece with the

15.28a Start off with a friction plate . . .

15.28b . . . followed by a plain plate

15.28c Install the special plain plate in the middle of the clutch pack

15.29a Slide the pushrod into the mainshaft

15.29b Pushrod end piece locates in the pressure plate bearing as shown

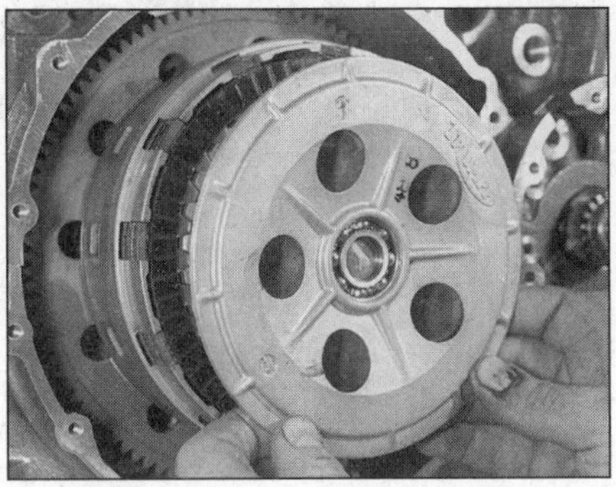

15.30a Install the pressure plate . . .

15.30b . . . the springs . . .

15.30c . . . bolts and washers

15.30d Tighten the bolts to the specified torque

15.31a A dowel (arrowed) is fitted at the bottom . . .

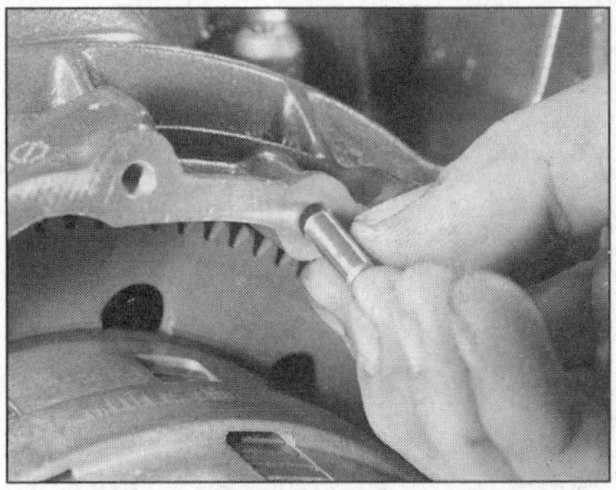

15.31b . . . and top of the crankcase

pushrod **(see illustration)**. Install the springs, washers and bolts and tighten them evenly in a criss-cross sequence to the specified torque setting **(see illustrations)**.

31 Insert the dowels in the crankcase **(see illustrations)**. Place a new gasket on the crankcase and install the cover **(see illustrations)**. Tighten the cover bolts evenly in a criss-cross sequence to the specified torque setting. Where applicable, reconnect the breather hose.

32 Install the crankshaft right end cover using a new gasket and tighten its bolts to the specified torque setting.

33 Refill the engine with oil (see Chapter 1).

34 Where applicable, install the fairing sections (see Chapter 8).

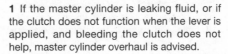

16 Clutch master cylinder – removal, overhaul and installation

1 If the master cylinder is leaking fluid, or if the clutch does not function when the lever is applied, and bleeding the clutch does not help, master cylinder overhaul is advised.

Removal

2 Remove the two screws holding the reservoir cap in place. Lift off the cap and diaphragm.

3 Pull the dust cap off the bleed valve on the release cylinder. Attach a length of clear tubing to the valve and direct its other end into a container. Pump the clutch lever until all fluid has drained from the reservoir. Tighten the bleed valve.

4 Remove the clutch lever pivot bolt, locknut and collar and withdraw the lever. On Tiger models this will also release the hand guard.

5 Disconnect the wire connectors from the clutch switch **(see illustration)**.

6 Pull back the rubber boot, loosen the banjo union bolt, and separate the clutch hose from the master cylinder. Wrap the hose end in a clean rag, then suspend it in an upright position or bend it down carefully and place the open end in a clean container. The objective is to prevent excessive loss of fluid, fluid spills and system contamination.

7 Remove the two master cylinder clamp

15.31c Install a new gasket (hold it in place with a dab of sealant if necessary) . . .

15.31d . . . and fit the clutch cover

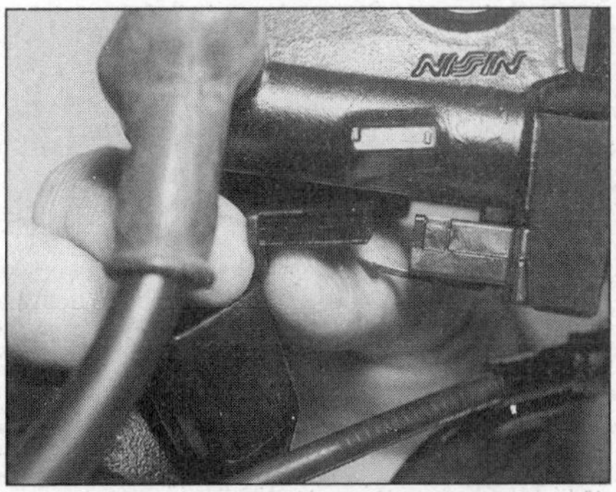

16.5 Pull back the dust boot and pull the wires off the clutch switch

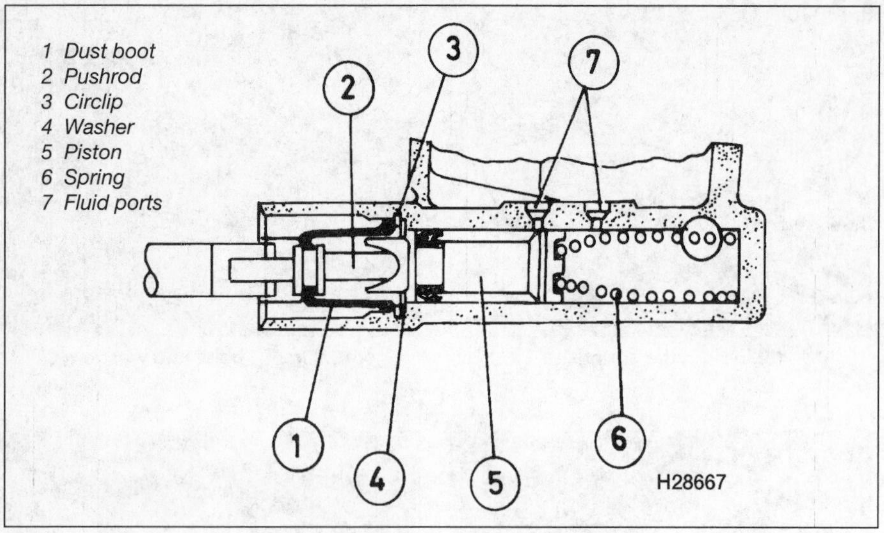

16.8 Master cylinder piston components

bolts and remove the unit from the handlebar.

Overhaul

8 Remove the dust boot from the end of the master cylinder piston. Using circlip pliers, release the circlip and withdraw the pushrod, washer, piston and spring **(see illustration)**. Lay the parts out in order on a clean surface.

9 Remove the screw to release the clutch switch from the base of the master cylinder.

16.14a Install clutch master cylinder clamp as shown . . .

10 Clean the piston and master cylinder bore with clean hydraulic fluid or brake system cleaner.

Caution: Do not, under any circumstances, use a petroleum-based solvent to clean hydraulic parts.

11 Inspect the piston and master cylinder bore for signs of corrosion, nicks and burrs and loss of plating. If surface defects are found, the piston and cylinder should be renewed. If the master cylinder is in poor condition the release cylinder should also be overhauled. Check that the fluid inlet and outlet ports in the master cylinder are clear.

12 Note the fitted position of the piston seal, then pry it off the piston and install a new seal in the same direction as the original.

13 Install the spring in the master cylinder so that its tapered end faces the piston. Lubricate the piston seal with clean hydraulic fluid and slip the piston into the master cylinder, followed by the washer and pushrod. Retain these components with the circlip, making sure that it locates in the master cylinder groove. Locate the dust boot in the bore and engage its outer end in the pushrod groove.

Installation

14 Position the master cylinder and its clamp on the handlebar with clamp arrow pointing upwards and the top edge of the clamp aligned with the punched dot on the handlebar **(see illustrations)**. Install the two clamp bolts, fully tighten the upper bolt first to the specified torque setting, then do the same with the lower.

15 Reconnect the wires to the clutch switch **(see illustration 16.5)**.

16 Using a new sealing washer on each side of the banjo union, bolt it into place on the master cylinder. Tighten the banjo bolt to the specified torque setting so that it abuts the lug on the master cylinder **(see illustration)**.

17 Install the clutch lever (and hand guard on Tiger models), locate the collar in the base of the pivot and secure with the bolt and locknut.

18 Fill the reservoir with new hydraulic fluid and bleed the clutch (see Section 18).

17 Clutch release cylinder – removal, overhaul and installation

Removal

1 On Trophy and Daytona models, remove the left lower fairing panel as described in Chapter 8.

2 Remove the clutch hose banjo union bolt and separate the hose from the release cylinder. Plug the hose end or wrap a plastic bag around it to minimise fluid loss and prevent dirt entering the system. Discard the sealing washers; new ones must be used on installation. **Note:** *If you're planning to overhaul the release cylinder and don't have a source of compressed air to blow out the piston, just loosen the banjo bolt at this stage and retighten it lightly. The bike's hydraulic system can then be used to force the piston out of the body once the cylinder has been unbolted. Disconnect the hose once the piston has been sufficiently displaced.*

3 Remove the three bolts and withdraw the release cylinder from the sprocket cover **(see illustration)**. If the release cylinder is not

16.14b . . . and align joint with dot on handlebar (arrowed)

16.16 Hydraulic hose banjo union must abut lug (arrowed) on master cylinder

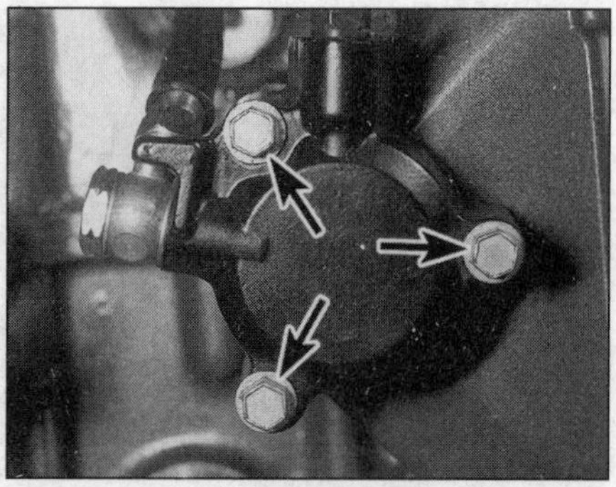

17.3 Clutch release cylinder is retained by three bolts (arrowed)

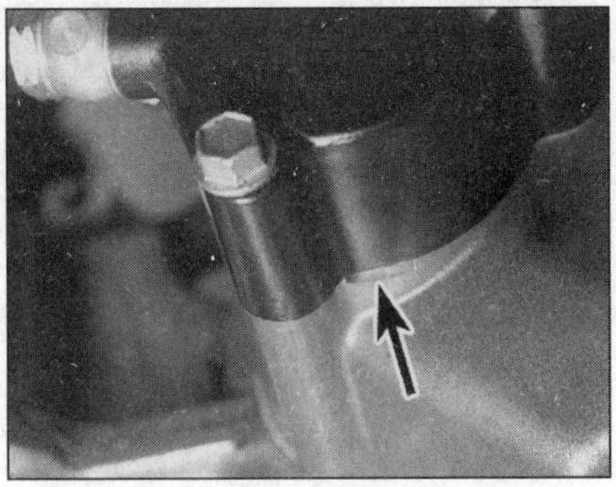

17.4 Fluid escape slot (arrowed) on underside of release cylinder

being disassembled, the piston can be prevented from creeping out of the release cylinder by restraining it with a couple of cable-ties **(see illustration 5.16)**. **Note:** *The hydraulic hose is routed behind the large coolant hose from the water pump to the cylinder block. The coolant must be drained and the coolant hose removed before the hydraulic hose can be freed.*

Overhaul

4 The release cylinder has a slot on its underside which allows the escape of hydraulic fluid in the event of the piston seal failing **(see illustration)**. Hydraulic fluid might otherwise be forced under pressure past the single-lipped pushrod seal and into the transmission.

5 Have a supply of clean rags on hand, then pump the clutch lever to expel the piston under hydraulic pressure. If the hose has already been detached, use a jet of compressed air directed into the fluid inlet to expel the piston.

Warning: Use only low air pressure, otherwise the piston may be forcibly expelled causing injury.

6 Recover the spring from the piston.

7 Using a plastic or wood tool, remove the piston seal from the piston groove.

8 Clean the piston and release cylinder bore with clean hydraulic fluid or brake system cleaner.

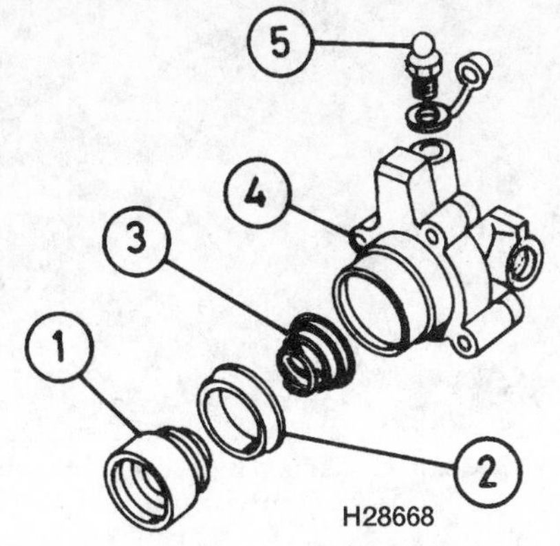

17.10 Release cylinder components

1 Piston
2 Piston seal
3 Spring
4 Release cylinder body
5 Bleed valve

Caution: Do not, under any circumstances, use a petroleum-based solvent to clean hydraulic parts.

9 Inspect the piston and release cylinder bore for signs of corrosion, nicks and burrs and loss of plating. If surface defects are found, the piston and cylinder should be renewed. If the release cylinder is in poor condition the master cylinder should also be overhauled.

10 Lubricate the new piston seal with clean hydraulic fluid and install it on the piston; make sure it is fitted the correct way round. Install the spring in the release cylinder so that its tapered end faces the piston **(see illustration)**. Lubricate the piston and seal with clean hydraulic fluid and insert the piston in the release cylinder. Use the thumbs to press it fully into the cylinder.

11 The pushrod can be withdrawn from the sprocket cover if required. If the pushrod oil seal requires renewal, remove the sprocket cover (see Chapter 6), slide out the pushrod, and prise the old seal out with a flat-bladed screwdriver **(see illustration)**. Press the new seal in using thumb pressure.

Installation

12 If the pushrod was removed smear it with engine oil and slide it back into the sprocket

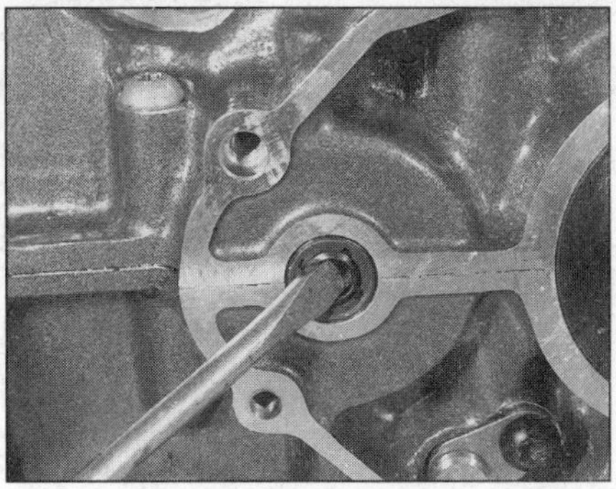

17.11 Pushrod oil seal can be prised out of the crankcase

cover. Apply a dab of grease to its end and install the release cylinder **(see illustration)**.

13 Install the two long retaining bolts in the left holes and the short bolt in the right hole; tighten them to the specified torque setting **(see illustration)**.

14 If the hydraulic hose was disconnected, use a new sealing washer on each side of the banjo union. Position the union so that its tab abuts the lug on the release cylinder and tighten the banjo bolt to the specified torque setting **(see illustration)**.

15 Remove the two screws and lift off the master cylinder reservoir cap and diaphragm. Fill the reservoir with new fluid and bleed the system as described in the next section.

18 Clutch - bleeding

1 Bleeding the clutch is simply the process of removing all the air bubbles from the clutch fluid reservoir, the hydraulic hose and the release cylinder. Bleeding is necessary whenever a clutch system hydraulic connection is loosened, when a component or hose is renewed, or when the master cylinder or release cylinder is overhauled. Leaks in the system may also allow air to enter, but leaking clutch fluid will reveal their presence and warn you of the need for repair.

2 To bleed the clutch, you will need some

17.12 Grease the end of the pushrod and install the release cylinder

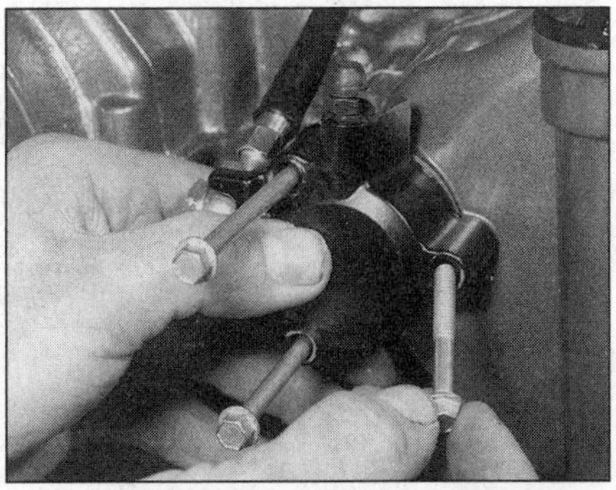

17.13 The shorter of the three retaining screws locates in the right-hand hole

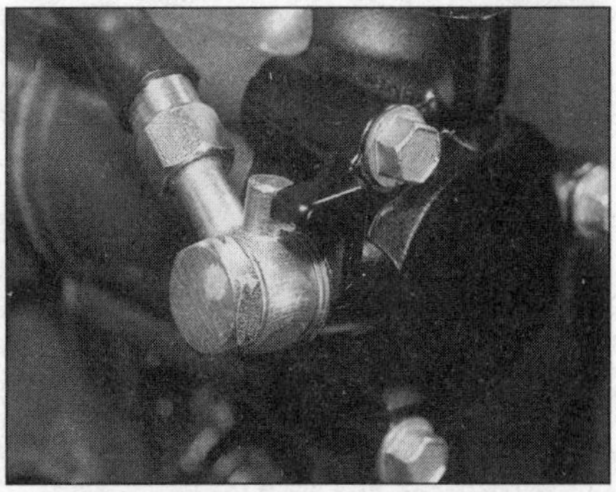

17.14 Ensure that the tab on the banjo union abuts the lug on the release cylinder

18.6 **Locate the spanner and tubing over the bleed valve on the release cylinder**

19.6 **Sump is retained by seventeen bolts on 3 cylinder engine**

19.8 **Internal oil pipe is retained by two bolts (arrowed) on 3 cylinder engine**

new, clean DOT 4 hydraulic fluid, a length of clear vinyl or plastic tubing, a small container partially filled with clean fluid, a supply of clean rags and a spanner to fit the bleed valve.

3 Cover the fuel tank and other painted components to prevent damage in the event that fluid is spilled.

4 On Trophy and Daytona models, remove the left lower fairing panel (see Chapter 8). On models so equipped, rotate the clutch lever span adjuster to position No. 1.

5 Position the bike on its centre stand, or where only a sidestand is fitted, have an assistant hold it upright so that the master cylinder is level. Remove the two screws retaining the master cylinder reservoir cap, then lift off the cap and diaphragm. Slowly pump the clutch lever a few times until no air bubbles can be seen floating up from the bottom of the reservoir. Doing this bleeds air from the master cylinder end of the hose.

6 Pull the dust cap off the bleed valve on the release cylinder and attach one end of the clear tubing to the valve **(see illustration)**. Submerge the other end in the fluid in the container. Check the fluid level in the reservoir. Do not allow it to drop below the lower mark during the bleeding process.

7 Pump the clutch lever three or four times and hold it in against the handlebar whilst opening the bleed valve. When the valve is opened, fluid will flow out of the release cylinder into the clear tubing.

8 Tighten the bleed valve, then release the lever gradually. Repeat the process until no air bubbles are visible in the fluid leaving the release cylinder and the clutch action feels smooth and progressive.

9 Ensure that the reservoir is topped up above the lower level mark on the sightglass, install the diaphragm and cap and secure with the two screws. Wipe up any spilled fluid and check that there are no leaks from the system. Refit the dust cap over the bleed valve.

10 Install the fairing panel (where applicable). Where applicable, return the front brake lever span adjuster to its original position.

19 Sump – removal and installation

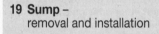

Note: *The sump can be removed with the engine in the frame. If work is being carried out with the engine removed ignore the steps which don't apply.*

Removal

1 On Trophy and Daytona models, remove the fairing lower panels (see Chapter 8). On Tiger models, remove the sump guard (see Chapter 8).

2 Where equipped, remove the oil cooler (see Section 21).

3 Remove the exhaust system (Chapter 4).

4 Drain the engine oil and remove the oil filter (see Chapter 1).

5 Disconnect the wires from the oil pressure switch. **Note:** *This only applies to early models with the switch mounted on the sump – later engines have the switch mounted on the upper crankcase.*

6 Remove all seventeen (3 cylinder) or twenty (4 cylinder) bolts, slackening them evenly in a criss-cross sequence to prevent distortion **(see illustration)**. Withdraw the sump and its gasket. **Note:** *On 3 cylinder engines, the internal oil pipes may stick in the sump – carefully ease them free with a long flat-bladed screwdriver rather than risk distorting them by pulling the sump off.*

7 Recover the large O-ring from the oil filter housing.

8 The internal oil pipe can be unbolted from the base of the crankcase if desired **(see illustration)**. Take note of the exact position of the bolts on 4 cylinder models – their hole diameters differ. Recover the O-rings from the oil pipe.

9 A gauze strainer is located in the sump. Clean the strainer whenever the sump is removed. Remove its five bolts to free the retaining plate and lift out the gauze **(see illustration)**. Wash the gauze in solvent. Four cylinder models have a second gauze strainer for the oil cooler; this can be removed after releasing its three bolts.

Installation

10 Remove all traces of gasket from the sump and crankcase mating surfaces.

11 Installed the cleaned oil strainer(s) and tighten the bolts securely **(see illustrations)**.

19.9 **Oil strainer is retained by five bolts**

19.11a **Clean the strainer gauze and locate it back in the sump**

19.11b **Secure the strainer with the retaining plate**

19.12a Use a new O-ring on the oil filter housing . . .

19.12b . . . and new sealing washers on the oil pipe banjo unions

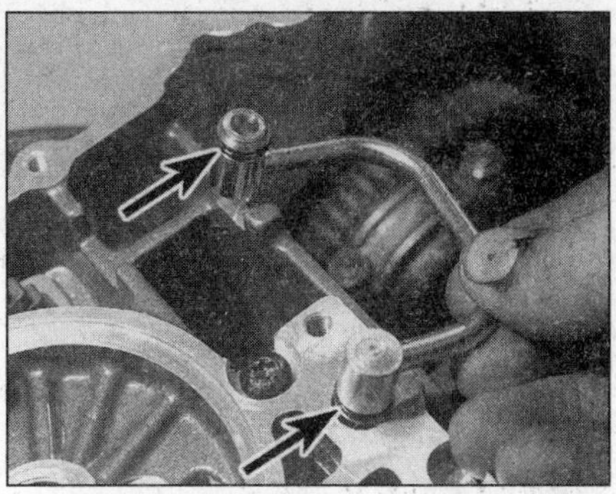

19.12c Use new O-rings (arrowed) on the small oil pipe (3 cylinder only)

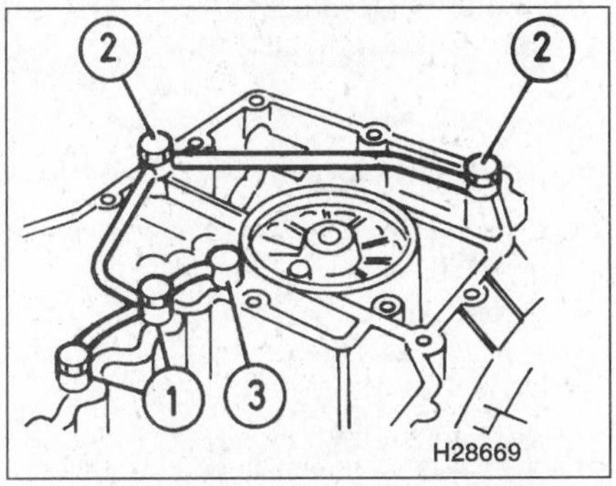

19.12d Ensure that the banjo bolts are fitted in the correct holes when installing the internal oil pipe on 4 cylinder engines

1 Banjo bolts with 1.5 mm holes
2 Banjo bolts with 3.0 mm holes
3 O-ring location

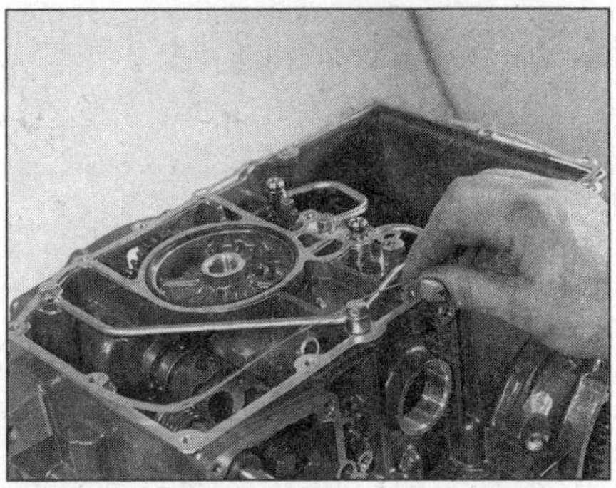

19.13a Always use a new sump gasket

19.13b Install the sump on the crankcase

12 Fit new O-rings to the internal oil pipe(s) and to the oil filter housing **(see illustration)**. Install the oil pipe using new sealing washers on each side of the banjo unions, and tighten the banjo bolts to the specified torque setting **(see illustration)**. On 4 cylinder engines, ensure that the bolts with the larger holes are fitted in their original locations **(see illustration)**.

13 Place a new gasket on the crankcase and install the sump; if the engine is in the frame, use a smear of grease on the gasket to hold it in place as the sump is installed **(see illustrations)**. Check that the bolts are returned to their original locations and tighten them evenly in a criss-cross sequence to the specified torque setting.

14 Reconnect the oil pressure switch wires (where applicable).

15 Install the oil cooler (see Section 21).

16 Install the exhaust system as described in Chapter 4.

17 Install a new oil filter, then fill the engine with the correct type and quantity of oil as described in Chapter 1 and *Daily (pre-ride) checks*. Start the engine and check that there are no leaks.

18 If all is well, fit the fairing lower panels (Trophy and Daytona models) or sump guard (Tiger) (see Chapter 8).

20 Oil pressure relief valve – removal, inspection and installation

Removal

1 Remove the sump (see Section 19). Use a socket to unscrew the relief valve from inside of the sump **(see illustration)**.

Inspection

2 Push the plunger into the relief valve body and check for free movement. If the valve operation is sticky it must be renewed (individual parts are not available).

Installation

3 Apply a drop of non-permanent thread locking compound to the pressure relief valve threads and tighten the valve to the specified torque setting **(see illustration)**.

4 Install the sump (see Section 19).

20.1 Pressure relief valve is located in sump

20.3 Apply thread lock to the relief valve threads on installation

21 Oil cooler – removal and installation (where fitted)

Note: *The oil cooler can be removed with the engine in the frame. If work is being carried out with the engine removed ignore the preliminary steps.*

Removal

1 Remove the fairing lower panels (see Chapter 8).

2 Drain the engine oil (see Chapter 1).

3 On 3 cylinder engines, remove the two

2

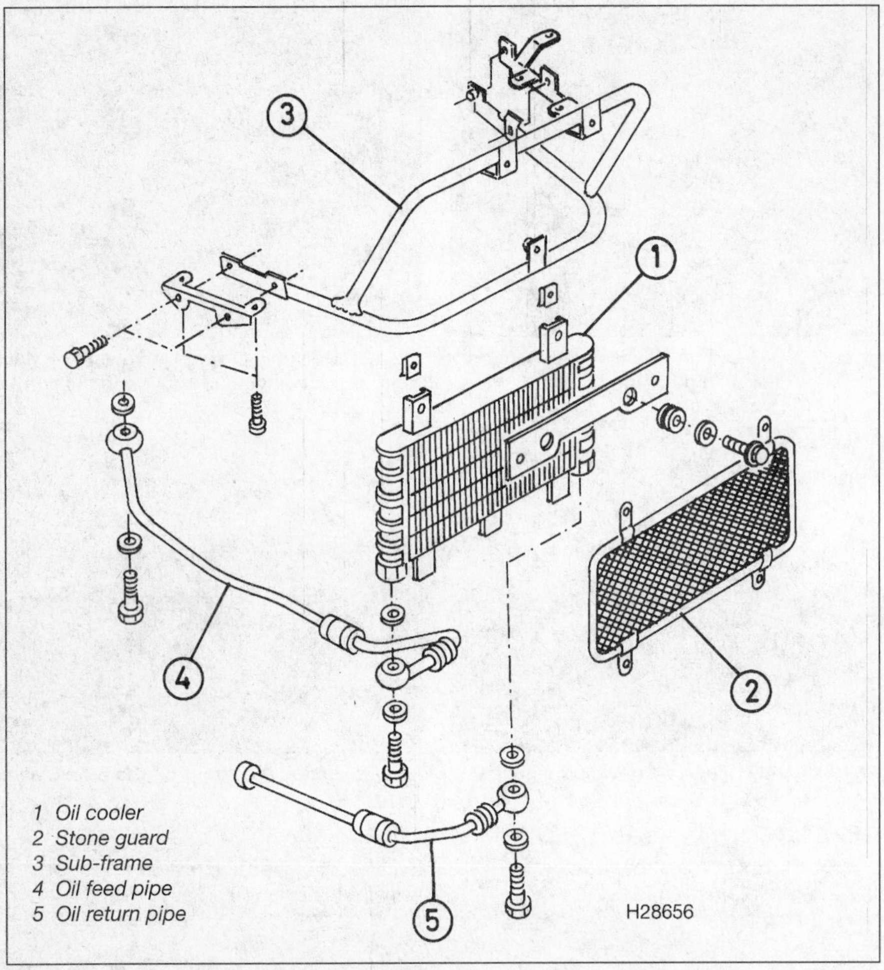

21.3 Oil cooler components – 4 cylinder engine

banjo union bolts and free the oil pipes from their connections on the sump. On 4 cylinder engines the oil feed pipe is retained by a banjo union bolt, and the oil return pipe by a gland nut on the union at the front of the sump; hold the union with an open-ended spanner whilst the gland nut is unscrewed **(see illustration)**.

4 Remove the three bolts, with their collars which retain the oil cooler to its sub-frame.

5 The oil pipes can be released from the oil cooler by removing their banjo union bolts. ***Caution: Always counterhold the hexagonal union of the oil cooler when slackening or tightening the banjo bolts.***

6 Remove the bolts to free the sub-frame from its mounting brackets on the engine. The oil cooler front stone guard is secured by four bolts.

Installation

7 Installation is a reverse of the removal procedure, noting the following:

a) Use new sealing washers on each side of the banjo unions.

b) Tighten the banjo union bolts to the specified torque settings.

c) On 4 cylinder models, counterhold the return pipe union on the sump whilst the gland nut is tightened.

d) Refill the engine with oil (see Chapter 1 and 'Daily (pre-ride) checks)' and check that there are no leaks from the oil cooler pipe connections when the engine is run.

22 Balancer – removal, inspection and installation

3 cylinder models

Note: *The balancer can be removed with the engine in the frame.*

Removal

1 On Trophy and Daytona models, remove the fairing lower panels (see Chapter 8).

2 Where fitted, free its clip and pull the breather hose off the union on the crankcase left cover **(see illustration)**. All early models (up to VIN 4338) have an external oil pipe to the crankcase left cover – remove the banjo union bolts and washers to free the pipe from the left cover.

3 On all models remove the ten bolts to free the crankcase left cover and gasket **(see illustration)**. On Thunderbird, Thunderbird Sport, Adventurer and Legend TT models, retrieve the cover dowels if they are loose. **Note:** *Have a drain tray ready to catch any escaping oil, particularly if the bike is on its sidestand.*

4 Moving to the other side of the engine. On Trident, Sprint, Trophy, Speed Triple, Daytona and Tiger models remove the balancer shaft end cover (three bolts) **(see illustration)** and the crankcase right end cover (seven bolts). On Thunderbird, Thunderbird Sport, Adventurer and Legend TT models, a

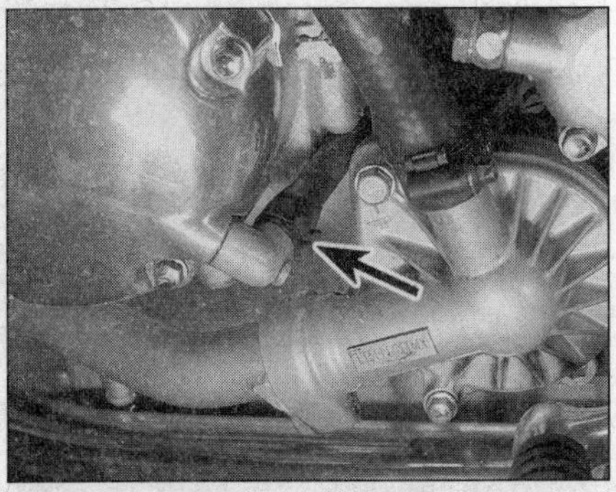

22.2 Release its clip and pull the breather hose off its union (arrowed) – Thunderbird model

22.3 Remove the ten bolts to free the crankshaft left end cover

22.4a Trident, Sprint, Trophy, Speed Triple, Daytona and Tiger models have a separate balancer end cover on the right side of the engine

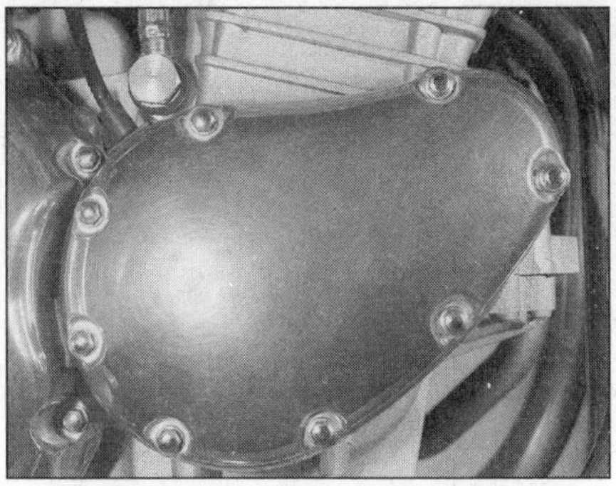

22.4b A combined cover is fitted to Thunderbird, Thunderbird Sport, Adventurer and Legend TT models

22.6 Balancer shaft gear can be disassembled after removal of the circlip

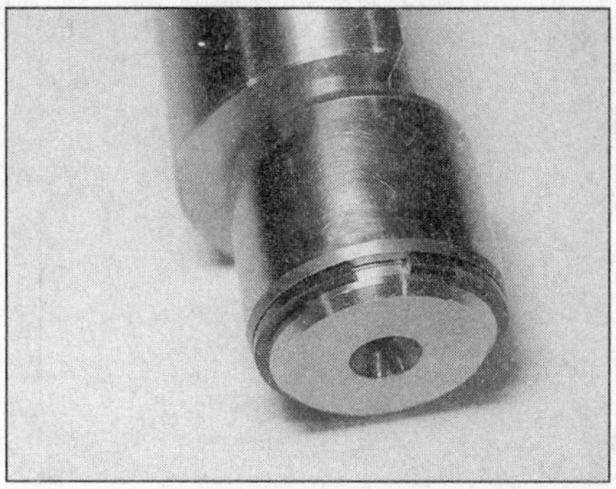

22.10a Needle roller bearing inner race is retained to balancer shaft by a circlip . . .

combined cover is fitted to the crankcase right side, retained by eight bolts **(see illustration)**.

5 Using a wrench on the large hexagon, rotate the crankshaft until the T mark for cylinder No. 1 aligns with the centre of the pick-up coil **(see illustration 9.2b)**. Observe the balancer gears on the left side of the engine. It will be seen that the drive gear on the crankshaft has two dots on consecutive teeth which will be in the 10 o'clock position. There is a similar dot on the balancer shaft outer gear, which when aligned between the two dots on the drive gear will permit access to the balancer shaft retaining plate screws through the holes in the gear.

6 The balancer shaft gear is a two-piece assembly, the main gear and the outer gear described above. Designed to prevent gear chatter, the outer gear has a different number of teeth to the main gear. Therefore, it is likely that when first inspected, the outer gear dot will not be in alignment with those on the drive gear. To correct this, rotate the crankshaft as necessary until its dot lies between the dots on the drive gear teeth, remembering at every stage to align the No. 1 T mark on the ignition rotor with the pick-up coil. Alternatively, remove the large circlip, convex washer and plain washer from the end of the balancer shaft and withdraw the outer gear **(see illustration)**.

7 With access to the balancer shaft retaining plate bolts, pass a Torx bit through the holes

22.10b . . . and the bearing itself is located in the crankcase

in the balancer gear and slacken the retaining plate bolts. Note that the screws will not withdraw through the gear – the objective is to slacken them just enough for the plate to drop down via its elongated holes.

8 When the retaining plate is heard to drop down out of engagement with the balancer shaft, withdraw the shaft from the crankcase.

Inspection

9 Inspect the teeth of all gears for signs of wear or damage. Early models (up to VIN 6957) were fitted with anti-backlash springs in the balancer shaft outer gear.

10 Check the ball bearing on the shaft left end, noting that if worn, the complete balancer shaft must be renewed. The bearing on the right end of the shaft is of the caged

22.10c The needle roller bearing can only be removed once the peg (arrowed) in the crankcase surface has been withdrawn

needle roller type; its inner race is secured by a circlip and its outer race by peg which can only be accessed after the crankcases have been separated **(see illustrations)**.

Installation

11 Clean the threads of the retaining plate screws and apply a drop of non-permanent thread locking compound to their them **(see illustration)**. Secure the retaining plate to the crankcase so that it is at its lowest setting, but leave the screws fairly loose **(see illustration)**.

12 Check that the crankshaft is positioned so that the No. 1 cylinder T mark on the ignition rotor aligns with centre of the pick-up coil. Install the balancer shaft in the crankcase, guiding its left end into the needle bearing **(see illustrations)**. Mesh the balancer shaft

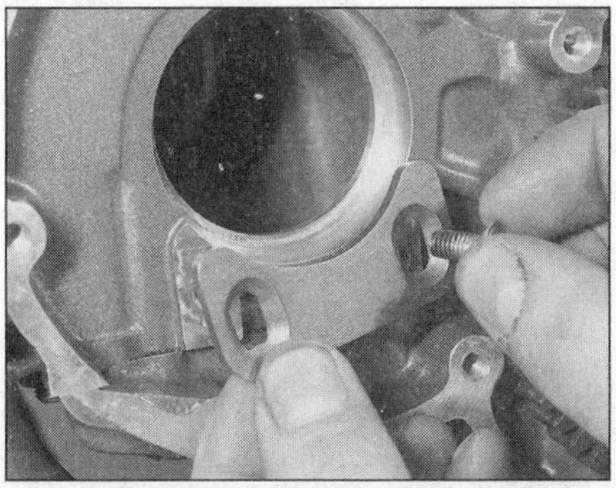

22.11a Apply thread lock to the retaining plate screws . . .

22.11b . . . and install them so that the plate is in the lowest position – leave the screws loose at this stage

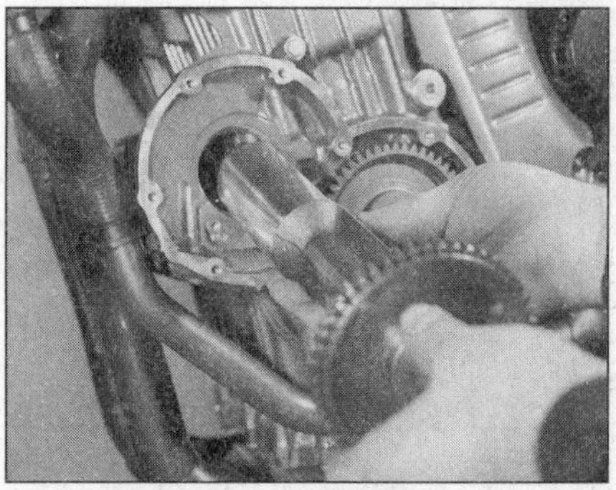

22.12a Install the balancer shaft . . .

22.12b . . . guiding it into the needle roller bearing

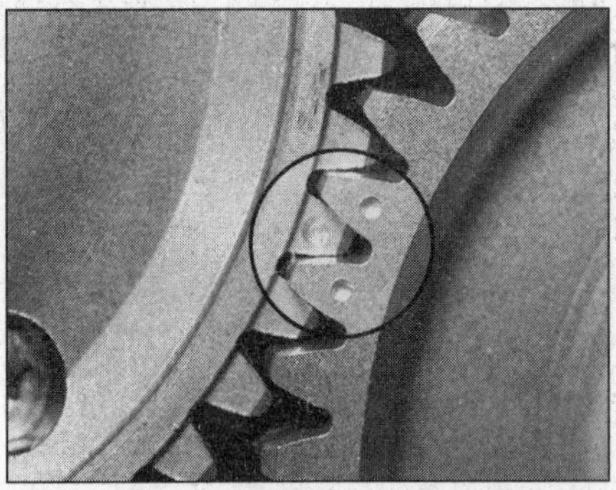

22.12c Mesh the balancer shaft gear with the drive gear so that the teeth dots align

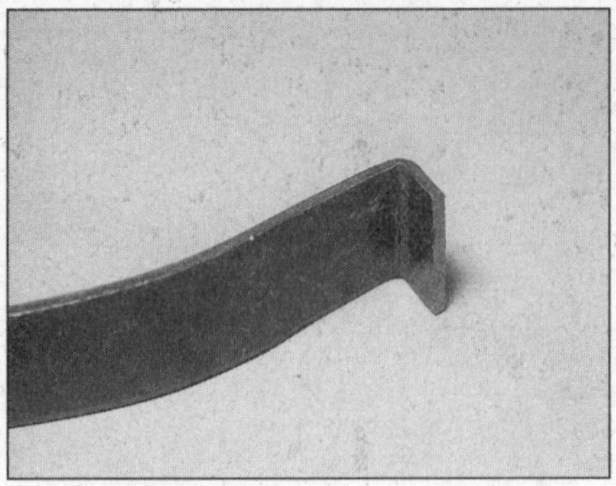

22.13a Make up a tool to access the retaining plate . . .

gear with the drive gear so that their dots align (see Step 5) **(see illustration)**. **Note:** *If the balancer outer gear is in place on the balancer shaft, use finger pressure only to hold the main gear and outer gear teeth in alignment while they are meshed with the drive gear teeth.*

13 Some means must now be devised to lift the retaining plate into engagement with the balancer shaft whilst the screws are tightened. We found a length of steel strip with the end bent over at a right angle, to be ideal **(see illustration)**. With the tool holding the retaining plate in position, tighten the screws to the specified torque **(see illustration)**.

14 If previously removed, install the outer gear, plain washer and convex washer (dished side facing inwards), then retain them with the large circlip **(see illustrations)**.

15 On Thunderbird, Thunderbird Sport, Adventurer and Legend TT models, the oil seal set in the crankshaft left end cover must be renewed whenever the cover is disturbed – failure to do so will prevent the engine breather from operating properly. Prise the old seal out with a flat-bladed screwdriver. The new seal is supplied complete with a shaped mandrel; press the seal into the cover so that it lies just below the face of the cover recess. Remove the mandrel from the seal immediately before the cover is fitted to the engine.

Caution: It is important that the seal is allowed 15 minutes to form on the breather tube before the crankshaft is rotated from its present position – the breather will not operate correctly if this precaution is not observed.

16 All models have sound absorbing material housed inside the crankcase cover; if required, this can be accessed by removing the retaining screws **(see illustration)**. Install a new gasket on the crankcase and on Thunderbird, Thunderbird Sport, Adventurer and Legend TT models only, install the two

22.13b . . . and lift the retaining plate into position whilst the screws are tightened through the access holes in the gear

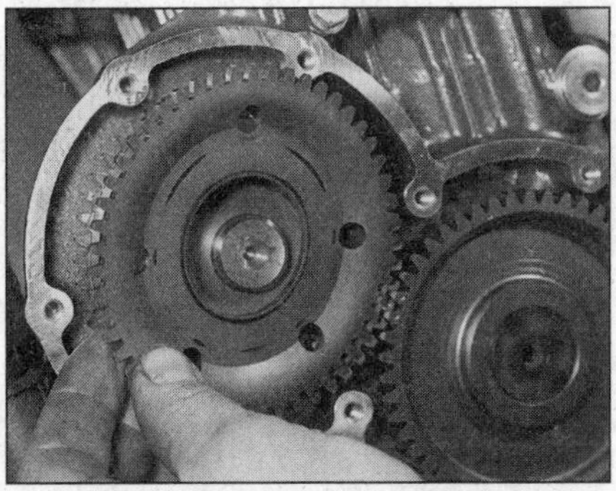

22.14a If removed, install the outer gear . . .

22.14b . . . followed by the washer . . .

22.14c . . . and convex washer

22.14d Secure the outer gear components with the circlip

22.16a Crankshaft left end cover noise damper is retained by six screws

dowels **(see illustration)**. Install the cover and tighten its bolts evenly in a criss-cross sequence to the specified torque setting. On early models, reconnect the external oil pipe using new sealing washers. Where fitted, reconnect the breather hose.

Caution: On Thunderbird, Thunderbird Sport, Adventurer and Legend TT models, make sure to observe the time requirement in Step 15.

17 Using new gaskets, install the crankcase right cover and balancer end cover (one-piece cover on Thunderbird, Thunderbird Sport, Adventurer and Legend TT models), tightening the bolts securely **(see illustration)**.

18 Check the oil level and top-up if any was lost whilst the covers were removed (see *'Daily (pre-ride) checks'*).

19 Install the fairing lower panels on Trophy and Daytona models.

4 cylinder models

Note: *It should be possible to remove the balancer shafts with the engine in the frame. However, working will be awkward and aligning the marks on the shafts may prove difficult due to limited access. Removal of the engine is advised.*

22.16b Use a new gasket when installing the crankshaft left end cover

Removal

20 Remove the sump (see Section 19). Where fitted, remove the oil cooler (see Section 21).

21 Remove the crankcase right cover and using a spanner on the engine turning hexagon, rotate the engine in the direction of the arrow on the ignition rotor so that the T 1.4 mark aligns with the centre of the ignition pick-up coil. Inspect both balancer weights for alignment marks **(see illustration 22.27)**. If they are indistinct or none are found, mark your own with white paint or a marker pen.

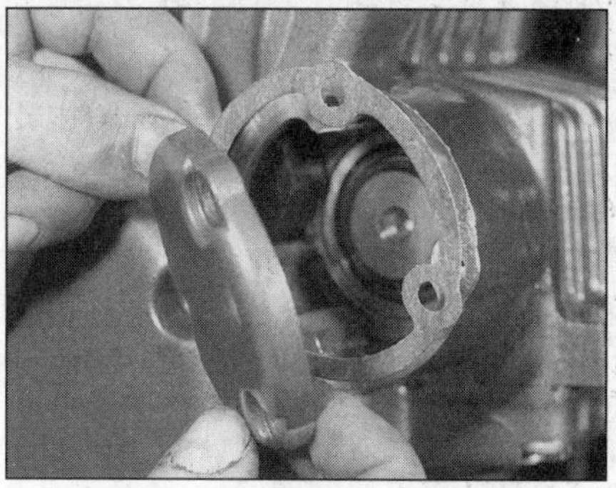

22.17 Fit a new gasket and install the balancer shaft end cover – where applicable

22 Slacken off the balancer shaft pinch bolts, and the two clamp retaining bolts, then pull the clamp off the shaft ends **(see illustration 22.24)**.

23 Hold the balancer weight from inside the sump area and withdraw the shaft from the side of the crankcase. Retrieve the thrustwashers from each end of the weight assembly. Label the shafts front and rear to ensure that they are returned to their original locations.

Inspection

24 Separate the balancer gear from the weight and inspect the rubber damping blocks; if damaged or deteriorated, these must be renewed **(see illustration)**.

25 Check the needle roller bearings in the weight. If damaged or worn they must be extracted and new ones pressed into place.

Installation

26 Install new O-rings on the end of each balancer shaft.

27 With the engine positioned as described in Step 21, install the first weight in the crankcase, complete with thrustwashers, so that its alignment mark corresponds with that on the casing **(see illustration)**. Holding the weight in this position, slide the balancer shaft into the crankcase so that the dot on its end is facing downwards (toward to the sump). Install the second weight and balancer shaft in the same way, making sure that the drive gears mesh correctly.

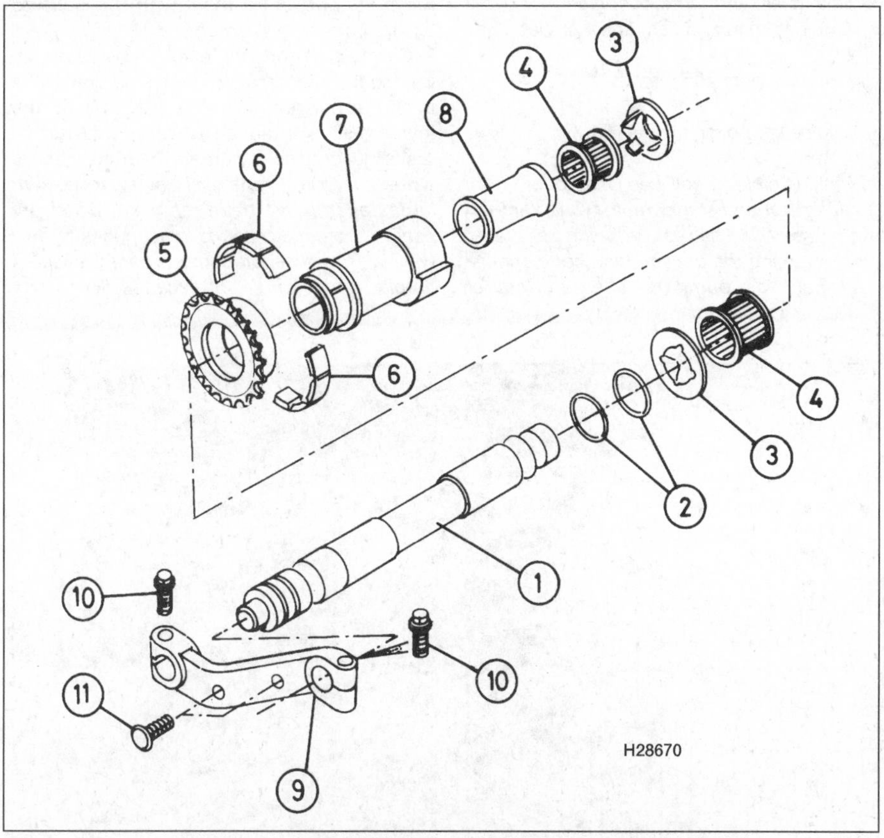

22.24 Balancer shaft components – 4 cylinder models

1 Balancer shaft
2 Shaft O-rings
3 Thrustwashers
4 Needle roller bearings
5 Drive gear
6 Rubber damping blocks
7 Balancer weight
8 Spacer
9 Clamp
10 Shaft pinch bolts
11 Clamp retaining bolts

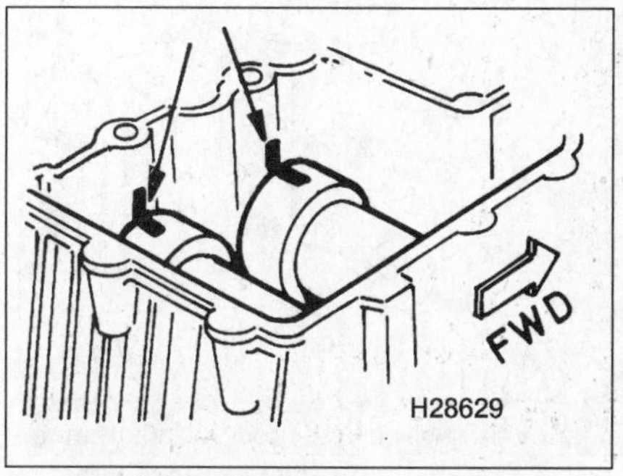

22.27 Balancer shaft weight and crankcase alignment marks (arrowed)

22.28 Balancer shaft adjustment

1 Clamp retaining bolts
2 Front balancer shaft
3 Rear balancer shaft
4 Shaft pinch bolts

28 Install the balancer clamp over the shaft ends and secure with its retaining screws. Using a flat-bladed screwdriver in the front balancer shaft, turn it clockwise until it will turn no further, then back it off a fraction; hold this position and tighten the shaft pinch bolt **(see illustration)**.
29 Using a flat-bladed screwdriver in the rear balancer shaft, turn it anti-clockwise until it will turn no further, then back it off a fraction; hold it here, and tighten the shaft pinch bolt.
30 Install the crankcase right cover using a new gasket. Install the sump (see Section 19), oil cooler (see Section 21) and refill the engine with oil (see Chapter 1 and *'Daily (pre-ride) checks'*).
31 Start the engine and whilst allowing it to idle, listen for any noise from the balancers. A rattle indicates that the balancer gears are too loosely meshed, whereas a whine indicates they are too tightly meshed. Make adjustment whilst the engine is idling, noting that only one balancer pinch bolt should be slackened and adjustment made at a time.

23 Crankcase – separation and reassembly

Separation

1 To gain access to the crankshaft and connecting rods, bearings, alternator/starter drive, oil pump and transmission components, the crankcase must be split into two parts. **Note:** *Early models have a detachable cover on the upper crankcase which permits removal of the alternator driveshaft and starter clutch (see Section 32). Later models do not have the detachable cover. Note that the crankcase bolt locations differ accordingly.*
2 To enable the crankcases to be separated, the engine must be removed from the frame (see Section 5) and the following components first removed with reference to the relevant Sections.

a) Camshafts and tappets
b) Cam chain and tensioner blade
*c) Cylinder head and cam chain guide blade**
*d) Cylinder liners and pistons**
e) Clutch
f) Engine left cover
g) Sump
h) Ignition pick-up coil (see Chapter 5)
i) Alternator and starter motor (Chapter 9)

**If the crankcase halves are being separated just to examine the transmission components, crankshaft, oil pump or alternator/starter clutch drive, then there is no need to remove the cylinder head.*

3 If a complete engine overhaul is planned, also remove the balancer(s) (see Section 22), the oil galley plug, the water pump (see Chapter 3), and the neutral switch (see Chapter 9).
4 On early engines (with an alternator driveshaft/starter clutch access cover), remove the nine bolts from the top of the crankcase, then withdraw the cover and gasket.
5 With the crankcase the right way up, slacken and remove all bolts from the top of the crankcase following the numbered sequence **(see illustrations)**. **Note:** *As each bolt is removed, store it in its relative position in a cardboard template of the crankcase halves. This will ensure that all bolts are installed in the correct location on reassembly.*
6 Turn the crankcase upside down. Again, following the numbered sequence, slacken and remove all bolts from the bottom of the crankcase **(see illustrations)**. **Note:** *As each bolt is removed, store it in its relative position in a cardboard template of the crankcase halves. This will ensure that all bolts are installed in the correct location on reassembly. Also, take note of any mounting brackets on the bolts and store them with the bolts to ensure correct reassembly.*
7 Carefully lift off the lower crankcase half, leaving the crankshaft and transmission shafts in the upper half of the crankcase. As the lower half is lifted away take care not to dislodge or lose any main bearing inserts. **Note:** *If it won't come easily away, make sure all fasteners have been removed. Don't pry against the crankcase mating surfaces or they will leak; initial separation can be achieved by tapping gently with a soft-faced mallet.*

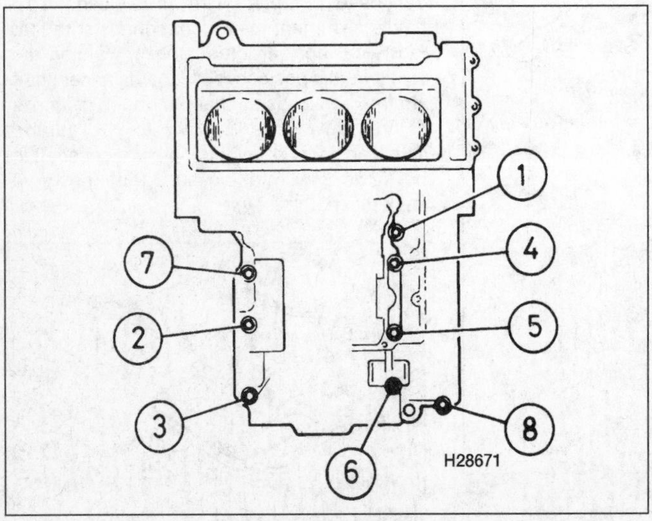

23.5a Upper crankcase bolt sequence – early engines with access cover (see text)
Bolt locations same for 4 cylinder engines

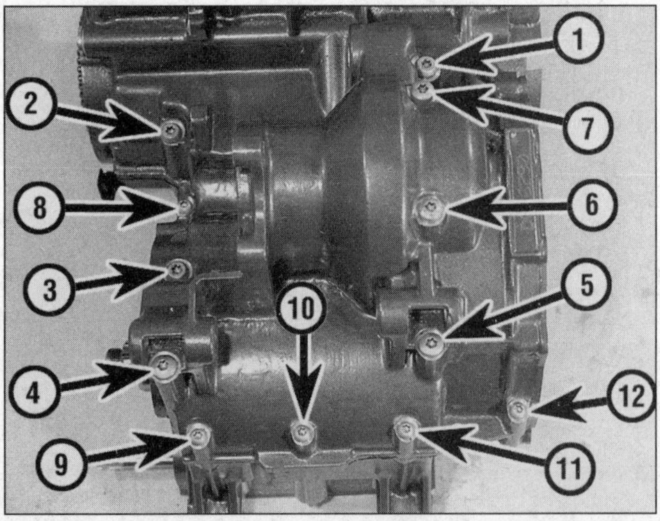

23.5b Upper crankcase bolt sequence – later engines (see text)
Bolt locations same for 4 cylinder engines

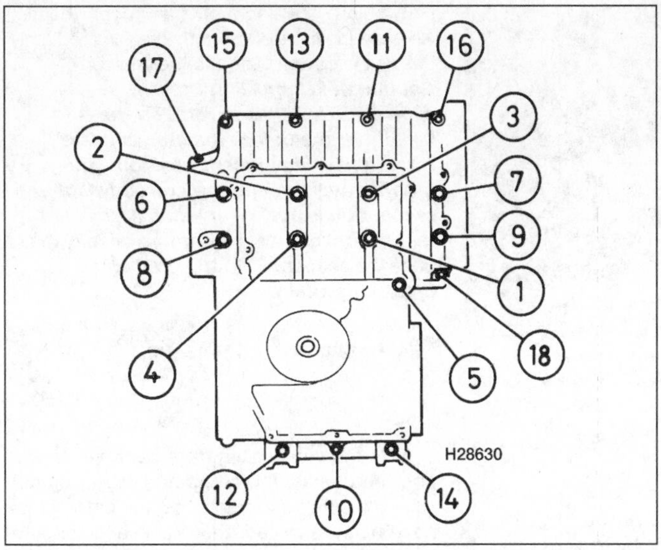

23.6a Lower crankcase bolt sequence – early 3 cylinder engines (see text)

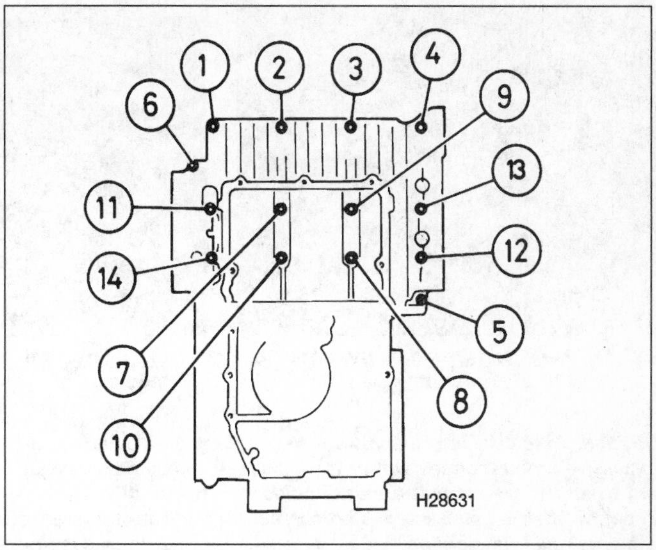

23.6b Lower crankcase bolt sequence – later 3 cylinder engines (see text)

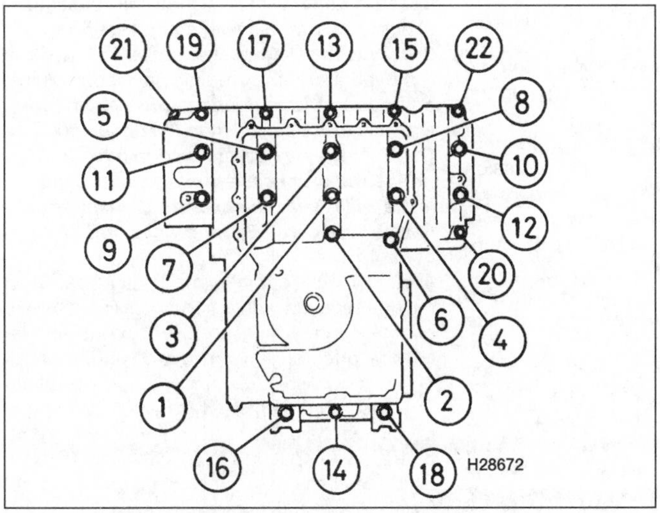

23.6c Lower crankcase bolt sequence – early 4 cylinder engines (see text)

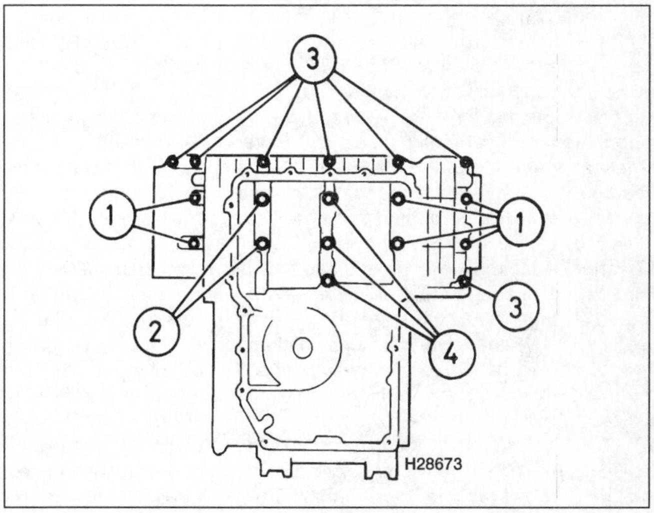

23.6d Lower crankcase bolt sequence – later 4 cylinder engines (see text)

8 Remove the three locating dowels from the upper crankcase half **(see illustration)**. Discard the clutch pushrod oil seal; it must be renewed on reassembly. Retrieve the O-ring from the oil pump outlet and obtain a new one for reassembly.

Reassembly

9 Remove all traces of sealant from the crankcase mating surfaces.

10 Ensure that all components are in place in the upper and lower crankcase halves. Note the instructions in Section 28 concerning applying thread lock to the transmission shaft bearing outer races.

11 Lubricate the transmission shafts and crankshaft with clean engine oil, then use a rag soaked in high flash-point solvent to wipe over the gasket surfaces of both halves to remove all traces of oil.

12 Install the three locating dowels in the upper crankcase half **(see illustration 23.8)**.

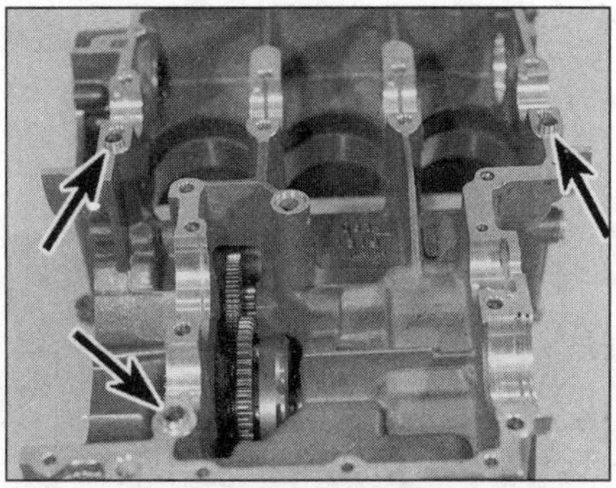

23.8 Three dowels are located in the crankcase mating surface (arrowed)

13 Apply a small amount of suitable sealant to the mating surface of the upper crankcase half **(see illustration)**.

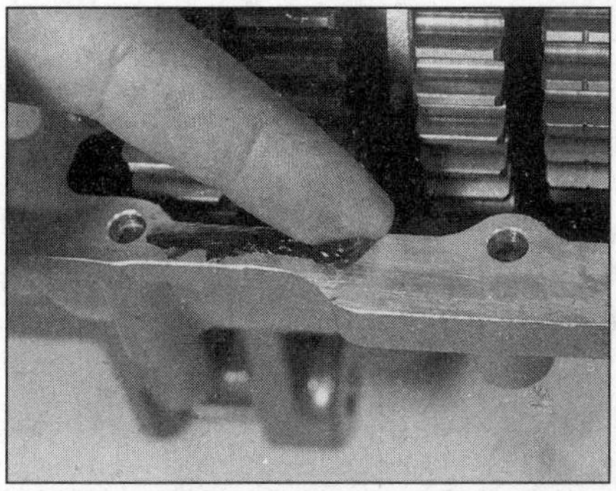

23.13 Smear sealant on the crankcase mating surfaces

2

23.14 Use a new O-ring on the oil pump outlet

23.16 Ensure that the selector forks engage the gear grooves correctly as the cases are joined (arrowed)

Caution: Take care not to apply an excessive amount of sealant, as it will ooze out when the case halves are assembled and may obstruct oil passages and prevent the bearings from seating.

14 Install a new O-ring to the oil pump outlet **(see illustration)**.

15 Check the position of the gearchange cam, gearchange forks and transmission shafts – make sure they're in the neutral position (ie the mainshaft and countershaft rotate independently of each other).

16 Make sure that the main bearing shells are in position and carefully guide the lower crankcase half onto the upper half. The gearchange forks must engage with their respective slots in the transmission gears as the halves are joined **(see illustration)**.

17 Check that the lower crankcase half is correctly seated and that all shafts are free to rotate. **Note:** *If the casings are not correctly seated, remove the lower crankcase half and investigate the problem. Do not attempt to pull them together using the crankcase bolts as the casing will crack and be ruined.*

18 Clean the threads of the lower crankcase bolts and insert them in their original locations, including any brackets **(see illustration)**. Secure all bolts hand-tight at this stage.

19 Turn the crankcase over so that it is upright. Clean the threads of the upper crankcase bolts and install them in their original locations. Secure all bolts hand-tight at this stage.

20 Turn the crankcase over and tighten the lower bolts to 12 Nm, working in the numbered sequence **(see illustrations 23.6a, b, c or d)**.

21 Turn the crankcase over and tighten all upper crankcase bolts to 12 Nm, working in the numbered sequence **(see illustrations 23.5a or 5b)**.

22 Turn the crankcase over and tighten the 8 mm lower crankcase bolts to 28 Nm in the numerical sequence.

23 Turn the crankcase over and tighten the 8 mm upper crankcase bolts to 28 Nm in the numerical sequence.

24 With all crankcase fasteners tightened, check that the crankshaft and transmission shafts rotate smoothly and easily. If there are any signs of undue stiffness or of any other problem, the fault must be rectified before proceeding further.

25 Using thumb pressure, push a new clutch pushrod oil seal in the left side of the crankcase **(see illustration)**.

26 Install all other removed assemblies in the reverse of the sequence in Steps 3 and 2.

27 When installing the crankshaft left end cover on Thunderbird, Thunderbird Sport, Adventurer and Legend TT models and all later 4 cylinder engined models (from VIN 2971 on), the oil seal set in the cover must be renewed. Failure to do so will prevent the crankcase breather from operating properly. Prise the old seal out with a flat-bladed screwdriver. The new seal is supplied complete with a shaped mandrel; leaving the mandrel in place, press the seal squarely into the cover so that it lies just below the face of the cover recess. Remove the mandrel from the seal immediately before the cover is fitted to the engine.

Caution: It is important that the seal is allowed 15 minutes to form on the breather tube before the crankshaft is rotated from its present position – the breather will not operate correctly is this precaution is not observed. If care is not taken with installation, engine oil may leak past the seal and into the crankcase breather system.

23.18 Check that any brackets are returned to their original locations

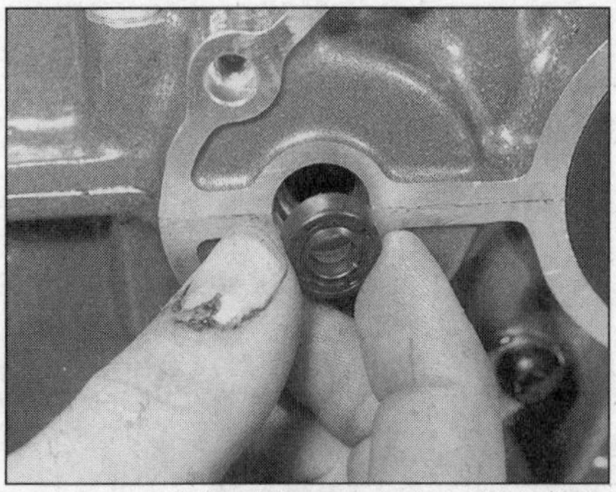

23.25 Press a new clutch pushrod oil seal into the crankcase joint

24 Crankcase – inspection

1 After the crankcases have been separated and the crankshaft, alternator/starter clutch drive, oil pump and transmission components have been removed, the crankcases should be cleaned thoroughly with new solvent and dried with compressed air.

2 Remove any oil gallery plugs that haven't already been removed. All oil passages should be blown out with compressed air.

3 All traces of old gasket sealant should be removed from the mating surfaces. Minor damage to the surfaces can be cleaned up with a fine sharpening stone or grindstone.

Caution: Be very careful not to nick or gouge the crankcase mating surfaces or leaks will result. Check both crankcase halves very carefully for cracks and other damage.

4 Small cracks or holes in aluminium castings may be repaired with an epoxy resin adhesive as a temporary measure. Permanent repairs can be effected by argon-arc welding, and only a specialist in this process is in a position to advise on the economy or practical aspect of such a repair. Alternatively you could try one of the low temperature aluminium welding kits available. If any damage is found that can't be repaired, renew the crankcase halves as a set.

5 Damaged threads can be economically reclaimed by using a diamond section wire insert, of the Helicoil type, which is easily fitted after drilling and re-tapping the affected thread.

6 Sheared studs or screws can usually be removed with screw extractors, which consist of a tapered, left thread screws of very hard steel. These are inserted into a pre-drilled hole in the stud, and usually succeed in dislodging the most stubborn stud or screw. If a problem arises which seems beyond your scope, it is worth consulting a professional engineering firm before condemning an otherwise sound casing. Many of these firms advertise regularly in the motorcycle press.

HAYNES HiNT ***Refer to 'Tools and Workshop Tips' in the Reference section for details of how to install a thread insert and use a screw extractor.***

25 Main and connecting rod bearings – general information

1 Even though main and connecting rod bearings are generally renewed during the engine overhaul, the old bearings should be retained for close examination as they may reveal valuable information about the condition of the engine.
2 Bearing failure occurs mainly because of lack of lubrication, the presence of dirt or other foreign particles, overloading the engine and/or corrosion. Regardless of the cause of bearing failure, it must be corrected before the engine is reassembled to prevent it from happening again.
3 When examining the bearings, remove the main bearings from the crankcase halves and the rod bearings from the connecting rods and caps and lay them out on a clean surface in the same general position as their location on the crankshaft journals. This will make it possible for you to match any noted bearing problems with the corresponding crankshaft journal.
4 Dirt and other foreign particles get into the engine in a variety of ways. It may be left in the engine during assembly or it may pass through filters or breathers. It may get into the oil and from there into the bearings. Metal chips from machining operations and normal engine wear are often present. Abrasives are sometimes left in engine components after reconditioning operations, especially when parts are not thoroughly cleaned using the proper cleaning methods. Whatever the source, these foreign objects often end up imbedded in the soft bearing material and are easily recognised. Large particles will not imbed in the bearing and will score or gouge the bearing and journal. The best prevention for this cause of bearing failure is to clean all parts thoroughly and keep everything spotlessly clean during engine reassembly. Frequent and regular oil and filter changes are also recommended.
5 Lack of lubrication or lubrication breakdown has a number of interrelated causes. Excessive heat (which thins the oil), overloading (which squeezes the oil from the bearing face) and oil leakage or throw off from excessive bearing clearances, worn oil pump or high engine speeds all contribute to lubrication breakdown. Blocked oil passages will also starve a bearing and destroy it. When lack of lubrication is the cause of bearing failure, the bearing material is wiped or extruded from the steel backing of the bearing. Temperatures may increase to the point where the steel backing and the journal turn blue from overheating.
6 Riding habits can have a definite effect on bearing life. Full throttle low speed operation, or labouring the engine, puts very high loads on bearings, which tend to squeeze out the oil film. These loads cause the bearings to flex, which produces fine cracks in the bearing face (fatigue failure). Eventually the bearing material will loosen in pieces and tear away from the steel backing. Short trip riding leads to corrosion of bearings, as insufficient engine heat is produced to drive off the condensed water and corrosive gases produced. These products collect in the engine oil, forming acid and sludge. As the oil is carried to the engine bearings, the acid attacks and corrodes the bearing material.
7 Incorrect bearing installation during engine assembly will lead to bearing failure as well. Tight fitting bearings which leave insufficient bearing oil clearances result in oil starvation. Dirt or foreign particles trapped behind a bearing insert result in high spots on the bearing which lead to failure.
8 To avoid bearing problems, clean all parts thoroughly before reassembly, double check all bearing clearance measurements and lubricate the new bearings with clean engine oil during installation.

26 Connecting rods – removal, inspection and installation

Removal

1 Separate the crankcase halves as described in Section 23. Note that the pistons must be removed (see Section 14) because they will not pass through the upper crankcase half with the connecting rods. Lift the crankshaft out of the upper crankcase.
2 Before removing the rods from the crankshaft, measure the side clearance on each rod with a feeler blade **(see illustration)**. If the clearance on any rod is greater than the service limit listed in this Chapter's Specifications, that rod will have to be renewed.
3 Using paint or a felt marker pen, mark the relevant cylinder number on each connecting rod and bearing cap (No. 1 cylinder on left end of crankshaft). Mark across the cap-to-connecting rod join to ensure that the cap is fitted the correct way around on reassembly.
4 Unscrew the big-end cap nuts and separate the connecting rod, cap and both bearing shells from the crankpin. Keep the cap, nuts and (if they are to be reused) the bearing shells together in their correct sequence.

Inspection

5 Check the connecting rods for cracks and other obvious damage Lubricate the piston pin for each rod, install it in its original rod and check for play **(see illustration)**. If it wobbles, renew the connecting rod and/or the pin. If the necessary measuring equipment is available measure the pin diameter and connecting rod bore and check the readings obtained do not exceed the limits given in this Chapter's Specifications. Renew components that are worn beyond the specified limit.
6 Refer to Section 25 and examine the connecting rod bearing shells. If they are scored, badly scuffed or appear to have seized, new shells must be installed. Always renew the shells in the connecting rods as a set. If they are badly damaged, check the corresponding crankpin. Evidence of extreme heat, such as discoloration, indicates that lubrication failure has occurred. Be sure to thoroughly check the oil pump and pressure relief valve as well as all oil holes and passages before reassembling the engine.
7 Have the rods checked for twist and bending by a Triumph dealer if you are in doubt about their straightness.

Bearing shell selection

8 The connecting rod bearing running clearance is controlled in production by selecting one of three grades of bearing shell. The grades are indicated by a colour-coding marked on the edge of each shell **(see illustration)**. In order,

2

26.2 Measuring connecting rod side clearance

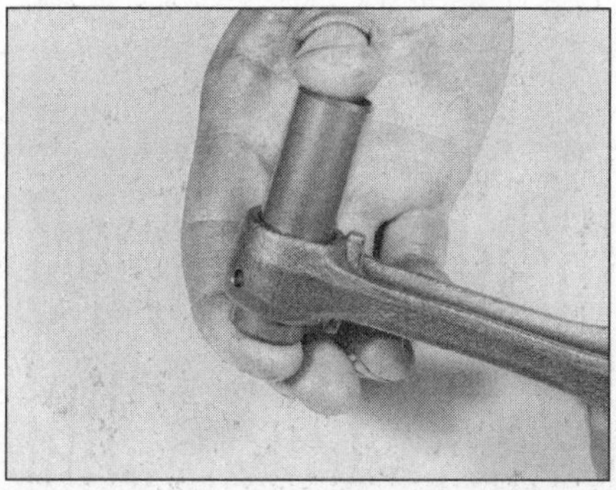

26.5 Slip the piston pin into the connecting rod small-end and feel for freeplay

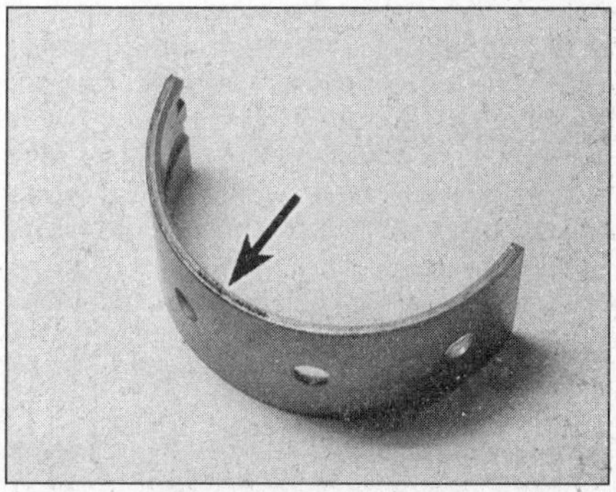

26.8 Bearing shells carry a colour code size marking (arrowed)

26.9 Connecting rod size marking is located on rod cap (arrowed)

26.14 Tighten the connecting rod nuts to the specified torque

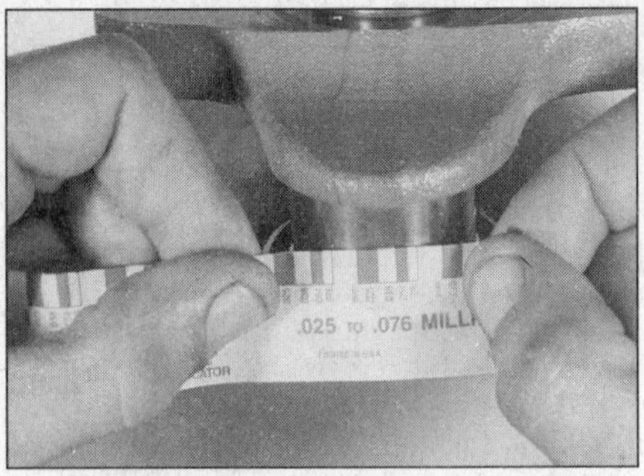

26.15 Place the Plastigauge scale next to the flattened Plastigauge to measure the bearing clearance

from the thickest to the thinnest, the insert grades are: blue, red, white. New bearing inserts are selected as follows using the crankpin journal diameter and connecting rod size marking.

9 Use a micrometer to determine the crankpin journal diameter. Inspect the connecting rod for its size marking, either the letter A or B **(see illustration)**.

10 Match the journal diameter with the rod marking and select a new set of bearing shells using the following table.

Con-rod marking	Crankpin journal diameter	Shell colour
A	40.954 to 40.960 mm	White
A	40.946 to 40.953 mm	Red
B	40.954 to 40.960 mm	Red
B	40.946 to 40.953 mm	Blue

Oil clearance check

11 Whether new bearing shells are being fitted or the original ones are being re-used, the connecting rod bearing oil clearance should be checked prior to reassembly.

12 Clean the backs of the bearing shells and the bearing locations in both the connecting rod and cap.

13 Press the bearing shells into their locations, ensuring that the tab on each shell engages the notch in the connecting rod/cap. Make sure the bearings are fitted in the correct locations and take care not to touch any shell's bearing surface with your fingers.

14 Cut several lengths of the appropriate size Plastigauge (they should be slightly shorter than the width of the crankpin). Place a strand of Plastigauge on each (cleaned) crankpin journal and fit the (clean) connecting rod assemblies, shells and caps. Make sure the cap is fitted the correct way around so the previously made markings align and tighten the bearing cap nuts to the specified torque wrench setting whilst ensuring that the connecting rod does not rotate **(see illustration)**. Take care not to disturb the Plastigauge. Slacken the cap nuts and remove the connecting rod assemblies, again taking great care not to rotate the crankshaft.

15 Compare the width of the crushed Plastigauge on each crankpin to the scale printed on the Plastigauge envelope to obtain the connecting rod bearing oil clearance **(see illustration)**.

16 If the clearance is not within the specified limits, the bearing shells may be the wrong grade (or excessively worn if the original shells are being reused). Before deciding that different grade shells are needed, make sure that no dirt or oil was trapped between the bearing shells and the connecting rod or cap when the clearance was measured. If the clearance is excessive, even with new shells (of the correct size), the crankpin is worn and the crankshaft should be renewed.

17 On completion carefully scrape away all traces of the Plastigauge material from the crankpin and bearing shells using a fingernail or other object which is unlikely to score the shells.

Installation

Note: *New connecting rod bolts and nuts must be used whenever the rods have been disassembled.*

18 Install the bearing shells in the connecting rods and caps. Lubricate the shells with new engine oil and assemble the components on the crankpin. **Note:** *The oilway in the rod must face to the rear of the engine when installed on the crankshaft* ***(see illustration 14.32a)***. Install the new connecting rod bolts and nuts, having applied a smear of molybdenum disulphide grease to the bolt threads and nut face; tighten them finger-tight at this stage. Check to make sure that all components have been returned to their original locations using the marks made on disassembly.

19 The connecting rod nuts must be tightened in the three stages specified (see Specifications) – do not tighten to the full setting in the first stage. Torque both nuts to the first setting, then both to the second and finally both to the third setting.

20 Check that the rod rotates freely on the crankpin, then install those for the other cylinders.

21 Install the crankshaft and assemble the crankcase halves (see Section 23).

27 Crankshaft and main bearings – removal, inspection and installation

Removal

1 Separate the crankcase halves as described in Section 23.

2 The crankshaft can be removed with the connecting rods attached if the pistons have previously been removed (see Section 14). Alternatively, the connecting rod caps can be removed, leaving the rods and pistons in the upper crankcase.

3 On all later 4 cylinder engined models (VIN 2971 on) and the Thunderbird, Thunderbird Sport, Adventurer and Legend TT models, unscrew the breather disc from the left end of the crankshaft and, where fitted, remove the locating dowel.

4 Lift the crankshaft out of the upper crankcase half, taking care not to dislodge the bearing shells **(see illustration)**.

5 The main bearing shells can be removed from the crankcase halves by pushing their centres to the side, then lifting them out **(see illustration)**.

27.4 Lift the crankshaft out of the upper crankcase

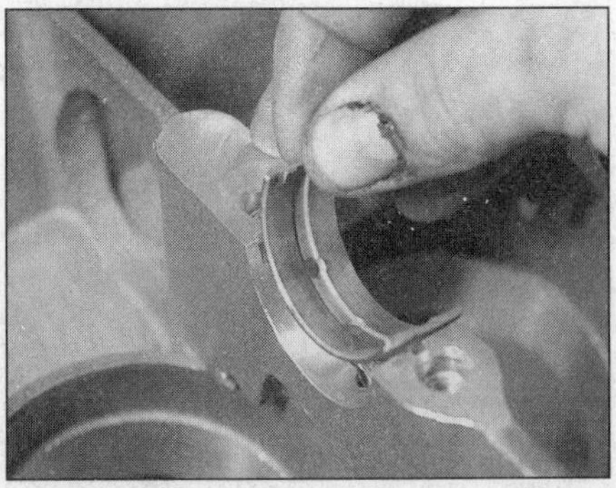

27.5 Slip the bearing shells to one side to remove them from their saddles

27.10 Measuring the crankshaft journal diameter

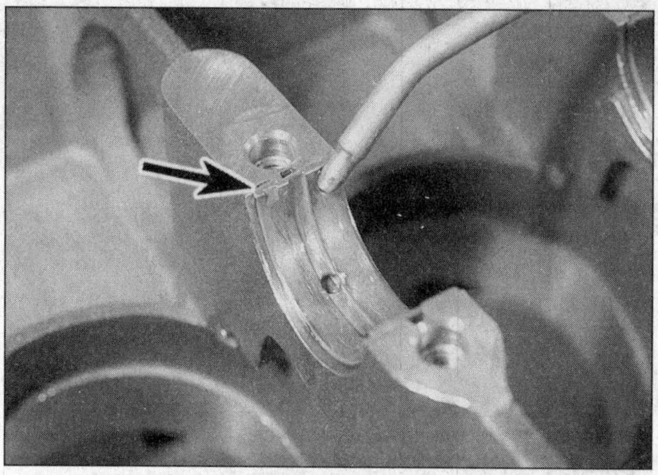

27.22 Engage the tab on the shell with the notch in the casing (arrowed). Lubricate the shells with engine oil

Keep the bearing shells in order. All shells are of the grooved type except for later 4 cylinder models, which have plain shells fitted to journals 1, 3 and 5.

Inspection

6 Clean the crankshaft with solvent, using a rifle-cleaning brush to scrub out the oil passages. If available, blow the crank dry with compressed air.

7 Refer to Section 25 and examine the main bearing shells. If they are scored, badly scuffed or appear to have been seized, new bearings must be installed. Always renew the main bearings as a set. If they are badly damaged, check the corresponding crankshaft journal. Evidence of extreme heat, such as discoloration, indicates that lubrication failure has occurred. Be sure to thoroughly check the oil pump and pressure relief valve as well as all oil holes and passages before reassembling the engine.

8 The crankshaft journals should be given a close visual examination, paying particular attention where damaged bearing shells have been discovered. If the journals are scored or pitted in any way a new crankshaft will be required. Note that undersizes are not available, precluding the option of re-grinding the crankshaft.

Bearing shell selection

9 The main bearing running clearance is controlled in production by selecting one of four grades of bearing shell. The grades are indicated by a colour-coding marked on the edge of each shell **(see illustration 26.8)**. In order, from the thickest to the thinnest, the insert grades are: Green, Blue, Red, White. New bearing inserts are selected with reference to the following chart, having measured the crankshaft journal diameter and the crankcase bore diameter.

10 Measure the crankshaft journal diameter with a micrometer **(see illustration)**. The crankcase bore diameter is measured with the shells removed and the crankcase halves bolted together – the bore diameters are then measured with a hole gauge and micrometer.

Crankcase bore diameter	Crankshaft journal dia.	Shell colour
41.118 to 41.126 mm	37.969 to 37.976 mm	White
41.118 to 41.126 mm	37.960 to 37.968 mm	Red
41.127 to 41.135 mm	37.969 to 37.976 mm	Red
41.127 to 41.135 mm	37.960 to 37.968 mm	Blue
41.136 to 41.144 mm	37.969 to 37.976 mm	Blue
41.136 to 41.144 mm	37.960 to 37.968 mm	Green

Oil clearance check

11 Whether new bearing shells are being fitted or the original ones are being re-used, the main bearing oil clearance should be checked prior to reassembly.

12 Clean the backs of the bearing shells and the bearing locations in both crankcase halves.

13 Press the bearing shells into their locations, ensuring that the tab on each shell engages in the notch in the crankcase. Make sure the bearings are fitted in the correct locations and take care not to touch any shell's bearing surface with your fingers.

14 Ensure that the shells and crankshaft are clean and dry. Lay the crankshaft in position in the upper crankcase.

15 Cut several lengths of the appropriate size Plastigauge (they should be slightly shorter than the width of the crankshaft journal). Place a strand of Plastigauge on each (cleaned) crankshaft journal.

16 Carefully install the lower crankcase half on to the upper half. Make sure that the gearchange forks (if fitted) engage with their respective slots in the transmission gears as the halves are joined. Check that the lower crankcase half is correctly seated. **Note:** *Do not tighten the crankcase bolts if the casing is not correctly seated.* Install the eight (3 cylinder) or ten (4 cylinder) 8 mm lower crankcase bolts in their original locations and, starting from the centre and working outwards in a criss-cross pattern, tighten them to the specified torque setting. Make sure that the crankshaft is not rotated as the bolts are tightened.

17 Slacken and remove the crankcase bolts, working in a criss-cross pattern from the outside in, then carefully lift off the lower crankcase half, making sure the Plastigauge is not disturbed.

18 Compare the width of the crushed Plastigauge on each crankshaft journal to the scale printed on the Plastigauge envelope to obtain the main bearing oil clearance **(see illustration 26.15)**.

19 If the clearance is not within the specified limits, the bearing shells may be the wrong grade (or excessively worn if the original inserts are being reused). Before deciding that different grade shells are needed, make sure that no dirt or oil was trapped between the bearing shells and the crankcase halves when the clearance was measured. If the clearance is excessive, even with new shells (of the correct size), the crankshaft journal is worn and the crankshaft should be renewed.

20 On completion carefully scrape away all traces of the Plastigauge material from the crankshaft journal and bearing shells; use a fingernail or other object which is unlikely to score them.

Installation

21 Clean the backs of the bearing shells and the bearing recesses in both crankcase halves. If new shells are being fitted, ensure that all traces of the protective grease are cleaned off using paraffin. Wipe dry the shells and crankcase halves with a lint-free cloth.

22 Press the bearing shells into their locations. Make sure the tab on each shell engages in the notch in the casing and lubricate the shell with clean engine oil **(see illustration)**. Make sure the bearings are fitted

28.5a Check that the needle roller bearing outer race dowels (arrowed) are in position in the upper crankcase

28.5b Smear locking compound on the bearing locations in the upper crankcase

28.6a Install the mainshaft so that the hole in the needle roller bearing outer race engages the dowel . . .

28.6b . . . and locate the ball bearing with the half ring

in the correct locations and take care not to touch any shell's bearing surface with your fingers.

23 Lower the crankshaft into position in the upper crankcase.

24 Fit the connecting rod caps to the crankshaft as described in Section 26 if they were disconnected.

25 On all later 4 cylinder engined models (VIN 2971 on) and Thunderbird, Thunderbird Sport, Adventurer and Legend TT models, install the breather disc (and its dowel, where fitted) to the left end of the crankshaft. Tighten the breather disc screws to the specified torque setting.

26 Reassemble the crankcase halves as described in Section 23.

28 Transmission shafts – removal and installation

Removal

1 Separate the crankcase halves as described in Section 23.

2 Lift the countershaft out of the lower crankcase half. Retrieve the bearing dowel pin from the needle bearing outer race location. The ball bearing on the left end of the shaft is located by a complete ring which remains on the shaft.

3 Lift the mainshaft out of the lower crankcase half. Recover the mainshaft bearing half ring from the right (clutch) end and the dowel pin from the left end. If the clutch outer drum was not removed prior to crankcase separation, it can be withdrawn at this stage.

4 If necessary, the transmission shafts can be disassembled and inspected for wear or damage as described in Section 29.

Installation

5 Ensure that the needle bearing outer race dowels are located in the upper crankcase **(see illustration)**. Apply a smear of bearing locking compound to the bearing locations in the upper crankcase **(see illustration)**.

6 Install the mainshaft, locating the hole in its needle bearing outer race with the dowel **(see illustration)**. Locate the bearing half ring in the ball bearing groove so that it bridges both casing halves when reassembled **(see illustration)**. The clutch can be installed on the mainshaft prior to crankcase reassembly or afterwards (see Section 15).

7 If not already done, slip the old oil seal off the countershaft left end and renew it **(see illustration 29.37e)**. Install the countershaft in the upper crankcase so that the hole in the needle bearing outer race locates over the dowel, and so that the bearing ring and oil seal lip both locate in their grooves **(see illustrations)**.

8 Ensure that the gears of both shafts mesh correct and position them so that they're in the neutral position (mainshaft can be turned whilst countershaft is held stationary).

28.7a Install the countershaft so that the hole in the needle roller bearing outer race engages the dowel . . .

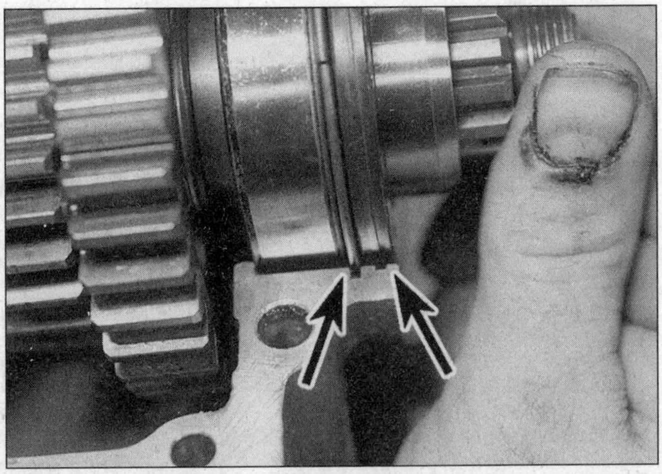

28.7b . . . and locate the bearing locating ring and oil seal lip with the grooves in the casing (arrowed)

29 Transmission shafts – disassembly, inspection and reassembly

1 Remove the shafts from the casing as described in Section 28.

Mainshaft

Disassembly

2 Slide off the needle roller bearing outer race from the left end of the shaft **(see illustration)**.
3 Remove the circlip from the shaft end and withdraw the needle roller bearing inner race and thrustwasher. Slide the second gear off the shaft.
4 On early Speed Triple and early Thunderbird models (5-speed transmission), slide the sleeve off the shaft. On all other models (6-speed transmission), slide the 6th gear and its bush off the shaft.

> **HAYNES HiNT** ***When disassembling the transmission shafts, place the parts on a long rod or thread a wire through them to keep them in order and facing the proper direction.***

5 Slide the thrustwasher off the shaft and remove the circlip to free the combined 3rd/4th gear.
6 Remove the circlip, followed by the thrustwasher and 5th gear.

Inspection

7 Wash all of the components in clean solvent and dry them off.
8 Check the gear teeth for cracking and other obvious damage. Check the 6th gear bush and the surface in the inner diameter of the gear for scoring or heat discoloration. If the gear or bush is damaged, renew it.
9 Inspect the dogs and the dog holes in the gears for excessive wear. Renew the paired gears as a set if necessary.
10 Measure the gearchange fork groove width in the 3rd/4th gear as described in Section 30.
11 The shaft is unlikely to sustain damage unless the engine has seized, placing an unusually high loading on the transmission, or the machine has covered a very high mileage. Check the surface of the shaft, especially where a pinion turns on it, and renew the shaft if it has scored or picked up. Damage of any kind can only be cured by renewal.
12 If the ball bearing requires renewal, a bearing puller will be required to extract the bearing from its shaft. Note the position of the locating groove in the outer race of the bearing prior to removing it and ensure that the new bearing is fitted with the groove in the same position. Pull the bearing off the shaft and install the new bearing using a press.

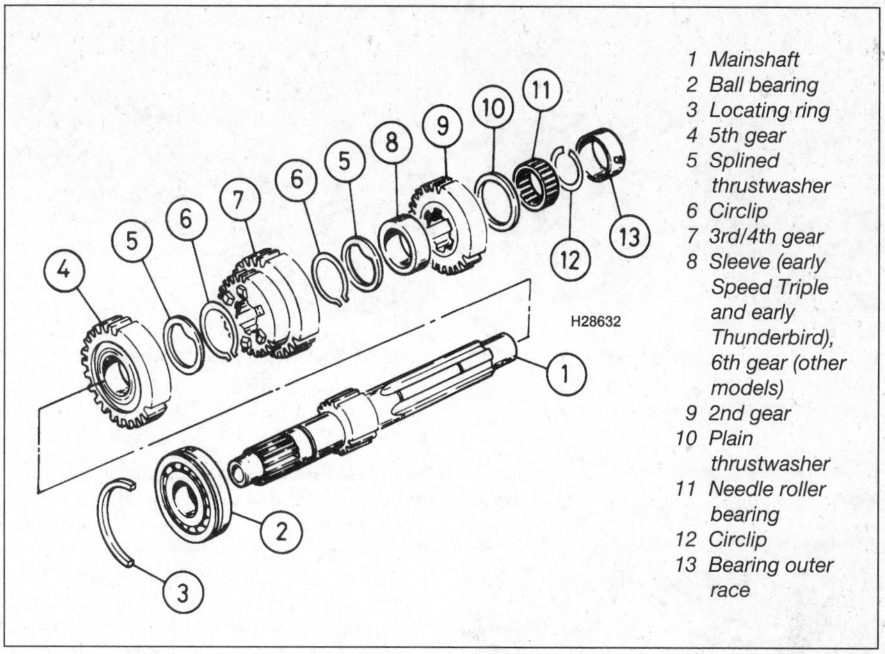

29.2 Mainshaft components

Reassembly

13 During reassembly, always use new circlips. Lubricate the components with the correct grade of engine oil before assembling them.
14 Slide on the 5th gear with its dogs facing away from the integral 1st gear **(see illustration)**. Install a thrustwasher and circlip, making sure that the circlip locates in the shaft groove **(see illustrations)**.
15 Install the combined 3rd/4th gear so that the smaller (3rd) gear faces the 5th gear and so that the oilway in the gearchange fork groove aligns with the two oilways in the shaft

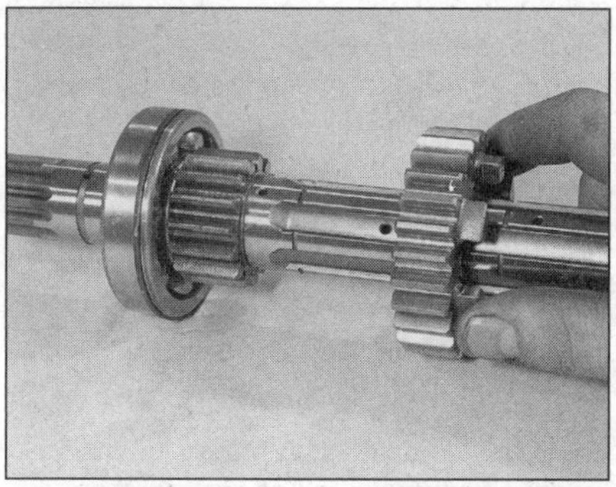
29.14a Slide 5th gear on the mainshaft so its dogs face away from integral 1st gear

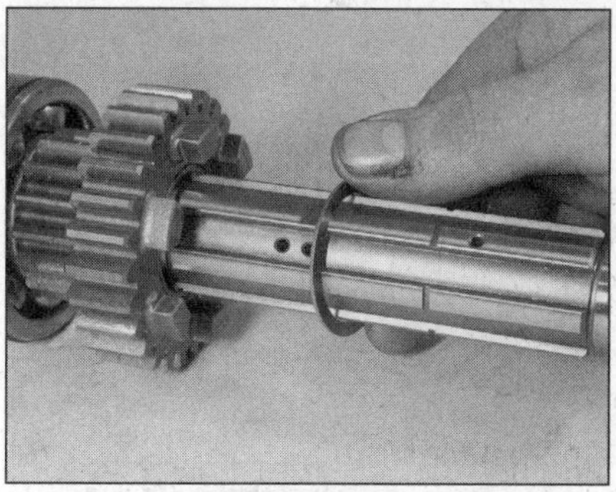
29.14b Install a thrustwasher . . .

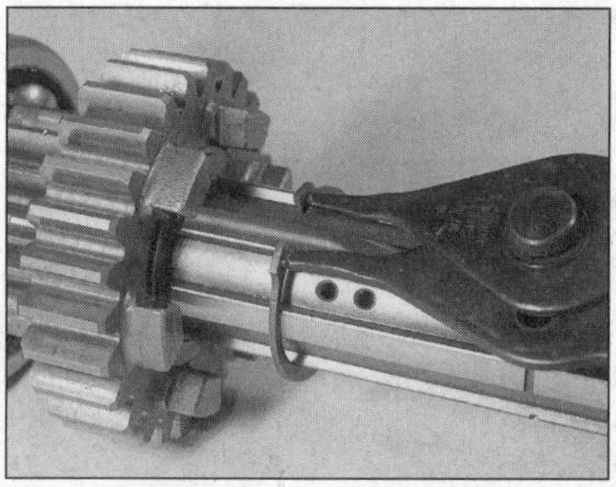
29.14c . . . and circlip

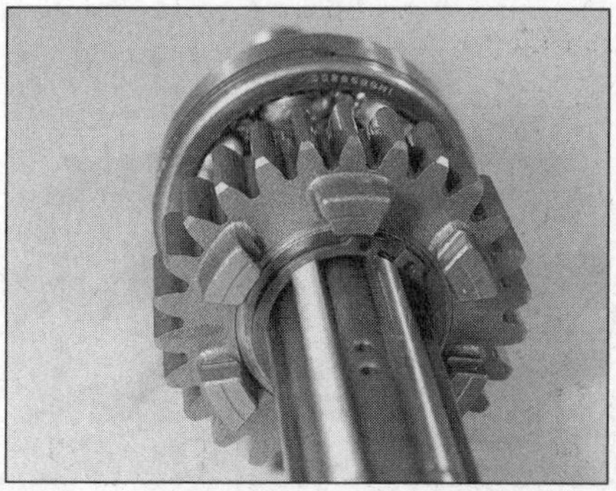
29.14d Ensure that the circlip locates in its groove

2

29.15a Combined 3rd/4th gear is installed with the smaller (3rd) gear facing 5th gear. Align the oil holes (arrowed)

29.15b Install a circlip in the shaft groove . . .

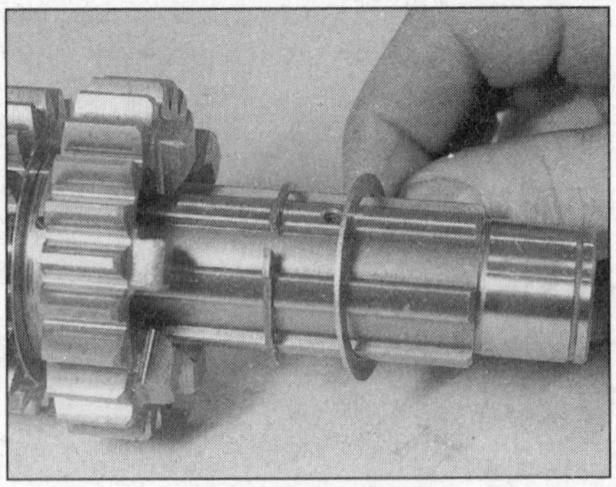

29.15c . . . and install a thrustwasher against the circlip

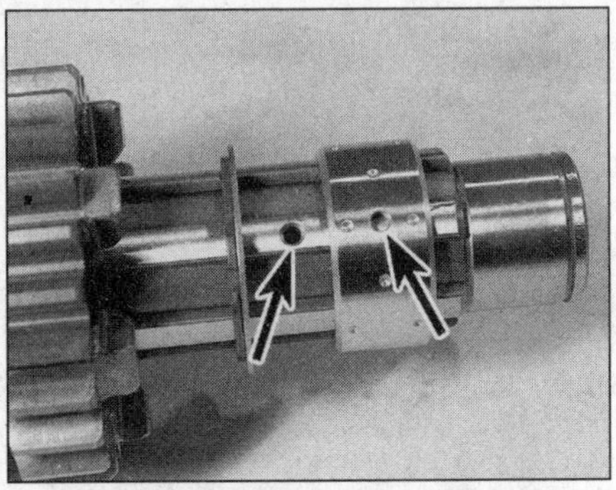

29.16a Slip the 6th gear bush on the mainshaft so that their oil holes align (arrowed) . . .

(see illustration). Locate a circlip in the shaft groove and slide a thrustwasher on the shaft so that it abuts the circlip **(see illustrations)**.

16 On early Speed Triple and early Thunderbird models (which have a 5-speed transmission), install the sleeve. On all other models, install the 6th gear bush so that its oilway aligns with the shaft oilway, then slide on the 6th gear with its dogs facing the 4th gear **(see illustrations)**.

17 Install 2nd gear with its stepped side facing away from 6th gear (or sleeve) **(see illustration)**. Slide on a thrustwasher and the needle roller bearing, then secure them with the circlip **(see illustrations)**. Install the bearing outer race on the shaft **(see illustration)**.

Countershaft

Disassembly

18 Remove the needle roller bearing outer race, inner race and thrustwasher from the shaft right end **(see illustration)**.

19 Make a paint mark on the outer face of the 1st gear, then slide it off the shaft, followed by the 5th gear.

20 Remove the circlip, then slide off the

29.16b . . . then install the 6th gear

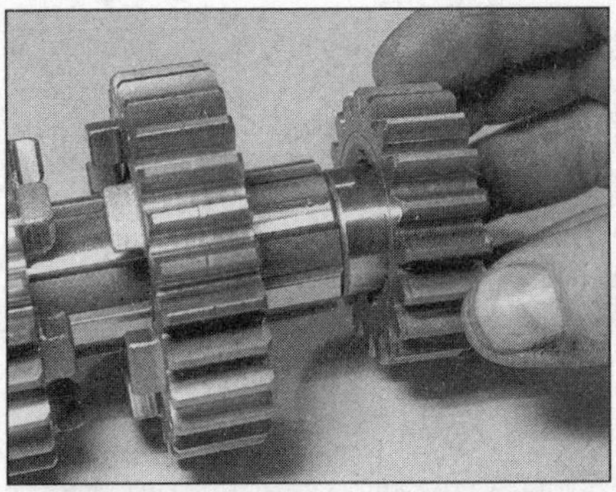

29.17a Install the 2nd gear with its stepped side facing away from 6th gear

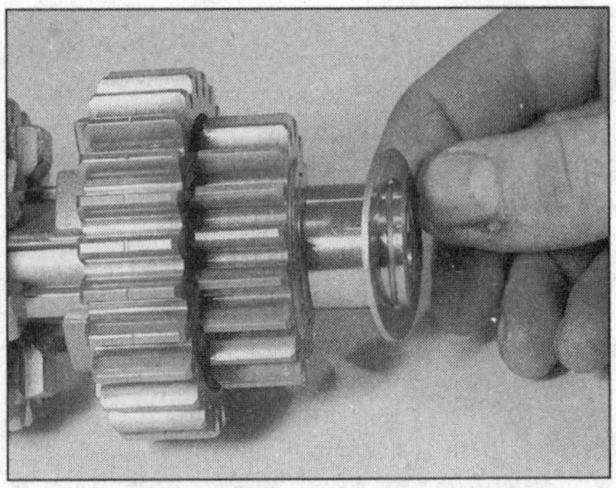

29.17b Slip a thrustwasher over the shaft . . .

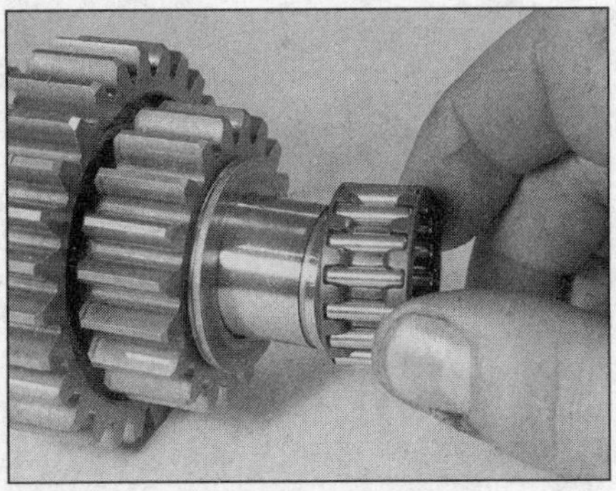

29.17c . . . followed by the needle roller bearing

29.17d Secure the bearing with a circlip (arrowed)

29.17e Finally, install the outer race over the bearing

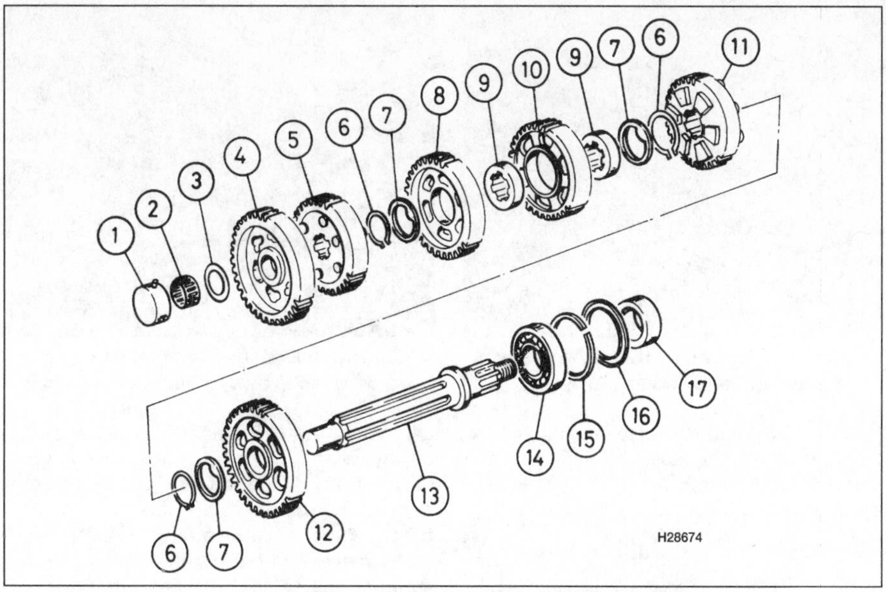

29.18 Countershaft components

1 *Bearing outer race*
2 *Needle roller bearing*
3 *Plain thrustwasher*
4 *1st gear*
5 *5th gear*
6 *Circlip*
7 *Splined thrustwasher*
8 *3rd gear*
9 *Bush*
10 *4th gear*
11 *6th gear*
12 *2nd gear*
13 *Countershaft*
14 *Bearing*
15 *Locating ring*
16 *Oil seal*
17 *Sleeve*

thrustwasher, 3rd gear, bush, 4th gear, bush and thrustwasher.

21 Remove the circlip and slide off 6th gear.

22 Remove the circlip, then slide off the thrustwasher and 2nd gear.

23 Moving to the left end of the shaft, remove the oil seal and discard it; a new seal must be installed on reassembly. Withdraw the sleeve and locating ring from the shaft. Slip the thick washer off the shaft, followed by the bearing. **Note:** *The bearing inner race is a press fit on the shaft and must not be disturbed unless renewal is required.*

Inspection

24 Wash all of the components in clean solvent and dry them off.

25 Check the gear teeth for cracking and other obvious damage. Check the 3rd and 4th gear bushes and the surface in the inner diameter of each gear for scoring or heat discoloration. If the gear or bush is damaged, renew it.

26 Inspect the dogs and the dog holes in the gears for excessive wear. Renew the paired gears as a set if necessary.

27 Measure the gearchange fork groove width in the 5th and 6th gears (see Section 30).

28 The shaft is unlikely to sustain damage unless the engine has seized, placing an unusually high loading on the transmission, or the machine has covered a very high mileage. Check the surface of the shaft, especially where a pinion turns on it, and renew the shaft if it has scored or picked up. Damage of any kind can only be cured by renewal.

29 The bearing inner race at the left end of the shaft is a press fit. Renewal necessitates splitting the inner race and pressing a new race on to the shaft; it is advised that this task be performed by a Triumph dealer.

Reassembly

30 During reassembly, always use new circlips. Lubricate the components with engine oil before assembling them.

31 Install the 2nd gear on the shaft with its dished side facing away from the ball bearing **(see illustration)**. Install a thrustwasher and secure with a circlip, making sure it seats in the shaft groove **(see illustrations)**.

32 Slide 6th gear on the shaft with its gearchange fork groove facing away from the 2nd gear, and so that the oilway in the fork groove aligns with the two oilways in the shaft **(see illustration)**. Secure the gear with the circlip, making sure it locates in the shaft groove **(see illustration)**.

29.31a Fit 2nd gear on countershaft with dished side facing away from ball bearing

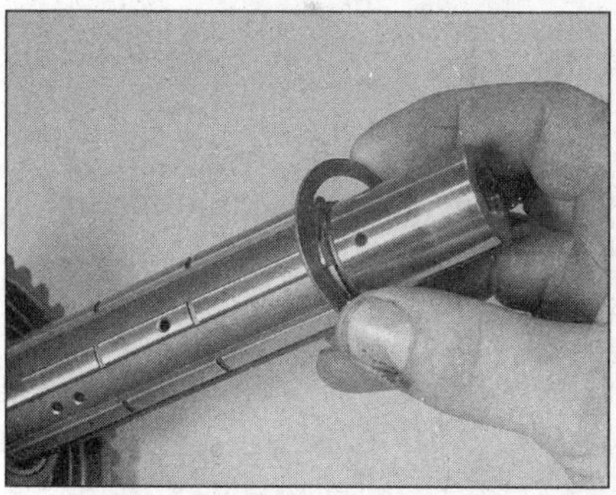

29.31b Install a thrustwasher . . .

29.31c . . . and secure the gear with the circlip (arrowed)

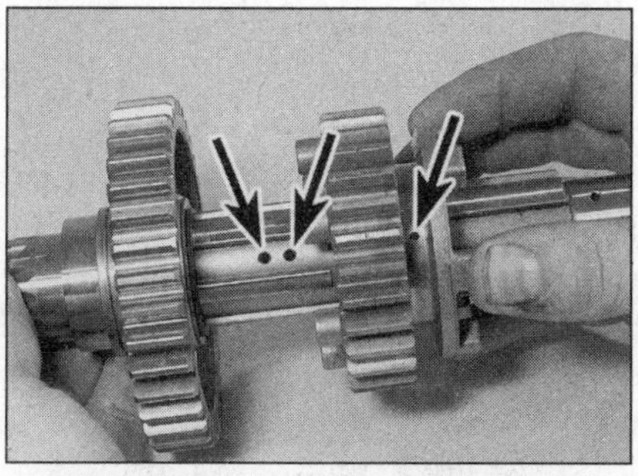

29.32a Install 6th gear so that its fork groove faces away from the 2nd gear and so that the oil holes align (arrowed)

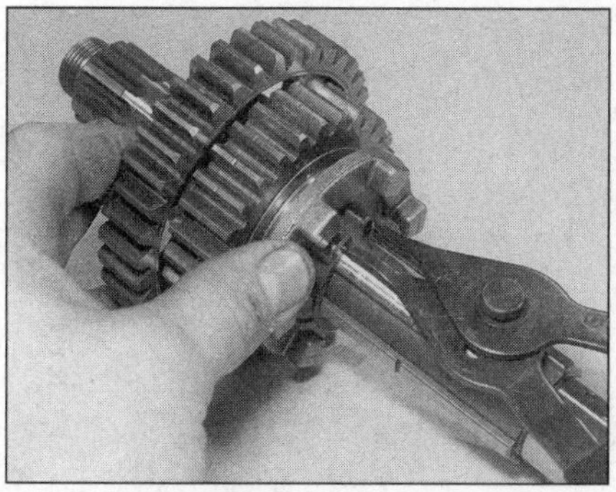

29.32b Insert a circlip into the countershaft groove

2

29.33a Slip a thrustwasher on the shaft . . .

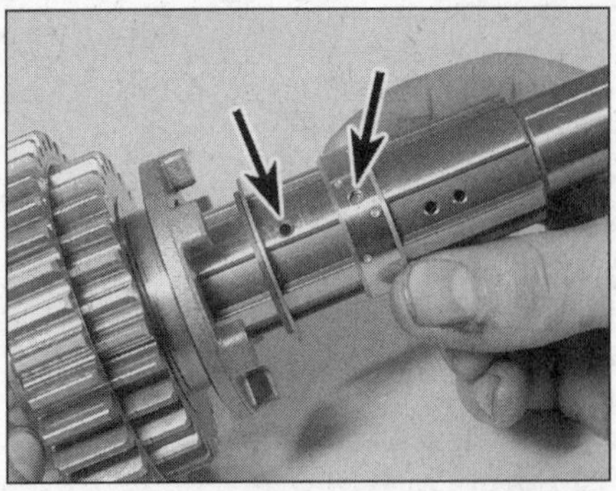
29.33b . . . followed by the 4th gear bush, aligning the oil holes (arrowed)

29.33c Install 4th gear so that its stepped centre faces away from the 6th gear

33 Install a thrustwasher on the shaft, followed by the 4th gear bush; align the bush oilway with the shaft oilway **(see illustrations)**. Slide 4th gear on the shaft so that its stepped side faces away from the 6th gear **(see illustration)**.

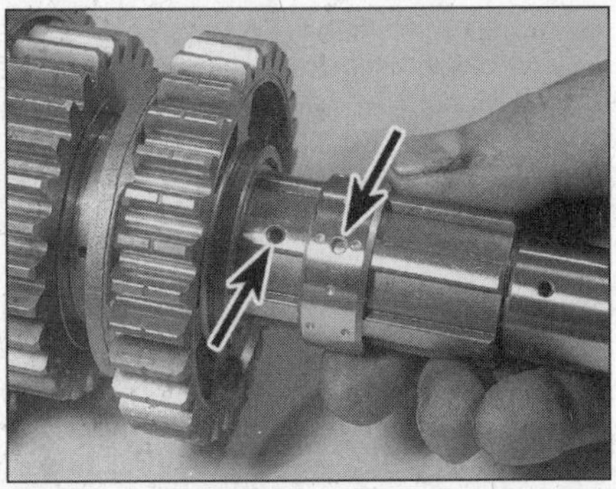
29.34a Align the 3rd gear bush oil hole with the shaft oil hole (arrowed) . . .

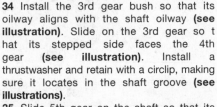

29.34b . . . then install the 3rd gear so that its stepped centre faces the 4th gear

34 Install the 3rd gear bush so that its oilway aligns with the shaft oilway **(see illustration)**. Slide on the 3rd gear so t hat its stepped side faces the 4th gear **(see illustration)**. Install a thrustwasher and retain with a circlip, making sure it locates in the shaft groove **(see illustrations)**.

35 Slide 5th gear on the shaft so that its gearchange fork groove faces the 3rd gear and so that the oilway in the groove aligns with the two oilways in the shaft **(see illustration)**.

36 Install 1st gear on the shaft as noted on removal **(see illustration)**. Install the thrustwasher, needle roller bearing and outer race **(see illustrations)**.

37 At the left end of the shaft, fit the bearing over its inner race on the shaft **(see**

29.34c Slip a thrustwasher on the shaft . . .

29.34d . . . and secure the gear with the circlip

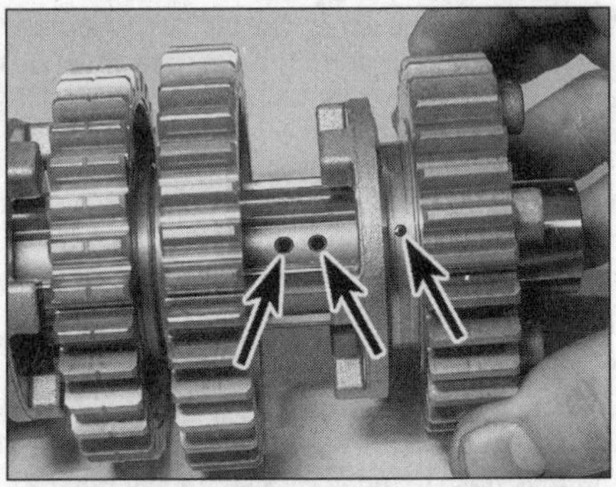
29.35 Install 5th gear with fork groove facing 3rd gear and oil holes aligned (arrowed)

29.36a Install the 1st gear in the direction noted on disassembly . . .

29.36b . . . install the thrustwasher . . .

29.36c . . . needle roller bearing and bearing outer race

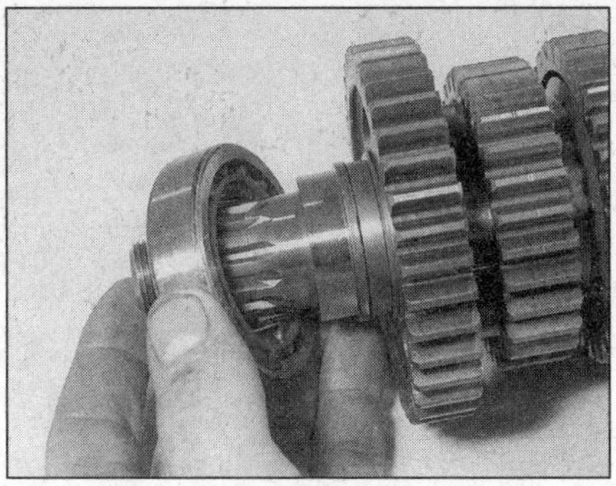

29.37a Slip on the bearing . . .

29.37b . . . followed by the thick washer . . .

29.37c . . . and sleeve (chamfered side out)

illustration). Slide the thick washer up against the bearing **(see illustration)**. Install the sleeve with its chamfered edge facing outwards then fit the bearing locating ring (the ring will float on the shaft until the countershaft is installed in the crankcase) **(see illustrations)**. Install a new oil seal over the sleeve **(see illustration)**.

30 Gearchange mechanism – removal, inspection and installation

Note: *Access can be gained to the detent cam and detent arms with the engine in the frame and the clutch outer drum removed (see Section 15). All other operations require the crankcases to be separated.*

Removal

1 Separate the crankcase halves (Section 23).
2 Remove the screw and retaining plate from the left side of the crankcase to free the gearchange fork rod. Slide the rod out of the crankcase and lift each fork out as it clears the rod. Install the forks back on the rod as a guide to reassembly **(see illustration)**.
3 Remove the circlip and washer from the outer end of the gearchange shaft, then remove the circlip, spring guide and return spring from the inner end of the shaft **(see illustration)**. Unscrew the quadrant stopper bolt from the crankcase and remove the two screws which retain the stopper plate to the crankcase. Rotate the stopper plate to allow

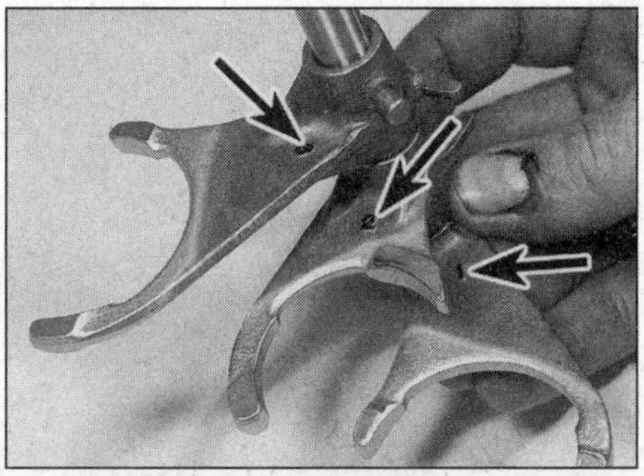

30.2 Install the selector forks back on the rod as a guide to reassembly. Note the identification numbers (arrowed)

29.37d Install the bearing locating ring over the shaft

29.37e Always use a new oil seal and install with its marked side outwards

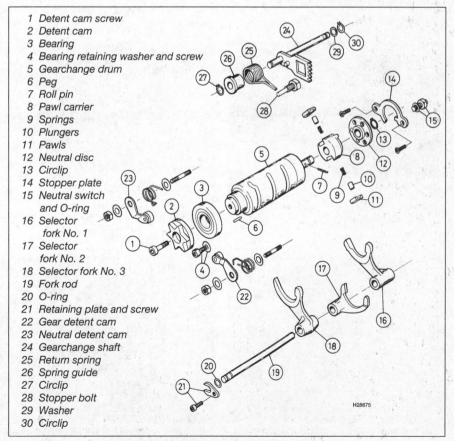

1 Detent cam screw
2 Detent cam
3 Bearing
4 Bearing retaining washer and screw
5 Gearchange drum
6 Peg
7 Roll pin
8 Pawl carrier
9 Springs
10 Plungers
11 Pawls
12 Neutral disc
13 Circlip
14 Stopper plate
15 Neutral switch and O-ring
16 Selector fork No. 1
17 Selector fork No. 2
18 Selector fork No. 3
19 Fork rod
20 O-ring
21 Retaining plate and screw
22 Gear detent cam
23 Neutral detent cam
24 Gearchange shaft
25 Return spring
26 Spring guide
27 Circlip
28 Stopper bolt
29 Washer
30 Circlip

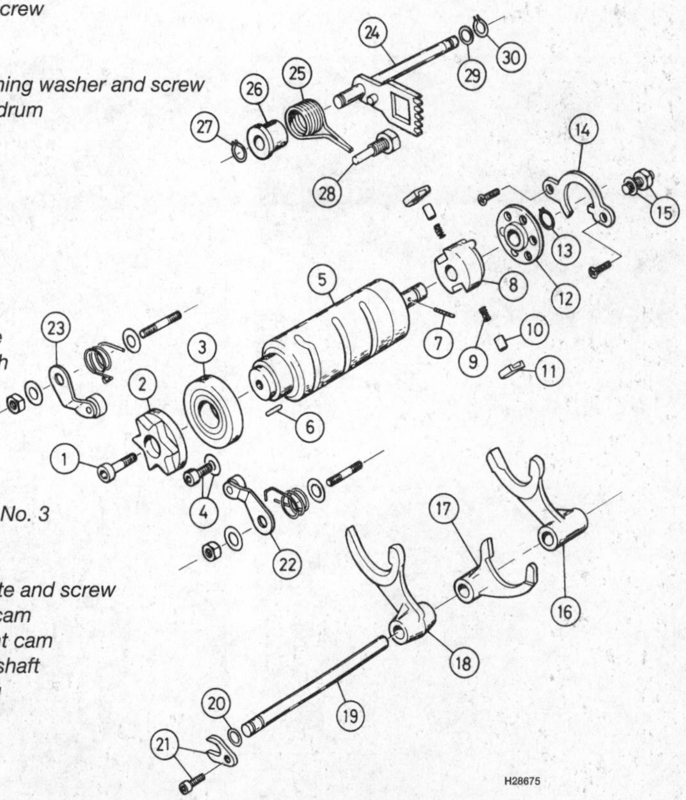

30.3 Gearchange mechanism components

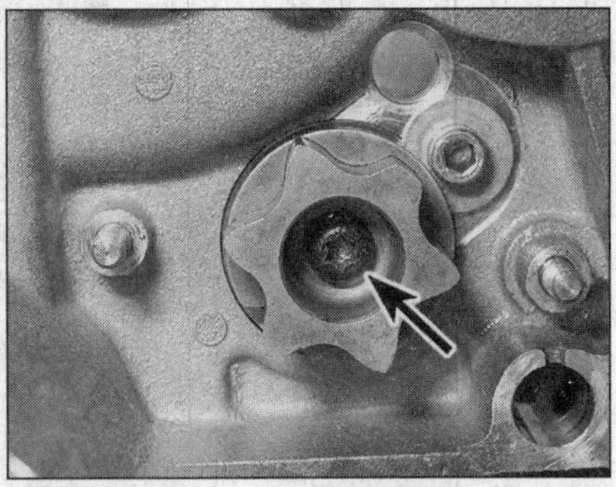

30.6 Detent cam is retained by a single screw (arrowed)

30.10a Measuring seletor fork-to-groove clearance

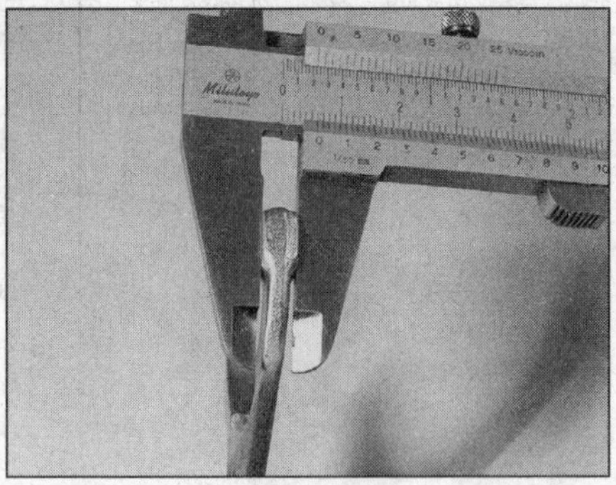

30.10b Measuring selector fork end thickness

the gearchange shaft quadrant to be disengaged from the pawl carrier teeth and withdrawn from the crankcase.

4 Remove the oil pump and its drive gear (see Section 31).

5 Working from the right side of the crankcase half. Remove the nuts securing the neutral and gear detent arm assemblies. Keep the components of each assembly separate to avoid their parts being interchanged.

6 Remove the screw from the end of the drum to free the detent cam **(see illustration)**.

7 Remove the screw and washer which retain the ball bearing in the right side of the crankcase. Push the bearing out from inside of the crankcase and lift out the gearchange drum.

8 If the pawl carrier requires removal from the gearchange drum, remove the circlip and lift off the neutral disc. Slip the stopper plate off the pawl assembly and drive out the roll pin in the shaft. Carefully withdraw the pawl carrier from the drum, taking care not to lose the spring-loaded pawls.

Inspection

9 The gearchange forks and rod should be closely inspected to ensure that they are not badly damaged or worn.

10 Locate each gearchange fork with its corresponding gear groove and measure the gearchange fork-to-groove clearance using feeler blades **(see illustration)**. If outside of the maximum clearance (see Specifications) either the gearchange fork or gear groove is worn. Using a vernier caliper measure the gearchange fork end widths and the gear groove **(see illustrations)**. Renew any component which is worn beyond the service limit (see Specifications).

11 The gearchange fork rod can be checked for trueness by rolling it along a flat surface. A bent rod will cause difficulty in selecting gears and make the gearchange action heavy.

12 Inspect the gearchange drum grooves and selector fork guide pins for signs of wear or damage. If either component shows signs of wear or damage the gearchange fork(s) and drum must be renewed.

13 Check that the gearchange drum bearing rotates freely and has no sign of freeplay between its inner and outer race. Renew the bearing if necessary.

Installation

14 If the pawl assembly was disturbed, install the pawls, plungers and springs on the carrier and hold them compressed whilst the carrier is inserted in the end of the gearchange drum. Drift the roll pin into the hole in the shaft to retain the carrier **(see illustration)**. Locate the stopper plate in the carrier and slip the neutral disc over the drum end so that its cutout aligns with the roll pin **(see illustrations)**. Secure the disc with the circlip.

15 Install the gearchange drum in the lower crankcase, locating its left end in the casing bore **(see illustration)**. Install the ball bearing

30.10c Measuring gear groove width

30.14a Retain the pawl carrier with the roll pin (arrowed)

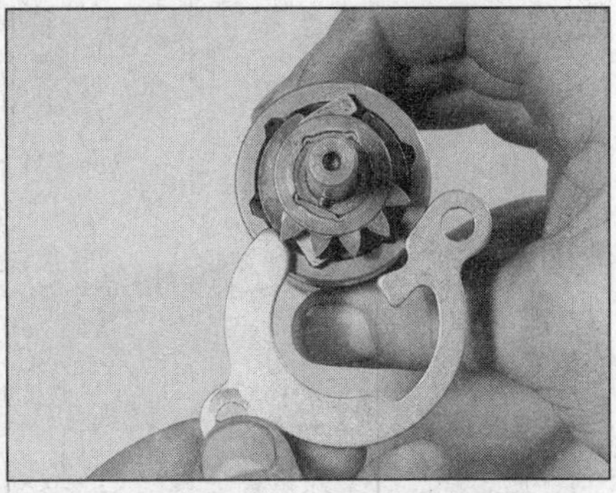

30.14b Engage the stopper plate with the pawl carrier . . .

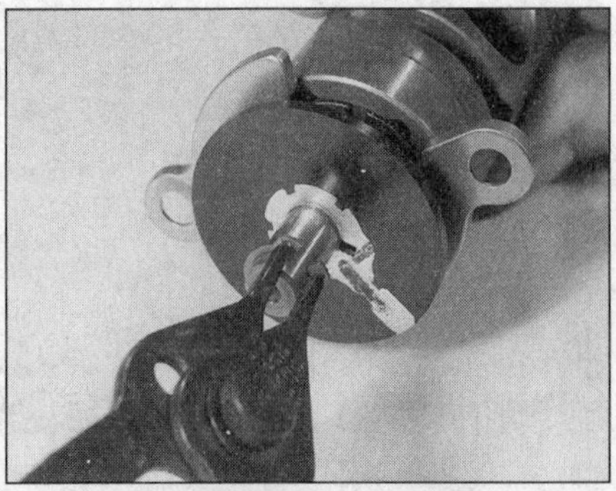

30.14c . . . then install the neutral disc and retain it with the circlip

30.15a Install the gearchange drum in the lower crankcase . . .

30.15b . . . and install the ball bearing over its right end

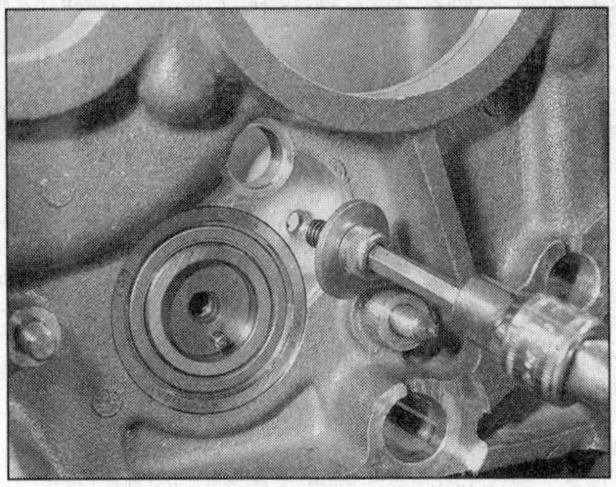

30.15c Retain the bearing with the screw and washer

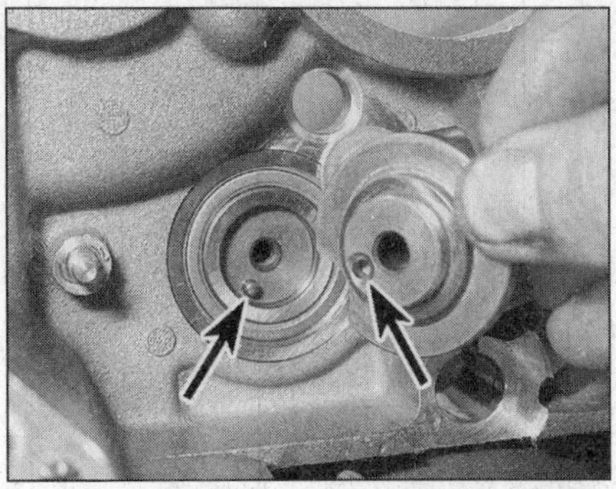

30.16a Engage the detent cam hole over the peg in the end of the drum (arrowed)

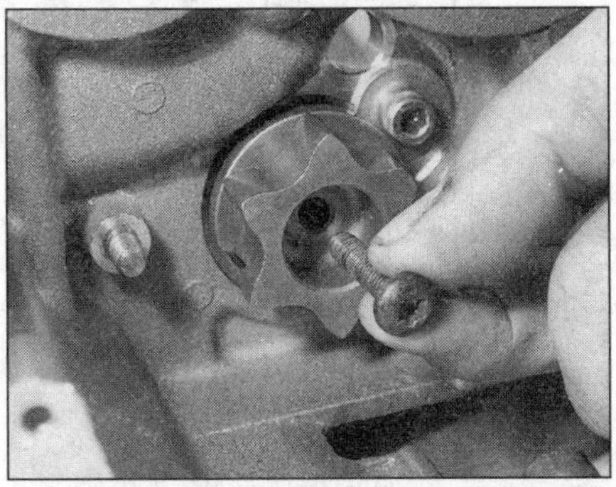

30.16b Secure the cam with the retaining screw

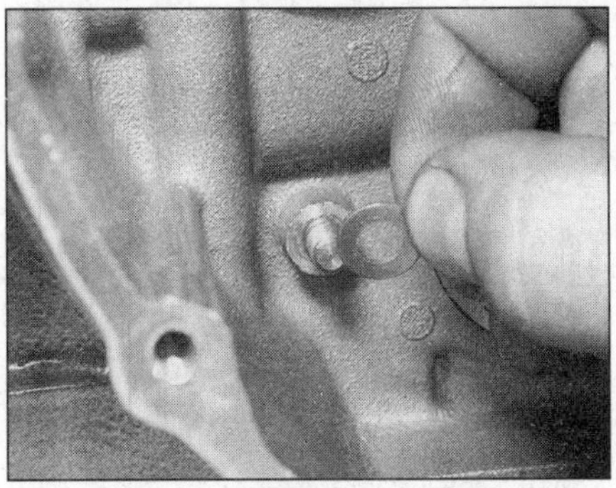

30.17a Install the washer . . .

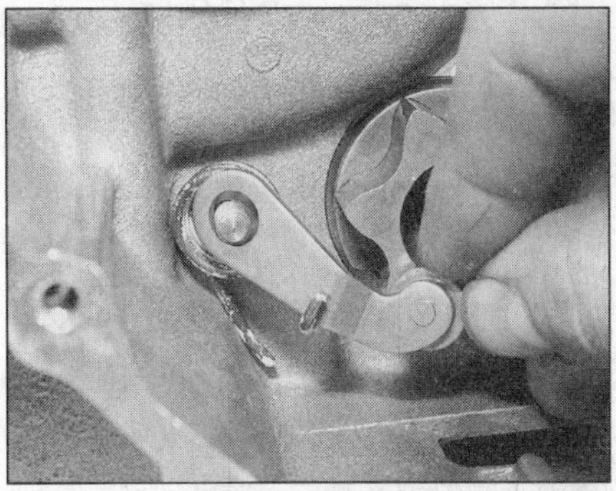

30.17b . . . spring and neutral detent arm

in the right side of the casing, noting that it must be installed from the outside **(see illustration)**. Retain the bearing with the screw and washer; a drop of non-permanent thread locking compound should be applied to the screw threads **(see illustration)**. Secure the screw to the specified torque

16 Locate the detent cam over the right end of the gearchange drum, aligning the hole in its rear face with the peg in the drum **(see illustration)**. Secure the cam with the retaining screw, having applied a drop of non-permanent thread locking compound to its threads, and tighten the screw to the specified torque setting **(see illustration)**.

17 Build up the neutral detent arm assembly, taking care not to interchange components with the gear detent arm; the neutral arm return spring can be identified by its white paint marking **(see illustrations)**. Tighten the retaining nut to the specified torque setting.

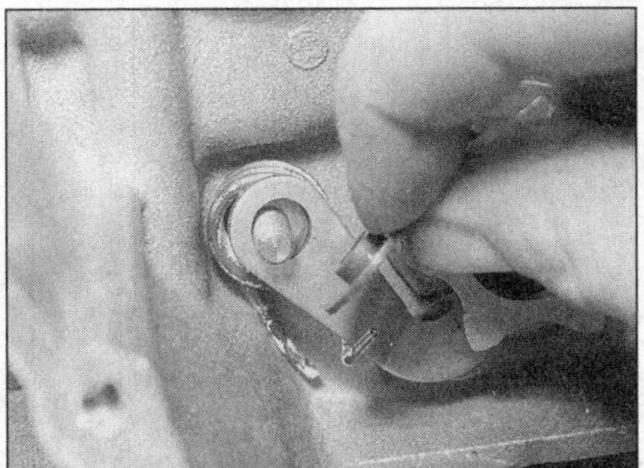

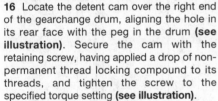

30.17c Fit the collar with its stepped side facing inwards

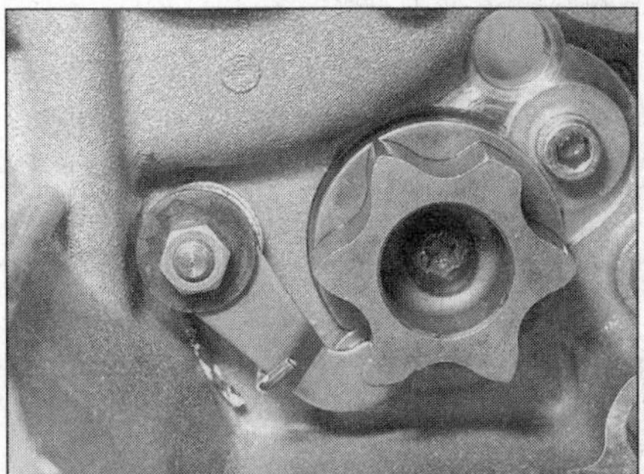

30.17d Secure the neutral detent arm pivot with the nut

18 Similarly build up the gear detent arm assembly **(see illustrations)**.

19 Install the gearchange shaft in the

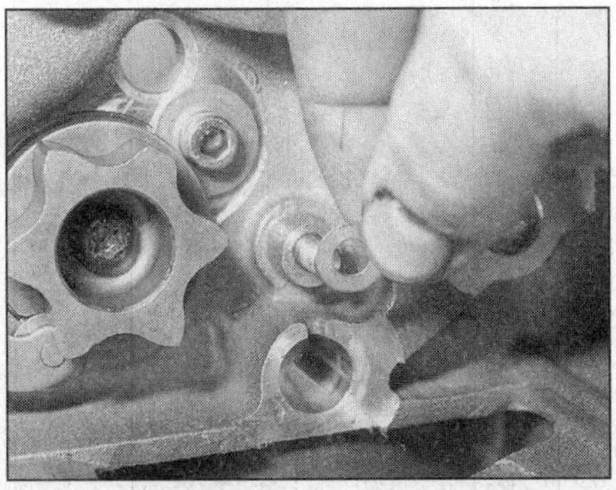

30.18a Build up the gear detent arm by installing the washer . . .

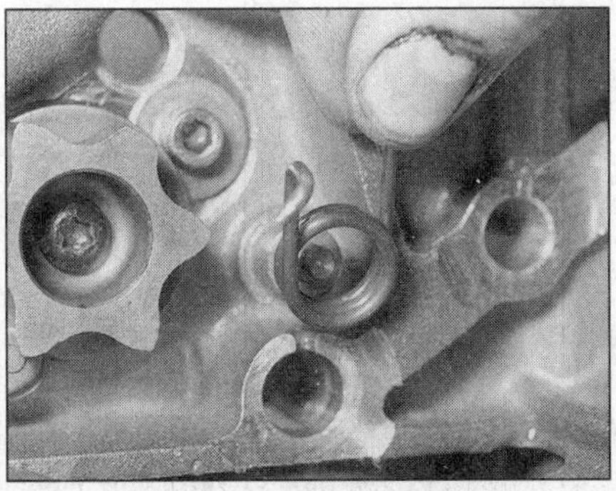

30.18b . . . return spring . . .

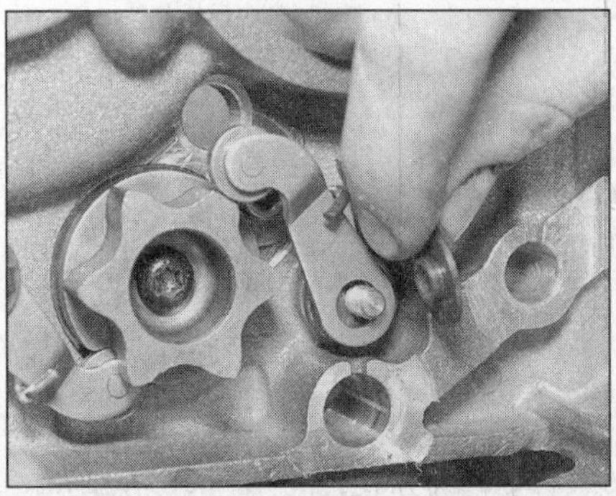

30.18c . . . gear detent arm and collar

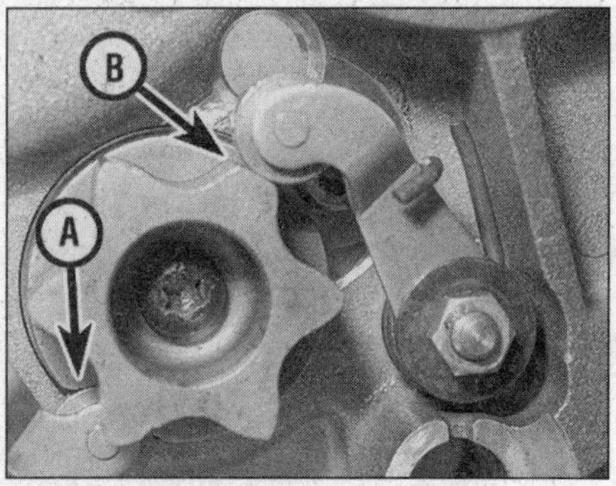

30.18d Secure with the nut. Detent cams are shown in neutral position

A Neutral detent B Gear detent

30.19a Install the gearchange shaft in the lower crankcase . . .

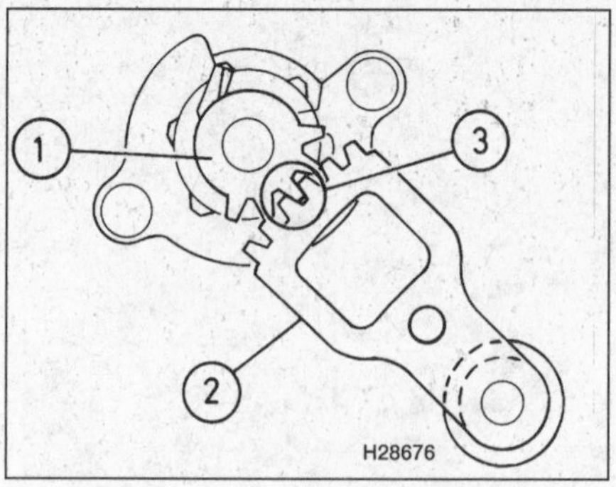

30.19b . . . and mesh its quadrant teeth with those of the pawl carrier

1 Pawl carrier
2 Quadrant
3 Centre tooth of pawl carrier meshed between 3rd and 4th teeth of quadrant

30.19c Secure the stopper plate with the two screws (arrowed)

crankcase and mesh its quadrant teeth with the pawl carrier teeth **(see illustration)**. Note that the stopper plate must be rotated out of the way to allow the teeth to engage. It is important that the centre tooth on the pawl carrier locates between the 3rd and 4th teeth of the quadrant **(see illustration)**. Align the stopper plate holes with those in the crankcase, apply a drop of non-permanent thread locking compound to the retaining screw threads and tighten them securely **(see illustration)**.

20 Install the quadrant stopper bolt in the crankcase and tighten it to the specified torque setting **(see illustration)**. Install the washer and circlip on the gearchange shaft to retain it in the crankcase **(see illustrations)**. Slip the return spring over the gearchange shaft, noting that its ends must locate over the quadrant peg and stopper bolt, then install the spring guide and secure with the circlip **(see illustrations)**.

21 Temporarily install the gearchange lever on the shaft end and rotate the gearchange drum fully in both directions. Check that when fully extended with the quadrant contacting the stopper bolt, the gear teeth engage as shown **(see illustration)**. If the teeth do not engage correctly, check the pawl carrier and quadrant teeth for accurate alignment as described in Step 19.

30.20a Install the stopper bolt in the crankcase

30.20b Slip the thrustwasher on the gearchange shaft . . .

30.20c . . . and retain the shaft with the circlip

30.20d Install the return spring, engaging its ends with the quadrant peg and stopper bolt. Slip the spring guide into place . . .

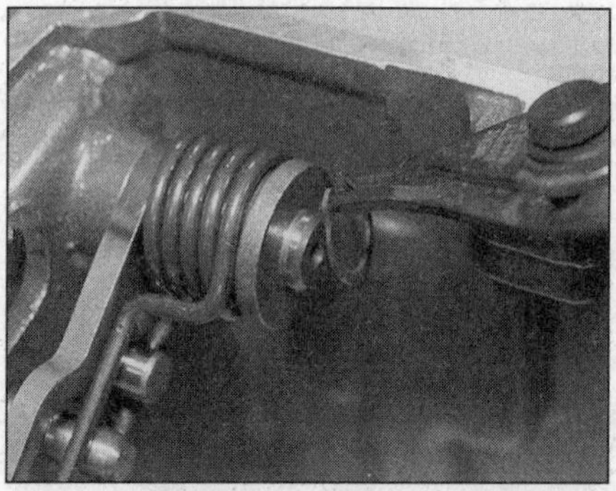

30.20e . . . and secure all components with the circlip

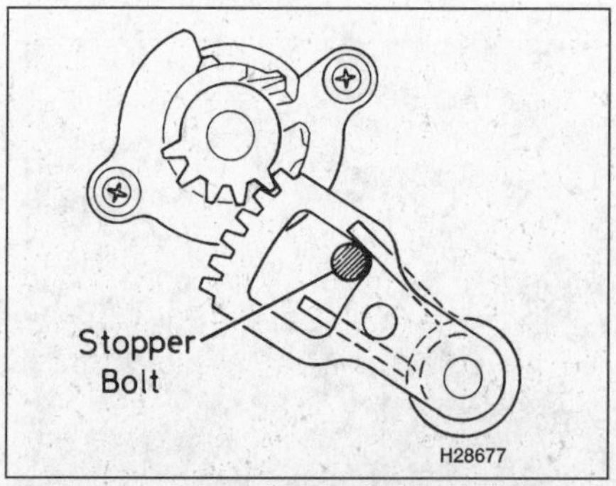

30.21 Check that pawl carrier and quadrant teeth still engage at the fullest extent of shifting

30.23a Slip the fork rod partway into the crankcase . . .

30.23b . . . and engage the left selector fork (No. 1) . . .

30.23c . . . then the centre selector fork (No. 2) . . .

30.23d . . . and finally the right selector fork (No. 3)

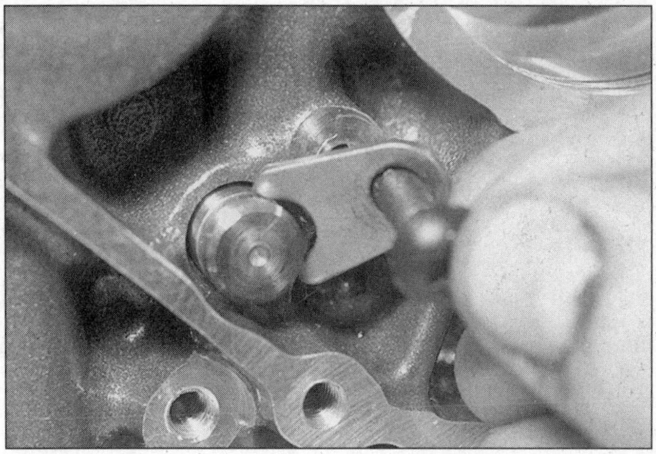

30.23e Secure the fork rod with the retaining plate and screw

22 Install the oil pump and its drive gear (see Section 31).

23 Slip the gearchange rod into its bore in the crankcase and engage the forks on the rod so that their guide pins locate in the drum tracks **(see illustrations)**. Note that the forks are marked 1, 2 and 3 to correspond with the cylinder numbers. Lock the rod in position with the retaining plate and screw, tightening it to the specified torque **(see illustration)**.

24 Position the gearchange drum in the neutral position, and assemble the crankcase halves (see Section 23).

31 Oil pump – pressure check, removal, inspection and installation

Pressure check

1 To check the oil pressure, a suitable gauge and the Triumph adapter (Pt. No. 3880095) will be needed.

2 Warm the engine up to normal operating temperature then stop it. Remove the right lower fairing panel on Trophy and Daytona models (see Chapter 8).

3 Swiftly unscrew the banjo bolt from the external oil pipe on the cylinder block and screw the adapter in its place **(see illustration 11.25)**. The Triumph adapter is drilled to accept the oil pipe banjo union and thus retain oil supply to the camshafts. Connect the gauge to the adapter.

4 Start the engine and increase the engine speed to 5000 rpm whilst watching the gauge reading. The oil pressure should be similar to that given in the Specifications at the start of this Chapter.

5 If the pressure is significantly lower than the standard, either the relief valve is stuck open, the oil pump is faulty, the oil pump pick-up strainer is blocked or there is other engine damage. Begin diagnosis by checking the oil pump pick-up strainer and relief valve (see Sections 19 and 20), then the oil pump. If those items check out okay, chances are the bearing oil clearances are excessive and the engine needs to be overhauled.

6 If the pressure is too high, the relief valve is stuck closed. To check it, see Section 20.

7 Stop the engine and unscrew the gauge and adapter from the crankcase. Install the banjo bolt using a new sealing washer on each side of the union, and tighten it to the specified torque setting.

8 On Trophy and Daytona models install the fairing panel (see Chapter 8).

Removal

9 Separate the crankcase halves (see Section 23). If not already done, remove the water pump (see Chapter 3).

10 The oil pump is housed in the crankcase lower half. Remove the screw and retaining plate from the left side of the crankcase to free the gearchange fork rod. Slide the rod out of the crankcase and lift each fork out as it clears the rod. Install the forks back on the rod as a guide to reassembly.

11 Remove the four screws from the base of the crankcase to free the oil pump **(see illustration)**.

31.11 Release four screws (arrowed) to free the oil pump from the lower crankcase

2

31.12a Free the circlip . . .

31.12b . . . and washer from the outside of the crankcase . . .

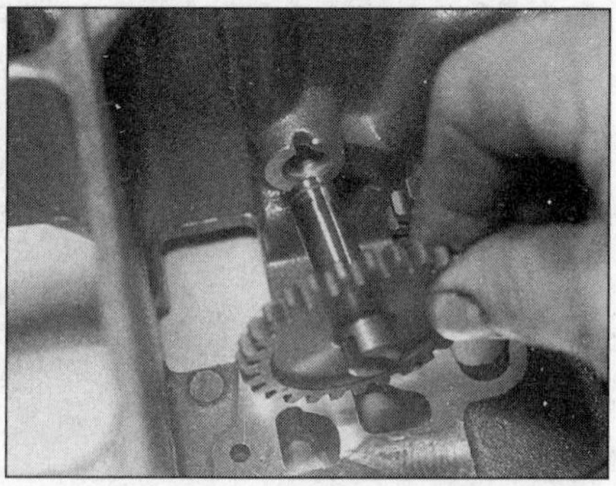

31.12c . . . then withdraw the driven gear from inside the crankcase

31.12d Remove the screw and washer . . .

31.12e . . . to free the drive gear from the outside of the crankcase

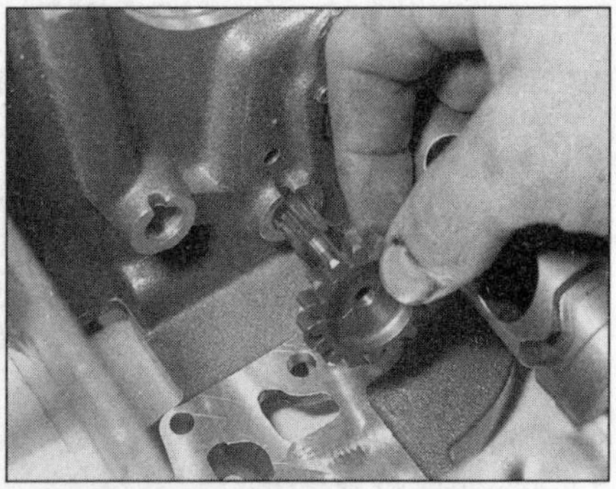

31.12f Withdraw the intermediate gear from inside the crankcase

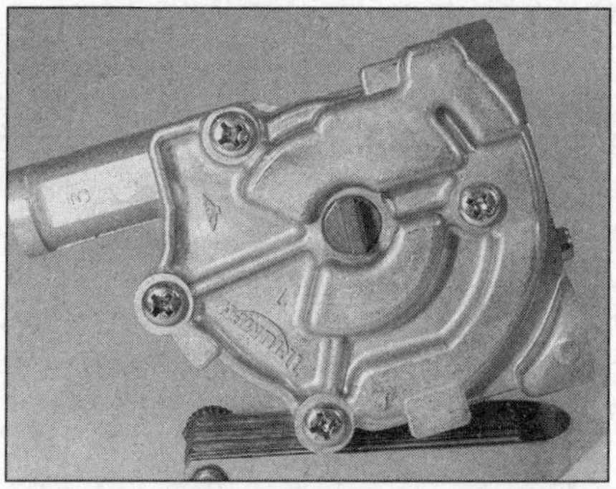

31.14 Remove the four screws to remove the pump cover

12 Release the circlip and washer and withdraw the driven gear from inside the crankcase **(see illustrations)**. Remove the oil pump drive gear retaining screw and washer, and withdraw the drive gear from its shaft **(see illustrations)**. The intermediate gear can be withdrawn from inside the crankcase **(see illustration)**.

Inspection

Note: *Individual parts are available for the oil pump; if the checks described below indicate that the pump is worn, it must be renewed as a complete unit.*

13 Wash the oil pump in solvent, then dry it off.

14 Remove the four screws to free the pump end cover **(see illustration)**. Recover the two dowels if they are loose.

15 Measure the clearance between the inner rotor tip and the outer rotor tip **(see illustration)**. Measure the clearance between the outer rotor and body with a feeler blade **(see illustration)**. Finally, lay a straightedge across the rotors and pump body and measure the rotor endfloat (gap between the rotors and pump body) with a feeler blade **(see illustration)**. If any of the results are outside the limits listed in this Chapter's Specifications, renew the pump.

16 Pick the inner and outer rotors out of the pump. Examine them for scoring and wear. Slip the inner rotor drive pin out of the shaft and withdraw the thrustwasher.

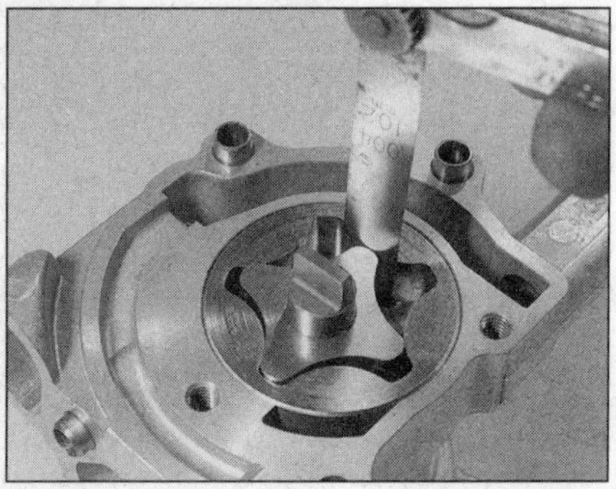

31.15a Measuring the rotor tip clearance

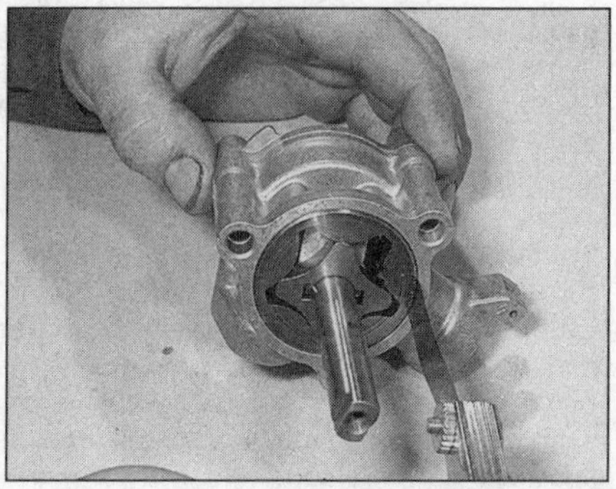

31.15b Measuring the outer rotor-to-body clearance

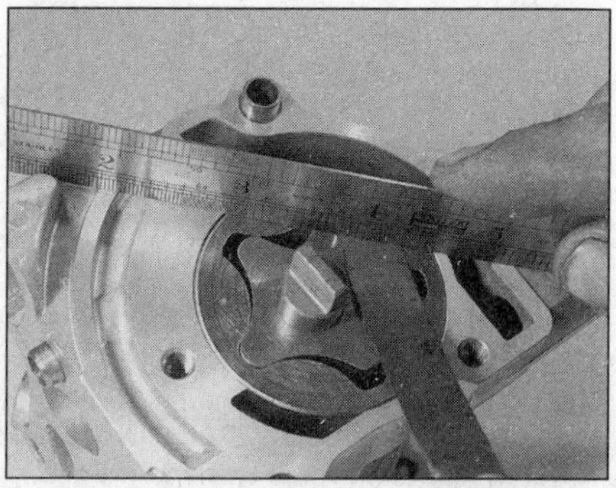

31.15c Measuring rotor endfloat

31.17 Remove three screws to remove the cover from the opposite end of the pump

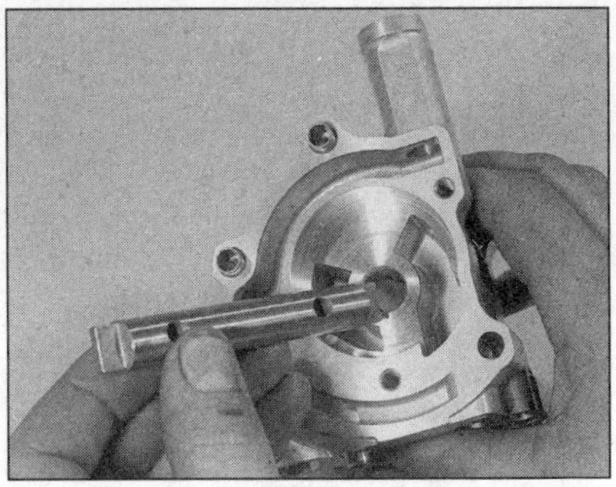

31.18a Install the driveshaft in the pump body . . .

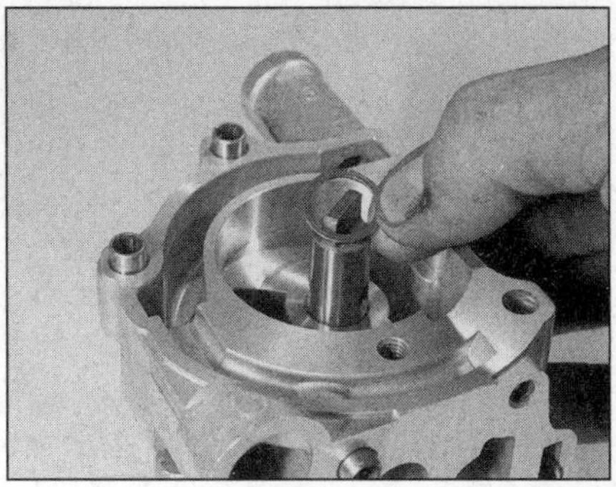

31.18b . . . followed by the thrustwasher

17 On 3 cylinder engines, the pump driveshaft can be withdrawn from the pump body. On 4 cylinder engines, another set of rotors is fitted to the back of the pump; remove the cover from the back of the pump and extract the other set of rotors (used to pump oil around the oil cooler) as described in Step 16 **(see illustration)**. **Note:** *Although largely of academic interest, the pump outlet has a cast number 3 or 4 to denote its engine application.*

18 Before reassembling the pump, make sure that all parts are clean. Have a supply of the correct grade of engine oil on hand to lubricate the rotors as they are installed. Insert the driveshaft into the body, followed by the thrustwasher **(see illustrations)**. Carefully install the drive pin and locate the cutouts in the back of the inner rotor over it **(see illustrations)**. Install the outer rotor so that the side with the dot faces outwards **(see illustration)**. If you are working on a 4 cylinder engine, build up the other set of rotors in the same way.

19 Secure the pump end cover(s) noting that the gold-coloured screws are located in the pump holes with dowels **(see illustrations)**.

20 Inspect the oil pump drive gear, intermediate gear and driven gear for signs of wear or damage.

Installation

21 Lubricate the shafts of the pump driven gear and intermediate gear and insert them in the crankcase **(see illustration)**. Position the drive slot in the driven gear vertically to allow engagement of the pump driveshaft tab.

22 Install the drive gear on the other end of the intermediate shaft and secure with its washer and screw, having applied a drop of non-permanent thread locking compound to its threads **(see illustration 31.12d)**. Tighten

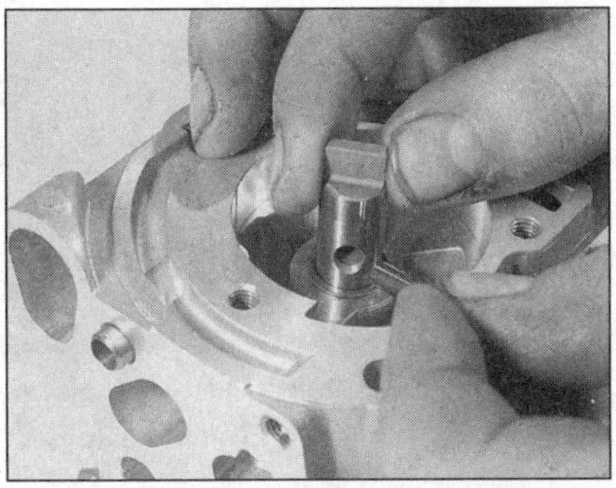

31.18c Insert the drive pin in the shaft . . .

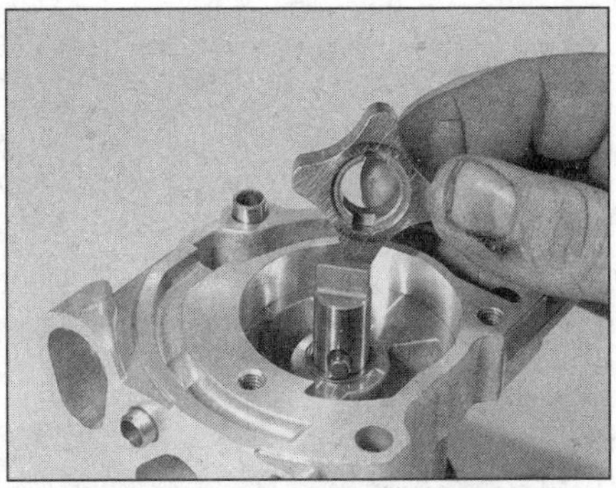

31.18d . . . and locate the cutouts in the rear of the inner rotor over the pin

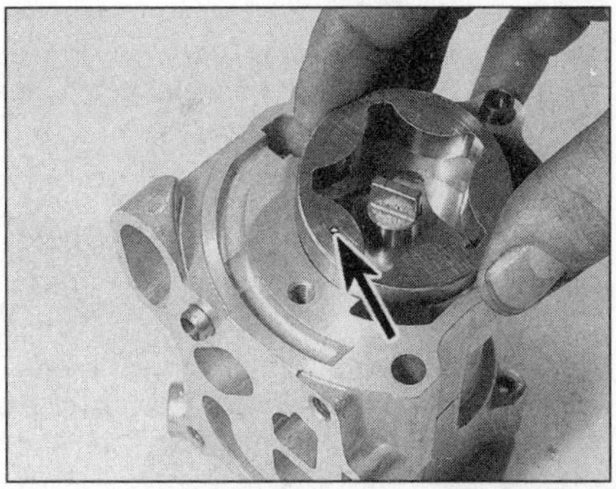

31.18e Install the outer rotor so that the side with the dot faces outwards (arrowed)

2

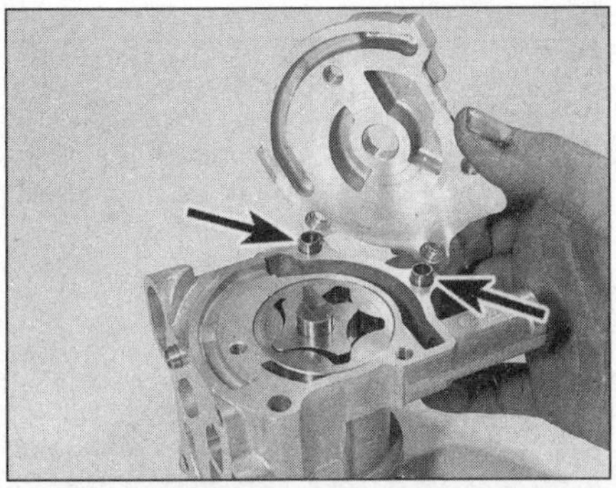

31.19a Check that the two dowels are in position (arrowed)

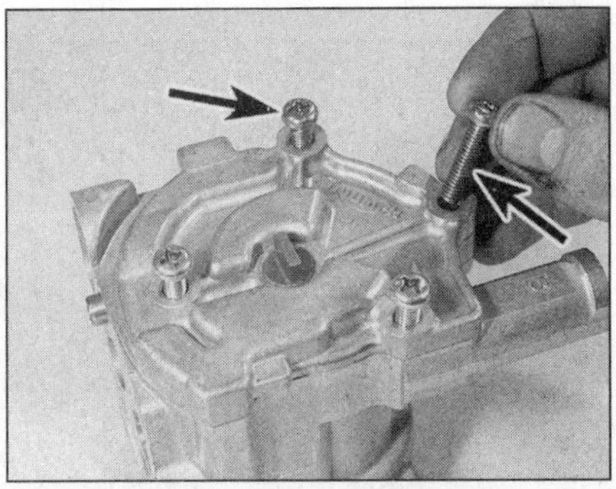

31.19b Install the gold-coloured screws in the holes with the dowels (arrowed)

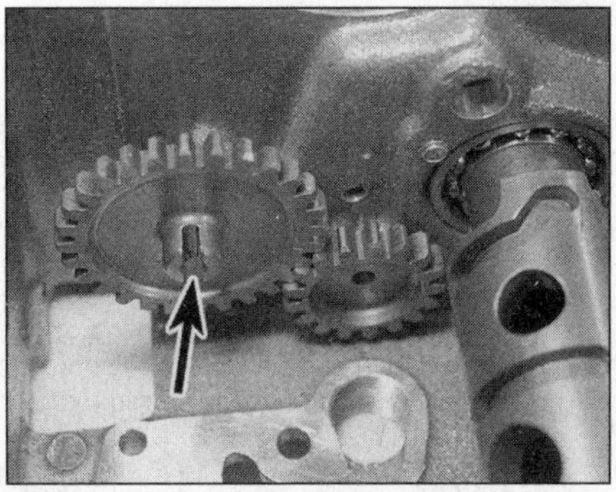

31.21 Fit the intermediate shaft and driven gear in the crankcase. Position the driven gear so that its slot is vertical (arrowed)

31.22 Retain the driven gear with the washer and circlip

the screw to the specified torque setting. Secure the end of the pump driven gear with the washer and circlip **(see illustration)**.

23 Check that the pump driveshaft rotates freely and that the two dowels are in place in the pump mating flange. Install the oil pump in the crankcase so that its tab engages the driven gear slot **(see illustration)**. Apply a drop of non-permanent thread locking compound to the four retaining screws and tighten them to the specified torque setting.

24 Slip the gearchange rod into its bore in the crankcase and engage the forks on the rod. Note that the forks are marked 1, 2 and 3 to correspond with the cylinder numbers. Lock the rod in position with the retaining plate and screw, tightening it to the specified torque setting.

25 Reassemble the crankcase halves (see Section 23) and install the water pump (see Chapter 3).

32 Alternator/starter clutch drive – removal, inspection and installation

Note: *These components can be accessed on early models via a cover in the top of the crankcase. On later models, crankcase separation is necessary.*

Removal

Early models (with access cover on the upper crankcase)

Note: *Extreme care must be taken not to allow any components to fall into the crankcase when carrying out this procedure. The procedure can also be carried out in full as described below for later models.*

1 On early models, the alternator/starter clutch drive and starter idler gear can be removed with the engine in the frame. The clutch outer drum (Section 15), alternator and starter motor (Chapter 9), carburettors and airbox (Chapter 4) must first be removed to gain the necessary access.

2 Remove the nine bolts to free the access cover from the top of the crankcase; withdraw the cover and gasket.

3 Proceed as described in Step 5.

31.23 Install the oil pump in the crankcase, aligning its drive tab (arrowed) with the slot in the driven gear

Later models

4 Separate the crankcase halves (Section 23) and remove the transmission shafts from the upper crankcase (see Section 28). The alternator/starter clutch drive is housed in the upper crankcase half.

5 The method of securing the alternator drive gear and shock absorber housing has been modified. On models up to VIN 56684 the drive gear and housing are retained by bolts which thread into the driveshaft. On models from VIN 56685, both components are retained by a single throughbolt which passes through the drive gear, driveshaft and housing, and is secured by a nut. Therefore on early models, remove the bolt and washer securing the alternator drive gear on the clutch side of the crankcase **(see illustration)**. You may need to counterhold the shock absorber housing bolt on the opposite end of the shaft whilst the drive gear bolt is slackened. A service tool (Pt. No. 3880040) is available which locates into one of the housing webs when the damping rubbers have been removed, although this was not found to be necessary on the machine featured. Slide the alternator driveshaft complete with shock absorber housing out of the left side of the crankcase **(see illustration)**. Recover the splined sleeve from the right side of the crankcase **(see illustration)**.

6 On later models, counterhold the drive gear bolt and unscrew the shock absorber housing nut. Remove the nut, washer and shock absorber housing. Withdraw the bolt, washer and drive gear from the other side of the casing, followed by the splined sleeve. Push the driveshaft out from either side. **Note:** *Triumph advise that the throughbolt and nut are renewed every time they are disturbed.*

7 On all models, lift out the starter clutch and recover the small spacer from its left side **(see illustration)**. On models fitted with the modified starter clutch (see **Note** at the beginning of Step 9) you may find that there is insufficient room to remove the starter clutch and spacer. In which case withdraw the ball bearing from the crankcase **(see illustration 32.16a)** and slip the spacer out via the bearing bore.

32.5a Remove the bolt and washer to free the alternator driveshaft gear from the clutch side of the upper crankcase

32.5b Withdraw the driveshaft complete with shock absorber housing from the alternator side of the upper crankcase

32.5c Slip the splined sleeve from the driveshaft as it is withdrawn

32.7 Lift the starter clutch out of the crankcase

32.8a Remove the bolt and washer . . .

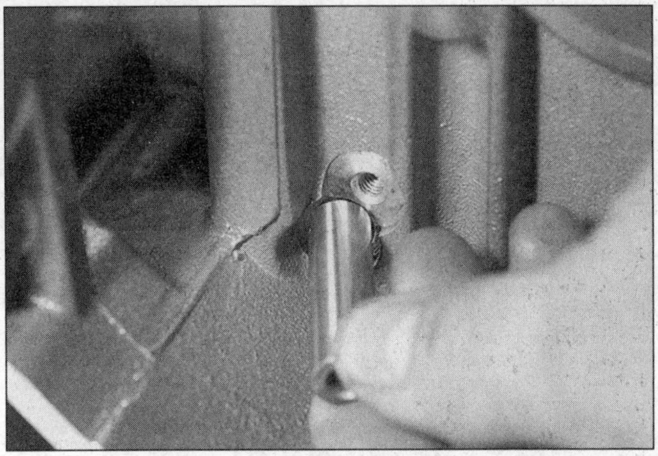

32.8b . . . and slip out the starter idler gear shaft

8 Remove the bolt and washer from the right side of the crankcase which retains the starter idler gear shaft **(see illustration)**. Support the idler gear from inside the crankcase and fully withdraw the shaft **(see illustration)**.

Inspection

Note: *The starter clutch components and starter idler gear were modified in late 1995. This modification was introduced on production models from engine no. 23707 (four cylinder grey-painted engines and all three cylinder engines) or engine no. 23681 (four cylinder black-painted engines) and the new components can be identified by the 15 tooth starter idler gear and 51 tooth starter clutch gear. On earlier engines, modified parts for the starter clutch and idler gear are available in the form of an assembly rather than individual parts; refer to a Triumph dealer for details and ensure that you purchase the 13 tooth idler gear and 53 tooth starter clutch gear set.*

9 Remove the circlip and thrustwasher to free the gear from the starter clutch **(see illustrations)**. Withdraw the needle roller bearing and second thrustwasher from the boss.

10 Examine the bearing surface of the starter clutch gear and the condition of the rollers inside the clutch body. If the gear surface shows signs of excessive wear or the rollers are damaged (especially if problems have been experienced in starting the engine), the starter clutch and idler gear should be renewed with the modified type – see **Note** above.

11 Extract the starter clutch caged roller assembly (termed a 'sprag') by removing the six screws **(see illustration)**.

12 To reassemble, insert the roller assembly into its housing, noting that its shoulder abuts the inner face of the housing **(see illustration)**. Insert the centre boss through the assembly **(see illustration)**. Apply non-permanent thread locking compound to the threads of the six screws and tighten them to the specified torque setting **(see illustration)**.

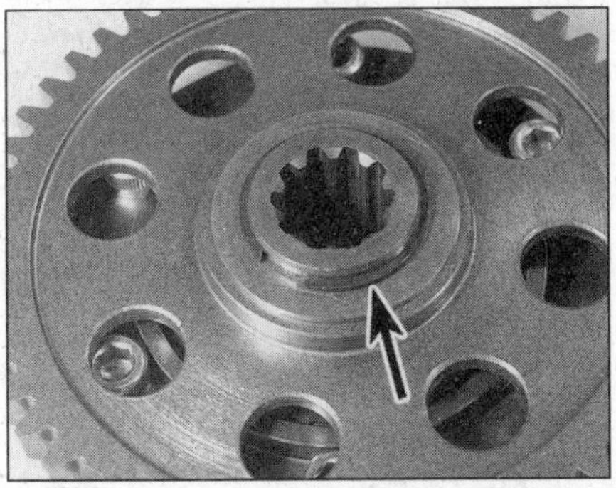

32.9a Remove the circlip (arrowed) . . .

32.9b . . . and thrustwasher from the starter clutch gear

32.11 Disassemble the starter clutch by removing the six screws

2

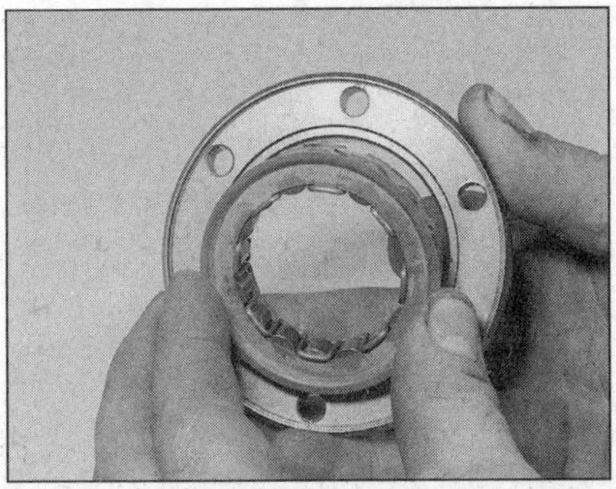

32.12a Install the roller assembly into the housing . . .

32.12b . . . and install the boss

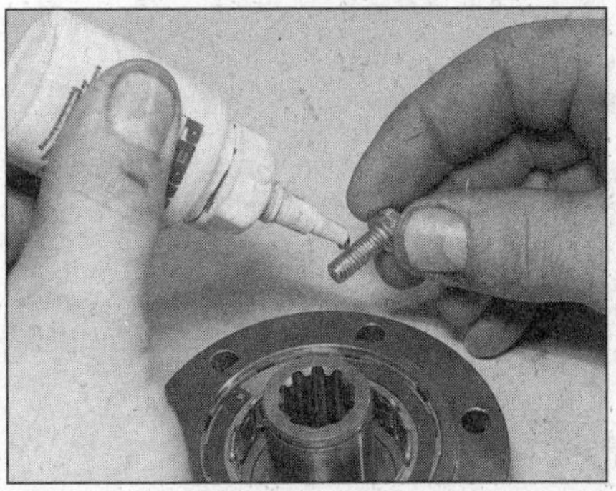

32.12c Apply thread lock to the starter clutch screws

32.13a Install the thrustwasher over the centre boss . . .

32.13b . . . followed by the needle roller bearing

32.13c Install the starter clutch gear

32.16a The ball bearing at the alternator end of the crankcase is retained by two screws and washers

32.16b The needle roller bearing at the clutch end of the crankcase has a screw and washer on each side of the casing

13 Slip the thrustwasher over the centre boss, followed by the needle roller bearing. Install the gear in the starter clutch, taking care not to damage the rollers as it is manoeuvred into position **(see illustrations)**.

14 Examine the teeth of the starter idler gear and the corresponding teeth of the starter clutch gear and starter motor gear. Also examine the alternator drive gear teeth and those of the clutch auxiliary gear. Renew the gears as a set if worn or chipped teeth are discovered.

15 Inspect the shock absorber rubbers in the alternator driveshaft housing. If compacted or deteriorated they should be renewed. The housing can be withdrawn from the driveshaft after the retaining bolt and washer have been removed.

16 The driveshaft locates in a ball bearing at its left end and by a needle roller bearing at its right end. The ball bearing is secured by two bolts and washers **(see illustration)**. The needle roller bearing is secured by a screw and washer on each side of the crankcase **(see illustration)**.

Installation

17 Position the starter idler gear in the crankcase with its larger gear against the side of the crankcase **(see illustration)**. Lubricate the idler gear shaft and slide it fully into place from the outside of the crankcase **(see illustration 32.8b)**. Secure the shaft with the washer and bolt, having applied a drop of non-permanent thread locking compound to the bolt threads **(see illustration 32.8a)**. Tighten the bolt to the specified torque setting.

18 Insert the assembled starter clutch in the crankcase and angle it to one side to allow the small spacer to locate in its left side **(see illustration)**. **Note:** *If working on an early model via the upper crankcase aperture take great care not to drop the spacer into the crankcase.* Holding the starter clutch steady, insert the driveshaft through the assembly from the left side of the crankcase **(see illustration 32.6a)**.

19 You may find that due to the increased thickness of the modified starter clutch assembly (see **Note** at the beginning of Step 9) there is insufficient room to fit the small spacer as described in Step 18. If this is the case, remove the ball bearing from the alternator end of the crankcase **(see illustration 32.16a)** and support the starter

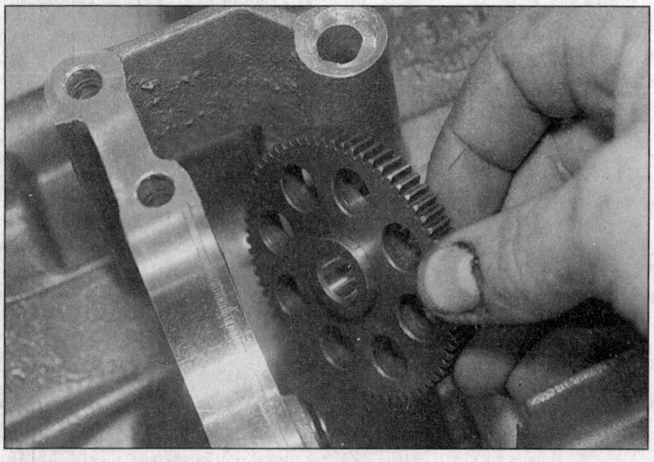

32.17 Starter idler gear is installed with the large gear against the crankcase

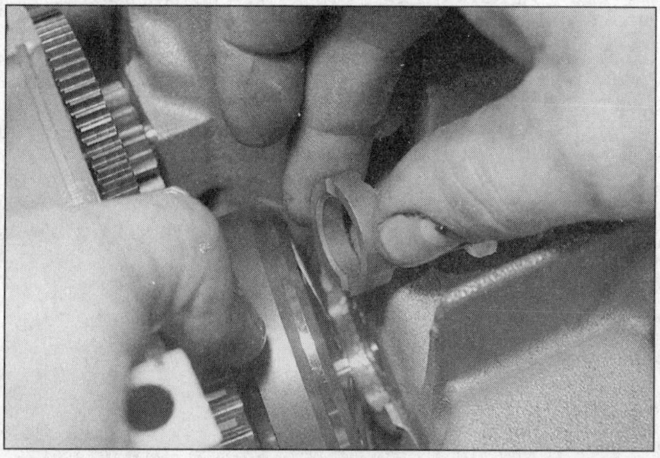

32.18 Tilt the starter clutch to one side to allow the spacer to be inserted

32.20a Tighten the drive gear bolt . . .

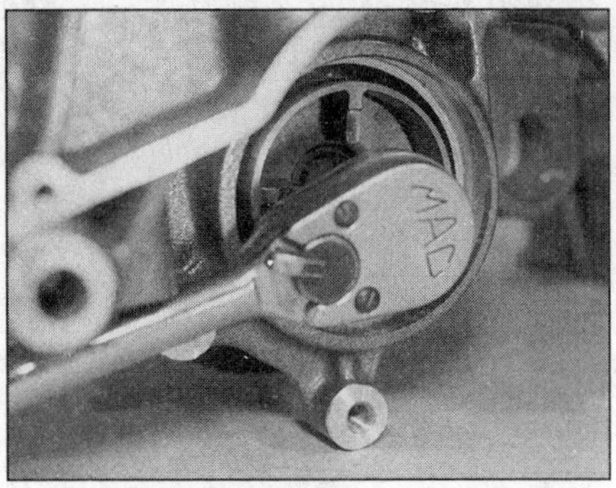

32.20b . . . and shock absorber housing bolt to the specified torque

clutch with a bar through its centre whilst the small spacer is inserted, followed by the bearing and driveshaft. Due to the increased thickness of the modified starter clutch, if fitting it to an early model with an access cover in the top of the crankcase check that the clutch body does not touch the crankcase wall by rotating it one full turn. There should be a minimum of 1 mm clearance between the clutch body and wall – if not, the high point on the crankcase must be carefully filed back. This will obviously require separation of the crankcase and thorough cleaning afterwards to remove all traces of swarf and it is advisable to have this done by a Triumph dealer.

20 On models up to VIN 56684, slip the splined sleeve over the right end of the driveshaft **(see illustration 32.6b)**. Install the drive gear over the driveshaft and secure with the washer and bolt. Tighten the bolt to the specified torque setting whilst counterholding the shock absorber housing at the other end of the shaft **(see illustration)**. Tighten the shock absorber housing bolt to the specified torque setting **(see illustration)**.

21 On models from VIN 56685, slip the splined sleeve over the right end of the driveshaft. Install the drive gear over the driveshaft and pass the bolt with its washer through the gear and shaft. **Note:** *Triumph advise that a new bolt and nut should be used.* Install the shock absorber housing and washer over the other end of the shaft and thread the nut into place. Counterhold the bolt head and tighten the nut to the specified torque setting.

22 On early models, install a new gasket on the crankcase and fit the cover, tightening its bolts evenly in a criss-cross sequence to the specified torque setting. Install all components described in Step 1.

23 On later models, install the transmission shafts (see Section 28) and reassemble the crankcase halves (see Section 23).

33 Initial start-up after overhaul

1 Make sure the engine oil and coolant levels are correct (see Chapter 1).

2 Make sure there is fuel in the tank, then turn the fuel tap to the ON position and operate the choke.

3 Start the engine and let it run at a moderately fast idle until it reaches operating temperature.

Warning: If the oil pressure indicator light doesn't go off, or it comes on while the engine is running, stop the engine immediately.

4 Check carefully for oil leaks and make sure the transmission and controls, especially the brakes, function properly before road testing the machine. Refer to Section 34 for the recommended running-in procedure.

5 Upon completion of the road test, and after the engine has cooled down completely, recheck the valve clearances and check the engine oil and coolant levels (see Chapter 1).

34 Recommended running-in procedure

1 Treat the machine gently for the first few miles to make sure oil has circulated throughout the engine and any new parts installed have started to seat.

2 Even greater care is necessary if new pistons and liners or a new crankshaft has been installed. In the case of new pistons and liners, the bike will have to be run in as when new. This means greater use of the transmission and a restraining hand on the throttle. There's no point in keeping to any set speed limit – the main idea is to keep from labouring the engine and to gradually increase performance. These recommendations can be lessened to an extent when only a new crankshaft is installed. Experience is the best guide, since it's easy to tell when an engine is running freely. The table shows maximum engine speed limitations, which Triumph provide for new motorcycles, and this can be used as a guide.

3 If a lubrication failure is suspected, stop the engine immediately and try to find the cause. If an engine is run without oil, even for a short period of time, severe damage will occur.

Maximum engine speeds when running-in

Up to 100 miles (160 km):	*3500 rpm max*
100 to 300 miles (160 to 480 km):	*5000 rpm max*
300 to 600 miles (480 to 965 km):	*6000 rpm max*
600 to 800 miles (965 to 1287 km):	*7000 rpm max*
800 to 1000 miles (1287 to 1609 km):	*8000 rpm max*

Notes

Chapter 3
Cooling system

Contents

Degrees of difficulty

Easy, suitable for novice with little experience	**Fairly easy,** suitable for beginner with some experience	**Fairly difficult,** suitable for competent DIY mechanic	**Difficult,** suitable for experienced DIY mechanic	**Very difficult,** suitable for expert DIY or professional

Specifications

Coolant

Mixture type and capacity	see Chapter 1

Radiator

Cap valve opening pressure	16 psi (1.1 Bar)

Thermostat

Opening temperature	83°C

Fan switch

Cooling fan cut-in temperature	
Trident, Sprint, Trophy, Speed Triple, Daytona, Tiger	99°C
Thunderbird, Thunderbird Sport, Adventurer, Legend TT	100°C

Temperature gauge sender unit

Resistance	255 to 310 ohms @ 60°C

Torque settings

Coolant drain plug	13 Nm
Coolant reservoir mounting bolts	
Trident, Sprint, Trophy, Speed Triple, Daytona, Tiger	4 Nm
Thunderbird, Thunderbird Sport, Adventurer, Legend TT	7 Nm
Coolant temperature sender unit	8 Nm
Radiator top mounting bolts	18 Nm
Radiator bottom bracket bolts	9 Nm
Radiator stone guard/electric fan mounting screws	2.5 Nm
Radiator end cover screws (Thunderbird, Thunderbird Sport, Adventurer, Legend TT)	7 Nm
Thermostat housing bolts (Thunderbird, Thunderbird Sport, Adventurer, Legend TT)	7 Nm
Water pump mounting bolts	12 Nm
Water pump inlet pipe bolt (at pump end)	8 Nm
Water pump inlet pipe bolt (at crankcase mounting)	10 Nm
Water pipe outlet union bolts (on cylinder head)	11 Nm
Water pipe inlet union bolts (on cylinder block)	11 Nm

3

1 General information

The cooling system uses a water/antifreeze coolant to carry away excess energy in the form of heat. The cylinders are surrounded by a water jacket from which the heated coolant is circulated by thermo-syphonic action in conjunction with a water pump, driven off the oil pump. The hot coolant passes upwards to the thermostat and through to the radiator. The coolant then flows across the radiator core, where it is cooled by the passing air, down to the water pump and back up to the engine where the cycle is repeated. On models fitted with fairings, air ducts direct the air flow to the radiator to ensure adequate cooling.

A thermostat is fitted in the system to prevent the coolant flowing through the radiator when the engine is cold, therefore accelerating the speed at which the engine reaches normal operating temperature. A thermostatically-controlled cooling fan is also fitted to aid cooling in extreme conditions.

The complete cooling system is partially sealed and pressurised, the pressure being controlled by a valve contained in the spring-loaded radiator cap. By pressurising the coolant the boiling point is raised, preventing premature boiling in adverse conditions. The overflow pipe from the system is connected to a reservoir into which excess coolant is expelled under pressure. The discharged coolant automatically returns to the radiator when the engine cools **(see illustrations)**.

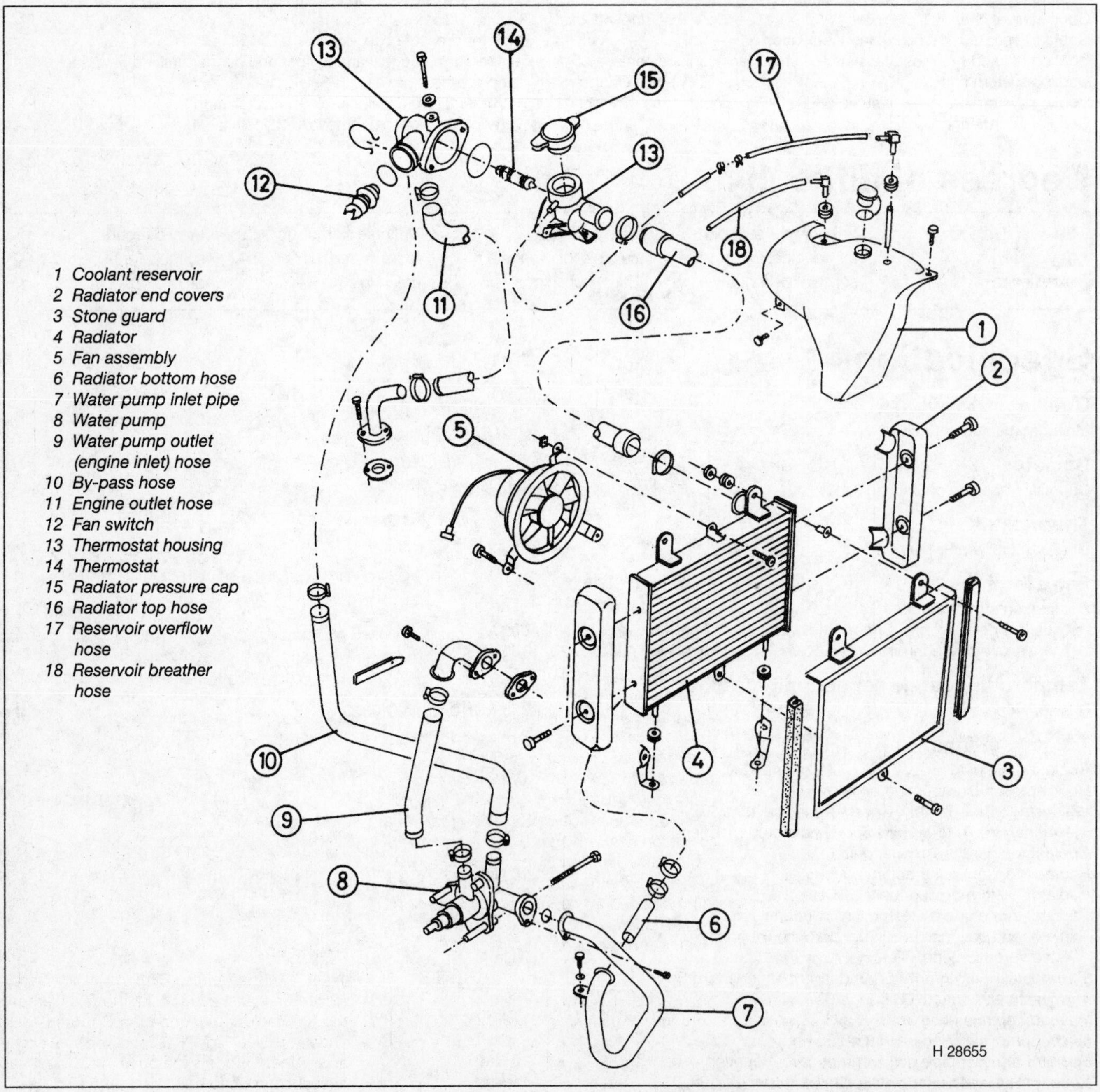

1.1a Cooling system components – Thunderbird, Thunderbird Sport, Adventurer and Legend TT models

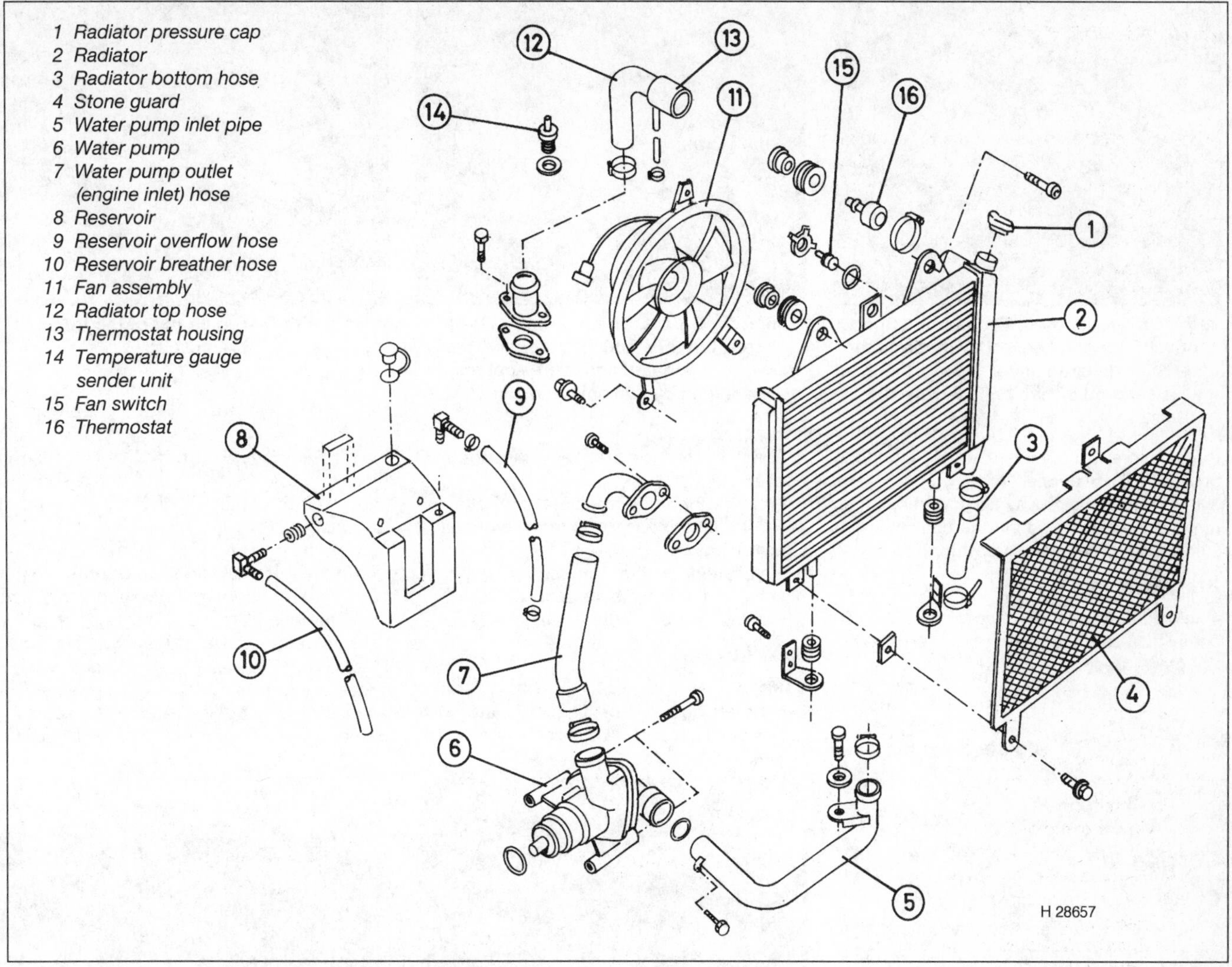

1.1b Cooling system components – Trident, Sprint, Trophy, Speed Triple, Daytona and Tiger models

Warning: Do not remove the pressure cap from the radiator when the engine is hot. Scalding hot coolant and steam may be blown out under pressure, which could cause serious injury. When the engine has cooled, place a thick rag, like a towel over the pressure cap; slowly rotate the cap anti-clockwise to the first stop. This procedure allows any residual pressure to escape. When the steam has stopped escaping, press down on the cap while turning it anti-clockwise and remove it.

Warning: Do not allow antifreeze to come in contact with your skin or painted surfaces of the motorcycle. Rinse off any spills immediately with plenty of water. Antifreeze is highly toxic if ingested. Never leave antifreeze lying around in an open container or in puddles on the floor; children and pets are attracted by its sweet smell and may drink it. Check with the local authorities about disposing of used antifreeze. Many communities will have collection centres which will see that antifreeze is disposed of safely.

Caution: At all times use the specified type of antifreeze, and always mix it with distilled water in the correct proportion. The antifreeze contains corrosion inhibitors which are essential to avoid damage to the cooling system. A lack of these inhibitors could lead to a build-up of corrosion which would block the coolant passages, resulting in overheating and severe engine damage. Distilled water must be used as opposed to tap water to avoid a build-up of scale which would also block the passages.

2 Radiator pressure cap – check

If problems such as overheating or loss of coolant occur, check the entire system as described in Chapter 1. The radiator cap opening pressure should be checked by a Triumph dealer with the special tester required to do the job. If the cap is defective, renew it with a new one.

3 Coolant reservoir – removal and installation

Removal

1 On Thunderbird, Thunderbird Sport, Adventurer and Legend TT models, remove the fuel tank as described in Chapter 4. On Trident, Sprint, Trophy, Speed Triple, Daytona and Tiger models remove the seat as described in Chapter 8.

2 Disconnect the hoses from the reservoir,

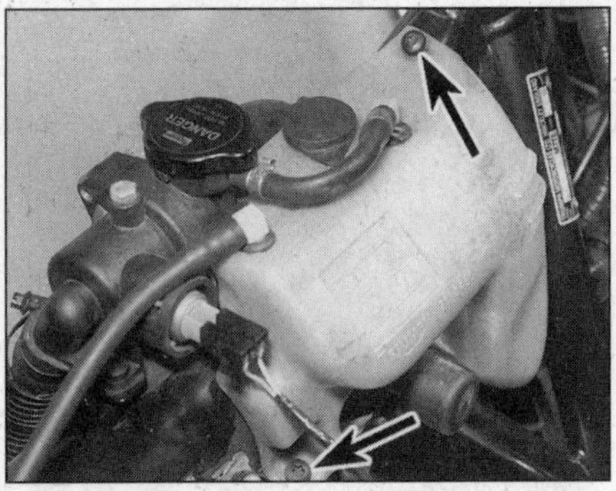

3.2a On Thunderbird, Thunderbird Sport, Adventurer and Legend TT models the reservoir is located under the fuel tank and is secured by two bolts (arrowed)

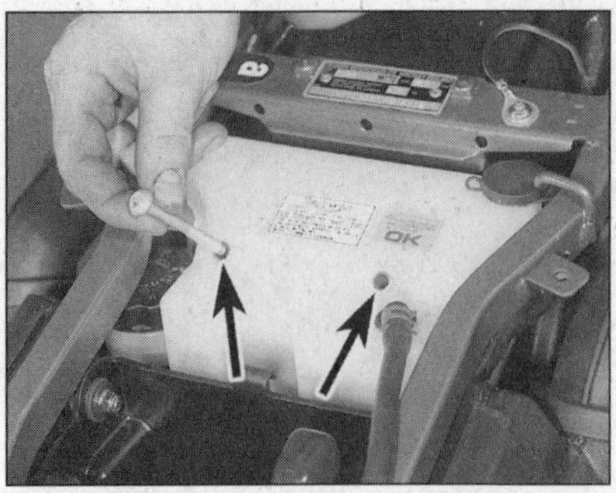

3.2b On Trident, Sprint, Trophy, Speed Triple, Daytona and Tiger models the reservoir is located under the seat and is secured by two bolts (arrowed)

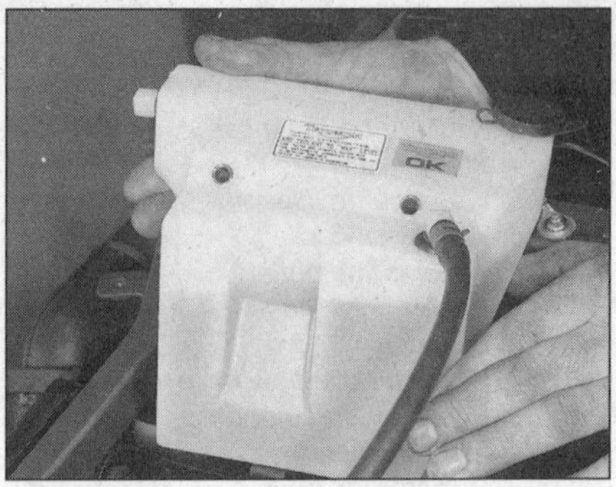

3.3 Lift the reservoir out of the frame to remove it

then unscrew the two reservoir mounting bolts **(see illustrations)**.

3 Lift the reservoir away from the bike, then remove the cap and drain the coolant into a suitable container **(see illustration)**.

Installation

4 Installation is the reverse of removal. On completion refill the reservoir as described in Chapter 1, Section 27.

4 Cooling fan and cooling fan switch - check and replacement

Cooling fan

Check

1 If the engine is overheating and the cooling fan isn't coming on, first check the cooling fan circuit fuse (see Chapter 9) and then the fan switch as described in Steps 8 to 12 below.

2 If the fan does not come on, (and the fan switch is good), the fault lies in either the cooling fan motor or the relevant wiring. Remove any fairing panels as necessary to gain access (requirements vary according to model and are described in Chapter 8), and test all the wiring and connections as described in Chapter 9.

3 To test the cooling fan motor, separate the two-pin fan wiring connector behind the radiator **(see illustration)**. Using a 12 volt battery and two jumper wires, connect the blue fan wire to the battery positive (+ve) lead and the black fan wire to the battery negative (-ve) lead. Once connected the fan should operate. If it does not, and the wiring is all good, then the fan is faulty. As no individual components are available for the fan assembly, if it is faulty it must be renewed as a unit.

Replacement

Warning: The engine must be completely cool before carrying out this procedure.

4 Remove the radiator as described in Section 7.

5 Unscrew the three fan mounting bolts and separate the fan assembly from the radiator **(see illustration)**.

6 Installation is the reverse of removal. Tighten the mounting bolts securely.

7 Install the radiator (refer to Section 7).

Cooling fan switch

Check

8 If the engine is overheating and the cooling fan isn't coming on, first check the cooling fan circuit fuse (see Chapter 9). If the fuse is blown, check the fan circuit for a short to earth (see the wiring diagrams at the end of this book).

9 If the fuse is good, disconnect the wires from the fan switch fitted to the thermostat housing (Thunderbird, Thunderbird Sport, Adventurer and Legend TT models), or to the left side of the radiator (all other models) **(see illustrations)**. Remove any fairing panels as necessary to gain access (requirements vary according to model – refer to Chapter 8). Using a jumper wire, connect between the

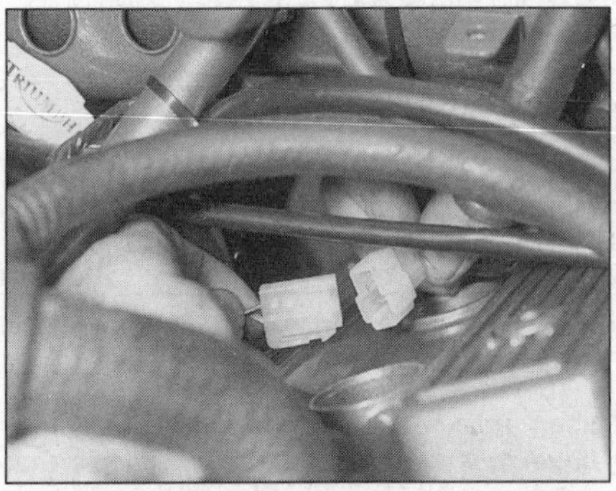

4.3 Trace the fan wiring to the connector behind the radiator and disconnect it

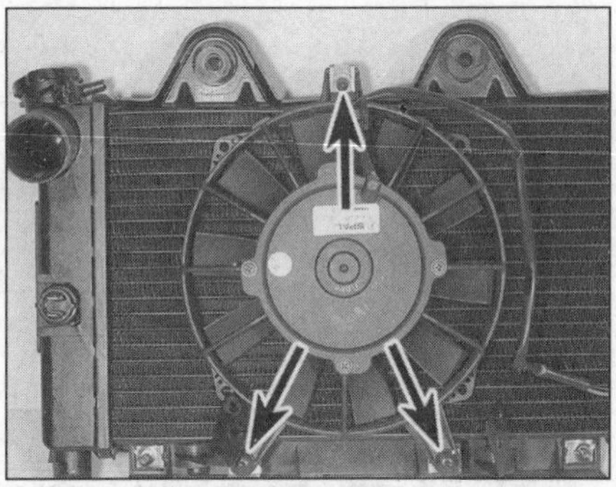

4.5 Remove the three bolts (arrowed) to separate the fan assembly from the radiator

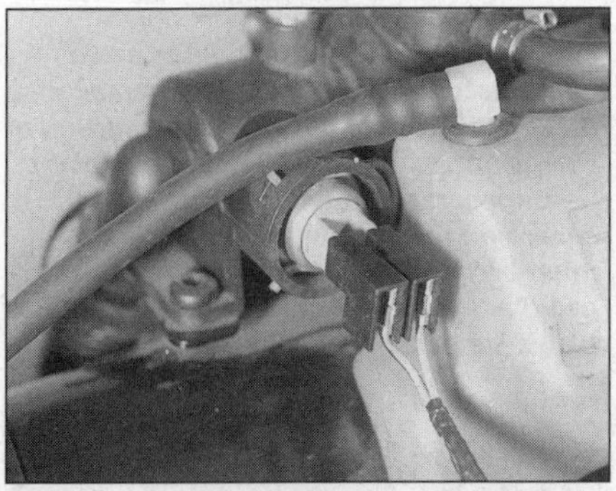

4.9a On Thunderbird, Thunderbird Sport, Adventurer and Legend TT models the fan switch is located in the thermostat housing under the tank

4.9b On Trident, Sprint, Trophy, Speed Triple, Daytona and Tiger models the fan switch is located on the left side of the radiator

two wires. The fan should come on. If it does, the fan switch is defective and must be renewed. If it does not come on, the fan should be tested as described in Step 3 above.

10 If the fan works but is suspected of cutting in at the wrong temperature, a more comprehensive test of the switch can be made as follows.

11 Remove the switch from the bike as described in Steps 13 to 16 or 19 to 22 below, according to model. Fill a small heatproof container with water and place it on a stove. Connect the probes of an ohmmeter to the terminals of the switch, and using some wire or other support suspend the switch in the water so that just the sensing portion and the threads are submerged. Also place a thermometer capable of reading temperatures up to 110°C in the water so that its bulb is close to the switch. The testing set-up is similar to that used for the temperature gauge sender unit **(see illustration 5.6)**. **Note:** *None of the components should be allowed to directly touch the container.*

12 Initially the ohmmeter reading should be very high indicating that the switch is open (OFF). Heat the water, stirring it gently.

> ***Warning: This must be done very carefully to avoid the risk of personal injury.***

When the temperature reaches around 99°C (100°C for Thunderbird, Thunderbird Sport, Adventurer and Legend TT models) the meter reading should drop to around zero ohms, indicating that the switch has closed (ON). Now turn the heat off. As the temperature falls below 99°C the meter reading should show infinite (very high) resistance, indicating that the switch has opened (OFF). If the meter readings obtained are different, or they are obtained at different temperatures, then the switch is faulty and must be renewed.

Replacement – Thunderbird, Thunderbird Sport, Adventurer and Legend TT models

> ***Warning: The engine must be completely cool before carrying out this procedure.***

13 Drain the cooling system (Chapter 1).

14 Remove the fuel tank (Chapter 4).

15 The fan switch is located in the thermostat housing underneath the fuel tank, and is secured in place by a clip **(see illustration 4.9a)**. Disconnect the wiring from the switch and pull off the clip using a pair of pliers.

16 Remove the switch by carefully pulling it out of the housing, and remove the rubber O-ring, which should be renewed.

17 Fit a new O-ring and install the switch in the housing, then fit the clip making sure it is properly secured. Reconnect the switch wiring.

18 Refill the cooling system (Chapter 1), and fit the fuel tank (Chapter 4).

Replacement – Trident, Sprint, Trophy, Speed Triple, Daytona and Tiger models

> ***Warning: The engine must be completely cool before carrying out this procedure.***

19 Remove any fairing panels necessary to gain access to the radiator (requirements vary according to the model – refer to Chapter 8).

20 Drain the cooling system (Chapter 1).

21 The fan switch is located in the left side of the radiator, and is secured by a locking ring **(see illustration 4.9b)**. Disconnect the wiring from the switch, then unscrew the locking ring.

22 Remove the switch by carefully pulling it out of the radiator, and remove the rubber O-ring, which should be renewed.

23 Fit a new O-ring and install the switch in the radiator, then fit the locking ring and tighten it securely. Reconnect the switch wiring.

24 Refill the cooling system as described in Chapter 1, then fit any fairing panels that have been removed as described in Chapter 8.

5 Temperature gauge/warning light and sender unit – check and replacement

Temperature gauge/warning light

Check

1 The circuit consists of the sender unit mounted in the left end of the cylinder head and the gauge assembly mounted in the instrument panel – on Speed Triple, Trophy (from VIN 29156), Thunderbird, Thunderbird Sport, Adventurer and Legend TT models, a warning light is fitted instead of the gauge. If the system malfunctions check first that the battery is fully charged and that the fuses are all good.

2 If the gauge is not working, first remove any fairing panels necessary to gain access to the temperature gauge sender unit (requirements vary according to model and are described in Chapter 8). Turn the ignition switch ON and disconnect the wire from the sender unit **(see illustration)**. The temperature gauge needle should be on the 'C' on the gauge or the warning light should remain extinguished (as applicable). Now earth the sender unit wire on the engine. The needle should swing immediately over to the 'H' on the gauge or the warning light should come on (as applicable). If the needle moves as described above, the sender unit is proven defective and must be renewed.

Caution: Do not earth the wire for any longer than is necessary to take the reading, or the gauge may be damaged.

3 If the needle movement is still faulty, or if it does not move at all, the fault lies in the wiring or the gauge/bulb itself. Remove the instrument cluster as described in Chapter 9 (if necessary), and check all the relevant wiring and wiring connectors. If all appears to be well, the gauge/bulb is defective and must be renewed.

Replacement

4 See Chapter 9.

Temperature gauge sender unit

Check

5 Remove the sender unit as described in Steps 8 to 10 below.

6 Fill a small heatproof container with water and place it on a stove. Using an ohmmeter, connect the positive (+ve) probe of the meter to the terminal on the sender unit, and the negative (-ve) probe to the body of the sender unit. Using some wire or other support suspend the sender unit in the water so that just the sensing portion and the threads are submerged. Also place a thermometer in the water so that its bulb is close to the sender unit **(see illustration)**. **Note:** *None of the components should be allowed to directly touch the container.*

7 Heat the water, stirring it gently. When the temperature reaches around 60°C the meter should read between 255 and 310 ohms. If the meter readings obtained are different, or they are obtained at different temperatures, then the sender unit is faulty and must be renewed.

3

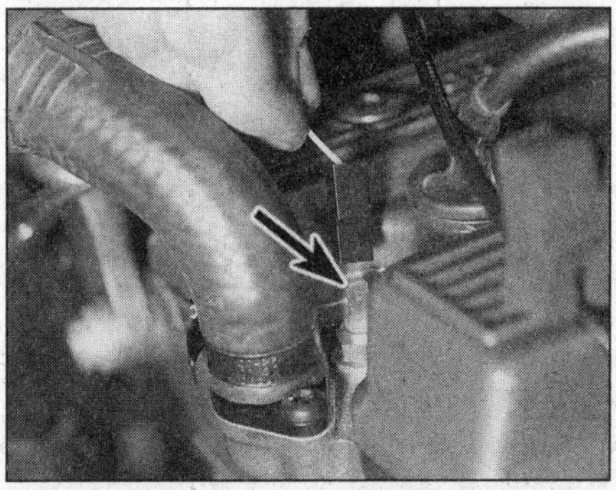

5.2 Disconnect the wire from the temperature gauge sender unit, located in the left side of the cylinder head

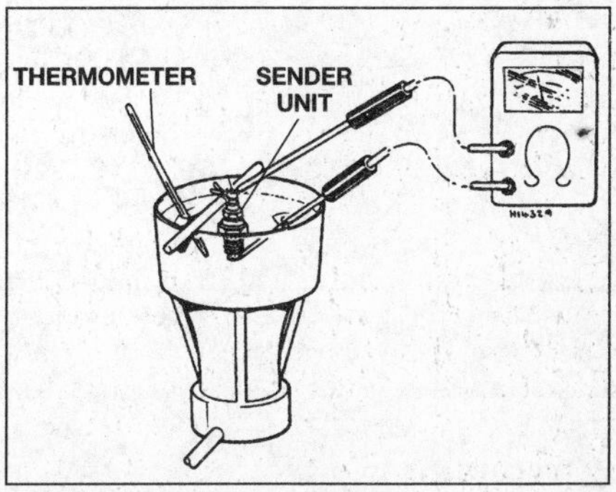

5.6 Temperature gauge sender unit testing set-up

Warning: This must be done very carefully to avoid the risk of personal injury.

Replacement

Warning: The engine must be completely cool before carrying out this procedure.

8 Drain the cooling system as described in Chapter 1.

9 If not already done, remove any fairing panels necessary to gain access to the sender unit which is fitted to the cylinder head on the left side (requirements vary according to model and are described in Chapter 8) and disconnect the sender unit wiring.

10 Unscrew the sender unit and remove it from the cylinder head.

11 Apply a smear of sealant to the threads of the new sender unit, then install it into the cylinder head and tighten it to the torque setting specified at the beginning of the Chapter.

12 Connect the wiring connector to the sender unit.

13 Refill the cooling system as described in Chapter 1, then install any fairing panels as described in Chapter 8.

6 Thermostat - removal, check and installation

Thunderbird, Thunderbird Sport, Adventurer and Legend TT models

Removal

Warning: The engine must be completely cool before carrying out this procedure.

1 The thermostat is automatic in operation and should give many years service without requiring attention. In the event of a failure, the valve will probably jam open, in which case the engine will take much longer than normal to warm up. Conversely, if the valve jams shut, the coolant will be unable to circulate and the engine will overheat. Neither condition is acceptable, and the fault must be investigated promptly.

2 Remove the fuel tank as described in Chapter 4 and drain the cooling system as described in Chapter 1.

3 The thermostat is located in the thermostat housing just behind the radiator pressure cap **(see illustration)**. Disconnect the fan switch wiring connector from the housing, then slacken the clamps securing the hoses to the housing and detach the hoses. Note that the crimp type clamps fitted to some models cannot be re-used and must be renewed.

4 Unscrew the two bolts securing the thermostat housing to the frame and remove the housing.

5 The housing is in two halves secured together by two bolts. Unscrew the bolts and separate the halves to gain access to the thermostat, then withdraw the thermostat, noting how it fits. Discard the O-ring from the housing as a new one must be fitted.

Check`

6 Examine the thermostat visually before carrying out the test. If it remains in the open position at room temperature, it should be renewed.

7 Suspend the thermostat by a piece of wire in a container of cold water. Place a thermometer in the water so that the bulb is close to the thermostat **(see illustration)**. Heat the water, noting the temperature when the thermostat opens, and compare the result with that given in the Specifications. If the reading obtained differs from that given, the thermostat is faulty and must be renewed.

8 In the event of thermostat failure, as an emergency measure only, it can be removed and the machine used without it. **Note:** *Take care when starting the engine from cold as it will take much longer than usual to warm up. Ensure that a new unit is installed as soon as possible.*

Installation

9 Fit the thermostat into the rear half of the housing, making sure that the base slots into the grooves in the housing.

10 Fit a new O-ring to the front half of the housing, then align the two halves, making sure that the point on the top of the thermostat fits into the recess in the front housing half.

11 Fit the halves together and install the two bolts, tightening them to the torque setting specified at the beginning of the Chapter.

12 Fit the housing to the frame and install the two mounting bolts, tightening them securely.

13 Fit the hoses to the housing and tighten their clamps, using new ones if necessary. Connect the fan switch wiring connector.

14 Refill the cooling system (Chapter 1).

15 Fit the fuel tank as described in Chapter 4.

Trident, Sprint, Trophy, Speed Triple, Daytona and Tiger models

Removal

Warning: The engine must be completely cool before carrying out this procedure.

16 The thermostat is automatic in operation and should give many years service without requiring attention. If it fails, the valve will probably jam open, in which case the engine will take much longer than normal to warm up. Conversely, if the valve jams shut, the coolant will be unable to circulate and the engine will overheat. Neither condition is acceptable, and the fault must be investigated promptly.

17 Remove any fairing panels necessary to gain access to the radiator (requirements vary according to model - refer to Chapter 8). Drain the cooling system as described in Chapter 1.

18 The thermostat is located inside the radiator top hose in the larger diameter portion which joins to the radiator. On Speed Triple and later Trident models, the radiator top hose cover screw can be accessed after removing the side cover from the radiator; peel off the reflector and remove the two screws to free the radiator side cover. Remove the clamp securing the hose to the radiator and detach the hose. Note that the

6.3 On Thunderbird, Thunderbird Sport, Adventurer and Legend TT models the thermostat housing (arrowed) is under the fuel tank

6.7 Thermostat opening check

6.18a Detach the top hose from the radiator to access the thermostat . . .

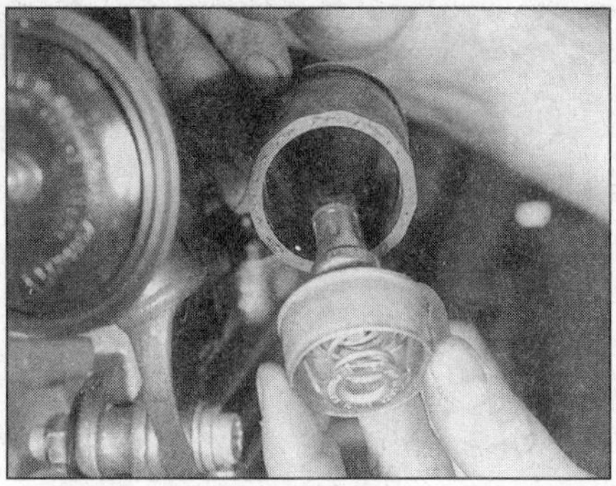

6.18b . . . and withdraw the thermostat from the hose

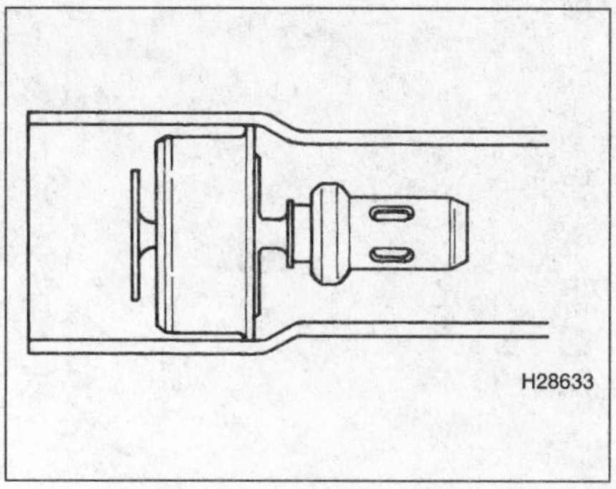

6.20 Make sure the thermostat fits correctly in the hose

crimp type clamps fitted to some models cannot be reused and must be renewed. Carefully withdraw the thermostat from inside the hose using a suitable pair of pliers, noting which way round it fits **(see illustrations)**.

Check

19 Refer to Steps 6, 7 and 8.

Installation

20 Install the thermostat in the radiator top hose, making sure it is the right way round and that it is inserted fully and squarely **(see illustration)**.

21 Fit the hose on the radiator and tighten the clamp, using a new one if necessary, to secure it in place. Install the top hose cover and radiator side cover on Speed Triple and later Trident models; use a new strip of adhesive on the reflector if necessary.

22 Refill the cooling system (Chapter 1).

23 Fit any fairing panels that have been removed as described in Chapter 8.

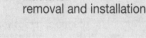

7 Radiator – removal and installation

Removal

Warning: The engine must be completely cool before carrying out this procedure.

1 Remove any fairing panels necessary to gain access to the radiator (requirements vary according to model – refer to Chapter 8).

2 Drain the cooling system (Chapter 1).

3 On Speed Triple and later Trident models, pull off the adhesive reflector strips fitted to the radiator end covers to access the end cover retaining screws. On these models and also on the Thunderbird, Thunderbird Sport, Adventurer and Legend TT, unscrew the screws and remove the end covers **(see illustration)**. Discard the adhesive strips as they will have to be renewed. On Speed Triple and later Trident models, release its retaining screw and clip, then remove the top hose cover.

4 On Trident, Sprint, Trophy, Speed Triple, Daytona and Tiger models, detach the reservoir hose from the radiator neck. On all models remove the clamps securing the top and bottom hoses to the radiator, and detach the hoses. The crimp type clamps fitted to some models cannot be re-used and must be renewed **(see illustrations)**.

5 Disconnect the cooling fan wiring at the connector, and on Trident, Sprint, Trophy, Speed Triple, Daytona and Tiger models also disconnect the fan switch wiring from the switch on the left side of the radiator **(see illustrations 4.3 and 4.9b)**.

6 Unscrew the two bolts securing the bottom mounting to the bracket on each side of the radiator. Make sure the radiator is supported, then remove the two top mounting bolts and withdraw the radiator assembly carefully from the side **(see illustrations)**.

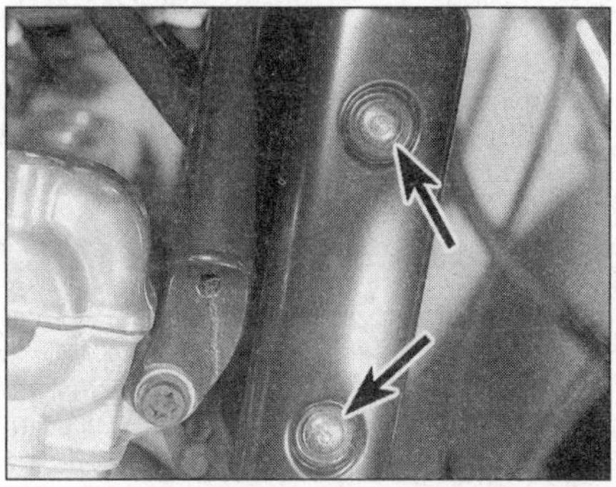

7.3 Radiator end cover mounting screws (arrowed)

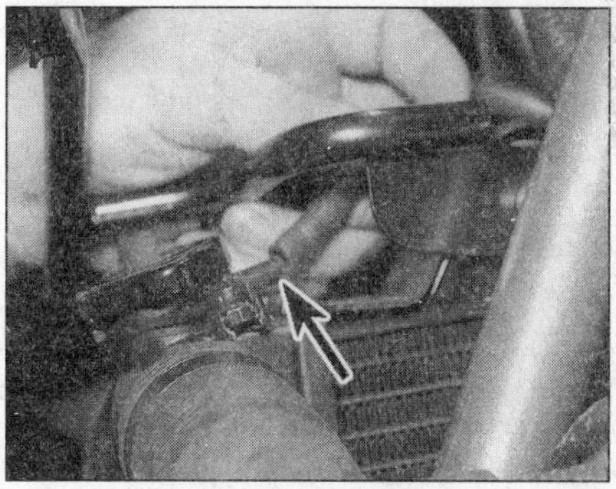

7.4a Detach the reservoir hose (arrowed) from the radiator filler neck

3

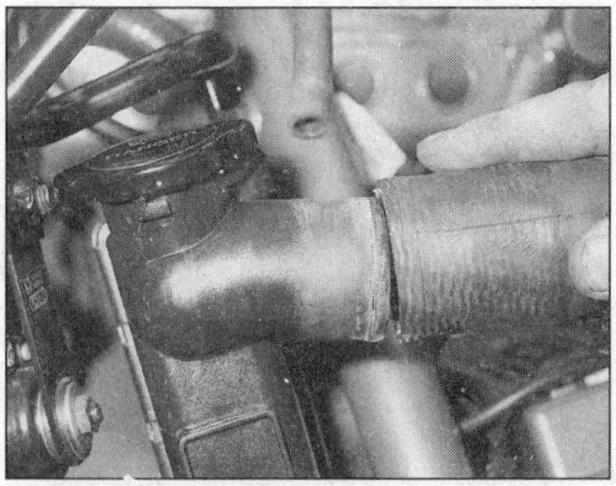

7.4b Release the clamp and detach the radiator top hose . . .

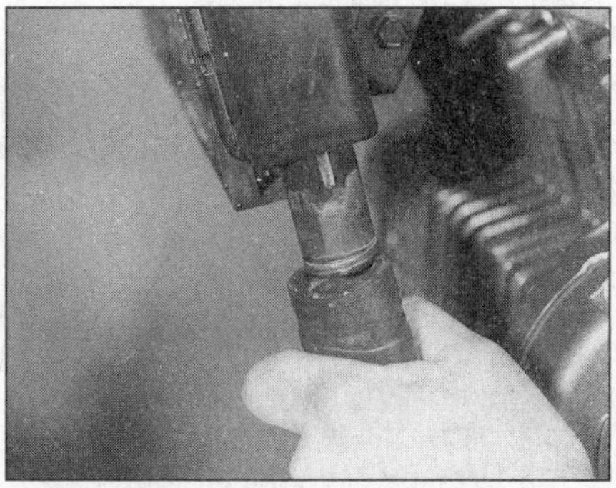

7.4c . . . and bottom hose

7.6a Unscrew the radiator bottom mounting bolts (arrowed) . . .

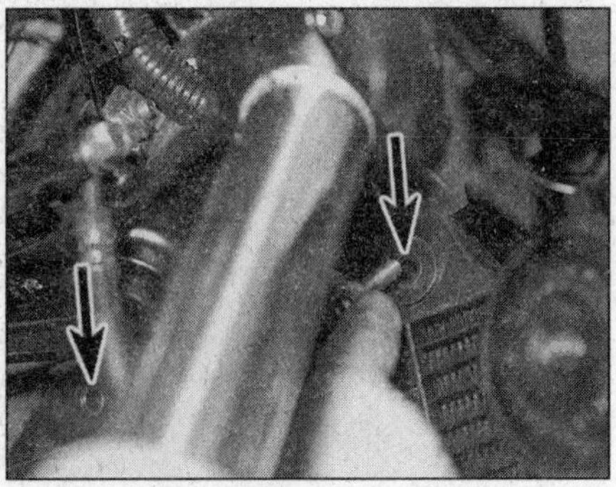

7.6b . . . then the top mounting bolts (arrowed)

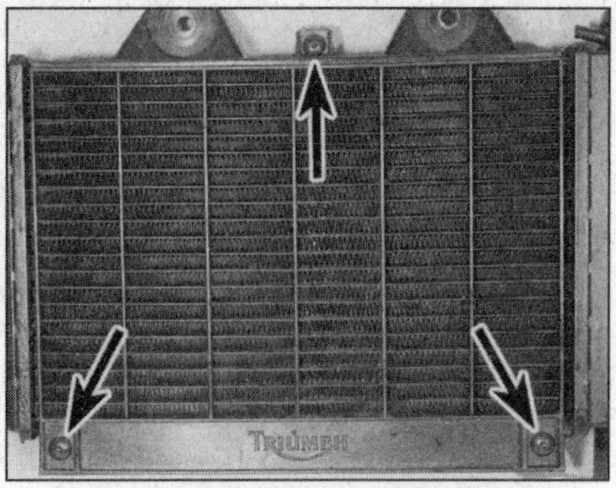

7.7 The stone guard is secured to the radiator by three screws (arrowed)

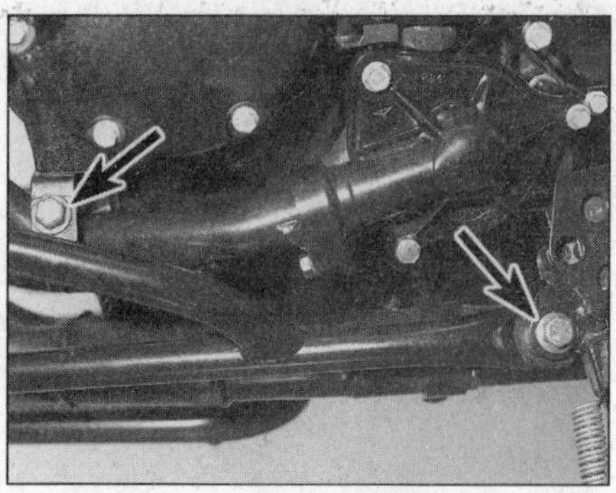

8.6 The sump guard (Tiger model) is secured by two bolts on each side (arrowed)

7 If necessary, unscrew the three screws to free the stone guard from the radiator **(see illustration)**. Note that the stone guard top mounting screw on Trident, Sprint, Trophy, Speed Triple, Daytona and Tiger models also secures the cooling fan top mounting. Take care not to lose the collars on the Thunderbird, Thunderbird Sport, Adventurer, Legend TT stone guard top mounting bolts, noting how they fit.

8 Check the stone guard and the radiator for signs of damage and clear any dirt or debris that might obstruct air flow and inhibit cooling. If the radiator fins are badly damaged or broken the radiator must be renewed. Also check the rubber mounting grommets, and renew them if necessary.

Installation

9 Installation is the reverse of removal, noting the following.

a) Install the radiator top mounting bolts first, but do not fully tighten them. Install the bottom bolts then tighten all the bolts to the specified torque setting.

b) Ensure the fan wiring is reconnected.

c) Ensure the coolant hoses are securely retained by their clamps, and use new ones if necessary.

d) On Speed Triple and later Trident models, do not forget to install the top hose cover and renew the adhesive reflector strips on the radiator end covers.

e) On completion refill the cooling system as described in Chapter 1.

8 Water pump – check, removal and installation

Check

1 The water pump is located on the lower left side of the engine. Visually check the area around the pump for signs of leakage. On Trophy and Daytona models, the fairing left lower panel will need to be removed for access (see Chapter 8).

2 To prevent leakage of water from the cooling system to the lubrication system and vice versa, two seals are fitted on the pump shaft. On the underside of the pump body there is also a drainage hole **(see Chapter 1, Section 14)**. If either seal fails, this hole should allow the coolant or oil to escape and prevent the oil and coolant mixing.

3 The seal on the water pump side is of the mechanical type which bears on the rear face of the impeller. The second seal, which is mounted behind the mechanical seal is of the normal feathered lip type. However, neither seal is available as a separate item as the pump is sold as an assembly. Therefore, if on inspection the drainage hole shows signs of leakage, the pump must be removed and renewed.

Removal

4 On Trophy and Daytona models, remove the fairing lower panels to gain access to the pump (see Chapter 8).

5 Drain the cooling system (Chapter 1).

6 On models fitted with lower fairing panels it is necessary to detach and support the oil cooler and its sub-frame and mounting brackets as an assembly (see Chapter 2). On Tiger models, unscrew the sump guard mounting bolts and remove the sump guard **(see illustration)**. On Thunderbird, Thunderbird Sport, Adventurer and Legend TT models remove the horn assembly (see Chapter 9).

7 On later models, unscrew the water pump hose cover retaining bolts and remove the cover **(see illustration)**.

8 On Thunderbird, Thunderbird Sport, Adventurer and Legend TT models only, remove the clamp securing the bypass hose to the pump and detach the hose, then do the same for the outlet hose behind it **(see illustration)**. On all other models, remove the clamp securing the outlet hose to the water pump and detach the hose from the pump **(see illustration)**. Some models use crimp type clamps which cannot be reused and must be renewed.

9 Unscrew and remove the bolt securing the

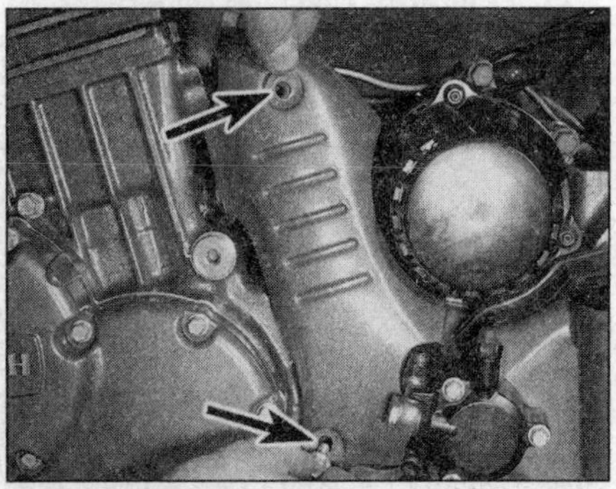

8.7 The water pump hose cover is secured by two bolts (arrowed)

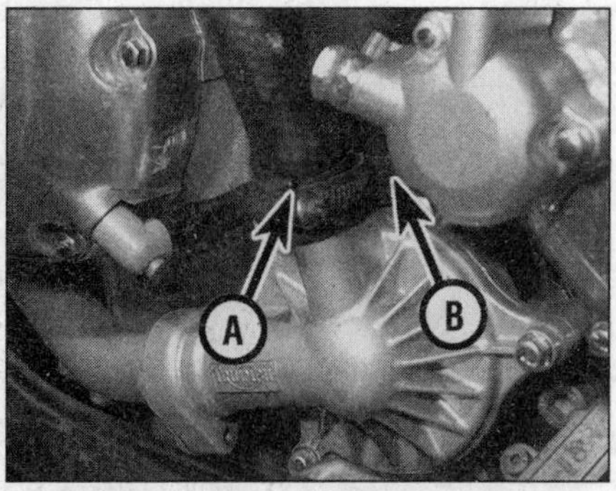

8.8a On Thunderbird, Thunderbird Sport, Adventurer and Legend TT models, remove the bypass hose (A) then the outlet hose behind it (B)

8.8b Release the clamp (arrowed) and detach the outlet hose from the pump

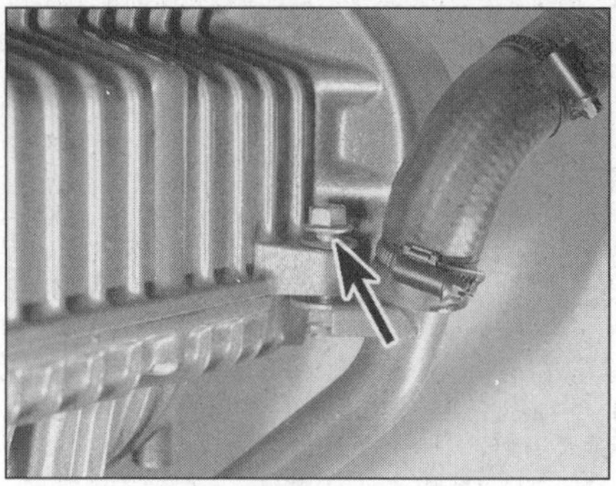

8.9a Unscrew the bolt securing the inlet pipe to the front of the crankcase (arrowed) . . .

8.9b . . . and the bolt securing the inlet pipe to the pump

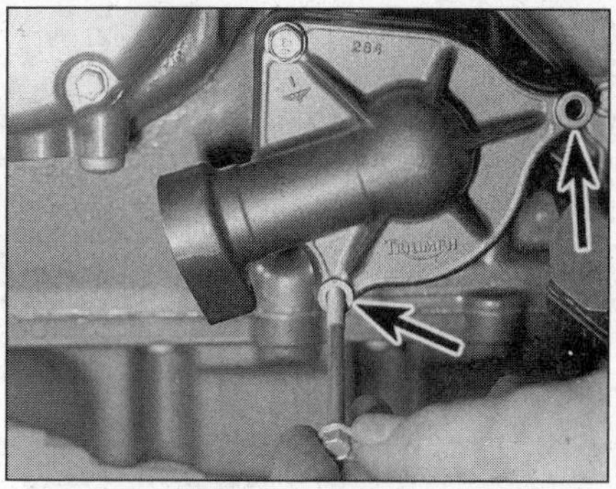

8.10 Unscrew the two bolts securing the water pump to the crankcase (arrowed) – third bolt secures the cover to the pump and also serves as the coolant drain plug

inlet pipe to the front of the crankcase, taking care not to lose or damage the fibre washer **(see illustration)**. Unscrew and remove the bolt securing the inlet pipe to the water pump and detach the pipe from the pump **(see illustration)**. Remove the rubber O-ring and discard it as a new one should be used.

10 Unscrew the two water pump mounting bolts and remove the pump from the crankcase **(see illustration)**. Remove the O-ring from the rear of the pump body and discard it as a new one must be used.

11 Unscrew the remaining bolt securing the pump cover to the body and remove the cover **(see illustrations)**.

12 Wiggle the water pump impeller back-and-forth and in-and-out. If there is excessive movement the pump must be renewed. Also check for corrosion or a build-up of scale in the pump body and clean or renew the pump as necessary.

Installation

13 Fit a new O-ring to the rear of the pump body and install the pump, aligning the slot in the impeller shaft with the tab on the oil pump shaft **(see illustrations)**.

14 Fit a new O-ring to the pump body and fit the cover.

15 Install the cover retaining bolt (using a new sealing washer) and the pump mounting bolts, and tighten them to the torque setting specified at the beginning of the Chapter.

16 Fit a new O-ring to the inlet pipe and install it into the pump **(see illustration)**. Tighten both pipe mounting bolts to the specified torque setting.

17 Fit the outlet hose to the pump and secure with its clamp; use a new clamp if necessary **(see illustration)**. On Thunderbird, Thunderbird Sport, Adventurer and Legend TT models also fit the bypass hose.

18 Install the hose cover (where fitted). On Thunderbird, Thunderbird Sport, Adventurer and Legend TT models install the horn assembly (see Chapter 9). On Tiger models fit the sump guard.

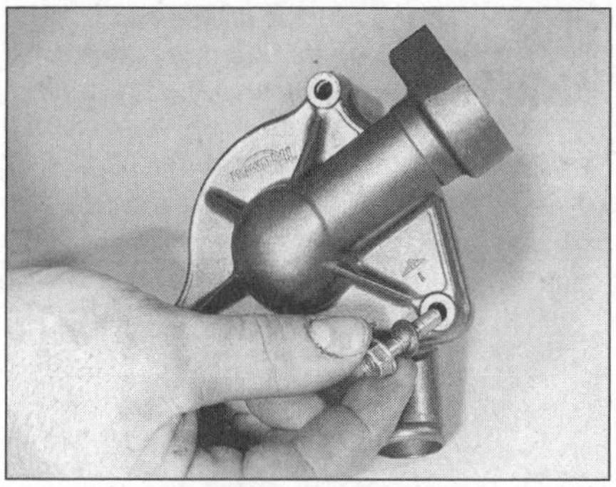

8.11a Unscrew the bolt securing the cover to the pump . . .

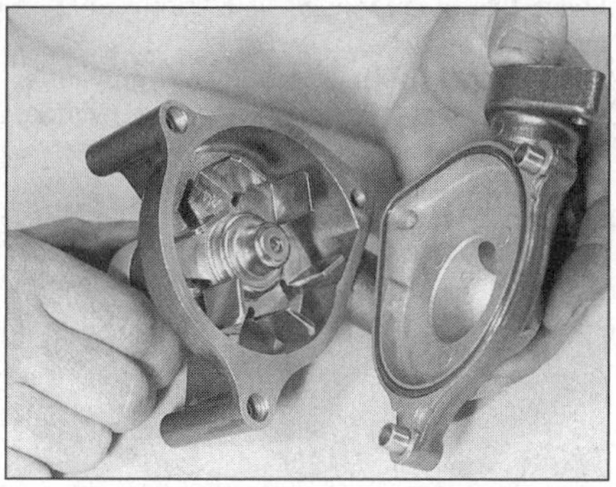

8.11b . . . and remove the cover

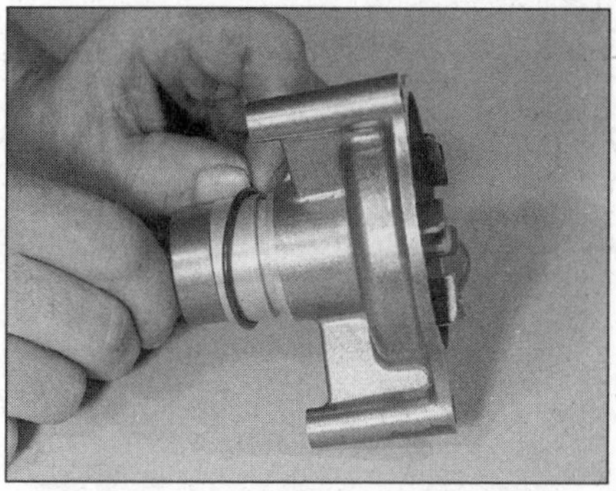

8.13a Fit a new O-ring to the rear of the pump body

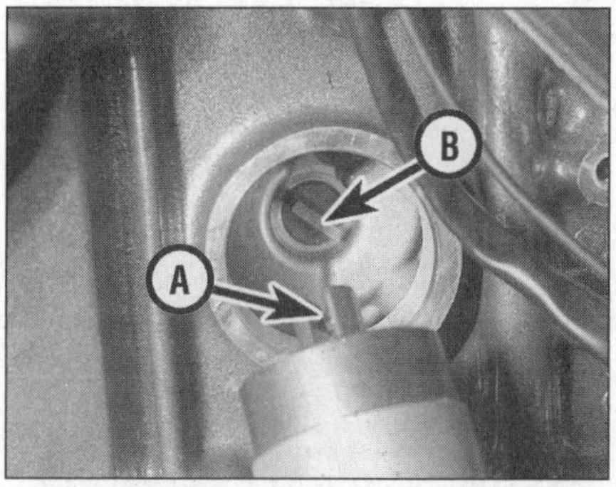

8.13b Fit the pump to the crankcase, aligning the slot in the water pump shaft (A) with the tab on the oil pump shaft (B)

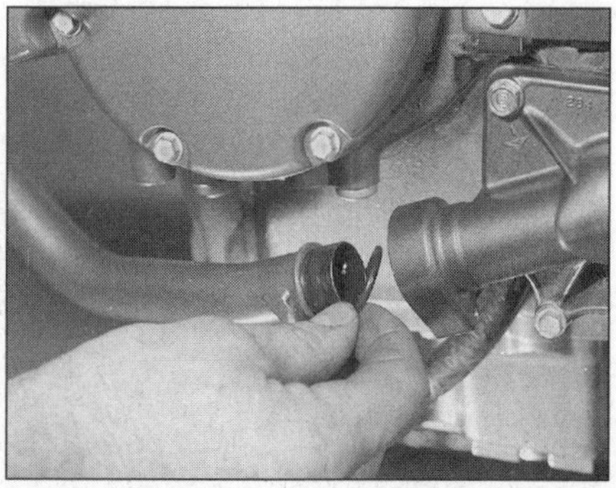

8.16 Fit a new O-ring to the inlet pipe before installing it in the pump

8.17 Securely tighten the outlet hose clamp

9.7a Fit a new gasket to the inlet union . . .

9.7b . . . and to the outlet union if they are removed

19 Install the oil cooler and sub-frame assembly (where fitted).
20 Refill the cooling system as described in Chapter 1.
21 Install the lower fairing panels (where applicable) as described in Chapter 8.

9 Coolant hoses – removal and installation

Removal

1 Before removing a hose, drain the coolant as described in Chapter 1.
2 Use a screwdriver to slacken the hose clamps, then slide them back along the hose and clear of the union spigot. Many of the smaller-bore hoses are secured by spring clamps which can be expanded by squeezing their ears together with pliers. Note that some models use crimp type clamps which cannot be reused and must be renewed.

Caution: The radiator unions are fragile. Do not use excessive force when attempting to remove the hoses.

3 If a hose proves stubborn, release it by rotating it on its union before working it off. If all else fails, cut the hose with a sharp knife then slit it at each union so that it can be peeled off in two pieces (see *Tools and Workshop Tips* in the Reference section). Whilst this is expensive it is preferable to buying a new radiator.
4 The water pipe inlet union to the cylinder block and the outlet union from the cylinder head can be removed by unscrewing the two retaining bolts. If they are removed, the gasket behind each must be renewed.

Installation

5 Slide the clips onto the hose and then work it on to its respective union.
6 Rotate the hose on its unions to settle it in position before sliding the clamps into place and tightening them securely.
7 If either the inlet union to the cylinder block or the outlet union from the cylinder head has been removed, fit a new gasket, then install the union and tighten the mounting bolts to the torque setting specified at the beginning of the Chapter **(see illustrations)**.

HAYNES HiNT

If the hose is difficult to push on its union, it can be softened by soaking it in very hot water, or alternatively a little soapy water can be used as a lubricant.

Chapter 4
Fuel and exhaust systems

Contents

Degrees of difficulty

Easy, suitable for novice with little experience	**Fairly easy,** suitable for beginner with some experience	**Fairly difficult,** suitable for competent DIY mechanic	**Difficult,** suitable for experienced DIY mechanic	**Very difficult,** suitable for expert DIY or professional

Specifications

Fuel

Grade	
UK models	Unleaded, minimum 95 RON (Research Octane Number)
US models	Unleaded, minimum 89 octane CLC and AKI
Fuel tank capacity	
Thunderbird, Thunderbird Sport, Adventurer, Legend TT	15 litres
Trident, Sprint, Trophy, Speed Triple, Daytona, Tiger	25 litres
Fuel tank reserve capacity	
Thunderbird, Thunderbird Sport, Adventurer, Legend TT	4 litres
Trident, Sprint, Trophy, Speed Triple, Daytona, Tiger	5 litres
Low fuel level warning light cut-in (where applicable)	7 litres

Carburettors and fuel system settings

Type	
All four cylinder models and early three cylinder models	Mikuni BST 36 mm
Later three cylinder models	Keihin CVK 36 mm
Float height (all models)	14.5 mm
Fuel level (above joint face) – see text	1.5 mm
Idle speed	see Chapter 1
CO content	
US models	1.0% @ 950 to 1050 rpm
All other models	2.5 to 4.5% @ 950 to 1050 rpm

Torque settings

Fuel tank-to-frame bolts – Tiger	9 Nm
Fuel tank bracket-to-frame bolts – all models except Tiger	12 Nm
Exhaust system	
Cylinder head clamps (see text)	
Stage one	8 Nm
Stage two	20 Nm
Gas analyser take-off plugs	7 Nm
Silencer mounting bolt or nut	
Tiger, Adventurer, Thunderbird Sport	27 Nm
Thunderbird, Legend TT	Not available
All other models	15 Nm

4

1 General information and precautions

General information

The fuel system consists of the fuel tank, the fuel tap and filter, the carburettors, fuel hoses and control cables.

The fuel tap is of the gravity-fed type on Thunderbird, Thunderbird Sport, Adventurer, Legend TT and Tiger models, and of the vacuum type on Trident, Sprint, Trophy, Speed Triple and Daytona models.

The carburettors used on all models are of the flat slide CV type, Mikuni on early three cylinder engines and all four cylinder engines, and Keihin on later three cylinder engines. On all models there is a carburettor for each cylinder. For cold starting, a choke lever mounted on the left handlebar and connected by a cable controls an enrichment circuit in the carburettor.

Air is drawn into the carburettors via air ducts and an airbox.

The exhaust system is either a four-into-two or a three-into-two design, depending on the engine. Certain California market models have a catalytic converter fitted in the exhaust downpipes, near the joint with the silencer.

Many of the fuel system service procedures are considered routine maintenance items and for that reason are included in Chapter 1.

Precautions

Warning: Petrol (gasoline) is extremely flammable, so take extra precautions when you work on any part of the fuel system. Don't smoke or allow open flames or bare light bulbs near the work area, and don't work in a garage where a natural gas-type appliance is present. If you spill any fuel on your skin, rinse it off with soap and water. When you perform any work on the fuel system, wear safety glasses and have a fire extinguisher suitable for a class B type fire (flammable liquids) on hand.

Always carry out any servicing work in a well-ventilated area to prevent a build-up of fumes.

Never work in a building containing a gas appliance with a pilot light, or any other form of naked flame. Ensure that there are no naked light bulbs or any sources of flame or sparks nearby.

Do not smoke (or allow anyone else to smoke) while in the vicinity of petrol or of components containing it. Remember the possible presence of vapour from these sources and move well clear before smoking.

Check all electrical equipment belonging to the house, garage or workshop where work is being undertaken (see the Safety first! section of this manual). Remember that certain electrical appliances such as drill, cutters etc create sparks in the normal course of operation and must not be used near petrol or any component containing it. Again, remember the possible presence of fumes before using electrical equipment.

Always mop up any spilt fuel and safely dispose of the rag used.

Any stored fuel that is drained off during servicing work, must be kept in sealed containers suitable for holding petrol, and clearly marked as such; the containers themselves should be kept in a safe place. This last point applies equally to the fuel tank, if it is removed from the machine; also remember to keep its cap closed at all times.

Note that the fuel system consists of the fuel tank and tap, with its cap and related hoses. On California models, this includes the evaporative loss system components.

Read the Safety first! section of this manual carefully before starting work.

Owners of machines used in the US, particularly California, should note that their machines must comply at all times with Federal or State legislation governing the permissible levels of noise and of pollutants such as unburnt hydrocarbons, carbon monoxide etc that can be emitted by those machines. All vehicles offered for sale must comply with legislation in force at the date of manufacture and must not subsequently be altered in any way which will affect their emission of noise or of pollutants.

In practice, this means that adjustments may not be made to any part of the fuel, ignition or exhaust systems by anyone who is not authorised or mechanically qualified to do so, or who does not have the tools, equipment and data necessary to properly carry out the task. Also if any part of these systems is to be renewed only genuine Triumph components or by components which are approved under the relevant legislation must be used. The machine must never be used with any part of these systems removed, modified or damaged.

2 Fuel tank and tap – removal and installation

Fuel tank

Warning: Refer to the precautions given in Section 1 before starting work.

Removal – Tiger

1 Make sure the fuel tap is turned to the OFF position and the fuel cap is secure.

2 Remove the seat as described in Chapter 8, then disconnect the battery, negative (-ve) terminal first.

3 Unscrew and remove the fasteners securing the fairing panels to the tank; don't lose the rubber washers **(see illustration)**.

4 Remove the screws securing the airbox end covers to the airbox and remove the covers.

5 Unscrew and remove the fuel tank front mounting bolt together with its sleeve and rubber, noting their order **(see illustration)**. Unscrew and remove the rear bolts together with their washers, noting their order. Don't lose the sleeve which houses the bolt and fits into the tank rubber mounting pad.

6 Partially raise the rear of the tank, supporting it if necessary, and disconnect the low fuel level sensor wires at the tank. Also release the fuel hose and the tank breather hose clamps and detach the hoses, having taken note of their routing and locations **(see illustration)**.

7 Remove the tank by carefully drawing it back and away from the bike. Take care not to

2.3 Remove the fasteners securing the fairing panels to the tank (arrowed)

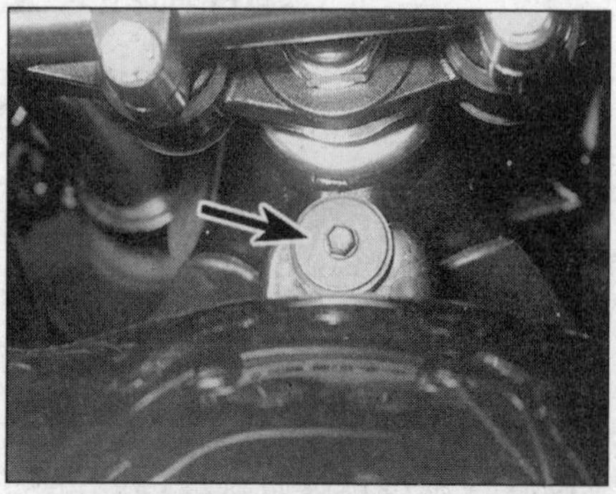

2.5 Unscrew the tank front mounting bolt (arrowed) and remove it with its sleeve and rubber

2.6 The fuel delivery pipe is secured to the fuel tap by a clamp (arrowed). Release the clamp and detach the pipe

displace the front mounting rubbers from the lugs on the frame and note how they fit into the grooves in the tank.

8 Inspect the tank mounting rubbers for signs of damage or deterioration and renew them if necessary.

Removal – Thunderbird, Thunderbird Sport, Adventurer and Legend TT

9 Make sure the fuel tap is turned to the OFF position and the fuel cap is secure.

10 Remove the seat (refer to Chapter 8), then disconnect the battery, removing the negative (-ve) terminal first.

11 Unscrew and remove the two bolts at the rear of the tank which secure the tank mounting bracket to the frame **(see illustrations)**.

12 Partially raise the rear of the tank, supporting it if necessary. Release the fuel hose clamp and detach the fuel hose from its union on the tap **(see illustration)**. The breather hose is a push fit on its union; either detach the hose or remove the tank with the hose and its roll-over valve still attached **(see illustrations)**.

13 Remove the tank by carefully drawing it back and away from the bike. Also take care not to displace the front mounting rubbers from the lugs on the frame and note how they fit into the grooves in the tank.

14 If necessary, unscrew the two bolts securing the tank mounting bracket to the underside of the tank and remove the bracket, taking care not to lose the sleeve or the rubber grommets and noting how they fit. Inspect the rubber grommets for damage or deterioration and renew them if necessary.

Removal – Trident, Sprint, Trophy, Speed Triple and Daytona

15 Make sure the fuel tap is turned to either the ON or RES position and the fuel cap is secure.

16 Remove the seat (refer to Chapter 8), then disconnect the battery, removing the negative (-ve) terminal first.

17 Remove the side panels (see Chapter 8).

18 Unscrew and remove the two bolts from each side of the tank which secure the tank mounting bracket to the frame **(see illustration)**.

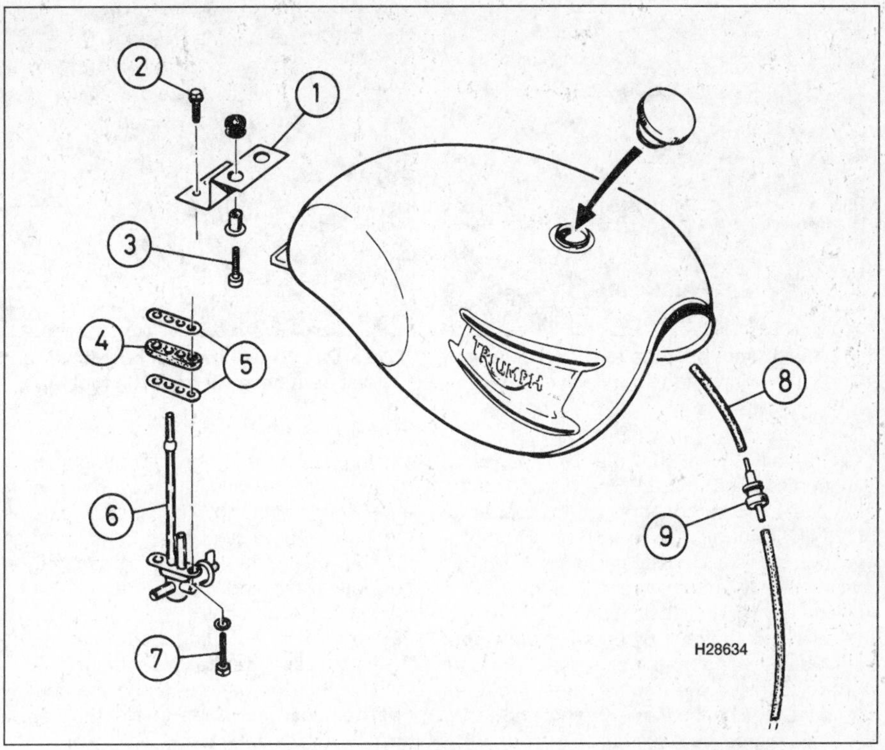

2.11a Fuel tank components – Thunderbird, Thunderbird Sport, Adventurer and Legend TT models

1 Mounting bracket
2 Bracket-to-frame bolt
3 Bracket-to-tank bolt
4 Spacer
5 Gaskets
6 Fuel tap
7 Tap mounting bolt
8 Breather hose
9 Roll-over valve

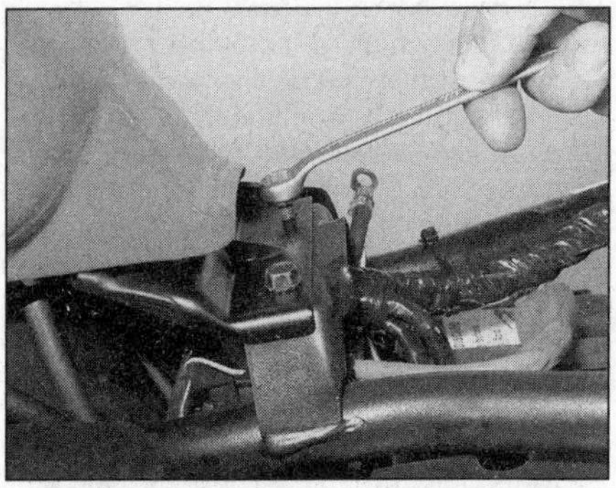

2.11b Fuel tank mounting bracket bolts

2.12a Fuel hose connection to tap (arrowed)

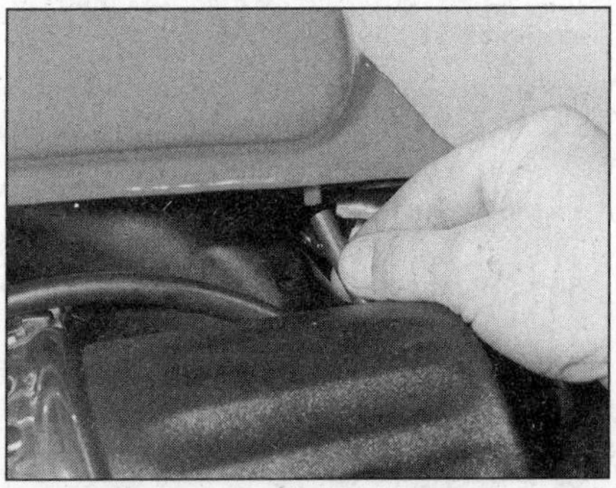

2.12b Breather hose is a push fit on its stub

2.12c Breather hose roll-over valve routing

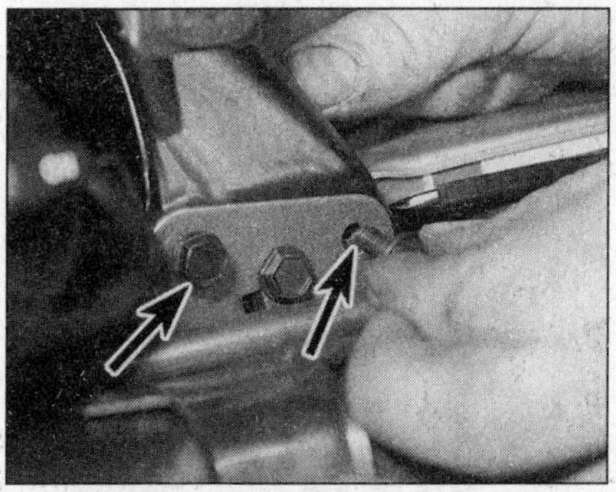

2.18 Unscrew the two tank bracket mounting bolts (arrowed)

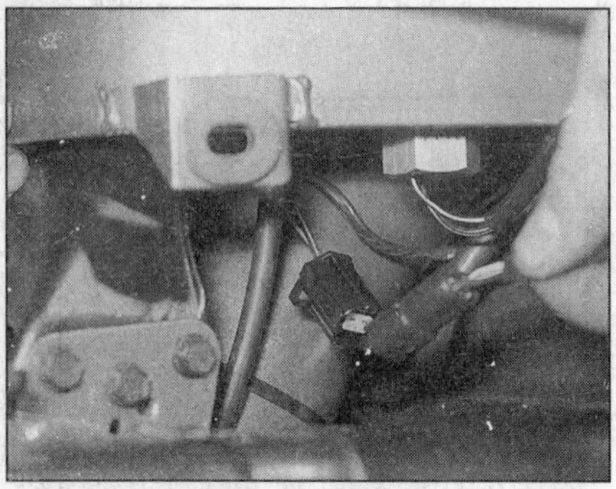

2.19a Disconnect the fuel level sensor wires at the connector

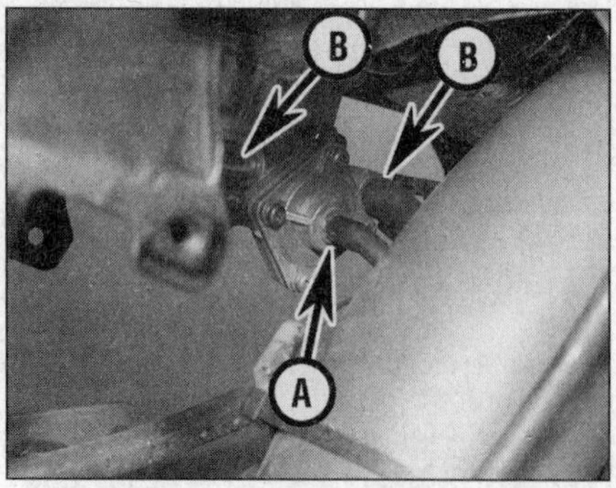

2.19b Disconnect the fuel hose(s) (B) and vacuum hose (A) from the fuel tap

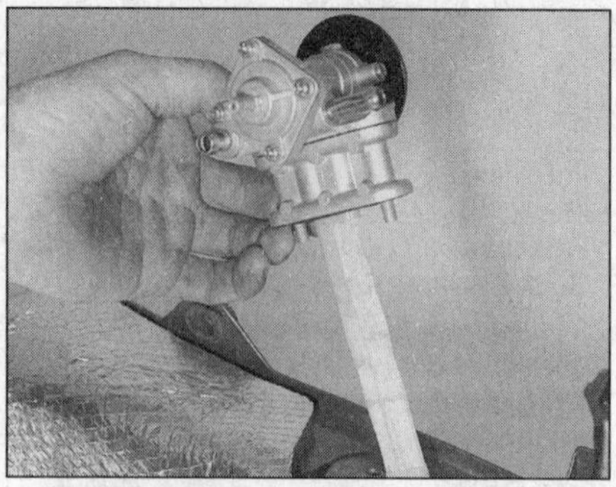

2.38 Withdraw the tap assembly carefully from the tank to avoid damaging the gauze filter

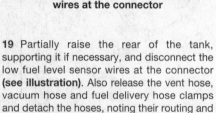

19 Partially raise the rear of the tank, supporting it if necessary, and disconnect the low fuel level sensor wires at the connector **(see illustration)**. Also release the vent hose, vacuum hose and fuel delivery hose clamps and detach the hoses, noting their routing and where they fit **(see illustration)**.

20 Remove the tank by carefully drawing it back and away from the bike. Also take care not to displace the front mounting rubbers from the lugs on the frame and note how they fit into the grooves in the tank.

21 If necessary, unscrew the two bolts securing the tank mounting bracket to the underside of the tank and remove the bracket, taking care not to lose the sleeve or the rubber grommets and noting how they fit. Inspect the rubber grommets for signs of damage or deterioration and renew them if necessary.

Installation – Tiger

22 Carefully lower the fuel tank into position, making sure the mounting rubbers remain in place. Partially raise the rear of the tank, supporting it if necessary, and reconnect the breather hose to its union and the fuel hose to the tap, making sure they are correctly fitted and routed. Secure them with their clamps. Also connect the low fuel level sensor wires to the tank.

23 Ensure that the sleeves are correctly positioned in the mounting rubbers, then install the mounting bolts and washers (where fitted), tightening them to the torque setting specified at the beginning of the Chapter.

24 Fit the airbox end covers and install the fasteners securing the fairing panels to the tank.

25 Connect the battery, fitting the negative (-ve) terminal last, then install the seat as described in Chapter 8.

26 Turn the fuel tap to the ON position and check that there is no sign of fuel leakage, then turn the tap back to the OFF position.

Installation – Thunderbird, Thunderbird Sport, Adventurer and Legend TT

27 If removed, fit the tank mounting bracket to the tank, making sure the sleeves and rubber grommets are correctly fitted.

28 Carefully lower the fuel tank into position, making sure the front mounting rubbers remain in place. Partially raise the rear of the tank, supporting it if necessary, and reconnect the breather hose to its union and the fuel hose to the tap, making sure they are correctly fitted and routed. Secure them in place with their clamps.

29 Install the mounting bolts and tighten them to the specified torque setting.

30 Connect the battery, fitting the negative (-ve) terminal last, then install the seat as described in Chapter 8.

31 Turn the fuel tap to the ON position and check that there is no sign of fuel leakage, then turn the tap back to the OFF position.

Installation – Trident, Sprint, Trophy, Speed Triple and Daytona

32 If removed, fit the tank mounting bracket to the tank, making sure the sleeves and rubber grommets are correctly fitted.

33 Carefully lower the fuel tank into position, making sure the front mounting rubbers remain in place. Partially raise the rear of the tank, supporting it if necessary, and reconnect the breather hose, the vacuum hose and the fuel delivery hoses, making sure they are correctly fitted and routed. Secure them in place with their clamps. Also connect the low fuel level sensor wires at the connector.

34 Install the four tank bracket mounting bolts and tighten them to the torque setting specified at the beginning of the Chapter.

35 Connect the battery, fitting the negative (-ve) terminal last, then install the seat as described in Chapter 8.

36 Start the engine and check that there is no sign of fuel leakage, then shut if off.

Fuel tap

Removal

37 Remove the fuel tank as described above. Connect a drain hose to the fuel tap stub and insert its end in a container suitable for storing petrol. Turn the fuel tap to the RES position on Tiger, Thunderbird, Thunderbird Sport, Adventurer and Legend TT models, or the PRI position on Trident, Sprint, Trophy, Speed Triple and Daytona models, and allow the tank to fully drain.

38 Unscrew the two bolts securing the tap to the tank and withdraw the tap assembly, taking care not to lose or damage any of the seals or the gauze filter **(see illustration)**.

39 Clean the gauze filter to remove all traces of dirt and fuel sediment.

40 Note that individual components are not available for the tap, including the rubber seals and the gauze filter. The tap should not be removed unnecessarily from the bike to prevent the possibility of damaging the seal or the filter, and the tap should not be dismantled – if it fails, or if the gauze filter is holed or torn, a new tap must be fitted.

Installation

41 Installation is the reverse of removal.

3 Fuel tank – cleaning and repair

1 All repairs to the fuel tank should be carried out by a professional who has experience in this critical and potentially dangerous work. Even after cleaning and flushing of the fuel system, explosive fumes can remain and ignite during repair of the tank.

2 If the fuel tank is removed from the bike, it should not be placed in an area where sparks or open flames could ignite the fumes coming out of the tank. Be especially careful inside garages where a natural gas-type appliance is located, because the pilot light could cause an explosion.

4 Idle fuel/air mixture adjustment – general information

Note: *Setting the fuel/air mixture accurately requires the use of equipment not likely to be available to the home mechanic; it is advised that the motorcycle is taken to a Triumph dealer for checking of the exhaust gas CO content and pilot screw adjustment.*

1 Due to the increased emphasis on controlling motorcycle exhaust emissions,

4.1 Exhaust gas analyser take-off points (arrowed)

certain governmental regulations have been formulated which directly affect the carburation of this machine. In order to comply with the regulations, the carburettor pilot screws on US models are sealed so they can't be tampered with. The pilot screws on other models are accessible, but the use of an exhaust gas analyser capable of taking readings from the exhaust downpipes rather than from the silencer is the only accurate way to check the CO and be sure the machine doesn't exceed the emissions regulations. Triumph exhaust systems are equipped with gas analyser take-off plugs in the exhaust downpipes **(see illustration)** – Triumph advise that exhaust gas CO content should not be measured by using a gas analyser which connects to the silencer end.

2 The pilot screws are set to their correct position by the manufacturer and should not be adjusted unless it is necessary to do so for a carburettor overhaul. If the screws have been renewed or disturbed for any reason they should be set to the base setting of 1.5 turns out, then the CO content should be measured as described above and further adjustment made to the pilot screw setting.

HAYNES HiNT ***A special adjusting tool (Part no 3880015) is available to aid adjustment of the screws whilst the carburettors are in situ.***

3 If the engine runs extremely rough at idle or continually stalls, and if a carburettor overhaul does not cure the problem, take the motorcycle to a Triumph dealer equipped with an exhaust gas analyser. They will be able to properly adjust the idle fuel/air mixture to achieve a smooth idle and restore low speed performance.

5 Carburettor overhaul – general information

1 Poor performance, hesitation, hard starting, stalling, flooding and backfiring are all signs that major carburettor work may be required.

2 Keep in mind that many so-called carburettor problems are really not carburettor problems at all, but mechanical problems within the engine or ignition system malfunctions. Try to establish for certain that the carburettors are in need of maintenance before beginning a major overhaul.

3 Check the fuel filters, the fuel hoses, the tank breather hose (except California models), the inlet manifold joint clamps, the airbox, the ignition system, the spark plugs and carburettor synchronisation before assuming that a carburettor overhaul is required.

4 Most carburettor problems are caused by dirt particles, varnish and other deposits which build up in and block the fuel and air passages. Also, in time, gaskets and O-rings shrink or deteriorate and cause fuel and air leaks which lead to poor performance.

5 When the carburettor is overhauled, it is generally disassembled completely and the parts are cleaned thoroughly with a carburettor cleaning solvent and dried with filtered, unlubricated compressed air. The fuel and air passages are also blown through with compressed air to force out any dirt that may have been loosened but not removed by the solvent. Once the cleaning process is complete, the carburettor is reassembled using new gaskets and O-rings.

6 Before disassembling the carburettors, make sure you have a carburettor rebuild kit (which will include all necessary O-rings and other parts), some carburettor cleaner, a supply of clean rags, some means of blowing out the carburettor passages and a clean place to work. It is recommended that only one carburettor be overhauled at a time to avoid mixing up parts.

6 Carburettors – removal and installation

Warning: Refer to the precautions given in Section 1 before starting work.

Removal

1 Referring to Chapter 8, remove the fairing on Sprint models, the fairing side panels on Tiger models, and the fairing lower panels on Trophy and Daytona models. On Thunderbird, Thunderbird Sport, Adventurer and Legend TT models, remove the horn (see Chapter 9).

2 On all models, remove the seat, side panels and fuel tank, referring to Chapter 8 and Section 2 of this Chapter.

3 Remove the auxiliary air chamber(s) (Section 12).

4 Release the clamps securing the airbox to the carburettors and carefully detach the airbox **(see illustration)**. Pull the airbox as far back as possible against the frame to make room for the carburettors to be removed **(see illustration)**.

5 To allow extra working space, remove the ignition HT coils from their mountings on the frame (see Chapter 5).

6 Detach the choke cable from the linkage on the carburettors as described in Section 11.

7 Release the clamps securing the rubber inlet manifolds to the cylinder head, leaving them attached to the carburettors **(see illustration)**. Ease the carburettors off the cylinder head stubs and out towards the left side of the frame, taking care not to damage the large coolant hose on Thunderbird, Thunderbird Sport, Adventurer and Legend TT models; support the carburettors in a position

6.4a Slacken the clamps which secure the airbox to the carburettors

6.4b Pull the airbox as far back as possible to allow room to remove the carburettors

6.7a Slacken the clamps which secure the inlet manifolds to the cylinder head

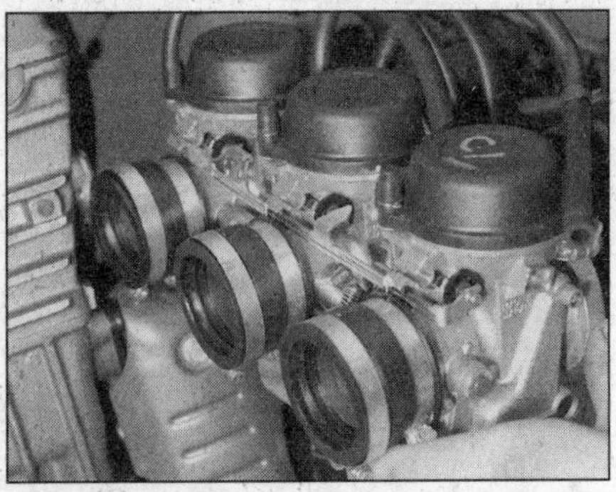

6.7b Ease the carburettors off the cylinder head with the rubber manifolds attached

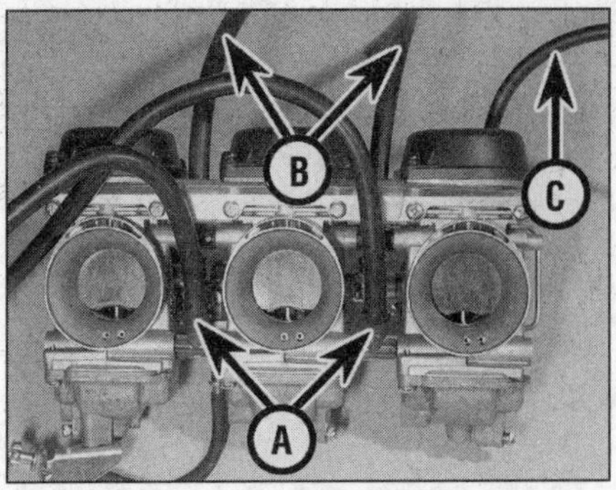

6.8a Fuel hoses (A), vent hoses (B), and vacuum hose (C) – Mikuni carburettors

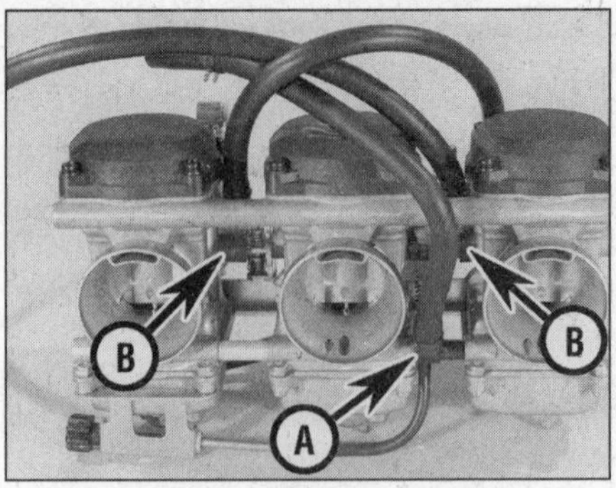

6.8b Fuel hose (A) and vent hoses (B) – Keihin carburettors

that gives access to the throttle cam **(see illustration)**. Release the throttle cable from the carburettors as described in Section 10. **Note:** *Keep the carburettors upright to prevent fuel spillage from the float chambers and the possibility of the piston diaphragms being damaged.*

8 Note the routing of the fuel hose(s), the vacuum hose (and on California models the evaporative loss system hoses) and the vent hoses, then withdraw the carburettors with the hoses attached **(see illustrations)**. Place a suitable container below the float chambers then slacken the drain screws and drain the fuel from the carburettors. Once all the fuel has been drained, tighten all the drain screws securely.

Installation

9 Installation is the reverse of removal. Check for cracks or splits in the rubber inlet manifolds. Make sure they are fully engaged with the cylinder head and their retaining clamps are securely tightened. Position the vent hoses in between the outer and inner carburettors. Prior to installing the airbox, adjust the throttle and choke cables as described in Chapter 1.

7 Carburettors – disassembly, cleaning and inspection

Warning: Refer to the precautions given in Section 1 before starting work.

Note: *All four cylinder engines and early three cylinder engines are fitted with Mikuni carburettors. Later three cylinder engines have Keihin carburettors. The carburettor manufacturer's name will be found cast into each carburettor body.*

Disassembly – Mikuni carburettor

1 Remove the carburettors from the machine as described in the previous Section. **Note:** *Do not separate the carburettors unless absolutely necessary; each carburettor can be dismantled sufficiently for all cleaning and adjustments while in place on the mounting brackets. Dismantle the carburettors separately to avoid interchanging parts* **(see illustration).**

2 Unscrew and remove the top cover retaining screws. Lift off the cover and remove the spring from inside the piston **(see illustration)**.

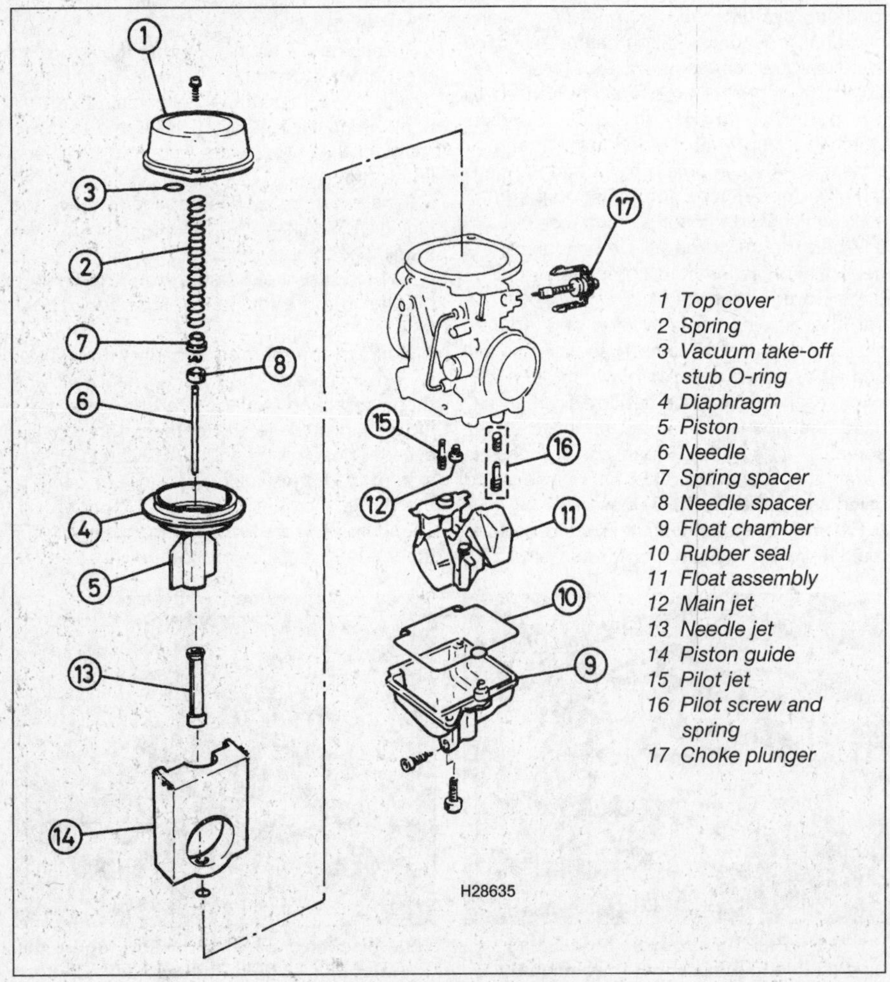

7.1 Carburettor detail – Mikuni

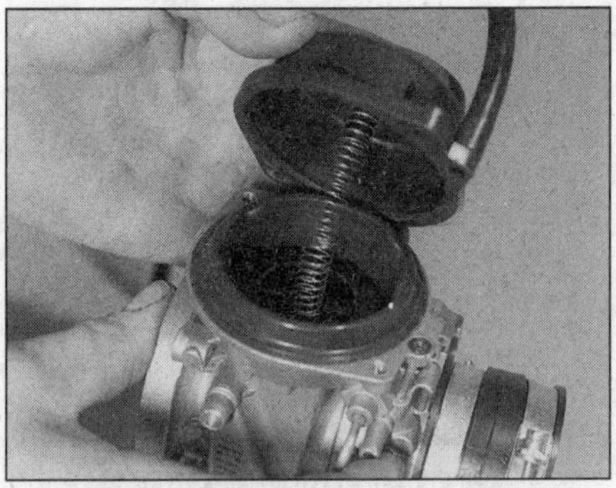

7.2 Unscrew the top cover screws and remove the top cover and spring

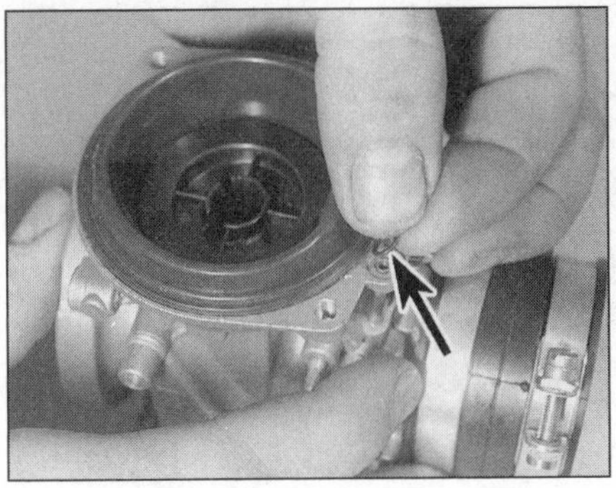

7.3 Remove the vacuum take-off stub O-ring (arrowed)

7.4 Withdraw the diaphragm and piston assembly from the carburettor

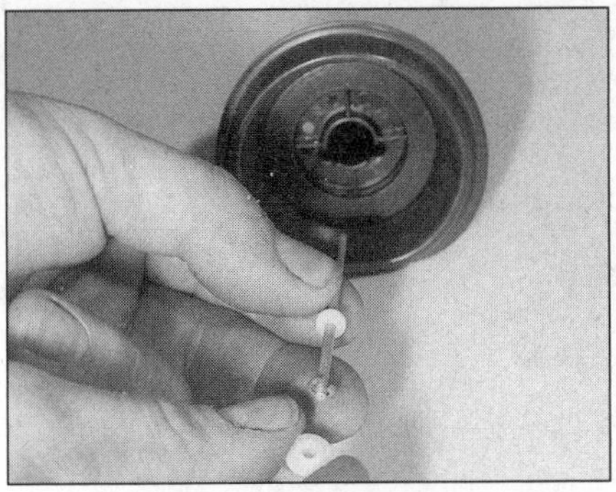

7.5 Withdraw the needle from the piston, noting how the spacers fit

3 Remove the vacuum take-off stub O-ring and discard it as a new one must be fitted **(see illustration)**.

4 Carefully peel the diaphragm away from its sealing groove in the carburettor. Carefully withdraw the diaphragm and piston assembly **(see illustration)**.

Caution: Do not use any sharp instruments to displace the diaphragm as it is delicate and easily damaged.

5 Push the needle from the bottom of the piston and remove it from the top. Don't lose any spacers – note how they fit **(see illustration)**.

6 Undo the screws and remove the float chamber from the base of the carburettor. Remove the rubber seal and discard it as a new one must be fitted **(see illustrations)**.

7 Carefully ease the float assembly out of the carburettor body **(see illustration)**. Remove the O-rings and discard them as new ones must be fitted on reassembly. Do not attempt to separate the needle valve from the float. If the needle valve is damaged or worn the float assembly must be renewed as a unit.

8 Unscrew the main jet **(see illustration)**.

9 With the main jet removed the needle jet can now be withdrawn from the body **(see illustration)**. Note the flat on the threaded end of the needle jet which has to align with the pin in the jet housing. Withdraw the piston guide from the carburettor **(see illustration)**.

10 Unscrew and remove the pilot jet, located next to the needle jet bore **(see illustration)**.

7.6a Unscrew the float chamber retaining screws . . .

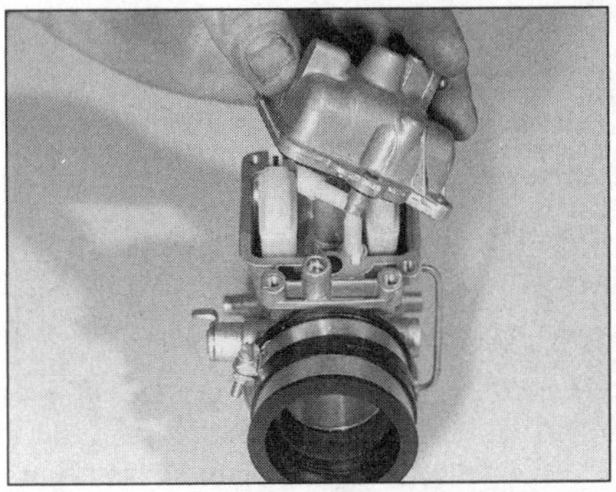

7.6b . . . and remove the float chamber

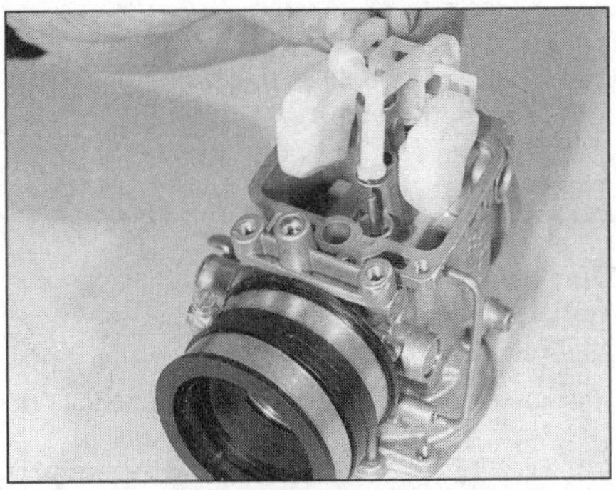

7.7 Carefully ease the float assembly out of the carburettor

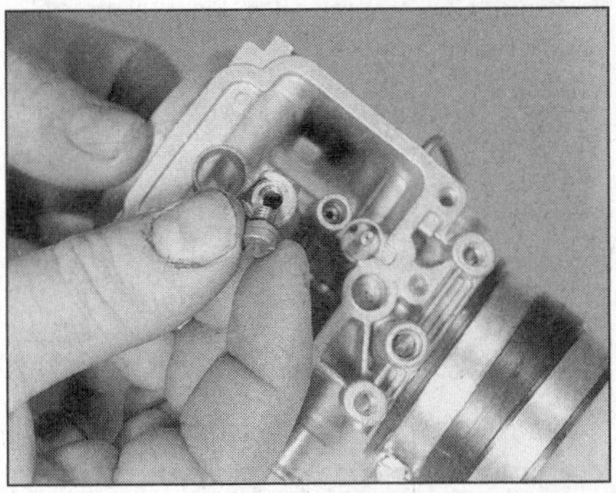

7.8 Unscrew and remove the main jet

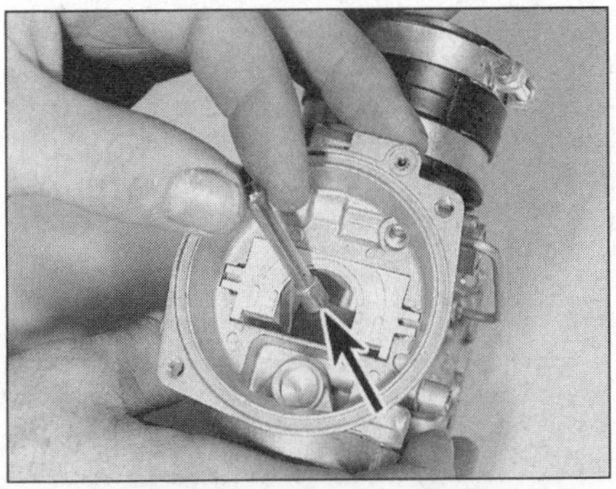

7.9a Withdraw the needle jet (noting its flat (arrowed)) . . .

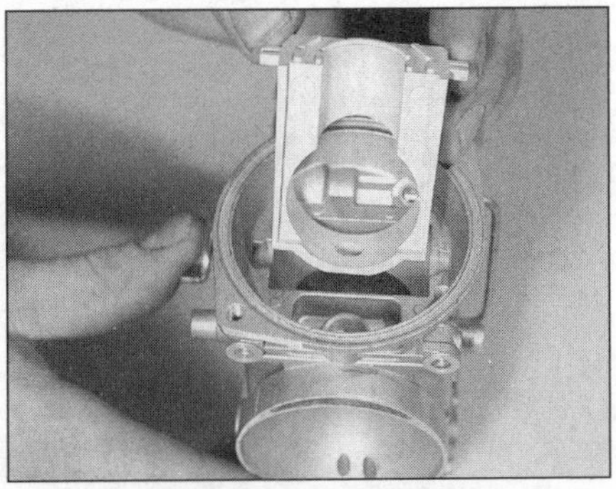

7.9b . . . and the piston guide from the carburettor body

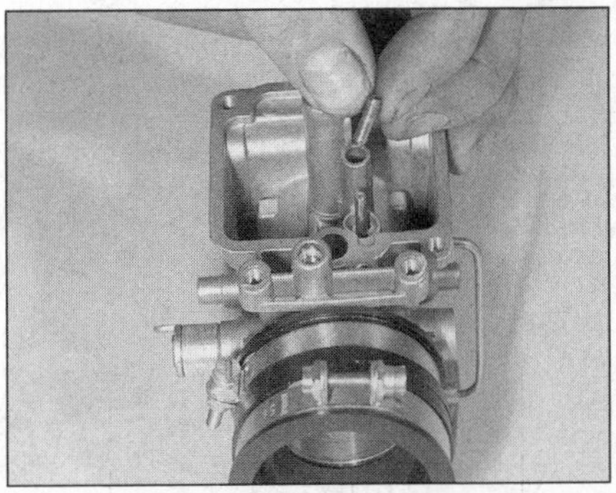

7.10 Unscrew the pilot jet from the carburettor

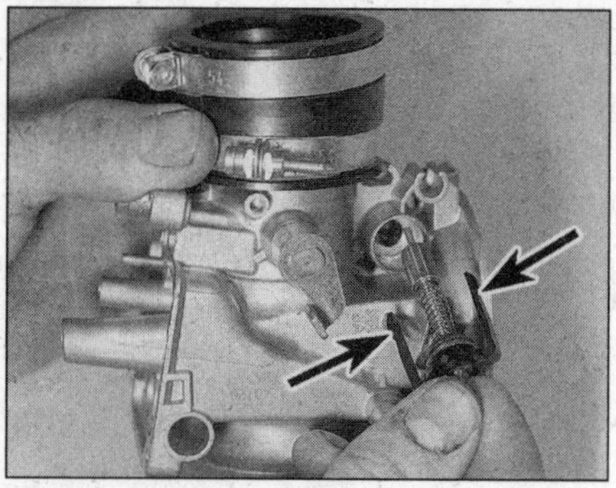

7.13 Press in the clips (arrowed) to release the choke plunger from the carburettor

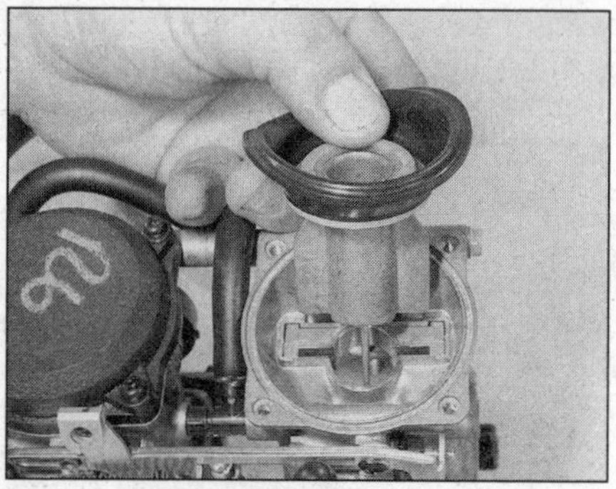

7.16 . . . followed by the piston/diaphragm

11 The pilot screw can be removed from the carburettor, but note that its setting will be disturbed. Remove the pilot screw along with its spring and O-ring.

HAYNES HiNT ***To record the pilot screw's current setting, turn the screw in until it seats lightly, counting the number of turns necessary to achieve this, then fully unscrew it. On installation, the screw is simply backed out the number of turns you've recorded.***

7.15a Carburettor top is retained by four screws (arrowed)

7.18 Float chamber is retained by four screws (arrowed)

12 If the carburettors have not been separated, ease the choke shaft sliders out of their retainers to release the choke shaft, then remove the choke shaft from the plungers **(see illustrations 8.3a and 8.3b)**.

13 Release the clips securing the choke plunger to the carburettor body and remove the plunger and spring **(see illustration)**.

Disassembly – Keihin carburettor

14 Remove the carburettors from the machine as described in the previous Section.

7.15b Withdraw the spring . . .

Note: *Do not separate the carburettors unless absolutely necessary; each carburettor can be dismantled sufficiently for all cleaning and adjustments while in place on the mounting brackets. Dismantle the carburettors separately to avoid interchanging parts.*

15 Unscrew and remove the top cover retaining screws **(see illustration)**. Lift off the cover and remove the spring from inside the piston **(see illustration)**.

16 Carefully peel the diaphragm away from its sealing groove in the carburettor. Withdraw the diaphragm and piston assembly **(see illustration)**.

Caution: Do not use any sharp instruments to displace the diaphragm as it is delicate and easily damaged.

17 Push the needle from the bottom of the piston and remove it from the top together with the holder.

18 Undo the screws and remove the float chamber from the base of the carburettor. Remove the rubber seal and discard it as a new one must be fitted **(see illustration)**.

19 Withdraw the float pivot pin and carefully ease the float assembly out of the carburettor body **(see illustration)**. Unhook the float needle from the float if necessary **(see illustration)**.

20 Unscrew the main jet from the needle jet

7.19a Withdraw the pivot pin to release the float

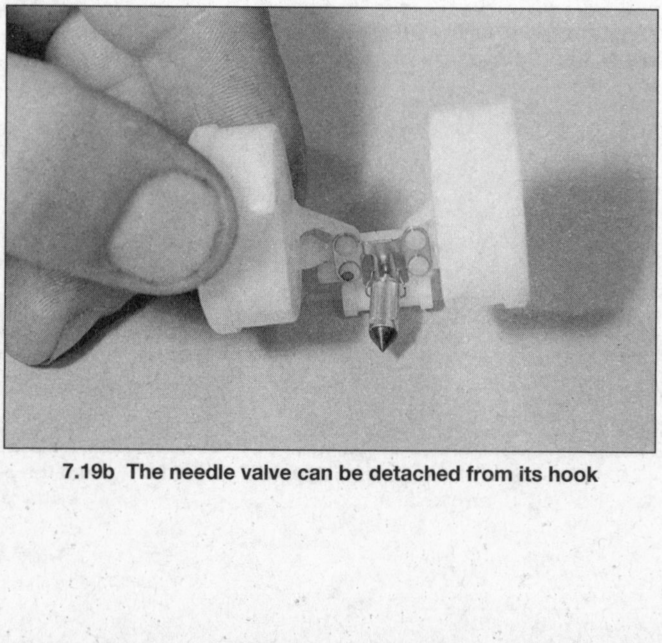

7.19b The needle valve can be detached from its hook

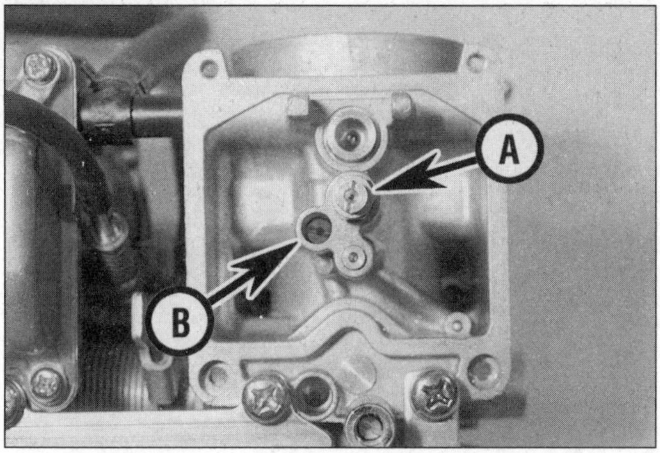

7.20 Main jet with needle jet below (A) and pilot jet (B)

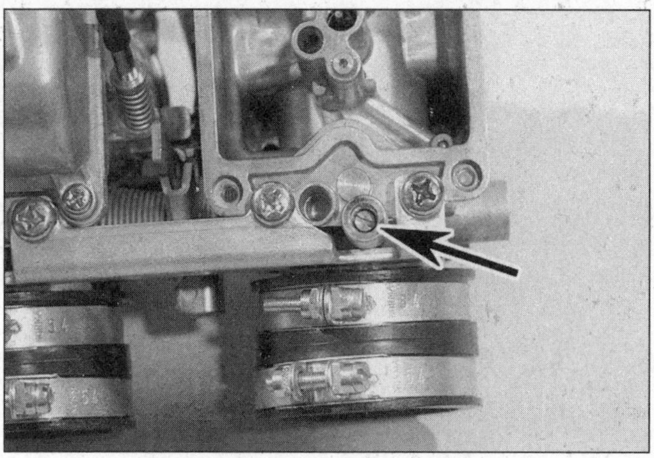

7.22 Pilot screw location (arrowed)

(see illustration). Unscrew the needle jet from the carburettor.

21 The pilot jet can be unscrewed using a thin flat-bladed screwdriver **(see illustration 7.20)**.

22 The pilot screw can be removed from the carburettor, but note that its setting will be disturbed **(see illustration)**. On some models, the pilot screw head may be fitted with a cap, designed to prevent tampering with the mixture. Record the pilot screw's position – see ***Haynes Hint***.

23 If the carburettor bodies have been separated, the choke plungers can simply be unscrewed from each body **(see illustration)**. If the carburettors have not been separated, disconnect the spring, then remove the two screws (with washers) which retain the choke linkage shaft, and detach the linkage shaft from the end of each choke plunger **(see illustrations 8.9a, b and c)**. Do not lose the two plastic washers on the inner side of the linkage shaft.

Cleaning

Caution: Use only a petroleum-based solvent for carburettor cleaning. Don't use caustic cleaners.

24 Submerge the metal components in the solvent for approximately thirty minutes (or longer, if the directions recommend it).

25 After the carburettor has soaked long enough for the cleaner to loosen and dissolve most of the varnish and other deposits, use a brush to remove the stubborn deposits. Rinse it again, then dry it with compressed air.

26 Use a jet of compressed air to blow out all of the fuel and air passages in the main and upper body.

Caution: Never clean the jets or passages with a piece of wire or a drill bit, as they will be enlarged, causing the fuel and air metering rates to be upset.

Inspection

27 Check the operation of the choke plunger. If it doesn't move smoothly, inspect the needle on the end of the choke plunger and the choke shaft. Renew either component if worn or bent **(see illustration)**.

28 Check the tapered portion of the pilot screw and the spring for wear or damage. Renew them if necessary.

29 Check the carburettor body, float chamber and top cover for cracks, distorted sealing surfaces and other damage. If any defects are found, renew the faulty component, although renewal of the entire carburettor will probably be necessary (check with a Triumph dealer on the availability of separate components).

30 Check the diaphragm for splits, holes and general deterioration. Holding it up to a light will help to reveal problems of this nature.

31 On Mikuni carburettors, insert the piston guide and piston in the carburettor body and check that the piston moves up-and-down smoothly. Check the surface of the piston for wear. If it's worn excessively or doesn't move smoothly in the guide, renew the components as necessary. On Keihin carburettors, insert the piston in the carburettor body and check that it moves up and down smoothly and that its surface is not worn.

32 Check the needle for straightness by rolling it on a flat surface (such as a piece of glass). Renew it if it's bent or if the tip is worn.

33 Check the tip of the float needle valve. If it

7.23 Choke plunger removal

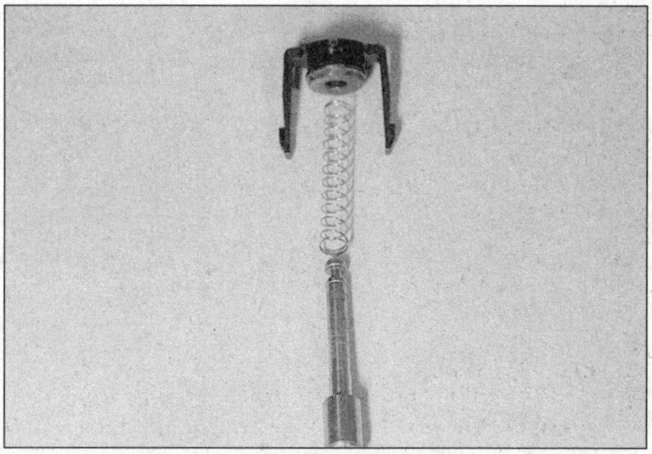

7.27 Check the choke plunger assembly for signs of wear or damage (Mikuni type shown)

has grooves or scratches in it, the float assembly must be renewed. If the needle valve seat is damaged the carburettor assembly must be renewed as it is not possible to obtain the seat individually.

34 Operate the throttle shaft to make sure that the throttle butterfly valve opens and closes smoothly. If it doesn't, renew the carburettor.

35 Check the floats for damage. This will usually be apparent by the presence of fuel inside one of the floats. If the floats are damaged, they must be renewed.

36 Clean the fuel filter set in the fuel hose T-piece(s) (see Chapter 1).

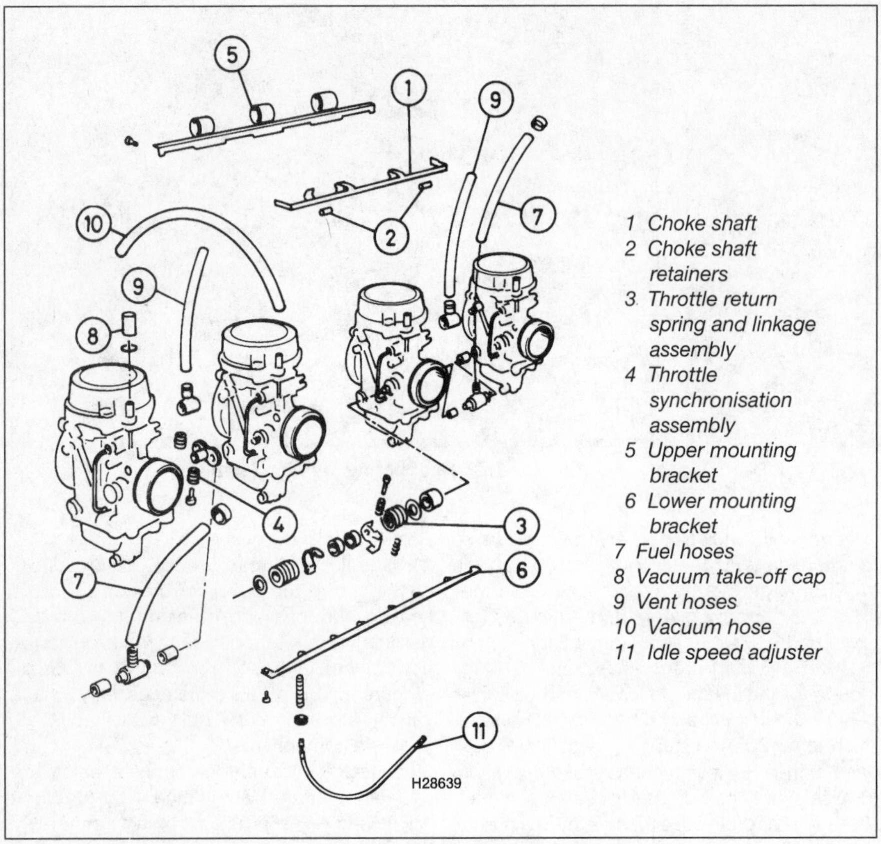

8.1 Carburettor linkage detail – Mikuni

8 Carburettors – separation and joining

Warning: Refer to the precautions given in Section 1 before starting work.

Separation – Mikuni carburettors

1 The carburettors do not need to be separated for normal overhaul. If you need to separate them (to renew a carburettor body, for example), refer to the following procedure **(see illustration)**.

2 Remove the carburettors from the machine as described in Section 6. Mark the body of each carburettor with its cylinder number to ensure that it is positioned correctly on reassembly.

3 Ease the choke shaft sliders out of their retainers to release the shaft, then remove the choke shaft from the plungers **(see illustrations)**.

4 Make a note of how the throttle return springs, linkage assembly and carburettor synchronisation springs are arranged to ensure that they are fitted correctly on reassembly **(see illustration)**.

5 Remove the screws securing the carburettors to the two mounting brackets and remove the brackets. If it is not essential to separate all the carburettors, only release those necessary and leave the others attached to the brackets **(see illustrations)**.

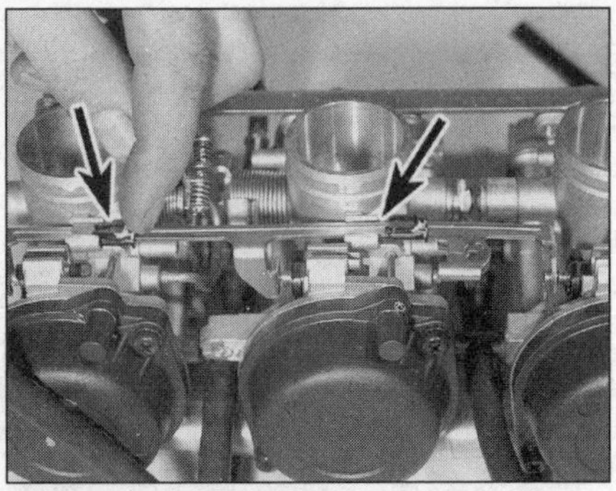

8.3a Ease the choke shaft sliders out of their retainers (arrowed) . . .

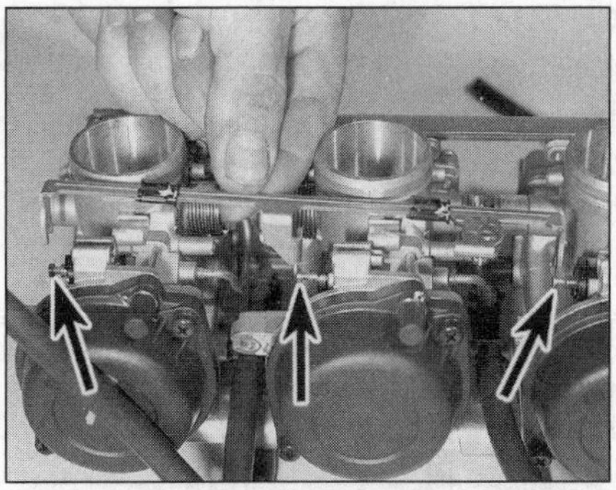

8.3b . . . then remove the shaft from the choke plungers (arrowed)

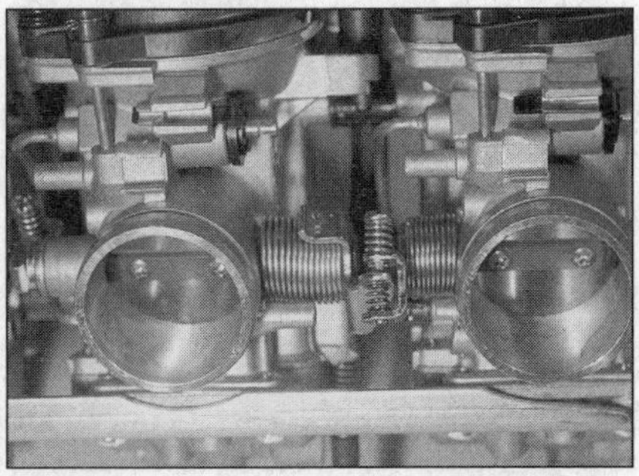

8.4 Note the arrangement of the linkage and synchronisation assembly springs before dismantling

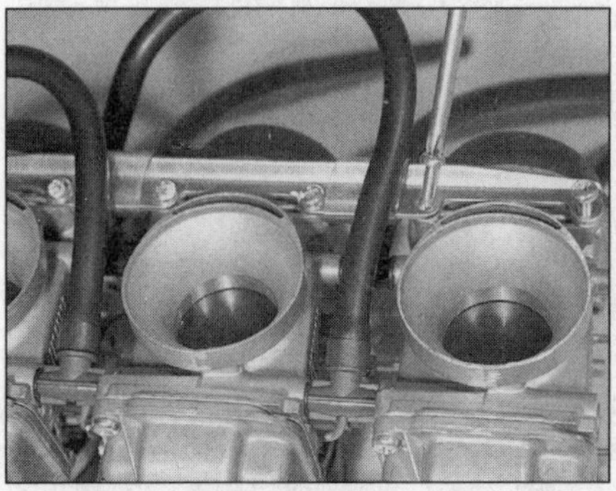

8.5a Unscrew the screws securing the carburettors to both the top . . .

8.5b . . . and the bottom mounting brackets

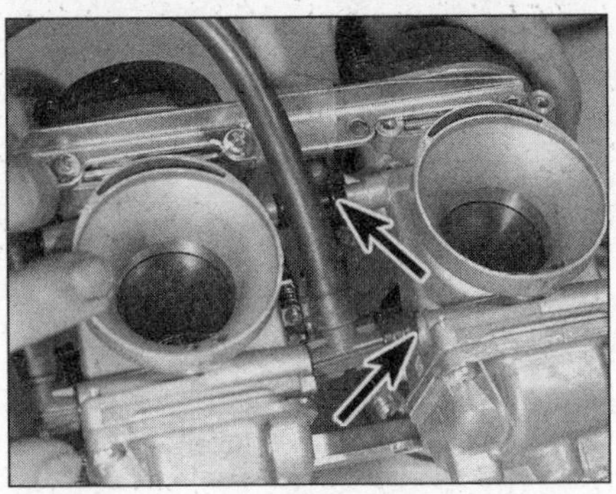

8.6 Separate the carburettors, noting how fuel and vent hose T-pieces fit (arrowed)

8.8 Release the idle speed adjuster bracket screws (arrowed)

8.9a Detach the choke linkage shaft return spring from its hook (arrowed)

8.9b Remove the two retaining screws with their washers (arrowed)

8.9c Retrieve the washers from the linkage shaft mounting points

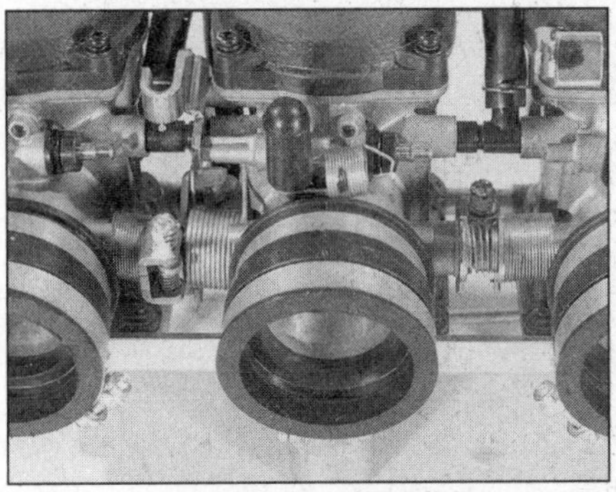

8.10 Throttle cam spring and synchronising screw spring arrangement

6 Carefully separate the carburettors. Retrieve the synchronisation springs and note the fitting of the fuel and vent hose T-pieces as they are separated **(see illustration)**.

Separation – Keihin carburettors

7 The carburettors do not need to be separated for normal overhaul. If you need to separate them (to renew a carburettor body, for example), refer to the following procedure.

8 Remove the carburettors from the machine as described in Section 6. Mark the body of each carburettor with its cylinder number to ensure that it is positioned correctly on reassembly. Remove the two screws which secure the idle speed adjuster bracket **(see illustration)**.

9 Disconnect the choke linkage shaft spring, then remove the two screws with plastic washers and disengage the linkage shaft from the choke plungers **(see illustrations)**. Retrieve the two plastic washers from the linkage shaft mounting points **(see illustration)**.

10 Make a note of how the throttle return springs, linkage assembly and carburettor synchronisation springs are arranged to ensure that they are fitted correctly on reassembly **(see illustration)**.

11 Remove the screws securing the mounting bracket to the base of each carburettor and withdraw the bracket **(see illustration)**. Now remove the long throughbolt and nut which passes through the carburettor bodies **(see illustration)**.

12 Carefully separate the carburettors. Retrieve the synchronisation springs and note the fitting of the fuel and vent hose T-pieces as they are separated.

Joining

13 Assembly is the reverse of the disassembly procedure, noting the following.

a) *Make sure the fuel and vent hose T-pieces are correctly and securely inserted into the carburettors **(see illustration)**.*

8.11a Mounting bracket screws (arrowed) . . .

8.11b . . . and throughbolt and nut (arrowed)

8.13a Make sure the hose T-pieces (arrowed) are securely fitted in the carburettors

8.13b Make sure the synchronisation springs (arrowed) sit squarely in the throttle linkage

b) Install the synchronisation springs after the carburettors are joined together. Make sure they are correctly and squarely seated ***(see illustration)****.*

c) Check the operation of both the choke and throttle linkages ensuring that both operate smoothly and return quickly under spring pressure before installing the carburettors on the machine.

d) Install the carburettors (see Section 6) and check carburettor synchronisation (see Chapter 1).

9 Carburettors – reassembly, float height check and fuel level check

Warning: Refer to the precautions given in Section 1 before starting work.

Reassembly and float height check – Mikuni carburettor

Note: *When reassembling the carburettors, be sure to use new O-rings and seals. Do not overtighten the carburettor jets and screws as they are easily damaged.*

1 Install the choke plunger assembly in its bore. Make sure the plunger retaining clips are securely in place **(see illustration 7.13)**.

2 Install the pilot screw (if removed) along with its spring and O-ring, turning it in until it seats lightly. Now, turn the screw out the number of turns previously recorded.

3 Fit a new O-ring to the base of the piston guide **(see illustration)**. Install the piston guide into the carburettor body, making sure it is the right way round **(see illustration 7.9b)**.

4 Install the needle jet through the piston guide and into the carburettor **(see illustration 7.9a)**. Align the flat in the needle jet with the pin in the jet housing **(see illustration)**. Hold the needle jet in place and screw the main jet into the end of the needle jet **(see illustration 7.8)**.

5 Screw the pilot jet into position next to the main jet.

6 Make sure the float assembly O-rings are seated properly in their grooves **(see illustration)**. Carefully press the assembly into position in the carburettor **(see illustration 7.7)**.

7 To check the float height, hold the carburettor so the float hangs down, then tilt it back until the needle valve is just seated, but not so far that the needle's spring-loaded tip is compressed. Measure the distance between the gasket face and the bottom of the float with an accurate ruler **(see illustration)**. The correct setting should be as given in the Specifications Section. If it is incorrect, adjust the float height by carefully bending the tab a little at a time until the correct height is obtained. Repeat the procedure for all carburettors.

8 With the float height checked, fit a new rubber seal to the float chamber and install the chamber on the carburettor **(see illustration)**.

9 Fit the spacers to the needle and insert the needle into the piston **(see illustration 7.5)**.

10 Insert the piston assembly into the carburettor body and lightly push it down, ensuring that the needle is correctly aligned with the needle jet. Press the diaphragm outer edge into its groove, making sure it is correctly seated. Check the diaphragm is not creased, and that the piston moves smoothly up and down in its guide.

11 Fit a new O-ring to the vacuum take-off stub, then insert the spring into the piston **(see illustration)**. Fit the top cover to the carburettor and tighten the screws securely.

12 If removed, fit the inlet manifold rubber to the carburettor. Note that the widest portion

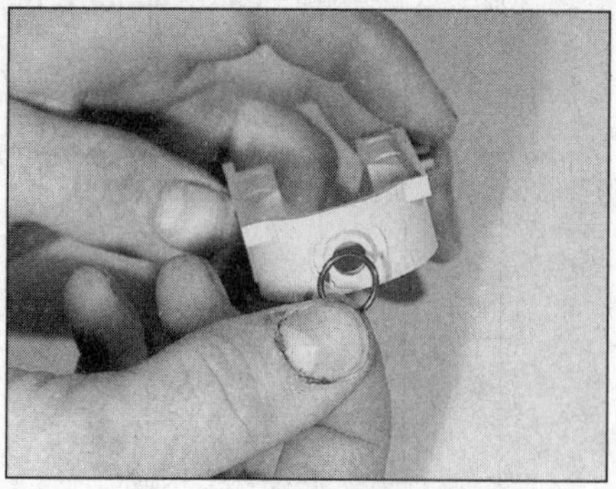

9.3 Fit a new O-ring to the base of the piston guide

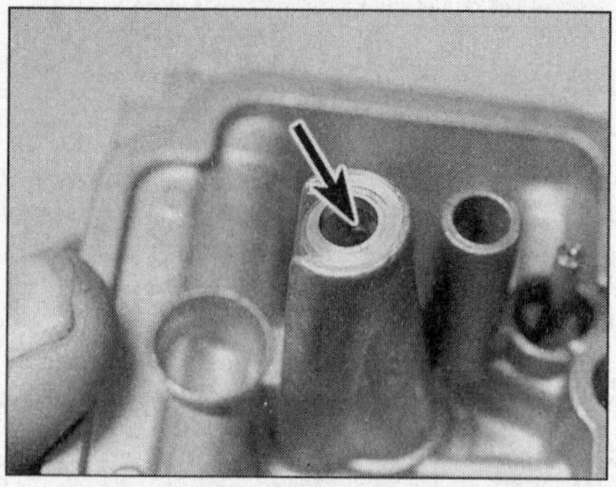

9.4 Align the flat on the needle jet with the pin in the jet housing (arrowed)

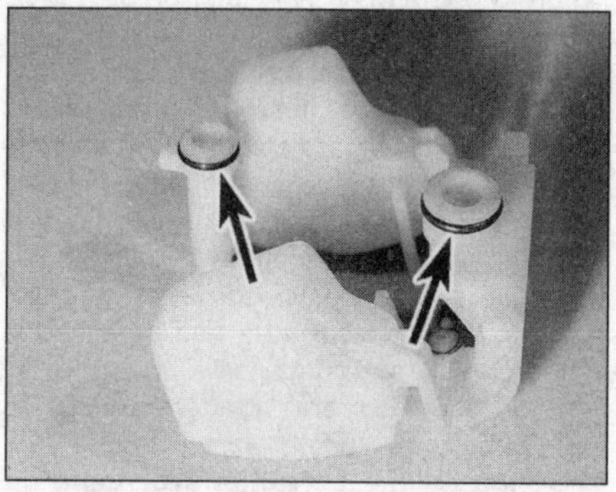

9.6 Fit new O-rings to the float assembly, making sure they are correctly seated in their grooves (arrowed)

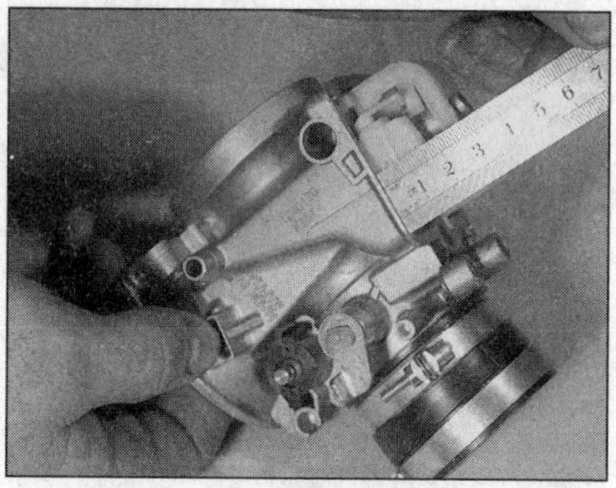

9.7 Check the float heights on all carburettors

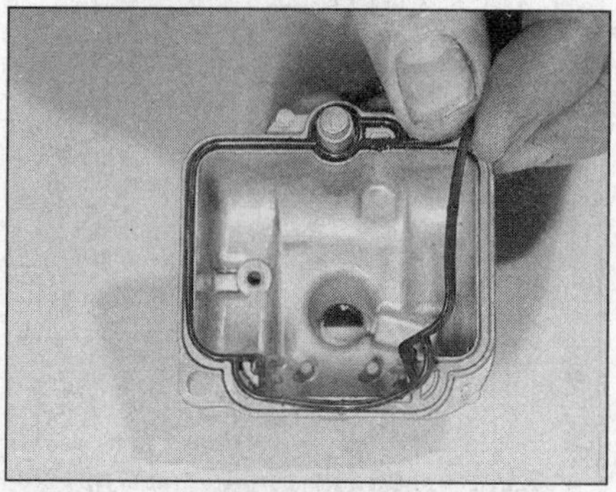

9.8 Fit a new rubber seal to the float chamber, ensuring it seats in the groove

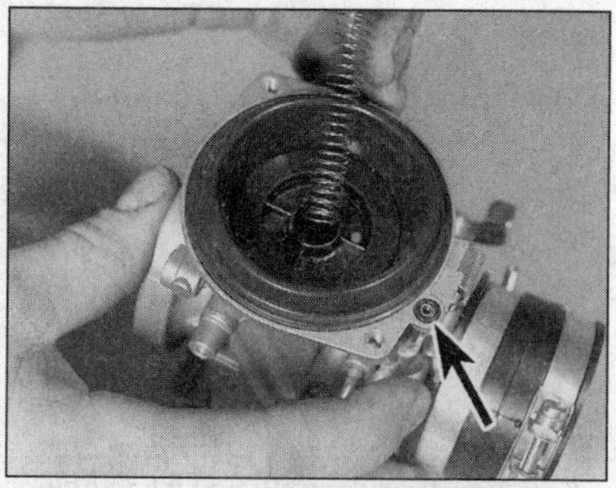

9.11 Fit a new O-ring to vacuum take-off stub (arrowed), then fit spring into piston

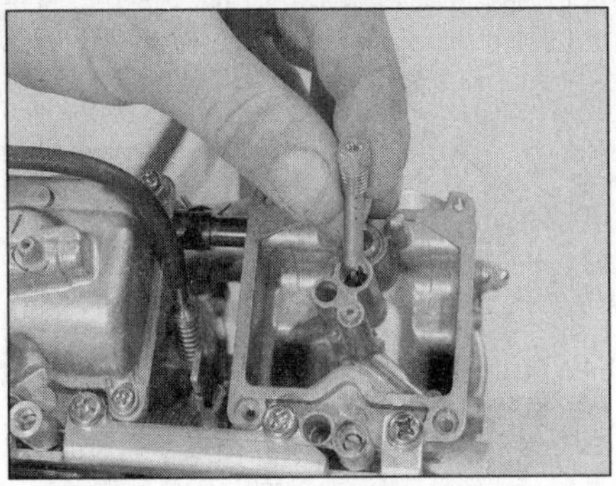

9.15a Screw the needle jet into the carburettor . . .

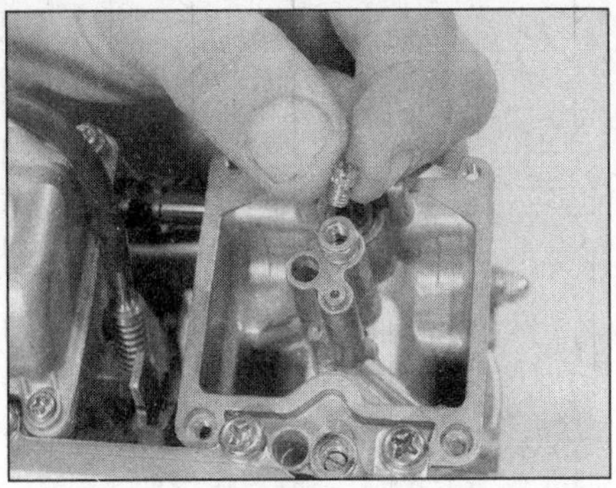

9.15b . . . then screw the main into the needle jet

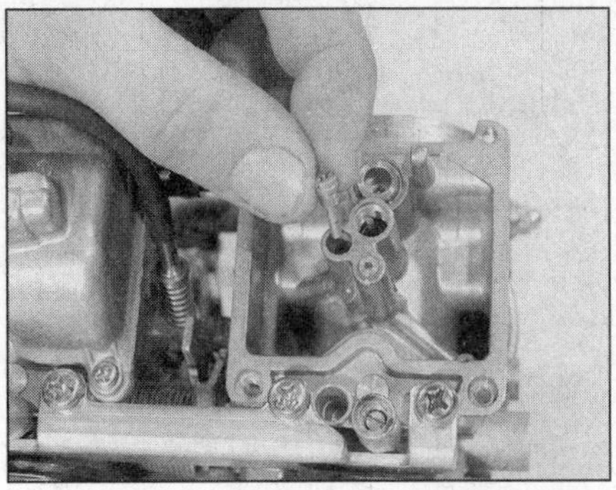

9.15c Screw the pilot jet into its bore

of the rubber must fit at the top and the narrowest at the bottom.

Reassembly and float height check – Keihin carburettor

Note: *When reassembling the carburettors, be sure to use new O-rings and seals. Do not overtighten the carburettor jets and screws as they are easily damaged.*

13 Install the choke plunger assembly in its bore, tightening its nut securely. If the carburettor bodies have not been separated, install the choke linkage shaft, making sure that its tangs engage the choke plunger ends and that a plastic washer is placed between the linkage shaft and carburettor bodies at each mounting point. Install the linkage shaft screws with their plastic washers and then reconnect the return spring. Operate the linkage shaft and make sure that each choke plunger is operated smoothly and returns easily.

14 Install the pilot screw (if removed), turning it in until it seats lightly. Now, turn the screw out the number of turns previously recorded, or if a new screw is being fitted, to the number of turns out specified at the beginning of this chapter.

15 Install the needle jet into the carburettor, then screw the main jet into the head of the needle jet **(see illustrations)**.

16 Hook the needle valve onto its tang on the float. Install the float carefully so that the needle valve fits into its seat **(see illustration)** and pass the pivot pin through its mountings to secure the float.

17 At this point, check the float height. Hold the carburettor so the float hangs down, then tilt it back until the needle valve is just seated, but not so far that the needle's spring-loaded tip is compressed. Measure the distance between the gasket face and the bottom of the float with an accurate ruler **(see illustration)**. The correct setting should be as given in the Specifications Section. If it is incorrect, adjust the float height by carefully bending the tab a little at a time until the correct height is obtained.

18 Fit a new rubber seal to the float chamber and install the chamber on the carburettor **(see illustration)**.

19 Install the jet needle in through the top of the piston, followed by the retainer **(see illustrations)**. Very carefully insert the piston into the carburettor, making sure that it is the correct way around (it will only fit one way), and that the jet needle passes through the needle jet. Press the diaphragm outer edge into its groove, making sure it is correctly seated. Check the diaphragm is not creased, and that the piston moves smoothly up and down in the carburettor.

20 Fit the spring into the piston so that its lower end locates over the retainer. Install the

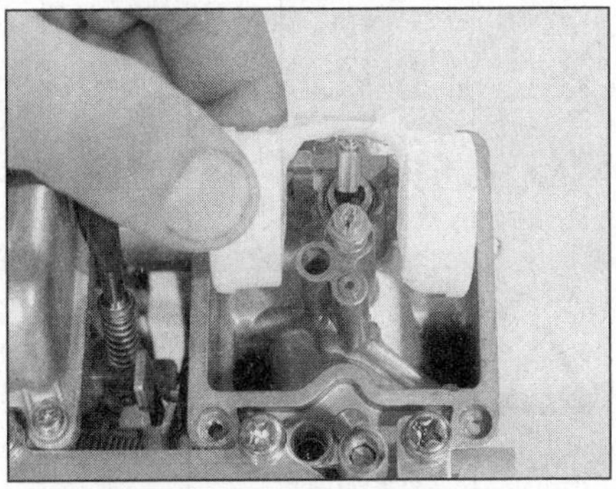

9.16 Carefully insert the float needle into its seat

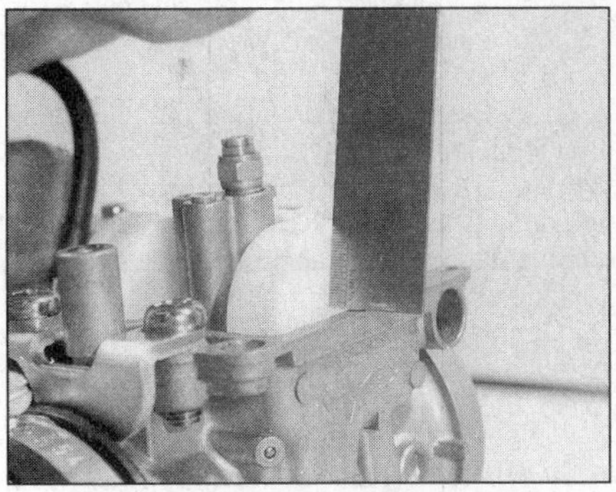

9.17 Measuring the float height

4

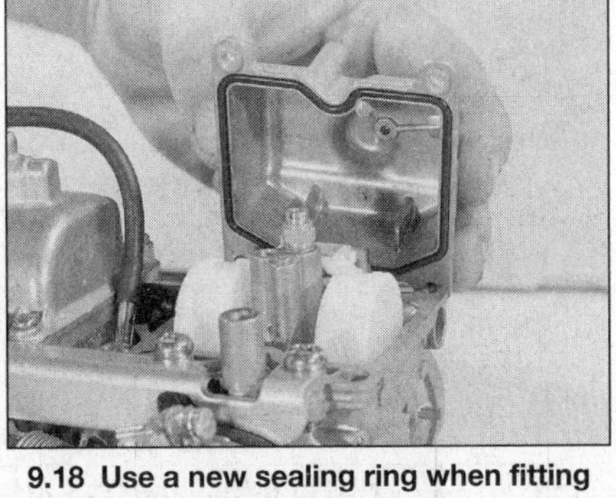

9.18 Use a new sealing ring when fitting the float chamber

9.19a Insert the jet needle into the piston . . .

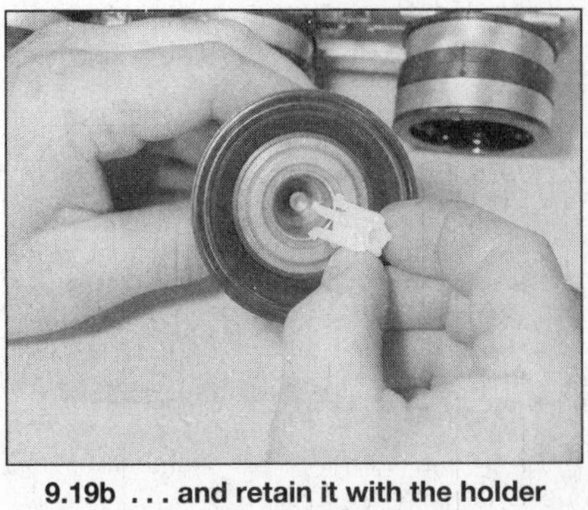

9.19b . . . and retain it with the holder

9.20 Ensure that you locate the spring over the stub on the inside of the cover

carburettor cover, engaging its stub in the top of the spring **(see illustration)** and tighten the cover screws – make sure that the diaphragm outer edge remains seated during this operation.

21 If removed, fit the inlet manifold rubber to the carburettor. Note that the widest portion of the rubber must fit at the top and the narrowest at the bottom.

Fuel level check

22 A check can be made of the fuel level in the carburettors without the need to remove and dismantle the carburettors to measure the float height. To perform the check, two special tools are needed, an adapter (Pt. No. 3880120) and a gauge (Pt. No. 3880125), together with a short length of fuel hose.

23 Make sure the bike is on level ground and place it on its centre stand. If no centre stand is fitted, use an auxiliary stand but make sure that the bike is upright and level.

24 On Thunderbird, Thunderbird Sport, Adventurer, Legend TT and Tiger models, turn the fuel tap OFF. On all other models turn the fuel tap ON.

25 On Mikuni carburettors, unscrew the drain screw on the bottom of the float chamber and drain the fuel from the carburettor into a suitable container. Thread the adapter into the float chamber in place of the drain screw, then attach the hose to the adapter and plug the gauge into the other end of the hose.

26 On Keihin carburettors, connect the hose to the drain point on the base of the float chamber, making sure that it is a good fit. Plug the gauge into the other end of the hose.

27 On all models, hold the gauge against the side of the carburettor body so that the bottom mark on its scale aligns with the joining faces of the float chamber and the carburettor, and so that it is vertical. Hold the gauge in this position whilst the fuel tap is turned ON (Thunderbird, Thunderbird Sport, Adventurer, Legend TT and Tiger models) or to the PRI position (all other models) – fuel will flow into the gauge **(see illustration)**; on models with Keihin carburettors, also unscrew the drain screw on the float chamber to allow fuel to flow into the gauge.

28 The fuel level should be the specified

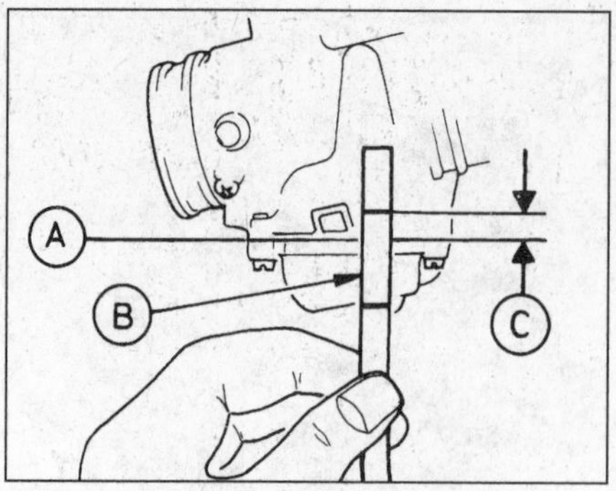

9.27 Fuel level measurement

A Joint face of carburettor
B Gauge
C Fuel level measurement

distance above the joint face of the carburettor (see Specifications at the beginning of this Chapter).

29 On completion, turn the fuel tap OFF (Thunderbird, Thunderbird Sport, Adventurer, Legend TT and Tiger models) or ON (all other models). On Mikuni carburettors, invert the gauge and drain the fuel into a suitable container, then remove the adapter and install the drain screw, tightening it securely. On Keihin carburettors, tighten the float chamber drain screw, pull off the hose and drain the fuel into a suitable container.

30 Check the other carburettors in the same way.

31 If the fuel level in any carburettor is incorrect, remove the float chambers (see Section 7) and adjust the float height as described in Step 7 or 17 above.

10 Throttle cable – removal and installation

Warning: Refer to the precautions given in Section 1 before starting work.

Removal

1 Detach the carburettors from the cylinder head as described in Section 6 and support them in a position that gives access to the throttle cable cam. **Note:** *Take care to keep the carburettors upright, to prevent fuel spillage from the float chambers and the possibility of the piston diaphragms being damaged.*

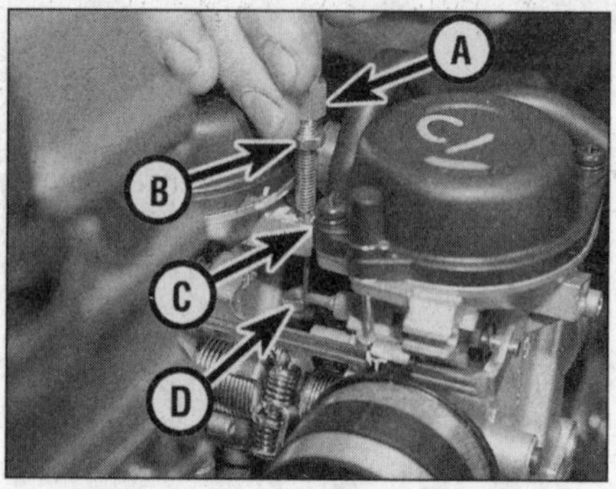

10.2 Throttle cable adjuster (A), upper locknut (B), adjuster housing (C), and lower locknut (D)

2 Back off the adjuster upper locknut and move the adjuster down in its housing to release the bottom locknut from the housing; where fitted, release the spring clip from the adjuster. Fully unscrew the lower locknut so that it comes off the adjuster **(see illustration)**.

3 Pull the adjuster up and out of the housing, then guide the cable through the slot to free it from the housing. If necessary, hold the throttle linkage open with a finger to aid removal of the adjuster from its housing.

4 Release the cable end from the throttle cam.

5 Unscrew the two right side handlebar switch/throttle pulley housing screws and separate the two halves. Remove the cable elbow from the housing, noting how it fits and hook the throttle cable end out of the pulley **(see illustration)**.

6 Remove the cable from the machine noting its routing.

Installation

7 Install the cable making sure it is correctly routed. The cable must not interfere with any other component and should not be kinked or bent sharply.

8 Lubricate the upper end of the cable with multi-purpose grease and install it into the throttle pulley. Install the cable elbow into the switch/throttle pulley housing **(see illustrations)**. Fit the two halves of the

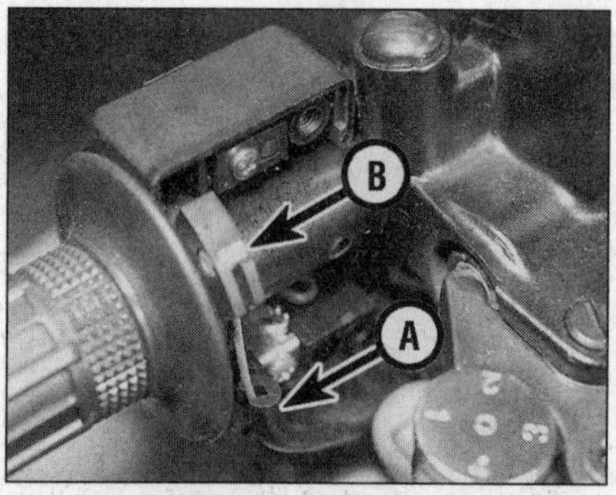

10.5 Remove the elbow (A) from the housing and unhook the cable end (B) from the pulley

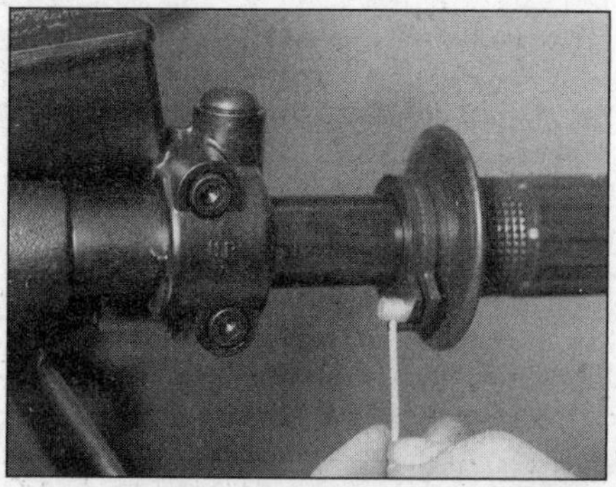

10.8a Fit the cable end into the throttle pulley . . .

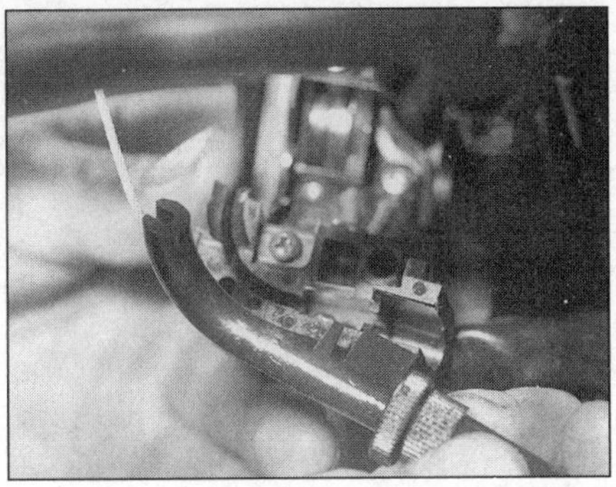

10.8b . . . and the cable elbow into the housing

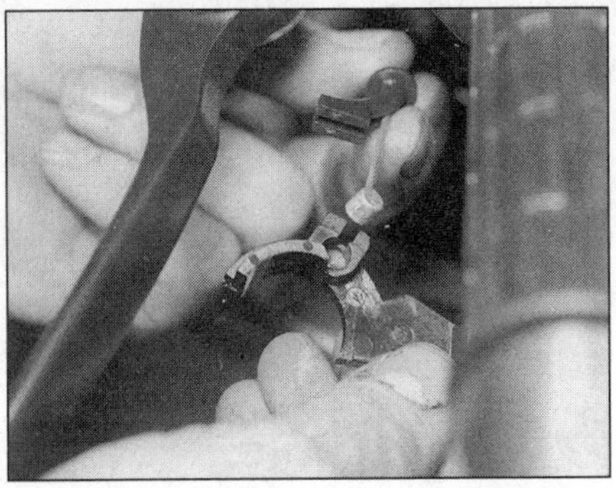

11.1 Remove the elbow from the housing and unhook the cable end from the lever

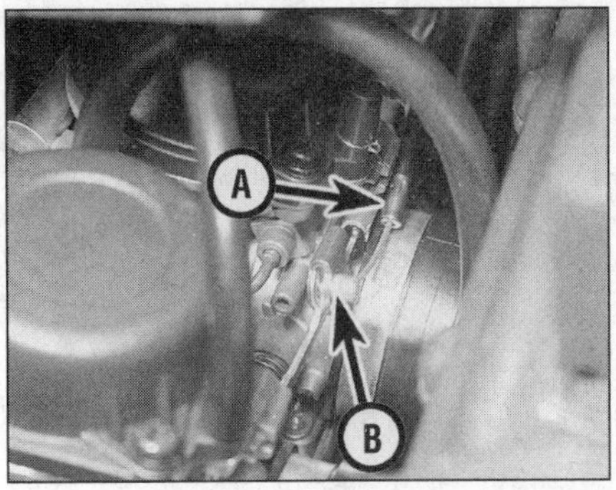

11.2 Free the outer cable from its housing (A) and the cable end from the choke shaft (B)

housing onto the handlebar and install the screws, tightening them securely.

9 Lubricate the lower end of the cable with multi-purpose grease and attach it to the carburettor throttle cam.

10 Make sure the cable is correctly connected, then lift the cable adjuster, slot the cable into the adjuster housing and allow the adjuster to be drawn into the housing by the pull of the throttle return spring.

11 Screw the bottom adjuster locknut onto the adjuster. Tighten the top adjuster locknut to secure the adjuster in place. Where fitted, install the spring clip. Operate the throttle to check that it opens and closes freely.

12 Check and adjust the throttle cable as described in Chapter 1. Turn the handlebars back and forth to make sure the cable doesn't cause the steering to bind.

13 Fit the carburettors to the cylinder head as described in Section 6.

14 Start the engine and check that the idle speed does not rise as the handlebars are turned. If it does, the cable is routed incorrectly; correct the problem before riding the motorcycle.

11 Choke cable – removal and installation

Removal

1 Unscrew the two left side handlebar switch/choke lever housing screws and separate the two halves. Remove the cable elbow from the housing, noting how it fits. Hook the choke cable end out of the lever **(see illustration)**.

2 Free the choke outer cable from its housing on the carburettor and detach the inner cable from the choke linkage **(see illustration)**.

3 Remove the cable from the machine noting its correct routing.

Installation

4 Install the cable, ensuring it is correctly routed. The cable must not interfere with any other components and should not be kinked or bent sharply.

5 Lubricate the lower cable end with multi-purpose grease and attach it to the choke shaft on the carburettor. Fit the outer cable into its housing.

6 Lubricate the upper cable end with multi-purpose grease and attach it to the choke lever. Install the choke lever and cable elbow into the left side handlebar switch/choke lever housing **(see illustration)**. Fit the two halves of the housing onto the handlebar and install the screws, tightening them securely.

7 Adjust the choke cable (see Chapter 1).

12 Auxiliary air chamber(s) and airbox – removal and installation

Auxiliary air chamber(s)

Removal – Trident, Sprint, Trophy, Speed Triple, Daytona and Tiger models

1 Remove the seat and the side panels (see Chapter 8), and the battery (Chapter 1).

2 Prise the air inlet ducts off the auxiliary air chambers (Tiger has one duct only, on the left side), then unscrew the air chamber mounting bolts **(see illustration)**. Note that the rear mounting bolts also secure the battery box to the frame and are held by nuts which locate on the inside of the battery box; the front mounting bolts screw directly into captive nuts on the frame. Remove the chamber from the bike. Remove the rubber gaiter from the airbox **(see illustration)**.

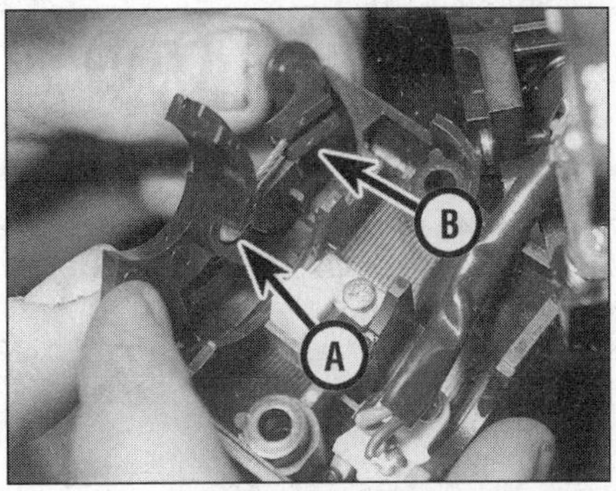

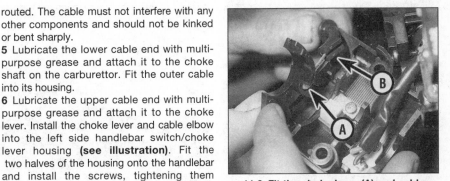

11.6 Fit the choke lever (A) and cable elbow (B) into the housing

Removal – Thunderbird, Thunderbird Sport, Adventurer and Legend TT models

3 Remove the seat and the side panels (see Chapter 8), and the battery (Chapter 1). On Thunderbird, Adventurer and Legend TT

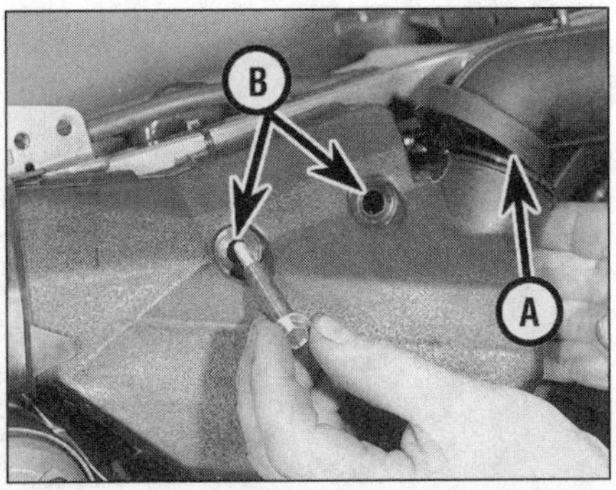

12.2a Prise off the air inlet duct (A), then unscrew the chamber mounting bolts (B)

12.2b Remove the rubber gaiter from the airbox inlet

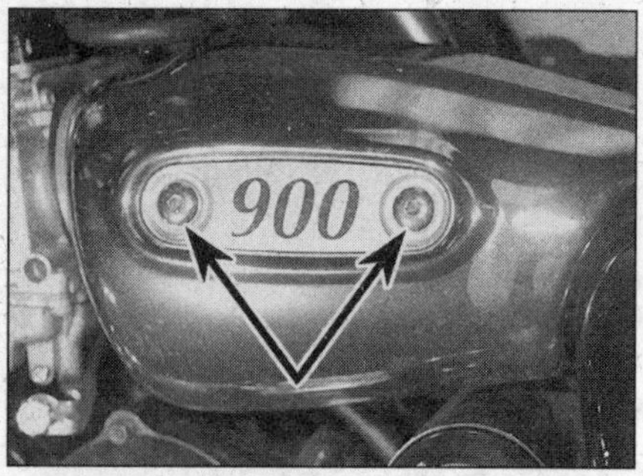

12.3a On Thunderbird, Adventurer and Legend TT models the airbox end covers have two screws (arrowed)

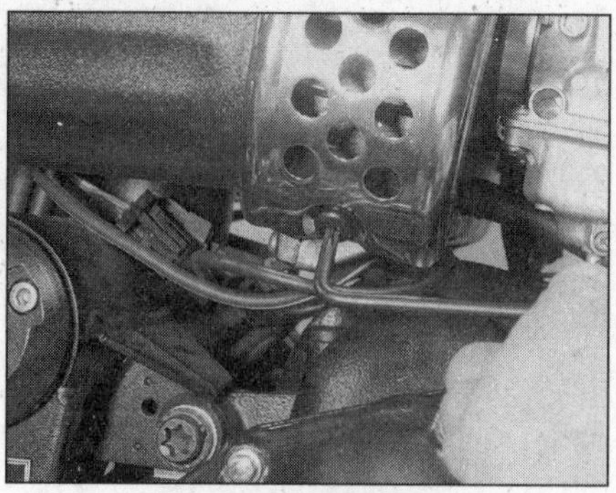

12.3b On Thunderbird Sport models, remove the screw . . .

12.3c . . . unhook the chrome trim . . .

models, remove the airbox end covers **(see illustration)**. On Thunderbird Sport models, remove the two airbox end covers on each side **(see illustrations)**. Remove the plastic cover from the right side of the frame top tube **(see illustration)**. On Thunderbird, Thunderbird Sport and Adventurer models, remove the two bolts to free the seat lock from the rear of the air chamber **(see illustration)**.

12.3d . . . and remove the rear section screw

12.3e Frame top tube cover is retained by a screw (A) and peg (B)

12.3f Seat lock is retained by two bolts

12.4a Slacken the air chamber hose clamp

4 Release the clamp securing the air chamber to the airbox, then remove the screw securing the air chamber to the frame **(see illustrations)**. Remove the chamber with the duct attached, noting how the air chamber locates over the peg on the frame **(see illustration)**. **Note:** *On California models, the evaporative loss system canister is housed inside the air chamber; remove the chamber lid and disconnect the canister hoses to permit removal.* The rubber joint can be removed from airbox if required after slackening its clamp.

Installation – all models

5 Installation is the reverse of removal. Ensure that the rubber gaiter/joint seals the joint between the air chamber and airbox.

Airbox

Removal

6 Remove the auxiliary air chamber(s) as described above.

7 Remove the carburettors (see Section 6).

8 Release the clip securing the breather hose to the front of the airbox and detach the hose **(see illustration)**. The breather hose is either routed off the clutch cover or the crankcase left cover, depending on the model.

9 Remove the airbox from the bike with its

12.4 b Air chamber retaining screw (arrowed) . . .

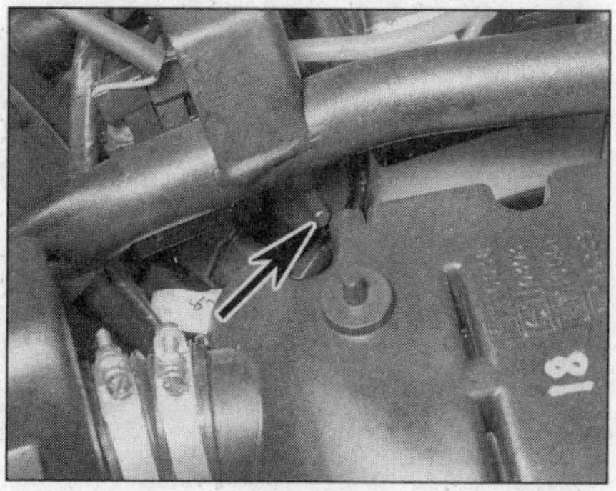

12.4c . . . and peg (arrowed)

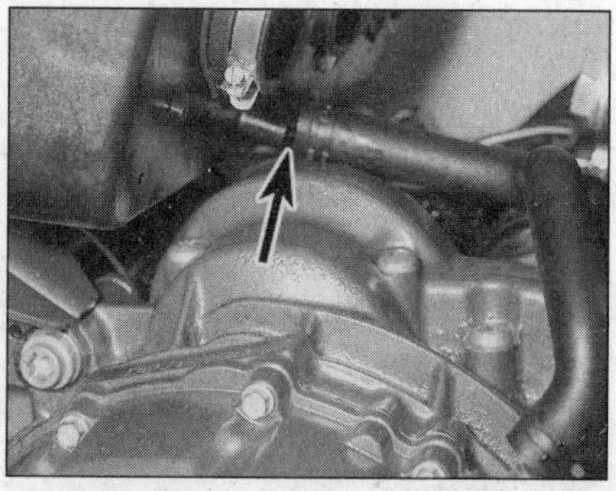

12.8 Detach the breather hose (arrowed) from the front of the airbox

12.9 Remove the airbox from the frame

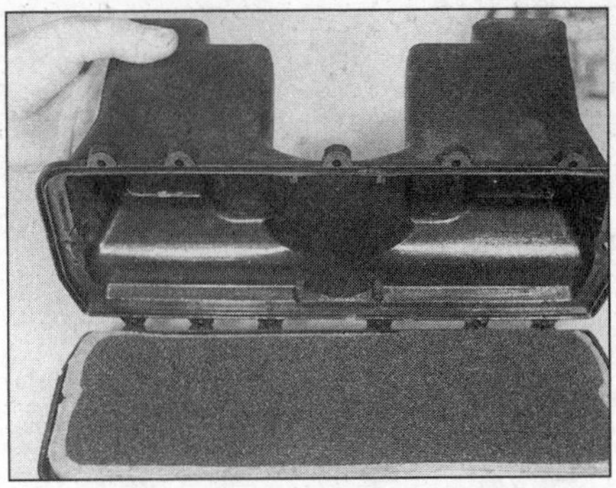

12.10a Remove the screws securing the airbox halves . . .

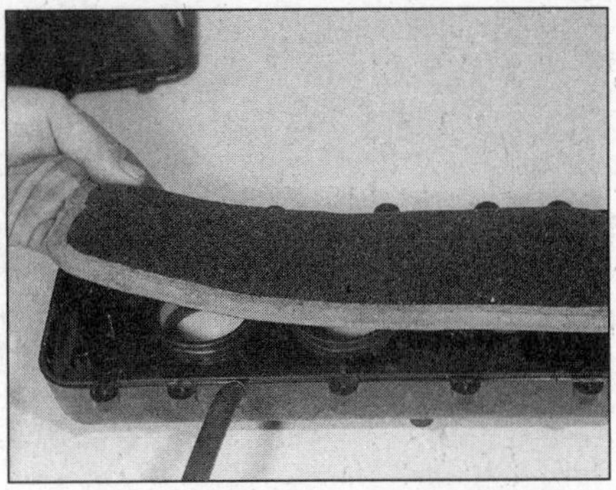

12.10b . . . and lift out the element

drain hose attached, noting its routing **(see illustration)**. Note the expansion rings fitted to the airbox/carburettor venturi and take care not to lose them.

10 Note that the airbox is sold as an assembly, it is not possible to purchase the element separately. There is however nothing to be lost by removing the element and cleaning it, but the airbox must be renewed at the interval specified in Chapter 1. Unscrew the screws securing the two halves of the airbox, then separate them to access the element **(see illustrations)**.

Installation

11 Installation is the reverse of removal. Make sure the expansion rings are installed correctly in the venturi, and that the drain pipe is correctly routed. Attach the breather pipe to the front of the airbox before installing the carburettors. Note that on Thunderbird, Thunderbird Sport, Adventurer and Legend TT models the airbox locates over the rear subframe mounting nuts; ensure that the rubber caps are in place over the nuts **(see illustration)**.

13 Exhaust system – removal and installation

Warning: If the engine has just been running, the exhaust system will be very hot. Allow the system time to cool before carrying out any work. This applies particularly to California market models due to the high operating temperature of the catalytic converter.

Silencer

Removal

1 On Tiger models, remove the side panels as described in Chapter 8.

2 Unscrew and remove the silencer mounting nut and bolt (nut only on Thunderbird, Thunderbird Sport, Adventurer and Legend TT models) and loosen the silencer clamp bolt, then release the silencer from the exhaust downpipe assembly using a twisting motion **(see illustration)**.

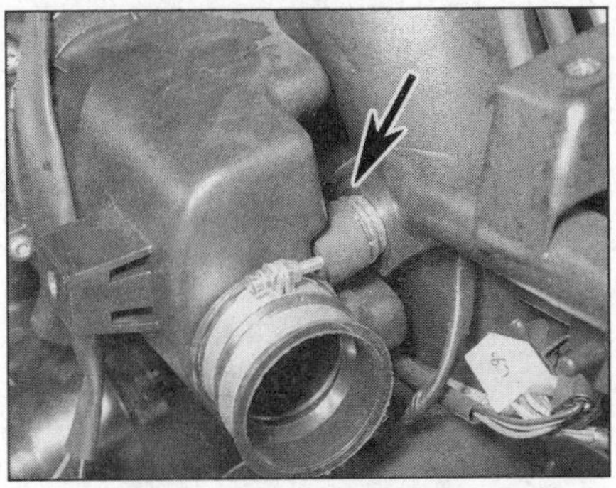

12.11 Locate airbox over rubber caps on subframe nuts (arrowed)

3 Recover the sleeves and rubber bushes, noting how they fit together **(see illustration)**. Inspect the bushes for signs of damage and renew them if necessary.

Installation

4 Install the silencer into the downpipe assembly. On Thunderbird, Thunderbird Sport, Adventurer and Legend TT models, the silencer mounting bracket fits to the inside of the carrier **(see illustration)**. On all other models the silencer bracket fits to the outside of the carrier **(see illustration)**. Ensure that the sleeves and bushes are in place, then install the bolt (not Thunderbird, Thunderbird Sport, Adventurer or Legend TT), washers and nut. Tighten the clamp bolt securely, and the

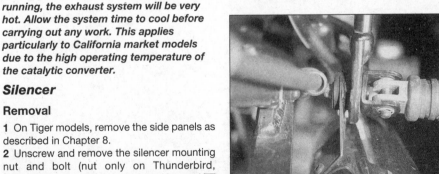

13.4a On the Thunderbird, Thunderbird Sport, Adventurer and Legend TT models, the silencer fits to the inside of the carrier and is secured by the footrest bracket bolt

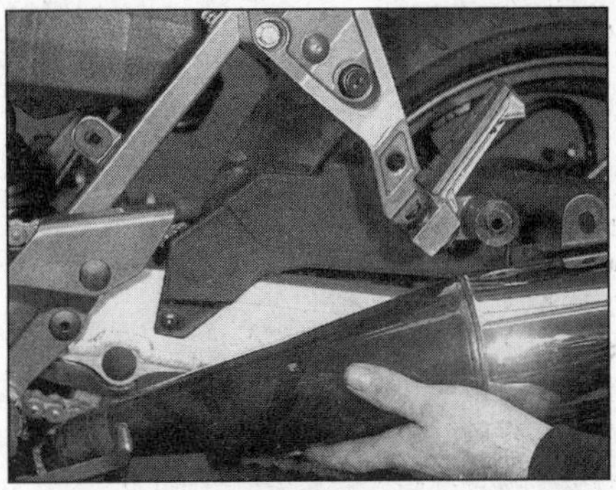

13.2 Release the silencer from the rest of the system using a twisting and pulling motion

13.3 Note how the sleeves fit into the bushes and how they both fit into the carrier

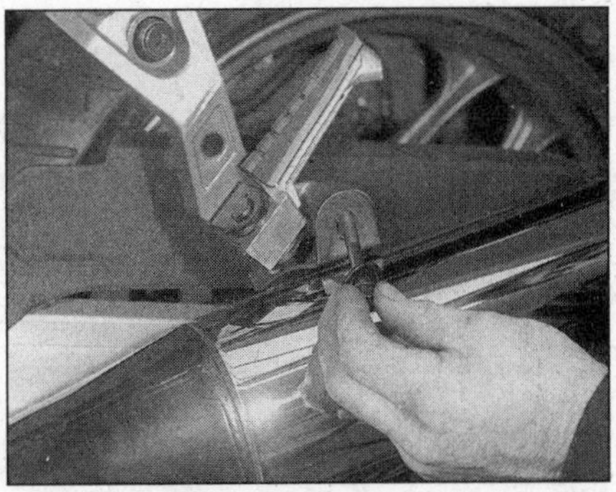

13.4b On all other models, the silencer fits outside of the carrier

13.10a Unscrew the downpipe clamp nuts . . .

13.10b . . . then remove the downpipe assembly from the bike

mounting bolt/nut to the torque setting specified at the beginning of the Chapter.

Complete system

Removal

5 On Daytona and Trophy models remove the lower fairing panels, on Tiger models remove the fairing side panels, and on Sprint models remove the fairing. All procedures are described in Chapter 8.

6 On Daytona and Trophy models, detach and support the oil cooler and its sub-frame as an assembly, referring to Chapter 2 for details.

7 On Tiger models, unscrew the sump guard mounting bolts and remove the sump guard **(see illustration 8.6 in Chapter 3)**.

8 Remove the silencers as described in Steps 1 to 3 above.

9 If fitted, unscrew the mounting bolt securing the balancer pipe to the rear of the engine and recover the bush.

10 Support the downpipe assembly, then unscrew the downpipe retaining nuts from the cylinder head studs and remove the assembly. Remove the gaskets from the cylinder head, noting how they fit, and discard them as new ones must be fitted **(see illustrations)**.

11 If necessary, the downpipe assembly can be split into its various parts by releasing the relevant clamp bolts and separating the components. The downpipe assemblies vary according to model **(see illustration)**.

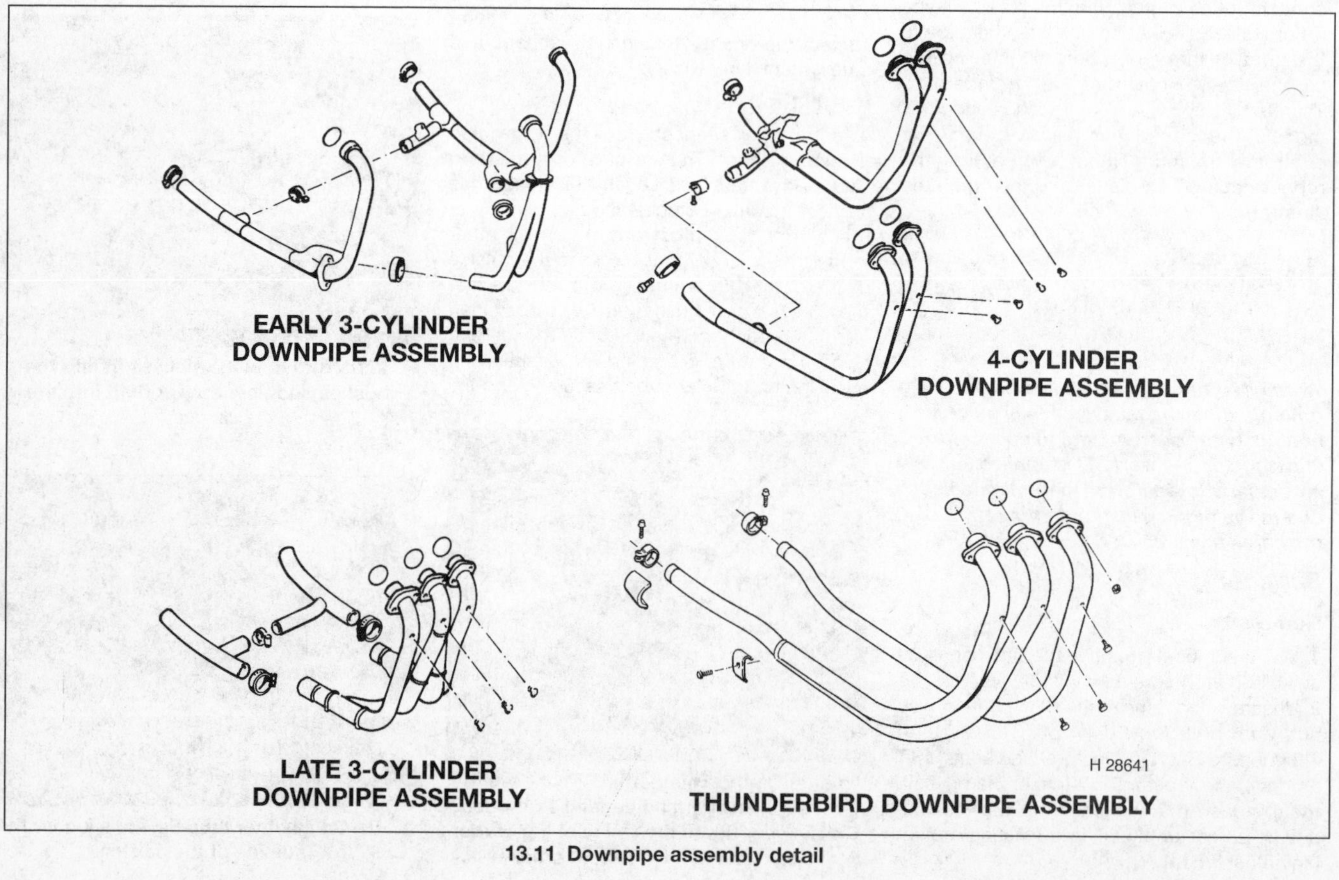

13.11 Downpipe assembly detail

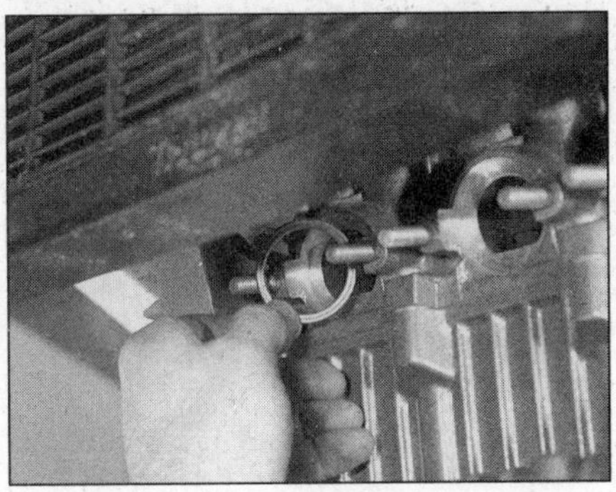

13.14 Fit a new gasket into each cylinder head port, with the flanged side inwards

Installation

12 If dismantled, reassemble the downpipe assembly, tightening all clamp bolts securely.

13 If fitted, inspect the balancer pipe rubber bush for signs of damage and renew it if necessary.

14 Fit a new gasket into each of the cylinder head ports with the flanged side inwards. Apply a smear of grease to the gaskets to keep them in place whilst fitting the downpipe assembly **(see illustration)**.

15 Install the exhaust downpipe assembly, aligning the pipes with the cylinder head ports. Support the assembly from underneath and slide the clamps on the cylinder head studs and fit the nuts. Tighten the downpipe nuts evenly and in two stages, first to the stage one torque setting and then to the stage two torque setting, as specified at the beginning of the Chapter.

16 If fitted, install the bush and the mounting bolt to secure the balancer pipe to the rear of the engine and tighten it securely.

17 Fit the silencers as described in Step 4 above.

18 On Daytona and Trophy models, install the oil cooler assembly as described in Chapter 2. On Tiger models, install the sump guard.

19 Install the fairing sections (where applicable) and side panels (Tiger only) as described in Chapter 8.

14 Evaporative loss system and catalytic converter (California only) – general information

Evaporative loss system

1 On all California models, an evaporative loss system is fitted to prevent the escape of fuel vapours into the atmosphere **(see illustration)**. The system functions as follows:

2 When the engine is stopped, fuel vapour from the tank and the carburettor float chambers is directed into a charcoal canister where it is absorbed and stored whilst the motorcycle is standing. When the engine is started, inlet manifold depression opens a vacuum switch in the canister and the vapours which are stored are drawn into the engine to be burned during the normal combustion process.

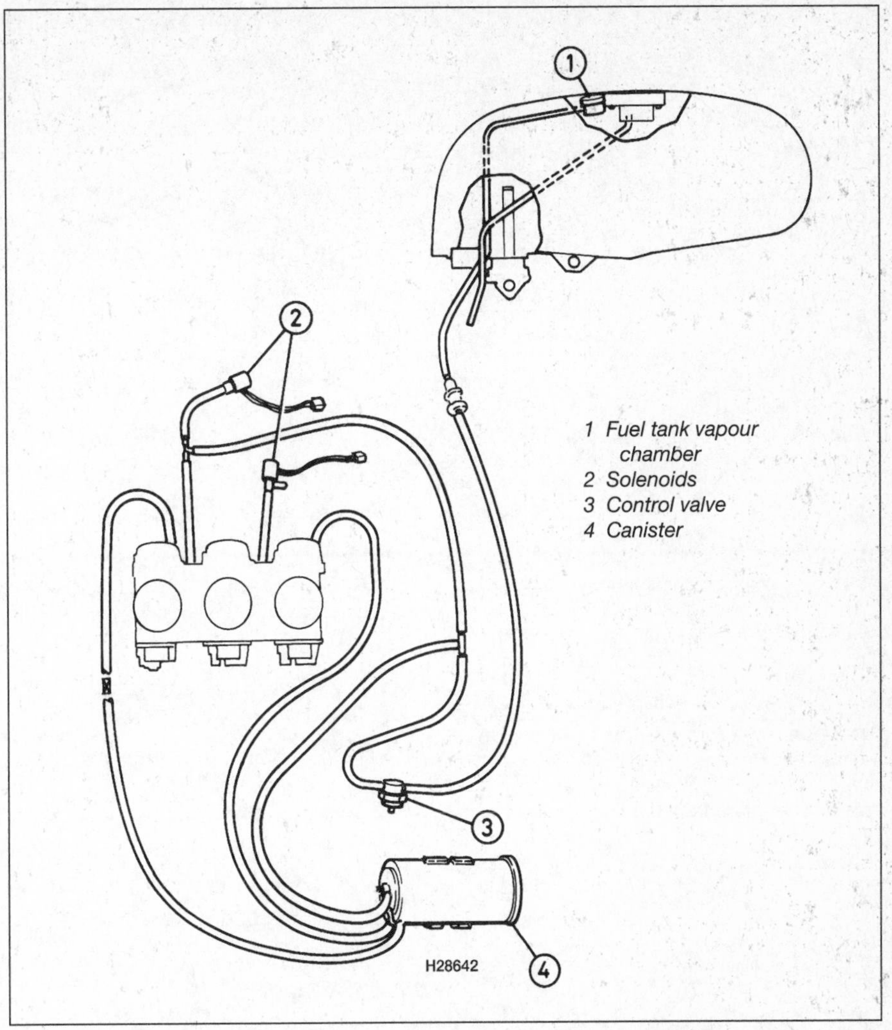

14.1 Evaporative loss system – US California models only

3 The fuel tank incorporates a special vapour chamber. When the pressure in the chamber rises above 0.75 psi (0.05 Bar) a pressure control valve in the vent pipe opens and allows the tank vapour to pass into the canister. The tank vent pipe also incorporates a roll-over valve which closes and prevents any fuel from escaping through it in the event of the bike falling over. The tank filler cap has a one way valve which allows air into the tank as the volume of fuel decreases, but prevents any fuel vapour from escaping.

4 A solenoid operated valve in the float chamber vent pipes allows air to flow into the float chamber whilst the engine is running. The fuel vapour cannot escape as it is being constantly drawn into the combustion chamber and burnt. When the engine is stopped the solenoid closes the vent to the air and any fuel vapour then passes down the vent pipe to the canister.

5 The system is not adjustable and can be tested only by a Triumph dealer. Checks which can be performed by the owner are given in Chapter 1.

Catalytic converter

6 Certain California market models have a catalytic converter located in the exhaust downpipes to minimise the amount of pollutants which escape into the atmosphere. It is an open-loop system, which has no link with the fuel and ignition system.

7 The catalytic converter is a simple device in operation and one which requires no routine maintenance.

8 Note the following points:

a) *Always use unleaded fuel – the use of leaded fuel will destroy the converter.*

b) *Do not use any fuel or oil additives.*

c) *Keep the fuel and ignition systems in good order – if the fuel/air mixture is suspected of being incorrect have it checked on an exhaust gas analyser.*

d) *If the catalytic converter is ever removed from the downpipes, handle it carefully and do not drop it.*

Notes

Chapter 5
Ignition system

Contents

Degrees of difficulty

Easy, suitable for novice with little experience	**Fairly easy,** suitable for beginner with some experience	**Fairly difficult,** suitable for competent DIY mechanic	**Difficult,** suitable for experienced DIY mechanic	**Very difficult,** suitable for expert DIY or professional

Specifications

General information

Firing order	
3 cylinder engines	1-2-3
4 cylinder engines	1-2-4-3
Cylinder identification	
3 cylinder engines	1-2-3 left to right
4 cylinder engines	1-2-3-4 left to right
Spark plugs	see Chapter 1

Ignition timing

At idle	5° BTDC @ 1000 rpm
Full advance	
1200 Trophy and Tiger	29° BTDC @ 6500 rpm
1000 Daytona	38° BTDC @ 6500 rpm
750 Daytona and 750 Trident	35° BTDC @ 6500 rpm
Thunderbird, Thunderbird Sport, Adventurer, Legend TT	30° BTDC @ 6500 rpm
900 Trident, Sprint, 900 Trophy, Speed Triple, 900/1200 Daytona	26° BTDC @ 6500 rpm
Electronic rev-limiter	
750/1000 Daytona and 750 Trident	11,000 rpm
Tiger, Thunderbird, Thunderbird Sport, Adventurer, Legend TT	8750 rpm
900 Trident, Sprint, Trophy, Speed Triple, 900/1200 Daytona	9700 rpm

Pick-up coil

Resistance	530 ohms ± 10%
Air gap	0.6 to 0.8 mm

Ignition HT coils

Primary winding resistance	0.63 ohms ± 10%
Secondary winding resistance	10.5 K-ohms ± 10%

Torque settings

Crankshaft right end cover retaining bolts	9 Nm
Ignition coil mounting bolts	5 Nm
Pick-up coil mounting bolts	10 Nm

5

1 General information

All models are fitted with an inductive transistorised digital electronic ignition system, which due to its lack of mechanical parts is totally maintenance free. The system comprises a rotor, pick-up coil, igniter and ignition HT coils (refer to the wiring diagrams at the end of Chapter 9 for details).

The triggers on the rotor, which is fitted to the right end of the crankshaft, magnetically operate the pick-up coil as the crankshaft rotates. The pick-up coil sends a signal to the igniter which then supplies the ignition HT coils with the power necessary to produce a spark at the plugs.

Three cylinder engines have one coil for each cylinder, whilst four cylinder engines have only two coils, with cylinders 1 and 4 operating off one coil and cylinders 2 and 3 off the other. Under the 4 cylinder arrangement each plug is fired twice for every engine cycle, but one of the sparks occurs during the exhaust stroke and therefore performs no useful function. This arrangement is usually known as a 'spare spark' or 'wasted spark' system.

Because of their nature, the individual ignition system components can be checked but not repaired. If ignition system troubles occur, and the faulty component can be isolated, the only cure for the problem is to renew the part. Keep in mind that most electrical parts, once purchased, cannot be returned. To avoid unnecessary expense, make very sure the faulty component has been positively identified before buying a new part.

2 Ignition system – check

Caution: The energy levels in electronic systems can be very high. On no account should the ignition be switched on whilst the plugs or plug caps are being held. Shocks from the HT circuit can be most unpleasant. Secondly, it is vital that the plugs are soundly earthed when the system is checked for sparking. The ignition system components can be seriously damaged if the HT circuit becomes isolated.

1 As no means of adjustment is available, any failure of the system can be traced to failure of a system component or a simple wiring fault. Of the two possibilities, the latter is far more likely. In the event of failure, check the system in a logical fashion, as described below.

2 On four cylinder engines disconnect the HT leads from No. 1 and No. 2 cylinder spark plugs, on three cylinder engines disconnect the HT leads from all three spark plugs. Connect each lead to a spare spark plug and lay each plug on the engine with the threads contacting the engine. If necessary, hold each spark plug with an insulated tool.

Warning: Do not remove any of the spark plugs from the engine to perform this check – atomised fuel being pumped out of the open spark plug hole could ignite, causing severe injury!

3 Having observed the above precautions, check that the kill switch is in the RUN position, turn the ignition switch ON and turn the engine over on the starter motor. If the system is in good condition a regular, fat blue spark should be evident at each plug electrode. If the spark appears thin or yellowish, or is non-existent, further investigation will be necessary. Before proceeding further, turn the ignition off and remove the key as a safety measure.

4 Ignition faults can be divided into two categories, namely those where the ignition system has failed completely, and those which are due to a partial failure. The likely faults are listed below, starting with the most probable source of failure. Work through the list systematically, referring to the subsequent sections for full details of the necessary checks and tests. **Note:** *Before checking the following items, ensure the battery is fully charged and all fuses are in good condition.*

a) Loose, corroded or damaged wiring connections, broken or shorted wiring between any of the component parts of the ignition system (see Chapter 9).
b) Faulty HT lead or spark plug cap, faulty spark plug, dirty, worn or corroded plug electrodes, or incorrect gap between electrodes.
c) Faulty ignition switch or engine kill switch (see Chapter 9).
d) Faulty sidestand switch/relay (see Chapter 9).
e) Faulty pick-up coil or damaged rotor.
f) Faulty ignition HT coil(s).
g) Faulty igniter.

5 If the above checks don't reveal the cause of the problem, have the ignition system tested by a Triumph dealer. Triumph produce a tester which can perform a complete diagnostic analysis of the ignition system.

3 Ignition HT coils – check, removal and installation

Check

1 In order to determine conclusively that the ignition coils are defective, they should be tested by a Triumph dealer equipped with the special diagnostic tester.

2 However, the coils can be checked visually (for cracks and other damage) and the primary and secondary coil resistance can be measured with an ohmmeter. If the coils are undamaged, and if the resistance readings are as specified at the beginning of the Chapter, they are probably capable of proper operation.

3 To gain access to the coils, remove the seat and disconnect the battery negative (-ve) lead, then remove the fuel tank as described in Chapter 4. The coils are mounted on the main frame tube **(see illustration)**. On Thunderbird, Thunderbird Sport, Adventurer and Legend TT models, remove the plastic cover from the right side of the frame top tube **(see illustration 12.3e in Chapter 4)**.

4 Disconnect the primary circuit electrical connectors and the HT lead(s) from the coil being tested **(see illustration)**. Mark the locations of all wires and leads before disconnecting them.

5 Set the meter to the ohms x 1 scale and measure the resistance between the primary circuit terminals **(see illustration)**. This will give a resistance reading of the primary windings and should be consistent with the value given in the Specifications at the beginning of the Chapter.

6 To check the condition of the secondary windings, set the meter to the K-ohm scale. On four cylinder engines, connect one meter probe to each HT lead socket. On three cylinder engines, connect one probe to one of the primary circuit terminals and the other probe to the HT lead socket **(see illustration)**.

3.3 Ignition HT coils are mounted on the main frame tube

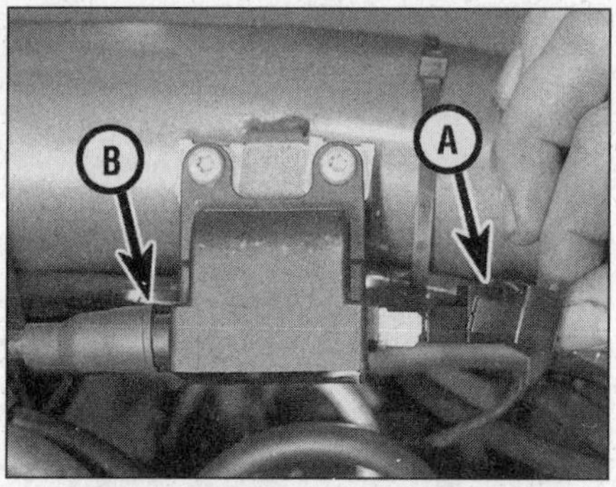

3.4 Disconnect the primary circuit connections (A) and HT lead (B) from coil

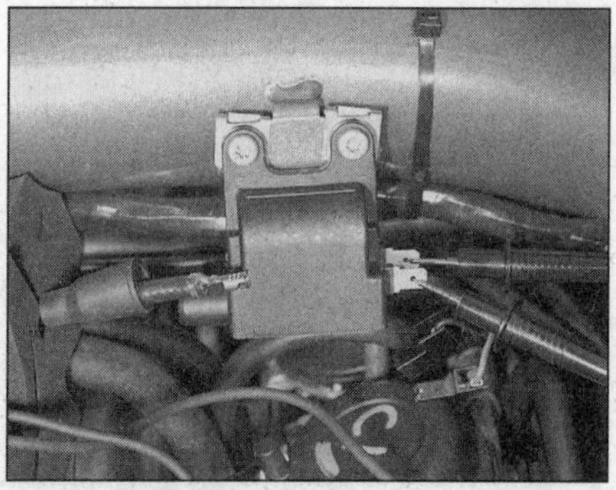

3.5 Measuring ignition HT coil primary winding resistance

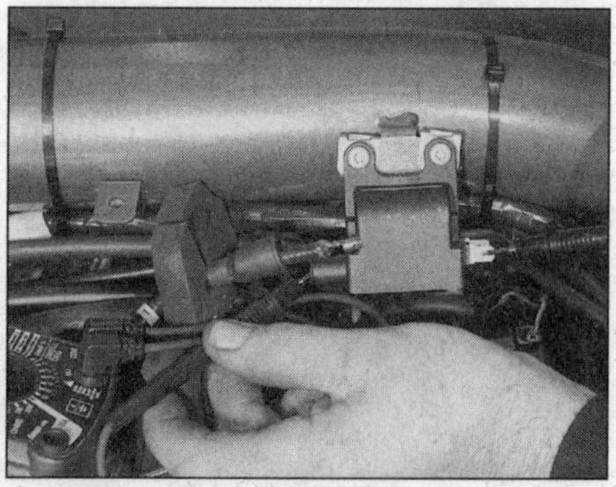

3.6 Measuring ignition HT coil secondary winding resistance (3 cylinder models)

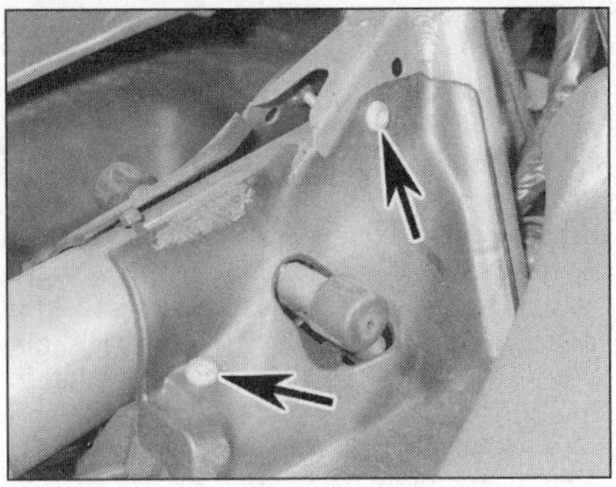

3.8 Valve cover cowls are retained by two screws (arrowed)

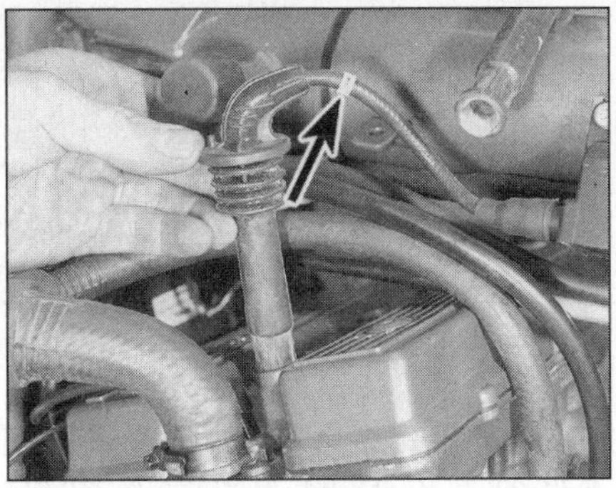

3.9 Each plug lead should be labelled with its cylinder number (arrowed)

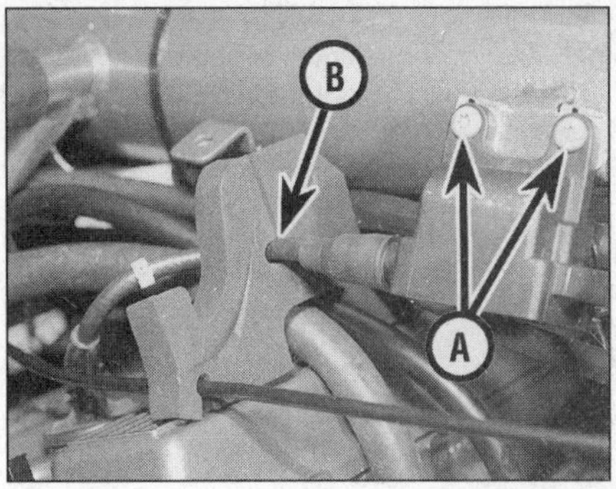

3.10 Unscrew the two coil mounting bolts (A). Note the routing of the HT leads through the separator (B)

If the reading obtained is not within the range shown in the Specifications, it is likely that the coil is defective.

7 Should any of the above checks not produce the expected result, have your findings confirmed on the diagnostic tester (see Step 1). If the coil is confirmed to be faulty, it must be renewed; the coil is a sealed unit and cannot therefore be repaired. Note that the HT leads can be unscrewed from the coils and renewed separately.

Removal

8 Remove the seat and disconnect the battery negative (-ve) lead, then remove the fuel tank as described in Chapter 4. On Trident, Sprint, Trophy, Speed Triple, Daytona and Tiger models, remove the valve cover cowls from each side of the frame; they are secured by two screws **(see illustration)**. On Thunderbird, Thunderbird Sport, Adventurer and Legend TT models, remove the plastic cover from the right side of the frame top tube **(see illustration 12.3e in Chapter 4)**.

9 Disconnect the primary circuit electrical connectors from the coil(s) and disconnect the HT lead(s) from the plug(s) that are connected to the coil being removed. Mark the locations of all wires and leads before disconnecting them **(see illustration)**.

10 Unscrew the two bolts securing each coil to the frame and remove the coil. Note the routing of the HT leads through the separator **(see illustration)**.

4.8 Pick-up coil is secured by two bolts (arrowed)

Installation

11 Installation is the reverse of removal. Make sure the wiring connectors and HT leads are securely connected. Tighten the coil mounting bolts to the torque setting specified at the beginning of the Chapter.

4 Pick-up coil – check, removal and installation

Check

1 Remove the seat as described in Chapter 8 and disconnect the battery negative (-ve) lead. On Trophy and Daytona models, remove the right side lower fairing panel (see Chapter 8).

2 Trace the pick-up coil wiring from the right side crankshaft end cover to the two-pin connector. Disconnect the connector and using a multimeter set to the ohms x 100 scale, measure the resistance between the black and red wires on the pick-up coil side of the connector. **Note:** *On certain models it may be impossible to access the pick-up coil connector without first removing the left air chamber.*

3 Compare the reading obtained with that given in the Specifications at the beginning of this Chapter. The pick-up coil must be renewed if the reading obtained differs greatly from that given, particularly if the meter indicates a short circuit (no measurable

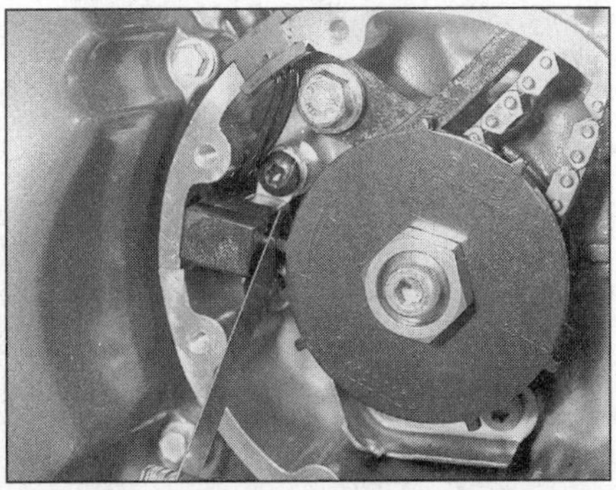

4.11 Measure the air gap between pick-up coil and rotor trigger using feeler blades

resistance) or an open circuit (infinite, or very high resistance).

4 If the pick-up coil is thought to be faulty, first check that this is not due to a damaged or broken wire from the coil to the connector; pinched or broken wires can usually be repaired.

Removal

5 Remove the seat as described in Chapter 8 and disconnect the battery negative (-ve) lead. On Trophy and Daytona models, remove the right side lower fairing panel (see Chapter 8).

6 Trace the pick-up coil wiring from the right side crankshaft end cover to the two-pin connector (see ***Haynes Hint***). Disconnect the connector and free the wiring from any relevant ties or clips.

7 Place a suitable container under the cover to catch any residual oil, then unscrew the retaining bolts and remove the cover squarely from the engine. Discard the gasket as a new one must be used.

8 Remove the two bolts which secure the pick-up coil to the crankcase and remove the coil, noting how it fits **(see illustration)**.

9 Examine the rotor triggers for signs of damage such as chipped or missing teeth and renew it if necessary (See Chapter 2).

Installation

10 Fit the pick-up coil to the crankcase and install the mounting bolts, but do not yet fully tighten them.

11 Rotate the crankshaft so that one of the triggers on the rotor is opposite the pick-up on the coil. Using feeler blades, measure the gap between the trigger and the pick-up coil and adjust as necessary until the gap is as specified at the beginning of the Chapter **(see illustration)**. When the gap is set, tighten the bolts to the specified torque setting.

12 Remove all traces of old gasket from the crankcase and cover mating surfaces and fit a new gasket to the crankcase.

13 Apply a smear of sealant to the end cover wiring grommet and fit the grommet in its recess in the crankcase.

14 Fit the cover to the engine and tighten the cover bolts to the specified torque setting.

15 Route the wiring up to the wire harness

and reconnect the two-pin connector. Secure the wiring in position with all the necessary clips and ties. Install the air chamber, where necessary.

16 Check the engine oil level as described in Chapter 1 and top-up if necessary.

17 Reconnect the battery negative (-ve) lead, then fit the seat and lower fairing panel as described in Chapter 8.

5 Igniter – removal, check and installation

Removal

1 Remove the seat as described in Chapter 8 and disconnect the battery negative (-ve) lead. On Tiger models, remove the fairing left side panel to gain access to the igniter. On later Trophy models (from VIN 29156) remove the main fairing to access the igniter which is mounted on the fairing stay **(see illustration)**. On Thunderbird, Thunderbird Sport, Adventurer and Legend TT models, remove the right side panel **(see illustration)**. On all other models the igniter is located under the seat on the rear mudguard.

2 Disconnect the igniter wiring at the connector **(see illustration)**.

3 Free the igniter from its mounting bracket and remove it from the bike **(see illustration)**.

Check

4 If the tests shown in the preceding Sections have failed to isolate the cause of an ignition fault, it is likely that the igniter itself is faulty. No test details are available with which the unit can be tested on home workshop equipment. Take the machine to a Triumph dealer for testing on the diagnostic tester.

Installation

5 Installation is the reverse of removal ensuring that the wiring connector is securely connected.

6 Ignition timing – general information and check

General information

1 Since no provision exists for adjusting the ignition timing and since no component is subject to mechanical wear, there is no need for regular checks; only if investigating a fault such as a loss of power or a misfire, should the ignition timing be checked.

2 The ignition timing is checked dynamically (engine running). Triumph produce a special tool which is basically a replacement crankshaft right end cover with an inspection hole to enable the timing marks to be viewed with the cover in place. Note that checking the timing without this cover is not possible due to the presence of engine oil in the casing.

3 Check the timing using a stroboscopic lamp. The inexpensive neon lamps should be adequate in theory, but in practice may produce a pulse of such low intensity that the timing mark remains indistinct. If possible, one of the more precise xenon tube lamps should be used, powered by an external source of the appropriate voltage. **Note:** *Do not use the machine's own battery as an incorrect reading may result from stray impulses within the machine's electrical system.*

Check

4 Warm the engine up to normal operating temperature then stop it.

5 On Daytona and Trophy models, remove the right side fairing lower panel as described in Chapter 8.

6 Place a suitable container under the rotor cover to catch any residual oil, then unscrew the retaining bolts and remove the cover squarely from the engine. Install the timing check cover in its place.

7 Identify the timing mark (the F next to the No. 1 (3 cylinder) or No. 1.4 (4 cylinder)) stamped on the rotor.

> **HAYNES HiNT** *The rotor timing mark can be highlighted with white paint to make it more visible under the stroboscopic light.*

8 Connect the timing light to the No. 1 cylinder HT lead as described in the manufacturer's instructions.

9 Start the engine and aim the light through the inspection hole.

10 With the machine idling at the specified speed, the timing mark should align with the pick-up coil centre.

11 Slowly increase the engine speed whilst observing the timing mark. The timing mark should move anti-clockwise, increasing in relation to the engine speed.

12 As already stated, there is no means of adjustment of the ignition timing on these machines. If the ignition timing is incorrect, or suspected of being incorrect, one of the ignition system components is at fault, and the system must be tested as described in the preceding Sections of this Chapter.

13 When the check is complete, fit the original rotor cover and top-up the engine oil if necessary (see Chapter 1).

14 Where applicable, install the fairing panel as described in Chapter 8.

5.1a Igniter location on later Trophy models

5.1b The igniter is located under the right side panel on Thunderbird, Thunderbird Sport, Adventurer and Legend TT models

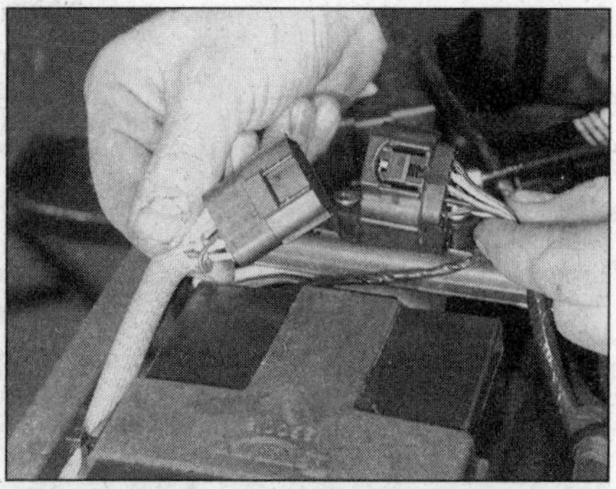

5.2 Disconnect the igniter at its wiring connector rather than at the igniter itself

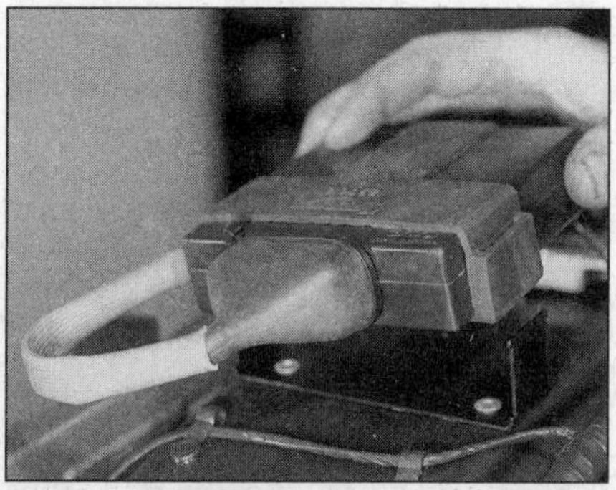

5.3 Free the igniter with its strap from the mounting bracket

Chapter 6
Frame, suspension and final drive

Contents

Degrees of difficulty

Easy, suitable for novice with little experience	**Fairly easy,** suitable for beginner with some experience	**Fairly difficult,** suitable for competent DIY mechanic	**Difficult,** suitable for experienced DIY mechanic	**Very difficult,** suitable for expert DIY or professional

Specifications

Front fork oil level and grade

Oil level is measured from the top of the tube with the fork spring removed and the leg fully compressed.

900 Trophy to VIN 4901*	84 mm, SAE 10
1200 Trophy to VIN 4901*	103 mm, SAE 10
900/1200 Trophy from VIN 4902 to 9082	117 mm (102 mm max), SAE 10
900/1200 Trophy from VIN 9083 to 29155	117 mm (102 mm max), SAE 15
900/1200 Trophy from VIN 29156 to 42274	105 mm, SAE 10
900/1200 Trophy from VIN 42275	133 mm, SAE 10W-20
750 Daytona	139 mm, SAE 10
900/1000/1200 Daytona to VIN 9082	132 mm, SAE 5
900/1200 Daytona from VIN 9083 to 29155	139 mm (132 mm max), SAE 5
900/1200 Daytona from VIN 29156 to 33785	128 mm, SAE 5
900/1200 Daytona from VIN 33786 to 36445	139 mm, SAE 5
900/1200 Daytona from VIN 36446	128 mm, SAE 5
Sprint to VIN 7491	109 mm (97 mm max), SAE 10
Sprint from VIN 7492 to 11541, Sprint Executive	117 mm (102 mm max), SAE 10
Sprint from VIN 11542	117 mm (102 mm max), SAE 15
Sprint Sport	139 mm, SAE 5
Trident to VIN 4901*	94 mm, SAE 10
Trident from VIN 4902 to 44301	109 mm (97 mm max), SAE 10
Trident from VIN 44302	141 mm, SAE 10W-20
750 Speed Triple, 900 Speed Triple up to VIN 29155	141 mm, SAE 10
900 Speed Triple from VIN 29156	130 mm, SAE 10
Thunderbird/Adventurer up to VIN 43509	109 mm, SAE 15
Thunderbird/Adventurer from VIN 43510, Legend TT	126 mm, SAE 10W-20
Thunderbird Sport	145 mm, SAE 5
Tiger up to VIN 43523	130 mm, SAE 10
Tiger from VIN 43524	144 mm, SAE 10W-20

**On Trophy and Trident models to VIN 4901, if Triumph fork modification kits have been fitted then VIN 4902-on oil levels apply.*

Torque settings

Handlebar clamp bolts	
Tiger	18 Nm
Thunderbird Sport	20 Nm
All other models	22 Nm
Yoke pinch bolts	
Top yoke	
Tiger	18 Nm
All other models	20 Nm
Bottom yoke	
Tiger	22 Nm
All other models	20 Nm
Bottom yoke brake hose union assembly bolts	9 Nm
Front forks	
Top bolt	23 Nm
Adjuster (Daytona, Speed Triple, Sprint Sport, Thunderbird Sport)	15 Nm
Damper rod/cartridge bolt	
Trophy, Trident, Sprint, Tiger	60 Nm
Daytona, Speed Triple, Sprint Sport	40 Nm
Thunderbird, Adventurer, Legend TT	20 Nm
Thunderbird Sport	43 Nm
Steering stem nut	65 Nm
Steering head bearing adjuster ring pinch bolt (early models)	7 Nm
Steering head bearing adjuster locknut (later models)	40 Nm
Rear shock absorber and linkage	
Thunderbird, Thunderbird Sport, Adventurer, Legend TT and Tiger	
Shock absorber top mounting bolt.	95 Nm
Shock absorber lower mounting bolt	55 Nm
Linkage connecting rod to swingarm mount	100 Nm
Linkage connecting rod to linkage arm mount	100 Nm
Linkage arm to frame mount	100 Nm
Trident, Trophy, Sprint, Speed Triple and Daytona	
Shock absorber top mounting bolt	95 Nm
Linkage spindle bolt	85 Nm
Linkage spindle clamp bolts	8 Nm
Linkage connecting rod to swingarm mount	55 Nm
Linkage arm to frame mount	100 Nm
Swingarm pivot shaft bolt	85 Nm
Front sprocket nut	132 Nm
Rear sprocket nuts	85 Nm
Centre stand pivot bolts (where applicable)	40 Nm
Sidestand pivot bolt	20 Nm
Sidestand pivot bolt locknut	25 Nm

1 General information

All models use a spine type frame made of micro alloyed high tensile steel, which uses the engine as a stressed member.

Front suspension on Trident, Trophy, Sprint, Thunderbird, Adventurer, Legend TT and Tiger models is by a pair of conventional oil-damped telescopic forks of either Showa or Kayaba manufacture. The Daytona, Speed Triple, Sprint Sport and Thunderbird Sport models have Kayaba cartridge forks, adjustable for preload, compression and rebound damping.

At the rear, an aluminium alloy swingarm acts on a single shock absorber via a two-piece linkage which provides a rising rate system.

Final drive to the rear wheel is by sealed chain. A rubber damper (often called a 'cush drive') is fitted between the rear wheel coupling and the wheel.

2 Frame – inspection and repair

1 The frame should not require attention unless accident damage has occurred. In most cases, frame renewal is the only satisfactory remedy for such damage. A few frame specialists have the jigs and other equipment necessary for straightening the frame to the required standard of accuracy, but even then there is no simple way of assessing to what extent the frame may have been over stressed.

2 After the machine has accumulated a lot of miles, the frame should be examined closely for signs of cracking or splitting at the welded joints. Loose engine mount bolts can cause ovaling or fracturing of the mounting tabs. Minor damage can often be repaired by welding, depending on the extent and nature of the damage.

3 Remember that a frame which is out of alignment will cause handling problems. If misalignment is suspected as the result of an accident, it will be necessary to strip the machine completely so the frame can be thoroughly checked.

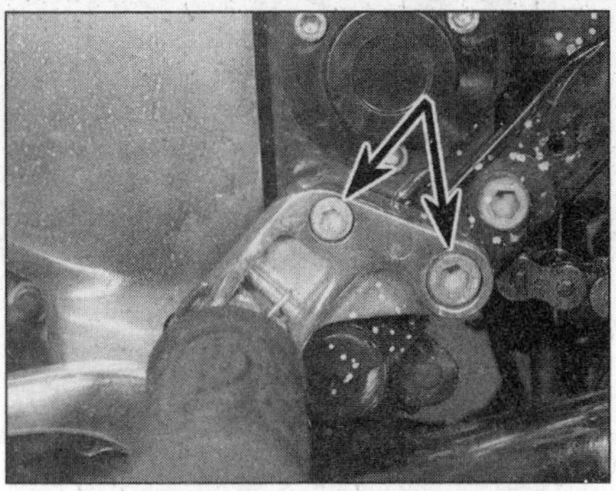

3.3 The left footrest bracket is secured to the frame by two bolts (arrowed)

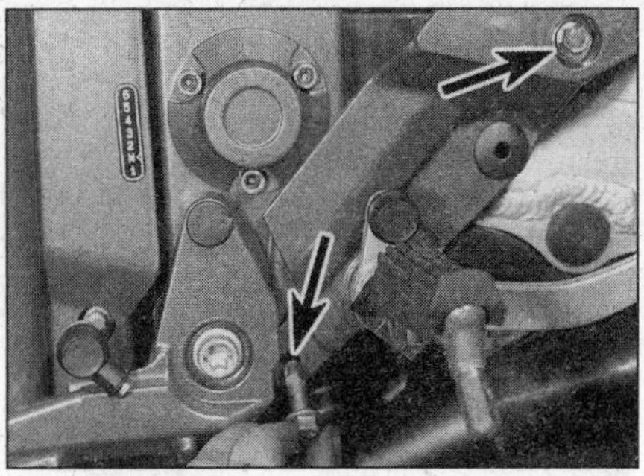

3.13 Remove the cap from the upper bolt, then unscrew both bolts (arrowed) and remove the carrier

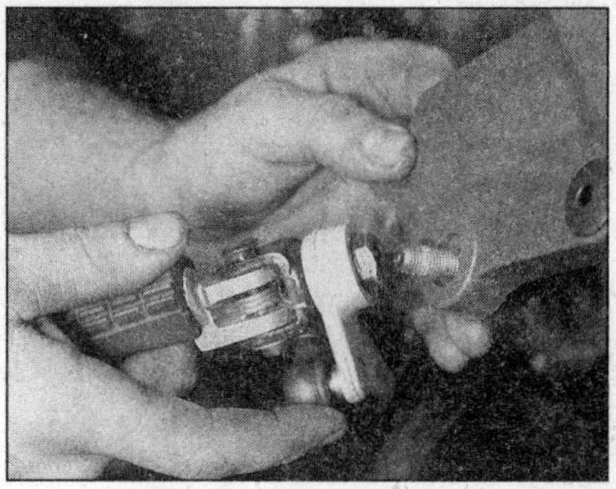

3.14 Unscrew the footrest bracket bolt from behind the carrier

3 Footrests and brackets/carriers – removal and installation

Rider's footrests

Removal

1 Remove the circlip from the end of the pivot pin, then slide out the pivot pin and remove the footrest from the footrest bracket along with its return spring. On Trident, Sprint, Trophy, Daytona, Speed Triple and Tiger models, the footrest rubber can be separated from the footrest by removing its retaining screws.

Installation

2 Installation is the reverse of removal.

Rider's left footrest bracket/carrier

Removal – Thunderbird, Adventurer and Legend TT models

3 Unscrew the two bracket-to-frame bolts, and remove the bracket **(see illustration)**.

Removal – Thunderbird Sport model

4 Detach the link rod from the gearchange shaft lever and pedal by slackening its locknuts and rotating the rod via its knurled centre section so that it unscrews from the lever and pedal at the same time.

5 Remove the two footrest bracket bolts to free the bracket from the frame. The footrest and gearchange pedal can be freed from the bracket by releasing the screw and washer from the inside of the bracket. Note the bush which locates inside the gearchange pedal bore.

Removal – Tiger model

6 On Tiger models the left footrest and the sidestand are mounted on the same bracket. To remove the bracket it is necessary to support the bike using an auxiliary stand. Make sure the bike is securely supported.

7 Detach the link rod from the gearchange pedal by slackening its locknuts and rotating the rod via its knurled centre section so that it unscrews from the lever and pedal at the same time.

8 Unscrew the two bolts securing the sidestand switch to the bracket and remove the switch.

9 Unhook the sidestand return spring, then unscrew the sidestand pivot bolt and remove the stand.

10 Unscrew the gearchange pedal-to-bracket pivot bolt, and remove the pedal.

11 Unscrew the two bolts securing the bracket to the frame and remove the bracket.

Removal – Trident, Sprint (not Executive), Trophy (up to VIN 29155), Daytona and Speed Triple models

12 Detach the link rod from the gearchange shaft lever and pedal by slackening its locknuts and rotating the rod via its knurled centre section so that it unscrews from the lever and pedal at the same time. On models with a dog-leg link rod, slacken off the locknut and unscrew the threaded sleeve to separate the link rod from the shaft lever.

13 Remove the cap from the upper carrier mounting bolt, then unscrew both mounting bolts and remove the carrier, gearchange pedal and footrest assembly **(see illustration)**.

14 Unscrew the bolt located on the back of the carrier and separate the gearchange pedal, pivot bracket and footrest from the carrier **(see illustration)**.

Removal – Sprint Executive and Trophy (from VIN 29156) models

15 Detach the pannier. Remove the two Torx bolts which retain the footrest carrier to the pannier bracket, followed by the bolt and nut which retain the silencer to the footrest carrier.

16 Detach the link rod from the gearchange shaft lever and pedal by slackening its locknuts and rotating the rod via its knurled centre section so that it unscrews from the lever and pedal at the same time **(see illustration)**.

17 The footrest carrier is retained by three bolts, the upper and middle bolt are hidden behind plastic caps and the lower bolt threads into a nut on the inside of the bracket **(see illustration)**. Take note of any washers as the footrest carrier is detached, complete with the gearchange pedal and footrests.

18 If required, the passenger footrest can be freed by removing the nut on the inside of the carrier, and the rider's footrest/gearchange pedal released by removing the bolt on the inside of the carrier. Do not lose the two damping rubbers from the silencer mounting point in the footrest carrier **(see illustration)**.

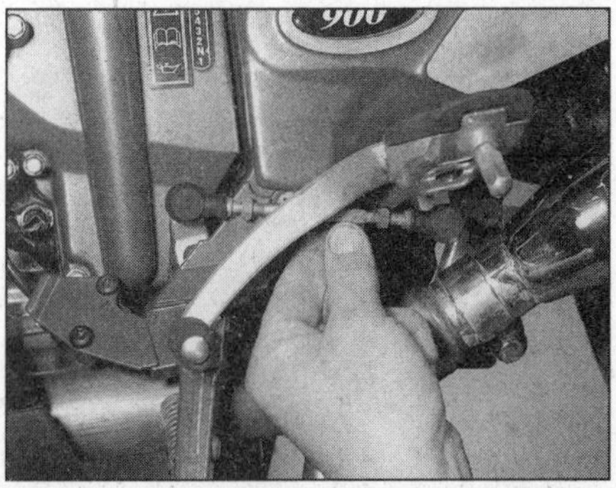

3.16 Unscrew the link rod by rotating its knurled section

3.17 Footrest carrier bolts (arrowed)

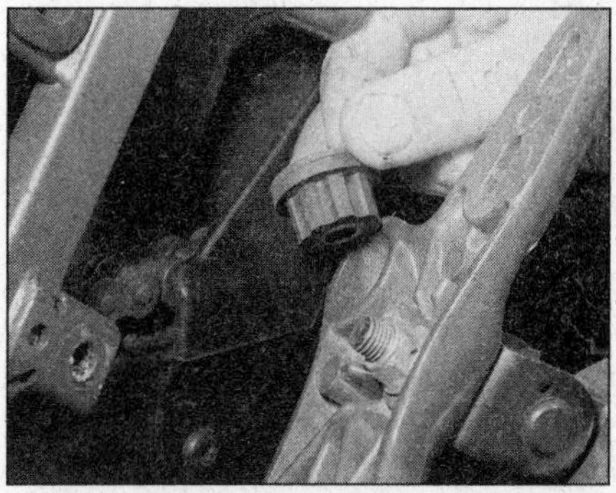

3.18 Damping rubbers locate in each side of silencer mounting point

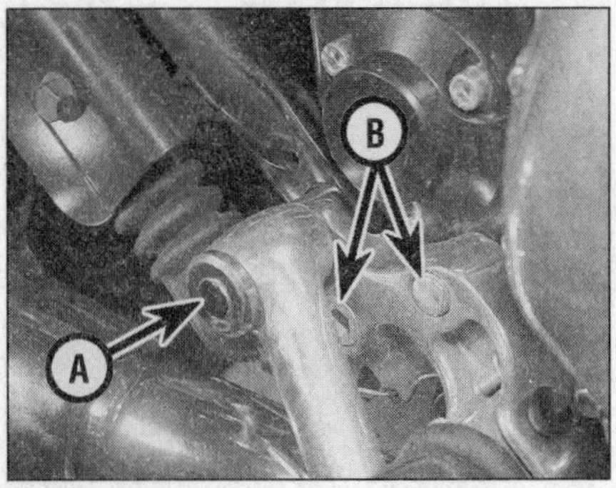

3.22 Remove the cap from the brake pedal pivot bolt (A), then unscrew the bolt and remove the pedal. Footrest bracket is secured by two bolts (B)

Installation – All models

19 Installation is the reverse of removal. On Tiger models, apply a smear of grease to the sidestand pivot bolt and the gearchange pedal pivot bolt. Tighten the bracket mounting bolts securely.

20 On all models except the Thunderbird, Adventurer, Legend TT and Tiger, apply a smear of grease to the bearing surface of the gearchange pedal pivot and a drop of non-permanent thread locking compound to the threads of the bolt.

Rider's right footrest bracket/carrier

Removal – Thunderbird, Adventurer and Legend TT models

21 Remove the split pin and washer (spring clip and washer on later models) and slip the clevis pin from the clevis joining the rear brake pedal to the rear brake master cylinder pushrod.

22 Unhook the brake pedal return spring. Remove the cap, then unscrew the brake pedal pivot bolt and remove the pedal from the bracket **(see illustration)**.

23 Unscrew the two footrest bracket mounting bolts and remove the bracket **(see illustration 3.22)**.

Removal – Thunderbird Sport model

24 Remove the spring clip and the clevis pin from the clevis joining the rear brake pedal to the rear brake master cylinder pushrod **(see illustrations)**.

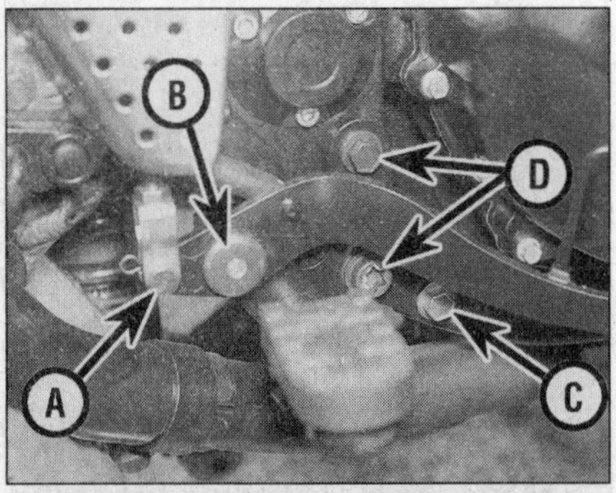

3.26 Release pushrod (A) from brake pedal, then unscrew pedal bolt (B). Sump guard is secured to bracket by bolt (C), and bracket to frame by two bolts (D)

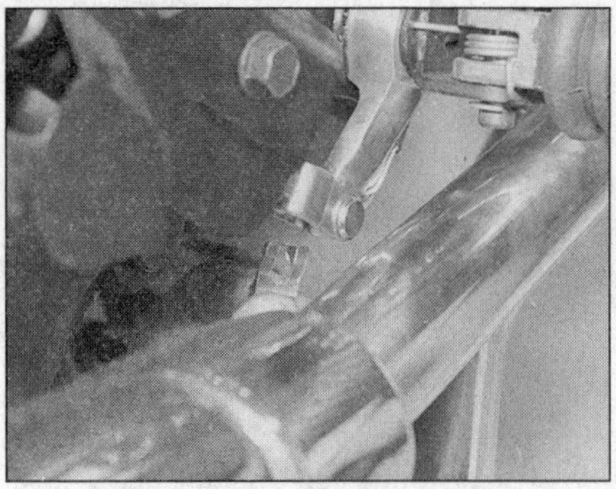

3.24a Prise off the spring clip . . .

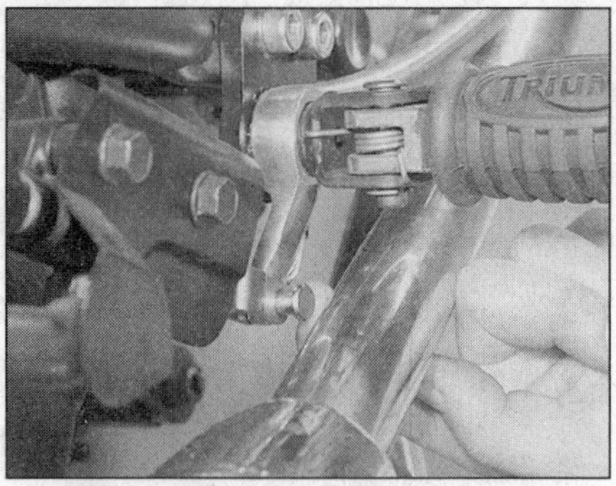

3.24b . . . to allow the clevis pin to be withdrawn

25 Unhook the brake pedal return spring. Remove the two footrest bracket bolts to free the bracket from the frame **(see illustration)**. The footrest and brake pedal can be freed from the bracket by releasing the bolt and washer from the inside of the bracket. Note the bush which locates inside the brake pedal bore.

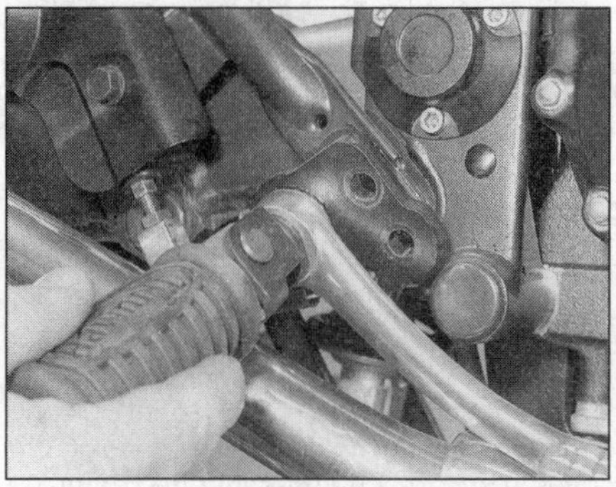

3.25 Remove the two bolts to free the bracket

Removal – Tiger

26 Remove the split pin and the clevis pin from the clevis joining the rear brake pedal to the rear brake master cylinder pushrod **(see illustration)**.

27 Unhook the brake pedal return spring. Unscrew the pivot bolt securing the brake pedal to the bracket and remove the pedal.

28 Unscrew the sump guard-to-bracket bolt, and the two bolts securing the bracket to the frame, and remove the bracket.

Removal – Trident, Sprint (not Executive), Trophy (up to VIN 29155), Daytona and Speed Triple models

29 Remove the split pin and the clevis pin from the clevis joining the rear brake pedal to the rear brake master cylinder pushrod.

30 Remove the cap from the upper footrest carrier mounting bolt, then unscrew both carrier mounting bolts and remove the carrier, brake pedal and footrest assembly.

31 Unhook the brake pedal return spring, then unscrew the pivot bolt on the back of the carrier and separate the rear brake pedal, pivot bracket and footrest from the carrier.

Removal – Sprint Executive and Trophy (from VIN 29156) models

32 Detach the pannier. Remove the two Torx bolts which retain the footrest carrier to the pannier bracket, followed by the bolt and nut which retain the silencer to the footrest carrier.

33 Remove the split pin and washer (or spring clip and washer) from the clevis pin joining the rear brake pedal to the rear brake master cylinder pushrod **(see illustrations)**. Slip the clevis pin our and separate the clevis

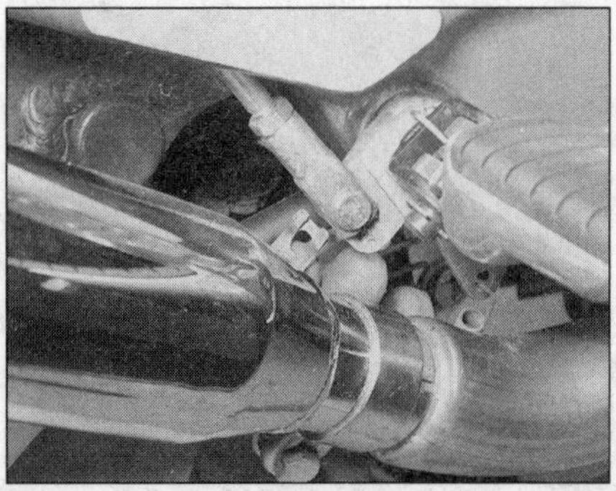

3.33a Withdraw the spring clip . . .

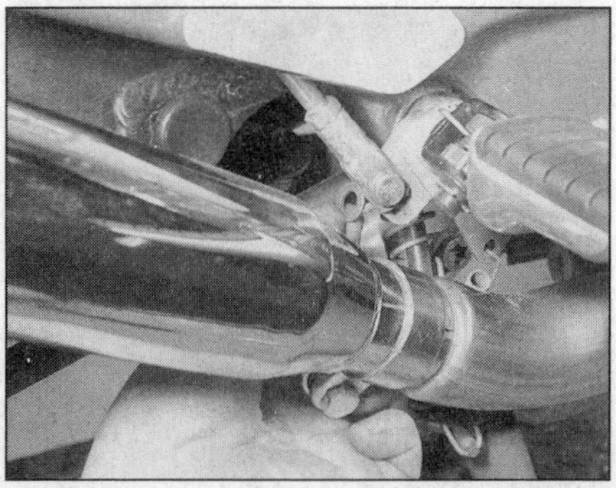

3.33b . . . and its washer . . .

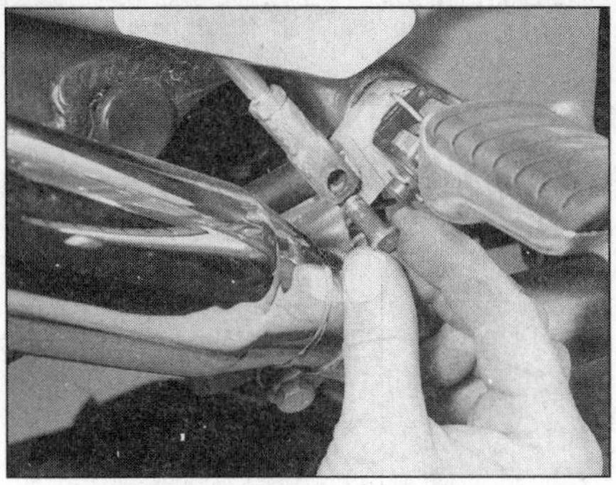

3.33c . . . to free the clevis pin

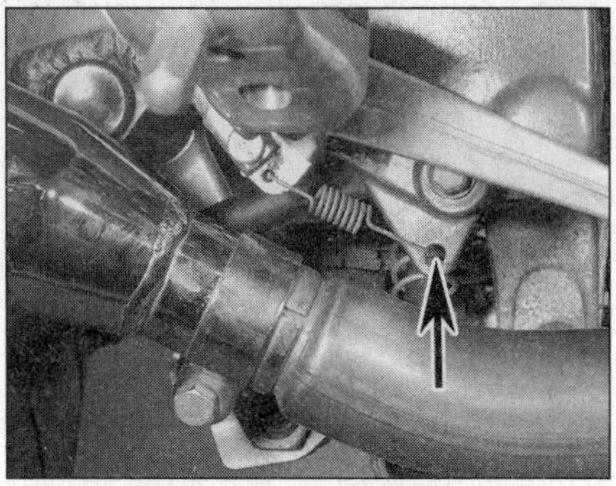

3.33d Disconnect the return spring from the brake pedal (arrowed)

3.34a Footrest carrier bolts (arrowed)

from the pedal. Unhook the brake pedal return spring **(see illustration)**.

34 The footrest carrier (control plate) is retained by three bolts, the upper and middle bolt are hidden behind plastic caps and the lower bolt threads into a nut on the inside of the bracket **(see illustrations)**. Take note of any washers as the footrest carrier is detached, complete with the brake pedal and footrests.

35 If required, the passenger footrest can be freed by removing the nut on the inside of the carrier, and the rider's footrest/brake pedal released by removing the screw on the inside of the carrier. Do not lose the two damping rubbers from the silencer mounting point in the footrest carrier **(see illustration 3.18)**.

Installation – all models

36 Installation is the reverse of removal. Apply a smear of grease to the bearing surface of the brake pedal pivot and a drop of non-permanent thread locking compound to the threads of the brake pedal pivot bolt (where applicable). Fit a new split pin to the brake pushrod clevis pin (early models), and do not forget to hook up the brake pedal return spring **(see illustration)**.

Passenger footrests

Removal

37 Remove the circlip from the end of the pivot pin, then slide out the pivot pin and remove the footrest from the pivot bracket. As the footrest is removed, recover the detent ball and spring, noting how they fit. On Trident, Sprint, Trophy, Daytona and Speed Triple models the footrest rubber can be separated from the footrest by unscrewing the retaining screws.

Installation

38 Installation is the reverse of removal using a new circlip.

Passenger footrest brackets/carriers

Removal

39 On Trident, Sprint, Trophy (up to VIN 29155), Daytona and Speed Triple models, remove the nut securing the footrest pivot bracket to the carrier and remove the bracket **(see illustration)**.

40 On later Trophy models (from VIN 29156) and the Sprint Executive, remove the footrest carrier as described for the rider's footrest bracket above. The passenger footrest bracket is retained to the carrier by a nut on the inside of the carrier.

41 On Thunderbird, Thunderbird Sport, Adventurer and Legend TT models, the footrest bracket is retained to the frame by a nut **(see illustration)**; if you're working on the side which also doubles as the mounting for the silencer, first support or tie the silencer to avoid putting too much strain on the rest of the system. On Tiger models the carrier can be removed if necessary by unscrewing the two mounting bolts, having first prised out their caps **(see illustration)**.

Installation

42 Installation is the reverse of removal.

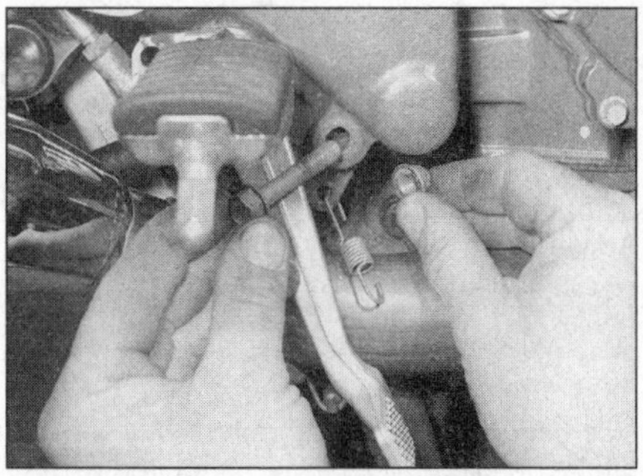

3.34b Note that the lower bolt threads into a nut on the inside

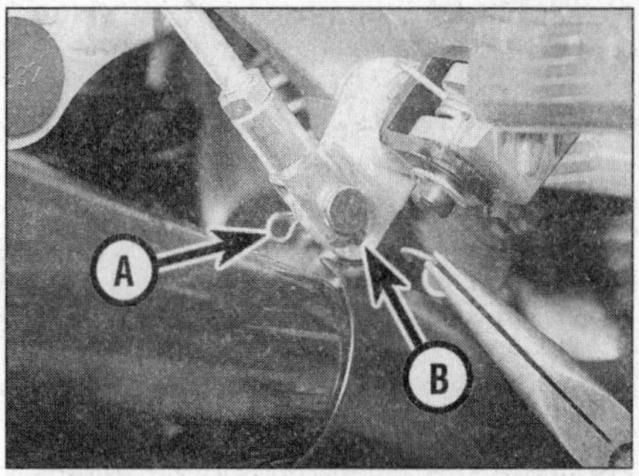

3.36 Fit a new split pin to the pushrod (A) and hook the return spring into the hole in the pedal (B)

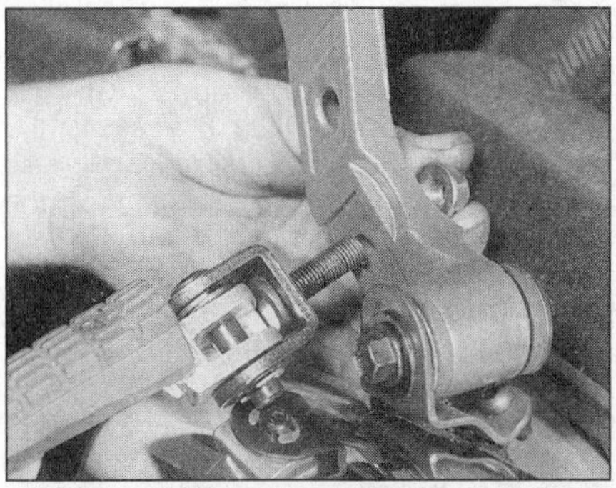

3.39 Unscrew the nut at the back of the carrier and remove the footrest pivot bracket

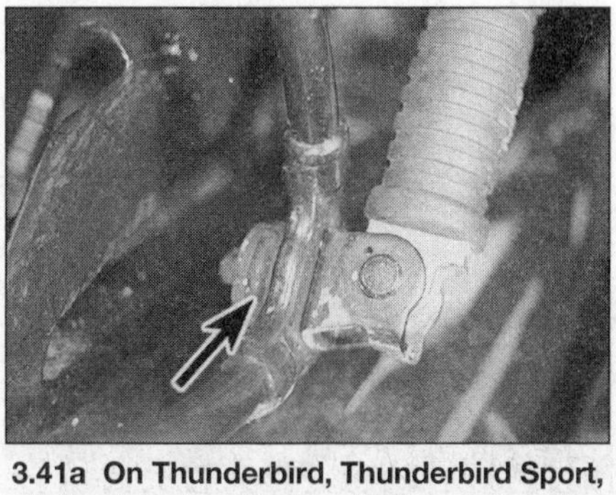

3.41a On Thunderbird, Thunderbird Sport, Adventurer and Legend TT models note that the footrest bracket bolt also secures the silencer (arrowed)

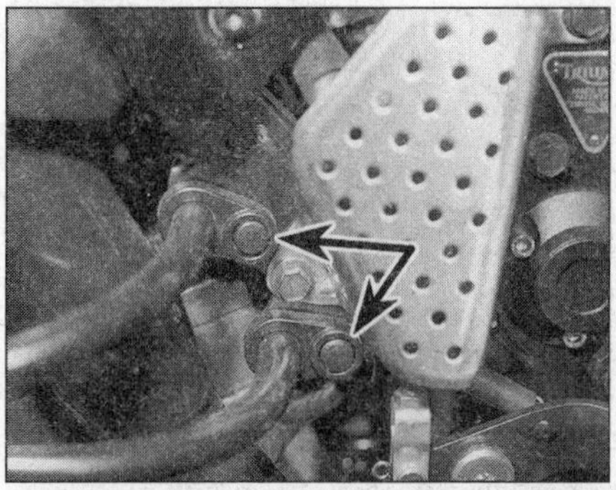

3.41b On Tiger models the footrest carrier is secured to the frame by two bolts (arrowed)

4 Stands – removal and installation

Centrestand – where fitted

1 The centre stand is attached to the frame and linkage carriers by two countersunk bolts passing through sleeves in the stand pivots. Support the bike on its sidestand and free one end of the centre stand return spring. Counterhold the pivot bolt nut and unscrew the pivot bolt from each side **(see illustration)**. Remove the stand and withdraw the sleeves from its pivot.

2 Inspect the stand, sleeves and bolts for signs of wear and renew if necessary. Apply a smear of grease to the sleeves and bolts and fit the stand back on the bike, tightening the bolts to the torque setting specified at the beginning of the Chapter. Reconnect the return spring.

3 Make sure the return spring is in good condition and is capable of holding the stand up when not in use. A broken or weak spring is an obvious safety hazard.

Sidestand – all models

4 The sidestand is attached to a bracket on the frame. An extension spring anchored to the bracket ensures that the stand is held in the retracted position. The sidestand incorporates a switch which is part of the ignition cut-out circuit. Certain models have a warning light on the instrument panel which illuminates when the ignition is ON and the sidestand is down.

5 Support the bike on its centre stand. Where no centre stand is fitted, use an auxiliary stand to support the bike.

6 Free the stand spring and unscrew the locknut from the pivot bolt. Unscrew the pivot bolt to free the stand from its bracket. On installation apply grease to the pivot bolt shank and tighten the pivot bolt, followed by the locknut, to their specified torque settings. Reconnect the sidestand spring and check that it holds the stand securely up when not in use – an accident is almost certain to occur if the stand extends while the bike is in motion.

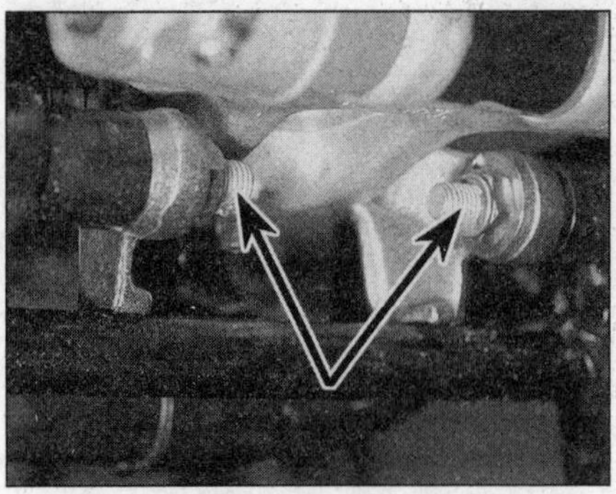

4.1 Centre stand pivot bolts are secured by nuts on inside of linkage carriers (arrowed)

7 For check and removal and installation of the sidestand switch see Chapter 9.

5 Handlebars – removal and installation

Thunderbird, Thunderbird Sport, Adventurer, Legend TT and Tiger models

Removal

1 Remove the left and right side handlebar switches as described in Chapter 9.

2 Detach the clutch and front brake master cylinders from the handlebar (see Chapters 2 and 7 respectively).

3 Unscrew the handlebar clamp bolts and remove the handlebars **(see illustration)**. Two handlebar clamps are used on the Tiger and Thunderbird Sport model, and a single combined clamp on the Thunderbird, Adventurer and Legend TT models. If necessary, unscrew the handlebar weight retaining screws, then remove the weight from the end of the handlebar. The throttle grip can be slid off the handlebar end, whereas the left side grip must be slit with a knife and peeled off the handlebar if renewal is required.

4 The handlebar clamp base is secured to the top yoke by a throughbolt and nut. Remove the R-pin (where fitted) from the bottom of the handlebar clamp base mounting bolt, then unscrew the nut (and where fitted, the washer) securing the clamp base to the top yoke and remove the base **(see illustration)**. Note the fitting of the rubber damper on each side of the top yoke on Thunderbird (up to VIN 45964), Adventurer (up to VIN 71698) and Tiger models; inspect the dampers for signs of wear or damage and renew them if necessary.

5.3 Tiger handlebar clamp bolts (arrowed)

Installation

5 Installation is the reverse of removal, noting the following.

a) *If the left side grip is being renewed, degrease the end of the handlebar and use adhesive to bond the new grip in place.*
b) *Align the punch mark(s) on the handlebar with the mating surfaces of the handlebar clamps* ***(see illustration)****.*
c) *Tighten the clamp bolts to the torque setting specified at the beginning of the Chapter.*

5.4 Remove the split pin from the clamp base mounting bolt (arrowed), then unscrew the nut and remove the base

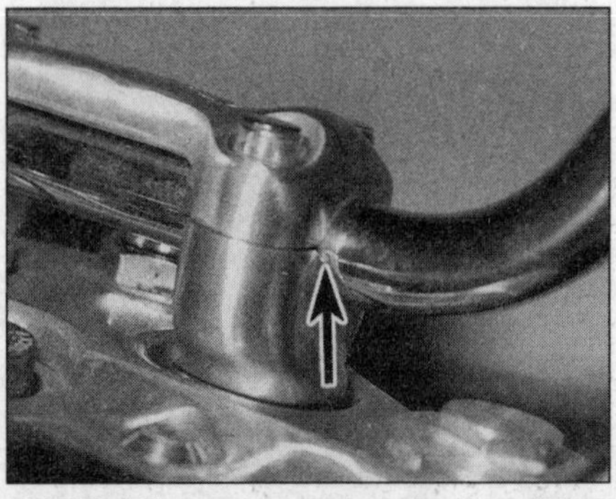

5.5 Align the punch mark on the handlebar (arrowed) with the clamp mating surfaces (Thunderbird shown)

Trophy, Trident and Sprint models

Right handlebar – removal

6 Remove the right side handlebar switch as described in Chapter 9.

7 Remove the front brake master cylinder assembly as described in Chapter 7.

8 On early Trophy (up to VIN 29155), all Trident and Sprint models, prise out the caps, then unscrew the bolts securing the handlebar to the top yoke and remove the handlebar **(see illustrations 5.12a, b and c)**. On later Trophy models (from VIN 29156), remove the top yoke cover (it is retained by two press studs at the front and a single stud on the inside **(see illustrations 5.12d and e)**), then slacken off the pinch bolt and remove the retaining bolt to free the handlebar **(see illustration 5.12f)**. If necessary, unscrew the handlebar weight retaining screw, then remove the weight from the end of the handlebar and slide off the throttle twistgrip.

Right handlebar – installation

9 Installation is the reverse of removal. If removed, apply a smear of grease to the

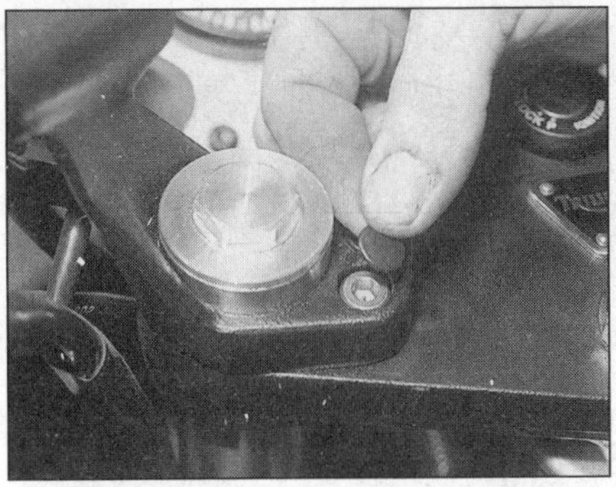

5.12a Prise out the caps . . .

5.12b . . . then unscrew the two handlebar clamp bolts . . .

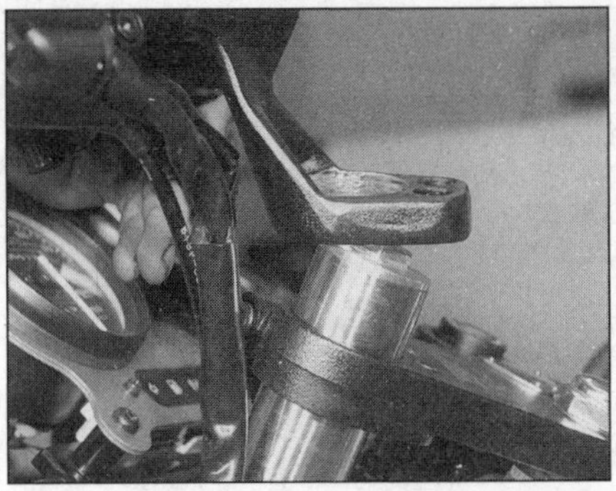

5.12c . . . and lift the handlebar off the fork

5.12d Remove the two press studs at the front of the cover . . .

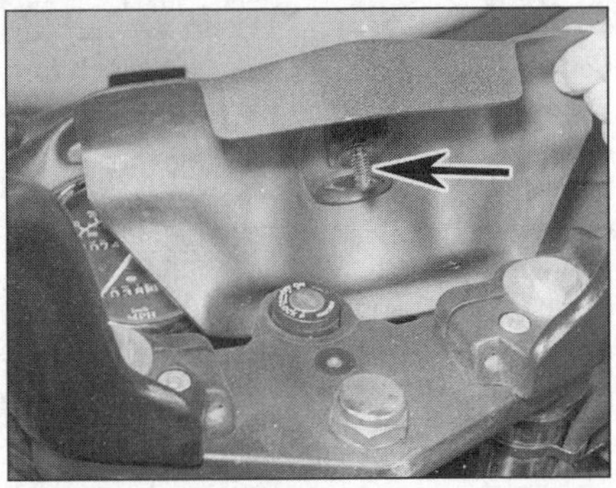

5.12e . . . and prise the inner stud out of the yoke

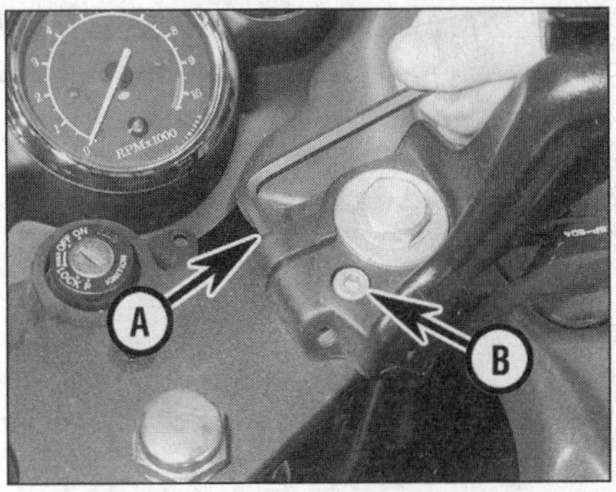

5.12f Slacken the pinch bolt (A) and remove the handlebar retaining bolt (B)

throttle twistgrip. Tighten the handlebar clamp bolts to the torque setting specified at the beginning of the Chapter.

Left handlebar – removal

10 Remove the left side handlebar switch as described in Chapter 9.

11 Remove the clutch master cylinder assembly as described in Chapter 2.

12 On early Trophy (up to VIN 29155), all Trident and Sprint models, prise out the caps, then unscrew the bolts securing the handlebar to the top yoke and remove the handlebar **(see illustrations)**. On later Trophy models (from VIN 29156), remove the top yoke cover (it is retained by two press studs at the front and a single stud on the inside **(see illustrations)**), then slacken off the pinch bolt and remove the retaining bolt to free the handlebar **(see illustration)**. If necessary, unscrew the handlebar weight retaining screw, then remove the weight from the end of the handlebar. If renewal of the handlebar grip is necessary, slit the grip with a knife and peel it off the handlebar.

Left handlebar – installation

13 Installation is the reverse of removal, noting that if the grip is being renewed, the handlebar end must be degreased and an adhesive applied to bond the grip in place. Tighten the handlebar clamp bolts to the torque setting specified at the beginning of the Chapter.

Daytona and Speed Triple models

Right handlebar – removal

14 Remove the right side handlebar switch as described in Chapter 9.

15 Remove the front brake master cylinder assembly as described in Chapter 7.

16 If necessary, unscrew the handlebar weight retaining screw, then remove the weight from the end of the handlebar and slide off the throttle twistgrip.

17 As it is not possible to remove the top yoke with the front forks in place, the right side fork must be lowered or removed to allow removal of the handlebar. See Section 6 for fork removal.

Right handlebar – installation

18 Install the handlebar and front fork as described in Section 6.

19 If removed, apply a smear of grease to the throttle twistgrip and slide the grip on the handlebar, then install the weight and securely tighten the screw.

20 Install the front brake master cylinder assembly as described in Chapter 7.

21 Install the handlebar switch (Chapter 9).

Left handlebar – removal

22 Remove the left side handlebar switch as described in Chapter 9.

23 Remove the clutch master cylinder assembly as described in Chapter 2.

24 If necessary, unscrew the handlebar weight retaining screw, then remove the weight from the end of the handlebar. If renewal of the handlebar grip is necessary, slit the grip with a knife and peel it off the handlebar.

25 As it is not possible to remove the top yoke with the front forks in place, the left side fork must be lowered or removed to allow removal of the handlebar. See Section 6 for fork removal.

Left handlebar – installation

26 Install the handlebar and front fork as described in Section 6.

27 If the grip is being renewed, the handlebar end must be degreased and an adhesive applied to bond the grip in place. Install the weight and securely tighten the screw.

28 Install the clutch master cylinder assembly as described in Chapter 2.

29 Install the handlebar switch (Chapter 9).

6 Forks – removal and installation

Removal

Caution: Although not strictly necessary, before removing the forks it is recommended that any fairing panels (where fitted) are removed. This should

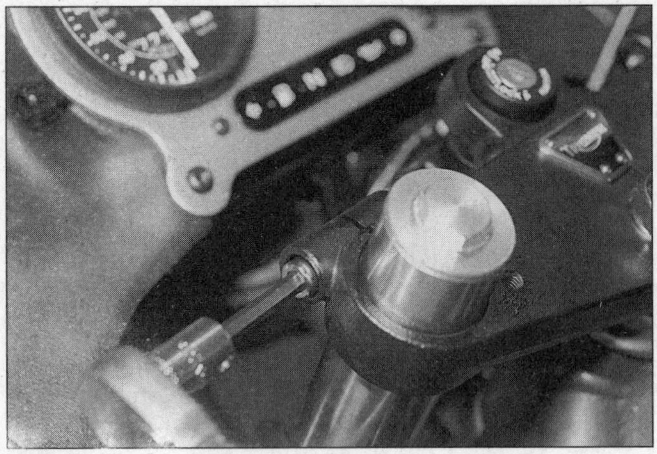

6.6 Slacken the top yoke pinch bolts

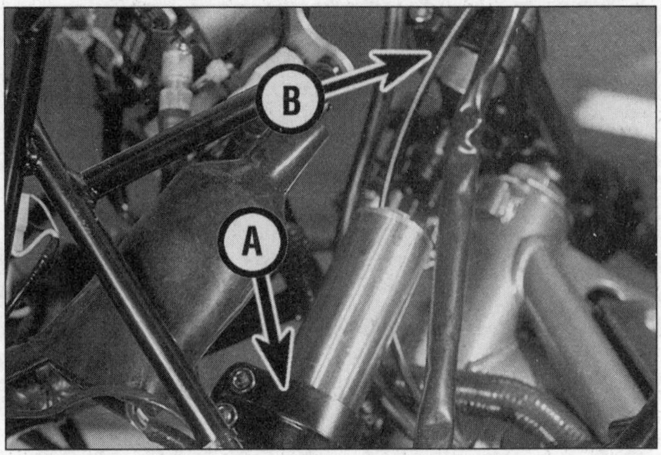

6.7 Slide each fork up through the bottom yoke (A) and the top yoke (B)

prevent any accidental damage to their finish (see Chapter 8).

Note: *If the fork legs are to be dismantled it is preferable to adjust the preload setting (where applicable) to minimum as described in Section 12, then slacken the top bolts whilst the forks are still held in the yokes.*

1 Remove the front wheel as described in Chapter 7.

2 Remove the front mudguard as described in Chapter 8.

3 Slacken, but do not remove, the bottom yoke pinch bolts.

4 On Daytona and Speed Triple models, slacken but do not remove both left and right handlebar clamp bolts.

5 On Trophy, Trident and Sprint models, detach the handlebars from the top yoke and move them aside, making sure they are supported so that the master cylinder reservoirs are upright and no strain is placed on the hoses (see Section 5).

6 Slacken but do not remove the top yoke pinch bolts, and remove the forks by twisting them and pulling them downwards **(see illustration)**. On Daytona and Speed Triple models, once the forks are removed, make sure the handlebars are supported so that the master cylinder reservoirs are upright and no strain is placed on their hoses. On Thunderbird, Thunderbird Sport, Adventurer, Legend TT, Speed Triple and later Trident models, the forks pass through the headlight mounting tubes. When removing the forks make sure the headlight is supported. Take care not to lose the mounting tube rubber grommets.

> **HAYNES HiNT** ***If the fork legs are seized in the yokes, spray the area with penetrating oil and allow time for it to soak in before trying again.***

Installation

7 Remove all traces of corrosion from the fork tubes and the yokes and slide the forks back into place **(see illustration)**. On Thunderbird, Thunderbird Sport, Adventurer, Legend TT, Speed Triple and later Trident models make sure the forks pass through the headlight mounting tubes and that the tube rubber grommets remain correctly in place. On Daytona and Speed Triple models make sure the forks pass through the handlebar clamps.

8 Position the top edge of each fork tube the specified distance above the top surface of the top yoke.

Trophy, Trident and Sprint up to VIN 29155	25 mm above
Trophy, Trident and Sprint from VIN 29156	20 mm above
Daytona and Speed Triple up to VIN 29155	28 mm above
Daytona and Speed Triple from VIN 29156	Level
Thunderbird, Thunderbird Sport, Adventurer, Legend TT and Tiger	Level

Note that the measurement is to the top of the fork tube, not to the top of the fork tube top bolt **(see illustration)**. Tighten the top and bottom yoke pinch bolts to the specified torque settings **(see illustration)**.

9 On Daytona and Speed Triple models, align

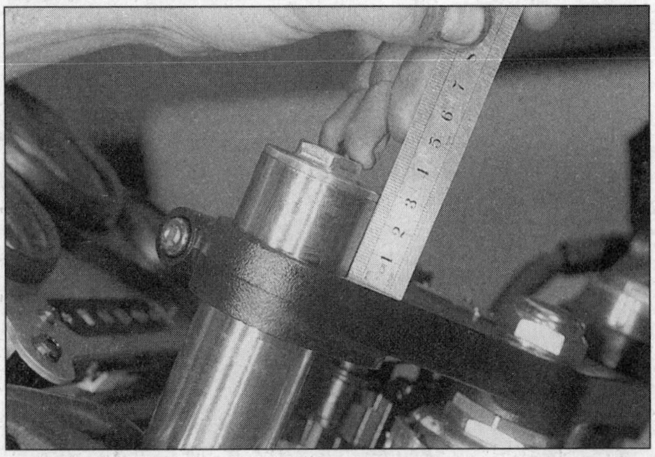

6.8a Set the height of the forks in the top yoke in accordance with the text

6.8b Tighten the bottom and top yoke pinch bolts to the specified torque setting

each handlebar so that it abuts the lug on the underside of the top yoke, then tighten their clamp bolts to the specified torque setting.

10 On Trophy, Trident and Sprint, mount the handlebars on the top yoke and tighten their bolts to the specified torque setting. Insert the caps into the bolt heads (on later Trophy models install the top yoke cover).

11 If the fork legs have been dismantled, the fork tube top bolts should now be tightened to the specified torque setting.

12 Install the front mudguard as described in Chapter 8.

13 Install the front wheel as described in Chapter 7.

14 Adjust the fork settings (where possible) as described in Section 12. Check the operation of the front forks and brake before taking the machine out on the road.

7 Forks – disassembly, inspection and reassembly

Trophy, Trident, Sprint (not Sprint Sport), Thunderbird, Adventurer, Legend TT and Tiger models

Disassembly

1 Always dismantle the fork legs separately to avoid mixing parts and causing accelerated wear. Store all components in separate, clearly marked containers **(see illustration)**.

2 Before dismantling the fork give some thought to the means of slackening the damper rod bolt. If the special tool or a home-made equivalent is not available (see Step 7), it is advised that the damper rod bolt be slackened at this stage. Compress the fork tube in the slider so that the spring exerts maximum pressure on the damper rod head, then have an assistant unscrew the damper rod bolt from the base of the fork slider. On Tiger models, free the gaiter clamps and slip the gaiter off the fork tube.

3 If the fork top bolt was not slackened with the fork in situ, carefully clamp the fork tube in a vice, taking care not to overtighten or score its surface, then slacken the fork top bolt.

4 Unscrew the fork top bolt from the top of the fork tube.

Warning: The fork spring is pressing on the fork top bolt with considerable pressure. Unscrew the bolt very carefully, keeping a downward pressure on it and release it slowly as it is likely to spring clear. It is advisable to wear eye and face protection when carrying out this task.

5 Remove the spacer, then slide the fork tube down into the slider and withdraw the spring seat and the spring from the tube, noting which way up they fit.

6 Invert the fork leg over a suitable container and pump the fork vigorously to expel as much fork oil as possible.

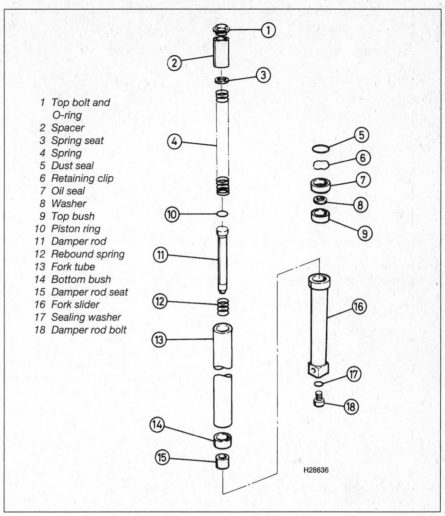

1 Top bolt and O-ring
2 Spacer
3 Spring seat
4 Spring
5 Dust seal
6 Retaining clip
7 Oil seal
8 Washer
9 Top bush
10 Piston ring
11 Damper rod
12 Rebound spring
13 Fork tube
14 Bottom bush
15 Damper rod seat
16 Fork slider
17 Sealing washer
18 Damper rod bolt

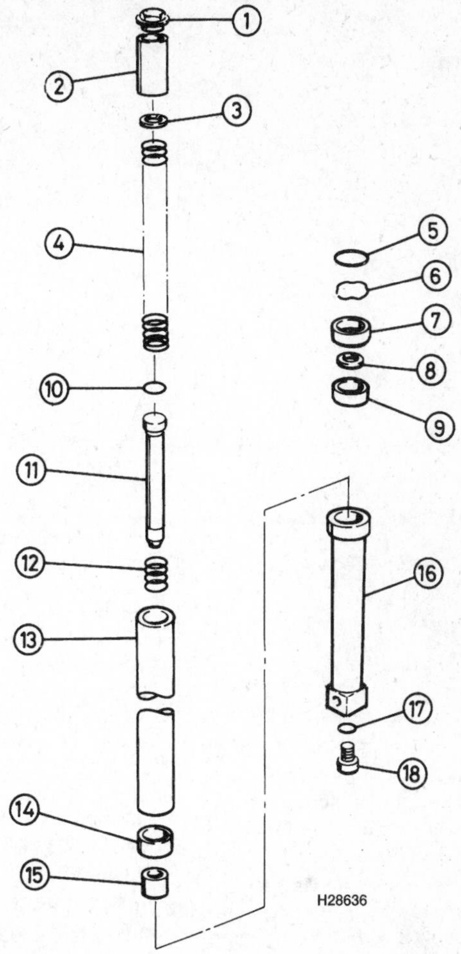

7.1 Front fork detail – Trophy, Trident, Sprint (not Sprint Sport), Thunderbird, Adventurer, Legend TT and Tiger models

7 Prise out the end cap (where fitted) from the base of the fork slider. If the damper rod bolt was not slackened before dismantling the fork, a special tool (Pt. No. 3880090) or home-made equivalent, will be needed to stop the damper rod from rotating inside the fork tube when the damper rod bolt is unscrewed. With the tool engaged in the head of the damper rod, remove the bolt and its copper sealing washer from the bottom of the slider **(see Tool Tip)**. Discard the sealing washer as a new one must be used on reassembly.

8 Withdraw the damper rod from the fork

TOOL TIP

A damper rod holding tool can be made quite easily by threading or pinning a 30 mm nut on the end of a steel bar about 14 inches long, then sawing or filing flats on the other end of the bar so that it can be held with an adjustable spanner.

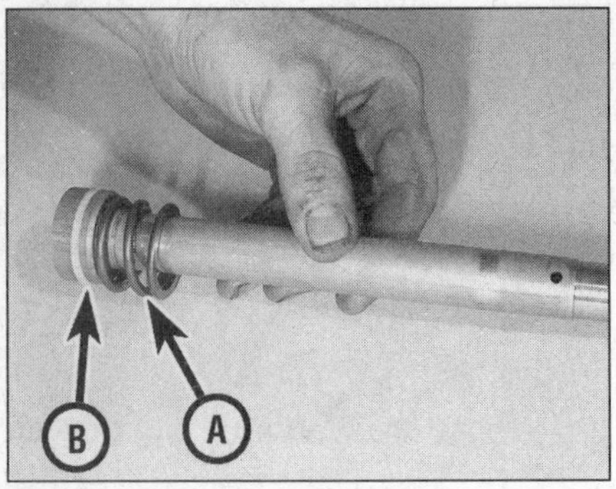

7.8 Withdraw the damper rod assembly, and remove the rebound spring (A) and the piston ring (B)

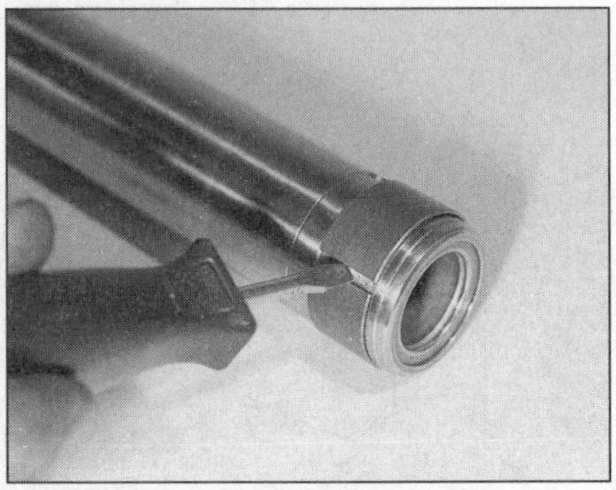

7.17 Prise the ends of the bottom bush apart with a flat-bladed screwdriver to remove it from the fork tube

tube **(see illustration)**. Remove the rebound spring, and remove the piston ring from the groove in the damper rod. Discard the piston ring – a new one must be used on reassembly.

9 Carefully prise out the dust seal from the top of the slider to gain access to the oil seal retaining clip **(see illustration)**. Discard the dust seal as a new one must be used.

10 Carefully remove the clip whilst taking care not to scratch the surface of the tube **(see illustration)**.

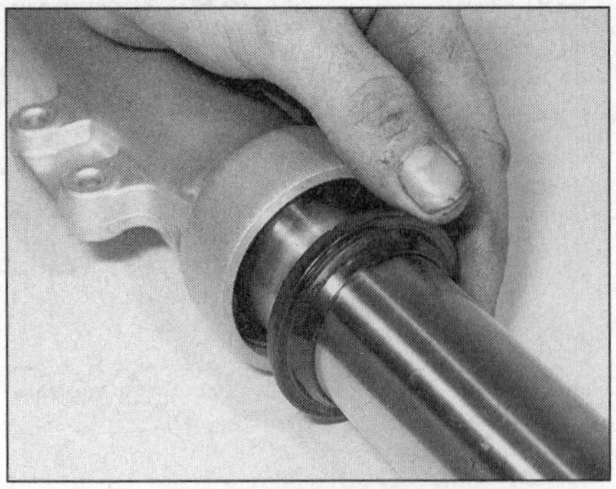

7.9 Use a flat-bladed screwdriver to prise out the dust seal . . .

11 To separate the tube from the slider it will be necessary to displace the top bush and oil seal. The bottom bush should not pass through the top bush, and this can be used to good effect. Push the tube gently inwards until it stops against the damper rod seat. Take care not to do this forcibly or the seat may be damaged. Then pull the tube sharply outwards until the bottom bush strikes the top bush. Repeat this operation until the top bush and seal have been displaced from the slider.

12 With the tube removed, slide off the oil seal and washer, noting which way up they fit. Discard the oil seal as a new one must be used. The top bush can then also be slid off its upper end.

13 Tip the damper rod seat out of the slider, noting which way up it fits.

Inspection

14 Clean all parts in solvent and blow them dry with compressed air, if available. Check the fork tube for score marks, scratches, flaking of the chrome finish and excessive or abnormal wear. Look for dents in the tube and renew the tube in both forks if any are found. Check the fork seal seat for nicks, gouges and scratches. If damage is evident, leaks will occur.

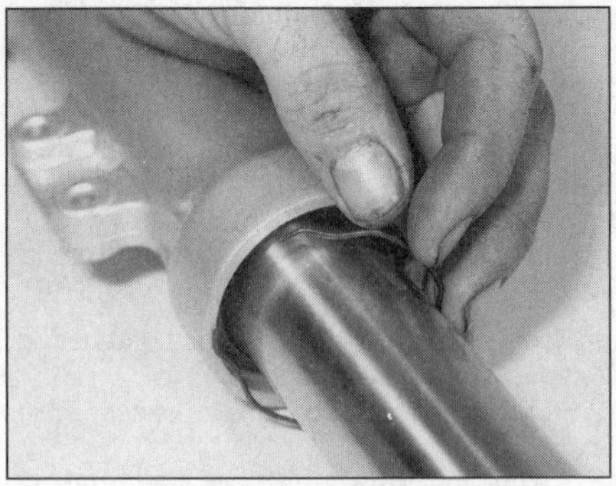

7.10 . . . and the retaining clip from the top of the fork slider

15 Have the fork tube checked for runout at a dealer service department or other repair shop.

Caution: If it is bent, the tube should not be straightened; renew it.

16 Check the spring for cracks and other damage. If it is defective or sagged, renew both fork springs. Never renew only one spring.

17 Examine the working surfaces of the two bushes; if worn they must be renewed. Before removing the bush from the fork tube check with a Triumph dealer whether the bush is available as a separate part. To remove the bush from the fork tube, prise it apart at the slit and slide it off. Make sure the new one seats properly **(see illustration)**.

Reassembly

18 Install a new piston ring into the groove in the damper rod head, and slide the rebound spring over the bottom of the assembly **(see illustrations)**.

19 Insert the damper rod into the fork tube and slide it into place so that it projects fully from the bottom of the tube. Install the seat on the bottom of the damper rod so that the

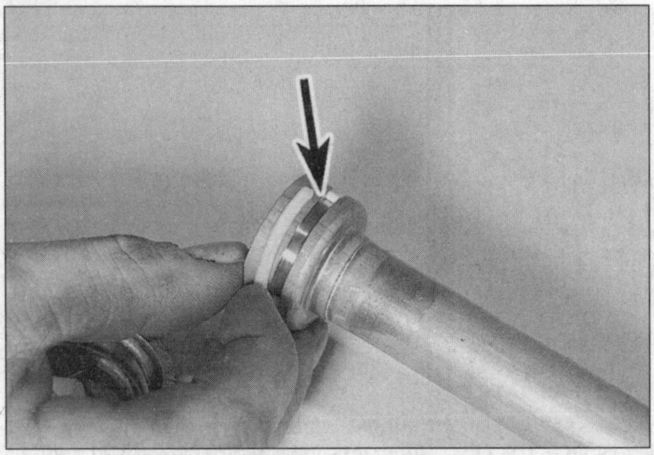

7.18a Fit a new piston ring into the groove in the damper assembly head (arrowed) . . .

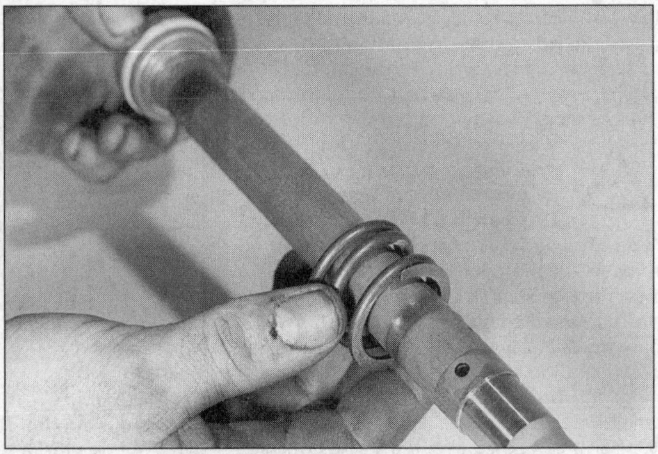

7.18b . . . and slide the rebound spring over the bottom of the assembly

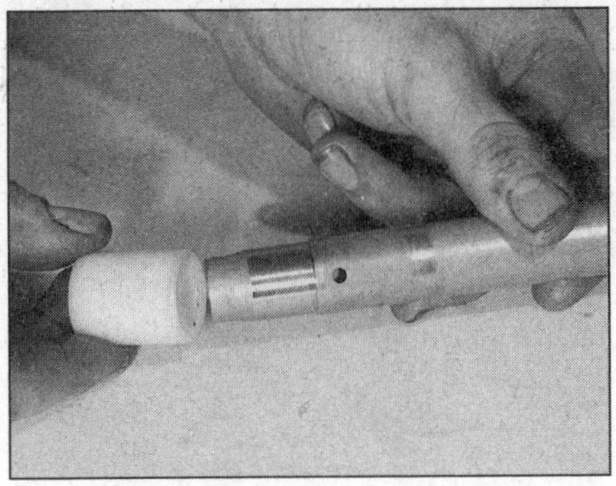

7.19 Slide damper assembly into the fork tube so that it protrudes, then fit the seat to the bottom of the damper assembly

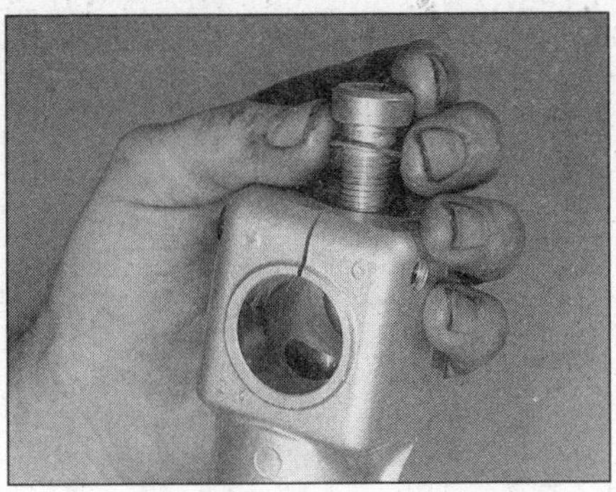

7.20a Fit a new sealing washer to the damper assembly bolt . . .

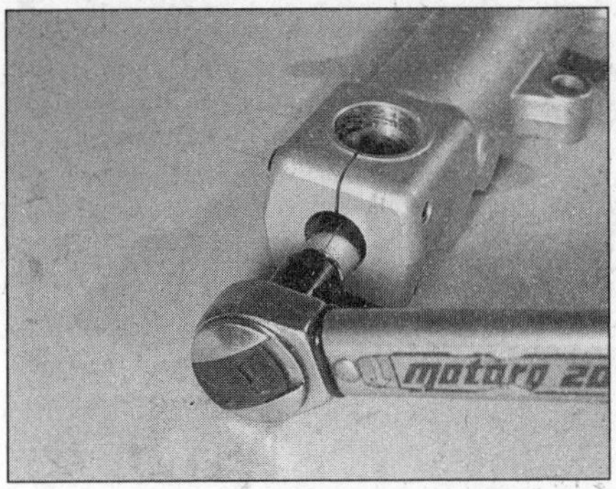

7.20b . . . then install the bolt and tighten it to the specified torque setting

lipped end of the seat faces the damper rod **(see illustration)**.

20 Oil the fork tube and bottom bush and insert the assembly into the slider. Fit a new copper sealing washer to the damper rod bolt and install the bolt into the bottom of the slider. Tighten the bolt to the specified torque setting **(see illustrations)**. Use the method employed on dismantling (see Step 7) to prevent the damper rod rotating inside the fork tube when the bolt is tightened. Alternatively, temporarily install the fork spring, spacer and top bolt (see Steps 26 and 27) to hold the damper rod.

21 Push the fork tube fully into the slider, then oil the top bush and slide it down over the tube. Press the bush squarely into its recess in the slider as far as possible, then install the washer **(see illustrations)**. Either use the service tool (Pt. No. 3880080) or a suitable piece of tubing to tap the bush fully into place; the tubing must be slightly larger in diameter than the fork tube and slightly smaller in diameter than the bush recess in the slider **(see illustration)**. Take care not to scratch the fork tube during this operation; it is best to make sure that the fork tube is pushed fully into the slider so that any accidental scratching is confined to the area above the oil seal.

22 When the bush is seated fully and squarely in its recess in the slider (remove the washer to check, wipe the recess clean, then reinstall the washer), install the new oil seal. Smear the seal's lips with fork oil and slide it over the tube so that its spring side faces downwards, towards the slider **(see illustration)**.

23 Place a large plain washer against the oil seal (to protect its surface) and drive the seal into place as described in Step 21 until the retaining clip groove is visible above the seal. Once the seal is correctly seated, remove the washer and fit the retaining clip, making sure it is correctly located in its groove **(see illustration 7.10)**.

24 Lubricate the lips of the new dust seal then slide it down the fork tube and press it into position **(see illustration 7.9)**.

25 Slowly pour in small quantities of the specified grade of fork oil at a time, and pump the fork to distribute the oil evenly. Note that specific oil quantities are not available; the oil level must be measured and adjustment made by adding or subtracting oil. Fully compress the fork tube into the slider and measure the fork oil level **(see illustration)**. Add or remove fork oil until the oil is at the level specified in the Specifications Section of this Chapter.

26 Clamp the slider in a vice via the brake caliper mounting lugs, taking care not to overtighten and damage them. Pull the fork tube out of the slider as far as possible then install the spring, with its closer-wound coils at the top, followed by the spring seat, with its

7.21a Slide the top bush down the fork tube and into the top of the slider . . .

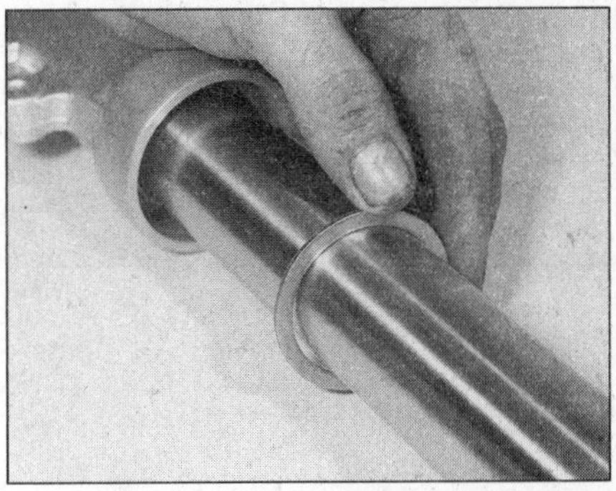

7.21b . . . followed by the washer

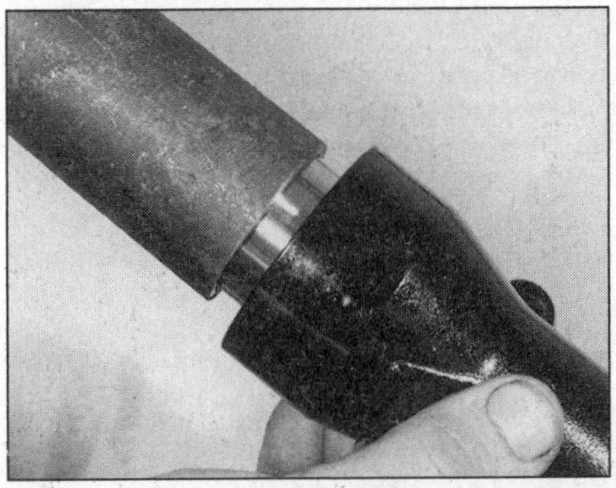

7.21c Use a piece of tubing as a drift to drive the top bush squarely into the slider

7.22 Remove the washer to check that the top bush is seated, then install the oil seal, with its spring side facing down

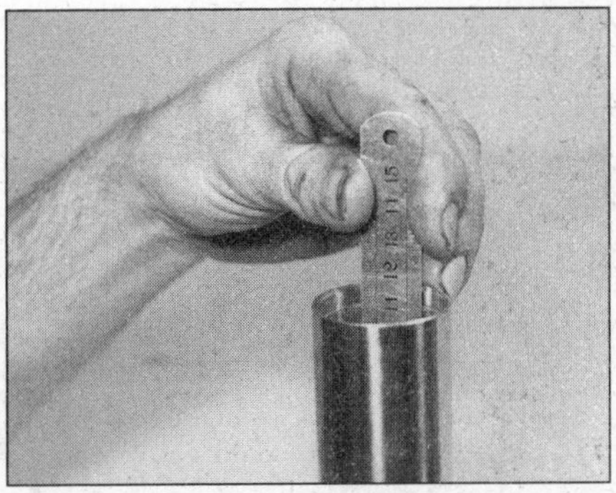

7.25 Check the oil level with the fork held vertical

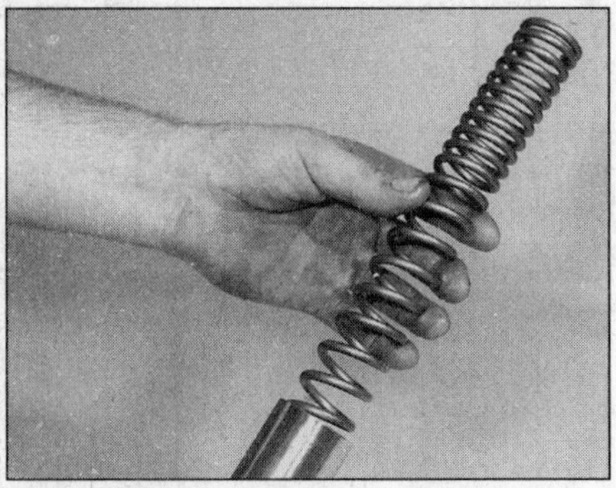

7.26a Install the fork spring making sure its closer-wound coils are at the top

7.26b Install the spring seat, with its shoulder fitting into the spring

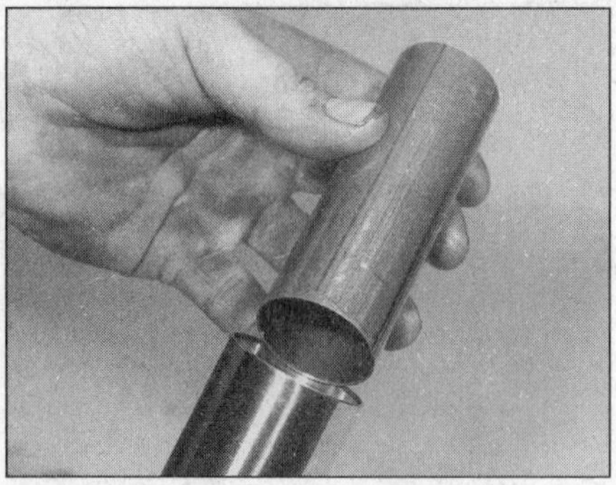

7.26c Fit the spacer into the fork tube

7.27 Fit a new O-ring to the top bolt, then install the bolt into the fork tube

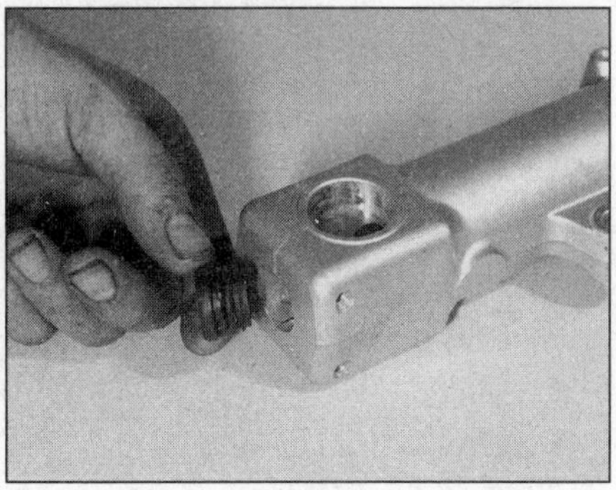

7.28 Fit the cap into the bottom of the fork

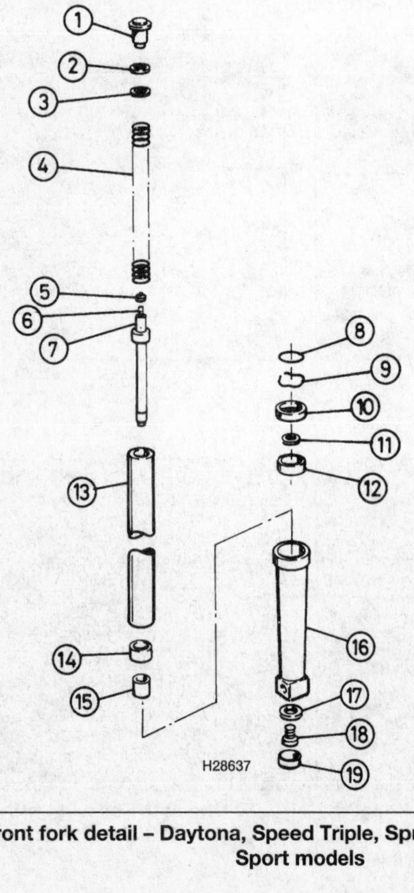

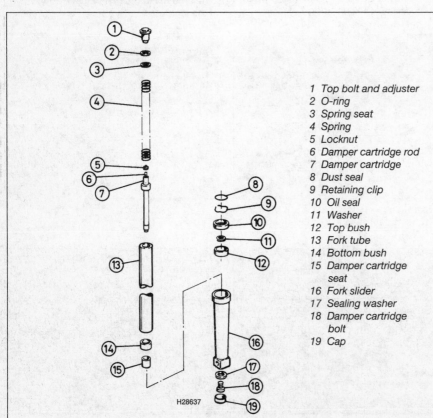

1 Top bolt and adjuster
2 O-ring
3 Spring seat
4 Spring
5 Locknut
6 Damper cartridge rod
7 Damper cartridge
8 Dust seal
9 Retaining clip
10 Oil seal
11 Washer
12 Top bush
13 Fork tube
14 Bottom bush
15 Damper cartridge seat
16 Fork slider
17 Sealing washer
18 Damper cartridge bolt
19 Cap

7.31 Front fork detail – Daytona, Speed Triple, Sprint Sport and Thunderbird Sport models

shoulder inserted into the spring, and the spacer **(see illustrations)**.

27 Fit a new O-ring to the fork top bolt and thread the bolt into the top of the fork tube **(see illustration)**.

Warning: It will be necessary to compress the spring by pressing it down using the top bolt to engage the threads of the top bolt with the fork tube. This is a potentially dangerous operation and should be performed with care, using an assistant if necessary.

Wipe off any excess oil before starting to prevent the possibility of slipping. Keep the fork tube fully extended whilst pressing on the spring. Screw the top bolt carefully into the fork tube making sure it is not cross-threaded. **Note:** *The top bolt can be tightened to the specified torque setting at this stage if the tube is held between the padded jaws of a vice, but do not risk distorting the tube by doing so. A better method is to tighten the top bolt when the fork has been installed in the bike and is securely held in the yokes.*

28 Fit the end cap (where fitted) into the bottom of the fork slider **(see illustration).**

29 On Tiger models, install the gaiter.

30 Install the forks as described in Section 6.

Daytona, Speed Triple, Sprint Sport and Thunderbird Sport models

Disassembly

31 Always dismantle the fork legs separately to avoid interchanging parts and thus causing an accelerated rate of wear. Store all components in separate, clearly marked containers **(see illustration)**.

32 Prise out the end cap from the base of the fork slider. Compress the fork tube in the slider so that the spring exerts maximum pressure on the damper cartridge, then have an assistant unscrew the damper cartridge bolt from the base of the fork slider.

33 If the fork top bolt was not slackened with the fork in situ, carefully clamp the fork tube in a vice, taking care not to overtighten or score its surface, then unscrew the fork top bolt/adjuster from the tube.

34 Hold the fork vertical and slide the fork tube down into the slider. Counterhold the locknut

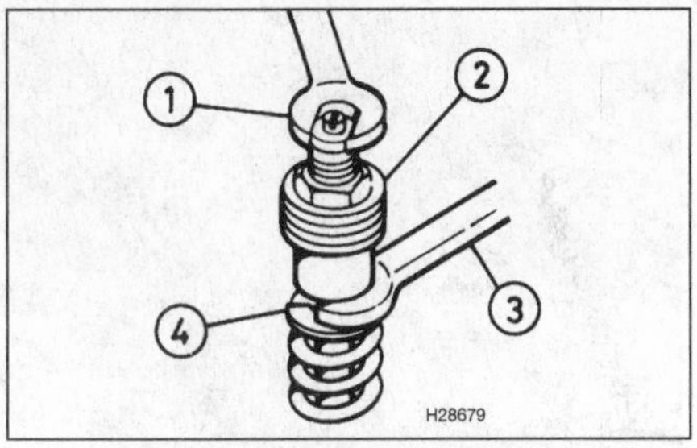

7.34 Releasing the top bolt from the damper cartridge rod

1 Open-ended spanner on preload adjuster flats
2 Top bolt
3 Open-ended spanner on locknut
4 Spring seat

just below the top bolt/adjuster with an open-ended spanner and unscrew the preload adjuster to release the top bolt from the damper cartridge rod **(see illustration)**. Unscrew the locknut from the damper cartridge rod.

Warning: The fork spring may be exerting considerable pressure on the spring seat, making this a potentially dangerous operation. Restrain the fork spring to prevent the locknut and spring seat from being sprung clear, and slowly release the spring once the locknut has been removed. Wipe off as much oil as possible to minimise the risk of your hands slipping on oily components and enlist the help of an assistant.

35 Withdraw the spring seat and the spring from the tube, noting which way up they fit. Invert the fork leg over a suitable container and pump the fork vigorously to expel as much fork oil as possible.

36 Remove the damper cartridge bolt with its copper washer from the end of the slider and withdraw the cartridge from the tube. Discard the copper washer as a new one must be used on reassembly.

37 Refer to Steps 9 to 13 above.

Inspection

38 Refer to Steps 14 to 17 above.

Reassembly

39 Insert the damper cartridge seat into the slider so that its larger diameter is

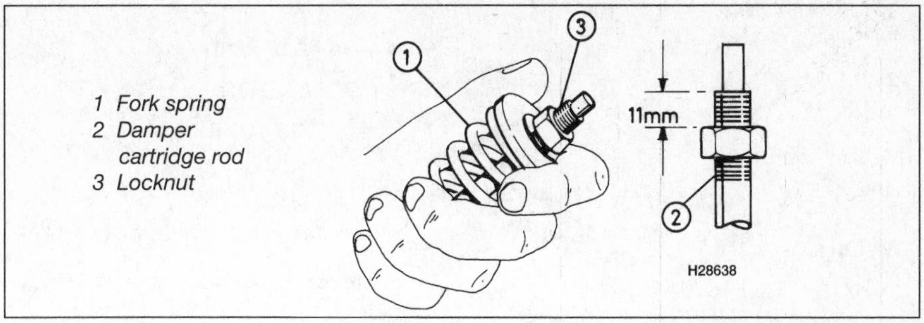

7.43 Screw the locknut onto the damper cartridge rod so that there is 11 mm of thread above the locknut

downwards. Apply fork oil to the damper cartridge and insert it into the fork tube.

40 Oil the fork tube and bottom bush and insert the fork tube into the slider. Fit a new copper sealing washer to the damper cartridge bolt and install the bolt in the bottom of the slider so that it screws into the base of the damper cartridge.

Caution: Do not attempt to hold the cartridge rod in order to tighten the bolt, temporarily refit the fork spring, spring seat and top bolt (see Steps 43 to 45) and compress the fork to hold the cartridge.

41 Refer to Steps 21 to 25 above.

42 Withdraw the damper cartridge rod as far as possible and install the spring, with its closer-wound coils at the top, followed by the spring seat, with its shoulder inserted into the spring.

43 Compress the spring and thread the locknut onto the damper cartridge rod until there is 11 mm of thread above the locknut **(see illustration)**.

Warning: This is a potentially dangerous operation and should be performed with care, using an assistant if necessary. Wipe any excess oil off the spring before starting to prevent the possibility of slipping.

44 Fit a new O-ring to the fork top bolt and lubricate it with a smear of fork oil. Screw the top bolt/adjuster onto the damper cartridge rod; counterhold the locknut with an open-ended spanner and tighten the adjuster. Watch carefully that the locknut and damper cartridge rod do not rotate as the adjuster is tightened – if they do, reposition the locknut on the rod as described in Step 43.

45 Carefully screw the top bolt into the fork tube making sure it is not cross-threaded. **Note:** *The top bolt can be tightened to the specified torque setting at this stage if the tube is held between the padded jaws of a vice, but do not risk distorting the tube by doing so. A better method is to tighten the top bolt when the fork leg has been installed and is securely held in the yokes.*

46 Fit the end cap (where fitted) into the bottom of the fork.

47 Install the forks as described in Section 6.

8 Steering stem – removal and installation

Caution: Although not strictly necessary, before removing the steering stem it is recommended that the fuel tank and fairing panels (if fitted) be removed. This will prevent accidental damage to the paintwork.

Removal

1 For improved access, remove the main fairing on Trophy, Sprint, Daytona and Tiger models (see Chapter 8). Remove the forks as described in Section 6 of this Chapter.

2 Unscrew the bolts securing the brake hose union assembly (where fitted) to the bottom yoke **(see illustration)**. Do not disconnect the hoses from the union assembly.

3 On Trident and Speed Triple models, disconnect the horn wires, then unscrew the horn mounting bolts and remove the horns from the bottom yoke.

4 On all models except the Daytona and Speed Triple, detach the handlebars from the top yoke (see Section 5 of this Chapter). If required, also remove, or detach and move aside, the instrument panel (see Chapter 9). This enables the top yoke to be moved further aside than would otherwise be allowed. If the top yoke is to be removed from the bike altogether, it is also necessary to disconnect the ignition switch wiring at its connector, and on Tiger models to remove the cable-ties from underneath the clamp.

5 Remove the steering stem nut and washer **(see illustration)**.

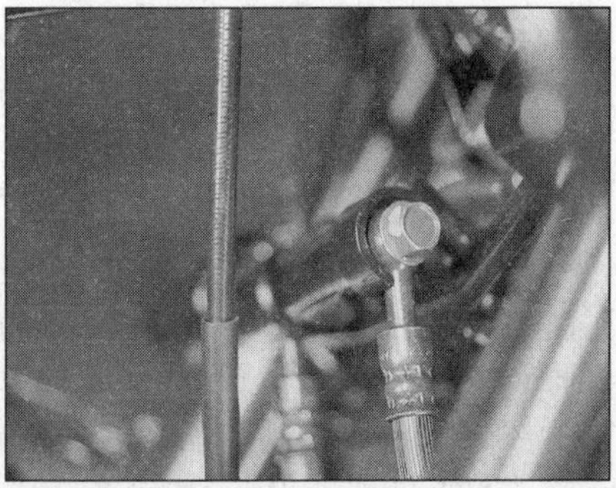

8.2 Remove the brake hose union from the bottom yoke with the hoses still connected

8.5 Unscrew the steering stem nut and remove the washer

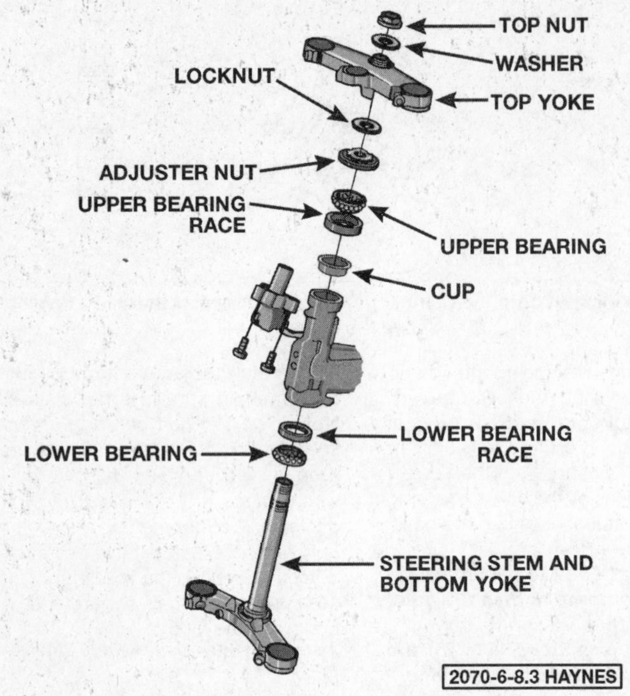

8.7 Steering stem detail

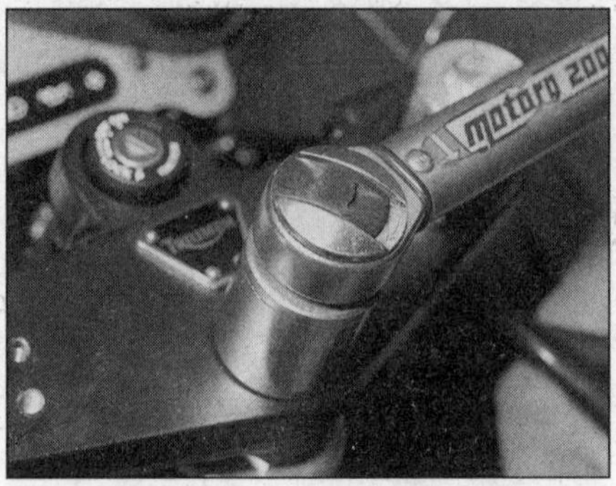

8.15 Tighten the steering stem nut to the specified torque setting

6 On early models, slacken off the pinch bolt in the side of the bearing adjuster ring **(see illustration 5.8 in Chapter 1)** and whilst supporting the bottom yoke, unscrew and remove the adjuster ring from the steering stem.

7 On later models unscrew the locknut and whilst supporting the bottom yoke, unscrew and remove the adjuster nut from the steering stem **(see illustration)**. These nuts are very narrow and whilst removal can be accomplished with normal DIY tools, subsequent tightening and bearing freeplay adjustment is made easier with the use of the Triumph service tools (Pt. No. 3880140).

8 Gently lower the bottom yoke and steering stem out of the frame. Move the top yoke forwards to disengage the ignition main switch from the steering lock bracket welded to the frame.

9 Remove the upper bearing from the top of the steering head. Remove all traces of old grease from the bearings and races and check them for wear or damage as described in Section 9. **Note:** *Do not attempt to remove the races from the frame or the lower bearing from the steering stem unless they are to be renewed.*

Installation

10 Smear a liberal quantity of grease on the bearing races in the frame. Work the grease well into both the upper and lower bearings. Install the upper bearing in the top of the steering head.

11 Install the top yoke on the steering head, engaging the ignition main switch with the steering lock bracket.

12 Carefully lift the steering stem/bottom yoke up through the frame. Thread the adjuster ring (early models) or adjuster nut (later models) on the steering stem before the stem passes up through the top yoke. Tighten the adjuster to preload the bearings, then turn the steering stem from lock to lock approximately 5 times to settle the bearings and races in position. After preloading the bearings, slacken the adjuster until pressure is just released, then turn it slowly clockwise until resistance is just evident. The object is to set the adjuster so that the bearings are under a very light loading, just enough to remove any freeplay.

Caution: Take great care not to apply excessive pressure because this will cause premature failure of the bearings.

13 On early models, when the setting is correct, tighten the pinch bolt to the specified torque setting to lock the adjuster ring's position.

14 On later models, when the setting is correct, hold the adjuster nut with one spanner and tighten the locknut against it with another spanner. **Note:** *The torque setting for the locknut can be applied if using the service tool (see Step 7); the torque wrench locates in the square machined in the tool* ***(see illustrations 5.17a and b in Chapter 1).***

15 Install the steering stem washer and nut to secure the top yoke, tightening the nut to the specified torque setting **(see illustration)**. If removed, fit the handlebars and instrument panel, connect the speedometer cable and the ignition switch wiring, and fit any cable-ties as necessary.

16 On Trident and Speed Triple models, install the horns on the bottom yoke and tighten their retaining bolts securely, then fit the horn wires.

17 Where applicable, fit the brake hose union assembly to the bottom yoke and tighten the retaining bolts to the specified torque setting.

18 Install the fork legs as described in Section 6 of this Chapter.

19 Carry out a check of the steering head bearing freeplay as described in Chapter 1, and if necessary re-adjust.

9 Steering head bearings – inspection and renewal

Inspection

1 Remove the steering stem as described in Section 8.

2 Remove all traces of old grease from the bearings and races and check them for wear or damage.

3 The races should be polished and free from indentations. Inspect the bearing rollers for signs of wear, damage or discoloration, and examine their retainer cage for signs of cracks or splits. If there are signs of wear on any of the above components both upper and lower bearing assemblies must be renewed as a set.

Renewal

4 The races are an interference fit in the steering head and can be tapped from position with a suitable drift. Prise out the plastic cap from the base of the steering head on later models. Tap firmly and evenly around each race to ensure that it is driven out squarely. It may prove advantageous to curve the end of the drift slightly to improve access.

5 Alternatively, the races can be removed using a slide-hammer type bearing extractor; these can often be hired from tool shops.

6 The new races can be pressed into the

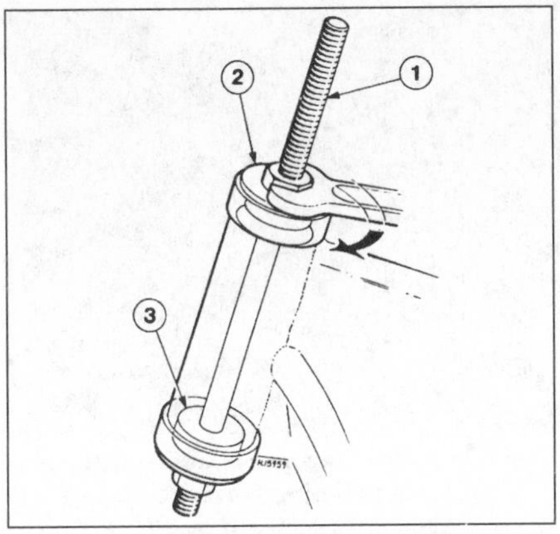

9.6 Drawbolt arrangement for fitting steering stem bearing races

1 Long bolt or threaded bar
2 Thick washer
3 Guide for lower race

head using a drawbolt arrangement **(see illustration)**, or by using a large diameter tubular drift which bears only on the outer edge of the race. Ensure that the drawbolt washer or drift (as applicable) bears only on the outer edge of the race and does not contact the working surface. Alternatively, have the races installed by a Triumph dealer equipped with the bearing race installing tools. Note that the cup must be in place in the frame before installing the upper bearing race.

7 To remove the lower bearing from the steering stem, use two screwdrivers placed on opposite sides of the race to work it free. If the bearing is firmly in place it will be necessary to use a bearing puller, or in extreme circumstances to split the bearing's inner section.

8 Fit the new lower bearing onto the steering stem. A length of tubing with an internal diameter slightly larger than the steering stem will be needed to tap the new bearing into position. Ensure that the drift bears only on the inner edge of the bearing and does not contact the rollers.

9 Install the steering stem as described in Section 8.

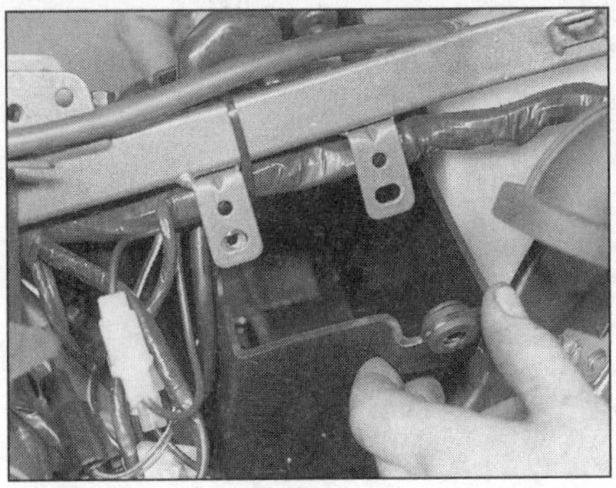

10.4a Move the battery box out to one side . . .

10 Rear shock absorber – removal and installation

Removal

1 In order to remove the shock absorber, it is necessary to support the bike securely in an upright position using an auxiliary stand or hoist. On Thunderbird, Thunderbird Sport, Adventurer, Legend TT and Tiger models the bike must be supported so that the rear wheel is just resting on the ground (ie so that the bike's weight is off the rear suspension), but also so that the rear suspension will not drop, with the possible risk of personal injury, when the shock absorber mounting bolts are removed. On all other models the bike must be supported so that the rear wheel is off the ground. This is to give room for the wheel to be lowered when the shock absorber top mounting bolt is removed so that the suspension linkage clears the exhaust system to enable the linkage spindle to be removed; it is advisable to place a block of wood or other support under the wheel to avoid having to manually support the wheel and so that the rear suspension will not drop, with the possible risk of personal injury, when the top shock absorber mounting bolt is removed. After the bolt is removed, take the weight of the wheel, remove the support and gently lower the wheel to the ground.

10.4b . . . then pull the inner end up and out from the top

2 Remove the seat and the side panels as described in Chapter 8.

3 Remove the battery as described in Chapter 1 and the auxiliary air chamber(s) as described in Chapter 4.

4 Remove the remaining battery box mounting bolt from the bottom of the box. The battery box comes out from the top, but first has to be twisted on its end by moving out to one side and then pulling the end up and out **(see illustrations)**.

5 On Tiger models, remove the fuel tank as described in Chapter 4, then unscrew the four bolts securing the fuel tank bracket to the frame and remove the bracket. Unscrew the retaining clamps securing the shock absorber reservoir to the left side of the cylinder head and remove the reservoir **(see illustration)**. On Thunderbird Sport models, release the clamps securing the shock absorber reservoir to the frame **(see illustration 12.37)**.

Caution: Do not attempt to separate the reservoir from the shock absorber.

6 On models which have a remote preload adjuster, unscrew the bolts securing the preload adjuster to the top of the frame **(see illustration)**. If a remote type damping adjuster is fitted, remove the screws securing the damping adjuster to the right side of the frame **(see illustration)**.

7 If fitted, remove the bolts securing the bottom of the mudflap to the swingarm.

8 On Thunderbird, Thunderbird Sport, Adventurer, Legend TT and Tiger models,

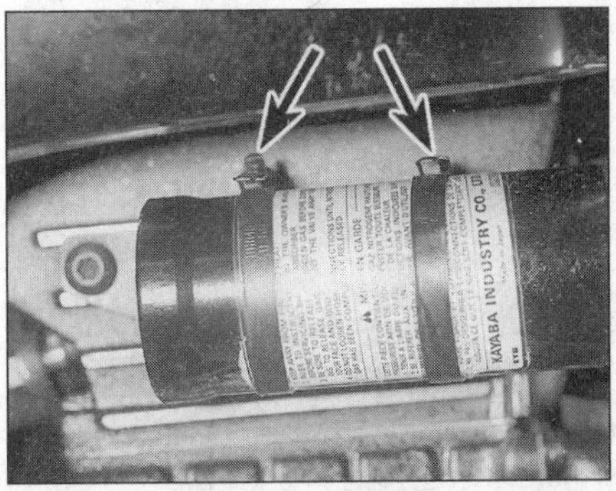

10.5 Release the reservoir from its retaining clamps (arrowed)

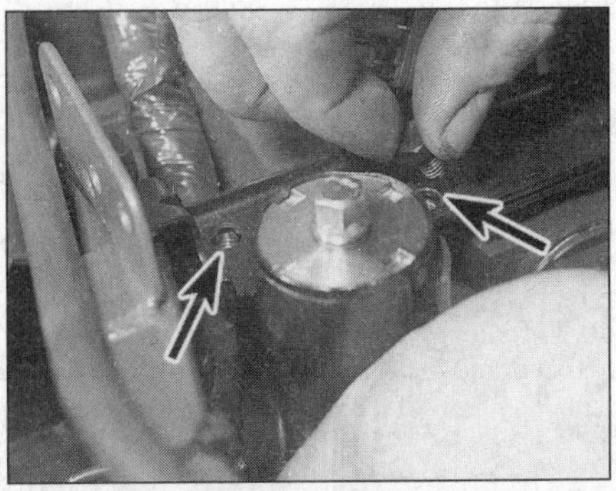

10.6a Unscrew the bolts securing the preload adjuster to the top of the frame (arrowed) . . .

10.6b . . . and the screws securing the damping adjuster to the right side of the frame (arrowed)

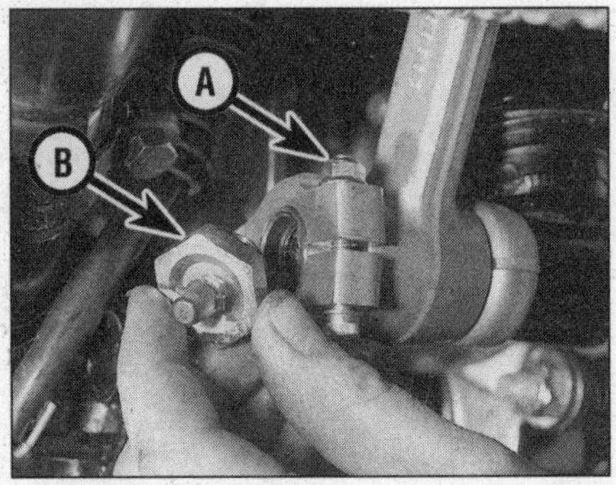

10.9 Slacken the spindle clamp bolts (A) and remove the spindle bolt (B)

10.10 Remove the shock absorber top mounting bolt (arrowed)

10.12 Withdraw linkage spindle to release the shock absorber from the linkage

unscrew the nut on the shock absorber lower mounting bolt but do not remove the bolt.

9 On Trident, Daytona, Trophy, Sprint and Speed Triple models, slacken but do not remove the suspension linkage spindle clamp bolts and unscrew the spindle bolt, but do not remove the spindle **(see illustration)**.

10 Unscrew and remove the shock absorber top mounting nut and bolt, making sure the rear wheel is adequately supported **(see illustration)**.

11 On Thunderbird, Thunderbird Sport, Adventurer, Legend TT and Tiger models, remove the shock absorber lower mounting bolt, then raise the wheel and manoeuvre the shock absorber carefully out of the frame, noting how and which way around it fits. On Tiger and Thunderbird Sport models, take care not to snag the reservoir.

12 On Trident, Daytona, Trophy, Sprint and Speed Triple models, carefully remove the support from under the wheel and gently lower the wheel to the ground. Withdraw the linkage spindle **(see illustration)**, then raise the rear wheel and manoeuvre the shock absorber carefully out of the frame, noting how and which way around it fits and taking care not to snag either the preload or the damping adjuster mechanisms, if fitted.

13 Inspect the bushes and seals (where fitted) for wear and renew worn components as necessary. Prise the seals out using a flat-bladed screwdriver. The bushes can be drifted out using a suitable drift or punch, or a drawbolt assembly (see Section 11).

Installation

14 Check that the mounting bolt and spindle are unworn (renew them if necessary); apply molybdenum grease to their shanks.

15 Raise the wheel and manoeuvre the shock absorber into place, making sure the preload and damping adjusters (if fitted) are correctly positioned. On Tiger and Thunderbird Sport models, make sure that the reservoir is correctly routed and positioned.

16 On Thunderbird, Thunderbird Sport, Adventurer, Legend TT and Tiger models, install the shock absorber lower mounting bolt, but do not yet fully tighten the nut.

17 On Trident, Daytona, Trophy, Sprint and Speed Triple models, install the linkage spindle through the linkage connecting rods and the shock absorber, but do not yet fully tighten the spindle bolt or the clamp bolts.

18 Raise the wheel if necessary and install the shock absorber top mounting bolt and nut and tighten to the torque setting specified at the beginning of the Chapter **(see illustration)**.

19 Tighten the shock absorber lower mounting bolt (Thunderbird, Thunderbird Sport, Adventurer, Legend TT and Tiger models) or the linkage spindle bolt and spindle clamp bolts (Trident, Daytona, Trophy, Sprint and Speed Triple models) to the specified torque setting **(see illustration)**.

20 If fitted, secure the mudflap to the swingarm.

21 If fitted, mount the preload adjuster to the top of the frame and the damping adjuster to the right side of the frame.

22 Install the battery box, not forgetting its bottom mounting bolt, and the auxiliary air chamber(s) as described in Chapter 4.

23 On Tiger and Thunderbird Sport models, fit the reservoir and tighten the retaining clamps securely. On the Tiger model, fit the tank mounting bracket to the frame and install the tank as described in Chapter 4.

24 Install and connect the battery, negative lead last, as described in Chapter 1.

25 Install the side panels and seat as described in Chapter 8.

26 Check the operation of the rear suspension and adjust the suspension settings as described in Section 12 before taking the bike on the road.

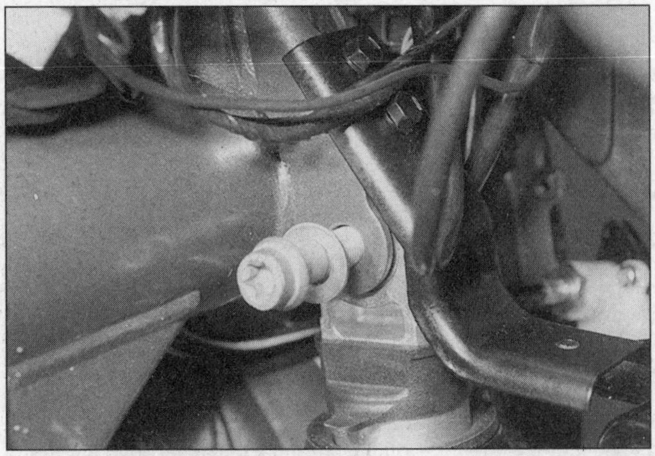

10.18 Install the shock absorber top mounting bolt

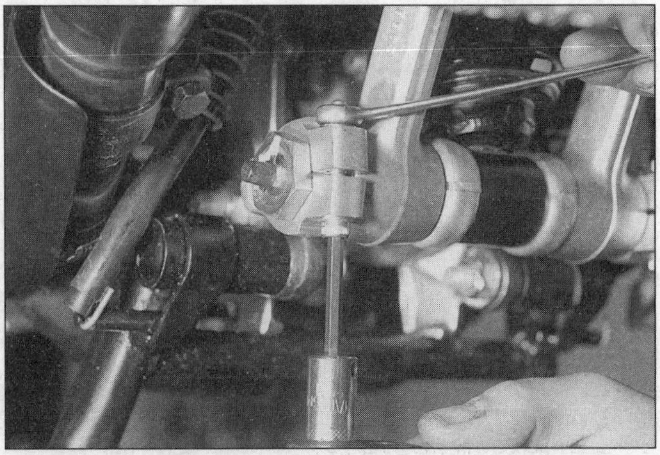

10.19 Tighten the spindle clamp bolts and the spindle bolt to the specified torque

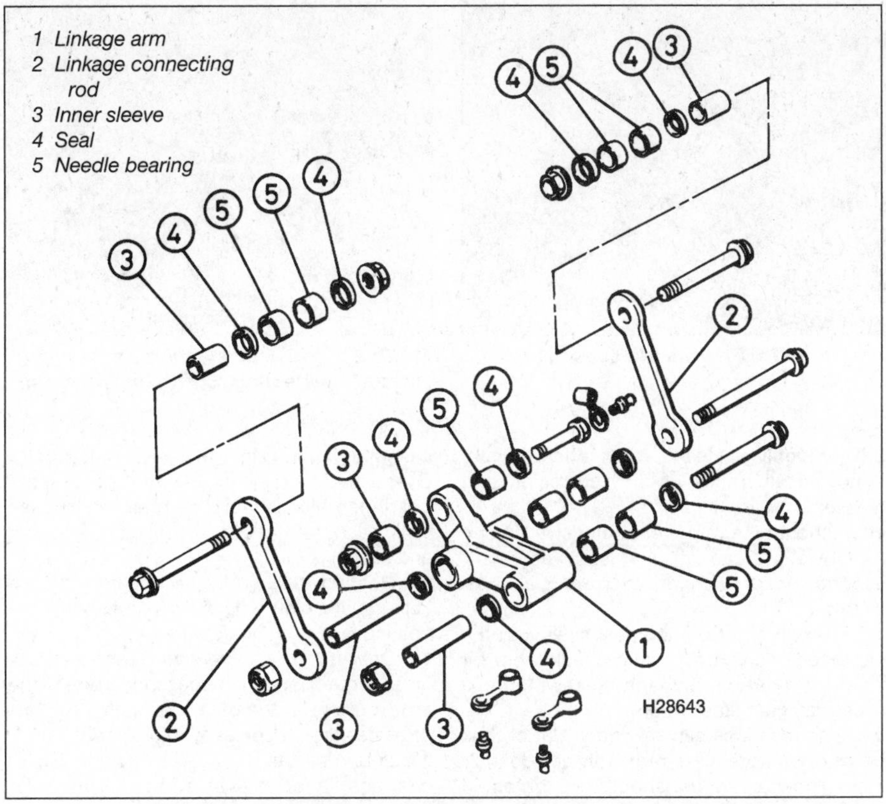

11.1a Suspension linkage detail – Thunderbird, Thunderbird Sport, Adventurer, Legend TT and Tiger models

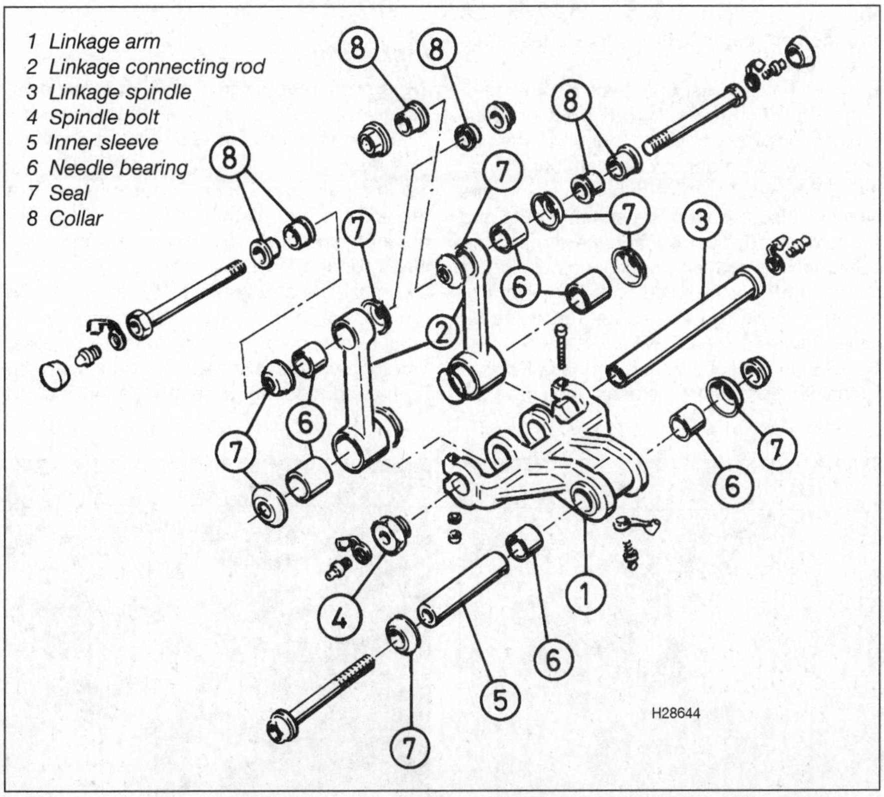

11.1b Suspension linkage detail – Trident, Sprint, Trophy, Speed Triple and Daytona models

11 Rear suspension linkage – removal, inspection and installation

Removal

1 In order to remove the rear suspension linkage, it is necessary to support the bike securely in an upright position using an auxiliary stand or hoist. The bike must be supported so that the bike's weight is off the rear suspension, but also so that the rear suspension will not drop, with the possible risk of personal injury, when the rear suspension lower mounting bolt is removed **(see illustrations).**

2 Remove the complete exhaust system as described in Chapter 4.

3 On Thunderbird, Thunderbird Sport, Adventurer, Legend TT and Tiger models, unscrew and remove the shock absorber lower mounting nut and bolt **(see illustration).**

4 On Trident, Daytona, Trophy, Sprint and Speed Triple models, slacken but do not remove the suspension linkage spindle clamp bolts, then unscrew the spindle bolt and withdraw the spindle **(see illustrations 10.9 and 10.12).**

5 Unscrew and remove the nut and pivot bolt securing the linkage arm to the linkage carriers. On Trident, Daytona, Trophy, Sprint and Speed Triple models, the linkage arm can now be removed **(see illustrations).**

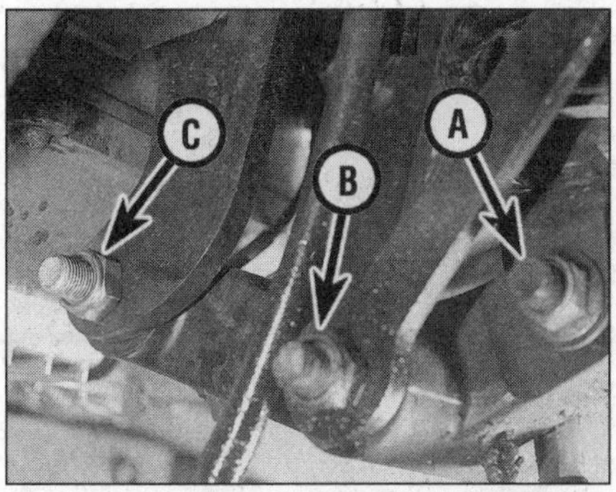

11.3 Thunderbird, Thunderbird Sport, Adventurer, Legend TT and Tiger suspension linkage: shock absorber lower mounting bolt (A), linkage connecting rod bolt (B), linkage arm to linkage carrier bolt (C)

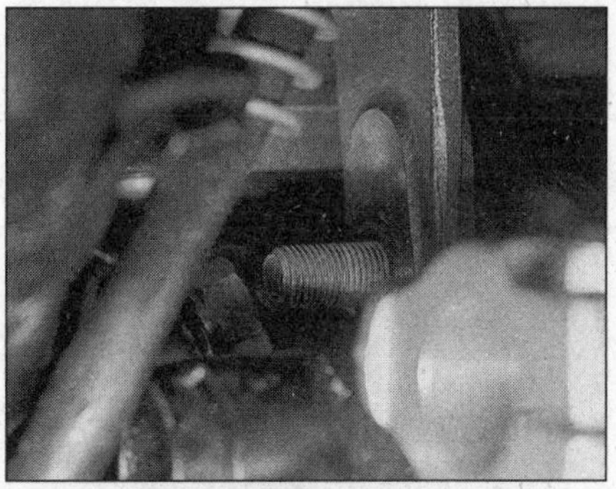

11.5a Unscrew the nut and remove the bolt securing the linkage arm to the linkage carrier . . .

11.5b ... then remove the linkage arm

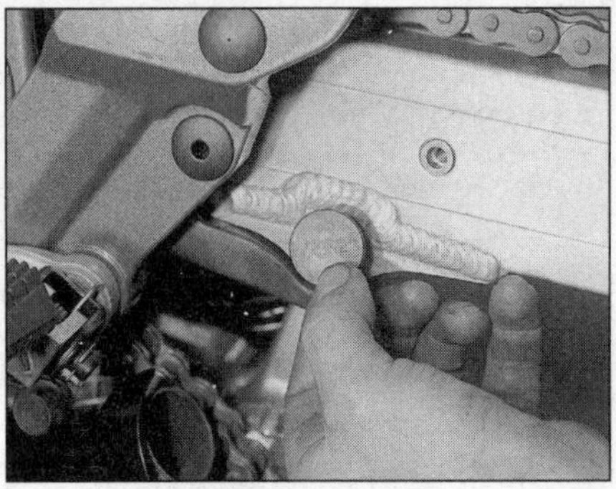
11.7a Remove the caps ...

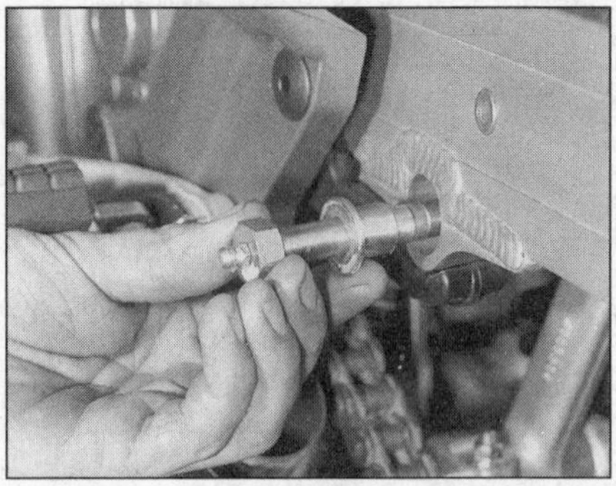
11.7b ... and unscrew the bolts securing linkage connecting rods to the swingarm

6 On Thunderbird, Thunderbird Sport, Adventurer, Legend TT and Tiger models, remove the nut and pivot bolt securing the linkage arm to the linkage connecting rods, and remove the arm **(see illustration 11.3)**.
7 Remove the caps on the bolts securing the linkage connecting rods to the swingarm, then unscrew the bolts and remove the connecting rods **(see illustrations)**. Note how the collars fit (Trident, Daytona, Trophy, Sprint and Speed Triple models).

Inspection

8 Remove the collars (where fitted), and withdraw the dust seals and inner sleeves from the linkage pivots **(see illustrations)**.

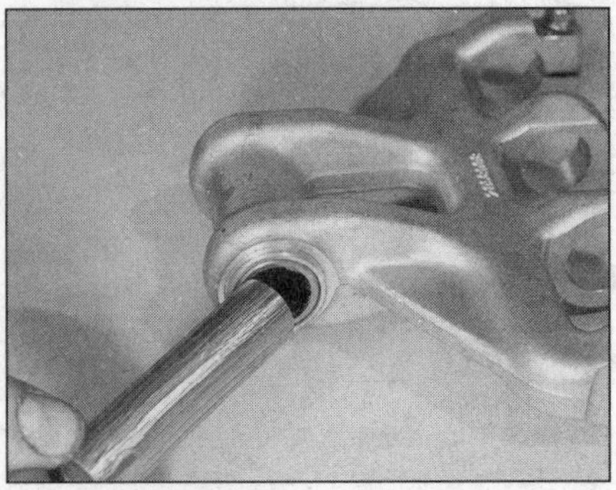
11.8a Withdraw the sleeves from the linkage arm ...

9 Thoroughly clean all components, removing all traces of dirt, corrosion and grease.
10 Inspect all components closely, looking for obvious signs of wear such as heavy scoring, or for damage such as cracks or distortion.
11 Carefully lever out the dust seals, using a flat-bladed screwdriver, and check them for signs of wear or damage; renew them if necessary **(see illustration)**.
12 Worn bearings can be drifted out of their bores, but note that removal will destroy them; new bearings should be obtained before work commences. The new bearings should be pressed or drawn into their bores rather than driven into position. In the absence of a press, a suitable drawbolt arrangement can be made up as described below.
13 It will be necessary to obtain a long bolt or a length of threaded rod from a local engineering works or similar supplier. The bolt or rod should be about one inch longer than the combined length of either link, and one bearing. Also required are suitable nuts and two large and robust washers having a larger outside diameter than the bearing housing. In the case of the threaded rod, fit one nut to one end of the rod and stake it in place for convenience.
14 Fit one of the washers over the bolt or rod so that it rests against the head, then pass the assembly through the relevant bore. Over the projecting end place the bearing, which should be greased to ease installation, followed by the remaining washer and nut.
15 Holding the bearing to ensure that it is kept square, slowly tighten the nut so that the bearing is drawn into its bore.
16 Once it is fully home, remove the drawbolt arrangement and, if necessary, repeat the procedure to fit the other bearings. The dust seals can then be pressed into place.
17 Lubricate all the seals, needle roller bearings, inner sleeves and the pivot bolts with molybdenum disulphide grease. Insert the inner sleeves into the bearings (where applicable).

Installation

18 If not already done, lubricate the seals, needle roller bearings, inner sleeves and the pivot bolts with molybdenum disulphide grease.
19 Install the seals in the linkage arm, then fit the linkage arm to the linkage carriers, but do not yet fully tighten the bolt **(see illustration)**.
20 Install the seals in the linkage connecting rod ends, and the collars into the swingarm mounts and onto the bolt (Trident, Daytona, Trophy, Sprint and Speed Triple models), then fit the connecting rods on the swingarm

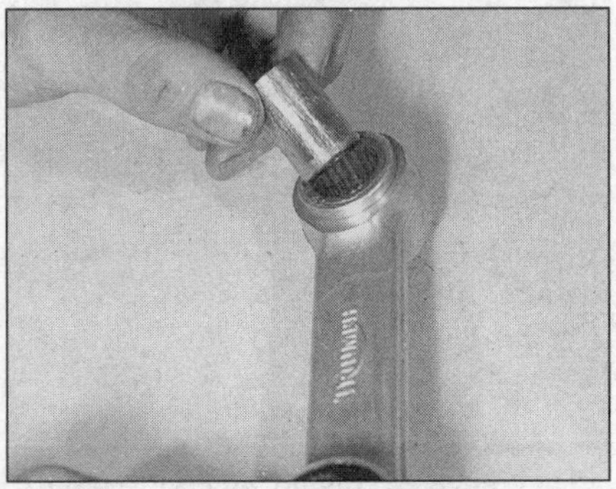
11.8b ... and from the connecting rod pivots

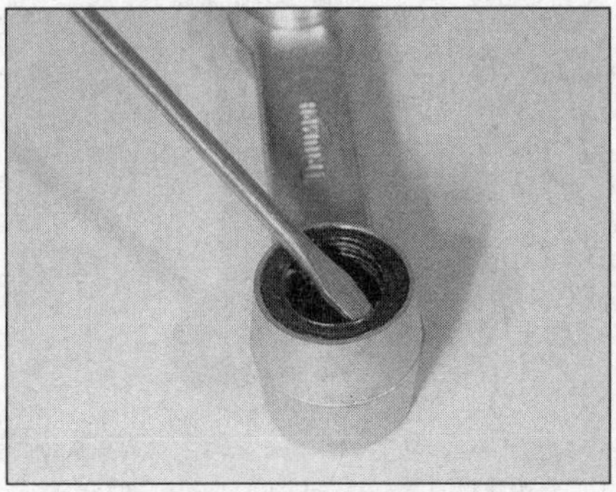
11.11 Lever out the dust seals using a flat-bladed screwdriver

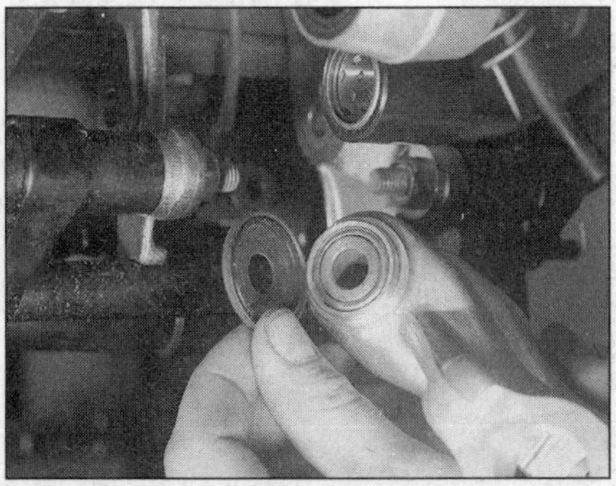
11.19 Do not forget to fit the seals before installing the linkage arm

mounts, but do not yet fully tighten the bolts **(see illustrations)**.

21 On Thunderbird, Thunderbird Sport, Adventurer, Legend TT and Tiger models, fit the linkage arm to the shock absorber lower mount, then fit the linkage arm to the linkage connecting rods, but do not yet fully tighten the bolts. Make a final check of the suspension linkage to ensure that all components are correctly fitted, then tighten all the linkage bolts to the torque settings specified at the beginning of the Chapter **(see illustration 11.3)**.

22 On Trident, Daytona, Trophy, Sprint and Speed Triple models, fit the linkage connecting rods and the shock absorber to the linkage arm and install the spindle and spindle bolt **(see illustrations 10.9 and 10.12)**. Make a final check of the suspension linkage to ensure that all components are correctly fitted, then tighten all the linkage bolts to the torque settings as specified at the beginning of the Chapter.

23 Install the exhaust system as described in Chapter 4.

24 Check the operation of the rear suspension before taking the machine on the road.

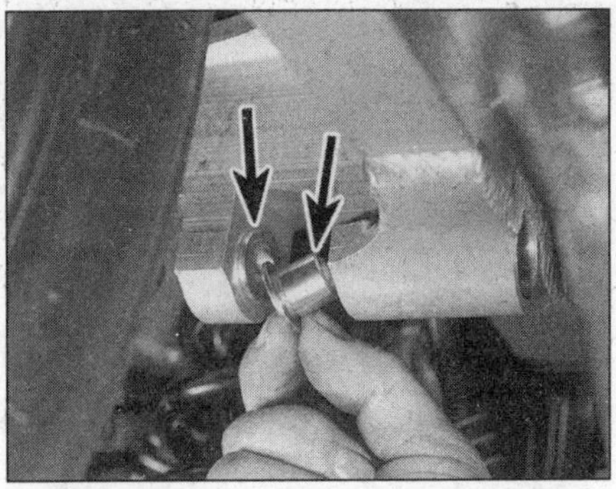

11.20a Fit the collars into the swingarm mounts (arrowed) . . .

11.20b . . . and the seals onto connecting rods

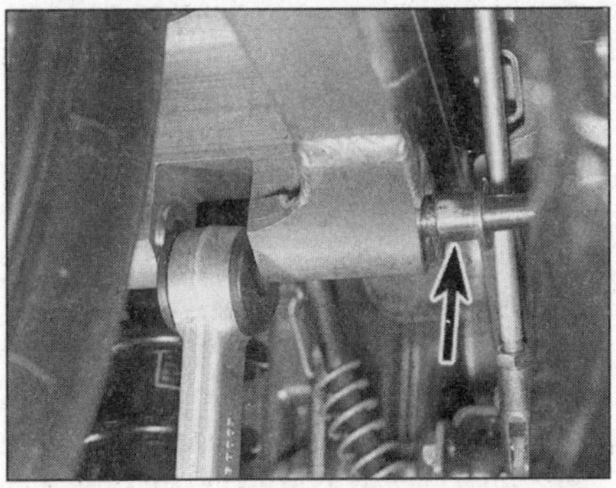

11.20c Fit connecting rod to swingarm, then install the bolt and collar (arrowed) . . .

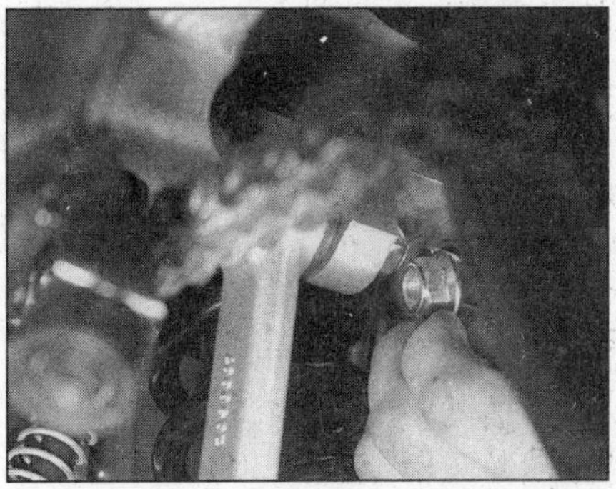

11.20d . . . and fit the nut to the bolt, but do not yet fully tighten it

12 Suspension – adjustments

Front forks – Daytona, Speed Triple, Sprint Sport and Thunderbird Sport only

Caution: Always ensure that both front fork settings are the same. Uneven settings will upset the handling of the machine and could cause it to become unstable. Also make sure you have the correct balance between front and rear suspension – refer to the suspension setting chart in your owners handbook or at the end of this Section.

Spring preload

1 The front fork spring preload adjuster is located in the centre of each fork top bolt and is adjusted using an open-ended spanner **(see illustration)**.

2 The amount of preload is indicated by the number of grooves which are visible on the adjuster above the top surface of the top bolt hexagon. There are eight grooves on the adjuster. To set the preload to the standard amount, turn the adjuster until the fifth (Daytona, Speed Triple and Sprint Sport) or sixth (Thunderbird Sport) groove from the top aligns with the top surface of the hexagon **(see illustration)**.

3 To reduce the preload (ie soften the ride), rotate the adjuster anti-clockwise.

4 To increase the preload (ie stiffen the ride), rotate the adjuster clockwise.

5 Always ensure both adjusters are set to the same position.

Rebound damping

6 The rebound damping adjuster is situated in the centre of the preload adjuster and is adjusted using a flat-bladed screwdriver **(see illustration 12.1)**.

7 Damping positions are identified by counting the number of clicks emitted by the adjuster when it is turned. There are twelve damping positions.

8 The standard setting recommended is six (Daytona, Speed Triple and Sprint Sport models) or four (Thunderbird Sport model) clicks anti-clockwise from the maximum damping setting. The maximum setting is when the adjuster is turned fully clockwise.

9 To establish the present setting, turn one of the adjusters fully clockwise whilst counting the number of clicks emitted, then rotate it back to its original position. Repeat the procedure on the other adjuster to ensure both are set to the same position.

10 To reduce the rebound damping, turn the adjuster anti-clockwise.

11 To increase the rebound damping, turn the adjuster clockwise.

12 Always ensure both adjusters are set to the same position.

Compression damping

13 The compression damping adjuster is situated at the bottom of each fork slider and

12.1 Adjust spring preload using an open-ended spanner. Damping adjustment is made with a flat-bladed screwdriver

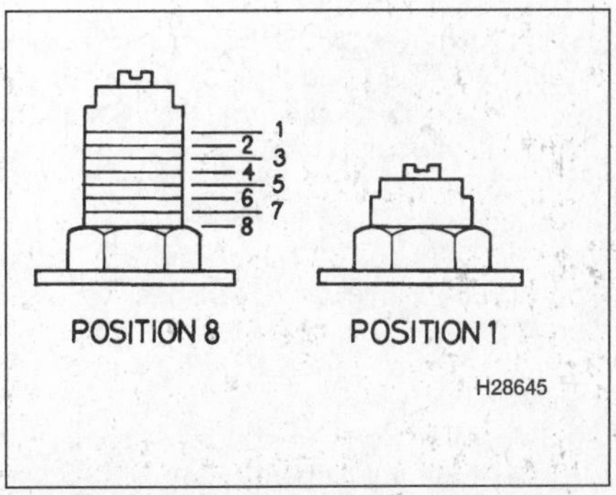

12.2 Front fork preload adjuster settings

6

12.13 The compression damping adjuster (arrowed) is situated in the bottom of the fork slider

is adjusted using a flat-bladed screwdriver **(see illustration)**.

14 Damping positions are indicated by counting the number of clicks emitted by the adjuster when it is turned. There are twelve damping positions. The standard setting recommended is six (Daytona, Speed Triple and Sprint Sport models) or four (Thunderbird Sport) clicks anti-clockwise from the maximum damping setting. The maximum setting is when the adjuster is turned fully clockwise.

15 To establish the present setting, rotate one of the adjusters fully clockwise whilst counting the number of clicks emitted, then rotate it back to its original position. Repeat the procedure on the other adjuster to ensure both are set in the same position.

16 To reduce the compression damping, turn the adjuster anti-clockwise.

17 To increase the compression damping, turn the adjuster clockwise.

18 Always ensure both adjusters are set to the same position.

Rear shock absorber

Spring preload – Trophy (VIN 29156 to 55071), 750 Trident, 900 Trident (up to VIN 9082 and from VIN 29156 to 51975), Speed Triple (from VIN 29156), Sprint (from VIN 29156), Daytona, Thunderbird, Adventurer, Legend TT and Tiger models

19 On Trophy (VIN 29156 to 55071), 900 Trident (VIN 29156 to 51975), Speed Triple (from VIN 29156), Sprint (from VIN 29156) and Daytona models, the shock absorber incorporates a preload adjuster in the form of a slotted collar. On Thunderbird, Adventurer, Legend TT, Tiger, 750 Trident and 900 Trident (to VIN 9082) models, the rear shock absorber spring preload adjuster is in the form of two locking rings threaded to the body of the shock absorber.

20 For each type of preload adjuster no details of the adjustment range or standard settings are available from the manufacturer. Refer to a Triumph dealer or suspension specialist for advice.

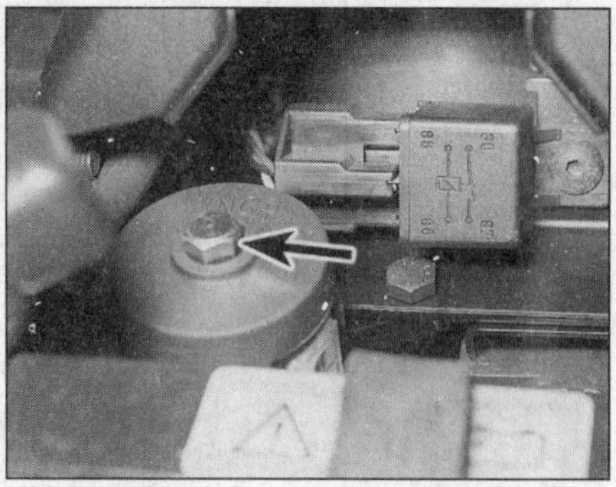

12.21 Rear shock absorber spring preload adjuster (arrowed)

Spring preload – Trophy (up to VIN 29155 and from VIN 55072), Daytona, 900 Trident (VIN 9083 to 29155 and from 51975), Sprint (up to VIN 29155), Speed Triple (up to VIN 29155), Sprint Sport and Sprint Executive models

Note: *It is important to obtain the correct balance between suspension settings – refer to the suspension setting chart in your owners handbook or at the end of this Section.*

21 The rear shock absorber spring preload adjuster is located on the frame under the seat, and is adjusted by rotating the hexagon on its top with a suitable spanner **(see illustration)**.

22 The preload adjuster has five positions marked on the window in the side of the adjuster; number 1 is the minimum (ie softest) setting and number five the maximum (hardest) setting. Triumph recommend position two as the standard setting for all models except the Daytona, which is set to position three as standard. A pointer indicates which position is set. To increase preload turn the adjuster clockwise. To reduce preload turn the adjuster anti-clockwise.

Rebound damping – 900 Trident (VIN 29156 to 51975), Trophy (VIN 29156 to 55071), Speed Triple (from VIN 29156), Daytona, Sprint (from VIN 29156), Tiger and Thunderbird Sport models

Note: *It is important to obtain the correct balance between suspension settings – refer to the suspension setting chart in your owners handbook or at the end of this Section.*

23 The rear suspension rebound damping adjuster is situated in the side of the shock absorber on its right side and is adjusted using a flat-bladed screwdriver **(see illustrations)**.

24 Damping positions are indicated by counting the number of clicks when it is turned. There are sixteen (Tiger models) or twelve (all other models) damping positions altogether.

25 The standard setting recommended is eight (Tiger models) or six (all other models) clicks anti-clockwise from the maximum damping setting. The maximum setting is when the adjuster is turned fully clockwise.

26 To establish the present setting, rotate the adjuster fully clockwise whilst counting the number of clicks, then rotate it back to its original position.

27 To reduce the rebound damping, turn the adjuster anti-clockwise.

28 To increase the rebound damping, turn the adjuster clockwise.

Rebound damping – 900 Trident (VIN 9084 to 29155 and from 51976), Trophy (up to VIN 29155), Speed Triple (up to VIN 29155), Daytona, Sprint (up to VIN 29155) and Sprint Sport

Note: *It is important to obtain the correct balance between suspension settings – refer to the suspension setting chart in your owners handbook or at the end of this Section.*

29 The rear suspension rebound damping adjuster is situated on the right side of the bike and is adjusted by turning the dial anti-clockwise only. The dial must not be rotated clockwise **(see illustration 10.6b)**.

30 There are four positions, as numbered on the dial and identified by a click. The position selected must align with the triangular index mark on the adjuster bracket. Number one is the softest setting and number four the hardest. The dial must be set in one of the four click positions only, not between them.

Compression damping – Tiger model only

Note: *It is important to obtain the correct balance between suspension settings – refer*

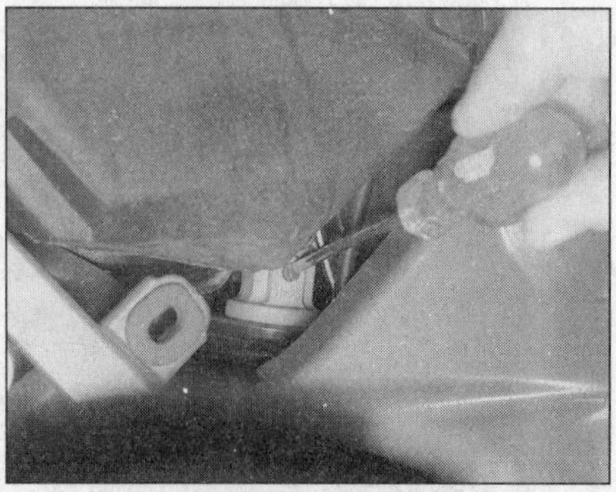

12.23a Rear shock absorber damping adjuster – Trophy model

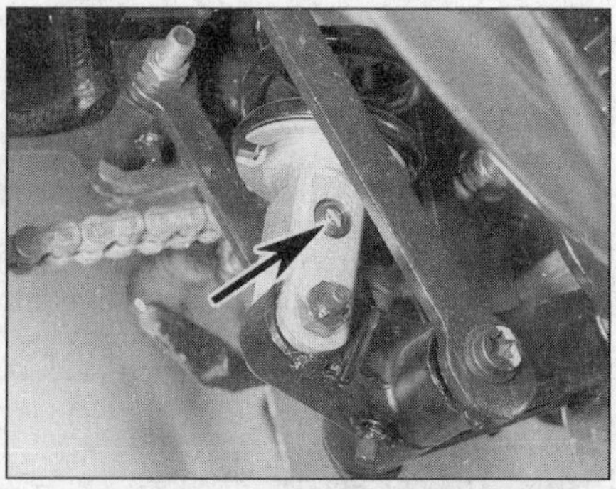

12.23b Rear shock absorber rebound damping adjuster (arrowed) – Thunderbird Sport model

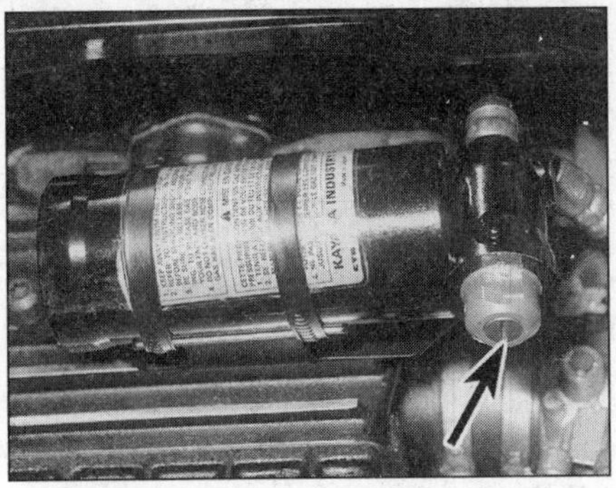

12.31 Compression damping adjuster on Tiger model (arrowed)

12.37 Compression damping adjuster on Thunderbird Sport

to the suspension setting chart in your owners handbook or at the end of this Section.

31 The rear suspension compression damping adjuster is situated on the shock absorber reservoir, mounted on the left side of the cylinder head, and is adjusted using a flat-bladed screwdriver **(see illustration)**.

32 Damping positions are indicated by counting the number of clicks when it is turned. There are twenty-four damping positions.

33 The standard setting recommended is six clicks anti-clockwise from the maximum damping setting. The maximum setting is when the adjuster is turned fully clockwise.

34 To establish the present setting, rotate the adjuster fully clockwise whilst counting the number of clicks, then rotate it back to its original position.

35 To reduce the compression damping, turn the adjuster anti-clockwise.

36 To increase the compression damping, turn the adjuster clockwise.

Compression damping – Thunderbird Sport model

37 The compression damping adjuster is situated on the shock absorber reservoir, mounted under the seat; it is adjusted using a flat-bladed screwdriver **(see illustration)**.

38 Damping positions are indicated by counting the number of clicks when it is turned. The standard position is six clicks anti-clockwise from the maximum damping setting. To establish the present setting, rotate the adjuster fully clockwise whilst counting the number of clicks, then rotate it back to its original position.

39 To reduce the compression damping, turn the adjuster anti-clockwise.

40 To increase the compression damping, turn the adjuster clockwise.

Suspension setting chart – Trophy (up to VIN 29155), Daytona, later 900 Trident, Sprint, Speed Triple and Thunderbird Sport models

Front fork (Daytona, Speed Triple, Sprint Sport)

	Preload	Rebound	Compression
Solo riding – standard	5	6	6
Solo riding – softer	6	9	8
Solo riding – firmer	4	4	3
With pillion	4 – 5	4 – 6	3 – 6
With pillion and luggage	1 – 4	1 – 4	1 – 3

Front fork (Thunderbird Sport)

	Preload	Rebound	Compression
Solo riding – standard	6	4	4
Solo riding – softer	7	6	6
Solo riding – firmer	5	2	2
With pillion	4 – 6	2 – 4	2 – 4
With pillion and luggage	1 – 4	1 – 3	1 – 3

Rear shock absorber – 900 Trident (VIN 9084 to 29155 and from 51976), Trophy (up to VIN 29155), Speed Triple (up to VIN 29155), Daytona, Sprint (up to VIN 29155) and Sprint Sport

	Preload	Damping
Solo riding – standard	2 or 3 (see text)	2
Solo riding – softer	2	1
Solo riding – firmer	4	3
With pillion	3 – 4	2 – 3
With pillion and luggage	3 – 4	3 – 4

Rear shock absorber (remote adjuster type) – Trophy (VIN 29156 to 55071), Daytona, 900 Trident (VIN 29156 to 51975), Sprint (from VIN 29156) and Speed Triple (from VIN 29156)

	Damping
Solo riding – standard	6
Solo riding – softer	8
Solo riding – firmer	4
With pillion	4
With pillion and luggage	1 – 3

Rear shock absorber – Thunderbird Sport

	Compression damping	Rebound damping
Solo riding – standard	6	6
Solo riding – softer	8	8
Solo riding – firmer	4	4
With pillion	4	4
With pillion and luggage	1 – 3	1 – 3

Rear shock absorber setting chart – Tiger models

	Compression damping	Rebound damping
Solo riding – standard	6	8
Solo riding – softer	8	10
Solo riding – firmer	4	6
With pillion	6	4
With pillion and luggage	6	4

13 Swingarm bearings – check

1 Remove the rear wheel as described in Chapter 7, then remove the rear shock absorber (see Section 10 of this Chapter).

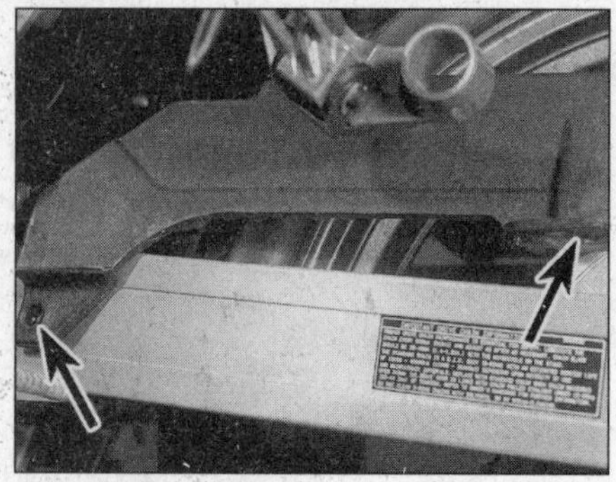

14.2 The chainguard is secured to the swingarm by two screws (arrowed)

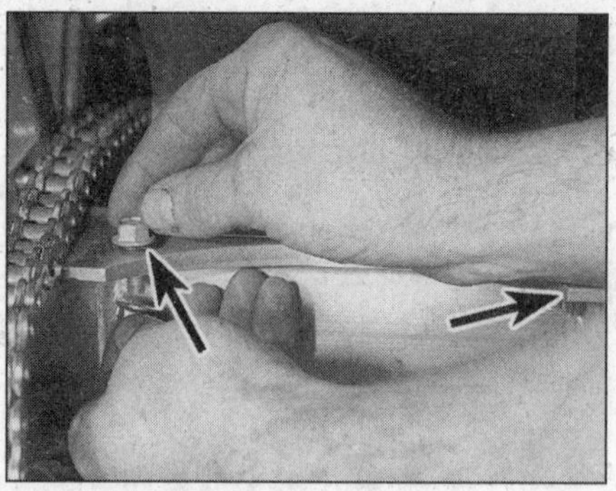

14.8 Unscrew the two bolts securing the mudflap to the swingarm

14.10 Remove the swingarm spindle end caps

2 Grasp the rear of the swingarm with one hand and place your other hand at the junction of the swingarm and the frame. Try to move the rear of the swingarm from side-to-side. Any wear (play) in the bearings should be felt as movement between the swingarm and the frame at the front. If there is any play the swingarm will be felt to move forward and backward at the front (not from side-to-side). If any play is noted, the bearings should be renewed (see Section 15).

3 Next, move the swingarm up and down through its full travel. It should move freely, without any binding or rough spots. If it does not move freely, remove the swingarm for inspection of its bearings (see Section 14).

14 Swingarm – removal and installation

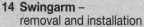

Removal

1 On Trident, Daytona, Trophy, Sprint and Speed Triple models, remove the side panels (Chapter 8).

2 Remove its mounting screws and lift off the chainguard on all models except the Speed Triple, later Trophy models (from VIN 29156), and early Daytona models (up to VIN 9082) and Super III **(see illustration)**.

3 On Speed Triple, later Trophy models (from VIN 29156), later Daytona models (from VIN 9083) and the Super III, remove the swingarm-mounted mudguard as described in Chapter 8.

4 On all models except the Tiger, remove the exhaust silencers as described in Chapter 4.

5 Remove the rear wheel as described in Chapter 7. Cover the drive chain with a rag to prevent it from resting directly on the ground or work surface and picking up any dirt.

6 Unscrew the bolt securing the brake torque arm to the swingarm and remove the sleeve. Discard the bolt as a new one must be used. Make sure the torque arm and brake caliper are adequately supported so that no strain is placed on the brake hose.

7 On models which have an underslung brake caliper (Daytona, Speed Triple and Trophy (from VIN 29156) models), remove the brake hose clamp from the right side of the swingarm.

8 If fitted, unscrew the bolts securing the bottom of the mudflap to the swingarm **(see illustration)**.

9 Remove the caps on the bolts securing the suspension linkage connecting rods to the swingarm, then support the swingarm and remove the bolts **(see illustrations 11.7a and 11.7b)**. On Thunderbird, Thunderbird Sport, Adventurer, Legend TT and Tiger models, remove the inner sleeves from the swingarm. On Trident, Daytona, Trophy, Sprint and Speed Triple models, remove the collars, noting how they fit.

10 On all models except the Sprint Executive and Trophy from VIN 29156, remove the caps covering the swingarm pivot ends on both sides of the bike. On early models the caps are a press fit and can be prised off. On later models the caps are secured by three bolts **(see illustration)**.

11 On Sprint Executive and Trophy from VIN 29156 models, remove the footrest carriers as described in Section 3.

12 Slacken, but do not remove the upper rear engine mounting bolts.

13 Using a flat-bladed screwdriver or a pair of pliers, remove the spring clips (where fitted) from each end of the swingarm pivot, taking care not to scratch any surfaces **(see illustration)**.

14 Unscrew and remove the swingarm pivot bolt and washer from the right side of the bike, then support the swingarm and withdraw the pivot shaft from the left side of the bike **(see illustrations)**. It may be necessary to drift the pivot shaft out using a suitable drift applied from the right side of the bike. Remove the spacer (Trident, Daytona, Trophy, Sprint, Speed Triple, Tiger models) from between the swingarm lugs as the spindle is withdrawn, noting how it fits. Take care not to lose the dust seals and shims fitted to the swingarm lugs. Note which seals and shims fit on which lug as they must not be mixed up.

15 Note the positions of any breather and drain pipes and move them aside if necessary, then carefully remove the swingarm from the frame.

16 Remove the drive chain slider and slider

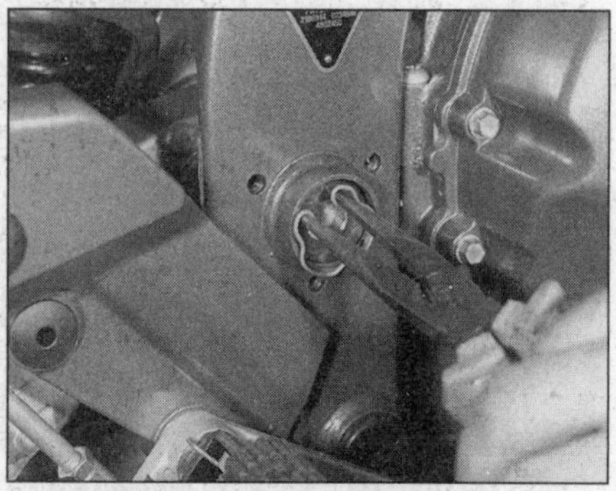

14.13 Remove the spring clip from both ends of the swingarm spindle

14.14a Unscrew the spindle bolt on the right side of the bike . . .

14.14b . . . and withdraw the spindle from the left side

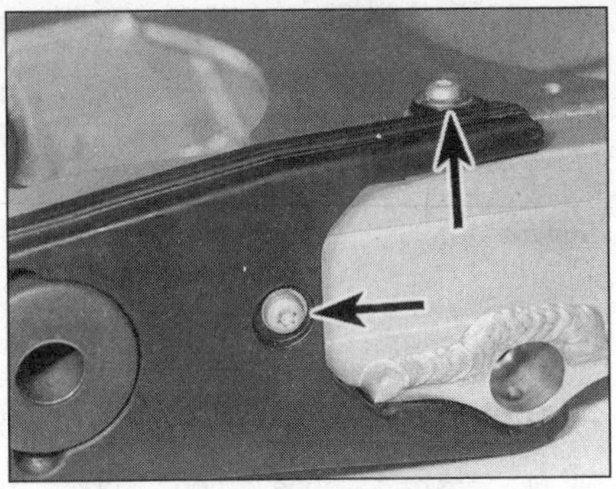
14.16 The drive chain slider is secured to the swingarm by two screws (arrowed)

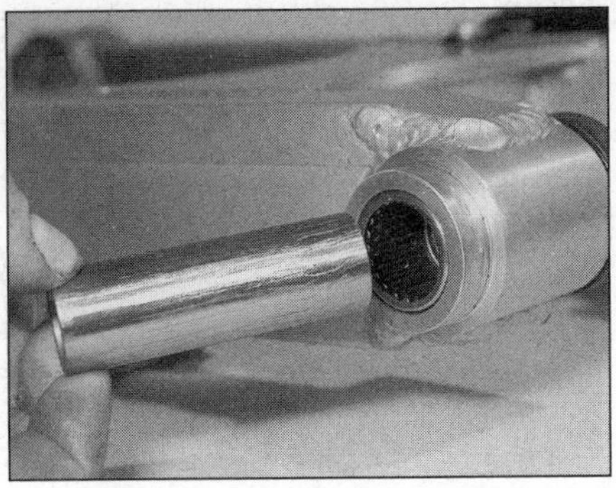
14.19a Fit the inner sleeve into the bearing . . .

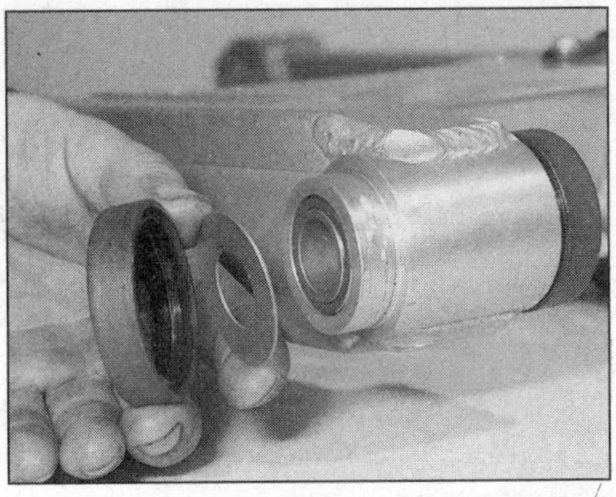
14.19b . . . and the shims and dust seals to the swingarm

block (Tiger only) from the swingarm if renewal is required **(see illustration)**.

17 Inspect all components for wear or damage as described in Section 15.

Installation

18 If removed, install the drive chain slider and slider block (Tiger only). Apply a drop of non-permanent locking compound to the threads of the chain slider mounting screws.

19 Remove the dust seals, shims and sleeves from the swingarm lugs, then lubricate the bearings, inner sleeves, centre spacer and the spindle with grease, and fit the inner sleeves back into the bearings. Fit the shims and dust seals, making sure they are each fitted in the same place from which they were removed **(see illustrations)**.

20 Loop the drive chain over the swingarm as it is offered up to the frame. Make sure the breather and drain pipes are correctly positioned behind and inside the front ends of the swingarm, and have an assistant hold the swingarm in place as the pivot shaft is fitted **(see illustration)**. Install the pivot shaft through the swingarm from the left side, not forgetting to install the centre spacer (Trident, Daytona, Trophy, Sprint, Speed Triple, Tiger models) in between the swingarm pivot lugs as the shaft passes through **(see illustration)**. If difficulty is experienced when installing the spacer between the lugs, the left side upper engine mounting bolt should be tightened after installing the swingarm pivot shaft into the left side lug to locate the swingarm in place. Alternatively, a special tool (Pt. No. 3880060) is available to align the spacer; this tool consists of a tapered nose cone that fits into the pivot shaft end to align the swingarm and spacer as the shaft passes through.

21 Install the swingarm pivot shaft bolt, but do not yet fully tighten it. Check the movement of the swingarm. Make sure any breather and drain pipes are correctly positioned.

22 Lubricate the suspension linkage seals, bearings and inner sleeves (where fitted) with grease. On Thunderbird, Thunderbird Sport, Adventurer, Legend TT and Tiger models the bearings are housed in the swingarm. On Trident, Daytona, Trophy, Sprint and Speed Triple models they are housed in the linkage connecting rod ends (see Section 11).

23 Fit the linkage connecting rods to the swingarm, not forgetting the collars on Trident, Daytona, Trophy, Sprint and Speed Triple models (see Section 11, Step 20, if necessary), and tighten the bolts to the torque setting specified at the beginning of the Chapter **(see illustration)**.

24 Tighten the pivot shaft bolt to the specified torque setting **(see illustration)**. Check the movement of the swingarm, then fit the spring clips (where fitted).

25 On Sprint Executive and Trophy from VIN 29156 models, install the footrest carriers. On all other models fit the caps covering the swingarm pivot ends **(see illustration 14.10)**.

26 Tighten the upper rear engine mounting bolts to the torque setting specified at the beginning of Chapter 2.

27 If fitted, install the bolts securing the bottom of the mudflap to the swingarm.

28 Install the brake torque arm on the swingarm, not forgetting the sleeve, and, using a new bolt, tighten to the torque setting

14.20a Breather and drain pipes fit inside the swingarm mounts so they are behind the swingarm spindle when it is installed

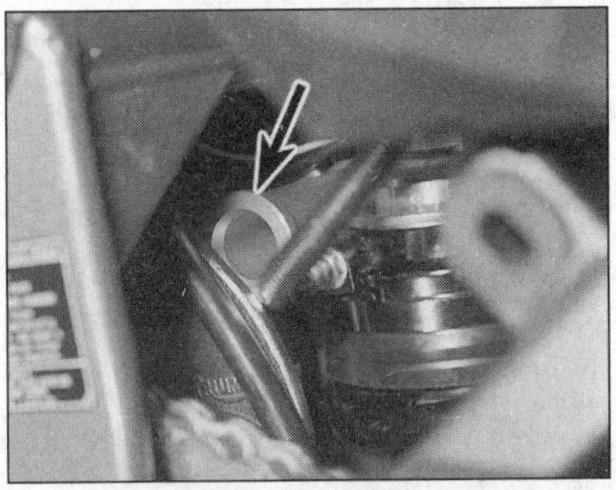
14.20b Install the spacer (arrowed) between the swingarm lugs before installing the spindle

14.23 Tighten the suspension linkage connecting rod bolts to the specified torque setting

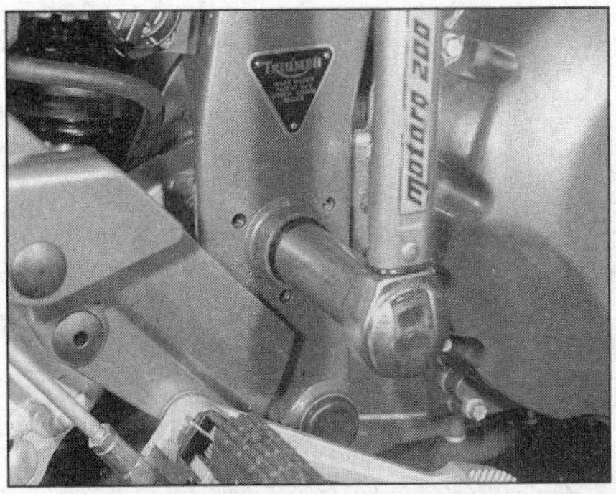
14.24 Tighten the swingarm spindle bolt to the specified torque setting

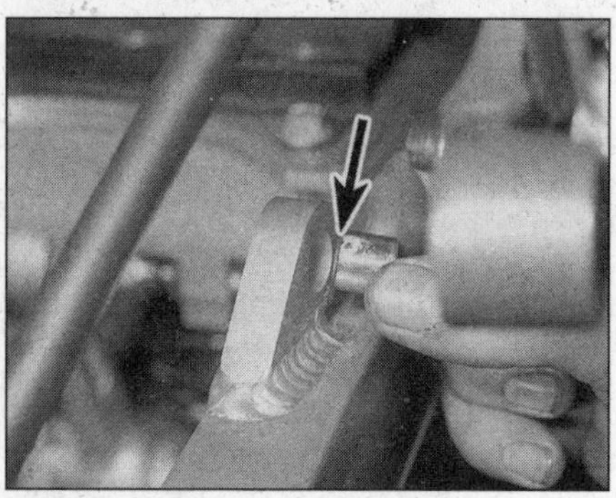

14.28a Fit the sleeve into the torque arm mount . . .

14.28b . . . then fit the torque arm and tighten the bolt to the specified torque

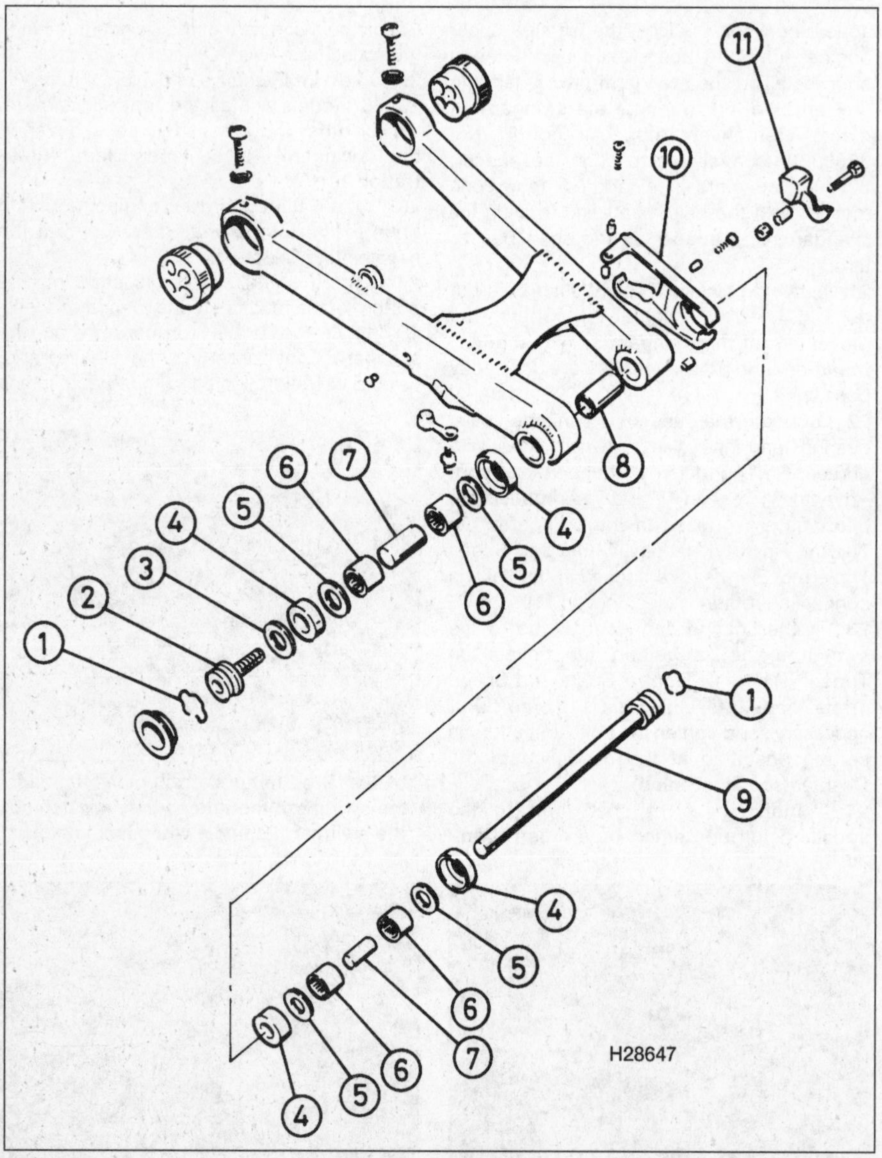

15.1 Swingarm detail

1 Spring clip
2 Spindle bolt
3 Washer
4 Dust seal
5 Shim
6 Needle bearing
7 Inner sleeve
8 Spacer
9 Spindle
10 Chain slider
11 Chain slider block (Tiger only)

specified at the beginning of Chapter 7 **(see illustrations)**.

29 Fit the brake hose clamp to the right side of the swingarm (models with an underslung brake caliper).

30 Install the rear wheel as described in Chapter 7.

31 Fit the exhaust silencers (not Tiger model).

32 On Daytona and Speed Triple models fit the swingarm-mounted mudguard as described In Chapter 8.

33 Fit the chainguard and tighten the screws securely.

34 On Trident, Daytona, Trophy, Sprint and Speed Triple models, fit the side panels as described in Chapter 8.

35 Check the operation of the rear suspension before taking the machine on the road.

15 Swingarm – inspection and bearing renewal

Inspection

1 Thoroughly clean all components, removing all dirt, corrosion or grease **(see illustration)**.

2 Inspect all components closely, looking for obvious signs of wear such as heavy scoring, and cracks or distortion due to accident damage. Inspect the drive chain slider and slider block (Tiger only). If they are worn they must be renewed. Any damaged or worn component must be renewed.

Bearing renewal

3 Remove the dust seals, shims and the inner sleeves, noting where each one fits as they must be installed in the same position. Inspect them for signs of wear or damage and renew them if necessary.

4 Worn bearings can be drifted out of their bores, but note that removal will destroy them; new bearings should be obtained before work commences. The new bearings should be pressed or drawn into their bores rather than driven into position. In the absence of a press, a suitable drawbolt arrangement can be made up (see Section 11 of this Chapter). Otherwise the bearings must be installed by a Triumph dealer.

16 Drive chain – removal, cleaning and installation

Removal – endless type chain

Note: *An endless chain doesn't have a joining link and therefore cannot be split. Removal requires the removal of the swingarm as detailed below.*

1 Remove the swingarm (see Section 14).

2 Remove the front sprocket cover as described in Section 17, Steps 1 to 9.

3 Slip the chain off the front sprocket and remove it from the bike.

Removal - riveted link chain

Note: *The riveted (soft) link can be identified by its identification markings on the side plate and usually slightly different colour. Also the staked ends of the link's two pins look as if they have been deeply centre-punched, instead of peened over as with all other pins.*

4 Locate the joining link in a suitable position to work on by rotating the back wheel; midway between the sprockets is ideal.

5 Slacken the drive chain as described in Chapter 1.

6 Split the chain at the joining link using an approved chain breaker tool intended for motorcycle use. There are a number of types available for motorcycle use and it is important to follow carefully the instructions supplied with the tool - see *Tools and Workshop Tips* in the Reference section for a typical example. Remove the chain from the bike, noting its routing around the swingarm.

Cleaning

7 Soak the chain in paraffin (kerosene) for approximately five or six minutes. If the chain is very dirty, use a soft-bristled brush to remove caked-on deposits, taking care to wear hand protection.

Caution: Don't use gasoline (petrol), solvent or other cleaning fluids. Don't use high-pressure water. Remove the chain, wipe it off, then blow dry it with compressed air immediately. The entire process shouldn't take longer than ten minutes - if it does, the O-rings in the chain rollers could be damaged.

Installation - endless chain

8 Installation is the reverse of removal, as described in Section 17, Steps 14 and 15.

9 On completion, adjust and lubricate the chain following the procedures in Chapter 1.

Installation - riveted link chain

Warning: NEVER install a drive chain which uses a clip-type master (split) link. If you do not have access to a chain riveting tool, have the chain fitted by a Triumph dealer.

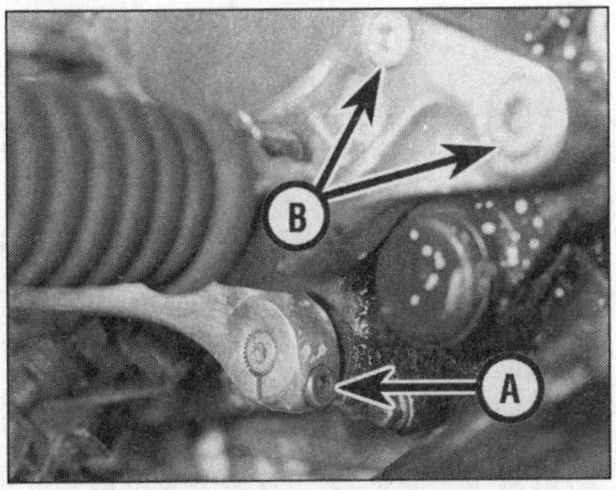

17.3 Unscrew the gearchange pedal pinch bolt (A) and the footrest bracket bolts (B)

10 Remove the front sprocket cover as described in Section 17, Steps 1 to 9.

11 Thread the chain into position, making sure that it takes the correct route around the swingarm and sprockets and leave the two ends in a convenient place to work on. Obtain a new soft link - never attempt to reuse an old link.

12 Install the new soft link complete with an O-ring on each of its pins through the chain ends from the inside of the chain. Install an O-ring over the pin ends and fit the side plate with its identification marks facing out; use the chain tool to press the side plate into position.

13 Stake the new link pins using the chain riveting tool, following carefully the instructions of both the chain manufacturer and the tool manufacturer. Refer to *Tools and Workshop Tips* in the Reference section for chain riveting details using a typical commercially available tool.

14 After riveting, check the soft link pin ends for any signs of cracking. If there is any evidence of cracking, the soft link, O-rings and side plate must be removed and the procedure repeated with a new soft link.

15 Install the sprocket cover, then lubricate and adjust the chain as described in Chapter 1.

17 Sprockets - check, removal and installation

Check

1 Place the bike on its centre stand. On models without a centre stand, it is necessary to support the bike using an auxiliary stand as the sidestand must be removed in order to remove the sprocket cover on Trident, Sprint, Trophy, Speed Triple and Daytona models.

2 Drain the engine oil (refer to Chapter 1); note that this is unnecessary on the later 1200 Trophy (with black engine) due to there being no oil contained in the sprocket cover.

Restrain the clutch release cylinder piston using cable-ties and a short spacer

3 On Thunderbird, Adventurer and Legend TT models, mark a line across the gearchange shaft end and lever as an aid to installation, then unscrew the gearchange pedal pinch bolt and remove the pedal. Unscrew the footrest bracket mounting bolts and remove the footrest with its bracket **(see illustration)**.

4 On Thunderbird Sport models, detach the link rod from the gearchange shaft lever and pedal by slackening its locknuts and rotating the rod via its knurled centre section so that it unscrews from the lever and pedal at the same time. Mark a line across the gearchange shaft end and shaft lever as an aid to installation, then remove the pinch bolt and withdraw the shaft lever.

5 On Tiger models, remove the rider's left footrest bracket (Section 3). Mark a line across the gearchange shaft end and shaft lever as an aid to installation, then remove the pinch bolt and withdraw the shaft lever.

6 On Trident, Sprint, Trophy, Speed Triple and Daytona models detach the link rod from the gearchange shaft lever and pedal by slackening its locknuts and rotating the rod via its knurled centre section so that it unscrews from the lever and pedal at the same time. Where a dog-leg link rod is fitted, slacken off the locknut and unscrew the threaded sleeve to separate the link rod from the shaft lever. Disconnect the sidestand switch wiring connector, then remove the sidestand bracket bolt and the engine left rear lower bolt **(see illustrations 5.10b and 5.10c in Chapter 2)**. Remove the sidestand with its bracket. Mark a line across the gearchange shaft end and shaft lever as an aid to installation, then remove the pinch bolt and withdraw the shaft lever.

7 If fitted, unscrew the bolts securing the water pump hose cover and remove the cover.

8 Unscrew the bolts securing the clutch release cylinder to the sprocket cover, noting the location of the shorter bolt, and remove the cylinder **(see illustration and Haynes Hint)**. Take care not to pull in the clutch lever with the cylinder removed. Withdraw the clutch pushrod.

9 Unscrew the sprocket cover bolts and

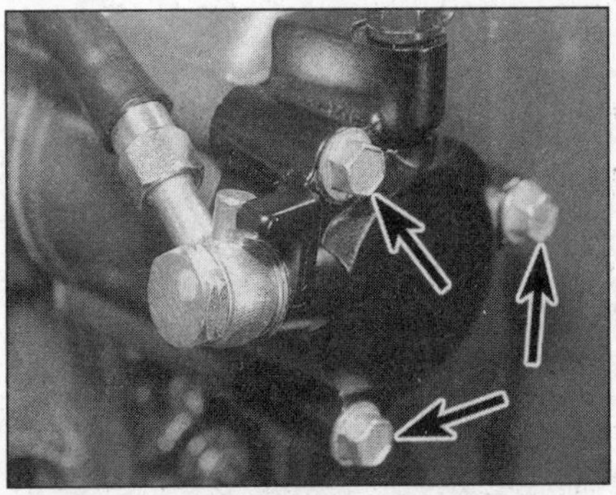

17.8 Unscrew the three clutch release cylinder mounting bolts (arrowed) and remove the cylinder

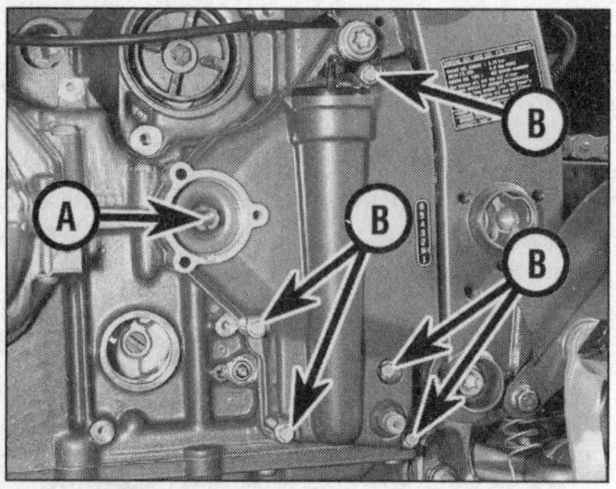

17.9 Remove the clutch pushrod (A), unscrew the remaining sprocket cover bolts (B) and remove the cover

17.11 Bend back the tabs on the lock washer (A), then unscrew the nut (B)

17.12 Remove the sprocket from the shaft with the chain attached

remove the cover **(see illustration)**. Take note of the bolt locations as they are of different lengths. Take care not to lose the locating dowels and note their positions. Discard the gasket as a new one must be used.

10 Check the wear pattern on both sprockets (see Chapter 1). If the sprocket teeth are worn excessively, renew the chain and both sprockets as a set. Whenever the drive chain is inspected, the sprockets should be inspected also. If you are renewing the chain, renew the sprockets as well.

Removal and installation

Front sprocket

10 Remove the sprocket cover as described in Steps 1 to 9 above.

11 Shift the transmission into gear and have an assistant sit on the seat and apply the rear brake hard. Bend the lock washer tabs away from the sprocket nut and unscrew the nut. Discard the lock washer as a new one must be used **(see illustration)**.

12 Slacken the drive chain adjusters if necessary (see Chapter 1), then pull the engine sprocket and chain off the shaft and separate the sprocket from the chain **(see illustration)**.

13 Engage the new sprocket with the chain and slide it on the shaft. Install the new lock washer and nut and tighten it to the specified torque setting whilst locking the transmission as described above. **Note:** *The nut should be installed with its recessed side towards the lock washer.* Bend the tabs on the lockwasher up against the nut **(see illustrations)**. Adjust the chain as necessary (see Chapter 1).

14 Install the engine sprocket cover and other components by reversing the removal procedure as described in Steps 1 to 9 above, noting the following:

*a) Fit a new oil seal to the gearchange shaft hole in the cover and a new gasket to the cover **(see illustrations)**. It is advisable to cover the gearchange shaft threads with tape to avoid damaging the lips of the new seal when fitting the cover.*

*b) Make sure all locating dowels are in place when fitting the cover and use a new gasket **(see illustration)**.*

c) Smear the pushrod with engine oil and

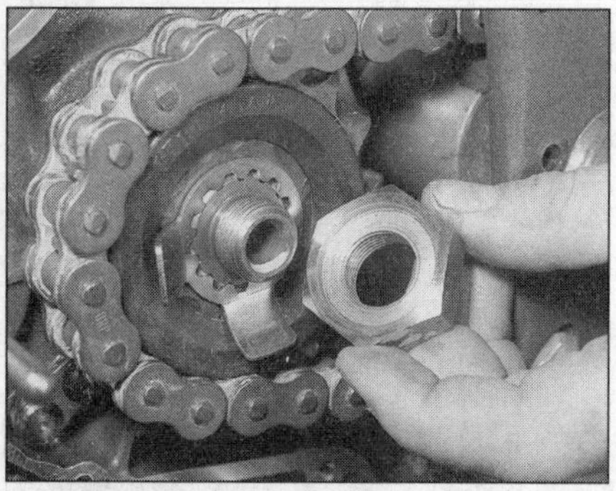
17.13a Fit a new lock washer to the shaft, then install the nut . . .

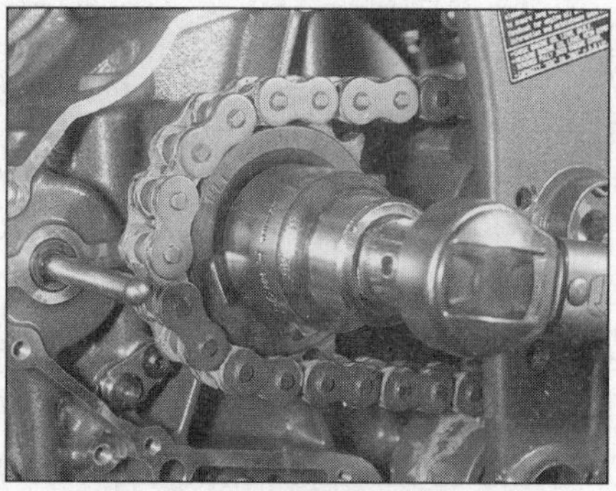
17.13b . . . tighten it to the specified torque setting . . .

17.13c . . . and then bend up the tabs of the washer to lock the nut in place

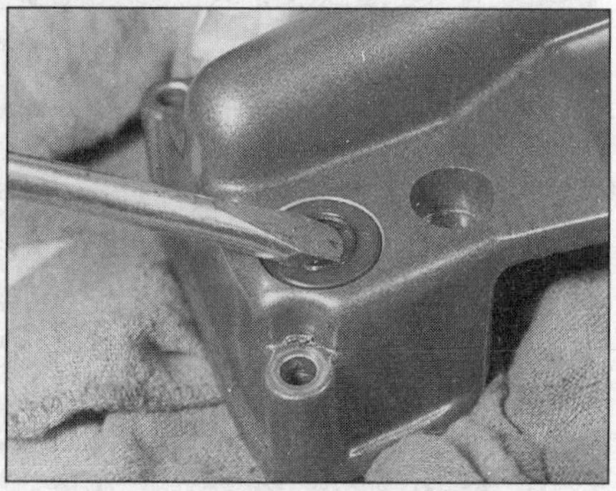
17.14a Lever the old gearchange shaft oil seal out of the cover . . .

17.14b . . . and press in a new seal

17.14c Make sure the two dowels are in position (arrowed), then fit a new gasket

17.17 The rear sprocket is held by five nuts

18.4 Remove the rubber dampers from the rear wheel and inspect them for wear and damage

slide it back into the sprocket cover. Apply a dab of grease to its end before installing the release cylinder

15 Fill the engine with oil (see Chapter 1).

Rear sprocket

16 To remove the rear sprocket, remove the rear wheel as described in Chapter 7.

Caution: Do not lay the wheel down on the disc as it could become warped. Lay the wheel on wooden blocks so that the disc is off the ground.

17 Unscrew the nuts holding the sprocket to the wheel coupling and lift it off, noting which way around it fits **(see illustration)**. Check the condition of the rubber damper under the rear wheel coupling (see Section 18).

18 Fit the new sprocket with the recess and No. of teeth marking facing outwards. Install the sprocket retaining nuts and tighten them to the torque setting specified at the beginning of the Chapter.

18 Rear wheel coupling/rubber damper - check and renewal

1 Remove the rear wheel as described in Chapter 7.

Caution: Do not lay the wheel down on the disc as it could become warped. Lay the wheel on wooden blocks so that the disc is off the ground.

2 If it has not already been removed, withdraw the spacer from the outside of the sprocket coupling.

3 Lift the sprocket coupling away from the wheel leaving the rubber dampers in position in the wheel. Take care not to lose the spacer from the inside of the coupling bearing.

4 Lift the rubber damper segments from the wheel and check them for cracks, hardening and general deterioration **(see illustration)**. Renew the rubber dampers as a set if necessary.

5 Checking and renewal procedures for the sprocket coupling bearing are described in Section 16 of Chapter 7.

6 Installation is the reverse of the removal procedure, making sure that the sprocket coupling spacers are correctly positioned.

7 Install the rear wheel as described in Chapter 7.

Notes

Chapter 7
Brakes, wheels and tyres

Contents

Degrees of difficulty

Easy, suitable for novice with little experience	**Fairly easy,** suitable for beginner with some experience	**Fairly difficult,** suitable for competent DIY mechanic	**Difficult,** suitable for experienced DIY mechanic	**Very difficult,** suitable for expert DIY or professional

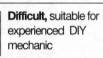

Specifications

Brakes

Brake fluid type	DOT 4
Brake pad minimum thickness	1.5 mm (see text)
Disc thickness:	
Front – all models except Tiger	
New	5.0 mm
Service limit	4.5 mm
Front – Tiger models	
New	4.0 mm
Service limit	3.5 mm
Rear – all models except Tiger	
New	6.0 mm
Service limit	5.0 mm
Rear – Tiger models	
New	5.0 mm
Service limit	4.0 mm
Disc maximum runout (front and rear)	0.3 mm
Caliper piston dimensions – refer to Section 1 for caliper identification	
Front	
Type A	33.96 mm and 30.23 mm
Types B, D and E	27.0 mm
Type C	30.2 mm, 25.4 mm and 22.0 mm
Rear – all types	27.0 mm
Master cylinder piston dimensions – refer to Section 1 for master cylinder identification	
Front	
Types A and C	15.8 mm
Type B	14.0 mm
Type D	11.0 mm
Type E	12.7 mm
Rear – all types	14.0 mm

Wheels

Maximum wheel runout (front and rear)	
Axial (side-to-side)	0.5 mm
Radial (out-of-round)	0.8 mm

Tyres

Tyre pressures and minimum tread depth	see Chapter 1
Tyre sizes*	
Front	
Trident, Sprint, Trophy, Speed Triple, Daytona	120/70 ZR 17
Thunderbird, Adventurer (up to VIN 71698)	110/80 ZR or VR 18
Adventurer (from VIN 71699)	100/90 ZR 19
Thunderbird Sport, Legend TT	120/70 R 17
Tiger	110/80 R 19
Rear	
Trident	160/60 ZR 18
Trophy and Sprint	170/60 ZR 17
Daytona and Speed Triple	180/55 ZR 17
Thunderbird, Adventurer (up to VIN 71698)	160/80 ZR 16 or 160/80 R 16
Adventurer (from VIN 71699)	150/80 ZR16
Thunderbird Sport, Legend TT	160/70 R 17
Tiger	140/80 R 17

**Refer to the owner's handbook or the tyre information label on the motorcycle for approved tyre brands.*

Torque settings

Front brake caliper	
Mounting bolts	
Type A, B, and C calipers	40 Nm
Type D and E calipers	28 Nm
Pad retaining pin	18 Nm
Pad pin plug (Type D and E calipers)	3 Nm
Caliper body joining bolts (Type A caliper)	25 Nm
Front brake disc retaining bolts	22 Nm
Front brake master cylinder clamp bolts	15 Nm
Front brake lever pivot bolt	
Tiger	6 Nm
All other models	1 Nm
Front brake lever pivot bolt locknut	6 Nm
Rear brake caliper	
Mounting bolt	
Type A and B calipers	40 Nm
Type C caliper	28 Nm
Pad retaining pin	18 Nm
Rear brake disc retaining bolts	22 Nm
Rear brake master cylinder mounting bolts	27 Nm
Rear brake light switch	15 Nm
Rear brake torque arm mounting bolts	28 Nm
Brake caliper bleed valves	5 Nm
Brake hose banjo union bolts	
Adapter at rear master cylinder (early models)	28 Nm
All other banjo union bolts	25 Nm
Front axle bolt (all models except Tiger)	60 Nm
Front axle clamp bolts (all models except Tiger)	20 Nm
Front axle nut (Tiger)	85 Nm
Rear axle bolt	85 Nm
Drive chain adjuster clamp bolts (Trident, Sprint, Trophy, Speed Triple, Daytona, Thunderbird (to VIN 29155), Tiger)	35 Nm

1 General information

Trident, Sprint, Trophy, Speed Triple and Daytona models are fitted with cast alloy wheels designed for tubeless tyres. The Thunderbird, Thunderbird Sport, Adventurer, Legend TT and Tiger models are fitted with spoked wheels using alloy rims and tubed tyres. Both front and rear brakes are hydraulically operated disc brakes. Four different set-ups are used across the range of models on the front, as described in Table 1.

On the rear, all models have 2 piston sliding calipers with a single fixed disc. Three different mounting set-ups are used throughout the range, as described in Table 2.

Caution: Disc brake components rarely require disassembly. Do not disassemble components unless absolutely necessary. If a hydraulic brake line is loosened, the entire system must be disassembled, drained, cleaned and then properly filled and bled upon reassembly. Do not use solvents on internal brake components. Solvents will cause the seals to swell and distort. Use only clean brake fluid or denatured alcohol for cleaning. Use care when working with brake fluid as it can injure your eyes and it will damage painted surfaces and plastic parts.

Table 1 – Front brake set-ups

Type A	4 piston opposed caliper with twin floating discs	Daytona (not Super III), Speed Triple, Sprint and 900 Trophy from VIN 9083, 1200 Trophy from VIN 4902
Type B	2 piston sliding caliper, with twin fixed discs	Trident, Tiger, Sprint and 900 Trophy to VIN 9082, 1200 Trophy to VIN 4901
Type C	6 piston opposed caliper, with twin floating discs	Daytona Super III
Type D	2 piston sliding caliper, with single fixed disc	Thunderbird, Adventurer, Legend TT
Type E	2 piston sliding caliper, with twin fixed discs	Thunderbird Sport

Table 2 – Rear brake set-ups

Type A	Caliper mounted below disc	Daytona, Speed Triple, Trophy from VIN 29156
Type B	Caliper mounted above disc, with torque arm mounted on caliper	Trophy to VIN 29155, Trident, Sprint and Tiger
Type C	Caliper mounted above disc, with torque arm mounted on caliper bracket	Thunderbird, Thunderbird Sport, Adventurer, Legend TT

2 Front brake pads – renewal

Note: *For brake caliper type applications, see Section 1.*

Warning: When renewing the front brake pads always renew the pads in BOTH calipers – never just on one side (not Thunderbird, Adventurer or Legend TT). The dust created by the brake system may contain asbestos, which is harmful to your health. Never blow it out with compressed air and don't inhale any of it. An approved filtering mask should be worn when working on the brakes.

1 On the Type A caliper, unscrew and remove the pad retaining pin from the caliper, then remove the pad spring, noting how it fits, and withdraw the pads from the caliper body **(see illustrations)**.

2 On the Type B caliper, slacken the pad retaining pins, then unscrew the caliper mounting bolts and remove the caliper from the disc. Support the caliper so that no strain is placed on its hose. Press down on the pads and remove the pad retaining pins. Withdraw the pads from the caliper body and remove the pad spring, noting how it fits.

3 On the Type C caliper, unscrew the caliper mounting bolts and remove the caliper from the disc **(see illustration)**. Support the caliper

2.1a Type A caliper – unscrew the pad retaining pin . . .

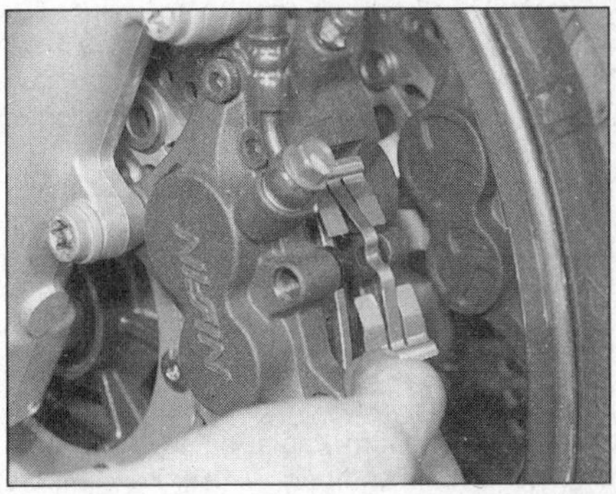

2.1b . . . remove the pad spring . . .

2.1c . . . and withdraw the brake pads

2.3 Caliper mounting bolts (arrows) – Type C caliper

7

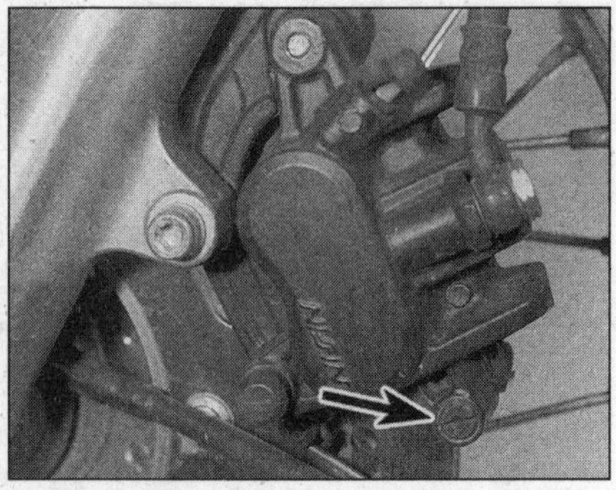

2.4 Unscrew the pad retaining pin plug (arrowed) to reveal pad pin – Type D caliper

so no strain is placed on the hose. Drive the pad retaining pins out using a suitable drift. Remove the pad spring, noting how it fits, and withdraw the pads from the caliper body.

4 On the Type D and E caliper, unscrew the pad retaining pin plug, then unscrew and remove the pad retaining pin from the caliper **(see illustration)**. Withdraw the pads from the lower end of the caliper body and remove the pad spring, noting how it fits.

5 On all types, inspect the surface of each pad for contamination and check that the friction material has not worn beyond its service limit **(see illustration)**. If either pad is worn down to, or beyond, the service limit specification or wear grooves (ie the grooves are no longer visible), fouled with oil or grease, or heavily scored or damaged by dirt and debris, both pads must be renewed as a set. Note that it is not possible to degrease the friction material; if the pads are contaminated in any way they must be renewed.

6 If the pads are in good condition clean them carefully, using a fine wire brush which is completely free of oil and grease to remove all traces of road dirt and corrosion. Using a pointed instrument, clean out the grooves in the friction material and dig out any embedded particles of foreign matter. Any areas of glazing may be removed using emery cloth.

7 Check the condition of the brake disc(s) (see Section 4).

8 Remove all traces of corrosion from the pad

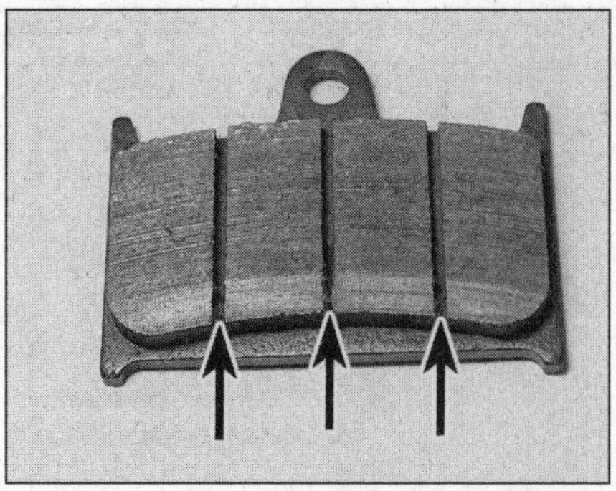

2.5 Brake pads must be renewed when the wear grooves (arrowed) are no longer visible (typical pad design shown)

pin(s). Inspect the pin(s) for signs of damage and renew if necessary.

9 Push the pistons as far back into the caliper as possible using hand pressure only. Due to the increased friction material thickness of new pads, it may be necessary to remove the master cylinder reservoir cover and diaphragm and siphon out some fluid.

10 Smear the backs of the pads and the shanks of the pad pins with copper-based grease, making sure that none gets on the front or sides of the pads.

11 Installation of the pads, pad springs and retaining pins is the reverse of removal for each type. Insert the pads into the caliper so that the friction material of each pad is facing the disc. On the type D and E caliper, ensure the upper end of each pad engages the anti-rattle spring on the caliper mounting bracket. Make sure the pad spring(s) is correctly positioned and the pin(s) fits correctly through the holes in the pads **(see illustrations)**. Tighten the pad retaining pins and caliper mounting bolts (if removed) to the specified torque setting.

12 Top-up the master cylinder reservoir if necessary (see *'Daily (pre-ride) checks'*), and refit the reservoir cover and diaphragm if removed.

13 Operate the brake lever several times to bring the pads into contact with the disc. Check the master cylinder fluid level (see *Daily (pre-ride) checks*) and the operation of the brake before riding the motorcycle.

3 Front brake caliper(s) – removal, overhaul and installation

Warning: If a caliper indicates the need for an overhaul (usually due to leaking fluid or sticky operation), all old brake fluid should be flushed from the system. Also, the dust created by the brake system may contain asbestos, which is harmful to your health. Never blow it out with compressed air and don't inhale any of it. An approved filtering mask should be worn when working on the brakes. Do not, under any circumstances, use petroleum-based solvents to clean brake parts. Use clean brake fluid, brake cleaner or denatured alcohol only.

Note: *For brake caliper type applications, see Table 1 in Section 1.*

Removal

1 Remove the brake hose banjo bolt, noting its position on the caliper, and separate the hose from the caliper. Plug the hose end or wrap a plastic bag tightly around it to minimise fluid loss and prevent dirt entering the system. Discard the sealing washers as new ones must be used on installation. **Note:** *If you are planning to overhaul the caliper and don't have a source of compressed air to blow out the pistons, just loosen the banjo bolt at this stage and retighten it lightly. The bike's hydraulic system can then be used to force the pistons out of the body once the pads have been removed. Disconnect the hose once the pistons have been sufficiently displaced.*

2 Unscrew the caliper mounting bolts, noting the spacers (where fitted) on the Type B caliper, and slide the caliper away from the disc **(see illustration)**. Remove the brake pads as described in Section 2. On the Type D and E caliper, unscrew the speedometer cable guide from the caliper.

Overhaul

3 Clean the exterior of the caliper with

2.11a Install the pads in the caliper . . .

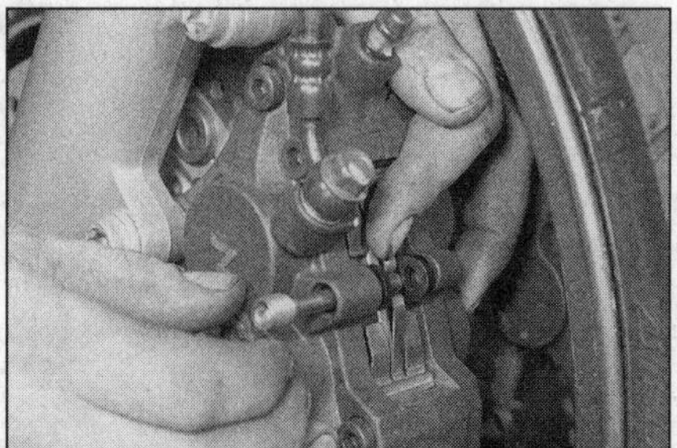

2.11b . . . then fit the pad pin and tighten it securely

3.2 Unscrew the caliper mounting bolts and slide the caliper off the disc

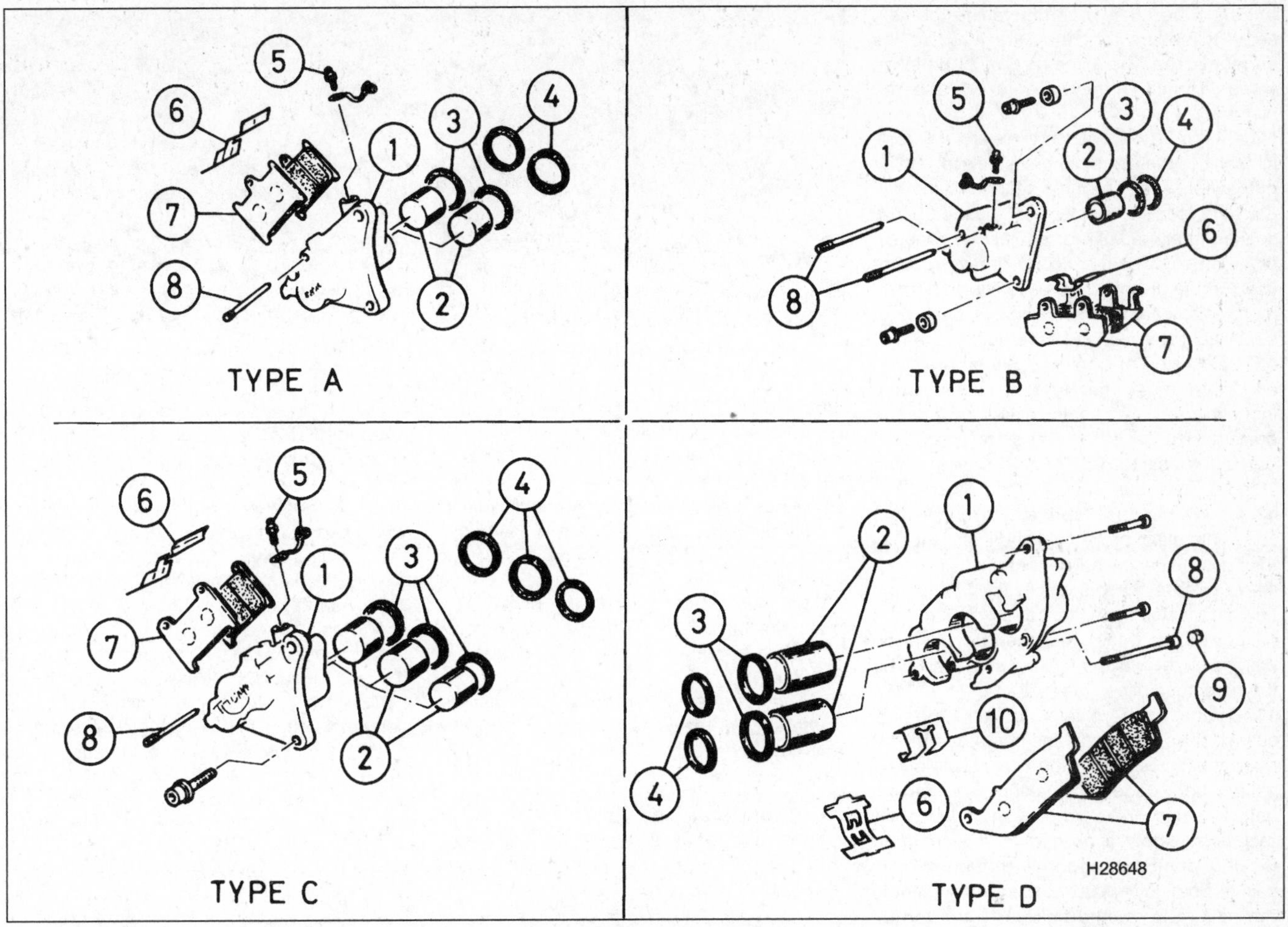

3.3 Front brake caliper detail

1 Caliper body
2 Piston
3 Piston seal
4 Dust seal
5 Bleed nipple
6 Pad spring
7 Brake pad
8 Pad pin
9 Pad pin plug
10 Anti-rattle spring

denatured alcohol or brake system cleaner **(see illustration)**.

4 Remove the pistons from the caliper body, either by pumping them out by operating the front brake lever until the pistons are displaced, or by forcing them out using compressed air. Mark each piston head and caliper body with a felt marker to ensure that the pistons can be matched to their original bores on reassembly. If the compressed air method is used, place a wad of rag between the opposed pistons (Types A and C) or between the pistons and caliper body (Types B, D and E) to act as a cushion, then use compressed air directed into the fluid inlet to force the pistons out of the body. Use only low pressure to ease the pistons out and make sure both pistons are displaced at the same time. If the air pressure is too high and the pistons are forced out, the caliper and/or pistons may be damaged. On the Type C caliper, even though the caliper body is manufactured in two halves and is bolted together, the two halves must not be split. Because of this it is not possible to remove all six pistons from the caliper at the same time. It is necessary to use a special tool (Pt. No. 3880185) which prevents the pistons in one half of the caliper from moving so that the pistons in the other half can be removed. When one side has been overhauled, reverse the tool and do the other side.

Warning: Never place your fingers in front of the pistons in an attempt to catch or protect them when applying compressed air, as serious injury could result.

5 On the Type A caliper, unscrew the caliper body joining bolts and split the caliper body into its two halves, and withdraw the pistons. Recover the seals between the caliper halves.

6 Using a wooden or plastic tool, remove the dust seals from the caliper bores and discard them. New seals must be used on installation. If a metal tool is being used, take great care not to damage the caliper bores.

7 Remove and discard the piston seals in the same way.

8 Clean the pistons and bores with denatured alcohol, clean brake fluid or brake system cleaner.

Caution: Do not, under any circumstances, use a petroleum-based solvent to clean brake parts. If compressed air is available, use it to dry the parts thoroughly (make sure it's filtered and unlubricated).

9 Inspect the caliper bores and pistons for signs of corrosion, nicks and burrs and loss of plating. If surface defects are present, the caliper assembly must be renewed. If the caliper is in bad shape the master cylinder should also be checked.

10 On Types B, D and E, check that the caliper body is able to slide on the mounting bracket pins. If seized due to corrosion, separate the two components and clean off all traces of corrosion and hardened grease. Apply a smear of copper-based grease to the mounting bracket pins and reassemble the two components. If the dust seals have deteriorated, they should be renewed; check first on their availability.

11 On Types A, B, D and E, lubricate the new piston seals with clean brake fluid and install them in their grooves in the caliper bores. Note that on the Type A caliper different sizes of bore and piston are used and care must therefore be taken when installing the new seals to ensure that they are fitted to the correct bores. The same care must be taken when fitting the new dust seals and the pistons.

12 On the Type C caliper, there are two seals in each cylinder, an inner pressure seal and an outer wiper seal. The inner seal is thicker than the outer seal. The inner seal must either be soaked in brake fluid for at least 10 minutes, or be smeared with silicone grease. Do not use a mineral-based grease. The outer seal must be smeared with silicone grease. Do not soak the outer seal in brake fluid. Note that different sizes of bore and piston are used and care must therefore be taken when installing the new seals to ensure that the correct size seals are fitted to the correct bores. The same care must be taken when fitting the new dust seals and the pistons.

13 On all models, lubricate the new dust seals with clean brake fluid and install them in their grooves in the caliper bores.

14 Lubricate the pistons with clean brake fluid and install them closed-end first into the caliper bores. Using your thumbs, push the pistons all the way in, making sure they enter the bore squarely.

15 On the Type A caliper, lubricate the new caliper seals and install them into one half of the caliper body. Join the two halves of the caliper body together, making sure that the caliper seals are correctly seated in their recesses. Apply a drop of non-permanent locking compound to the threads of the caliper body joining bolts, then install them in the caliper body and tighten to the torque setting specified at the beginning of the Chapter.

Installation

16 Install the brake pads as described in Section 2.

17 Install the caliper on the brake disc making sure the pads sit squarely either side of the disc **(see illustration)**.

18 Install the caliper mounting bolts, not forgetting the spacers on the Type B caliper, and tighten them to the torque setting specified at the beginning of this Chapter **(see illustration)**. On the Type D and E caliper secure the speedometer cable guide to the caliper.

3.17 Install the caliper on the disc

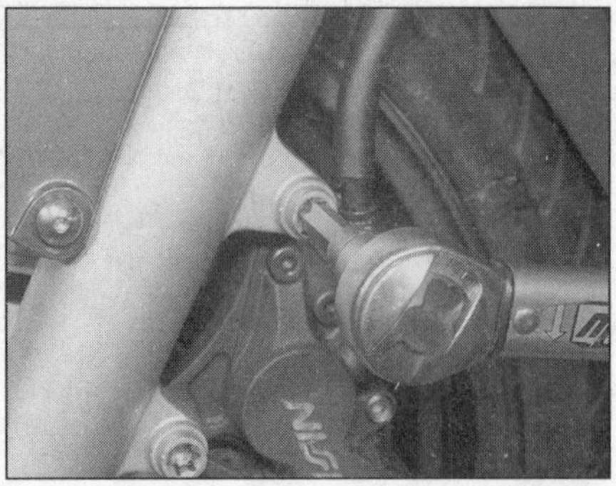

3.18 Tighten the caliper mounting bolts to the specified torque setting

19 Connect the brake hose to the caliper, using new sealing washers on each side of the fitting. Tighten the banjo bolt to the torque setting specified at the beginning of the Chapter.

20 Fill the master cylinder with new DOT 4 brake fluid (see *'Daily (pre-ride) checks'*) and bleed the hydraulic system as described in Section 11.

21 Check for leaks and thoroughly test the operation of the brake before riding the motorcycle.

4 Front brake disc(s) – inspection, removal and installation

Inspection

1 Visually inspect the surface of the disc(s) for score marks and other damage. Light scratches are normal after use and won't affect brake operation, but deep grooves and heavy score marks will reduce braking efficiency and accelerate pad wear. If a disc is badly grooved it must be machined or renewed.

2 To check disc runout, position the bike on its centre stand and support it so that the front wheel is raised off the ground. Where only a sidestand is fitted, the front wheel must be raised off the ground using an auxiliary stand – always make sure that the bike is properly supported. Mount a dial gauge to the fork slider, with the gauge plunger touching the surface of the disc about 10 mm (1/2 inch) from the outer edge **(see illustration)**. Rotate the wheel and watch the gauge needle, comparing the reading with the limit listed in the Specifications at the beginning of the Chapter. If the runout is greater than the service limit, check the hub bearings for play. If the bearings are worn, renew them and repeat this check. If the disc runout is still excessive, it will have to be renewed, although machining by a competent engineering shop may be possible.

3 The disc must not be machined or allowed to wear down to a thickness less than the service limit as listed in this Chapter's Specifications and as stamped on the outside of the disc itself. The thickness of the disc can be checked with a micrometer **(see illustration)**. If the thickness of the disc is less than the service limit, it must be renewed.

Removal

4 Remove the wheel (refer to Section 14). ***Caution: Do not lay the wheel down and allow it to rest on one of the discs – the disc could become warped. Set the wheel on wood blocks so the disc doesn't support the weight of the wheel.***

5 Mark the relationship of the disc to the wheel, so it can be installed in the same position. Remove the disc retaining bolt caps (if fitted), then unscrew the bolts and remove the disc from the wheel **(see illustration)**.

4.2 Using a dial gauge to measure disc runout

4.3 Using a micrometer to measure disc thickness

4.5 Unscrew the disc bolts a little at a time and in a criss-cross pattern to avoid distorting the disc

5.3 Loosen the reservoir cover screws

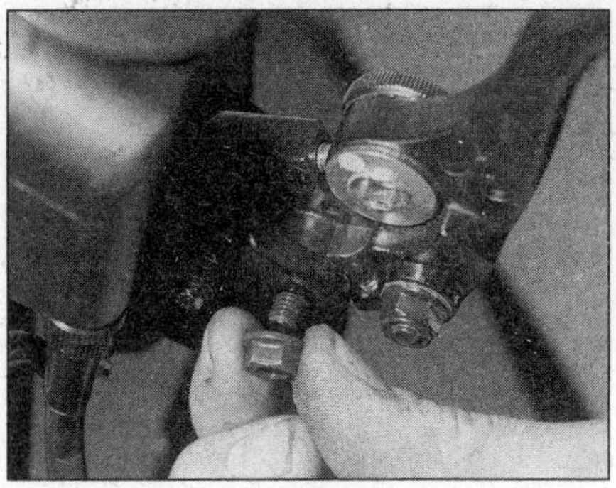

5.5a Unscrew the brake lever pivot bolt locknut

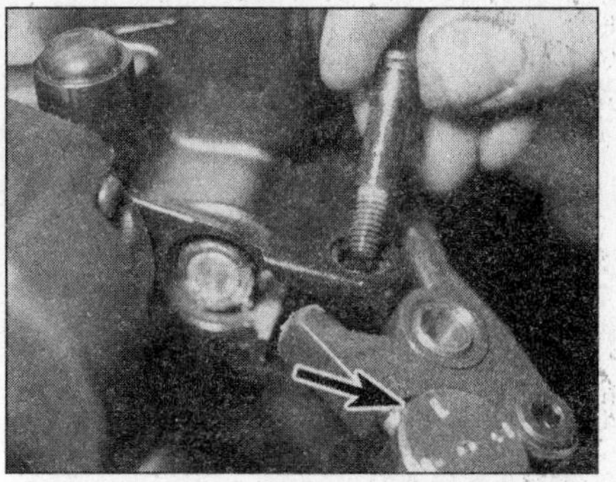

5.5b Unscrew and remove the pivot bolt, then remove the lever. Note the setting on the span adjuster (arrowed)

Loosen the bolts a little at a time, in a criss-cross pattern, to avoid distorting the disc.

6 On all models except the Thunderbird, Adventurer and Legend TT, if both discs are to be removed mark them LEFT and RIGHT to ensure that they are correctly positioned on installation.

Installation

7 Install the disc on the wheel, aligning the previously applied matchmarks (if you're reinstalling the original disc).

8 Install the bolts and tighten them in a criss-cross pattern evenly and progressively to the torque setting specified at the beginning of the Chapter. Install the bolt caps, if fitted. Clean off all grease from the brake disc(s) using acetone or brake system cleaner. If a new brake disc has been installed, remove any protective coating from its working surfaces.

9 Install the wheel as described in Section 14.

10 Operate the brake lever several times to bring the pads into contact with the disc. Check the operation of the brakes carefully before riding the bike.

5 Front brake master cylinder – removal, overhaul and installation

1 If the master cylinder is leaking fluid, or if the lever does not produce a firm feel when the brake is applied, and bleeding the brakes does not help (see Section 11), and the hydraulic hoses are all in good condition, then master cylinder overhaul is recommended.

2 Before disassembling the master cylinder, read through the entire procedure and make sure that you obtain all new parts required. Also, you will need some new, clean brake fluid of the recommended type, some clean rags and internal circlip pliers. **Note:** *To prevent damage to the paint from spilled brake fluid, always cover the fuel tank when working on the master cylinder.*

Caution: Disassembly, overhaul and reassembly of the brake master cylinder must be done in a spotlessly clean work area to avoid contamination and possible failure of the brake hydraulic system components.

Removal

3 Loosen, but do not remove, the screws holding the reservoir cover in place **(see illustration)**.

4 Disconnect the electrical connectors from the brake light switch.

5 Remove the locknut from the underside of the brake lever pivot bolt, then unscrew the bolt (on Tiger remove the bolt cap first) and remove the brake lever **(see illustrations)**. On Tiger models, the plastic hand guard will be freed as the brake lever pivot bolt is withdrawn; retrieve the collar from the pivot bolt. If fitted, note the setting of the lever span adjuster.

6 Remove the rubber boot then unscrew the banjo bolt and separate the brake hose from the master cylinder. Note the alignment of the hose. Discard the two sealing washers as these must be renewed. Wrap the end of the hose in a clean rag and suspend the hose in an upright position or bend it down carefully and place the open end in a clean container. The objective is to prevent excessive loss of brake fluid, fluid spills and system contamination.

7 Remove the master cylinder mounting bolts to free the clamp, then lift the master cylinder and reservoir away from the handlebar **(see illustration)**.

Overhaul

8 Remove its retaining screws and lift off the reservoir cover and the rubber diaphragm **(see illustration)**. Drain the brake fluid from

5.7 Remove the clamp bolts (arrowed) to free the master cylinder

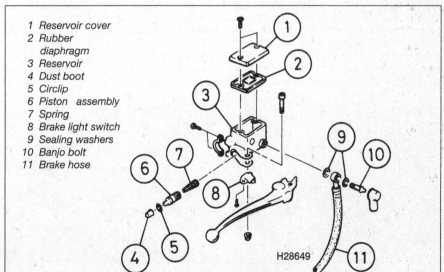

1 *Reservoir cover*
2 *Rubber diaphragm*
3 *Reservoir*
4 *Dust boot*
5 *Circlip*
6 *Piston assembly*
7 *Spring*
8 *Brake light switch*
9 *Sealing washers*
10 *Banjo bolt*
11 *Brake hose*

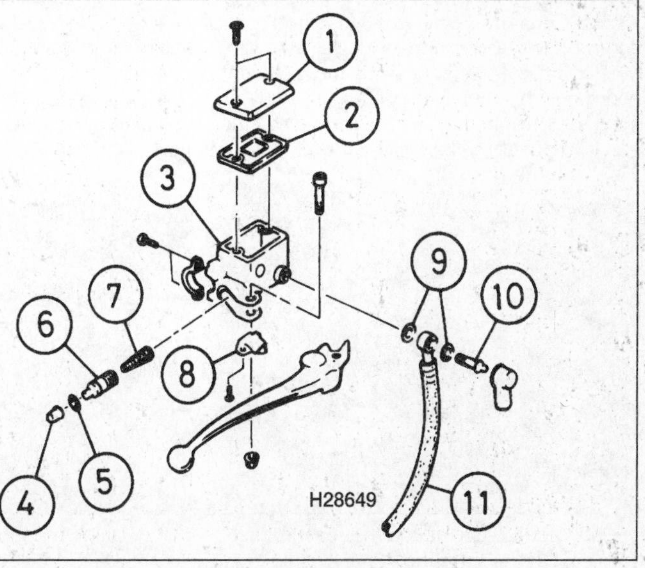

5.8 Front brake master cylinder detail

7

5.20a Fit the master cylinder and clamp to the handlebar making sure they are correctly aligned

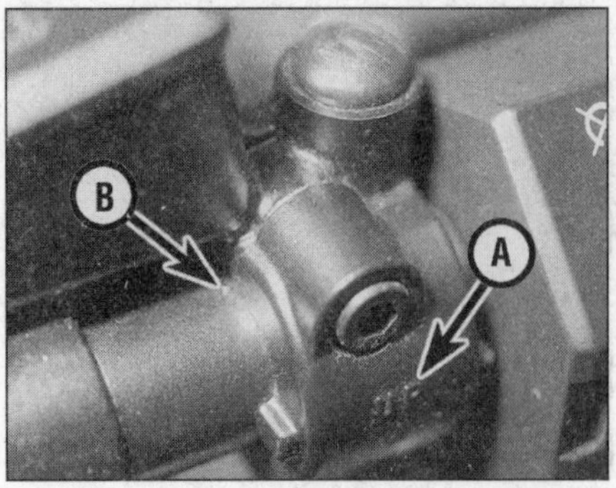

5.20b Note the UP mark on the clamp (A) and the punch mark on the handlebar (B)

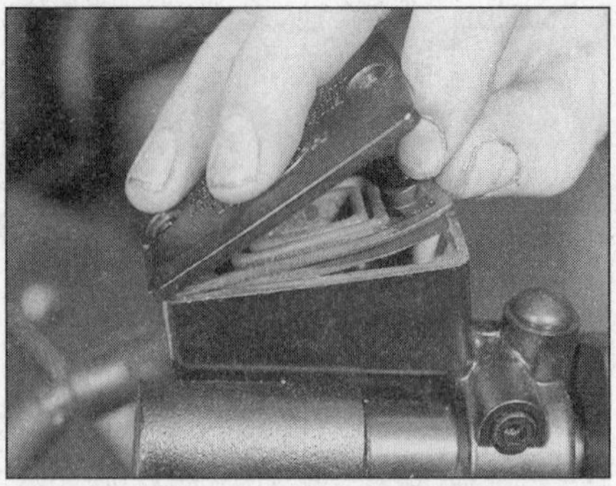

5.25 Make sure the diaphragm is properly seated, then fit the reservoir cover

the reservoir into a suitable container. Wipe any remaining fluid out of the reservoir with a clean rag.

9 Undo the brake light switch retaining screw and remove the switch.

10 Carefully remove the dust boot from the end of the piston.

11 Using circlip pliers, remove the circlip and slide out the piston assembly and the spring, noting how they fit. Lay the parts out in the proper order to prevent confusion during reassembly. Triumph advise that the piston, seals and circlip assembly be renewed when disturbed.

12 Clean all parts with clean brake fluid or denatured alcohol.

Caution: Do not, under any circumstances, use a petroleum-based solvent to clean brake parts. If compressed air is available, use it to dry the parts thoroughly (make sure it's filtered and unlubricated).

13 Check the master cylinder bore for corrosion, scratches, nicks and score marks. If damage is evident, the master cylinder must be renewed. If the master cylinder is in poor condition, then the caliper(s) should be checked as well. Check that the fluid inlet and outlet ports in the master cylinder are clear.

14 The dust boot, piston assembly and spring are included in the rebuild kit. Use all of the new parts, regardless of the apparent condition of the old ones.

15 Install the spring in the master cylinder so that its tapered end faces the piston.

16 Lubricate the piston seal with clean hydraulic fluid and slip the piston into the master cylinder. Depress the piston and install the new circlip, making sure that it locates in the master cylinder groove.

17 Locate the dust boot in the bore and engage its outer end in the piston groove.

18 Install the brake light switch and securely tighten its retaining screw.

19 Inspect the reservoir cover rubber diaphragm and renew it if damaged or deteriorated.

Installation

20 Attach the master cylinder to the handlebar and fit the clamp making sure the 'UP' mark is facing upwards **(see illustration)**. Align the upper mating surfaces of the clamp with the punch mark on the handlebar, then tighten the upper clamp bolt first followed by the lower one **(see illustration)**.

21 Connect the brake hose to the master cylinder, using new sealing washers on each side of the union. Tighten the banjo bolt to the torque setting specified at the beginning of this Chapter.

22 Install the brake lever and pivot bolt and tighten the bolt to the specified torque setting. On Tiger models also fit the hand guard and collar. On all models, install the pivot bolt locknut and tighten it to the specified torque setting. Install the pivot bolt cap on Tiger models. The front brake lever has an adjuster mechanism which alters the span of the lever from the handlebar according to the rider's requirements. Adjust this as necessary by turning the adjuster either clockwise or anti-clockwise until the desired position is achieved (see Chapter 1).

23 Connect the brake light switch wiring.

24 Fill the fluid reservoir with new DOT 4 brake fluid as described in *Daily (pre-ride) checks*. Refer to Section 11 of this Chapter and bleed the air from the system.

25 Carefully fit the rubber diaphragm, making sure that it is correctly seated, and the cover on the master cylinder reservoir **(see illustration)**.

6 Rear brake pads – renewal

Warning: The dust created by the brake system may contain asbestos, which is harmful to your health. Never blow it out with compressed air and don't inhale any of it. An approved filtering mask should be worn when working on the brakes.

Note: *For brake caliper type applications, see Section 1.*

1 On models where the exhaust silencer restricts access to the brake caliper, remove the silencer (Chapter 4).

2 On Type A and B calipers, slacken the pad retaining pins, then unscrew the caliper mounting bolts and remove the caliper from the disc **(see illustrations)**. Support the caliper so that no strain is placed on the hose.

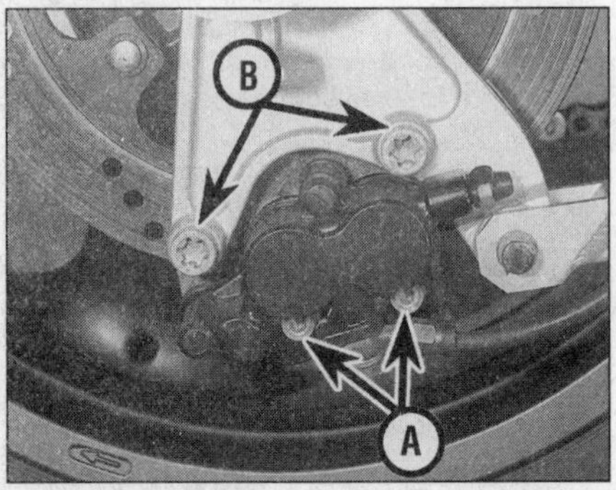

6.2a Type A caliper – Pad retaining pins (A), caliper mounting bolts (B)

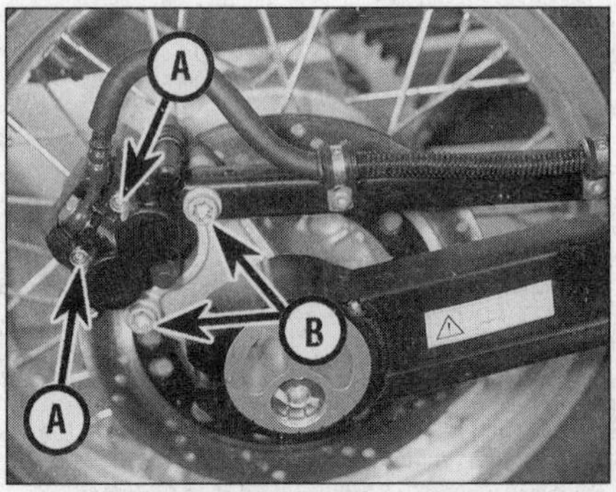

6.2b Type B caliper – Pad retaining pins (A), caliper mounting bolts (B)

6.2c Slacken the pad retaining pins . . .

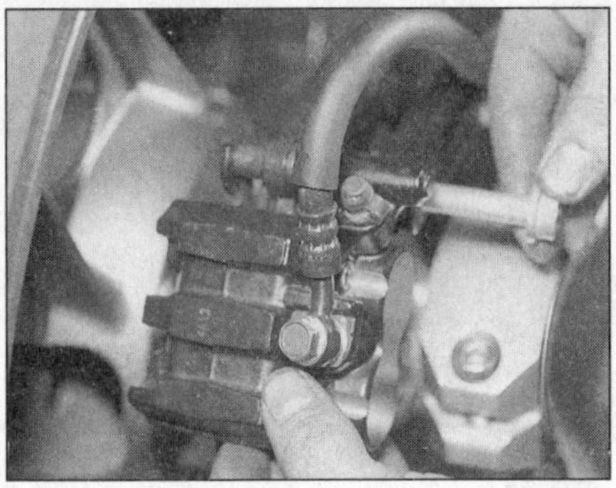

6.2d . . . unscrew the caliper mounting bolts . . .

6.2e . . . and remove the caliper from the disc

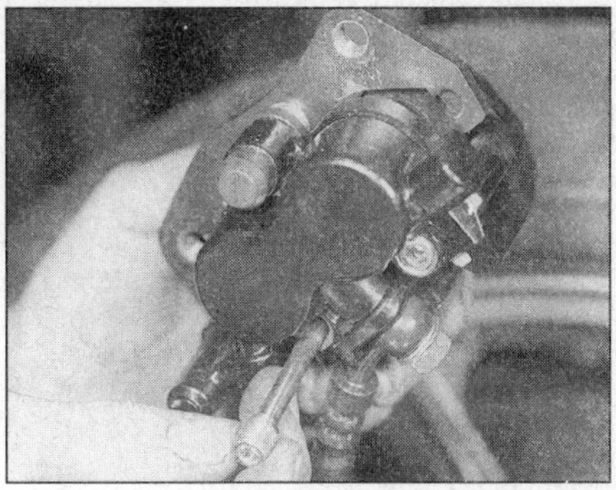

6.2f Unscrew the pad retaining pins . . .

6.2g . . . and remove the pads, noting how they fit against the lug (arrowed)

6.2h Note the fitting of the pad spring (arrowed)

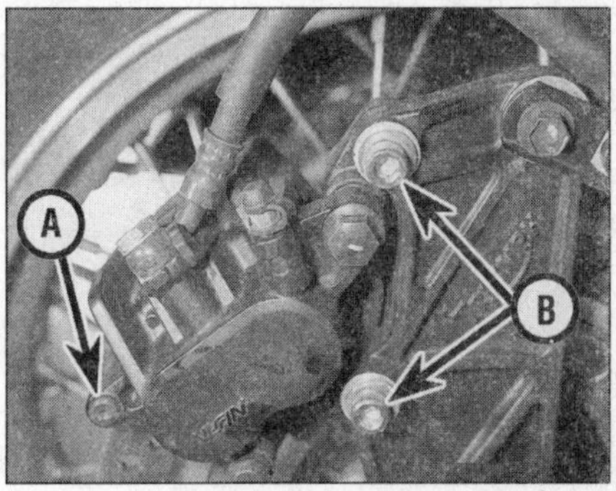

6.3 Type C caliper – Pad retaining pin plug and pin (A), caliper mounting bolts (B)

Press down on the pads and remove the pad retaining pins. Withdraw the pads from the caliper body and remove the pad spring, if necessary, noting how it fits **(see illustrations)**.

3 On the Type C caliper, unscrew the pad retaining pin plug, then unscrew and remove the pad retaining pin from the caliper **(see illustration)**. Withdraw the pads from the lower end of the caliper body and remove the pad spring, noting how it fits.

4 Inspect the brake pads and associated components as described in Steps 5 through 8 of Section 2.

5 Push the pistons as far back into the caliper as possible using hand pressure only. Due to the increased friction material thickness of new pads, it may be necessary to remove the master cylinder reservoir cover and diaphragm and siphon out some fluid.

6 Smear the backs of the pads and the shanks of the pad pins with copper-based grease, making sure that none gets on the front or sides of the pads.

7 Installation of the pads, pad springs and retaining pins is the reverse of removal for each type. Insert the pads into the caliper so that the friction material of each pad is facing the disc. On the Type C caliper, ensure that the upper end of each pad engages the anti-rattle spring on the caliper slider bracket. Make sure the pad spring is correctly positioned and the pins fit correctly through the holes in the pads. Tighten the pad retaining pins and caliper mounting bolts (if removed) to the specified torque setting.

8 Top-up the master cylinder reservoir if necessary (see *Daily (pre-ride) checks*), and refit the reservoir cap and diaphragm if removed.

9 Operate the brake pedal several times to bring the pads into contact with the disc. Check the master cylinder fluid level (see *Daily (pre-ride) checks*) and the operation of the brake before riding the motorcycle.

10 Check that the brake hose is located in the retaining clamp on the swingarm.

11 If removed, fit the exhaust silencer.

7 Rear brake caliper – removal, overhaul and installation

Warning: If the caliper indicates the need for an overhaul (usually due to leaking fluid or sticky operation), all old brake fluid should be flushed from the system. Also, the dust created by the brake system may contain asbestos, which is harmful to your health. Never blow it out with compressed air and don't inhale any of it. An approved filtering mask should be worn when working on the brakes.

Caution: Do not, under any circumstances, use petroleum-based solvents to clean brake parts. Use clean brake fluid or denatured alcohol only.

Note: *For brake caliper type applications, see Table 2 in Section 1.*

Removal

1 On models where the exhaust silencer restricts access to the brake caliper, remove the silencer (Chapter 4).

2 Remove the brake hose banjo bolt and separate the hose from the caliper. Plug the hose end or wrap a plastic bag tightly around it to minimise fluid loss and prevent dirt entering the system. Discard the sealing washers; new ones must be used on installation. **Note:** *If you are planning to overhaul the caliper and don't have a source of compressed air to blow out the pistons, just loosen the banjo bolt at this stage and retighten it lightly. The bike's hydraulic system can then be used to force the pistons out of the body once the pads have been removed. Disconnect the hose once the pistons have been sufficiently displaced.*

3 Remove the caliper mounting bolts and slip the caliper off the disc **(see illustrations 6.2a, 6.2b and 6.3)**.

4 Remove the brake pads as described in Section 6.

Overhaul

5 Clean the exterior of the caliper with clean

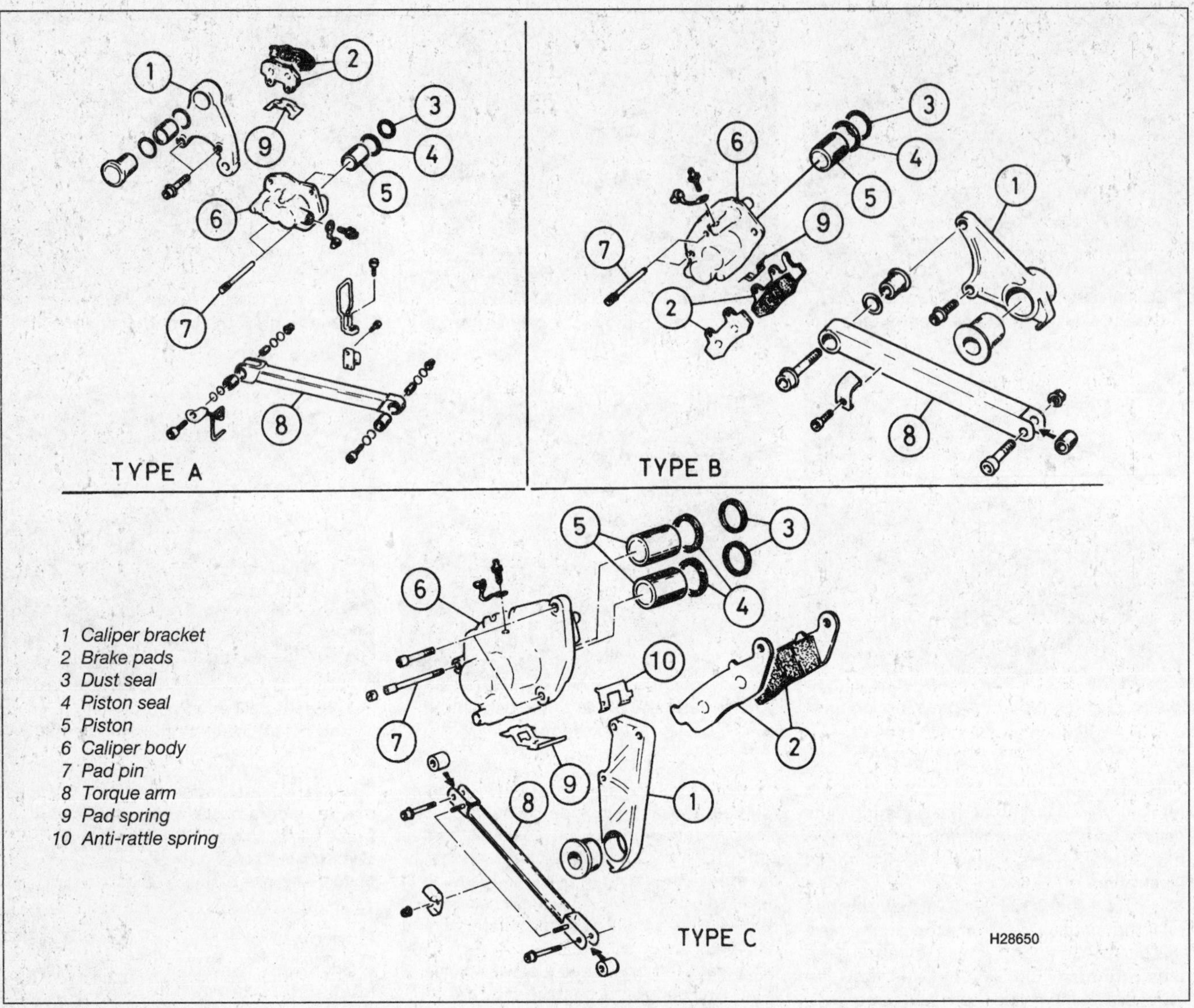

7.5 Rear brake caliper detail

brake fluid or denatured alcohol **(see illustration)**.

6 If the pistons weren't forced out using the bike's hydraulic system, place a wad of rag between the piston and caliper body to act as a cushion, then use compressed air directed into the fluid inlet to force the piston out of the body. Use only low pressure to ease the piston out. If the air pressure is too high and the piston is forced out, the caliper and/or piston may be damaged.

Warning: Never place your fingers in front of the piston in an attempt to catch or protect it when applying compressed air, as serious injury could result. Label the piston heads and caliper bores with a felt marker pen so that each piston can be returned to its original bore on reassembly.

7 Using a wooden or plastic tool, remove the dust seal from each caliper bore. If a metal tool is being used, take great care not to damage the caliper bore.

8 Remove the piston seals in the same way.

9 Clean the piston and bore with clean brake fluid or denatured alcohol.

Caution: Do not, under any circumstances, use a petroleum-based solvent to clean brake parts. If compressed air is available, use it to dry the parts thoroughly (make sure it's filtered and unlubricated).

10 Inspect the caliper bore and piston for signs of corrosion, nicks and burrs and loss of plating. If surface defects are present, the caliper assembly must be renewed. If the caliper is in bad shape the master cylinder should also be checked.

11 Check that the caliper body is able to slide on the slider bracket pins. If seized due to corrosion, separate the slider bracket from the caliper body and clean off all traces of corrosion and hardened grease. Apply a smear of copper-based grease to the slider bracket pins and reassemble the two components. If the dust seals have deteriorated, they should be renewed; check first on their availability.

12 Lubricate the new piston seals with clean brake fluid and install them in the grooves in the caliper bores.

13 Lubricate the new dust seals with clean brake fluid and install them in the grooves in the caliper bores.

14 Lubricate the pistons with clean brake fluid and install them, closed-end first, in their original bores in the caliper. Using your thumbs, push the pistons all the way in, making sure they enter the bores squarely.

Installation

15 Install the brake pads as described in Section 6.

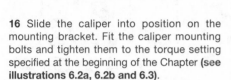

8.3 Rear brake disc mounting bolts

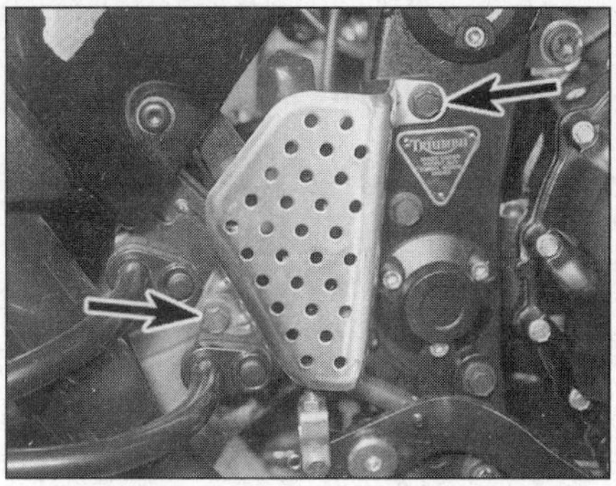
9.4 Remove two retaining bolts (arrowed) and remove the master cylinder cover

9.5 Remove the brake light switch cover and disconnect the wiring

16 Slide the caliper into position on the mounting bracket. Fit the caliper mounting bolts and tighten them to the torque setting specified at the beginning of the Chapter **(see illustrations 6.2a, 6.2b and 6.3)**.
17 Connect the brake hose to the caliper, using new sealing washers on each side of the union. Tighten the banjo bolt to the specified torque setting. Check that the brake hose is located in the retaining clamp on the swingarm.
18 Fill the master cylinder with the recommended brake fluid (see *Daily (pre-ride) checks*) and bleed the hydraulic system as described in Section 11.
19 Check that there are no leaks and thoroughly test the operation of the brake before riding the motorcycle.

8 Rear brake disc – inspection, removal and installation

Inspection

1 Refer to Section 4 of this Chapter, noting that the dial gauge should be attached to the swingarm.

Removal

2 Remove the wheel (see Section 15).
3 Mark the relationship of the disc to the wheel so it can be installed in the same position. Remove the disc retaining bolt caps (if fitted), then unscrew the bolts and remove the disc **(see illustration)**. Loosen the bolts a little at a time, in a criss-cross pattern, to avoid distorting the disc.

Installation

4 Position the disc on the wheel, aligning the previously applied matchmarks (if you're reinstalling the original disc).
5 Install the bolts and tighten them in a criss-cross pattern evenly and progressively to the torque setting specified at the beginning of this Chapter. Install the bolt caps, if fitted. Clean off all grease from the brake disc using acetone or brake system cleaner. If a new brake disc has been installed, remove any protective coating from its working surfaces.
6 Install the wheel as described in Section 15.
7 Operate the brake pedal several times to bring the pads into contact with the disc. Check the operation of the brake carefully before riding the motorcycle.

9 Rear brake master cylinder – removal, overhaul and installation

1 If the master cylinder is leaking fluid, or if the pedal does not produce a firm feel when the brake is applied, and bleeding the brakes does not help (see Section 11), and the hydraulic hoses are all in good condition, then master cylinder overhaul is recommended.
2 Before disassembling the master cylinder, read through the entire procedure and make sure that you obtain any new parts required. Also, you will need some new, clean DOT 4 brake fluid, some clean rags and internal circlip pliers.

Caution: Disassembly, overhaul and reassembly of the brake master cylinder must be done in a spotlessly clean work area to avoid contamination and possible failure of the brake hydraulic system components.

Removal

3 On Trident, Sprint, Trophy, Daytona and Speed Triple models, remove the seat and right side panel as described in Chapter 8. On Thunderbird, Thunderbird Sport, Adventurer and Legend TT models, remove the right side panel as described in Chapter 8.
4 On Tiger models, unscrew the bolts securing the master cylinder cover to the frame and remove the cover **(see illustration)**.
5 Peel back the rubber cover and disconnect the brake light switch wiring from the switch on top of the master cylinder **(see illustration)**. The brake hose union is secured by a union bolt on early models and by the brake light switch on later models. Therefore, on early models, first unscrew the brake light switch from the union bolt, then unscrew the union bolt to release the brake hose. On later models, simply unscrew the brake light switch to release the brake hose. Take note of the alignment of the brake hose union, and remove from the cylinder. Discard the sealing washers as new ones must be fitted. Wrap the end of the hose in a clean rag to prevent fluid spills and system contamination.
6 Remove the split pin and washer (spring clip and washer on later models) and withdraw the clevis pin which secures the master cylinder pushrod to the brake pedal **(see illustration)**.
7 Remove the screw securing the master cylinder fluid reservoir, then unscrew the reservoir cap and pour the fluid into a container **(see illustration)**.
8 Remove the bolts securing the master cylinder and cover (not Tiger model) to the

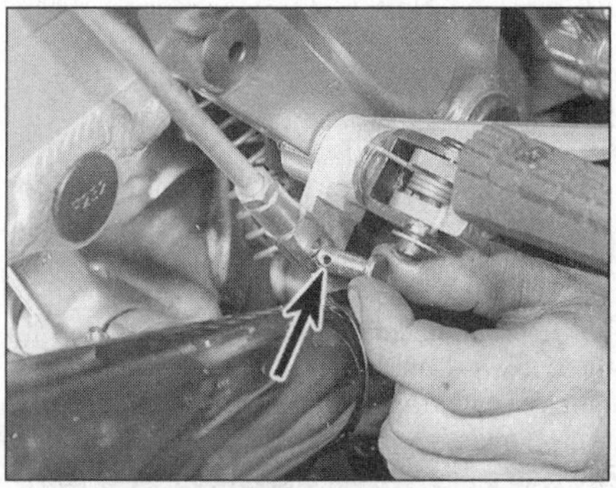
9.6 Remove the clevis pin (arrowed) to release the pushrod from the brake pedal

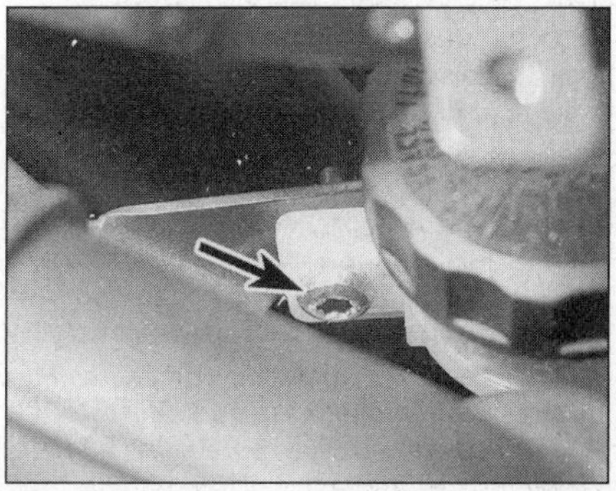
9.7 The reservoir is located behind the left side air duct and is secured to the frame by a screw (arrowed)

9.8 Remove the two bolts to release the master cylinder from the frame

frame, and remove the master cylinder assembly **(see illustration)**.

9 Separate the fluid reservoir hose from the elbow on the master cylinder by releasing the hose clamp.

Overhaul

10 Dislodge the rubber dust boot from the base of the master cylinder to reveal the pushrod retaining circlip **(see illustration)**.

11 Depress the pushrod and, using circlip pliers, remove the circlip. Slide out the piston assembly and spring. Lay the parts out in the proper order to prevent confusion during reassembly. Triumph advise that the circlip and piston seals be renewed when disturbed.

12 Clean all of the parts with clean brake fluid or denatured alcohol.

Caution: Do not, under any circumstances, use a petroleum-based solvent to clean brake parts. If compressed air is available, use it to dry the parts thoroughly (make sure it's filtered and unlubricated).

13 Check the master cylinder bore for corrosion, scratches, nicks and score marks. If damage is evident, the master cylinder must be renewed. If the master cylinder is in poor condition, then the caliper should be checked as well.

14 If required, the fluid reservoir hose elbow can be detached from the master cylinder once the circlip has been removed. Discard the O-ring as a new one must be fitted on installation. Inspect the reservoir hose for cracks or splits and renew it if necessary.

15 Before reassembling the master cylinder, soak the piston and its new seals in clean brake fluid for 10 or 15 minutes. Lubricate the master cylinder bore with clean brake fluid, then carefully insert the parts in the reverse order of disassembly, ensuring the tapered end of the spring is facing the piston. Make sure the lips on the cup seals do not turn inside out when they are slipped into the bore.

16 Install and depress the pushrod, then install a new circlip, making sure it is properly seated in the groove.

17 Install the rubber dust boot, making sure the lip is seated properly in the groove.

18 If removed, fit a new O-ring to the fluid reservoir hose elbow and retain the elbow to the master cylinder with the circlip. Reconnect the fluid reservoir hose and secure with its clip.

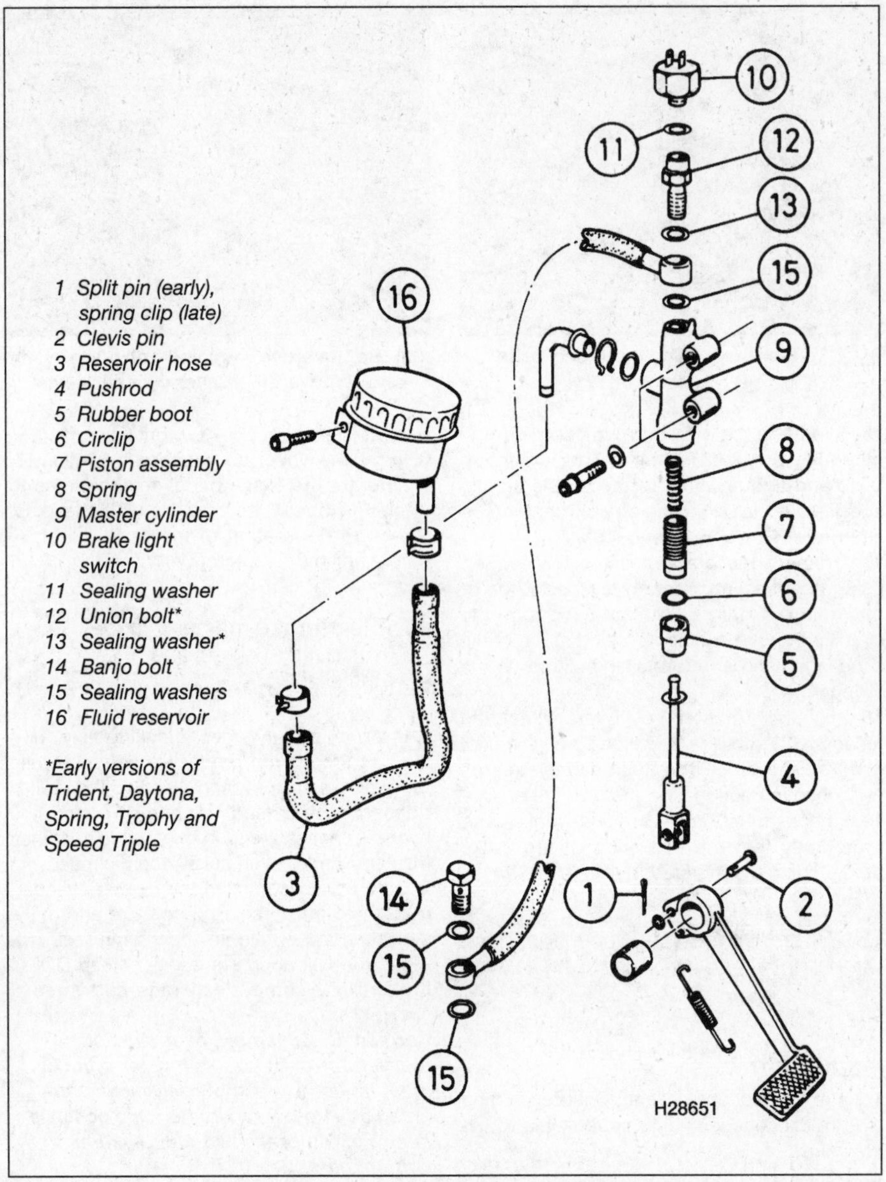

9.10 Rear brake master cylinder detail

Installation

19 Install the mounting bolts through the cover (not Tiger model) and master cylinder and attach the assembly to the frame, tightening the bolts to the specified torque setting **(see illustration 9.8)**.

20 Secure the fluid reservoir to the frame with its screw. Ensure the hose between the master cylinder and reservoir is correctly routed and secured by clamps at each end. If the clamps have weakened, use new ones.

21 On early models, connect the brake hose banjo bolt to the top of the master cylinder, using a new sealing washer on each side of the banjo union. Ensure that the hose is positioned at the correct angle and tighten the banjo bolt to the specified torque setting. Using a new sealing washer, screw the brake light switch into the banjo bolt and tighten it to the specified torque setting. Reconnect the brake light switch wires and slip the rubber cover into place.

22 On later models, position the brake hose banjo union on the top of the master cylinder, using a new sealing washer on each side of it. Ensure that the hose is positioned at the correct angle and screw the brake light switch into place, tightening it to the specified torque setting. Reconnect the brake light switch wires and slip the rubber cover into place.

23 On all models, align the brake pedal with the master cylinder pushrod clevis and slide in the clevis pin. Secure the clevis pin with a new split pin on early models, or with the spring clip on later models **(see illustration)**.

24 If the clevis position on the pushrod was disturbed during overhaul, the brake pedal height should be reset. On Thunderbird, Thunderbird Sport, Adventurer, Legend TT and Tiger models, adjustment is made via the locknut and adjusting nut on the clevis; peel up the gaiter (Thunderbird, Thunderbird Sport, Adventurer and Legend TT only) on the threaded pushrod to access the adjuster nut and tighten the locknut when adjustment is complete **(see illustration)**. On Trident, Sprint, Trophy, Speed Triple and Daytona models, slacken the locknut at the top of the clevis and rotate the pushrod to make adjustment; tighten the locknut when complete.

Warning: The master cylinder pushrod must have at least 10 mm of thread engaged in the clevis

25 Fill the fluid reservoir with the specified fluid (see *Daily (pre-ride) checks*) and bleed the system following the procedure in Section 11.

26 On Tiger models, fit the master cylinder cover.

27 Check the operation of the brake carefully before riding the motorcycle. Ensure that the pedal height is a comfortable distance below the top of the footrest, and if necessary readjust as described in Step 24.

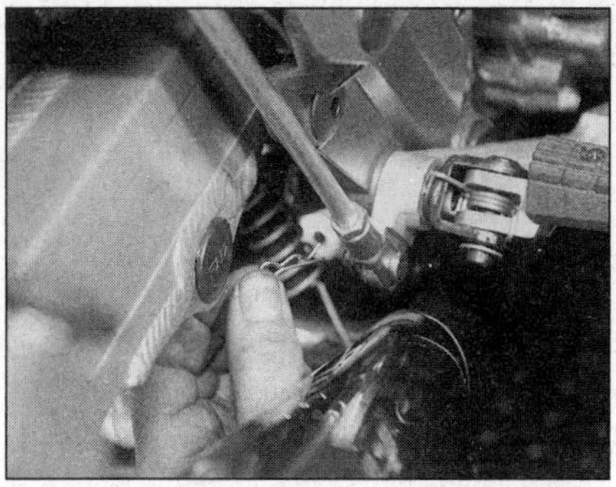

9.23 Fit a new split pin to secure the clevis pin

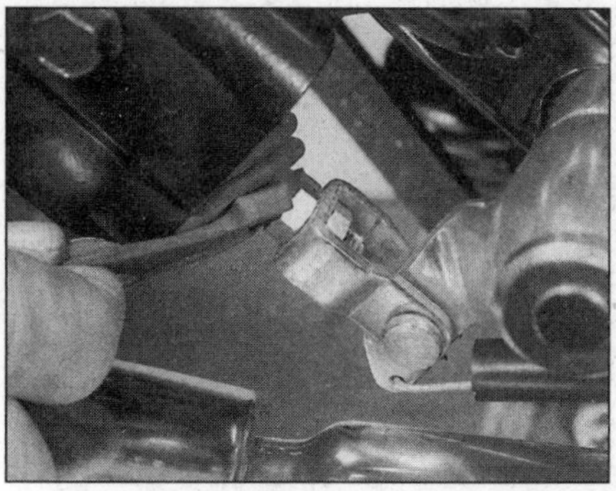

9.24 On Thunderbird and Tiger, pedal height adjustment is made at clevis

10 Brake hoses and unions – inspection and renewal

Inspection

1 Brake hose condition should be checked regularly and the hoses renewed at the specified interval (see Chapter 1).

2 Twist and flex the rubber hoses while looking for cracks, bulges and seeping fluid. Check extra carefully around the areas where the hoses connect with the banjo fittings, as these are common areas for hose failure.

3 Inspect the metal banjo fittings connected to the brake hoses. If the fittings are rusted, scratched or cracked, renew them.

Renewal

4 The brake hoses have banjo union fittings on each end. Cover the surrounding area with plenty of rags and unscrew the banjo bolt on each end of the hose. Detach the hose from any clips that may be present and remove the hose. Discard the sealing washers.

5 Position the new hose, making sure it isn't twisted or otherwise strained, and abut the tab on the hose union with the lug on the component casting. Install the banjo bolts, using new sealing washers on both sides of the unions, and tighten them to the torque setting specified at the beginning of this Chapter. Make sure they are correctly aligned and routed clear of all moving components.

6 Flush the old brake fluid from the system, refill with new DOT 4 brake fluid (see *Daily (pre-ride) checks*) and bleed the air from the system (see Section 11). Check the operation of the brakes carefully before riding the motorcycle.

11 Brake system – bleeding

1 Bleeding the brakes is simply the process of removing all the air bubbles from the brake fluid reservoirs, the hoses and the brake calipers. Bleeding is necessary whenever a brake system hydraulic connection is loosened, when a component or hose is renewed, or when the master cylinder or caliper is overhauled. Leaks in the system may also allow air to enter, but leaking brake fluid will reveal their presence and warn you of the need for repair.

2 To bleed the brakes, you will need some new, clean DOT 4 brake fluid, a length of clear vinyl or plastic tubing, a small container partially filled with clean brake fluid, some rags and a spanner to fit the brake caliper bleed valves.

3 Cover the fuel tank and other painted components to prevent damage in the event that brake fluid is spilled.

4 If the front brake lever is equipped with a span adjuster, set it to position No. 1.

5 If bleeding the rear brake, remove the right side panel and pull off the air intake duct for access to the fluid reservoir.

6 Remove the reservoir cap/cover and diaphragm and slowly pump the brake lever or pedal a few times, until no air bubbles can be seen floating up from the holes in the bottom of the reservoir. Doing this bleeds the air from the master cylinder end of the line. Loosely refit the reservoir cap/cover.

7 Pull the dust cap off the bleed valve. Attach one end of the clear vinyl or plastic tubing to the bleed valve and submerge the other end in the brake fluid in the container.

8 Remove the reservoir cap/cover and check the fluid level. Do not allow the fluid level to drop below the lower mark during the bleeding process.

9 Carefully pump the brake lever or pedal three or four times and hold it in (front) or down (rear) while opening the caliper bleed valve. When the valve is opened, brake fluid will flow out of the caliper into the clear tubing and the lever will move toward the handlebar or the pedal will move down.

10 Retighten the bleed valve (note the torque setting in the Specifications of this Chapter), then release the brake lever or pedal gradually. Repeat the process until no air bubbles are visible in the brake fluid leaving the caliper and the lever or pedal is firm when applied. Disconnect the bleeding equipment and install the dust cap on the bleed valve.

11 Install the diaphragm and cap/cover assembly, wipe up any spilled brake fluid and check the entire system for leaks.

12 Where applicable, return the front brake lever span adjuster to its original position.

HAYNES HiNT ***If it's not possible to produce a firm feel to the lever or pedal the fluid may be aerated. Let the brake fluid in the system stabilise for a few hours and then repeat the procedure when the tiny bubbles in the system have settled out.***

12 Wheels – inspection and repair

1 In order to carry out a proper inspection of the wheels, it is necessary to support the bike upright so that the wheel being inspected is raised off the ground. Position the motorcycle on its centre stand or an auxiliary stand. Clean the wheels thoroughly to remove mud and dirt that may interfere with the inspection procedure or mask defects. Make a general check of the wheels and tyres as described in Chapter 1.

2 Attach a dial gauge to the fork slider or the swingarm and position its stem against the

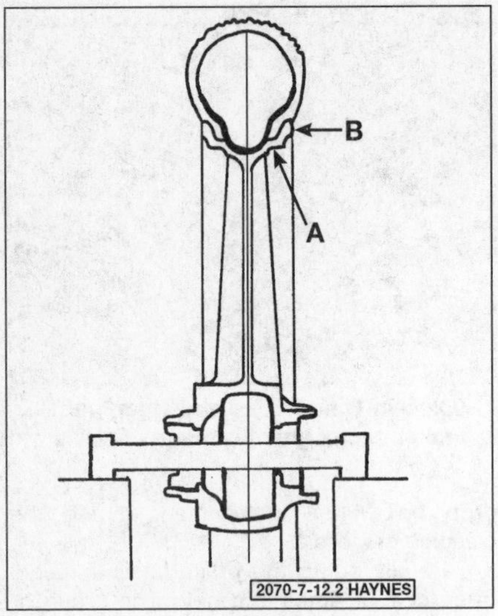

12.2 Use a dial gauge to measure wheel runout

A Radial runout B Axial runout

side of the rim **(see illustration)**. Spin the wheel slowly and check the side-to-side (axial) runout of the rim. In order to accurately check radial runout with the dial gauge, the wheel would have to be removed from the machine. With the axle clamped in a vice, the wheel can be rotated to check the runout.

3 An easier, though slightly less accurate, method is to attach a stiff wire pointer to the fork slider or the swingarm and position the end a fraction of an inch from the wheel (where the wheel and tyre join). If the wheel is true, the distance from the pointer to the rim will be constant as the wheel is rotated. **Note:** *If wheel runout is excessive, check the wheel bearings very carefully before renewing the wheel (cast wheels) or having it retensioned (spoked wheels).*

4 The wheels should also be visually inspected for cracks, flat spots on the rim and other damage. On all cast alloy wheels, look very closely for dents in the area where the tyre bead contacts the rim. Dents in this area may prevent complete sealing of the tyre against the rim, which leads to deflation of the tyre over a period of time. If damage is evident, or if runout in either direction is excessive, the wheel will have to be renewed. Never attempt to repair a damaged cast alloy wheel.

5 On spoked wheels, check for loose or broken spokes as described in Chapter 1. Spoke renewal and tensioning must be carried out by a wheel building specialist.

13 Wheels – alignment check

1 Misalignment of the wheels, which may be due to a cocked rear wheel or a bent frame or fork yokes, can cause strange and possibly serious handling problems. If the frame or yokes are at fault, repair by a frame specialist or renewal are the only alternatives.

2 To check the alignment you will need an assistant, a length of string or a perfectly straight piece of wood and a ruler. A plumb bob or other suitable weight will also be required.

3 In order to make a proper check of the wheels it is necessary to support the bike in an upright position, using an auxiliary stand. Measure the width of both tyres at their widest points. Subtract the smaller measurement from the larger measurement, then divide the difference by two. The result is the amount of offset that should exist between the front and rear tyres on both sides.

4 If a string is used, have your assistant hold one end of it about halfway between the floor and the rear axle, touching the rear sidewall of the tyre.

5 Run the other end of the string forward and pull it tight so that it is roughly parallel to the floor **(see illustration)**. Slowly bring the string into contact with the front sidewall of the rear tyre, then turn the front wheel until it is parallel with the string. Measure the distance from the front tyre sidewall to the string.

6 Repeat the procedure on the other side of the motorcycle. The distance from the front tyre sidewall to the string should be equal on both sides.

7 As was previously pointed out, a perfectly straight length of wood or metal bar may be substituted for the string **(see illustration)**. The procedure is the same.

8 If the distance between the string and tyre is greater on one side, or if the rear wheel appears to be cocked, refer to Chapter 1, Section 2 and check that the chain adjuster markings coincide on each side of the swingarm.

9 If the front-to-back alignment is correct, the wheels still may be out of alignment vertically.

10 Using the plumb bob, or other suitable weight, and a length of string, check the rear wheel to make sure it is vertical. To do this, hold the string against the tyre upper sidewall and allow the weight to settle just off the floor. When the string touches both the upper and lower tyre sidewalls and is perfectly straight, the wheel is vertical. If it is not, place thin spacers under one leg of the stand.

11 Once the rear wheel is vertical, check the front wheel in the same manner. If both wheels are not perfectly vertical, the frame and/or major suspension components are bent.

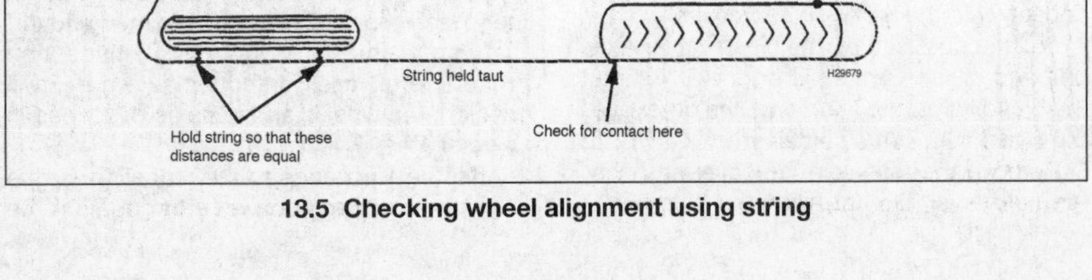

13.5 Checking wheel alignment using string

14 Front wheel – removal and installation

Removal

1 Where equipped, position the motorcycle on its centre stand and support it under the crankcase so that the front wheel is off the ground; use an auxiliary stand on models not equipped with a centre stand. Always make sure the motorcycle is properly supported.

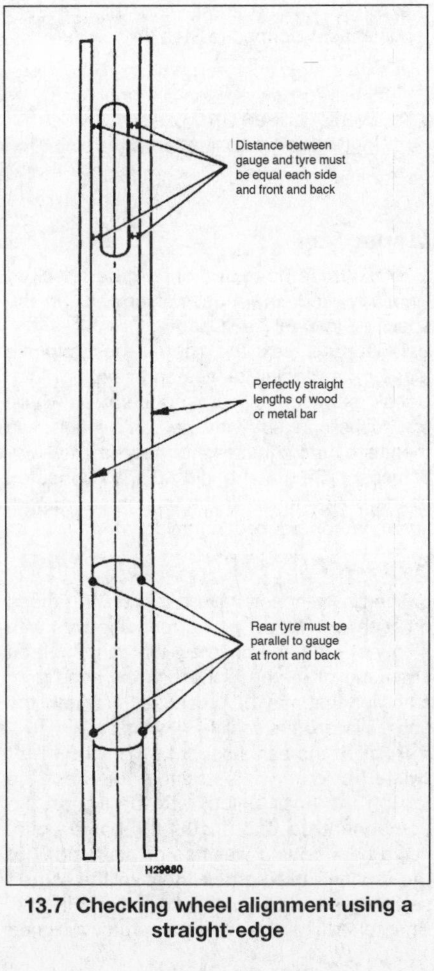

13.7 Checking wheel alignment using a straight-edge

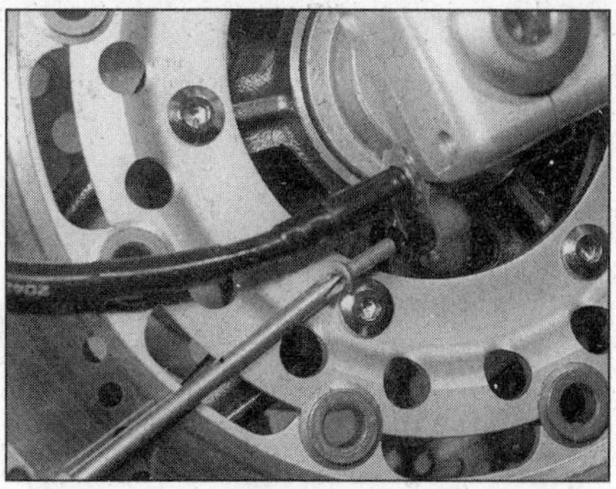

14.3 Remove the speedometer cable retaining screw and withdraw the cable

14.4a On Tiger the axle is secured by a domed nut

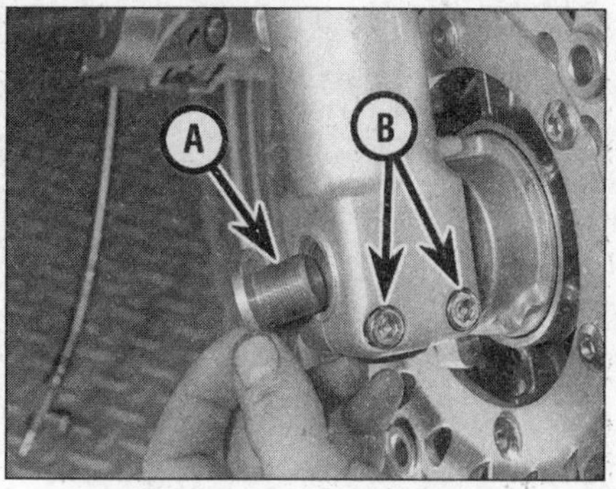

14.4b Unscrew the axle bolt (A), and loosen the axle clamp bolts (B)

2 Remove the brake caliper mounting bolts and slide the caliper(s) off the disc(s). Support each caliper with a piece of wire or a bungee cord so that no strain is placed on its hydraulic hose. There is no need to disconnect the brake hose from the caliper(s).

3 Remove the speedometer cable retaining screw on the right side of the wheel hub (left side on Thunderbird, Adventurer, Legend TT and Tiger) and detach the cable from its drive unit **(see illustration)**.

4 On Tiger models, remove the domed nut and washer from the wheel axle **(see illustration)**. On all other models, remove the axle bolt and loosen the four axle clamp bolts **(see illustration)**.

5 Support the wheel, then withdraw the axle and carefully lower the wheel **(see illustration)**.

6 Remove the spacer from the left side of the wheel (right side on Tiger models), and the speedometer drive from the right side (left side on Thunderbird, Adventurer, Legend TT and Tiger).

Caution: Don't lay the wheel down and allow it to rest on one of the discs – the disc could become warped. Set the wheel on wood blocks so the disc doesn't support the weight of the wheel. Do not operate the front brake lever with the wheel removed.

7 Check the axle for straightness by rolling it on a flat surface such as a piece of plate glass (first wipe off all old grease and remove any corrosion using fine emery cloth). If the axle is bent, renew it.

8 Check the condition of the wheel bearings (see Section 16).

Installation

9 Fit the speedometer drive to the wheel's right side (left on Thunderbird, Adventurer, Legend TT and Tiger), aligning its drive gear slots with the driveplate tabs **(see illustration)**.

10 Apply a smear of grease to the outer surface of the spacer (where it contacts the grease seal) and install the spacer in the left side of the wheel (right side on Thunderbird, Adventurer, Legend TT and Tiger) **(see illustration)**.

11 Manoeuvre the wheel into position. Apply a thin coat of grease to the axle.

12 Lift the wheel into position making sure the spacer remains in place. Position the speedometer drive lug against the rear of the lug on the fork slider **(see illustration)**.

13 Slide the axle into position from the right side on Tiger models. On all other models, slide it in from the left side.

14 On Tiger models, install the washer and domed axle nut. Tighten the nut to the specified torque setting.

15 On models except the Tiger, install the axle bolt and tighten it to the specified torque setting **(see illustration)**. Make sure the groove in the axle head aligns with the outside of the fork slider. Tighten all four axle clamp

14.5 Support the wheel and withdraw the axle

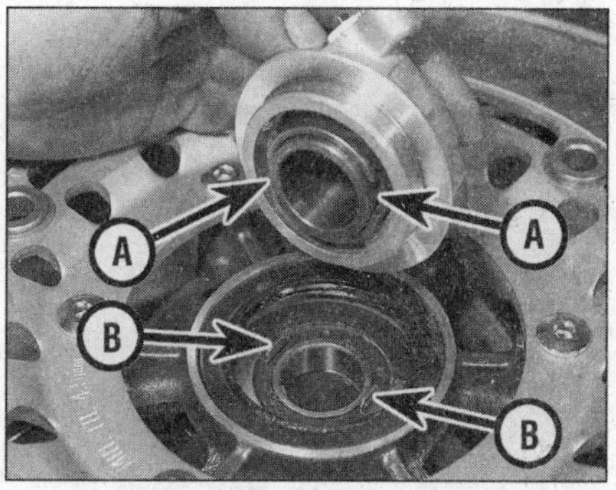

14.9 Align the slots in the speedometer drive gear (A) with the tabs on the driveplate (B)

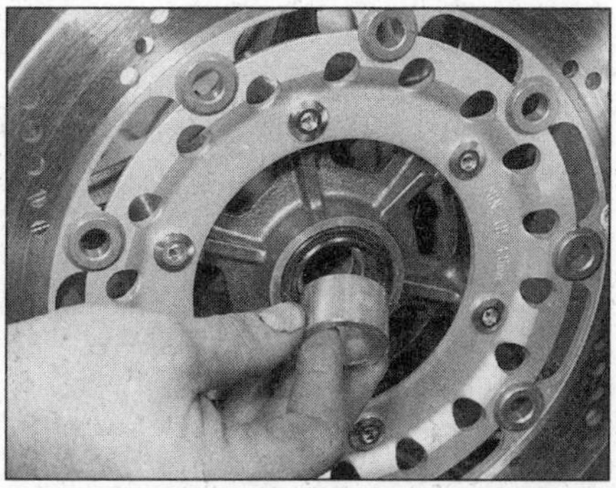

14.10 Fit the spacer into the wheel

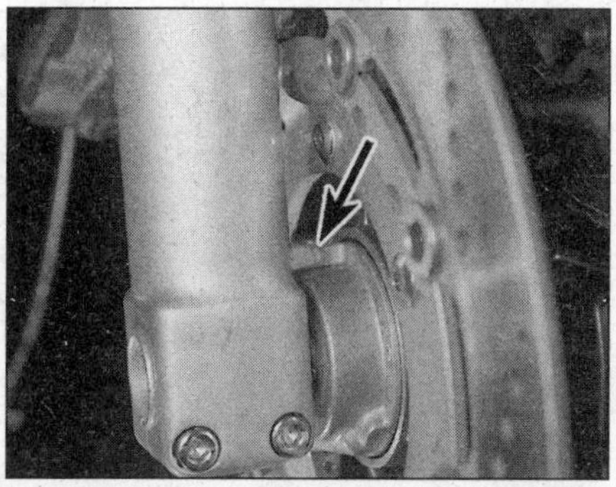

14.12 Lug on speedometer drive must abut rear of lug on fork slider (arrowed)

14.15a Tighten the axle bolt to the specified torque setting

14.15b Tighten the axle clamp bolts on both fork sliders to the specified torque

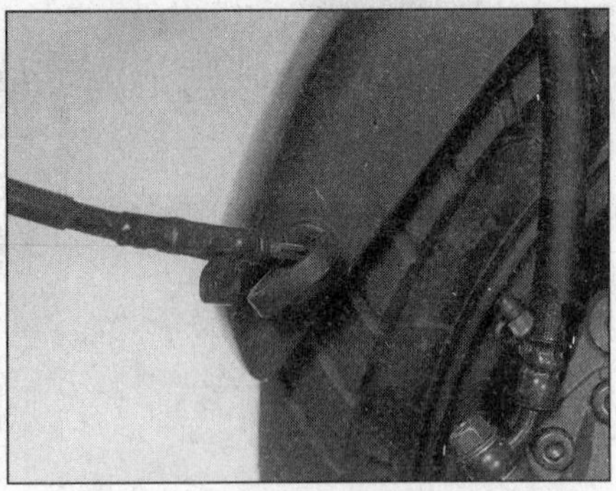

14.17a Pass the speedometer cable through its guide . . .

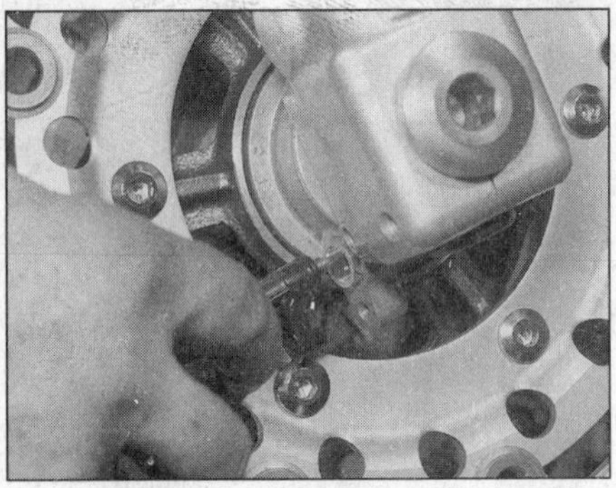

14.17b . . . and connect it to the speedometer drive

bolts to the specified torque setting **(see illustration)**.

16 Install the brake calipers making sure the pads sit squarely on either side of the disc. Fit the caliper mounting bolts and tighten them to the torque setting specified at the beginning of this Chapter.

17 Pass the speedometer cable through its guide, then connect the cable to the drive, aligning the inner cable slot with the drive dog, and securely tighten its retaining screw **(see illustrations)**.

18 Apply the front brake a few times to bring the pads back into contact with the disc(s). Move the motorcycle off its stand, apply the front brake and pump the front forks a few times to settle all components in position. Check for correct operation of the front brake before riding the motorcycle.

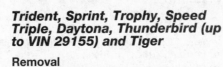

15 Rear wheel – removal and installation

Trident, Sprint, Trophy, Speed Triple, Daytona, Thunderbird (up to VIN 29155) and Tiger

Removal

1 Position the motorcycle on its centre stand. On models without a centre stand, use an auxiliary stand to hold the motorcycle upright and the rear wheel off the ground. Always make sure the bike is properly supported.

2 Unscrew the bolts securing the chainguard and remove it from the swingarm.

3 Remove the spring clips on each end of the axle **(see illustration)**. Remove the axle bolt from the right side **(see illustration)**.

15.3a Remove the spring clip from each end of the axle . . .

15.3b . . . and unscrew the axle bolt from the right side

4 Support the wheel, then slide out the axle and lower the wheel down **(see illustration)**. Depending on the type of brake caliper fitted, the caliper/torque arm assembly should be raised or lowered to ease wheel removal.

5 Disengage the chain from the sprocket and remove the wheel from the swingarm. Note which spacer fits on which side of the wheel, and remove them from the wheel. Also note, and take care not to lose, the spacer in the brake caliper bracket.

Caution: Do not lay the wheel down and allow it to rest on the disc or the sprocket – they could become warped. Set the wheel on wood blocks so that neither component supports the weight of the wheel. Do not operate the brake pedal with the wheel removed.

6 Check the axle for straightness by rolling it on a flat surface such as a piece of plate glass (first wipe off all old grease and remove any corrosion using fine emery cloth). If the axle is bent, renew it.

7 Check the condition of the wheel bearings (see Section 16).

Installation

8 Apply a thin coat of grease to the seal lips, then slide the spacers into their proper positions on both sides of the hub. Fit the spacer in the caliper bracket, making sure it is fitted the right way round **(see illustrations)**.

9 Apply a thin coat of grease to the axle.

15.4 Support the wheel and withdraw the axle

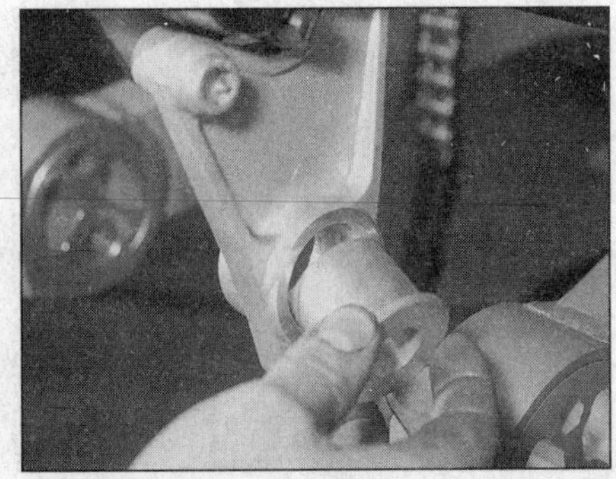

15.8a Fit the spacer into the brake caliper bracket . . .

15.8b . . . and the wheel spacers into each side of the wheel

15.11 Tighten the axle bolt to the specified torque

15.17a Chainguard retaining screws (arrowed)

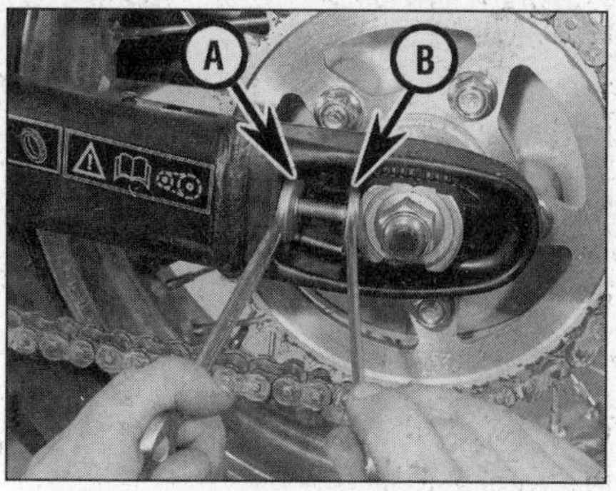

15.17b Locknut (A) and chain adjuster bolt (B)

10 Engage the drive chain with the sprocket and lift the wheel into position. Make sure both spacers remain in the wheel and that the disc fits correctly in the caliper, with the brake pads sitting squarely on each side of the disc, when the caliper assembly is moved down or up into position (as applicable).

11 Slacken the chain adjuster clamp bolts and rotate the adjusters via the Allen key slots so that the wheel axle hole is positioned further forward in the swingarm – this will relax chain tension and allow easy insertion of the axle. Slide the axle fully into position from the left side, making sure that it passes through the caliper mounting bracket. Synchronise each chain adjuster so that its index mark aligns with the same mark on each side of the swingarm, then tighten the adjuster clamp bolts – this will ensure correct wheel alignment when the axle is later tightened. Fit the axle bolt and tighten it to the specified torque setting **(see illustration)**. Fit new spring clips to both ends of the axle **(see illustration 15.3a)**.

15.18 Remove the axle nut and adjuster collar

12 Install the chainguard.

13 Apply the rear brake a few times to bring the pads back into contact with the disc. Move the motorcycle off its stand.

14 Adjust drive chain freeplay as described in Chapter 1.

15 Check for correct operation of the rear brake before riding the motorcycle.

Thunderbird (from VIN 29156), Thunderbird Sport, Adventurer and Legend TT models

Removal

16 Position the motorcycle upright on an auxiliary stand so that the rear wheel is off the ground. Always make sure the bike is properly supported.

17 Remove the two screws securing the chainguard and remove it from the swingarm **(see illustration)**. Slacken off the chain adjuster locknuts and screw the adjuster bolts into the swingarm by two or three turns **(see illustration)**.

18 Remove the axle nut and adjuster collar from the left side of the wheel and withdraw the axle from the right side complete with its adjuster collar **(see illustration)**. On models where the silencer impedes removal of the axle, remove the silencer (Chapter 4).

19 Push the wheel fully forwards in the swingarm and slip the drive chain off the sprocket **(see illustration)**. Withdraw the rear wheel from the swingarm.

20 Remove the headed spacer from the wheel hub right side and the thin spacer from its left side **(see illustrations)**. Take care not to lose the headed spacer in the brake caliper bracket.

Caution: Do not lay the wheel down and allow it to rest on the disc or the sprocket – they could become warped. Set the wheel on wood blocks so that neither component supports the weight of the wheel. Do not operate the brake pedal with the wheel removed.

21 Check the axle for straightness by rolling it on a flat surface such as a piece of plate glass (first wipe off all old grease and remove any corrosion using fine emery cloth). If the axle is bent, renew it.

22 Check the condition of the wheel bearings (see Section 16).

Installation

23 Apply a thin coat of grease to the seal lips, then slide the spacers into their proper positions on both sides of the hub. Fit the spacer in the caliper bracket, making sure it is fitted the right way round.

24 Apply a thin coat of grease to the axle.

25 Move the wheel into position and slip the drive chain over the sprocket. Make sure that the spacer is still in position in the caliper bracket and that the wheel spacers are

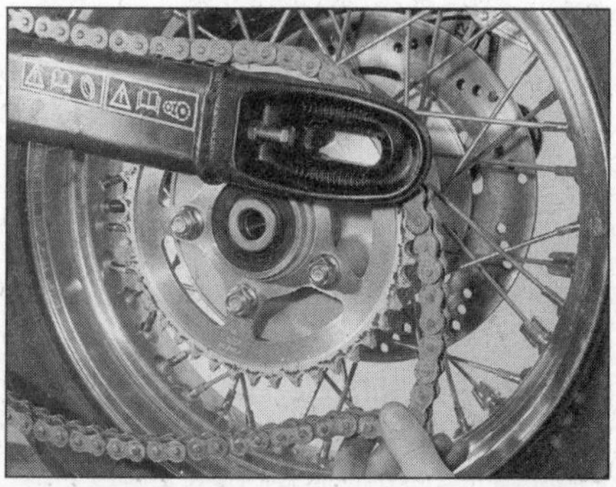

15.19 Slip the drive chain off the sprocket

15.20a Remove the headed spacer from the right side . . .

15.20b . . . and the thin spacer from the left side

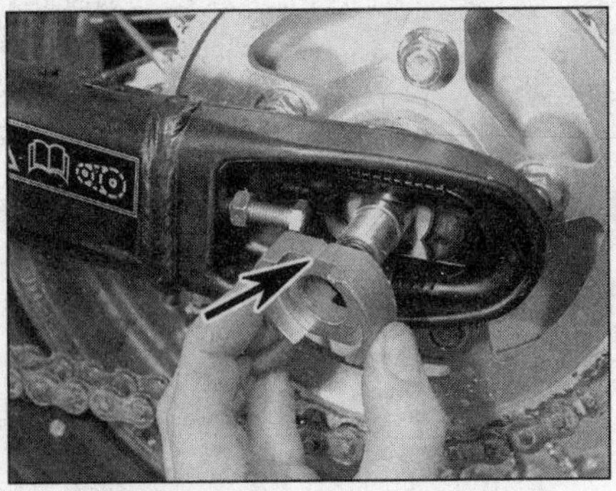

15.25 Adjuster collar index groove (arrowed) must be uppermost

15.28 Axle nut must be tightened to the specified torque

located each side of the hub **(see illustrations 15.20a and b)**. Slip the adjuster collar over the axle (make sure it is positioned so that the index groove is at the top), then lift the wheel and insert the axle through the swingarm and wheel from the right side. Check that the axle has passed through both hub spacers and the caliper bracket. Fit the adjuster collar on the end of the axle, followed by the axle nut. Note that the adjuster collar index groove must be at the top **(see illustration)**.

26 Secure the axle nut hand-tight.

27 Apply the rear brake a few times to bring the pads back into contact with the disc.

28 Adjust the drive chain freeplay as described in Chapter 1, then tighten the axle nut to the specified torque **(see illustration)**.

29 Install the chainguard.

30 Check for correct operation of the rear brake before riding the motorcycle.

16 Wheel bearings – removal, inspection and installation

Front wheel bearings

Note: *Always renew the wheel bearings in pairs. Never renew the bearings individually. Avoid using a high pressure cleaner on the wheel bearing area.*

1 Remove the wheel (see Section 14).

2 Set the wheel on blocks so as not to allow the weight of the wheel to rest on the brake discs.

3 Using a flat-bladed screwdriver, prise out the grease seals from both sides of the wheel **(see illustrations)**.

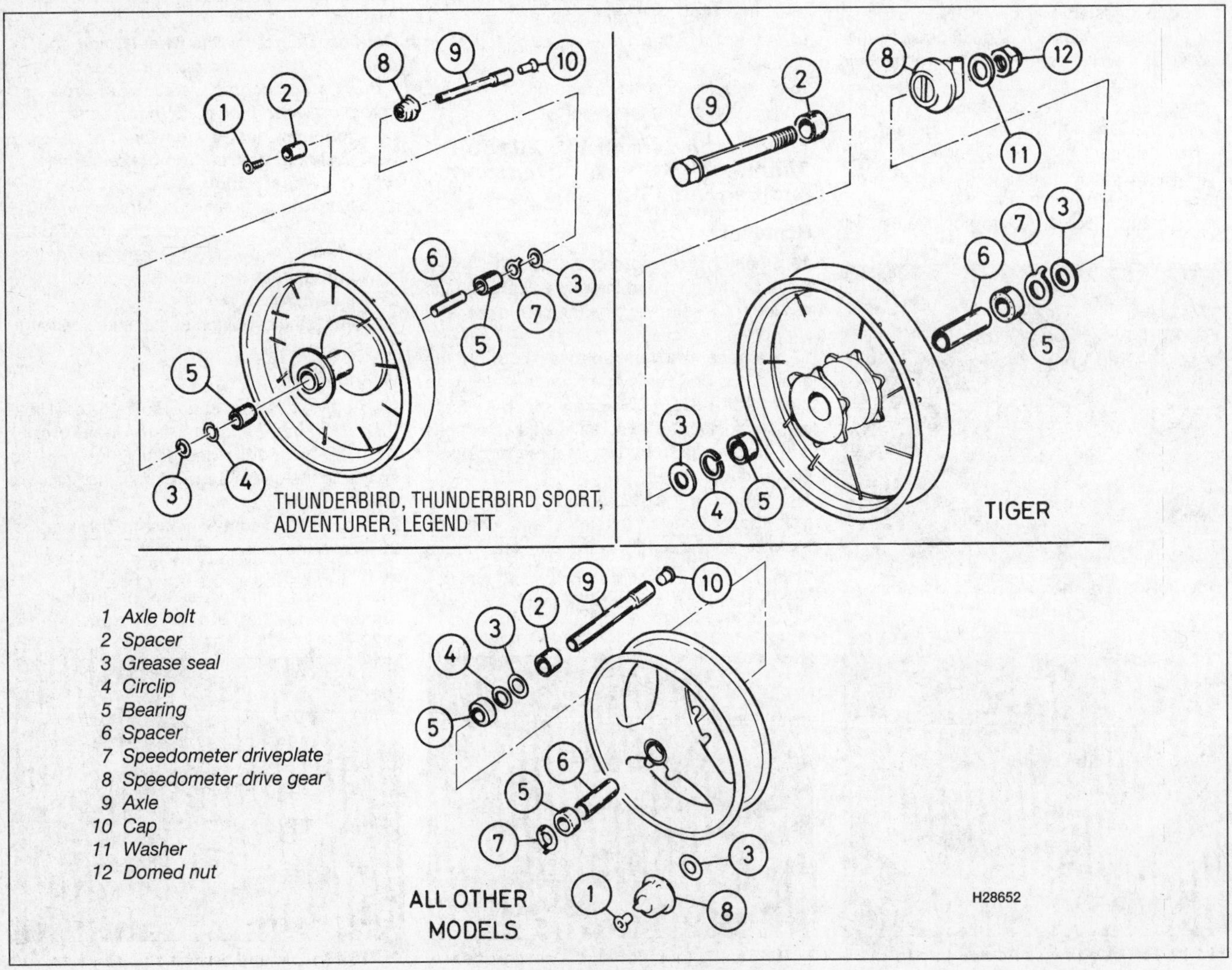

16.3a Front wheel detail

16.3b Prise out the grease seal using a flat-bladed screwdriver

16.4 Remove the circlip from the wheel

16.5 Drift the first wheel bearing out using a metal rod passed through from the opposite side of the wheel

4 Withdraw the speedometer driveplate from the right side of the wheel (left side on Thunderbird, Adventurer, Legend TT and Tiger), noting how it fits. Remove the circlip from the other side of the wheel **(see illustration)**.

5 Using a metal rod (preferably a brass drift punch) inserted through the centre of the hub bearing, tap evenly around the inner race of the opposite bearing to drive it from the hub **(see illustration)**. The bearing spacer will also come out.

6 Lay the wheel on its other side and remove the other bearing using the same technique.

7 If the bearings are of the unsealed type or are only sealed on one side, clean them with a high flash-point solvent (one which won't leave any residue) and blow them dry with compressed air (don't let the bearings spin as you dry them). Apply a few drops of oil to the bearing. **Note:** *If the bearing is sealed on both sides don't attempt to clean it.*

8 Hold the outer race of the bearing and rotate the inner race – if the bearing doesn't turn smoothly, has rough spots or is noisy, renew it.

9 If the bearing is good and can be re-used, wash it in solvent once again and dry it, then pack the bearing with high-quality wheel bearing grease.

10 Thoroughly clean the hub area of the wheel. Install a bearing into the recess in the hub, with the marked or sealed side facing outwards. Using a bearing driver or a socket large enough to contact the outer race of the bearing, drive it in until it's completely seated **(see illustrations)**.

11 Turn the wheel over and install the bearing spacer **(see illustration)**. Drive the other bearing into place as described above.

12 Fit the speedometer driveplate to the right side of the wheel (left side on Thunderbird, Adventurer, Legend TT and Tiger); ensure its locating tangs are correctly located in the hub slots **(see illustration)**. Fit the circlip to the other side of the wheel, making sure it is properly seated in its groove.

13 Install new grease seals, using a seal driver, large socket or a flat piece of wood to drive them into place **(see illustrations)**.

16.10a Install the bearing with the marked or sealed side facing out . . .

16.10b . . . then drive the bearing squarely into the hub using a drift or socket which bears only on the bearing's outer race

16.11 Install the spacer into the wheel before fitting the other bearing

16.12 Fit speedometer driveplate to the left side of wheel, making sure its tangs are seated in the hub slots (arrowed) . . .

16.13a . . . then press in a new grease seal . . .

16.13b . . . and drive it squarely into position using a suitably sized drift or socket

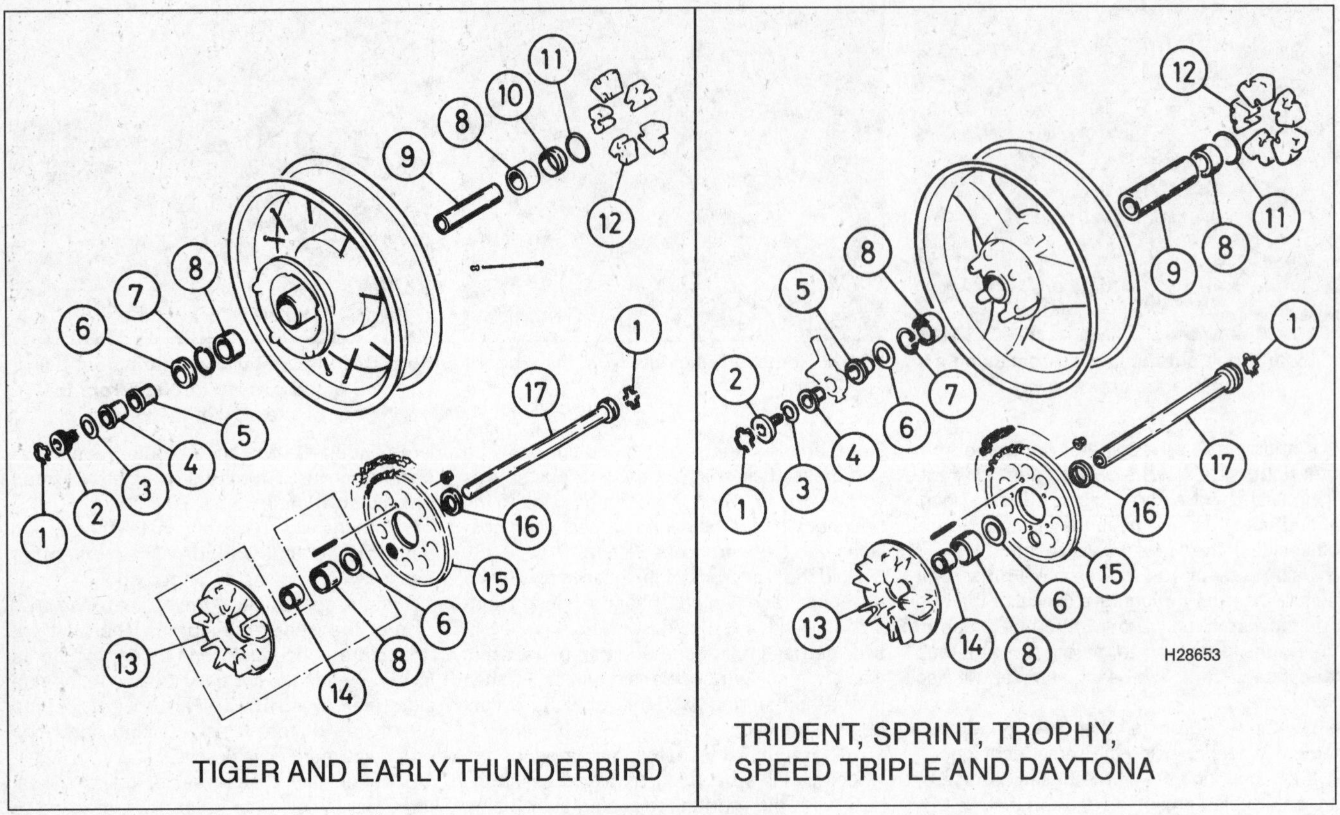

16.15 Rear wheel detail

1 *Spring clip*
2 *Axle bolt*
3 *Washer*
4 *Brake caliper bracket spacer*
5 *Spacer*
6 *Grease seal*
7 *Circlip*
8 *Bearing*
9 *Spacer*
10 *O-ring carrier*
11 *O-ring*
12 *Rubber damper*
13 *Sprocket coupling*
14 *Spacer*
15 *Sprocket*
16 *Spacer*
17 *Axle*

14 Clean off all traces of grease from the brake disc(s) using acetone or brake system cleaner, then install the wheel as described in Section 14.

Sprocket coupling bearing

15 Remove the rear wheel as described in Section 15 and remove the spacer from the left side of the wheel **(see illustration)**.

16 Lift the sprocket coupling away from the wheel leaving the rubber dampers in position in the wheel. Remove the spacer from the inside of the coupling bearing **(see illustration)**.

17 Prise out the grease seal from the outside of the coupling **(see illustration)**.

18 Support the coupling on blocks of wood and drive the bearing out from the inside with a bearing driver or socket **(see illustration)**.

19 Inspect the bearing as described above in Steps 7 through 9.

20 Thoroughly clean the bearing recess then install the bearing into the recess in the coupling, with the marked or sealed side facing out. Using a bearing driver or a socket large enough to contact the outer race of the

16.16 Lift the sprocket coupling out of the wheel and remove the spacer

16.17 Lever out the seal – use a flat-bladed screwdriver if necessary

16.18 Support the coupling and drive the bearing out from the inside using a hammer and bearing driver or socket

16.20 Drive the new coupling bearing into position using a large tubular drift which bears only on the bearing's outer race

16.22 Ensure the hub O-ring (arrowed) is in position on the wheel and apply a smear of grease to it to aid installation

16.26a Lever out the seal – use a flat-bladed screwdriver if necessary . . .

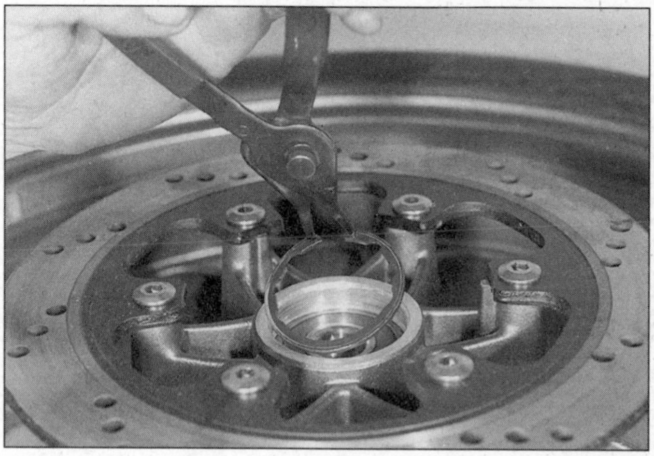

16.26b . . . and remove the circlip

bearing, drive it in until it's completely seated **(see illustration)**.

21 Install a new grease seal, using a seal driver, large socket or a flat piece of wood to drive it into place. Fit the spacer to the inside of the coupling bearing **(see illustration 16.16)**.

22 Apply a smear of grease to the hub O-ring and fit the sprocket coupling to the wheel **(see illustration)**.

23 Clean off all grease from the brake disc using acetone or brake system cleaner then install the wheel as described in Section 15.

Rear wheel bearings

Note: *Always renew the wheel bearings in pairs. Never renew the bearings individually. Avoid using a high pressure cleaner on the wheel bearing area.*

24 Remove the rear wheel as described in Section 15.

25 Lift the sprocket coupling away from the wheel leaving the rubber dampers in position in the wheel. Take care not to lose the spacer from inside the sprocket coupling, and note how it fits **(see illustration 16.16)**.

26 Prise out the grease seal from the right side of the wheel and remove the circlip **(see illustrations)**.

27 Set the wheel on blocks so as not to allow the weight of the wheel to rest on the brake disc or sprocket.

28 Remove, inspect and install the bearings as described above in Steps 5 through 11.

29 Fit the circlip to the right side of the wheel, making sure it is properly seated in its groove, and then install a new grease seal, using a seal driver, large socket or a flat piece of wood to drive it into place.

30 Install a new hub O-ring and smear it with grease **(see illustration 16.22)**. Fit the sprocket coupling to the wheel, making sure both the spacers are in position.

31 Clean off all grease from the brake disc using acetone or brake system cleaner then install the wheel as described in Section 15.

17 Tyres – general information and fitting

General information

1 Thunderbird, Thunderbird Sport, Adventurer, Legend TT and Tiger models have tubed-type tyres, due to their spoked wheel design. Trident, Sprint, Trophy, Speed Triple and Daytona models use tubeless tyres.

2 Refer to the *'Daily (pre-ride) checks'* listed at the beginning of this manual, and to the scheduled checks in Chapter 1 for tyre and wheel maintenance.

Fitting new tyres

3 When selecting new tyres, refer to the tyre information label on the motorcycle and the tyre options listed in the owners handbook and the in the Specifications at the beginning of this Chapter. Ensure that front and rear tyre types are compatible, the correct size and correct speed rating; if necessary seek advice from a Triumph dealer or tyre fitting specialist **(see illustration)**.

4 It is recommended that tyres are fitted by a motorcycle tyre specialist rather than attempted in the home workshop. This is particularly relevant in the case of tubeless tyres because the force required to break the seal between the wheel rim and tyre bead is substantial, and is usually beyond the capabilities of an individual working with normal tyre levers. Additionally, the specialist will be able to balance the wheels after tyre fitting.

5 Note that although punctured tyres can in some cases be repaired, Triumph do not recommend it.

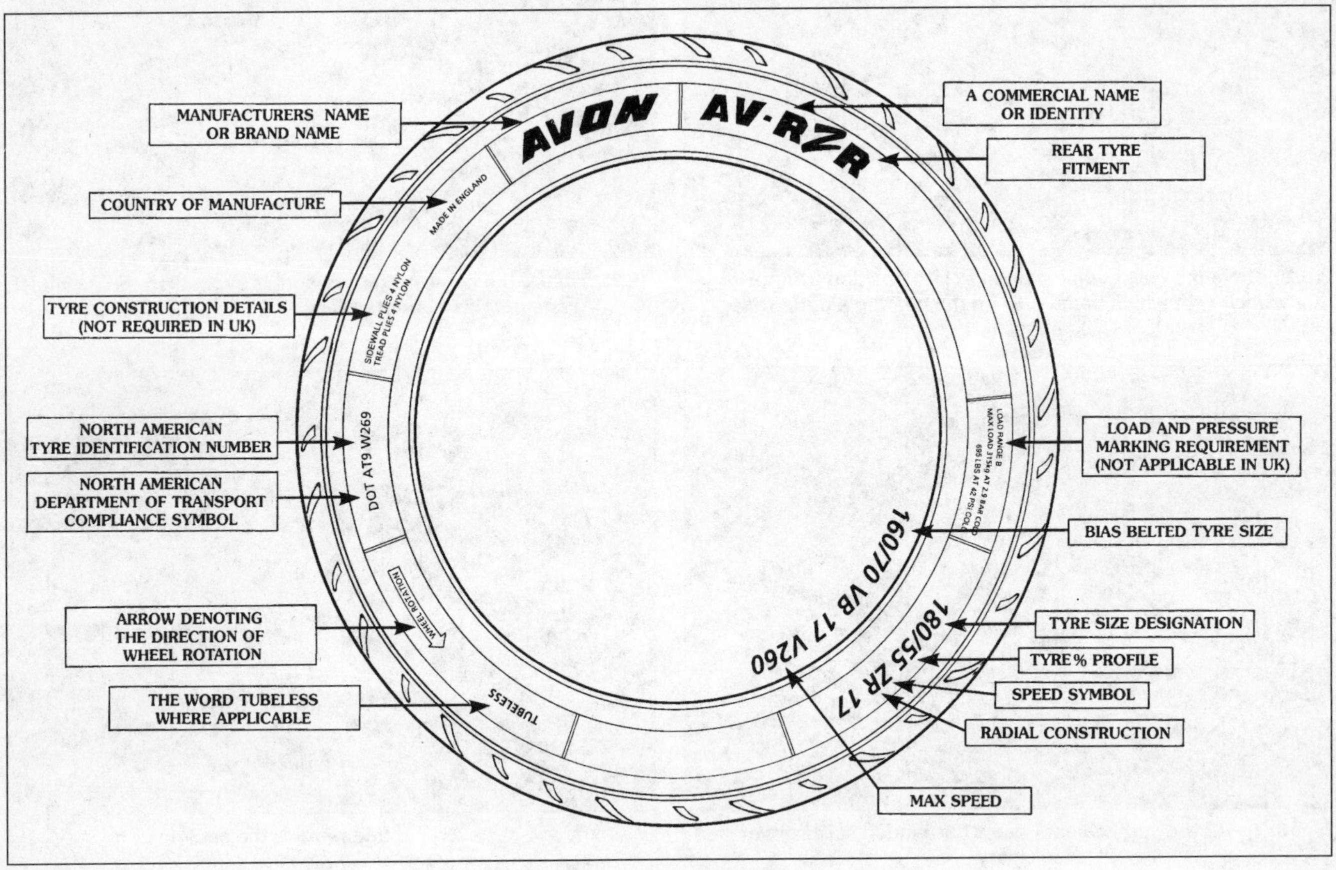

17.3 Common tyre sidewall markings

Chapter 8
Bodywork

Contents

Degrees of difficulty

Easy, suitable for novice with little experience	**Fairly easy,** suitable for beginner with some experience	**Fairly difficult,** suitable for competent DIY mechanic	**Difficult,** suitable for experienced DIY mechanic	**Very difficult,** suitable for expert DIY or professional

1 General information

This Chapter covers the procedures necessary to remove and install the fairing and other body parts. Since many service and repair operations on these motorcycles require the removal of the fairing and/or other body parts, the procedures are grouped here and referred to from other Chapters.

In the case of damage to the fairing or other body parts, it is usually necessary to remove the broken component and replace it with a new (or used) one. The material that the fairing and other body parts are composed of doesn't lend itself to conventional repair techniques. Note that there are however some companies that specialise in 'plastic welding' and there are a number of bodywork repair kits now available for motorcycles. The Daytona Super III model has a carbon fibre front mudguard and fairing facia panels.

When attempting to remove any fairing panel, first study it closely, noting any fasteners and associated fittings, to be sure of returning everything to its correct place on installation. In most cases the aid of an assistant will be required when removing panels, to help avoid the risk of damage to paintwork. Once the evident fasteners have been removed, try to withdraw the panel as described but DO NOT FORCE IT – if it will not release, check that all fasteners have been removed and try again. Where a panel engages another by means of tabs, be careful not to break the tab or its mating slot or to damage the paintwork. Remember that a few moments of patience at this stage will save you a lot of money in replacing broken fairing panels!

When installing a fairing panel, first study it closely, noting any fasteners and associated fittings removed with it, to be sure of returning everything to its correct place. Check that all fasteners are in good condition, including all trim nuts or clips and damping/rubber mounts; any of these must be renewed if faulty before the panel is reassembled. Check also that all mounting brackets are straight and repair or renew them if necessary before attempting to install the panel. Where assistance was required to remove a panel, make sure your assistant is on hand to install it.

Carefully settle the panel in place, following the instructions provided, and check that it engages correctly with its partners (where applicable) before tightening any of the fasteners. Where a panel engages another by means of tabs, be careful not to break the tab or its mating slot.

Tighten the fasteners securely, but be careful not to overtighten any of them or the panel may break (not always immediately) due to the uneven stress.

2 Fairing panels – removal and installation

Main fairing – removal

Trophy (up to VIN 29155) and Daytona models

1 Remove the seat (Section 9) and disconnect the battery negative (-ve) terminal. Unscrew the screws securing both left and right side instrument facia panels to the fairing. Carefully raise the right side facia panel and disconnect the clock wiring, then remove the panels from the fairing, noting

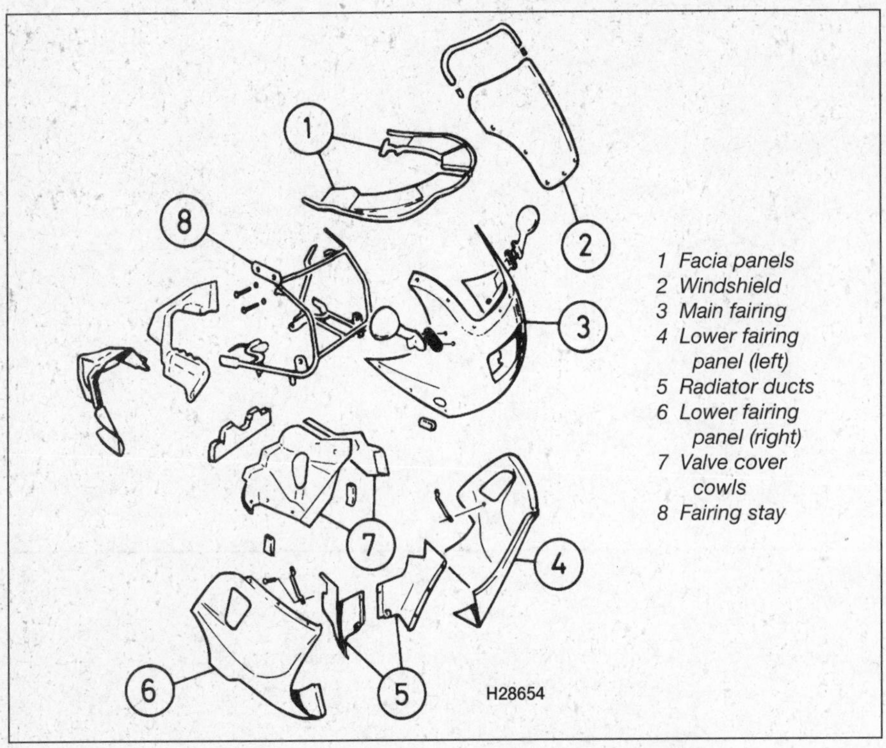

2.1a Fairing panel detail – Trophy and Daytona models

how they fit to each other, to the fairing, and around the instrument panel **(see illustrations)**.

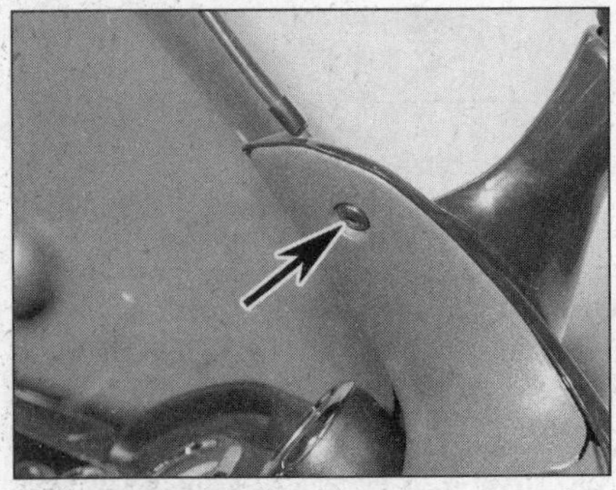

2.8a Inner trim panel screw (arrowed)

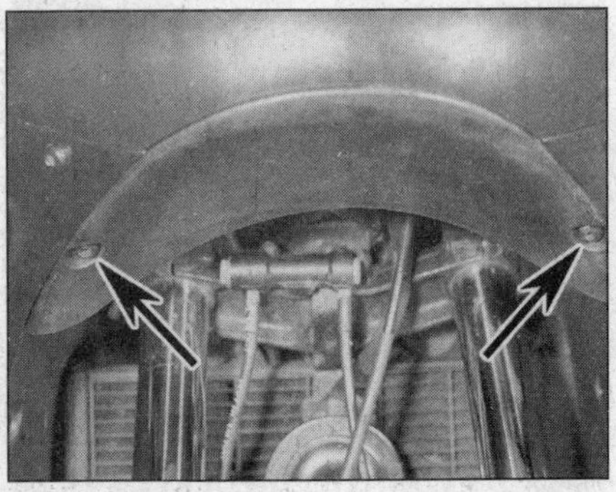

2.9 Chin panel retaining screws (arrowed)

2 Remove the front turn signal assemblies as described in Chapter 9.

3 Unscrew the three screws securing each

2.8b Headlight beam adjuster is retained by a knurled nut (arrowed)

2.10 Main-to-lower fairing screws (arrowed)

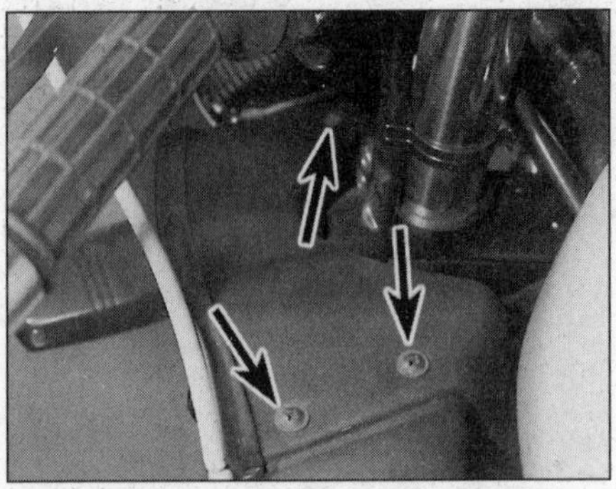

2.1b Instrument facia panels are secured by three screws (arrows) – Daytona shown

side of the fairing to the lower fairing panels **(see illustration 2.22)**. Where fitted, recover the nuts from these screws.

4 Remove the rear view mirrors as described in Section 4.

5 On Trophy models, move the fairing forward slightly if necessary and disconnect the headlight and sidelight wiring connectors. On all models, release any other wiring clips and cable guides and check that the fairing is free from all restraints. Carefully remove the fairing from the bike.

Trophy (from VIN 29156) models

6 Remove the seat (Section 9) and disconnect the battery negative (-ve) terminal.

7 Remove the rear view mirrors as described in Section 4.

8 Remove the screw from each inner trim panel – do not try to remove the panel **(see illustration)**. Open the right storage box and unscrew the headlight beam height adjuster retaining ring **(see illustration)**.

9 Remove the chin panel from the fairing underside; it is retained by two screws **(see illustration)**.

10 Remove the four screws on each side which secure the main fairing to each lower fairing panel **(see illustration)**.

11 Remove the two bolts underneath the headlight unit to free the main fairing from its stay **(see illustration)**. As the fairing it withdrawn forwards, disconnect the wiring

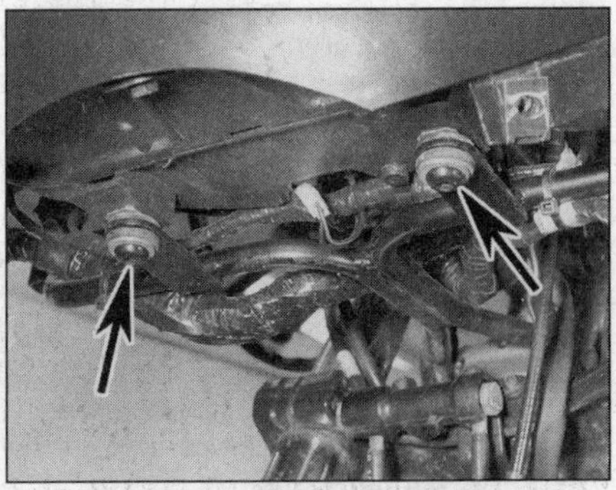

2.11a Main fairing mounting bolts (arrowed)

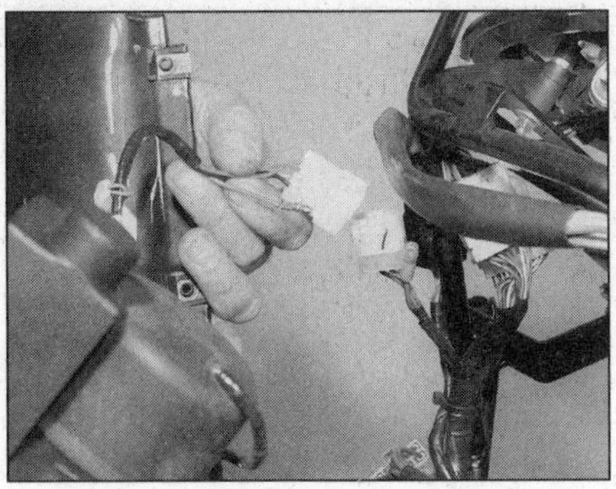
2.11b Headlight wiring connectors

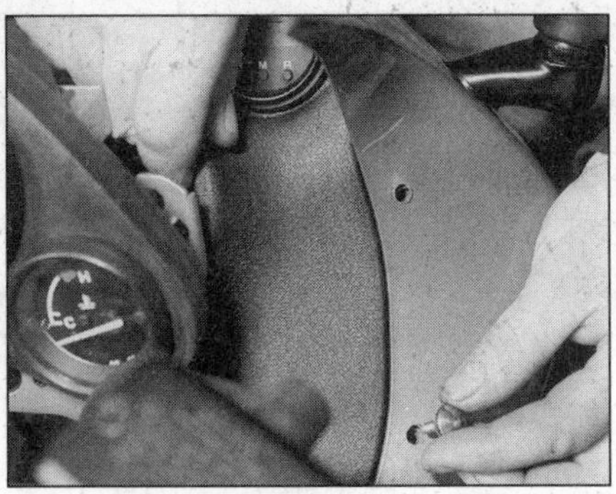
2.12a Unscrew the instrument facia panel retaining screws

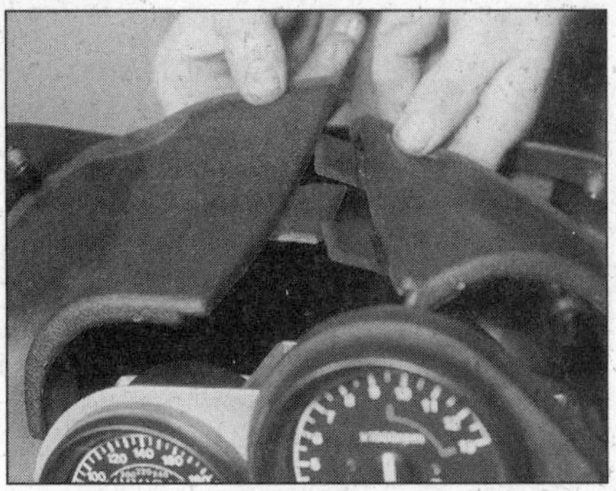
2.12b Note how the facia panels join together

connectors for the headlight **(see illustration)**.

Sprint model

12 Remove the seat (Section 9) and disconnect the battery negative (-ve) terminal. Unscrew the screws securing both left and right side instrument facia panels to the fairing. Carefully raise the right side facia panel and disconnect the clock wiring, then remove the panels from the fairing, noting how they fit to each other, to the fairing, and around the instrument panel **(see illustrations)**.

13 Remove the front turn signal assemblies as described in Chapter 9.

14 Remove the rear view mirrors as described in Section 4.

15 Unscrew the three fairing mounting screws on each side of the fairing **(see illustration)**.

16 Release any other wiring clips and cable guides and check that the fairing is free from all restraints. Carefully remove the fairing by drawing it forwards from the bike **(see illustration)**.

Tiger model

17 Remove the eleven screws (four on each side, and three along the bottom) securing the fairing front panel to the fairing side panels, and remove the front panel **(see illustration)**. Note how the instrument facia fits against the front fairing panel and around the instruments.

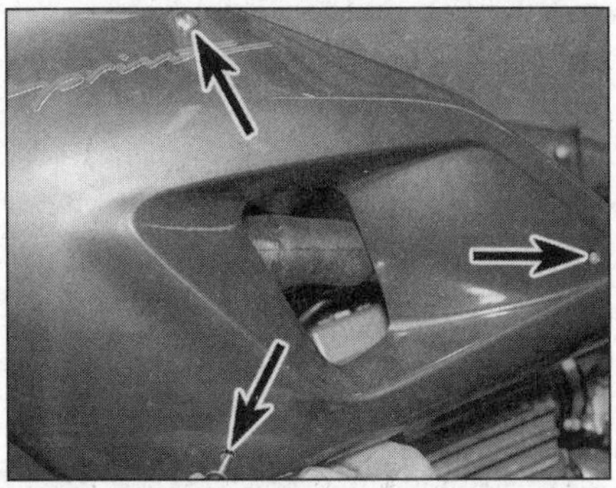
2.15 Unscrew the fairing mounting screws (arrowed)

2.16 Remove the fairing by carefully drawing it forwards from the bike

18 Remove the screws securing each fairing side panel to the fuel tank and to the radiator bottom bracket, and carefully remove the panel **(see illustration)**.

Main fairing – installation

19 Installation on all models is the reverse of removal. Make sure that all cables and wires are correctly routed and connected, and secured by any clips or ties. Reconnect the battery negative terminal. On completion, check the headlight aim as described in Chapter 9, and check that the turn signals, headlights and instruments all function correctly.

Lower fairing panels – removal

Trophy (up to VIN 29155) and Daytona models

20 Where fitted, remove the screws securing the instrument facia panel to the lower fairing panel.

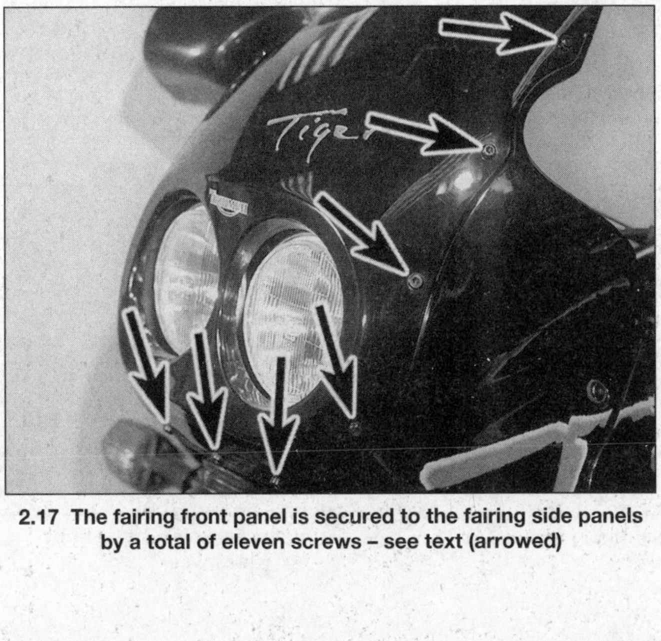
2.17 The fairing front panel is secured to the fairing side panels by a total of eleven screws – see text (arrowed)

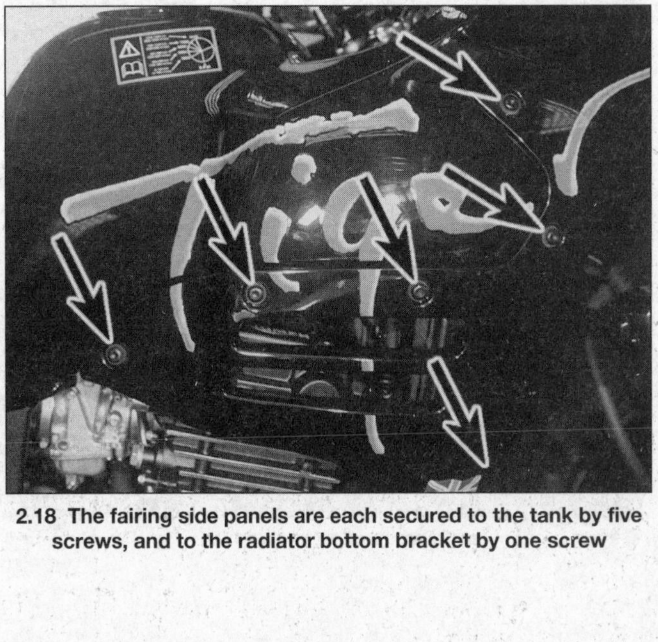
2.18 The fairing side panels are each secured to the tank by five screws, and to the radiator bottom bracket by one screw

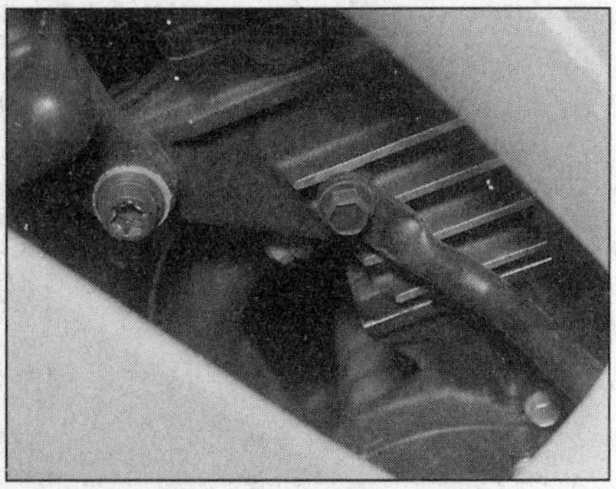

2.21 Lower panel bracket-to-cylinder head bolt is accessed through aperture

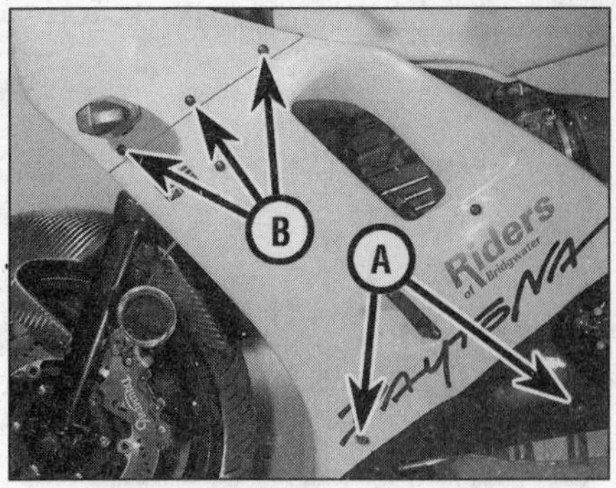

2.22 Lower panel fixings to sub-frame (A) and to main fairing (B)

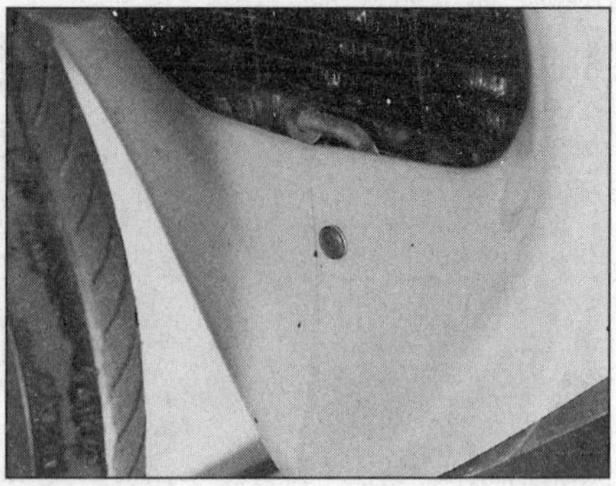

2.24a Lower panels are joined together by a single screw at the front . . .

21 Unscrew the bolt securing the lower fairing panel bracket to the cylinder head. This bolt is accessed via the aperture in the panel **(see illustration)**.
22 Remove the screws securing the bottom of the lower fairing panel to the sub-frame **(see illustration)**.
23 On early models, unscrew the screws securing the left and right side radiator ducts to the oil cooler and to each other.
24 Remove the screws joining the lower fairing panels to each other at the bottom and on the underside of the panels **(see illustrations)**.
25 Support the lower fairing panel, then remove the screws securing the panel to the main fairing and carefully remove the panel. Where fitted, recover the nuts from these screws.

Trophy (from VIN 29156) models

26 Remove the seat (Section 9) and disconnect the battery negative (-ve) terminal.
27 Remove the five screws from each side of the belly pan and remove it from the lower fairing panels **(see illustration)**.
28 Open the storage compartment and remove the screw on its inner side **(see illustration)**. If you're removing the right side panel, also thread the knurled nut off the beam adjuster and push the adjuster through into the panel.
29 Remove the two screws retaining the chin panel to the underside of the main fairing **(see illustration 2.9)**. Remove the four screws which retain the lower panel to the main fairing **(see illustration 2.31b)**.
30 Remove the screw from each inner trim panel – do not try to remove the panel **(see illustration 2.8a)**.
31 Remove the single screw from the rear inner section of the lower panel **(see illustration)** – this screw is only fitted to three-cylinder models. Remove the four screws which retain the lower panel to its mountings on the engine **(see illustration)**. Withdraw the panel far enough to access the turn signal wire connector and the fuse wire connector block (right side only) **(see illustration)**.

Lower fairing panels – installation

32 Installation is the reverse of removal.

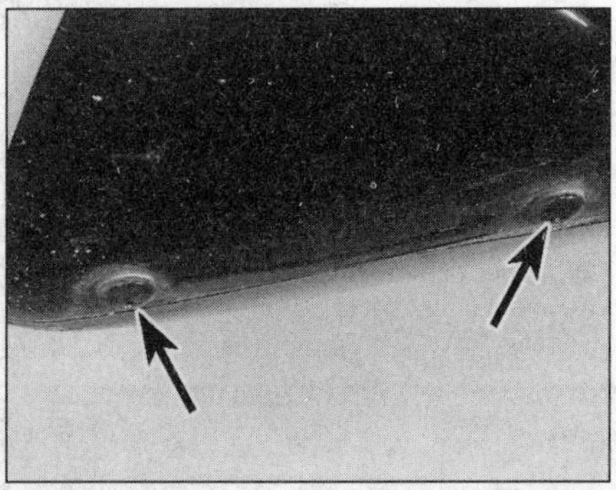

2.24b . . . and by two screws at the bottom

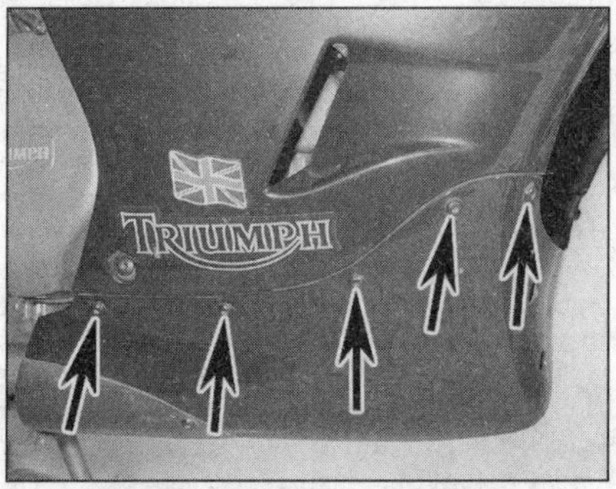

2.27 Belly pan is retained by five screws (arrowed) on each side

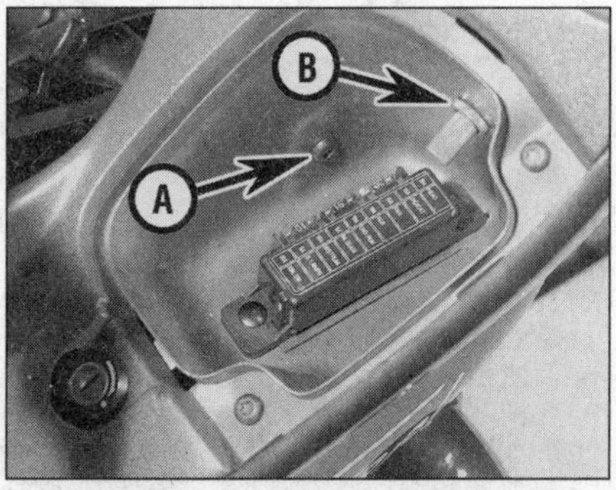

2.28 Screw inside storage compartment (A) and beam adjuster knurled nut (B)

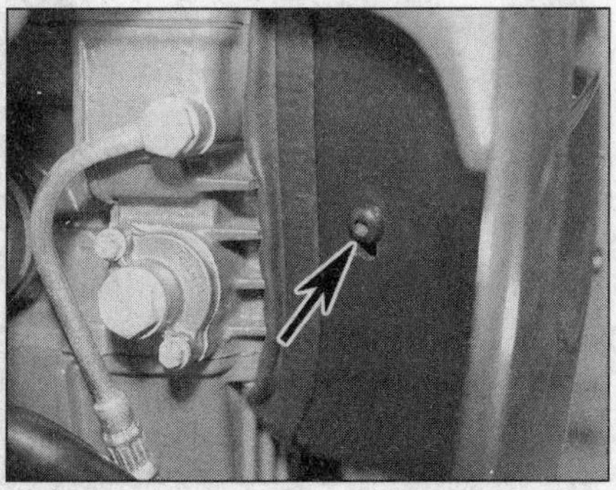

2.31a Inner rear section screw (arrowed)

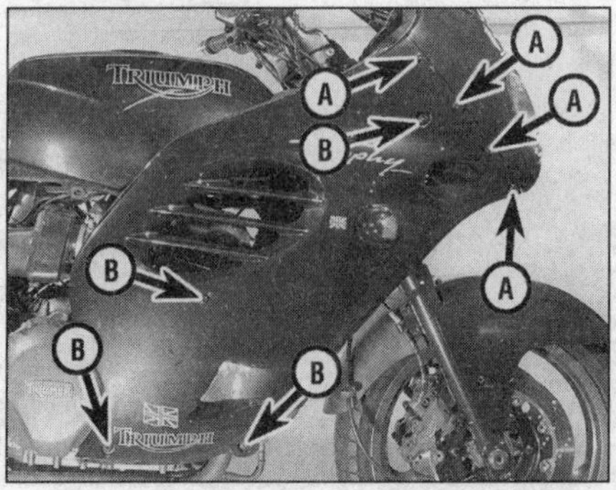

2.31b Lower-to-main fairing screws (A) and lower fairing-to-engine screws (B)

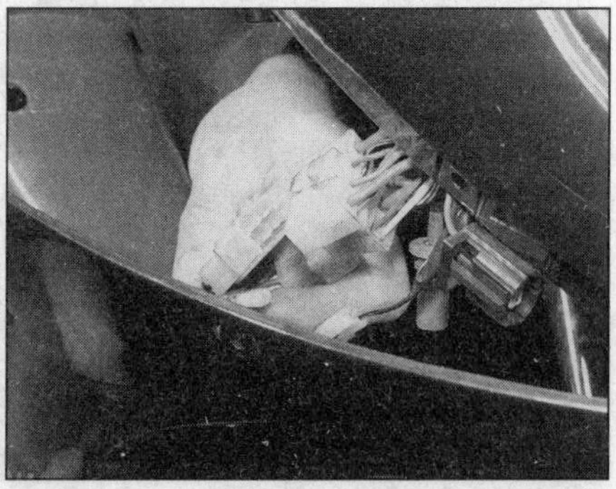

2.31c Disconnect the wiring as the panel is withdrawn

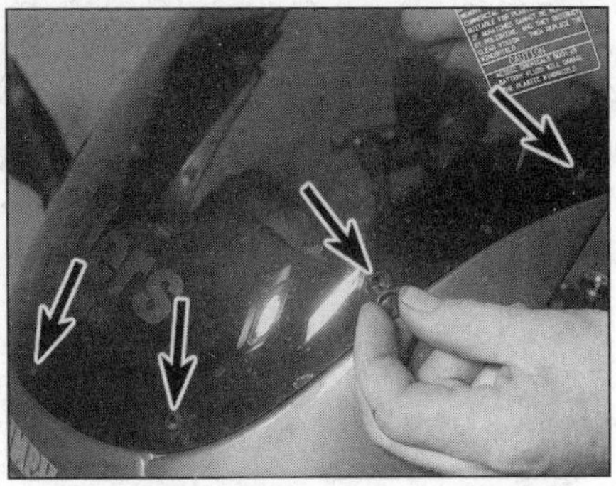

3.1a Unscrew the windshield fasteners (arrowed) – Sprint shown

3.1b Tiger windshield fasteners (arrowed)

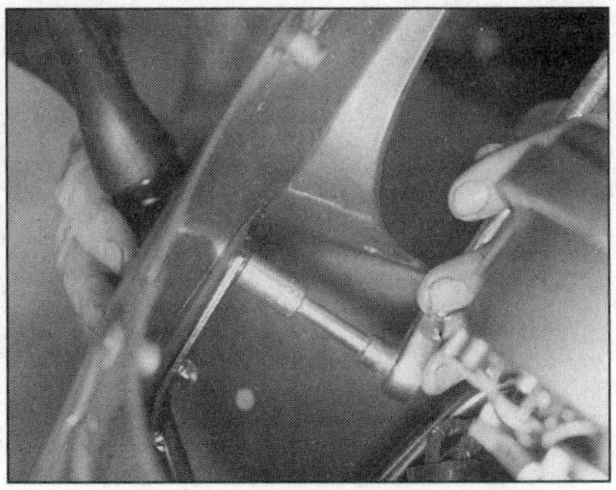

4.1a Unscrew the two nuts from inside of the main fairing . . .

3 Windshield – removal and installation

Removal

1 Remove the fasteners securing the windshield to the upper fairing assembly, noting how they fit, then lift the windshield away from the bike **(see illustrations)**.

Installation

2 Installation is the reverse of removal. Make sure the fasteners are correctly and securely fitted.

4 Rear view mirrors – removal and installation

Removal

1 On Daytona, Sprint and early Trophy models, remove the caps from the nuts securing the mirror to the upper fairing assembly. Unscrew the nuts, then carefully remove the mirror along with its mounting pad **(see illustrations)**.

2 On later Trophy models (from VIN 29156), peel back the rubber cover from the mirror base. Remove the two bolts and withdraw the mirror from the main fairing **(see illustration)**. The mounting rubber and collars should remain in place on the mirror.

3 On Trident, Speed Triple, Thunderbird, Thunderbird Sport, Adventurer, Legend TT and Tiger models, simply unscrew the mirror from its mounting on the handlebar.

Installation

4 Installation is the reverse of removal. Make sure the components are fitted in the correct order.

5 Fairing stay – removal and installation

Removal – Sprint, Trophy (up to VIN 29155), Daytona and Tiger

1 Remove the main fairing and the lower fairing panels (Trophy and Daytona models) as described in Section 2.

2 Remove the headlight assembly as described in Chapter 9.

3 Remove the instrument cluster as described in Chapter 9.

4 Disconnect and remove the horns as described in Chapter 9.

5 On Tiger models, remove the turn signals as described in Chapter 9.

6 Unscrew the radiator top mounting bolts.

7 Note the routing of all the wiring and cables, and release them from any ties or clips necessary, noting their positions.

8 Unscrew the two bolts securing the fairing stay to the frame headstock and carefully remove the stay, taking care not to snag any wiring **(see illustration)**.

Removal – Trophy (from VIN 29156)

9 Remove the main fairing.

10 Disconnect all wiring connectors and cut any cable ties securing the wiring to the stay. Disconnect the wires from the turn signal relay having first taken note of their locations.

11 Disconnect the speedometer cable from the instruments.

12 Remove the two bolts which retain the stay to the steering head and remove the stay, taking care not to snag any wiring.

Installation

13 Installation is the reverse of removal. Make sure that the wiring and cables are correctly routed and secured with ties and clips as required.

6 Side panels – removal and installation

Removal

Thunderbird, Thunderbird Sport, Adventurer and Legend TT models

1 Remove the seat as described in Section 9.

2 Remove the screw securing the bottom of the side panel to the frame, taking care not to

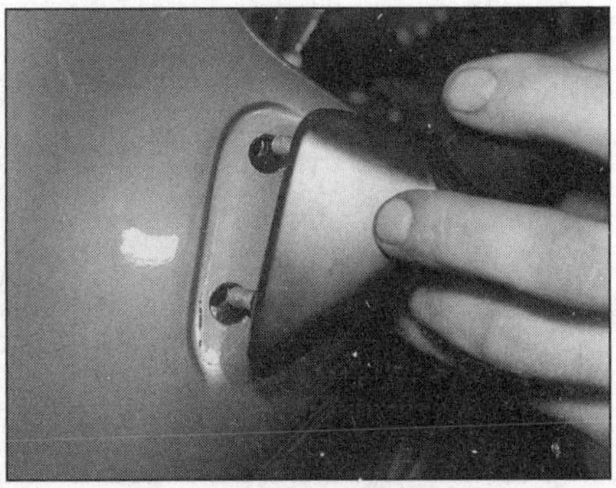

4.1b . . . and remove the mirror

4.2 Mirror is retained by two bolts on later Trophy

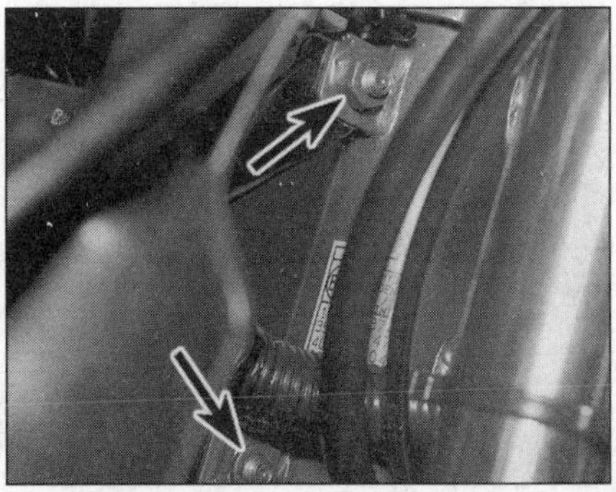

5.8 Unscrew the two bolts securing the fairing stay to the frame (arrowed)

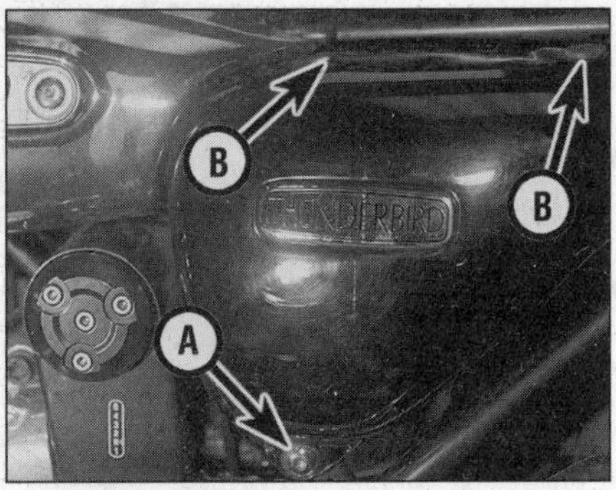

6.2 Side panel is retained by a screw (A) and fits over two lugs (B) on top frame rail

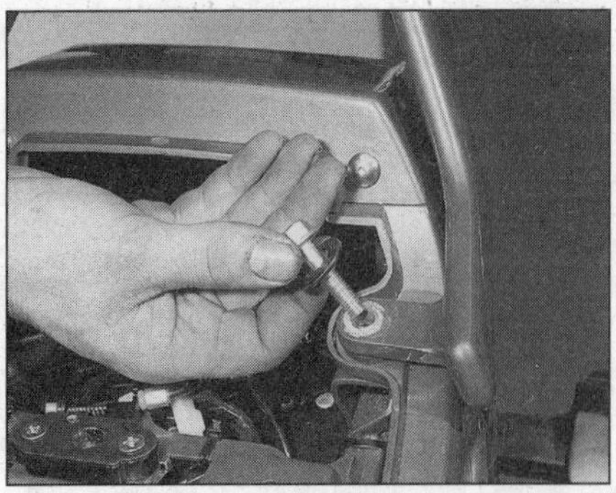

6.6 Unscrew the bolts securing the grab rail

6.7a The tail light assembly is secured by two nuts (arrowed)

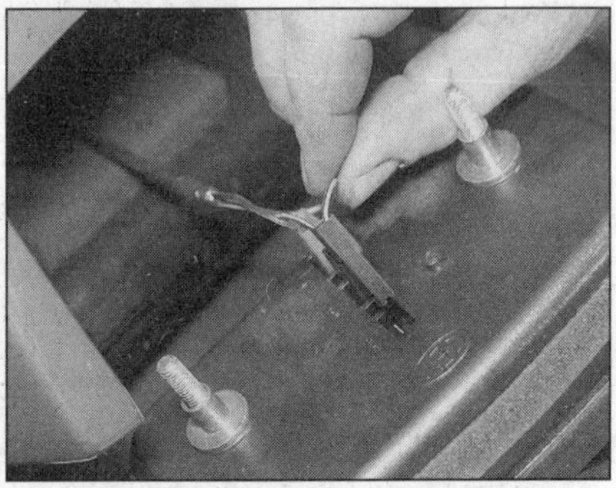

6.7b Disconnect the tail light wiring connectors

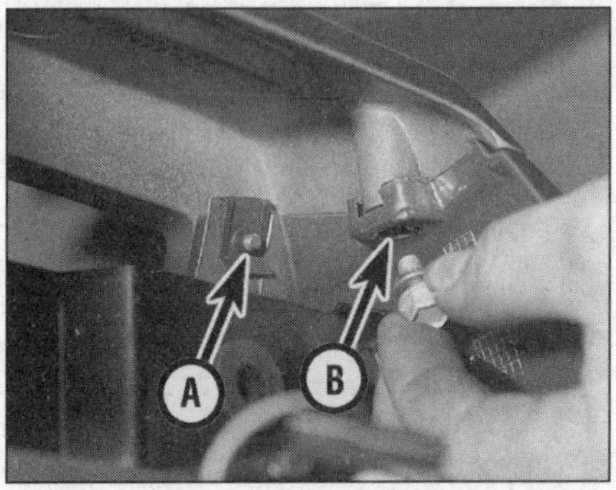

6.8a Remove screw at front (A) and bolt at the rear (B) on each side of top cover . . .

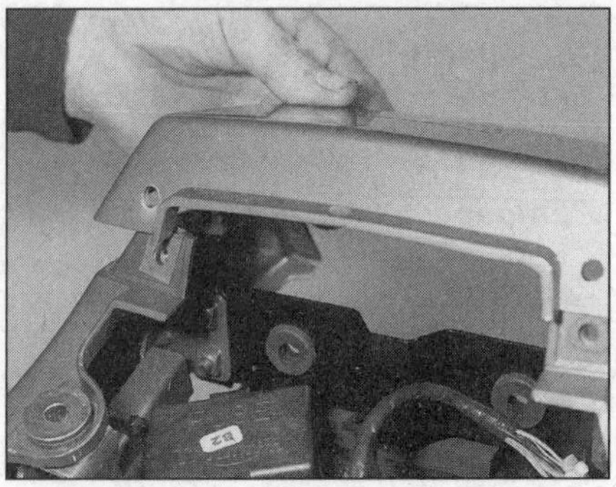

6.8b . . . and lift the top cover away

lose the sleeve and noting how it fits, then lift the side panel clear of its two mounting lugs on the frame top rail **(see illustration)**. Check the condition of the two rubber mounting grommets and renew them if necessary.

Tiger model

3 Remove the seat as described in Section 9.

4 Remove the three screws securing the side panel and carefully remove the panel, noting how it fits.

Trident (up to VIN 55071), Sprint (up to VIN 16921), Trophy (up to VIN 29155), Speed Triple and Daytona models

5 Remove the seat as described in Section 9. Where fitted, remove the panniers as described in Section 10.

6 Remove the two bolts securing the grab rail and lift it clear (not applicable to Daytona or Speed Triple models when using the seat hump) **(see illustration)**.

7 Unscrew the two nuts securing the tail light assembly, noting the order of the washers, then withdraw the assembly a little way and disconnect the wiring connectors, noting their positions **(see illustrations)**.

8 Unscrew the four screws securing the top cover to the side panels and remove the cover **(see illustrations)**.

9 Remove the screw securing the side panel to the frame **(see illustration)**.

10 The side panel has four lugs which fit into rubber grommets on the frame **(see illustration)**. Gently ease the side panel outwards to release it from the grommets.

11 The above procedure details separate removal of the right and left side panels. However, if care is taken not to overstress the plastic, both side panels and top cover can be removed as an assembly without disturbing the tail light.

Trident (from VIN 55072), Sprint (from VIN 16922) and Trophy (from VIN 29156) models

Note: *The side panels are removed as a single unit. If required, the two side sections can be separated from the top cover after removal from the machine.*

12 Remove the seat as described in Section 9. On Trophy and Sprint Executive models, remove the panniers as described in Section 10.

13 Remove the grab rails, each is secured by two bolts **(see illustrations)**.

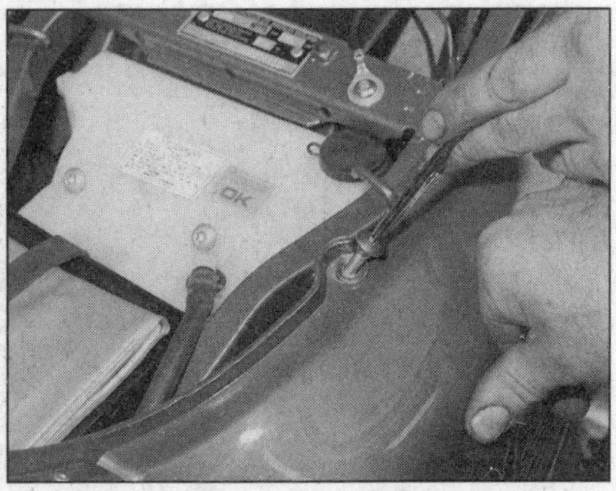

6.9 Remove the screw securing the side panel to the frame

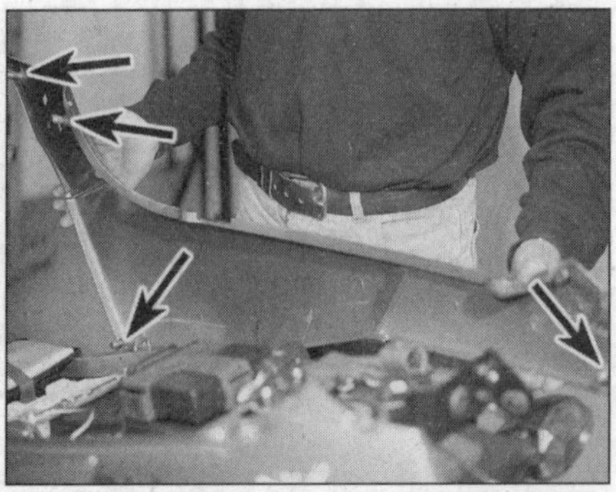

6.10 Gently ease the lugs (arrowed) out of their mounting grommets

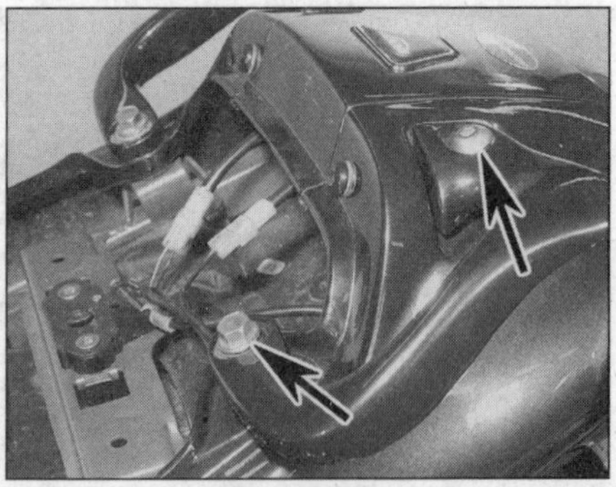

6.13a Grab rails are retained by two bolts (arrowed)

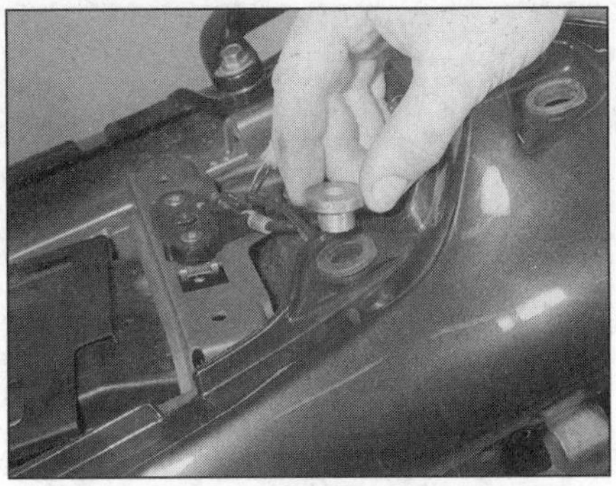

6.13b Take note of the collar position

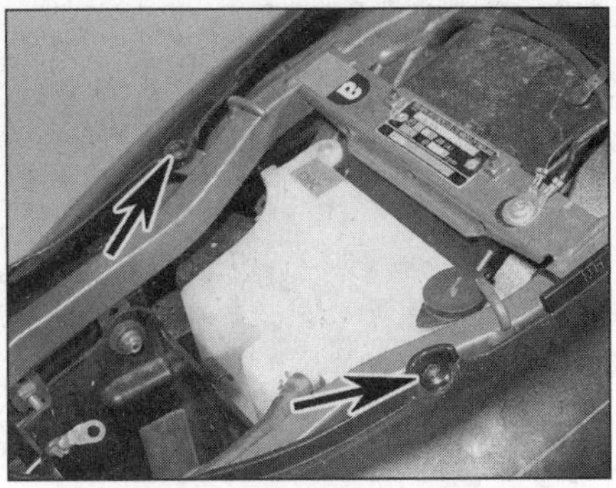

6.14a Remove the single screw along each top edge (arrowed) . . .

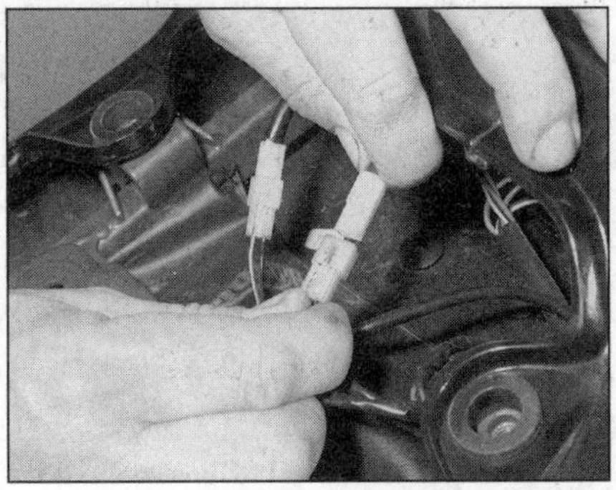

6.14b . . . disconnect the turn signal wiring . . .

6.14c . . . ease the lugs out of their grommets at the top (arrowed) . . .

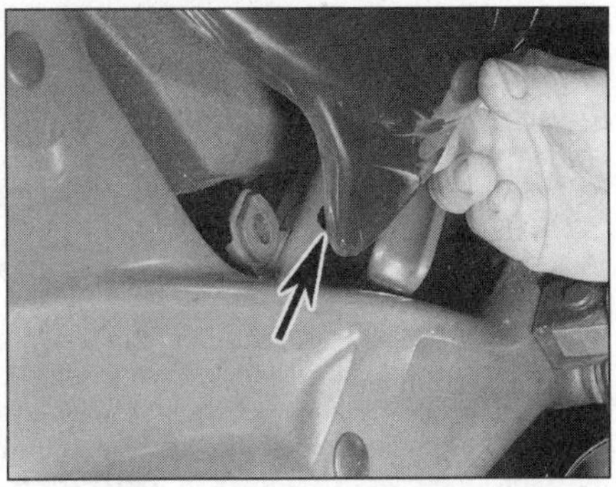

6.14d . . . and bottom (arrowed) . . .

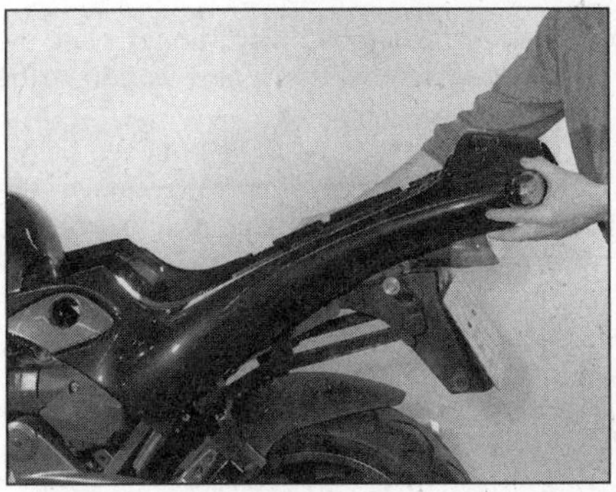

6.14e . . . then ease the sidepanel off the frame

14 Remove the single screw along the top edge of each side panel **(see illustration)**. Disconnect the two turn signal wire connectors **(see illustration)**. Gently ease the side panel lugs out of their grommets in the frame, then ease the complete sidepanel assembly rearwards off the motorcycle, taking care as it is eased over the pannier carrier bracket bolts on Trophy and Sprint Executive models **(see illustrations)**.

Installation

15 Installation is the reverse of removal.

> **HAYNES HiNT** *A smear of liquid soap applied to the mounting grommets will help the side panel lugs engage without the need for undue pressure.*

7 Front mudguard – removal and installation

Removal

Thunderbird, Thunderbird Sport, Adventurer and Legend TT model

1 Remove the four bolts securing the mudguard to the inside of the fork sliders (if they can't be withdrawn fully with the wheel in place, remove the front wheel as described in Chapter 7). Carefully remove the mudguard by drawing it forwards through the forks. Note that the rear left mudguard bolt also secures the brake hose guide. On US models, both rear bolts retain the reflector mounting brackets.

Tiger model

2 Unscrew the bolts securing the mudguard side panels to the mudguard and the forks. Remove the side panels, then carefully remove the mudguard by drawing it forwards through the forks.

Trident, Sprint, Trophy (up to VIN 29155), Speed Triple and Daytona models

3 Remove the speedometer cable retaining screw on the right side of the wheel hub and withdraw the cable, slipping it through the guide on the mudguard **(see illustration 14.3 in Chapter 7)**. Unscrew the bolts securing the mudguard to the forks, noting the positions of the brake hose clamps on the upper mountings and the rubber washers on the lower mountings **(see illustrations)**.

Trophy model (from VIN 29156)

4 To release the front section, remove the single screw on each side and the two screws

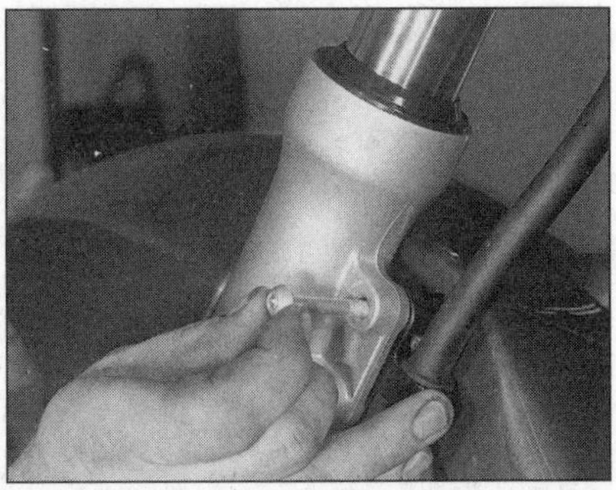

7.3a The mudguard is secured on each side by two bolts at the top . . .

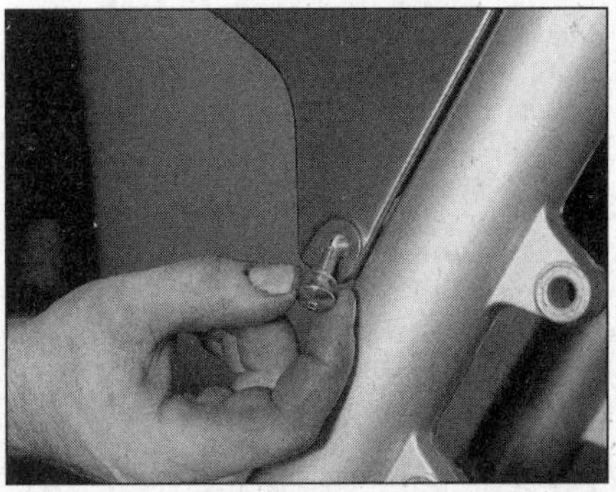

7.3b . . . and one at the bottom

8

7.4a Remove the single screw on each side (arrowed) . . .

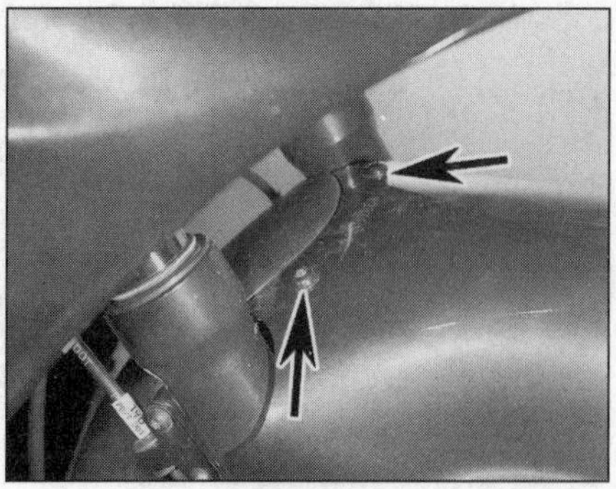

7.4b . . . and the two screws at the top (arrowed)

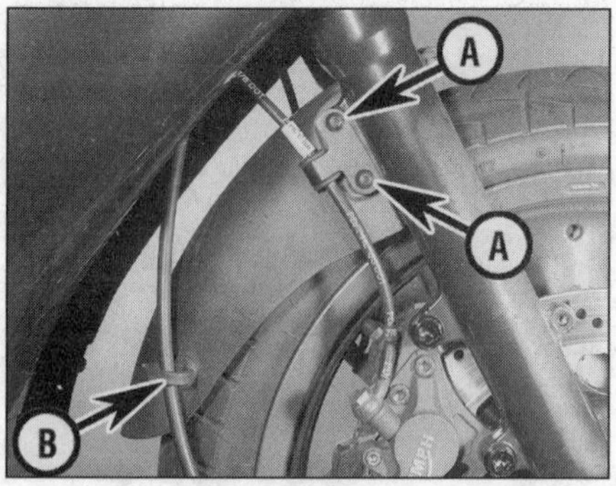

7.5 Rear section is retained by the brake hose clamps (A); note the speedometer cable guide (B)

on the top face **(see illustrations)**. Note the position of any washers and withdraw the front section.

5 The front section must be removed before removing the rear section. Remove the speedometer cable retaining screw on the right side of the wheel hub and withdraw the cable, slipping it through the guide on the mudguard. Remove the two screws on each side which retain the brake hose clamps and mudguard to the fork slider **(see illustration)**.

Installation

6 Installation is the reverse of removal. Make sure the speedometer cable and brake hoses are correctly routed and secured by their clamps. On Daytona Super III models, the front mudguard is made of carbon-fibre; take care not to crack or overstress this material.

8 Rear mudguard – removal and installation

Frame-mounted mudguard

Removal – Thunderbird, Thunderbird Sport, Adventurer and Legend TT models

1 Remove the seat as described in Section 9.

2 Where fitted, unscrew the bolts securing the mudflap at the front of the mudguard to the swingarm **(see Chapter 6, illustration 14.8)**.

3 Disconnect the wiring to the rear turn signals, tail light assembly and, where fitted, the licence plate light. Release the wiring from any clips or ties on the mudguard.

4 Unscrew the nuts securing the tail light assembly to the mudguard, noting the positions of the sleeves and grommets, and remove the assembly.

5 Remove the rear turn signals as described in Chapter 9.

6 Unscrew the bolts securing the mudguard to the frame, and carefully remove the mudguard.

Removal – Trident, Sprint, Trophy, Speed Triple, Daytona and Tiger models

7 Remove the seat as described in Section 9, the panniers (where fitted) and the side panels as described in Section 6.

8 Remove the coolant reservoir as described in Chapter 3.

9 Unscrew the two nuts securing the tail light assembly, noting the order of the washers, then withdraw the assembly a little way and disconnect the wiring connectors, noting their positions **(see illustrations 6.7a and 6.7b)**.

10 Disconnect the wiring connectors from the rear turn signal assemblies (not necessary on Trident (from VIN 55072), Sprint (from VIN 16922) and Trophy (from VIN 29156) models).

11 Remove the igniter from its mounts and disconnect it at the connector block (not applicable to later Trophy models and Tiger models) **(see Chapter 5, illustrations 5.2 and 5.3)**.

12 Disconnect the fusebox wiring connector, then unscrew the fusebox mounting bolts and remove it from the mudguard **(see illustration)** (not applicable to Trophy from VIN 29156).

13 Disconnect the turn signal relay wiring connectors, then release the relay from its clamp **(see illustration 8.12)** (not applicable to Trophy from VIN 29156).

14 Release the wire clips from the mudguard **(see illustration)**.

15 Unscrew the bolts securing the mudflap at the front of the mudguard to the swingarm **(see Chapter 6, illustration 14.8)**. Unscrew the rear mudguard mounting bolts, noting how the sleeves and grommets fit. Lower the mudguard and carefully draw it back away from the machine, taking care not to snag any wiring.

Installation – all models

16 Installation is the reverse of removal. Make sure that all wires are correctly reconnected and routed, and test the turn signals, rear light and brake light before riding the bike.

Swingarm-mounted mudguard – 900 Speed Triple, Trophy from VIN 29156 and Daytona from VIN 9083 (including the Super III)

Removal

17 The chainguard is integral with a swingarm-mounted mudguard. Remove the two screws from the chainguard, the single screw from the rear of the mudguard, followed by the two throughbolts and nuts which secure the mudguard to the front of the swingarm. Carefully withdraw the mudguard from the swingarm.

Installation

18 Installation is the reverse of removal. On Daytona Super III models, the mudguard is made of carbon-fibre; take care not to crack or overstress this material.

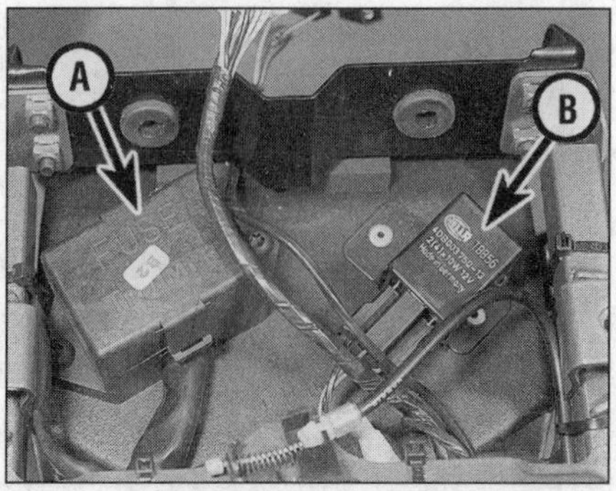

8.12 Fusebox (A) and turn signal relay (B) locations on rear mudguard

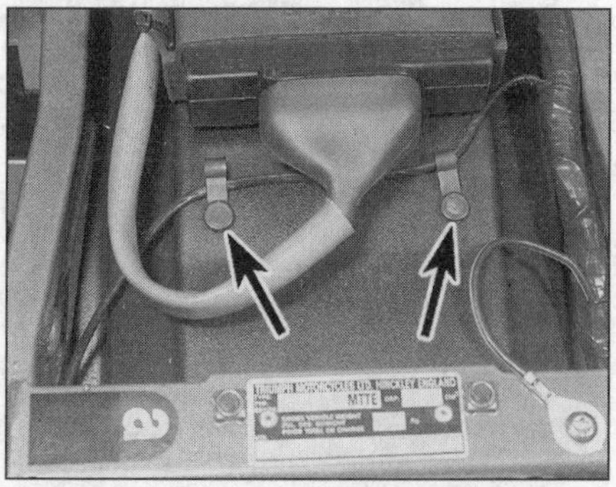

8.14 Release the two wiring clips from the mudguard (arrowed)

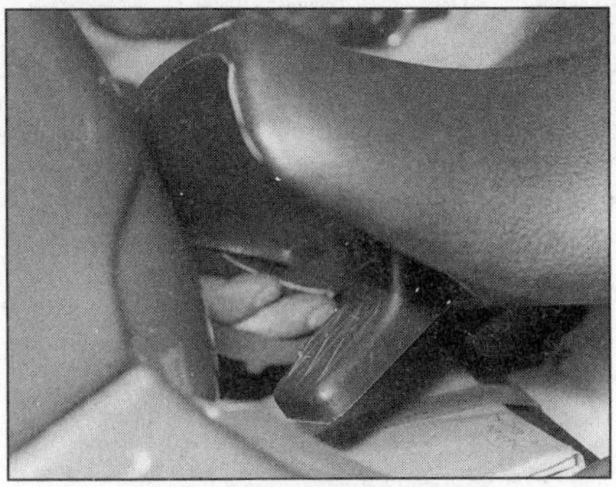

9.2a Locate the tab at the front of the seat under the tank . . .

9.2b . . . and the brackets in the middle of the seat under the frame rail

9 Seat - removal and installation

Seat

Removal

1 On all models except the Adventurer (from VIN 71699) and the Legend TT, insert the ignition key into the seat lock and unlock the seat. On Thunderbird, Thunderbird Sport and Adventurer, the seat lock is located in the left side cover; note that on the Adventurer the ring on the left side of the seat must be pulled before the seat lock is operated. On Tiger models the lock is located on the left side of the seat end cover, underneath the luggage rack. On Trident, Sprint, Trophy, Speed Triple and Daytona models the seat lock is located in the left side silencer carrier.

2 Lift the rear of the seat and draw it back and away from the bike. Note how the tab at the front of the seat locates under the tank mounting bracket, and also how the two brackets locate under the frame rail **(see illustrations)**. The seat locking device is mounted to the frame rail under the seat, and is connected to the lock by a cable. Check that the locking device works smoothly and apply some general purpose grease to the moving parts.

3 On the Adventurer (from VIN 71699) and the Legend TT models, the seat is bolted to the frame. Remove the bolts and disengage the tab at the front of the seat from the fuel tank bracket.

Installation

4 Locate the tab at the front of the seat under the fuel tank mounting bracket. Align the seat at the rear and push down on it to engage it with the lock (where applicable).

Single seat conversion - Daytona and Speed Triple

Removal

5 The single seat conversion hump is fitted as standard to the Daytona Super III and can be fitted as an option on the Speed Triple and other Daytona models.

6 To remove the hump from the seat, unscrew the two bolts securing the sides of the hump to the seat, then lift the hump up at the front and draw it back from the seat. Note how the hump locates under the rear edge of the seat. When the hump is not fitted, fit the trim to the end cover, then install the grab rail and tighten its mounting bolts securely.

Installation

7 Open the seat and remove the grab rail and trim. Locate the rear edge of the hump under the rear edge of the seat, and drop the front of the hump down so that its mounting holes align correctly. Install the bolts and tighten them securely.

10 Panniers - removal and installation

Panniers

1 Unlock and release the pannier latch **(see illustration)**. Slide the pannier back to release its hooks from the mounting bracket rail **(see illustration)**.

2 Installation is a reverse of removal.

Pannier brackets

3 Remove the panniers. Remove the side panels (Section 6).

4 The pannier brackets are retained to the footrest carriers by two Torx bolts and to the frame by two hex-head bolts. Take note of all washer and damping rubber positions as the bolts are withdrawn and if removing the left-hand bracket disconnect the seat lock from the bracket.

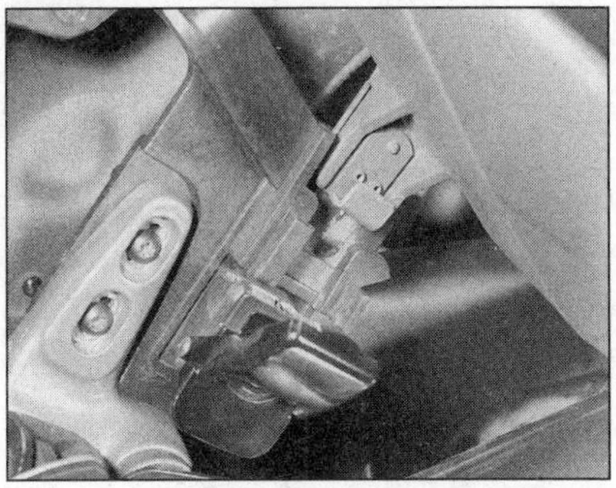

10.1a Unlatch the pannier . . .

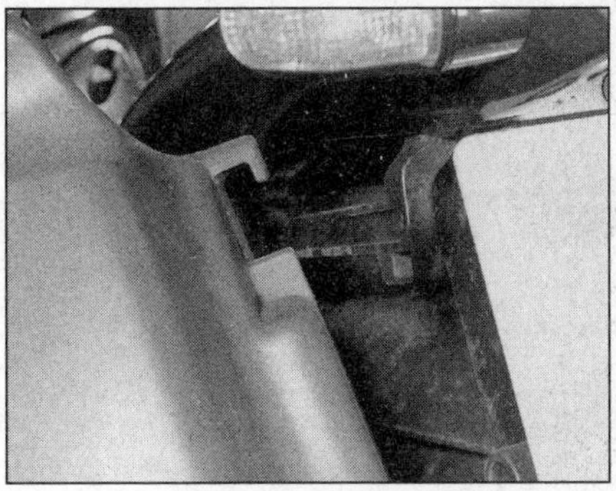

10.1b . . . slide the pannier rearwards and lift it off the rail

Notes

Chapter 9
Electrical system

Contents

Degrees of difficulty

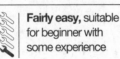

Easy, suitable for novice with little experience	**Fairly easy,** suitable for beginner with some experience	**Fairly difficult,** suitable for competent DIY mechanic	**Difficult,** suitable for experienced DIY mechanic	**Very difficult,** suitable for expert DIY or professional

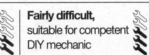

Specifications

Battery

Capacity	12V, 14Ah

Alternator

Rating	12V, 25A
Regulated voltage	14.5 volts @ 5500 rpm
Stator coil resistance	1.0 ohm maximum
Brush length	
New	10.5 mm
Service limit	4.5 mm
Slip ring diameter	
New	14.4 mm
Service limit	14.0 mm

Starter motor

Brush length	
New	12.0 mm
Service limit	8.5 mm
Commutator diameter	
New	28.0 mm
Service limit	27.0 mm
Commutator groove depth	
New	0.7 mm
Service limit	0.2 mm

Fusebox fuses

Trophy from VIN 29156	
Headlight, alternator	30A
Turn signals, clock and alarm	15A
Radiator fan	15A
Accessory circuit	10A
Starting circuit	15A
Headlight relay and alarm	5A
Instruments, brake lights and horn	10A
Instrument illumination and side lights	5A
Ignition switch (main)	30A
All models except Trophy from VIN 29156	
Headlight	10A
Tail light	10A
Main fuse	30A
Radiator fan	15A (10A up to VIN 4901)
Alarm/clock (where fitted)	10A

In-line fuses

Brake light (1995-on Trident, Sprint, Trophy (up to VIN 29155), Speed Triple, Daytona and Tiger models)	5A
Starter relay, ignition (and emission system solenoids on US models) – Thunderbird, Thunderbird Sport, Adventurer and Legend TT only	15A

Bulbs

Headlight	60/55W H4 halogen
Sidelight	4W
Brake/tail light	21/5W
Turn signal lights	10W
Licence plate light (Thunderbird, Thunderbird Sport and Legend TT)	5W
Clock (where fitted)	1.2W
Instrument cluster	Refer to existing bulb ratings

Torque settings

Neutral switch	14 Nm
Oil pressure switch	8 Nm
Rear brake light switch	15 Nm
Starter motor retaining bolts	10 Nm

1 General information

All models have a 12-volt electrical system. The components include a three-phase alternator unit with integral regulator and rectifier units.

The regulator maintains the charging system output within the specified range to prevent overcharging, and the rectifier converts the ac (alternating current) output of the alternator to dc (direct current) to power the lights and other components and to charge the battery. The alternator is driven off the alternator driveshaft in the upper crankcase; a shock absorber on the end of the driveshaft cushions the drive to the alternator.

The starter motor is mounted on the crankcase behind the cylinders. The starting system includes the motor, the battery, the relay and the various relevant wires and switches. If the engine stop switch and the ignition (main) switch are both in the 'Run' or 'On' position, the starter relay allows the starter motor to operate only if the transmission is in neutral (neutral switch on) or, if the transmission is in gear and the clutch lever is pulled into the handlebar (clutch switch on).

The wiring harness includes a take-off point for the Triumph alarm system; refer to a Triumph dealer for details.

Note: *Keep in mind that electrical parts, once purchased, cannot usually be returned (unless an agreement is made when such parts are bought). To avoid unnecessary expense, make absolutely certain that the faulty component has been positively identified before buying a new part.*

2 Electrical system – fault finding

Warning: To prevent the risk of short circuits, the ignition (main) switch must always be OFF and the battery negative (-ve) terminal should be disconnected before any of the bike's other electrical components are disturbed. Don't forget to reconnect the terminal securely once work is finished or if battery power is needed for circuit testing.

1 A typical electrical circuit consists of an electrical component, the switches, relays, etc. related to that component and the wiring and connectors that hook the component to both the battery and the frame. To aid in locating a problem in any electrical circuit, refer to the wiring diagrams at the end of this Chapter.

2 Before tackling any troublesome electrical circuit, first study the wiring diagram (see end of Chapter) thoroughly to get a complete picture of what makes up that individual circuit. Trouble spots, for instance, can often be narrowed down by noting if other components related to that circuit are operating properly or not. If several components or circuits fail at one time, chances are the fault lies in the fuse or earth (ground) connection, as several circuits often are routed through the same fuse and earth (ground) connections.

3 Electrical problems often stem from simple causes, such as loose or corroded connections or a blown fuse. Prior to any electrical fault finding, always visually check the condition of the fuse, wires and connections in the problem circuit. Intermittent failures can be especially frustrating, since you can't always duplicate the failure when it's convenient to test. In such situations, a good practice is to clean all connections in the affected circuit, whether or not they appear to be good. All of the connections and wires should also be wiggled to check for looseness which can cause intermittent failure.

4 If testing instruments are going to be utilised, use the wiring diagram to plan where you will make the necessary connections in order to accurately pinpoint the trouble spot.

5 The basic tools needed for electrical fault finding include a battery and bulb test circuit, a continuity tester, a test light, and a jumper wire. A multimeter capable of reading volts, ohms and amps is also very useful as an alternative to the above, and is necessary for performing more extensive tests and checks.

HAYNES HiNT ***Refer to Fault Finding Equipment in the Reference section for details of how to use electrical test equipment.***

3 Battery - inspection and checks

1 The battery is of the conventional lead/acid type on all models except the later Trophy (from VIN 71699), requiring regular checks of the electrolyte level, as described in Chapter 1, in addition to those detailed below. Trophy models from VIN 71699 are fitted with maintenance-free batteries; these batteries are sealed and thus do not require regular electrolyte level checks, although the following information on terminal condition and voltage checks is applicable.

2 The battery removal procedure is described in Chapter 1.

3 Check the battery terminals and leads for tightness and corrosion. If corrosion is evident, disconnect the leads from the battery, disconnecting the negative (-ve) terminal first, and clean the terminals and lead ends with a wire brush or knife and emery paper. Reconnect the leads, connecting the negative (-ve) terminal last, and apply a thin coat of petroleum jelly to the connections to slow further corrosion.

4 The battery case should be kept clean to prevent current leakage, which can discharge the battery over a period of time (especially when it sits unused). Wash the outside of the case with a solution of baking soda and water. Rinse the battery thoroughly, then dry it.

5 Look for cracks in the case and renew the battery if any are found. If acid has been spilled on the frame or battery holder, neutralise it with a baking soda and water solution, dry it thoroughly, then touch up any damaged paint. Make sure the battery vent tube is routed correctly and is not kinked or pinched.

6 If the motorcycle sits unused for long periods of time, disconnect the cables from the battery terminals. Refer to Section 4 and charge the battery approximately once every month.

7 The condition of the battery can be assessed by measuring the voltage present at the battery terminals. Connect the voltmeter positive (+ve) probe to the battery positive (+ve) terminal and the negative (-ve) probe to the battery negative (-ve) terminal. When fully charged there should be approximately 13 volts present. If the voltage falls below 12.3 volts the battery must be removed, disconnecting the negative (-ve) terminal first, and recharged as described in Section 4.

4 Battery - charging

Warning: Be extremely careful when handling or working around the battery. The electrolyte is very caustic and an explosive gas (hydrogen) is given off when the battery is charging.

1 To charge the battery it is first necessary to remove it from the motorcycle, as described in Chapter 1.

2 Triumph recommend that the battery is charged at a maximum rate of 1.4 amps (1.2 amps for the maintenance-free battery fitted to later Trophy models). Exceeding this figure can cause the battery to overheat, buckling the plates and rendering it useless. Few owners will have access to an expensive current controlled charger, so if a normal domestic charger is used check that after a possible initial peak, the charge rate falls to a safe level **(see illustration)**. If the battery becomes hot during charging stop. Further charging will cause damage. **Note:** *In emergencies the battery can be charged at a higher rate for a period of 1 hour. However, this is not recommended and the low amp charge is by far the safer method of charging the battery.*

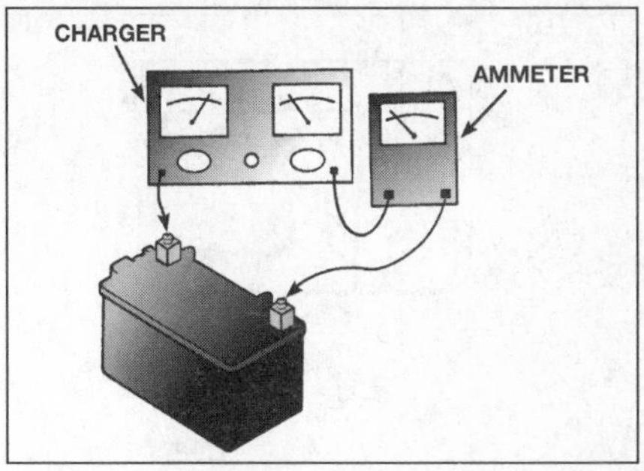

4.2 If the charger doesn't have an ammeter built in, connect one in series as shown; DO NOT connect the ammeter between the battery terminals or it will be ruined

3 If the recharged battery discharges rapidly if left disconnected it is likely that an internal short caused by physical damage or sulphation has occurred. A new battery will be required. A sound item will tend to lose its charge at about 1% per day.

4 Install the battery (refer to Chapter 1).

5 Fuses - check and renewal

1 The fusebox is located under the seat on Trident, Sprint, Trophy (up to VIN 29155), Speed Triple, Daytona and Tiger models. On later Trophy models (from VIN 29156) the fusebox is located in the fairing storage box on the right side. On Thunderbird, Thunderbird Sport, Adventurer and Legend TT models the fusebox is situated under the right side panel. Tiger models also have an in-line fuse in the brake circuit which is located under the seat on the seat left mounting rail.

2 To gain access to the fuses unclip and remove the fusebox lid **(see illustrations)**. The fuses are labelled for easy identification.

5.2a Fusebox location - Thunderbird, Thunderbird Sport, Adventurer and Legend TT

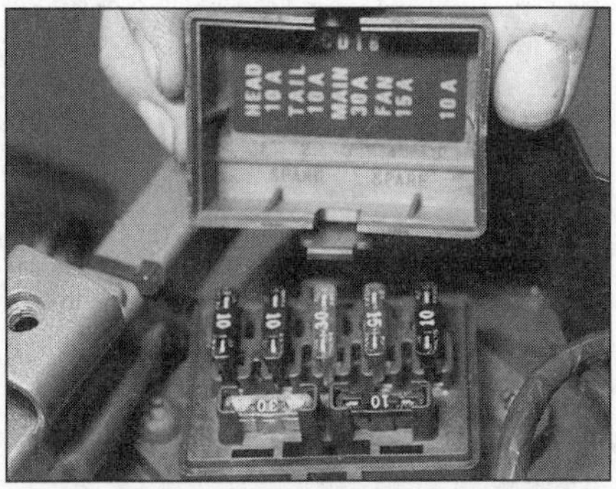

5.2b Fusebox location - Trident, Sprint, early Trophy, Speed Triple, Daytona and Tiger

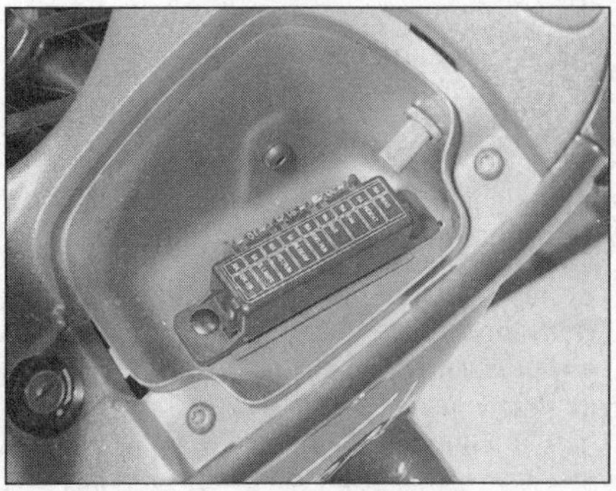

5.2c Fusebox location - later Trophy

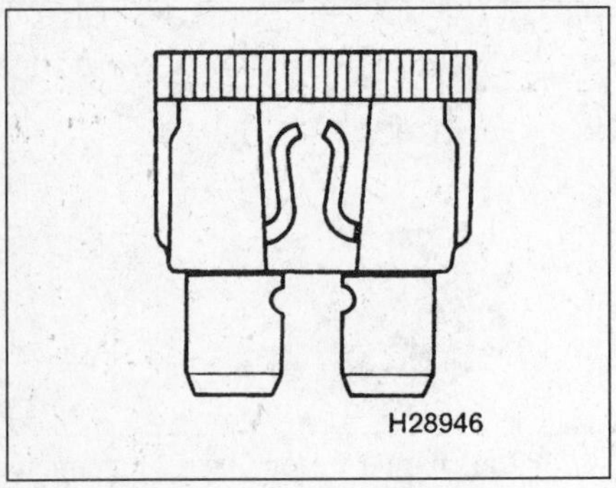

5.3 A blown fuse is easily identified by a break in its element

3 The fuses can be removed and checked visually. If you can't pull the fuse out with your fingertips, use a pair of needle-nose pliers. A blown fuse is easily identified by a break in the element **(see illustration)**. Each fuse is clearly marked with its rating and must only be replaced by a fuse of the correct rating. If the spare fuses are used, always renew them so that a spare fuse of each rating is carried on the bike at all times.

Caution: Never put in a fuse of a higher rating or bridge the terminals with any other substitute, however temporary it may be. Serious damage may be done to the circuit, or a fire may start.

4 If a fuse blows, be sure to check the wiring circuit very carefully for evidence of a short-circuit. Look for bare wires and chafed, melted or burned insulation. If a fuse is renewed before the cause is located, the new fuse will blow immediately.

5 Occasionally a fuse will blow or cause an open-circuit for no obvious reason. Corrosion of the fuse ends and fusebox terminals may occur and cause poor fuse contact. If this happens, remove the corrosion with a wire brush or emery paper, then spray the fuse end and terminals with electrical contact cleaner.

6 Lighting system – check

1 The battery provides power for operation of the headlight, tail light, brake light, licence plate light and instrument cluster lights. If none of the lights operate, always check battery voltage before proceeding. Low battery voltage indicates either a faulty battery or a defective charging system. Refer to Section 3 for battery checks and Sections 29 and 30 for charging system tests. Also, check the condition of the fuses and renew any blown fuses with new ones.

Headlight

2 If the headlight fails to work, check the fuse first with the key 'ON' (see Section 5), then unplug the electrical connector for the headlight and use jumper wires to connect the bulb directly to the battery terminals. If the light comes on, the problem lies in the wiring or one of the switches in the circuit or the headlight relay (twin headlight models only). Refer to Section 19 for the switch testing procedures, and also the wiring diagrams at the end of this Chapter. On models with twin headlights, if one of the relays is suspected of being faulty, substitute it with the other relay **(see illustration)**. If the headlight then works, the faulty relay must be renewed.

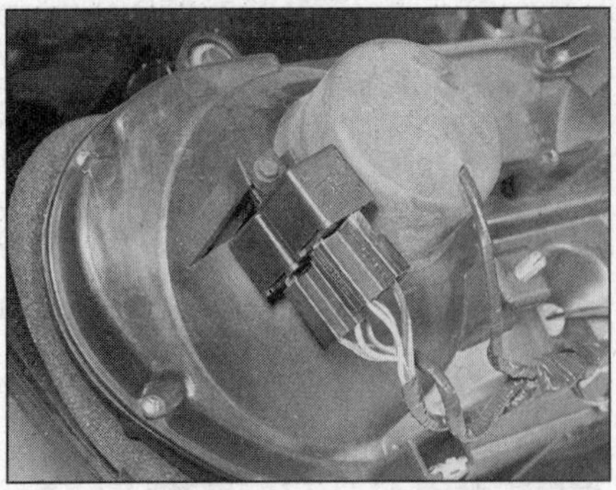

6.2 Headlight relay – later Trophy models

Tail light and licence plate light

3 If the tail light fails to work, check the bulbs and the bulb terminals first, then the fuses, then check for battery voltage at the tail light electrical connector. If voltage is present, check the earth circuit for an open or poor connection.

4 If no voltage is indicated, check the wiring between the tail light and the ignition switch, then check the switch. Also check the lighting switch.

5 The licence plate light fitted to Thunderbird, Thunderbird Sport and Legend TT models only can be checked in the same way as the tail light (see the wiring diagram at the end of this Chapter).

Brake light

6 See Section 13 for the brake light switch checking procedure.

Neutral indicator light

7 If the neutral light fails to operate when the transmission is in neutral, first check the fuses and the bulb (see Sections 5 and 16). If they are in good condition, check for battery voltage at the connector attached to the neutral switch on the left side of the engine. If battery voltage is present, refer to Section 21 for the neutral switch check procedure.

8 If no voltage is indicated, check the wiring between the switch and the bulb for open-circuits and poor connections.

Oil pressure warning light

9 See Section 17 for the oil pressure switch check.

Sidestand warning light (Trophy and Trident models)

10 If the sidestand light fails to operate when the stand is down (extended), check the fuses and the bulb (see Sections 5 and 16). If they are in good condition, check for battery voltage at the switch wiring connector. If battery voltage is present, refer to Section 22 for the sidestand switch check procedure.

11 If no voltage is indicated, check the wiring between the switch and the bulb for open-circuits and poor connections.

Low fuel level warning light (Trident, Sprint, Trophy (up to VIN 29155), Speed Triple, Daytona and Tiger)

12 If the low fuel level warning light has not come on by the time the reserve fuel tank is needed, check the fuses and the bulb (see Sections 5 and 16). If the fuses and bulb are in good condition, check for battery voltage at the low fuel level sensor wiring connector. If battery voltage is present, refer to Section 25 for the low fuel level sensor check procedure.

13 If no voltage is indicated, check the wiring between the switch and the bulb for open-circuits and poor connections.

High coolant temperature warning light (Speed Triple, Trophy (from VIN 29156), Thunderbird, Thunderbird Sport, Adventurer, Legend TT)

14 If you suspect that the warning light circuit is faulty, first check the fuse.

15 If the fuse is sound, check whether the bulb has blown (see Section 16).

16 Check the coolant temperature sender as described in Chapter 3.

7 Headlight bulb and sidelight bulb – renewal

Note: *The headlight bulb is of the quartz-halogen type. Do not touch the bulb glass with your fingers, as skin acids will shorten the bulb's service life. If the bulb is accidentally touched, it should be wiped carefully when cold with a rag soaked in methylated spirit and dried before fitting.*

Warning: Allow the bulb time to cool before removing it if the headlight has just been on.

Headlight

Trophy (up to VIN 29155), Daytona, Sprint and Tiger models

1 Access to the headlight bulb(s) is possible, though restricted, from underneath the fairing. It is better to access the bulb(s) by removing the instrument facia panels and, if necessary, removing the windshield as described in Chapter 8. On Trophy models, if access is still restricted, the fairing must be detached and moved forward (though not entirely removed) as described in Chapter 8.

2 Disconnect the wiring connector from the

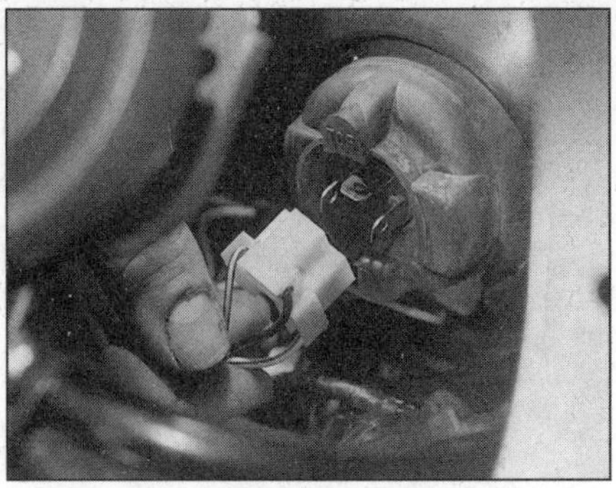

7.2a Disconnect the wiring connector from the headlight bulb . . .

7.2b . . . and pull off the rubber cover

7.3a Unhook the bulb retaining clip ears from the headlight . . .

headlight bulb and remove the rubber dust cover **(see illustrations)**.

3 On Daytona, Sprint and Tiger models, release the bulb retaining clip and swing it away, then remove the bulb **(see illustrations)**.

4 On Trophy models, turn the bulb retaining ring anti-clockwise, then remove the bulb.

5 Fit the new bulb, bearing in mind the information in the **Note** above, and secure it in position with the retaining clip or ring.

6 Install the dust cover, making sure it is correctly seated and with the 'TOP' mark facing up.

7 Reconnect the wiring connector and check the operation of the headlight(s).

8 If removed, fit the fairing, windshield, and facia panels as described in Chapter 8.

Trident, Speed Triple, Thunderbird, Thunderbird Sport, Adventurer and Legend TT models

9 Remove the two rim retaining screws and ease the rim out of the headlight shell **(see illustration)**.

10 Disconnect the wire connector to the headlight bulb, peel off the dust cover, and ease the sidelight bulbholder out of the headlight **(see illustration)**.

11 Release the bulb retaining clip and swing it away, then remove the bulb.

12 Fit the new bulb, bearing in mind the information in the previous **Note**, and secure it in position with the retaining clip.

13 Fit the sidelight bulbholder back into the headlight. Install the dust cover, making sure it is correctly seated and with the 'TOP' mark facing up **(see illustration)**.

14 Reconnect the wiring and operate the light.

15 When installing the headlight, engage the cut-out in the rim with the lip on the shell and secure with the two screws **(see illustration)**.

Trophy (from VIN 29156)

16 Access to the headlight bulbs is possible, though severely restricted, by removing the chin panel from the underside of the main fairing **(see illustration 2.9 in Chapter 8)**. Easier access is obtained by removing the fairing lower panel on the required side (see Chapter 8).

17 Slip off the rubber dust cover and pull off the wire connector to the bulb **(see illustration)**.

7.3b . . . then swing the clip away and remove the bulb

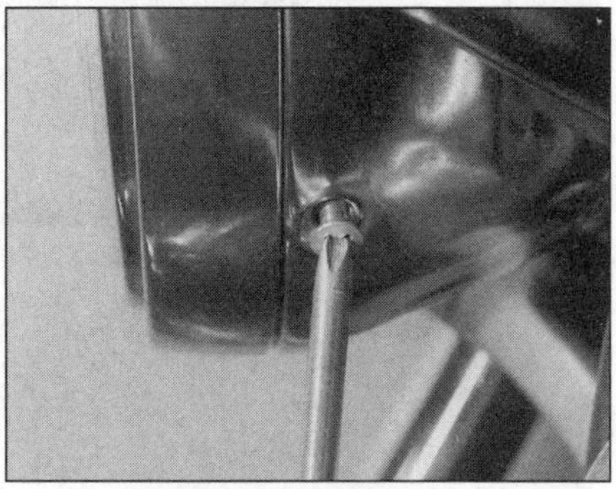

7.9 Headlight rim is retained by a screw on each side

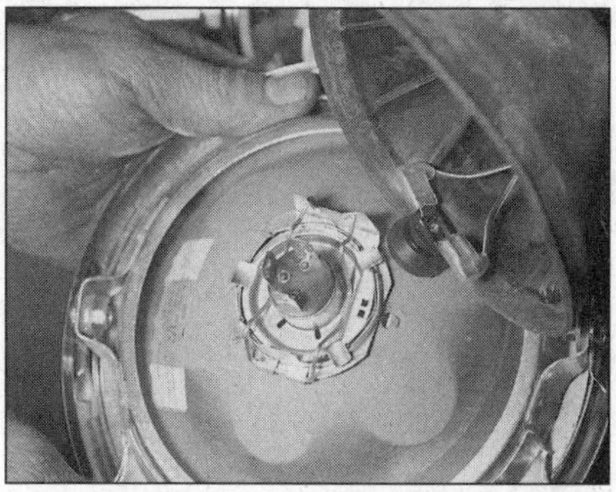

7.10 Separate dust cover from headlight to access the bulb

7.13 Ensure that the TOP marking faces upwards when fitting dust cover

7.15 Cut-out in headlight rim must engage lip at top of shell

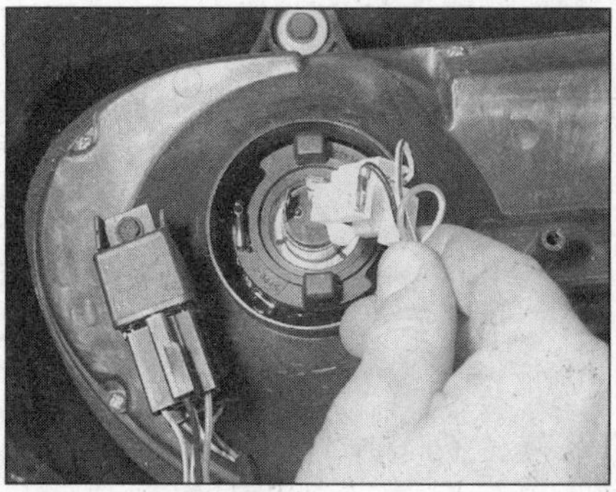

7.17 Pull off the wire connector

7.18a Release the retaining ring . . .

7.18b . . . and lift out the bulb

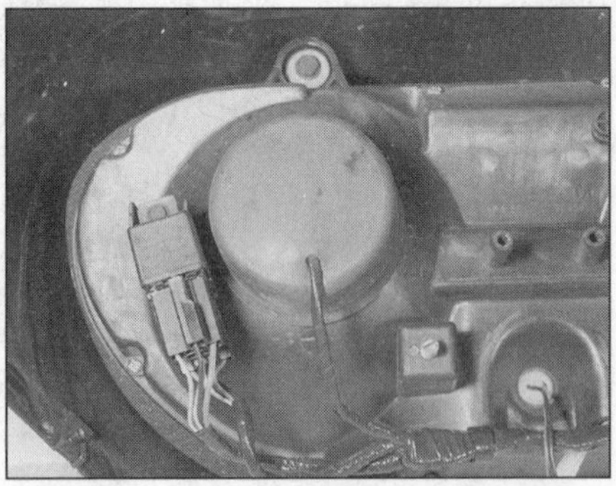
7.20 Make sure that the dust cover seats correctly

18 Turn the bulb retaining ring anticlockwise, then lift out the bulb **(see illustrations)**.

19 Fit the new bulb so that its two small tangs engage the cutout in the headlight, bearing in mind the information in the **Note** above. Secure the bulb in position with the retaining ring.

20 Push the wire connector on and slide the dust cover back over the headlight **(see illustration)**.

21 Check that the headlight works, then turn the ignition OFF again and install any removed fairing panels.

Sidelight

22 On all models the sidelight bulb is situated just below the headlight bulb. Access to the bulb is as described for the headlight above.

23 Pull the bulbholder out from the base of the headlight **(see illustration)**. If a bayonet type bulb is fitted, push the bulb inwards and twist it anti-clockwise to release it from the bulbholder. Capless bulbs should by carefully pulled out of the bulbholder **(see illustration)**.

24 If the socket contacts are dirty or corroded, they should be scraped clean and sprayed with electrical contact cleaner before the new bulb is installed. To install a new bayonet fitting bulb, pressing it into the bulbholder and twist it clockwise. To install a capless bulb simply press it into the bulbholder. Press the bulbholder back into the headlight.

25 Check the operation of the sidelight then install the headlight or fit the bodywork as described above, according to model.

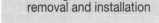

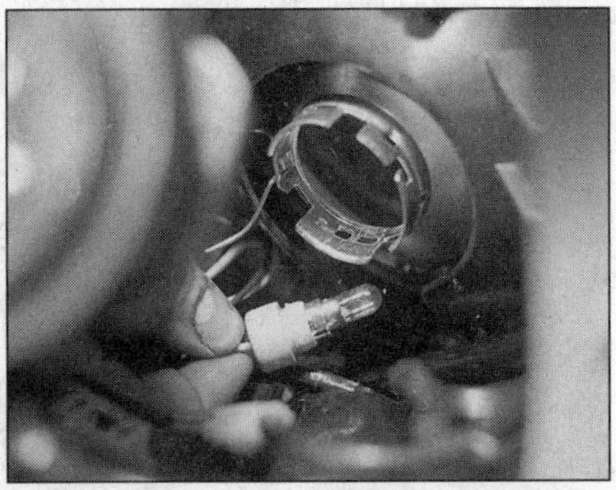
7.23a Gently pull the sidelight bulb out of its holder just below the headlight (bayonet bulb)

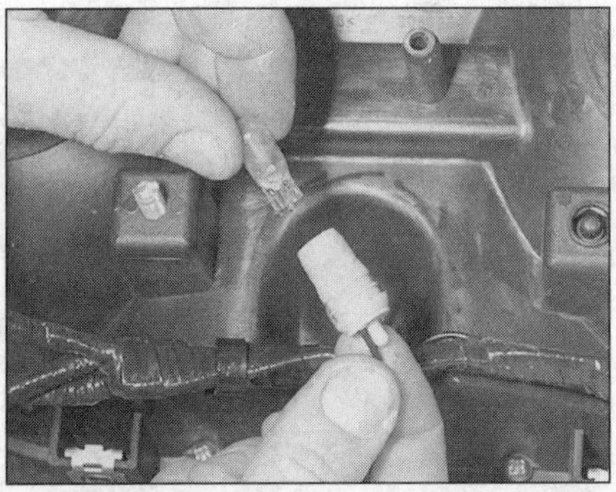
7.23b Removing a capless bulb from its holder

8 Headlight unit – removal and installation

Removal

Daytona, Sprint and Tiger models

1 Remove the main fairing (Chapter 8).

2 Disconnect the headlight wiring connectors from the headlights. Trace the sidelight wiring to the connector block and disconnect it.

3 Disconnect the headlight relay wiring connectors from the relays **(see illustration)**.

4 Unscrew the three screws securing the headlight assembly to the fairing stay and remove the assembly **(see illustrations)**.

Trophy models up to VIN 29155

5 Remove the main fairing as described in Chapter 8.

6 Unscrew the four screws securing the headlight to the fairing and remove the headlight.

Trophy models from VIN 29156

7 Remove the main fairing (see Chapter 8).

8 The headlight unit is retained by three bolts **(see illustration)**. Note the exact position of the washers, collars and grommets when removing the headlight from the fairing and retrieve the foam seal if it is loose.

Trident, Speed Triple, Thunderbird, Thunderbird Sport, Adventurer and Legend TT models

9 Remove the two rim retaining screws and ease the rim out of the headlight shell **(see**

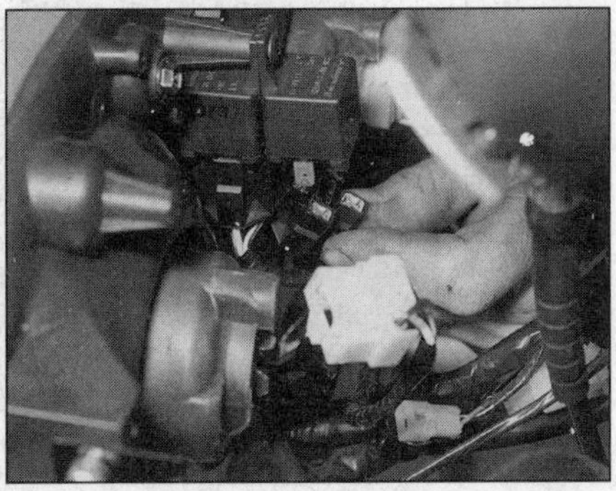
8.3 Disconnect the headlight relay wiring connectors

8.4a The headlight assembly is secured to the fairing stay by a bolt on each side . . .

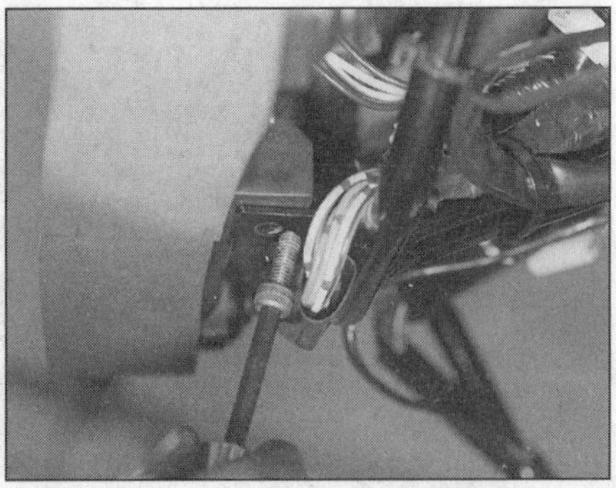
8.4b . . . and one underneath

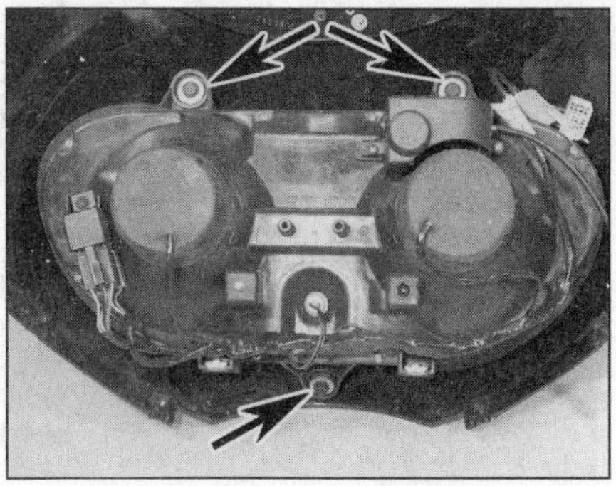

8.8 Headlight unit retaining bolts (arrowed)

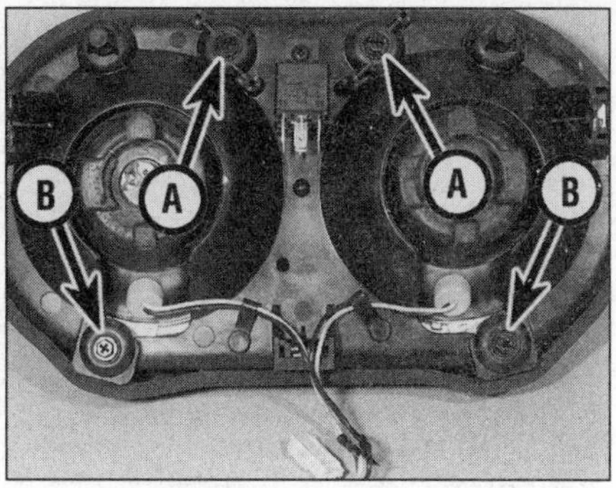

9.1 Beam adjusting screws on Daytona, Sprint and Tiger – horizontal (A), vertical (B)

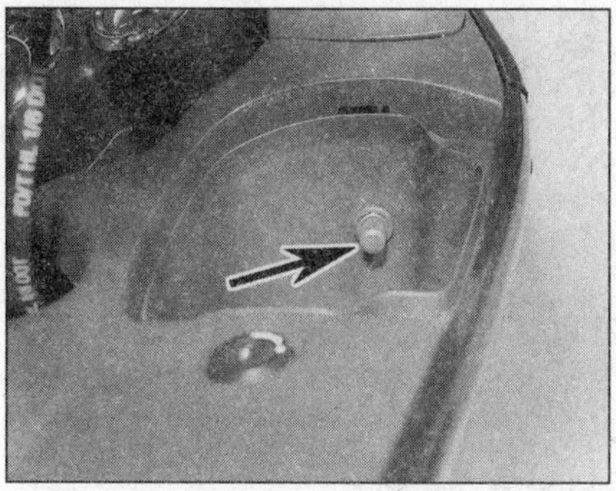

9.9 Vertical adjuster knob – later Trophy

illustration 7.9). Disconnect the wire connector to the headlight bulb, peel off the dust cover, and ease the sidelight bulbholder out of the headlight **(see illustration 7.10)**.

10 To remove the headlight shell, remove the bolts securing it to the headlight brackets, then carefully withdraw the shell from the brackets. Free the wiring inside the shell from the clamps and ease it out the back of the shell.

> **HAYNES HiNT** *When disconnecting wiring, label the wire connectors to aid easy reconnection*

Installation – all models

11 Installation is the reverse of removal. Check the operation of the headlight and sidelight. Check the headlight aim (see Section 9).

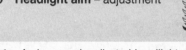

9 Headlight aim – adjustment

Note: *An improperly adjusted headlight may cause problems for oncoming traffic or provide poor, unsafe illumination of the road ahead. Before adjusting the headlight aim, be sure to consult with local traffic laws and regulations. Riders of machines in the UK should refer to MOT Test Checks in the Reference section of this manual.*

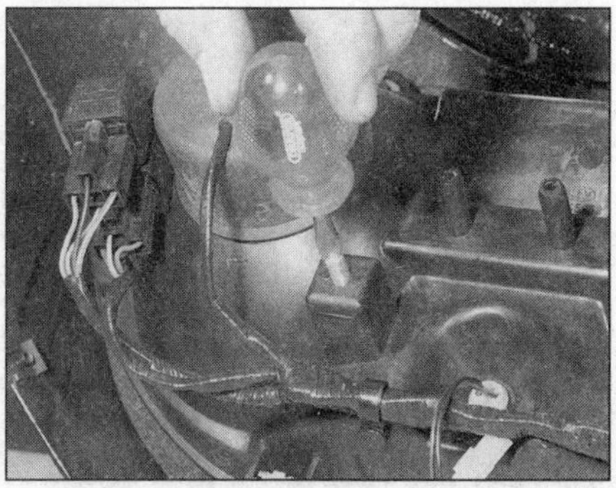

9.10 Horizontal adjuster screw – later Trophy

Daytona, Sprint and Tiger models

1 Horizontal (side-to-side) adjustment is made via the adjusters at the top of each headlight. Vertical adjustment of the headlight aim is made via the screws at the bottom of each headlight **(see illustration)**.

2 Adjustment is made using a stubby cross-head screwdriver passed up through the bottom of the upper fairing.

3 On the right side light, turn the horizontal adjuster anti-clockwise to adjust the beam to the right, and clockwise to adjust the beam to the left.

4 On the left side light, turn the horizontal adjuster clockwise to adjust the beam to the right, and anti-clockwise to adjust the beam to the left.

5 On both lights, turn the vertical adjuster clockwise to adjust the beam down, and anti-clockwise to adjust the beam up.

Trophy models up to VIN 29155

6 Adjustment is made either manually or using a suitable spanner passed up through the bottom of the main fairing. Remove the instrument facia panels (three screws) for access to the back of the headlight.

7 Horizontal (side-to-side) adjustment is made by turning the adjuster screws on either side of the light in opposite directions. To adjust the beam to the right, turn the right side adjuster anti-clockwise and the left side adjuster clockwise. To adjust the beam to the left, turn the right side adjuster clockwise and the left side adjuster anti-clockwise.

8 Vertical adjustment is made by turning both adjusters an equal amount in the same direction. To adjust the beam up, turn the adjusters anti-clockwise. To adjust the beam down, turn the adjusters clockwise.

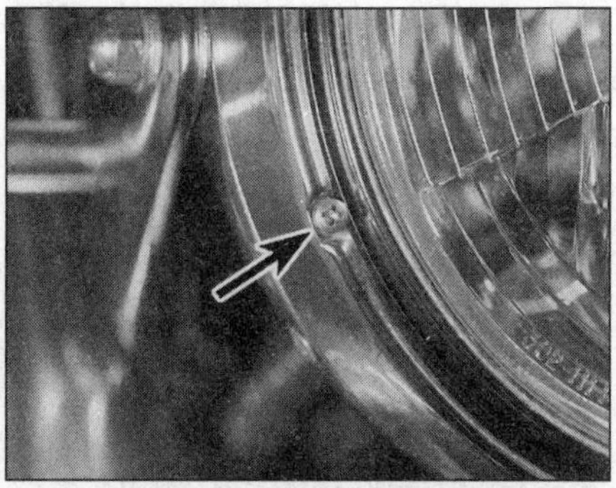

9.11 Beam horizontal adjustment screw (arrowed) – Thunderbird, Thunderbird Sport, Adventurer, Legend TT, Trident and Speed Triple

Trophy models from VIN 29156

Note: *In each case the beam adjuster controls both headlights.*

9 Vertical adjustment is made by turning the beam adjusting knob inside the storage box in the fairing right side **(see illustration)**. Turn the knob clockwise to raise the beam and anti-clockwise to lower it.

10 Horizontal adjustment is made by turning the adjuster screw on the back of the left side headlight using a stubby flat-blade screwdriver **(see illustration)**. Remove the fairing chin panel for access **(see illustration 2.9 in Chapter 8)**. Turn the screw clockwise to move the beam to the right and anti-clockwise to move it to the left.

Trident, Speed Triple, Thunderbird, Thunderbird Sport, Adventurer and Legend TT models

11 Horizontal adjustment is made by turning the adjuster screw in the rim on the left side of the headlight **(see illustration)**.

12 Vertical adjustment is made by loosening the headlight shell mounting bolts and manually moving the headlight up or down in the brackets **(see illustration)**. Tighten the bolts after adjustment has been made.

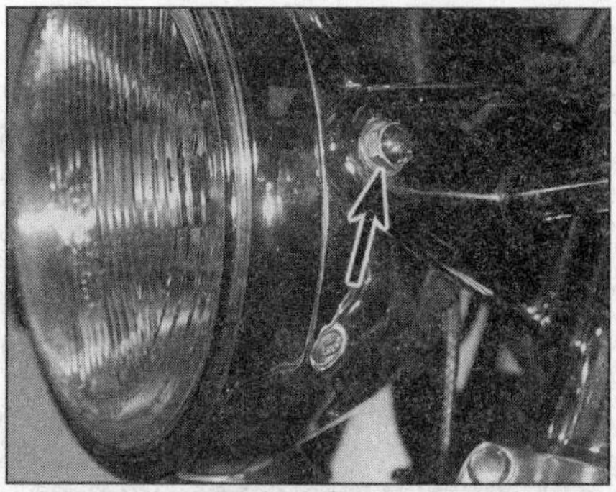

9.12 Beam vertical adjustment is made by loosening shell mounting bolts – Thunderbird, Thunderbird Sport, Adventurer, Legend TT, Trident and Speed Triple

10.2a Unscrew the lens retaining screw from the back of the turn signal . . .

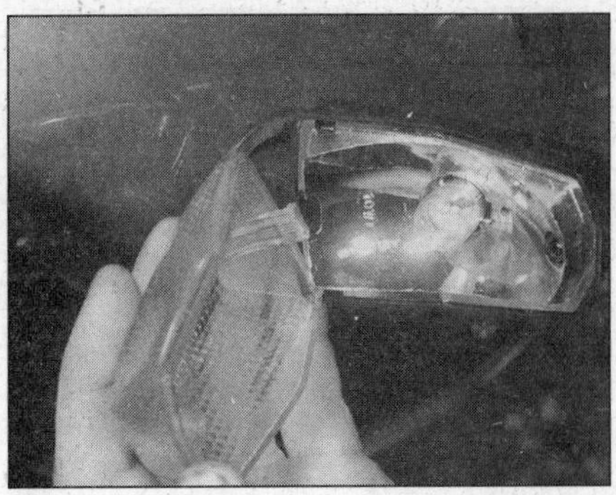
10.2b . . . and remove the lens, noting how it fits

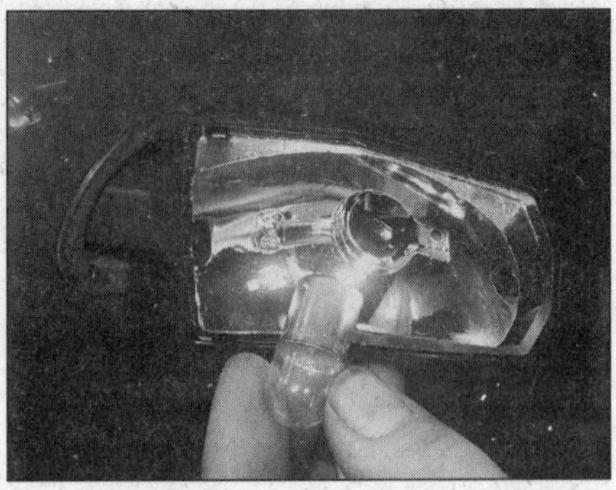
10.3 To release the bulb gently push it in and twist it anti-clockwise

10 Turn signal, tail light and licence plate bulbs – renewal

Turn signal bulbs

1 On Thunderbird, Thunderbird Sport, Adventurer and Legend TT models, unscrew the turn signal lens retaining screws from the front of the turn signal and withdraw the lens. Note the drain hole on the bottom of the lens – this must face downwards.

2 On Trident, Sprint, Trophy, Speed Triple, Daytona and Tiger models, unscrew the turn signal lens retaining screw from the back of the turn signal and withdraw the lens **(see illustrations)**.

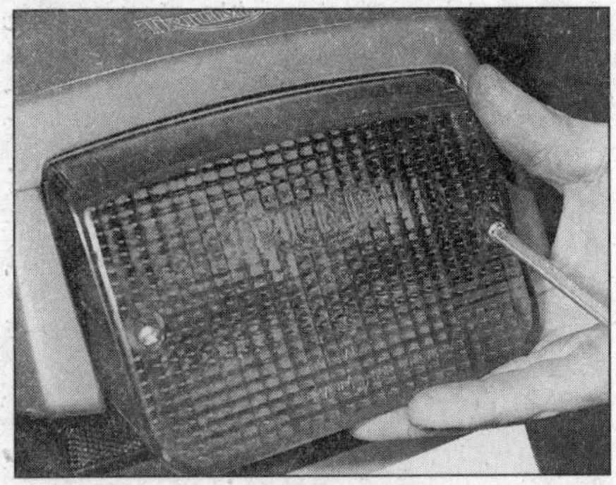
10.5 The tail light lens is secured by two screws

3 Push the bulb into the holder and twist it anti-clockwise to remove it **(see illustration)**. Check the socket terminals for corrosion and clean them if necessary. Line up the pins of the new bulb with the slots in the socket, then push the bulb in and turn it clockwise until it locks into place. **Note:** *It is a good idea to use a paper towel or dry cloth when handling the new bulb to prevent injury if the bulb should break and to increase bulb life.*

4 Install the lens back into the turn signal and securely tighten the retaining screw(s). Take care not to overtighten the screw(s) as the lens is easily cracked.

HAYNES HiNT *If the socket contacts are dirty or corroded, scrape them clean and spray with electrical contact cleaner before a new bulb is fitted.*

Tail light bulbs

5 Unscrew the tail light lens retaining screws and remove the lens **(see illustration)**.

6 Push each bulb into the holder and twist it anti-clockwise to remove it **(see illustration)**. Check the socket terminals for corrosion and clean them if necessary. Line up the pins of the new bulb with the slots in the socket, then push the bulb in and turn it clockwise until it locks into place. **Note:** *The pins on the bulb are offset so it can only be installed one way. Use a paper towel or dry cloth when handling the new bulb to prevent injury if the bulb should break and to increase bulb life.*

7 Install the lens back onto the tail light and securely tighten the retaining screws. Take care not to overtighten the screws as the lens is easily cracked.

Licence plate bulb – Thunderbird, Thunderbird Sport and Legend TT

8 The bulbholder is accessed from inside the rear mudguard. Scrub any dirt from the surrounding area and pull the bulbholder out of the light unit **(see illustration)**.

9 The bulb is of the capless type – simply pull it out of the holder. Take care not to break the new bulb when installing it in the bulbholder. Push the bulbholder back into place.

11 Turn signal assemblies – removal and installation

Front turn signals

Removal – Trophy (up to VIN 29155), Daytona, Sprint and Tiger models

1 Trace the turn signal wiring back from the turn signal and disconnect it at the connectors inside the fairing **(see illustration)**.

2 Carefully pull the wiring through to the turn signal mounting, noting its routing for use when refitting. Remove the rubber boot and

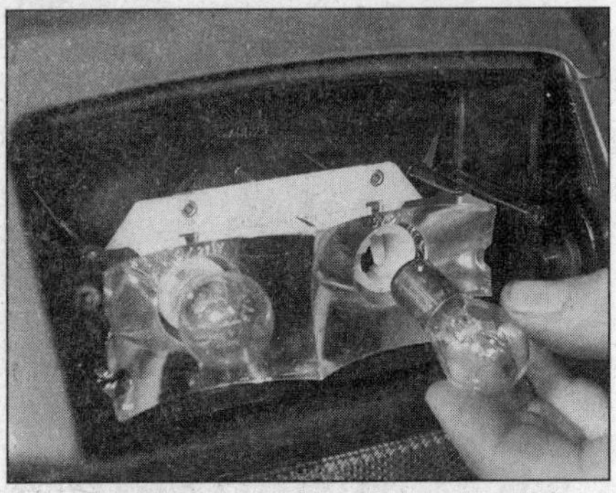
10.6 Twist the bulb anti-clockwise to release it from the tail light unit

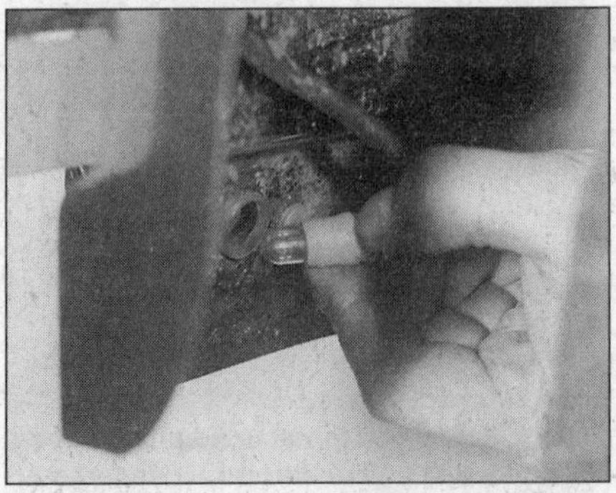
10.8 Pull licence plate light bulbholder out from inside rear mudguard

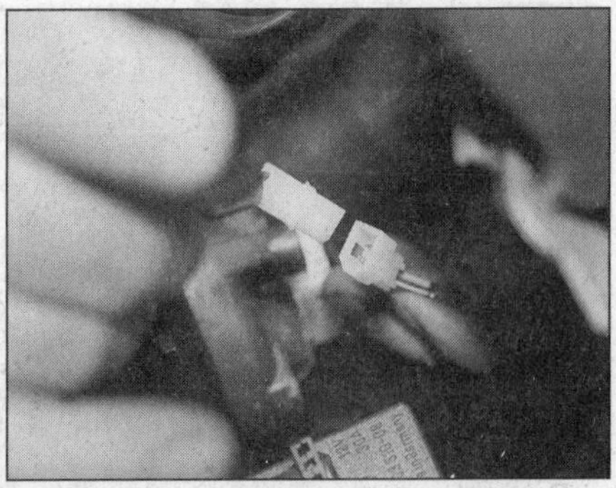
11.1 Disconnect the turn signal wiring

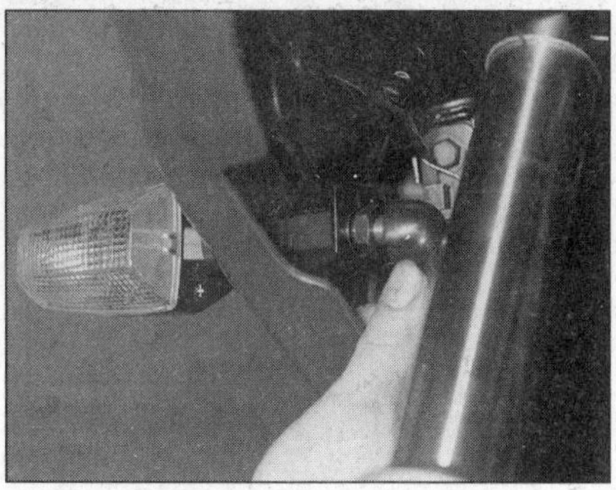

11.2a Remove the rubber boot . . .

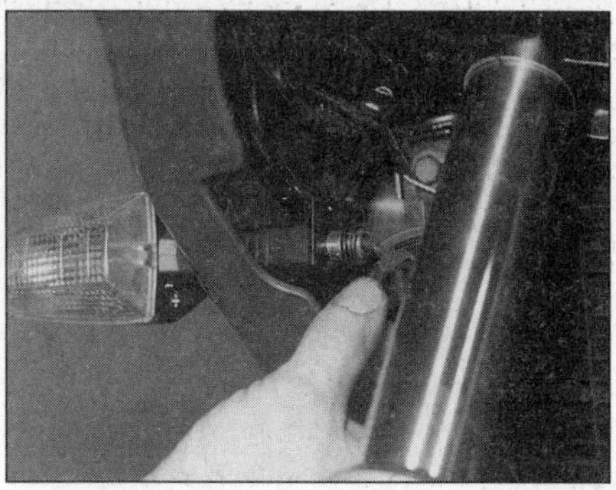

11.2b . . . and unscrew the turn signal nut

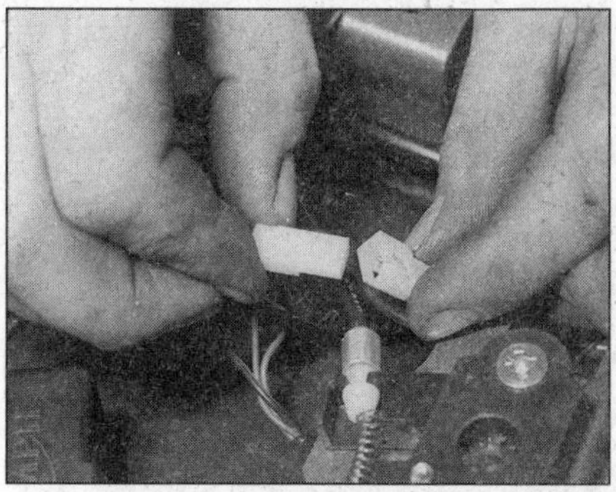

11.12 Disconnect the turn signal wiring at the connectors

unscrew the turn signal mounting nut, noting the order of the washers **(see illustrations)**. Slip the nut, spring washer and washer off the wiring and withdraw the turn signal from the fairing.

Removal – Trophy models from VIN 29156

3 Remove the fairing lower panel on the side concerned (see Chapter 8).

4 From the inside of the lower panel remove the upper inner section/storage box, followed by the lower inner section. The turn signal is retained by two bolts.

Removal – Trident, Speed Triple, Thunderbird, Thunderbird Sport, Adventurer and Legend TT models

5 Unscrew the two screws securing the headlight rim to the shell, then carefully withdraw the headlight from the shell, noting how it fits. Trace the wiring back from the turn signal and disconnect it at the connectors inside the headlight shell.

6 Pull the wiring through to the turn signal mounting, noting its routing, then remove the rubber boot and unscrew the turn signal mounting nut, noting the order of the washers (where fitted). Slip the nut, spring washer and washer (where fitted) off the wiring and remove the turn signal from the bracket.

Installation – all models

7 Installation is the reverse of removal.

Rear turn signals

Removal – Thunderbird, Thunderbird Sport, Adventurer and Legend TT models

8 Remove the seat as described in Chapter 8. Trace the turn signal wiring back from the turn signal and disconnect it at the connector.

9 Pull the wiring through to the turn signal mounting, noting its routing, then unscrew the turn signal mounting nut on the inside of the rear mudguard, and remove the turn signal from the mudguard.

Removal – Tiger model

10 Remove the seat as described in Chapter 8. Release its six retaining screws and remove the top cover for access to the turn signal mounting. Trace the turn signal wiring back from the turn signal and disconnect it at the connector.

11 Slip the rubber boot off the turn signal mounting, and unscrew the mounting nut, noting the order of the washers. Remove the nut, spring washer and washer from the wiring and remove the turn signal from the bracket.

Removal – Trident, Sprint, Trophy (up to VIN 29155), Speed Triple and Daytona models

12 Remove the seat and the side panel as described in Chapter 8. Trace the turn signal wiring back from the turn signal and disconnect it at the connector **(see illustration)**.

13 Release the wiring from its tie and note its routing, then unscrew the bolt securing the turn signal mounting bracket to the frame **(see illustration)**. Remove the bracket and turn signal from the frame. If necessary, remove the rubber boot and unscrew the turn signal mounting nut, noting the order of the washers. Slip the nut, spring washer and washer off the wiring and remove the turn signal from the bracket.

Removal – Trophy models from VIN 29156

14 Remove the side panels (see Chapter 8). Remove the two screws to free the turn signal from the side panel.

Installation – all models

15 Installation is the reverse of removal.

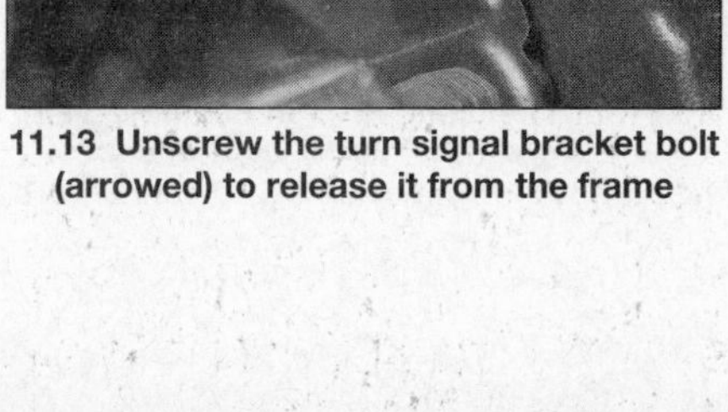

11.13 Unscrew the turn signal bracket bolt (arrowed) to release it from the frame

12 Turn signal circuit – check

1 The battery provides power for operation of the turn signal lights, so if they do not operate, always check the battery voltage first. Low battery voltage indicates either a faulty battery or a defective charging system. Refer to Section 3 for battery checks and Sections 29 and 30 for charging system tests. Also, check the fuses (see Section 5) and the switch (see Section 19).

2 Most turn signal problems are the result of a burned out bulb or corroded socket. This is especially true when the turn signals function properly in one direction, but fail to flash in the other direction. Check the bulbs and the sockets (see Section 10).

3 If the bulbs and sockets are good, check for power at the turn signal relay orange/green wire (all models except Trophy from VIN 29156) or green/grey wire (Trophy from VIN 29156) with the ignition 'ON'. The relay is mounted below the fusebox behind the right side panel on Thunderbird, Thunderbird Sport, Adventurer and Legend TT models, next to the fusebox under the seat on Trident, Sprint Trophy (up to VIN 29155), Speed Triple, Daytona and Tiger models, and on the main fairing stay on Trophy models from VIN 29156 **(see illustrations)**. Turn the ignition OFF when the check is complete.

4 If no power was present at the relay, check

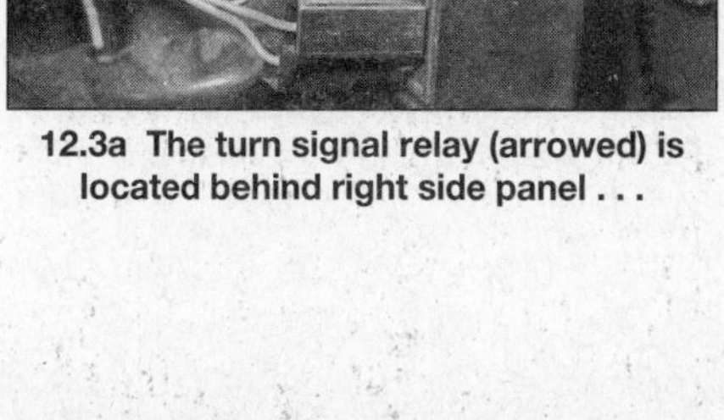

12.3a The turn signal relay (arrowed) is located behind right side panel . . .

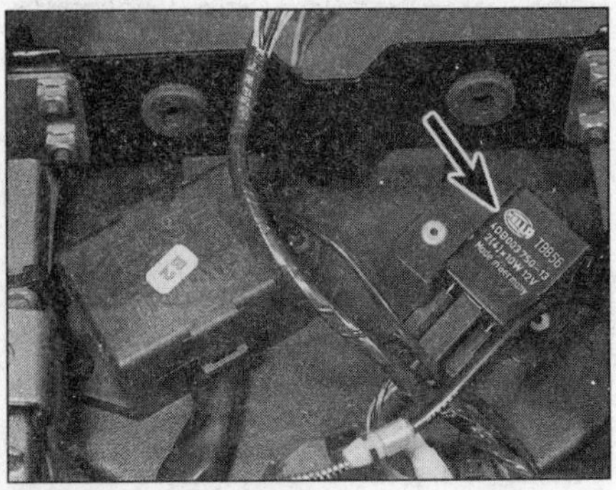

12.3b . . . or under the seat (arrowed) . . .

the wiring from the relay to the ignition (main) switch for continuity.

5 If power was present at the relay, using the appropriate wiring diagram at the end of this Chapter, check the wiring between the relay, turn signal switch and turn signal lights for continuity. If the wiring and switch are sound, renew the relay.

6 The turn signal circuit includes a hazard warning switch which, when operated, flashes all four turn signals simultaneously. If the turn signals do not all flash when the switch is operated, yet function normally otherwise, check the hazard switch for continuity.

13 Brake light switches – check, removal and installation

Circuit check

1 Before checking any electrical circuit, check the bulb (see Section 10) and fuses (see Section 5).

2 Using a test light connected to a good earth, check for voltage at the brake light switch wiring connector. If there's no voltage present, check the wire between the switch and the fusebox (see the wiring diagrams at the end of this Chapter).

3 If voltage is available, touch the probe of the test light to the other terminal of the switch, then pull the brake lever in or depress

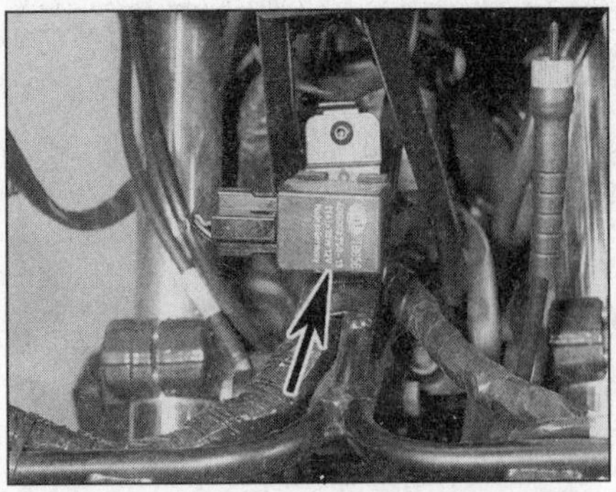

12.3c . . . or on the fairing stay (arrowed) – according to model

the brake pedal. If the test light doesn't light up, renew the switch.

4 If the test light does light, check the wiring between the switch and the brake lights (see the wiring diagrams at the end of this Chapter).

Switch removal and installation

Front brake lever switch

5 Remove the mounting screw and unplug the electrical connectors from the switch **(see illustration)**.

6 Detach the switch from the bottom of the front brake master cylinder.

7 Installation is the reverse of the removal procedure. The switch isn't adjustable.

Rear brake pedal switch

Caution: The rear brake switch is of the pressure type and screws into the top of the master cylinder. Take care when the switch is removed to protect the surrounding components from contact with brake fluid spills.

8 Prise up the rubber boot and disconnect the wiring from the switch mounted to the top of the rear brake master cylinder **(see illustration)**.

9 Wrap a rag around the master cylinder to catch any brake fluid that escapes, then unscrew the switch from the top of the cylinder. Discard the sealing washer as a new one must be used. **Note:** *Do not operate the brake pedal with the switch removed.*

10 Fit a new sealing washer to the switch, then install the switch and tighten it to the specified torque setting. Note that on later models, the brake light switch secures the hydraulic hose to the top of the master cylinder; a new sealing washer should be used between the union and master cylinder and the union positioned at the correct angle.

11 Bleed the hydraulic system as described in Chapter 7. Check that the rear brake works properly before riding the motorcycle and that there is no sign of hydraulic fluid leakage from the disturbed joint.

14 Instrument cluster and speedometer cable – removal and installation

Instrument cluster

Removal

1 On Trophy (up to VIN 29155), Daytona and Sprint models remove the instrument facia panels, on later Trophy models (from VIN 29156) remove the main fairing, and on Tiger models remove the fairing front panel (see Chapter 8, Section 2). On Thunderbird, Thunderbird Sport, Adventurer, Legend TT, Speed Triple and Trident models, remove the headlight from its shell to access the wiring connectors (see Section 7).

2 Unscrew the speedometer cable retaining ring from the rear of the instrument cluster and detach the cable.

3 Disconnect the instrument cluster wiring at the connectors, and release the wiring from any ties.

4 On Trophy and Trident models, remove the mounting nuts underneath the instrument cluster and lift the assembly off its mounting bracket **(see illustration)**. On all other models, unscrew the two main instrument cluster mounting screws from the top of the instruments and carefully lift the instrument cluster off the mounting bracket **(see illustrations)**.

Installation

5 Installation is the reverse of removal. Make sure that the speedometer cable and wiring are correctly routed and secured.

13.5 Remove the single screw to free front brake light switch from the master cylinder

13.8 Prise off the rubber boot to access the rear brake light switch wire connectors

14.4a Instrument cluster nuts (arrowed) – later Trophy

14.4b Instrument cluster mounting screws (arrowed) – Thunderbird, Thunderbird Sport, Adventurer, Legend TT and Speed Triple

14.4c Instrument cluster mounting screws (arrowed) – Daytona, Sprint, and Tiger

14.7 Unscrew the cable retaining ring and detach the cable

Speedometer cable

Removal

6 On Trophy, Daytona and Sprint models remove the instrument facia panels, and on Tiger models remove the fairing front panel (see Chapter 8, Section 2).

7 Unscrew the speedometer cable retaining ring from the rear of the instrument cluster and detach the cable **(see illustration)**.

8 Remove the screw securing the lower end of the cable to the drive unit on the wheel and detach the cable **(refer to Chapter 7, illustration 14.3)**.

9 Slip the cable out of its retaining guide on the brake caliper (Thunderbird, Thunderbird Sport, Adventurer and Legend TT), brake hose clamp (Tiger) or front mudguard (all other models) and remove it from the bike, noting its correct routing.

Installation

10 Route the cable correctly and install it in its retaining guide.

11 Align the inner cable slot at the lower end of the cable with the drive gear dog on the front wheel and connect the cable to the drive **(see Chapter 7, illustration 14.17b)**. Install the cable retaining screw and tighten it securely.

12 Connect the cable upper end to the instrument cluster and tighten the retaining ring securely.

13 Check that the cable doesn't restrict steering movement or interfere with any other components.

14 On Trophy, Daytona, Sprint and Tiger models, install the panels as described in Chapter 8.

15 Meters and gauges – check, removal and installation

Coolant temperature gauge (where fitted)

Check

1 The temperature gauge check is described in Chapter 3.

Removal and installation

2 Remove the instrument cluster from the bike as described in Section 14. On Trophy and Trident models, remove the instrument lower cover; it is retained by two screws.

3 Unscrew the nuts securing the temperature gauge to the casing and withdraw it far enough out of the casing to gain access to the wiring **(see illustration)**.

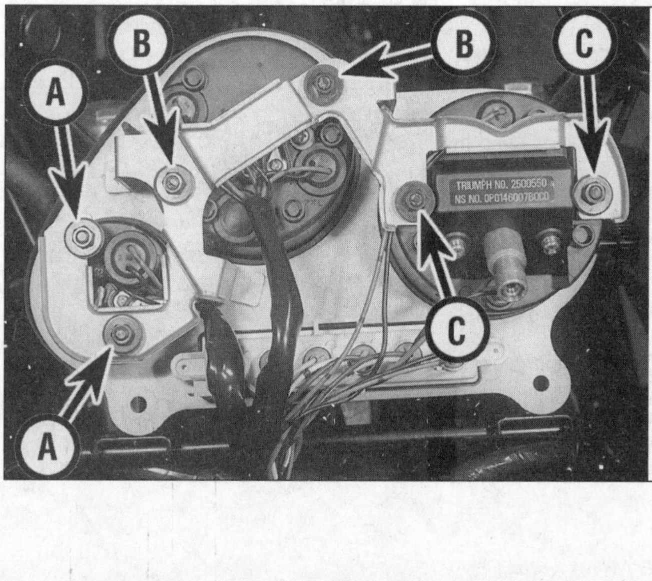

15.3 Rear view of instrument cluster fitted to Daytona, Sprint, and Tiger models – temperature gauge mountings (A), tachometer mountings (B), speedometer mountings (C)

4 Note the correct fitted position of the temperature gauge wires, then unscrew the wire retaining screws and detach the wires. Carefully pull the bulbholder out from its socket. The temperature gauge can now be fully removed from the casing.

5 Install the temperature gauge by reversing the removal sequence.

Tachometer

Check

6 On Trophy (up to VIN 29155), Daytona and Sprint models remove the instrument facia panels, and on Tiger models remove the fairing front panel (see Chapter 8, Section 2). On later Trophy models (from VIN 29156) remove the main fairing to locate the instrument wiring connector (see Chapter 8). On Thunderbird, Thunderbird Sport, Adventurer, Legend TT, Speed Triple and Trident models, remove the headlight from its casing to access the wiring connectors (see Section 8). Carefully disconnect the instrument cluster wiring connector.

7 Disconnect the igniter wiring connector (see Chapter 5).

8 Using an ohmmeter or continuity tester, check for continuity between the black/blue (orange/pink wire on Trophy from VIN 29156) wire terminal on the instrument cluster connector and its terminal on the igniter connector. If no continuity is obtained, check the wiring between the two connectors (refer to the wiring diagrams at the end of this Chapter), and repair the wiring if an open circuit is indicated. If continuity is indicated but the tachometer does not work, then it is probably faulty and should be taken to a Triumph dealer for further testing.

Removal and installation – Speed Triple, Thunderbird, Thunderbird Sport, Adventurer and Legend TT models

9 Remove the two domed nuts with washers from the base of the tachometer; this will free the baseplate (where fitted) and instrument pod **(see illustrations 16.1a and 16.1b)**. Pull the bulbholders from the base of the

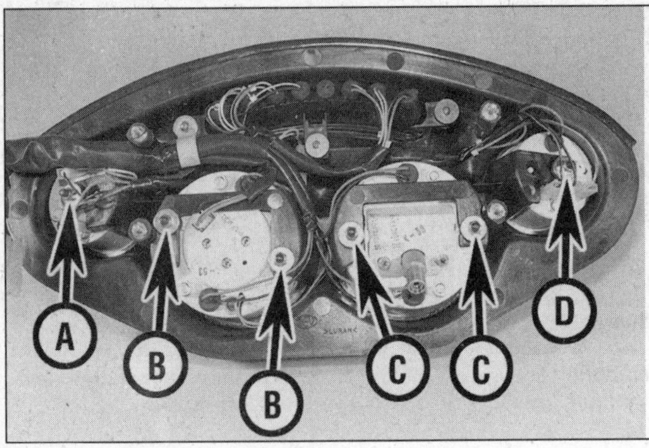

15.12 Rear view of the instrument cluster fitted to later Trophy – clock mounting (A), tachometer mountings (B), speedometer mountings (C) and fuel gauge mounting (D)

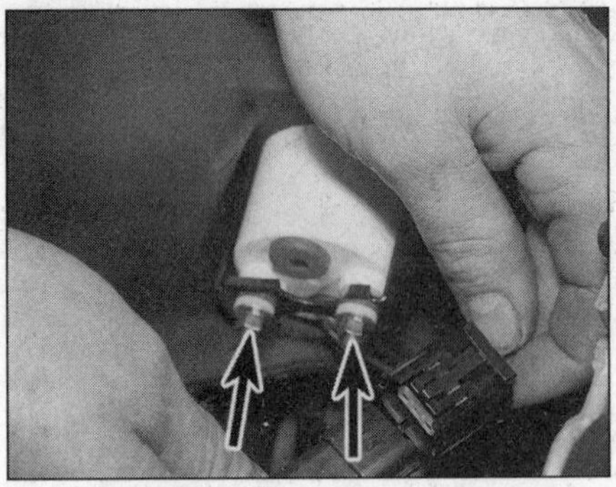

15.22 Disconnect the wiring at the connector, then unscrew the two nuts (arrowed) to release the clock

tachometer and disconnect the wire connector **(see illustration 16.1c)**. Lift the tachometer out of the instrument cluster.

10 Install the tachometer by reversing the removal sequence.

Removal and installation – Trident, Sprint, Trophy, Daytona and Tiger models

11 Remove the instrument cluster as described in Section 14. On Trophy (up to VIN 29155) and Trident models, also remove the two screws to free the bottom cover from the instruments.

12 Unscrew the nuts securing the tachometer to the casing and withdraw it far enough out of the casing to gain access to the wiring **(see accompanying illustration and illustration 15.3)**. Note the correct fitted position of the tachometer wires, then remove the wire retaining screws and carefully detach the wires. Carefully pull the bulbholders out from their sockets. The tachometer can now be fully removed from the instrument cluster.

13 Install the tachometer by reversing the removal sequence.

Speedometer

Check

14 Special instruments are required to properly check the operation of this meter. Seek the advice of a Triumph dealer for diagnosis.

Removal and installation – Speed Triple, Thunderbird, Thunderbird Sport, Adventurer and Legend TT models

15 Remove the two domed nuts with washers from the base of the speedometer; this will free the baseplate (where fitted) and instrument pod. Pull the bulbholders from the base of the speedometer and lift it out of the instrument cluster.

16 Install the speedometer by reversing the removal sequence.

Removal and installation – Trident, Sprint, Trophy, Daytona and Tiger models

17 Remove the instrument cluster from the bike as described in Section 14. On Trophy and Trident models, also remove the two screws to free the bottom cover from the instruments.

18 Unplug the bulbholders from the speedometer. Remove the retaining screw from the centre of the odometer trip knob. Unscrew the nuts securing the speedometer to the casing and withdraw it from the instrument cluster **(see illustrations 15.3 and 15.12)**.

19 Install the speedometer by reversing the removal sequence.

Clock (where fitted)

Check

20 If the clock does not work, check the fuse (see Section 5). If the fuse is in good condition, remove the instrument facia panel (or fairing side panel on Tiger models) as described in Chapter 8, Section 2 and check for battery voltage at the clock red wire connector. If battery voltage is present, the clock is faulty and must be renewed.

21 If no voltage is indicated, check the wiring between the clock and the fusebox for open-circuits and poor connections.

Removal and installation

22 Remove the instrument facia panel (or fairing side panel on Tiger models) as described in Chapter 8, Section 2; on later Trophy models (from VIN 29156) remove the instrument cluster (see Section 14). Gently pull the bulbholder from the base of the clock. Disconnect the clock wiring at the connector, then unscrew the nut(s) securing the clock to its bracket and remove the clock **(see illustration)**.

23 Install the clock by reversing the removal procedure.

Fuel gauge (Trophy from VIN 29156)

Check

24 The fuel gauge check is described in Section 25.

Removal and installation

25 Remove the instrument cluster (see Section 14).

26 Make a written note of their positions, then disconnect the three wires from the gauge **(see illustration)**. Gently pull the bulbholder from the base of the gauge **(see illustration)**.

27 Release the single nut with its washer and

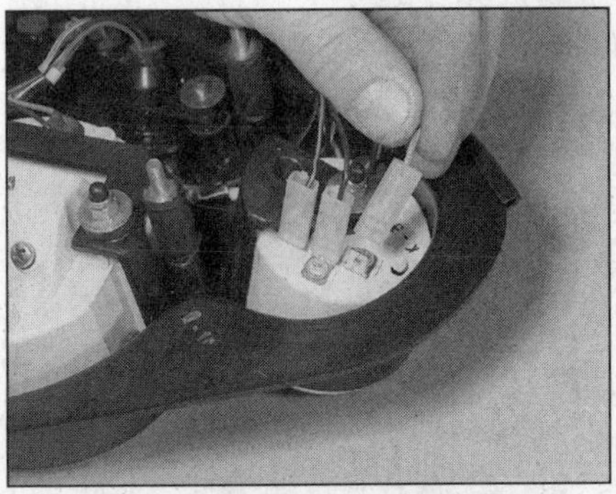

15.26a Detach the fuel gauge wire connectors . . .

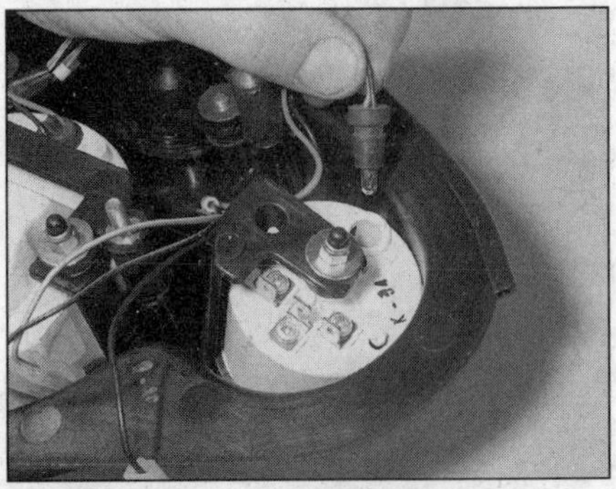

15.26b . . . pull out the bulbholder

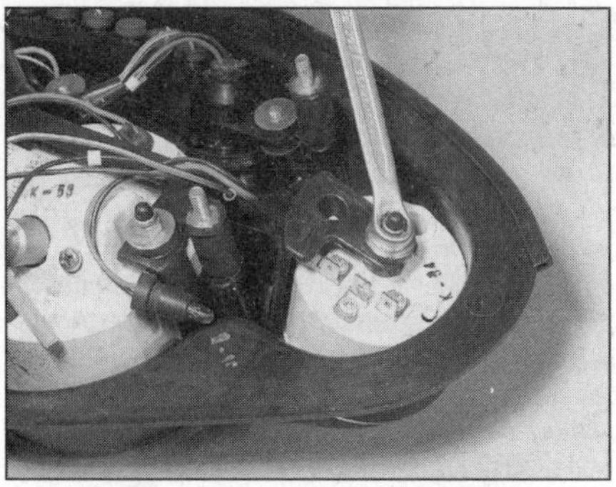

15.27a Remove the mounting nut . . .

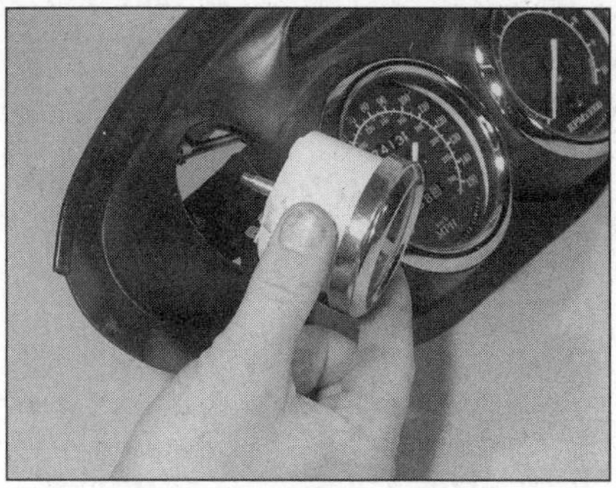

15.27b . . . and lift the gauge out

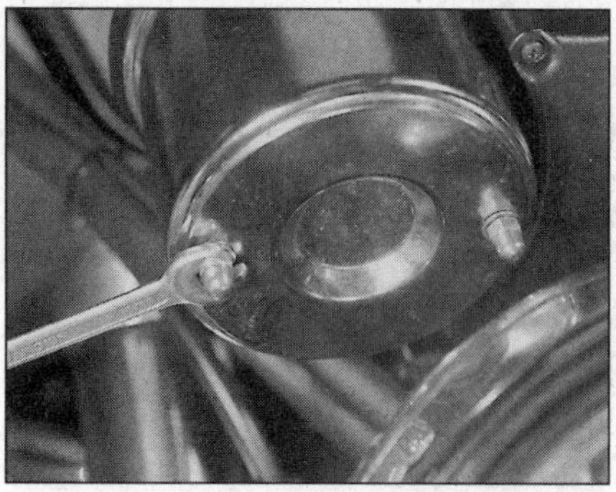

16.1a Remove the two domed nuts and washers to free the baseplate . . .

lift the gauge out from the top of the instrument cluster **(see illustrations)**.

28 When installing the gauge, ensure that the locating peg on its base engages the hole in the bracket and that the wires are reconnected to their original terminals.

16 Instrument and warning light bulbs – renewal

Speed Triple, Thunderbird, Thunderbird Sport, Adventurer and Legend TT models

1 Remove the two domed nuts with washers from the base of the meter; this will free the baseplate (where fitted) and instrument pod **(see illustrations)**. Pull the bulbholders from the base of the meter and gently pull the bulbs out of their holders **(see illustration)**.

2 The warning light bulbs are housed in the display unit between the meters. Remove the retaining screws to free the bottom cover and access the bulbholders **(see illustration)**. Gently pull the bulbs out of their holders **(see illustration)**.

Trident, Sprint, Trophy, Daytona and Tiger models

Note: *The instrument and warning light bulb wattages differ; examine the existing bulb and make sure the new bulb is of the same size and wattage.*

3 Remove the instrument cluster as described in Section 14 and on Trophy (up to VIN 29155) and Trident models also remove the bottom cover (retained by two screws). **Note:** *Depending on your dexterity, you may be able to access certain bulbholders without removing the instruments.*

4 Pull the relevant bulbholder out of the back of the cluster then gently pull the bulb out of its holder **(see illustrations)**.

5 Carefully push the new bulb into position, then push the bulbholder back into the rear of the cluster.

6 Install the bottom cover (Trophy and Trident) and install instrument cluster as described in Section 14.

17 Oil pressure switch – check, removal and installation

Check

1 The oil pressure warning light should come on when the ignition (main) switch is turned

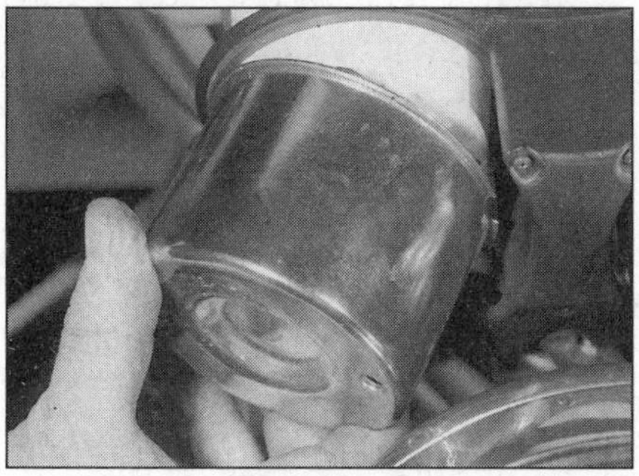

16.1b . . . then withdraw the instrument pod

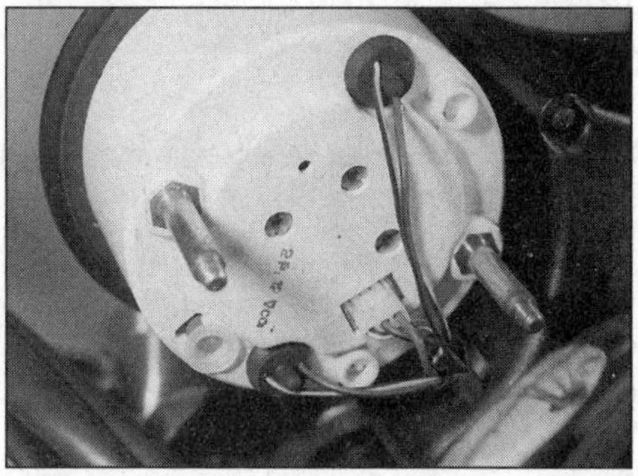

16.1c Bulbholders are a push fit in back of meter

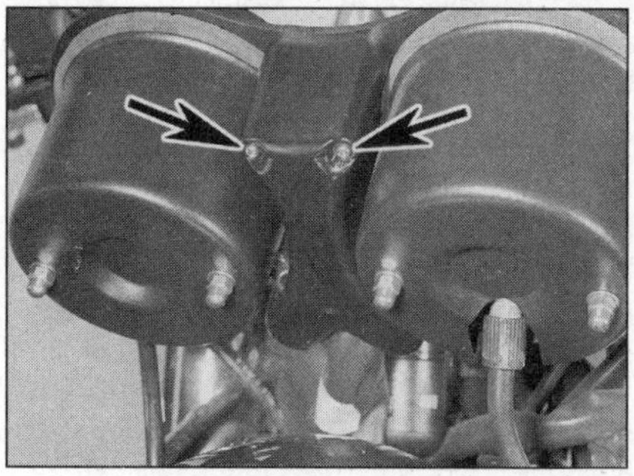

16.2a Bottom cover is retained by two screws (arrowed)

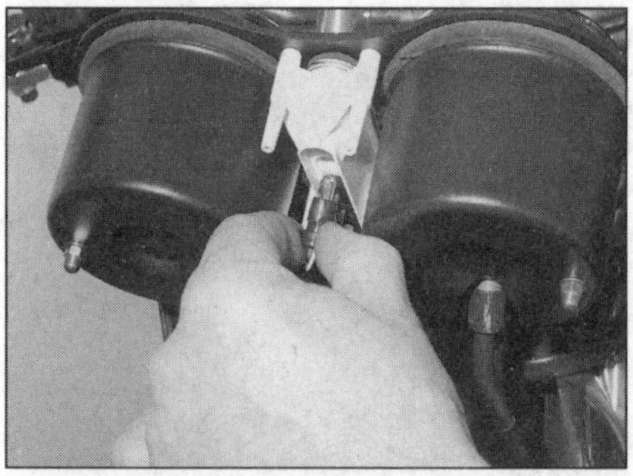

16.2b Bulbs can simply be pulled out of their holders

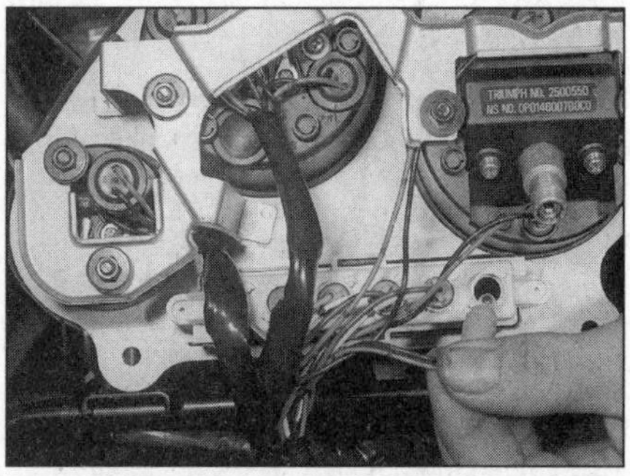

16.4a Pull the relevant bulbholder out of the casing . . .

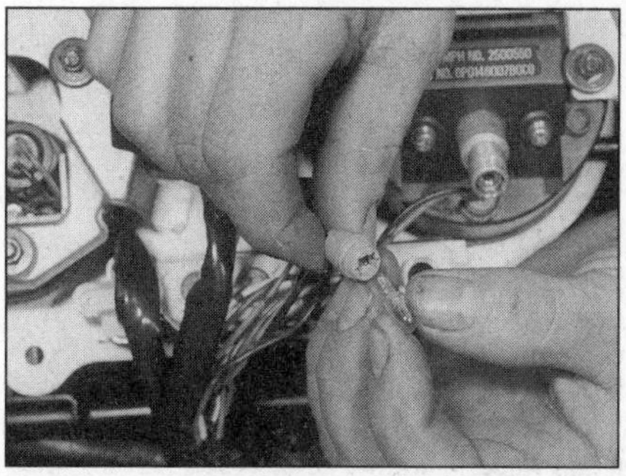

16.4b . . . and gently ease the bulb out of the bulbholder

17.3a The oil pressure switch is screwed into the back of the sump on early engines . . .

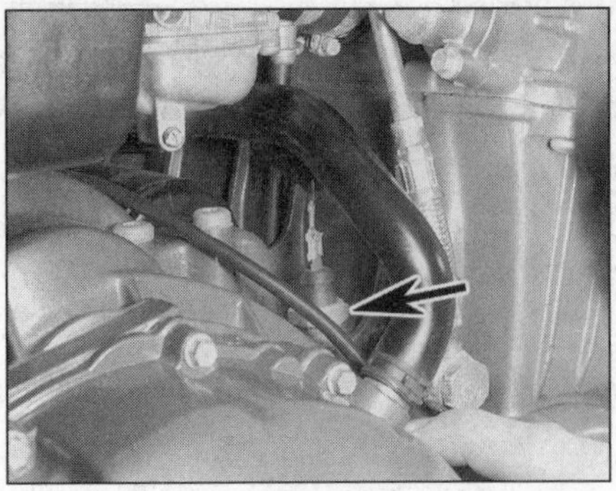

17.3b . . . and into the top of the crankcase on later engines (arrowed)

ON and extinguish a few seconds after the engine is started. If the oil pressure light comes on whilst the engine is running, stop the engine immediately and carry out an oil pressure check (see Chapter 2).

2 If the oil pressure warning light does not come on when the ignition is turned on, check the bulb (see Section 16) and fuses (see Section 5).

3 The oil pressure switch is screwed into the back of the sump on early engines **(see illustration)** and into the top of the crankcase on later engines **(see illustration)**. Slip the protective sleeve back and detach the wiring connector from the switch. With the ignition switched ON, earth the wire on the crankcase and check that the warning light comes on. If the light comes on, the switch is confirmed defective and must be renewed.

4 If the light still does not come on, check for voltage at the wire terminal using a test light. If there is no voltage present, switch the ignition OFF and using an ohmmeter or continuity tester check the pink (white/brown on later Trophy from VIN 29156) wire from the switch to the instrument cluster for continuity (see the wiring diagrams at the end of this Chapter).

5 If the warning light comes on whilst the engine is running, yet the oil pressure is satisfactory, remove the wire from the oil pressure switch. With the wire detached and the ignition switched ON the light should be out. If it is illuminated, the pink (white/brown on later Trophy from VIN 29156) wire between the switch and instrument cluster must be earthed at some point. If the wiring is good, the switch must be assumed faulty and renewed.

Removal and installation

6 Slip the protective sleeve back and detach the wiring connector from the switch.

7 Drain the engine oil (see Chapter 1).

8 Unscrew the switch from the sump (early engines) or upper crankcase (later engines) and wipe the oil from the hole threads.

9 Apply a few drops of non-permanent thread locking compound to the threads of the new switch and screw it into the sump, tightening it to the specified torque. Reconnect the wire connector and slip the sleeve back into place.

10 Refill the engine oil (see Chapter 1).

11 Check that the oil pressure warning light illuminates when the ignition is turned ON, then extinguishes a few seconds after the engine is started.

18 Ignition (main) switch – check, removal and installation

Check

1 Trace the ignition (main) switch wiring back from the base of the switch and disconnect it at the connector. On Trident, Speed Triple, Thunderbird, Thunderbird Sport, Adventurer and Legend TT models the connector is located inside the headlight shell (see Section 7). On Trophy (up to VIN 29155), Daytona and Sprint models remove the instrument facia panels to trace the connector, on later Trophy models (from VIN 29156) remove the main fairing to access the connector, and on Tiger models remove the fairing front panel (see Chapter 8, Section 2).

2 Using an ohmmeter or a continuity tester, check the continuity of the terminal pairs (see the wiring diagrams at the end of this Chapter). Continuity should exist between the terminals connected by a solid line on the diagram when the switch is in the indicated position.

3 If the switch fails any of the tests, renew it.

Removal and installation

Note: *It is strongly recommended that this task be carried out by a Triumph dealer.*

4 The ignition (main) switch is attached to the top yoke by two shear-head bolts, designed to shear off at the head when they are tightened sufficiently. This is a security measure designed to make it very difficult to remove the ignition switch.

5 If the switch has to be renewed, the top yoke (complete with switch) must be removed (see Chapter 6, Section 8) and the switch retaining bolts drilled out. Apply a few drops of non-permanent thread locking compound to the threads of the new shear-head bolts, then tighten them until their heads shear off.

6 Install all disturbed components in a reverse of the removal procedure.

19 Handlebar switches – check

1 Generally speaking, the switches are reliable and trouble-free. Most troubles, when they do occur, are caused by dirty or corroded contacts, but wear and breakage of internal parts is a possibility that should not be overlooked. If breakage does occur, the entire switch and related wiring harness will have to be renewed, since individual parts are not available.

2 The switches can be checked for continuity using an ohmmeter or a continuity test light. Always disconnect the battery negative (-ve) cable, which will prevent the possibility of a short circuit, before making the checks.

3 Trace the wiring harness of the switch in question back to its connector(s) and disconnect it.

4 Using the ohmmeter or test light, check for continuity between the terminals of the switch harness with the switch in the various positions (see the wiring diagrams at the end of this Chapter).

5 If the continuity check indicates a problem exists, refer to Section 20, remove the switch and spray the switch contacts with electrical contact cleaner. If they are accessible, the contacts can be scraped clean with a knife or polished with crocus cloth. If switch components are damaged or broken, it will be obvious when the switch is disassembled.

20 Handlebar switches – removal and installation

Right handlebar switch

Removal

1 Trace the wiring harness back from the switch to the wiring connector, and then disconnect it.

2 Work back along the harness, freeing it from all the relevant clips and ties, whilst noting its correct routing.

3 Unscrew the two switch screws and remove the switch from the handlebar **(see illustration)**. Disconnect the two wires from

20.3 Unscrew the two right handlebar switch retaining screws

20.4 When installing the right switch, locate the peg on the switch (A) in the hole in the handlebar (arrowed)

20.7 Unscrew the two left handlebar switch retaining screws

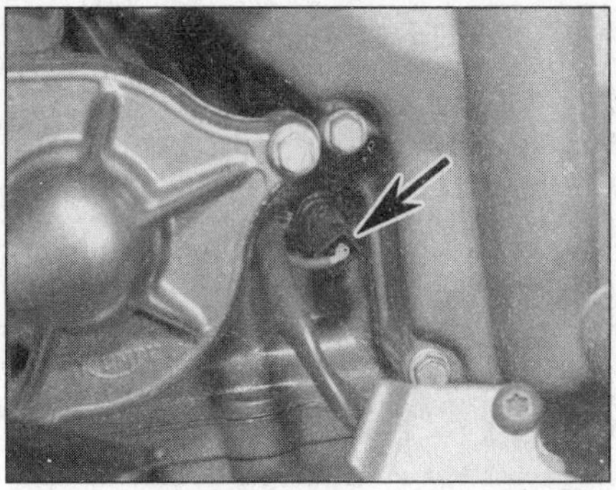

21.2 The neutral switch (arrowed) is located between the water pump and sprocket cover

the brake light switch and remove the throttle cable and cable elbow from the switch.

Installation

4 Installation is a reversal of the removal procedure, making sure that the locating peg on the back half of the switch is correctly located in the hole in the handlebar **(see illustration)**. If necessary, refer to Chapter 4 for installation of the throttle cable.

Left handlebar switch

Removal

5 Trace the wiring harness back from the switch to the connector and disconnect it.

6 Work back along the harness, freeing it from all the relevant clips and ties, whilst noting its correct routing.

7 Unscrew the two switch retaining screws and remove the switch from the handlebar **(see illustration)**. Disconnect the two wires from the clutch switch, and remove the choke cable, complete with its elbow and lever, from the switch.

Installation

8 Installation is a reversal of the removal procedure, making sure that the locating peg on the back half of the switch is correctly located in the hole in the handlebar. If necessary, refer to Chapter 4 for installation of the choke cable.

21 Neutral switch - check, removal and installation

Check

1 Before checking the electrical circuit, check the bulb (see Section 16) and fuse (see Section 5).

2 The switch is screwed into the left side of the crankcase, between the water pump and sprocket cover **(see illustration)**. Access can be improved on Trophy and Daytona models by removing the fairing left lower panel (see Chapter 8).

3 Disconnect the wiring connector from the switch. Make sure the transmission is in neutral.

4 With the wire detached and the ignition switched ON, the neutral light should be out. If not, the wire between the switch and instrument cluster must be earthed at some point.

5 Earth the wire on the crankcase and check that the neutral light comes on. If the light comes on, but doesn't when connected to the switch, the switch is confirmed defective.

6 If the light does not come on when the wire is earthed, check for voltage at the wire terminal using a test light. If there's no voltage present, check the wire between the switch, the instrument cluster and fusebox (see the wiring diagrams at the end of this Chapter).

Removal and installation

7 Disconnect the wiring connector from the switch **(see illustration 21.2)**. Remove the fairing left lower panel if necessary for access on Trophy and Daytona models (refer to Chapter 8).

8 Unscrew the switch from the crankcase. Recover the sealing washer and plug the switch opening to minimise oil loss whilst the switch is removed.

9 Clean the threads of the switch and fit a new sealing washer to it.

10 Remove the plug from the crankcase and install the switch. Tighten the switch to the specified torque setting, then reconnect the wiring connector.

11 Check the operation of the neutral light.

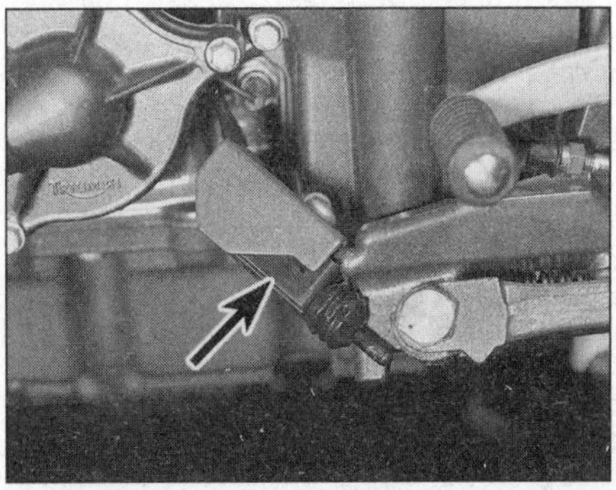

22.2a Sidestand switch location (arrowed)

12 Check the oil level as described in *'Daily (pre-ride) checks'* and top-up if necessary.

13 If removed, install the fairing panel on Trophy and Daytona models (see Chapter 8).

22 Sidestand switch - check, removal and installation

Check

Sidestand warning light - Trophy and Trident models

1 The warning light in the instrument cluster should illuminate with the ignition switched ON and the sidestand down (extended). If it doesn't, first check the bulb (Section 16).

2 Trace the wiring from the sidestand switch up to its connector behind the left side panel and disconnect it **(see illustrations)**. Note that it was found necessary on the machine photographed, to remove the left auxiliary air chamber for access to the wire connector (see Chapter 4 for air chamber removal).

3 Check the operation of the switch using an ohmmeter or continuity test light. Set the meter to the ohms x 1 scale and connect its probes between the blue and green (black and green on Trophy models from VIN 29156) wires on the switch side of the wiring connector. With the sidestand down (extended) there should be continuity between

22.2b Disconnect the sidestand switch wiring at the connector behind the left side panel (air chamber removed for access)

22.11 Sidestand relay is located under fuel tank's rear mounting on Sprint model

the terminals, and with the stand up there should be no continuity (infinite resistance).

4 If the switch does not perform as expected, it is defective and must be renewed. Check first that the fault is not caused by a sticking switch plunger due to the ingress of road dirt; spray the switch with a water dispersant aerosol.

5 If the switch is good, check the brown/red (yellow/black on Trophy models from VIN 29156) wire between the wiring connector and the instrument cluster for continuity (refer to the wiring diagrams at the end of this book).

Sidestand switch (ignition cut-out)

6 Depending on the type of circuit fitted, the ignition will be cut out if the sidestand is extended, or if the machine is put into gear while the sidestand is extended. Make the following checks using the appropriate wiring diagram at the end of this Chapter.

7 Trace the wiring from the switch on the sidestand to its connector behind the left side panel and disconnect it **(see illustration 22.2b)**. Note that it was found necessary on the machine photographed, to remove the left auxiliary air chamber for access to the wire connector (see Chapter 4 for air chamber removal).

8 Check the operation of the switch using an ohmmeter or continuity test light. Connect the meter to the blue and brown (black and brown on Trophy models from VIN 29156) wires on the switch side of the connector. With the sidestand up there should be continuity between the terminals; with the stand down there should be no continuity (infinite resistance).

9 If the switch does not perform as expected, it is defective and must be renewed. Check first that the fault is not caused by a sticking switch plunger due to ingress of road dirt; spray the switch with a water dispersant aerosol.

10 If the switch checks out OK, but the circuit fails to function correctly, use the appropriate wiring diagram at the end of this Chapter to trace all wires from the switch. Make continuity checks (see *Fault Finding Equipment* in the Reference section) to check whether any of the wires or connectors are broken.

23.5 Removing the clutch switch from the clutch master cylinder

11 Certain models are fitted with a sidestand relay, whereas on others the relay is incorporated in the ignition igniter unit. No test details are available for the relay; if it fails it can only be tested by the substitution of a new relay. The relay is located in the vicinity of the battery **(see illustration)**.

Removal and installation

12 Disconnect the switch wiring connector as described above in Step 2.

13 Work back along the switch wiring, freeing it from any relevant retaining clips and ties, noting its correct routing. On later models, remove the water pump hose cover for access. On Trophy and Daytona models, access to the wiring can be improved by removing the fairing left lower panel as described in Chapter 8.

14 Unscrew the bolts securing the switch to the sidestand mounting bracket **(see illustration 22.2a)**. **Note:** *It may be found that the wiring will not pass between the water pump and sprocket cover, necessitating the removal of either component (see Chapter 3 for the water pump or Chapter 6 for the sprocket cover).*

15 Fit the new switch to the sidestand bracket and install the retaining bolts, tightening them securely.

16 Make sure the wiring is correctly routed up to the connector and retained by all the necessary clips and ties. If removed, install the water pump or sprocket cover. On later models, install the water pump hose cover.

17 Reconnect the wiring connector and check the operation of the sidestand switch and, where fitted, the warning light.

18 If removed on Trophy and Daytona models, fit the fairing panel as described in Chapter 8.

23 Clutch switch – check, removal and installation

Check

1 The clutch switch is situated on the base of the clutch master cylinder. The switch is part of the starter safety circuit which prevents the starter motor operating whilst the transmission is in gear unless the clutch lever is pulled in. If the starter circuit is faulty, first check the fuse (see Section 5).

2 To check the switch, disconnect the wiring connector from the switch. Connect the probes of an ohmmeter or a continuity test light between the two switch terminals which connect with the black/red and black wires of the connector. With the clutch lever at rest, continuity should be indicated. No continuity (infinite resistance) should be indicated when the clutch lever is pulled into the handlebar.

3 Now connect the meter probes across the switch terminals which connect with the black/yellow and black wires. With the clutch lever at rest, no continuity (infinite resistance) should be indicated. Continuity (0 ohms) should be indicated when the lever is pulled in to the handlebar.

4 If the switch is satisfactory, check the remaining components in the starter circuit (neutral switch and starter relay) as described in the relevant sections of this Chapter. If all components are good, check the wiring between the various components (refer to the wiring diagrams at the end of this Chapter).

Removal and installation

5 Disconnect the wiring connector from the clutch switch. Unscrew the screw securing the switch to the base of the master cylinder and remove the switch, noting how it fits **(see illustration)**.

6 Install the new switch and connect the wiring connector.

24 Horn – check, removal and installation

Check

1 On Trophy (up to VIN 29155), Daytona, Sprint and Tiger models, the horns are mounted to the bottom of the fairing stay **(see illustration)**. On later Trophy (from VIN 29156) the horn is mounted to the front of the frame, below the head stock. On Trident and Speed Triple models, the horns are mounted on the

24.1a On Trophy, Daytona, Sprint and Tiger models the horns are mounted on the fairing stay

24.1b On Thunderbird models the horn is mounted on the left side of the cylinder head

bottom yoke. On Thunderbird, Thunderbird Sport, Adventurer and Legend TT models, the horn is mounted to the left side of the cylinder head **(see illustration)**.

2 Unplug the wiring connectors from the horn. Using two jumper wires, apply battery voltage directly to the terminals on the horn. If the horn sounds, check the switch (see Section 19) and the wiring between the switch and the horn (see the wiring diagrams at the end of this Chapter).

3 If the horn doesn't sound, check first that the battery is in good condition. If the battery is fully charged, and the horn still does not sound, renew the horn.

Removal and installation

4 Unplug the wiring connectors from the horn then unscrew the bolt securing the horn to its mounting bracket and remove it from the bike.

5 Connect the wiring connectors to the new horn and securely tighten its retaining bolt.

25 Fuel level sensor – check, removal and installation

Warning: Petrol (gasoline) is extremely flammable, so take extra precautions when you work on any part of the fuel system. Don't smoke or allow open flames or bare light bulbs near the work area, and don't work in a garage where a natural gas-type appliance is present. If you spill any fuel on your skin, rinse it off immediately with soap and water. When you perform any kind of work on the fuel system, wear safety glasses and have a fire extinguisher suitable for a class B type fire (flammable liquids) on hand.

Low fuel level sensor and warning light – Trident, Sprint, Trophy (up to VIN 29155), Speed Triple, Daytona and Tiger

Check

1 If the low fuel level warning light has not come on by the time the reserve fuel is needed (see Chapter 4 Specifications), check the fuses and the bulb (see Sections 5 and 16). If the fuses and bulb are good, check for battery voltage at the low fuel level sensor wiring connector blue/orange wire terminal using a test light.

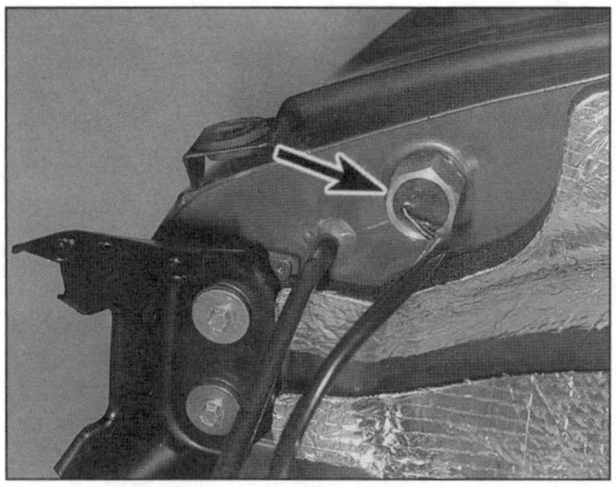

25.6 The low fuel level sensor is mounted in the bottom of the tank

2 If no voltage is indicated, check the blue/orange wire between the sensor and the warning light bulb for open-circuits and poor connections (see the wiring diagrams at the end of this Chapter).

3 If the light still does not come on, and voltage is present at the connector, the sensor is faulty and must be renewed.

4 If the warning light comes on when the tank is full, disconnect the sensor wiring at the connector (at the sensor on Tiger models). The warning light should be out. If it is illuminated, the blue/orange wire between the sensor and warning light bulb must be earthed at some point. If the light goes out when the wiring is disconnected, the sensor must be assumed faulty and renewed.

Removal and installation

5 Drain and remove the fuel tank (Chapter 4).

6 Unscrew the sensor from the base of the tank and withdraw it **(see illustration)**. Discard the sealing washer as a new one must be used.

7 Install the sensor by reversing the removal process and use a new sealing washer.

Fuel level sender and gauge – Trophy (from VIN 29156)

Check

8 If the fuel level gauge does not work, first check the fuse (S.LAMPS). Note that the tachometer, oil pressure warning light, neutral light, sidestand warning light and coolant warning light all share the same power supply wire from the fusebox, so if they are also not working the fault must lie between the instrument wiring connector and the fusebox. Check for battery voltage at the green/yellow wire of the instrument connector.

9 Remove the sender unit from the tank as described below.

10 Reconnect the sender wiring, then turn the ignition ON and manually raise its float. With the float fully raised the gauge needle should swing over to the F on the gauge. Now lower the float and check that the needle swings over to the E on the gauge. Turn the ignition OFF when the check is complete. If the gauge does not operate as described either the gauge or the sender is faulty. Unfortunately Triumph do not supply further test details for either unit.

25.13 Fuel level sender is retained by four screws

11 Before renewing the fuel gauge or the sender unit, check that the fault is not due to a poor wire connection or break in the green/black wire between the gauge and sender unit.

Removal and installation

12 Drain and remove the fuel tank (Chapter 4).

13 Remove the four Torx screws with their washers and withdraw the fuel level sender from the tank, noting that it must be rotated to allow the float arm to pass through the hole without bending it **(see illustration)**.

14 Peel the gasket off the tank or sender unit base. Inspect the float on the end of the sender unit arm; if the float is punctured the sender unit must be renewed.

15 Install the sender by reversing the removal process. Always use a new gasket between the sender and the tank and if the sealing washers on any of the four retaining screws are damaged renew them.

26 Starter relay – check, removal and installation

Check

1 If the starter circuit is faulty, check the fuses (see Section 5). The starter relay is under the seat, in front of the battery **(see illustration)**.

26.1 The starter relay is located in front of the battery, under the seat (arrowed)

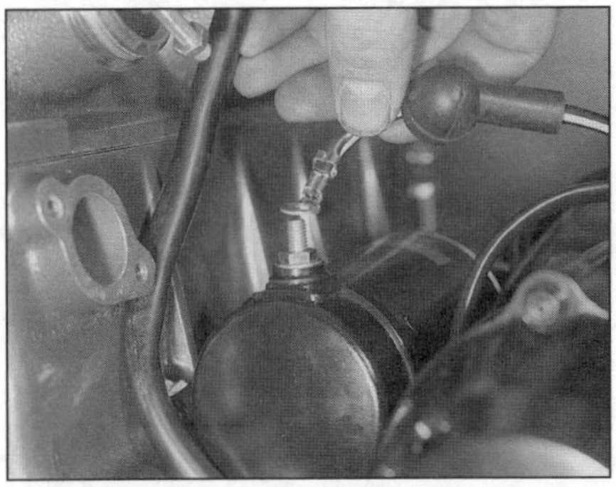

27.5 Peel back the rubber cover, then unscrew the nut and disconnect the starter cable from the motor

27.6 Unscrew the starter motor retaining bolts

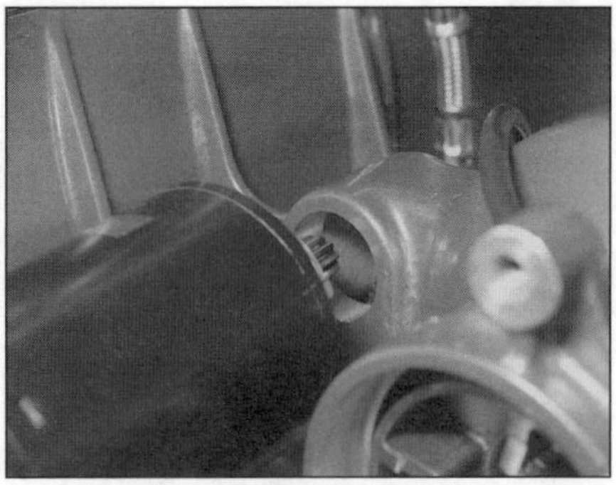

27.10 Slide the starter motor into position in the crankcase

2 With the ignition switch ON, the engine kill switch in RUN and the transmission in neutral, press the starter switch. The relay should click.
3 If the relay doesn't click, switch off the ignition and remove the relay; test it as follows.
4 Set a multimeter to the ohms x 1 scale and connect it across the relay's starter motor and battery lead terminals. Using a fully-charged 12 volt battery and two insulated jumper wires, connect the positive (+ve) terminal of the battery to the black/red (white/red on Trophy from VIN 29156) wire terminal of the relay, and the negative (-ve) terminal to the yellow/green (black/pink on Trophy from VIN 29156) wire terminal of the relay. At this point the relay should click and the multimeter read 0 ohms (continuity). If this is the case the relay is proved good and the fault lies in the starter switch circuit (check the clutch switch and neutral switch as described elsewhere in this Chapter); if the relay does not click when battery voltage is applied and indicates no continuity (infinite resistance) across its terminals, it is faulty and must be renewed.

Removal and installation

5 Remove the seat as described in Chapter 8.
6 Disconnect the battery terminals, remembering to disconnect the negative (-ve) terminal first.
7 Disconnect the relay wiring connectors and remove the relay with its rubber sleeve from the mounting lugs.
8 Peel back the rubber boots from the relay terminals, then unscrew the two nuts securing the starter motor and battery leads to the relay and detach the leads.
9 Installation is the reverse of removal ensuring that the terminal screws are securely tightened. Connect the negative (-ve) lead last when reconnecting the battery.

27 Starter motor – removal and installation

Removal

1 Remove the seat and side panels (see Chapter 8). Disconnect the battery negative (-ve) lead.
2 Referring to Chapter 8, remove the fairing lower panels on Trophy and Daytona models, the fairing on Sprint models, and the fairing side panels on Tiger models. On Thunderbird, Thunderbird Sport, Adventurer and Legend TT models remove the horn as described in Section 24 of this Chapter.
3 Remove the fuel tank and the carburettors as described in Chapter 4. On models which have the crankcase breather hose connected to the engine left end cover, detach the hose.
4 Drain the cooling system as described in Chapter 1, then remove the water pump outlet pipe as described in Chapter 3.
5 Peel back the rubber cover and unscrew the nut securing the starter cable to the motor **(see illustration)**.
6 Unscrew the starter motor retaining bolts **(see illustration)**.
7 Slide the starter motor out from the crankcase and remove it from the left side of the machine.
8 Remove the O-ring on the end of the starter motor; a new one will be needed for installation.

Installation

9 Install a new O-ring on the end of the starter motor and ensure it is seated in its groove; apply a smear of engine oil to the O-ring to aid installation.
10 Manoeuvre the motor into position and slide it into the crankcase **(see illustration)**. Ensure that the starter motor teeth mesh correctly with those of the starter idler gear.
11 Fit the retaining bolts and tighten them to the specified torque setting.
12 Connect the cable and spring washer, and secure with the nut. Make sure the rubber cover is correctly seated over the terminal.
13 Install the remaining components in a reverse of the removal procedure.
14 Refill the cooling system (see Chapter 1).
15 Connect the battery negative (-ve) lead.

28 Starter motor – disassembly, inspection and reassembly

Disassembly

1 Remove the starter motor (see Section 27).
2 Make alignment marks between the housing and end covers **(see illustrations)**.
3 Unscrew the two long bolts then remove the left end cover from the motor along with its O-ring.
4 Wrap insulating tape around the teeth of the starter motor gear – this will protect the oil seal from damage as the right end cover is withdrawn. Remove the right end cover from the motor along with its O-ring.
5 Withdraw the armature from the housing.
6 Unscrew the nut from the terminal bolt and

28.2a Make alignment marks (arrowed) between the housing . . .

28.2b . . . and the end covers before disassembly (arrowed)

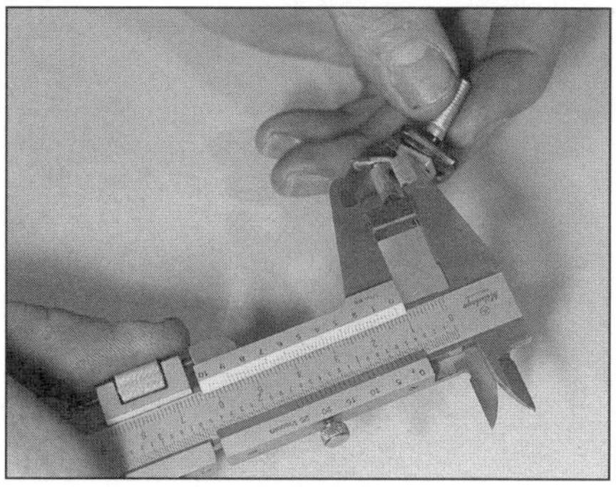

28.8 Measuring brush length

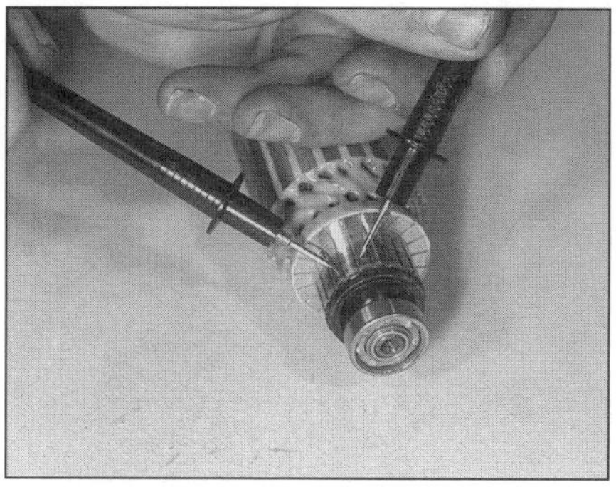

28.10 Inspect the commutator bars for wear and test as described in the text

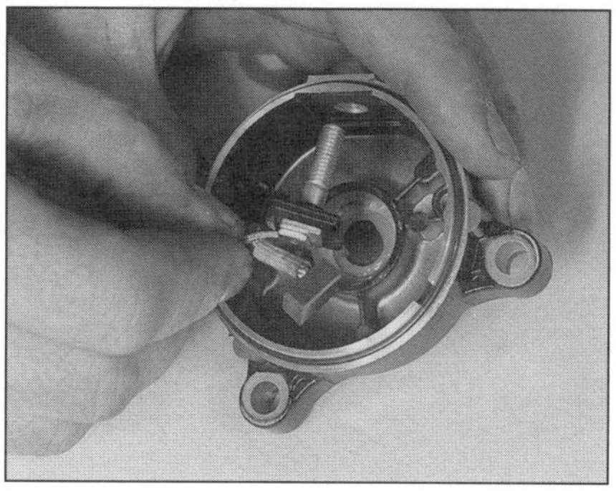

28.14a Install the terminal bolt in the rear cover . . .

remove the insulating washer and the O-ring. Withdraw the terminal bolt and brushplate assembly from the housing.

7 Lift the brush springs and slide the brushes out from their holders.

Inspection

Note: *No replacement parts are available from Triumph for the starter motor. If the following checks indicate a worn or faulty internal component, seek the advice of a Triumph dealer or auto electrical specialist before buying a new starter motor.*

8 The parts of the starter motor that are most likely to wear are the brushes. Measure the length of the brushes and compare the results to the service limit in this Chapter's Specifications **(see illustration)**. If the brushes are not worn excessively, nor cracked, chipped, or otherwise damaged, they may be re-used.

9 Inspect the commutator for scoring, scratches and discoloration. The commutator can be cleaned and polished with crocus cloth, but do not use sandpaper or emery paper. After cleaning, wipe away any residue with a cloth soaked in electrical system cleaner or denatured alcohol. Measure the diameter of the commutator and compare the reading with the service limit in the Specifications.

10 Using an ohmmeter or a continuity test light, check for continuity between the commutator bars **(see illustration)**. Continuity should exist between each bar and all of the others. Also, check for continuity between the commutator bars and the armature shaft. There should be no continuity (infinite resistance) between the commutator and the shaft. If the checks indicate otherwise, the armature is defective.

11 Check for continuity between each brush and the brushplate, and between the brush and its terminal bolt. There should be continuity in both cases.

12 Check the starter gear for worn, cracked, chipped and broken teeth. If the gear is damaged or worn, renew the starter motor.

13 Inspect the end covers for signs of cracks or wear. Inspect the magnets in the main housing and the housing itself for cracks.

Reassembly

14 Ensure that the rubber insulating washer is in place on the terminal bolt, then insert the bolt through the rear cover **(see illustration)**. Fit the O-ring and the insulating washer and secure them in place with the nut **(see illustrations)**.

15 Lift the brush springs on the brushplate and slide the brushes back into position in their holders, then install the brushplate assembly in the rear cover making sure its tab is correctly located in the slot in the cover. Make sure the O-ring is fitted to the cover **(see illustration)**.

16 Insert the armature into the rear end cover taking care not to damage the brushes. As it is inserted, locate the brushes on the commutator bars. Check that each brush is securely pressed against the commutator by its spring and is free to move easily in its holder **(see illustration)**.

17 Fit the main housing over the armature,

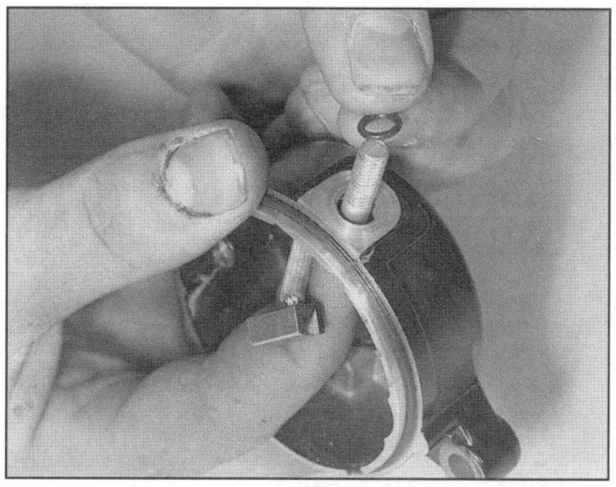

28.14b . . . fit the O-ring . . .

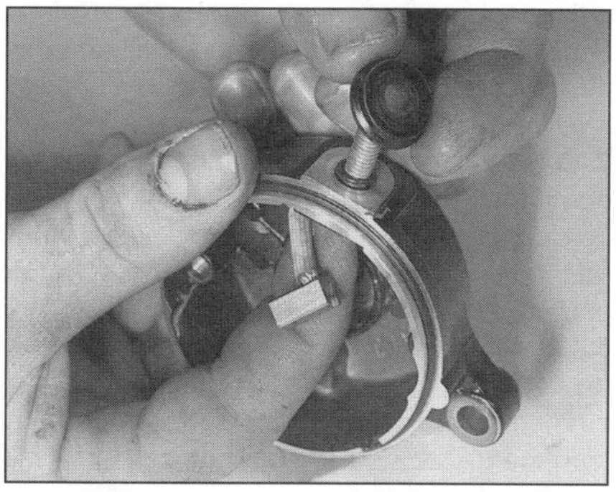

28.14c . . . the insulating washer . . .

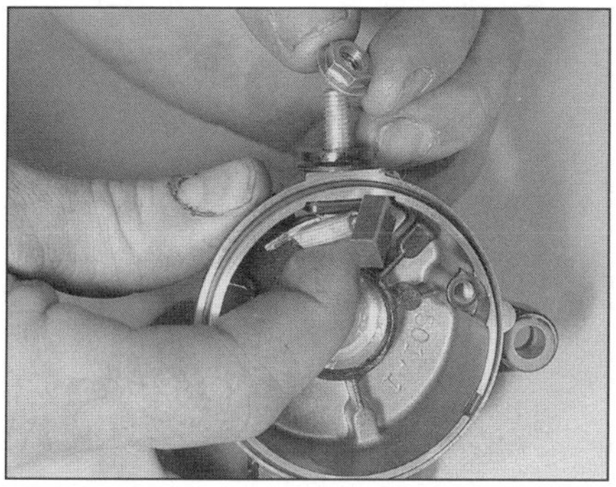

28.14d . . . and the terminal nut

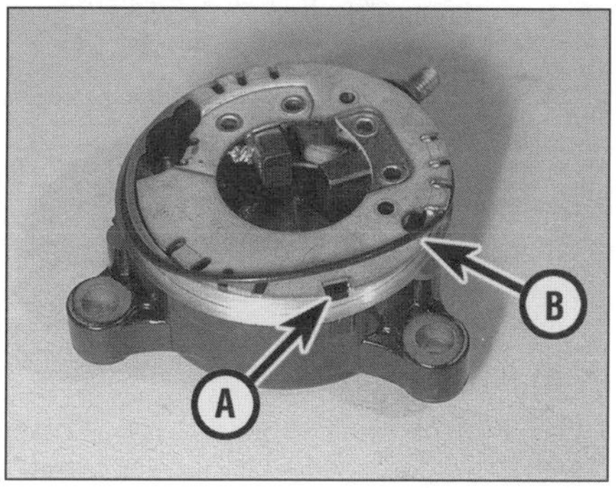

28.15 Align brushplate tab with slot in the rear cover (A) and fit the cover O-ring (B)

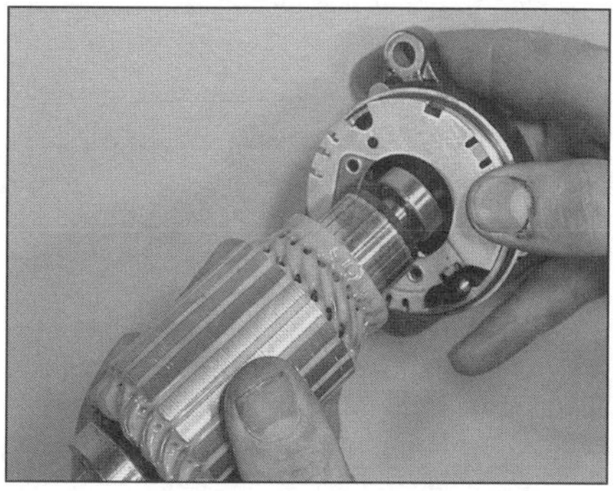

28.16 Fit the armature into the rear cover . . .

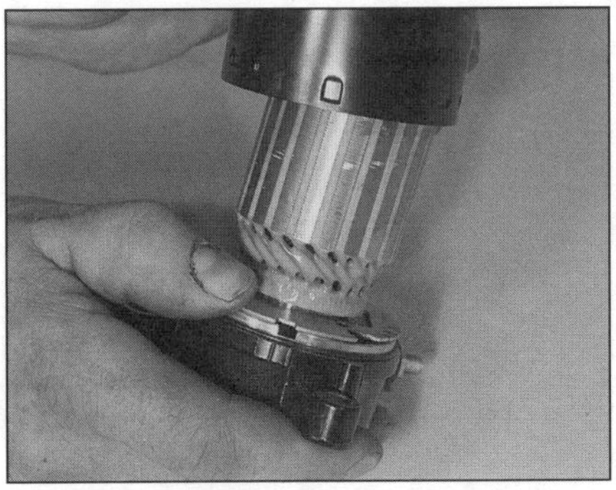

28.17 . . . and fit the main housing over the armature

28.19 Install the long bolts and tighten them securely

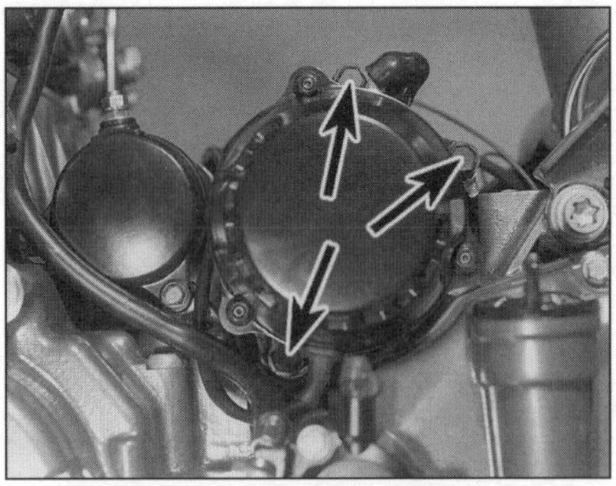

31.3 The alternator is secured to the crankcase by three bolts (arrowed)

aligning the marks made on removal **(see illustration)**.

18 Fit the O-ring to the front end cover and carefully slide the cover into position, aligning the marks made on removal. Remove any protective tape from the gear teeth.

19 Check the marks made on removal are correctly aligned then fit the long bolts and tighten them securely **(see illustration)**.

20 Install the starter motor (see Section 27).

29 Charging system testing – general information and precautions

1 If the performance of the charging system is suspect, the system as a whole should be checked first, followed by testing of the individual components. **Note:** *Before beginning the checks, make sure the battery is fully charged and that all system connections are clean and tight.*

2 Checking the output of the charging system and the performance of the various components within the charging system requires the use of a multimeter (with voltage, current and resistance checking facilities).

3 When making the checks, follow the procedures carefully to prevent incorrect connections or short circuits, as irreparable damage to electrical system components may result if short circuits occur.

4 If a multimeter is not available, the job of checking the charging system should be left to a Triumph dealer.

30 Charging system – output test

1 Remove the seat (see Chapter 8).

2 Remove the three nuts from the alternator end cover and lift off the cover **(see illustration 31.5)**. Make a visual check of the alternator leads and connections; repair or clean as required. If all appears to be in order, proceed as follows.

3 Connect a multimeter set to the dc 0 – 20 volts scale across the terminals of the battery (positive (+ve) meter lead to battery positive (+ve) terminal, negative (-ve) meter lead to battery negative (-ve) terminal). Start the engine and take note of the voltage reading. If the alternator is in good condition, the measured voltage should be higher than 13.5 volts, although not excessively high. If the voltage is lower than 13.5 volts, stop the engine and repeat the test having first earthed the F terminal of the regulator (see illustration 31.9 for terminal identification) to the frame using an insulated auxiliary wire; if the voltage reading obtained when the engine is running is now higher than 13.5 volts, the regulator is faulty – confirm this with the check described in Section 31. If the reading is still below 13.5 volts the fault must lie in either the brushes and slip rings, the rectifier, stator coil or rotor coil (see Section 31).

4 Occasionally the condition may arise where the alternator output is excessive. This condition is probably due to a faulty regulator – confirm this with the check in Section 31.

5 If the alternator has become noisy whilst the engine is running it is most likely that its bearings are worn. Check also the condition of the shock absorber dampers in the alternator drive.

HAYNES HiNT ***Clues to a faulty regulator are constantly blowing bulbs, with brightness varying considerably with engine speed, and battery overheating, necessitating frequent topping up of the electrolyte level.***

31 Alternator components – removal, testing and installation

Removal

1 On Thunderbird, Thunderbird Sport, Adventurer and Legend TT models, remove the horn as described in Section 24.

2 Trace the alternator wiring to its connector behind the left side panel and disconnect it. **Note:** *It was found necessary on the machine photographed, to remove the left auxiliary air chamber for access to the wire connector (see Chapter 4 for air chamber removal).*

3 Unscrew the three alternator mounting bolts, noting that the upper bolt secures the alternator earth lead **(see illustration)**. Withdraw the alternator from the engine, leaving the shock absorber rubbers in the driveshaft housing.

Testing

Note: *No replacement parts are available from Triumph for the alternator. If the following checks indicate a worn or faulty internal component, seek the advice of a Triumph dealer or auto electrical specialist before buying a new alternator.*

4 The following checks can be made without removing the alternator from the engine, although the alternator wiring must first be disconnected as described in Step 2.

5 Unscrew the three nuts securing the alternator end cover and remove the cover **(see illustration)**.

Brushes and slip rings

6 Remove the three screws securing the brush holder and remove the holder **(see illustration)**. Inspect the holder for any signs of damage. Measure the brush lengths (ie the

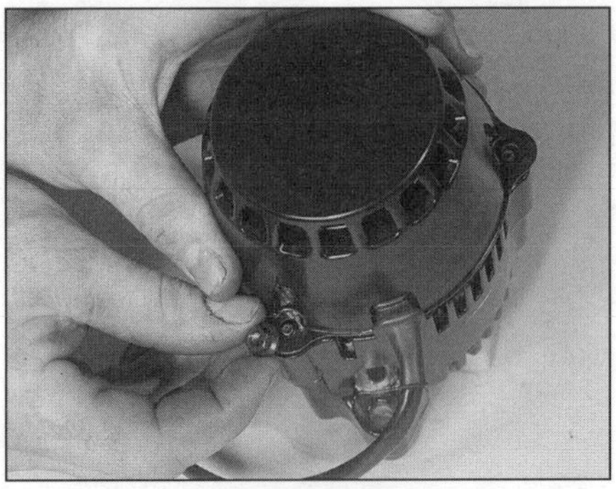

31.5 Unscrew the three nuts and detach the alternator end cover

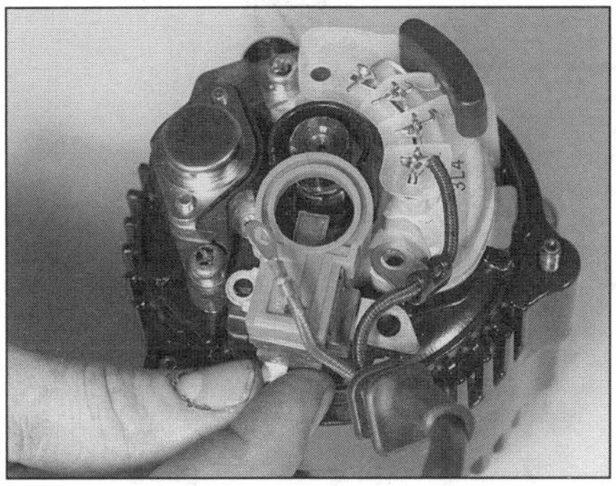

31.6a Remove the brush holder screws and remove the holder

31.6b Inspect the brush holder for damage and measure the brush lengths

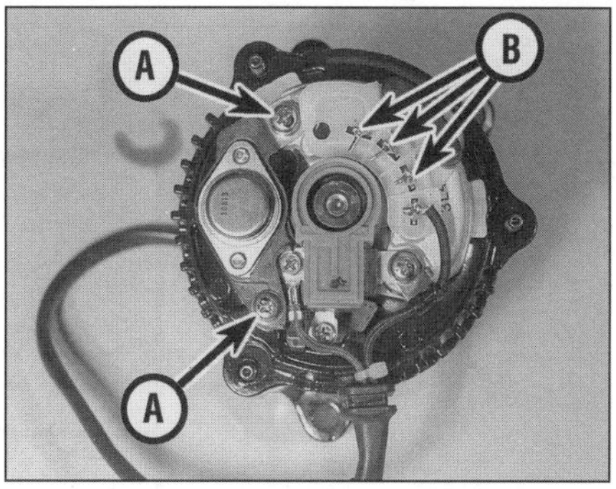

31.8 The regulator is secured to the alternator by two screws (A). Rectifier diode terminals are shown by arrows (B)

amount of brush extending from the holder) and compare the measurements with the figures given in the Specifications at the beginning of the Chapter **(see illustration)**.

7 Whilst the brush holder is removed, clean the slip rings with a rag moistened with solvent. If they are badly marked, tidy them up with very fine emery cloth. Using a vernier caliper, measure the diameter of both slip rings and check that they have not worn down past the service limit (see Specifications).

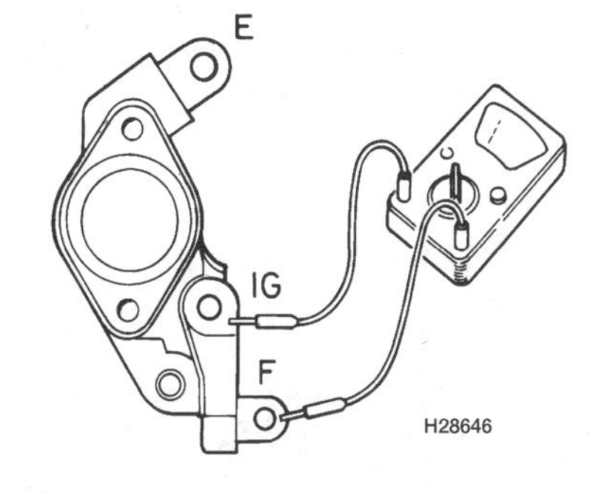

METER RANGE	CONNECTIONS		READING
	METER(+)TO	METER(-)TO	
x100Ω	F	E	170Ω
x1kΩ	E	F	4kΩ
x100Ω	IG	E	800Ω
x1kΩ	E	IG	2kΩ
x1kΩ	F	IG	2kΩ
x100Ω	IG	F	150Ω

31.9 Regulator resistance tests

Regulator

8 Remove the brush holder as described above. Remove the two screws securing the regulator to the alternator and remove the regulator **(see illustration)**.

9 Using a multimeter set to the required ohms range, test the internal resistances of the regulator in accordance with the diagram **(see illustration)**. Further testing of the regulator isn't possible with home workshop equipment – have your findings confirmed by a Triumph dealer before replacing the regulator with a new one.

Rectifier

10 The rectifier connections require unsoldering before it can be fully removed from the alternator. Since there is a risk of damaging the rectifier diodes if excess heat is applied, it is recommended that the rectifier be tested by a Triumph dealer or auto electrician.

Further checks and overhaul

11 Further testing of the alternator components should be left to a Triumph dealer or auto electrician. This also applies to removal of the rotor and bearing renewal.

Installation

12 If removed, install the rubbers into the shock absorber housing, using a smear of grease to secure them in place if necessary **(see illustration)**.

13 Fit a new O-ring to the alternator and smear it with oil.

14 Install the alternator on the engine and fit the mounting bolts, not forgetting to connect the earth lead **(see illustration)**. Fit the rubber boot over the earth connection.

15 Reconnect the alternator wiring at the connector. On Thunderbird models, Thunderbird Sport, Adventurer and Legend TT models, fit the horn as described in Section 24.

31.12 Install the rubbers into the shock absorber housing

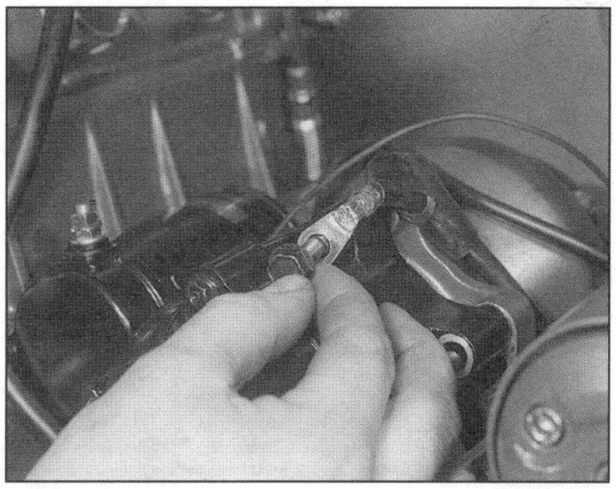

31.14 Install the alternator and fit the earth lead

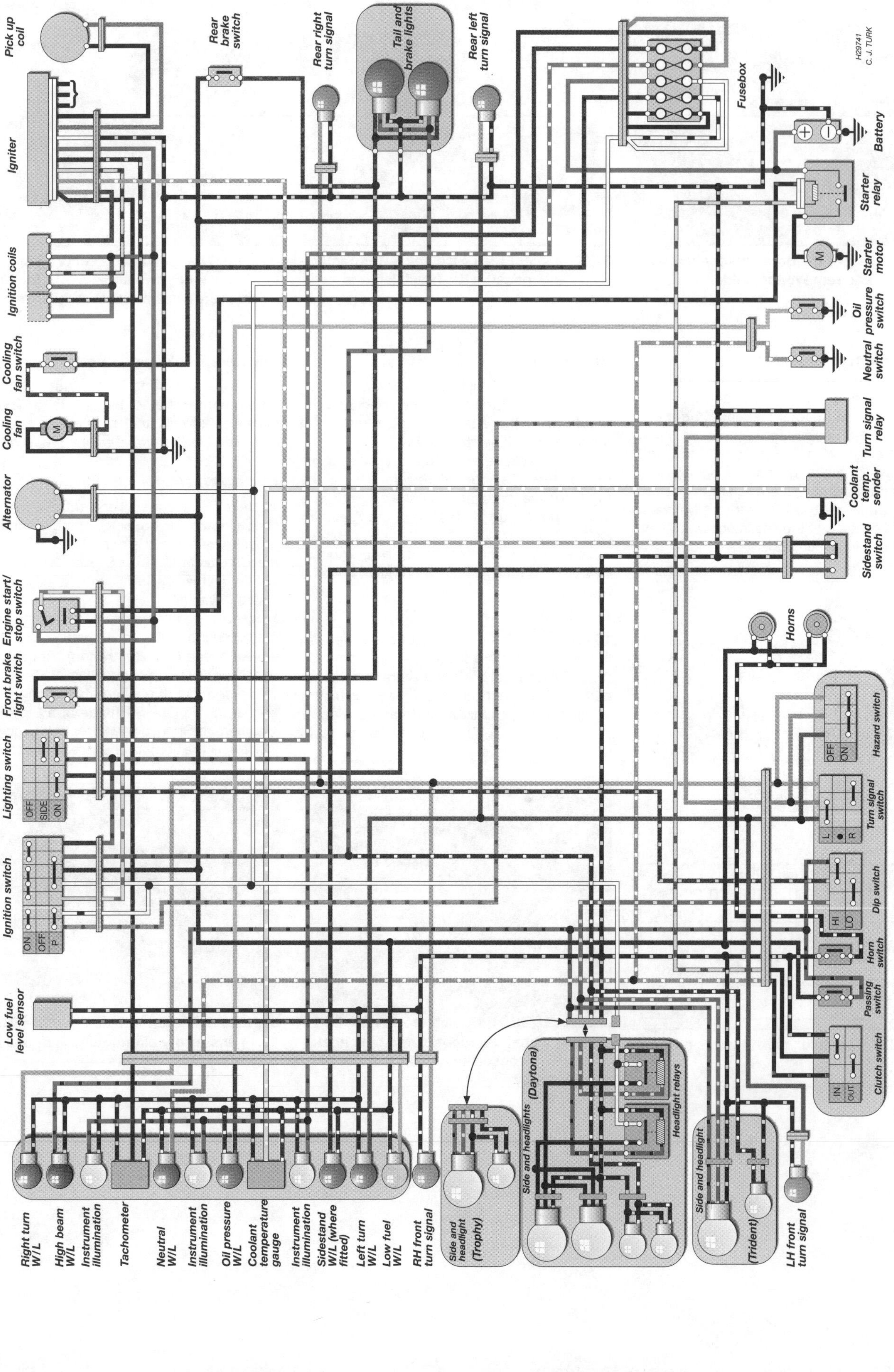

Trophy, Trident and Daytona - 1991/92 models

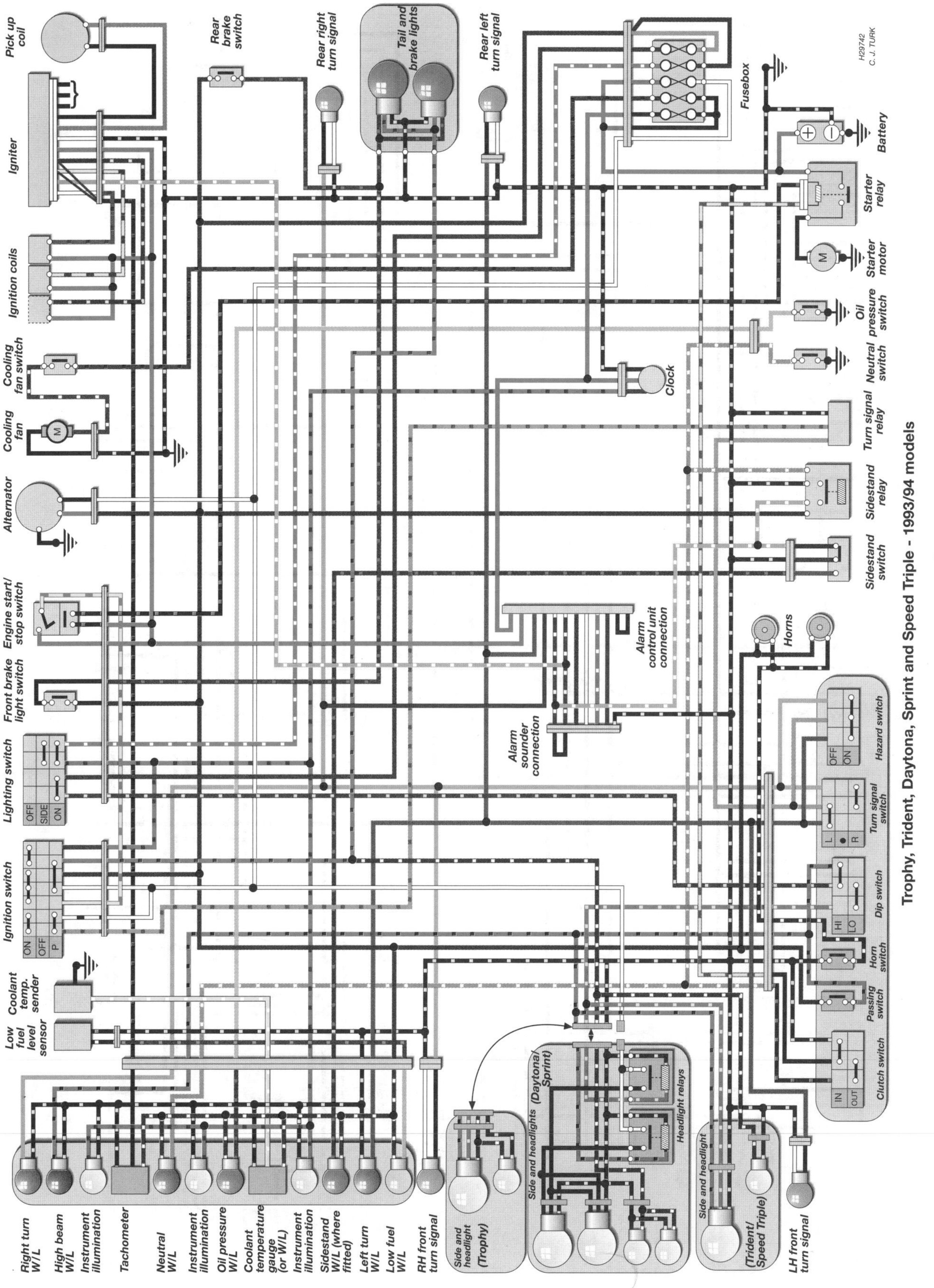

Trophy, Trident, Daytona, Sprint and Speed Triple - 1993/94 models

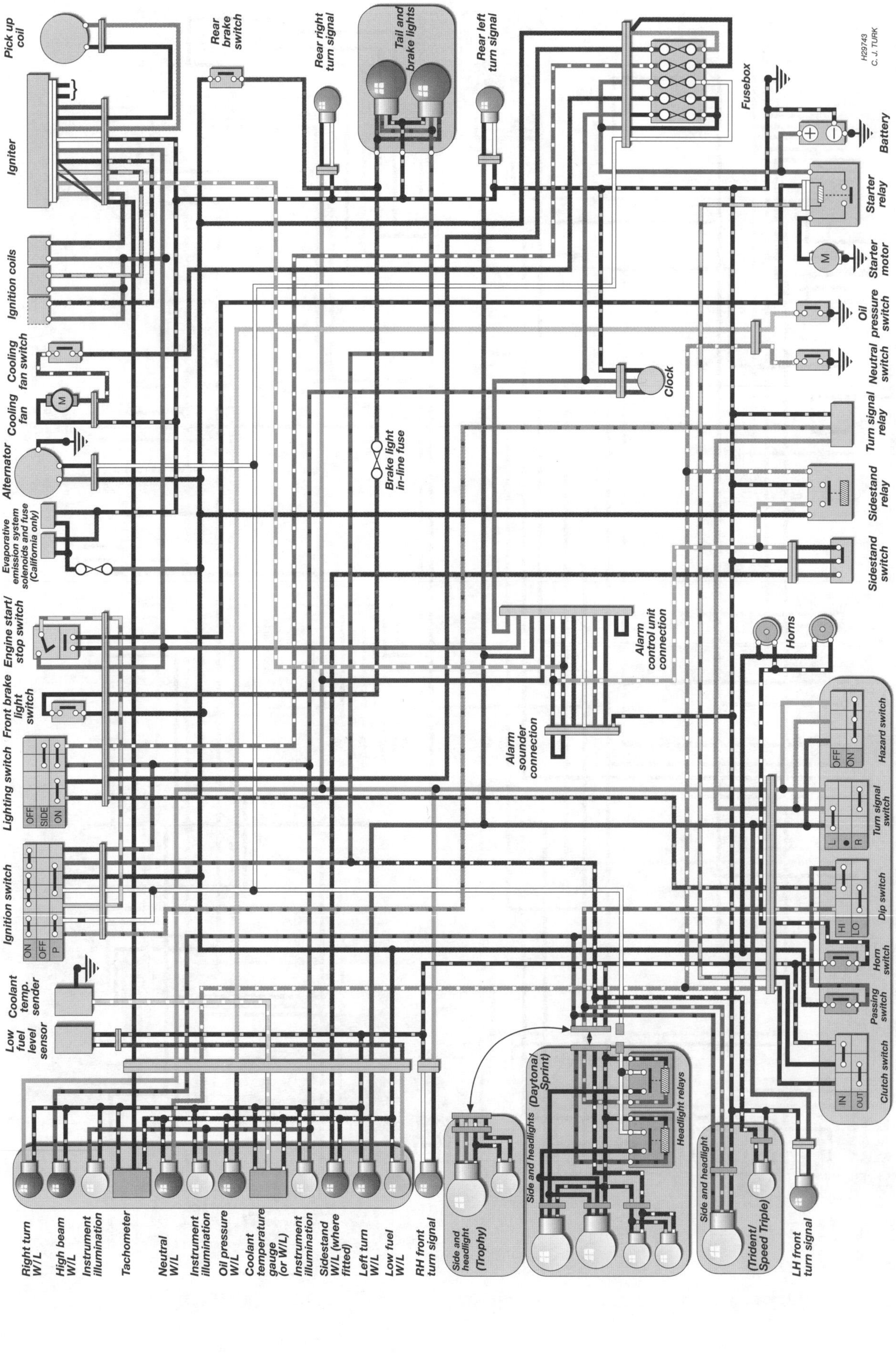

Trident, Sprint, Speed Triple and Daytona - 1995-on models. Trophy 1995 model (up to VIN 29155)

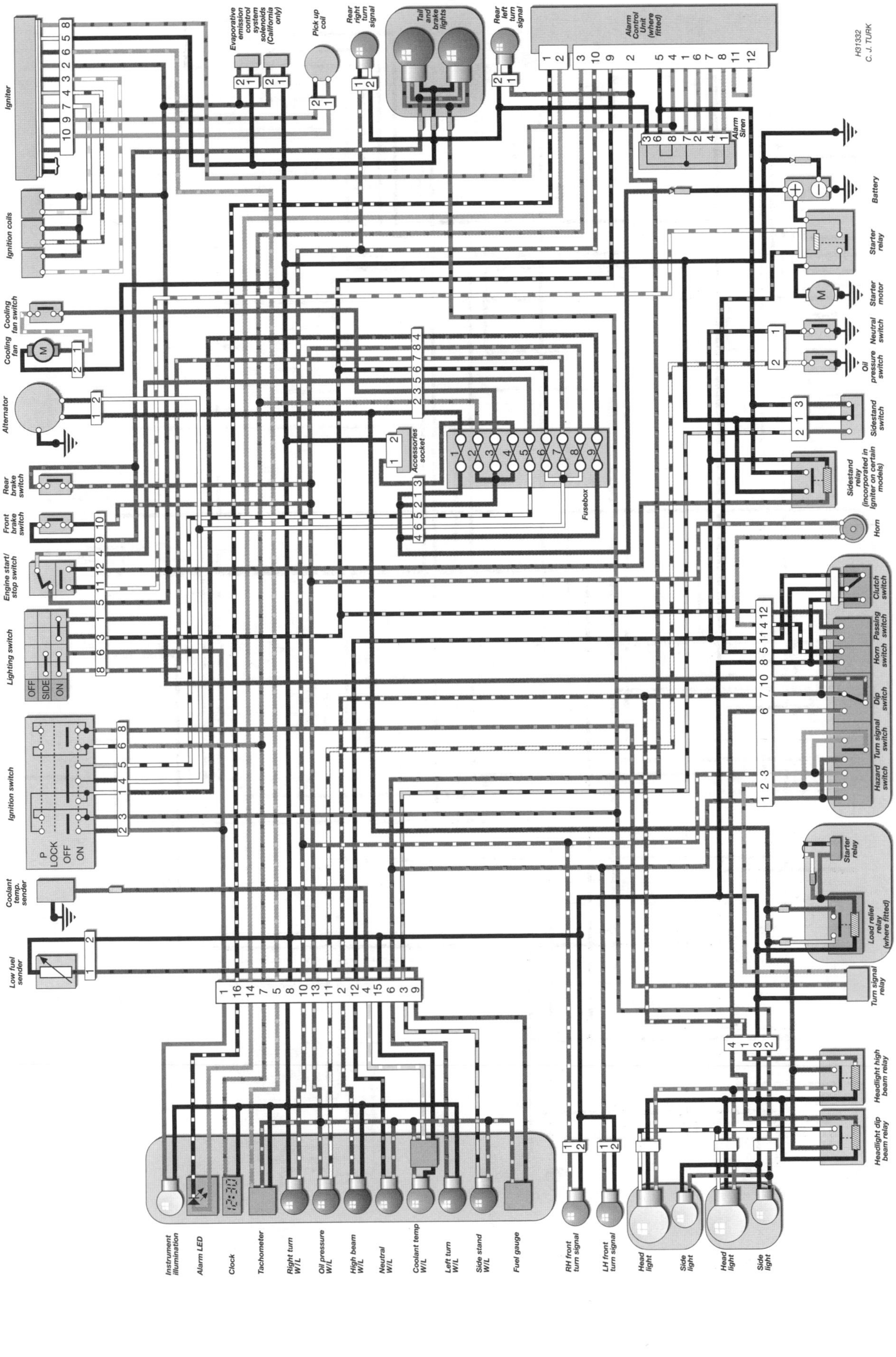

Trophy - 1996-on (from VIN 29156) models

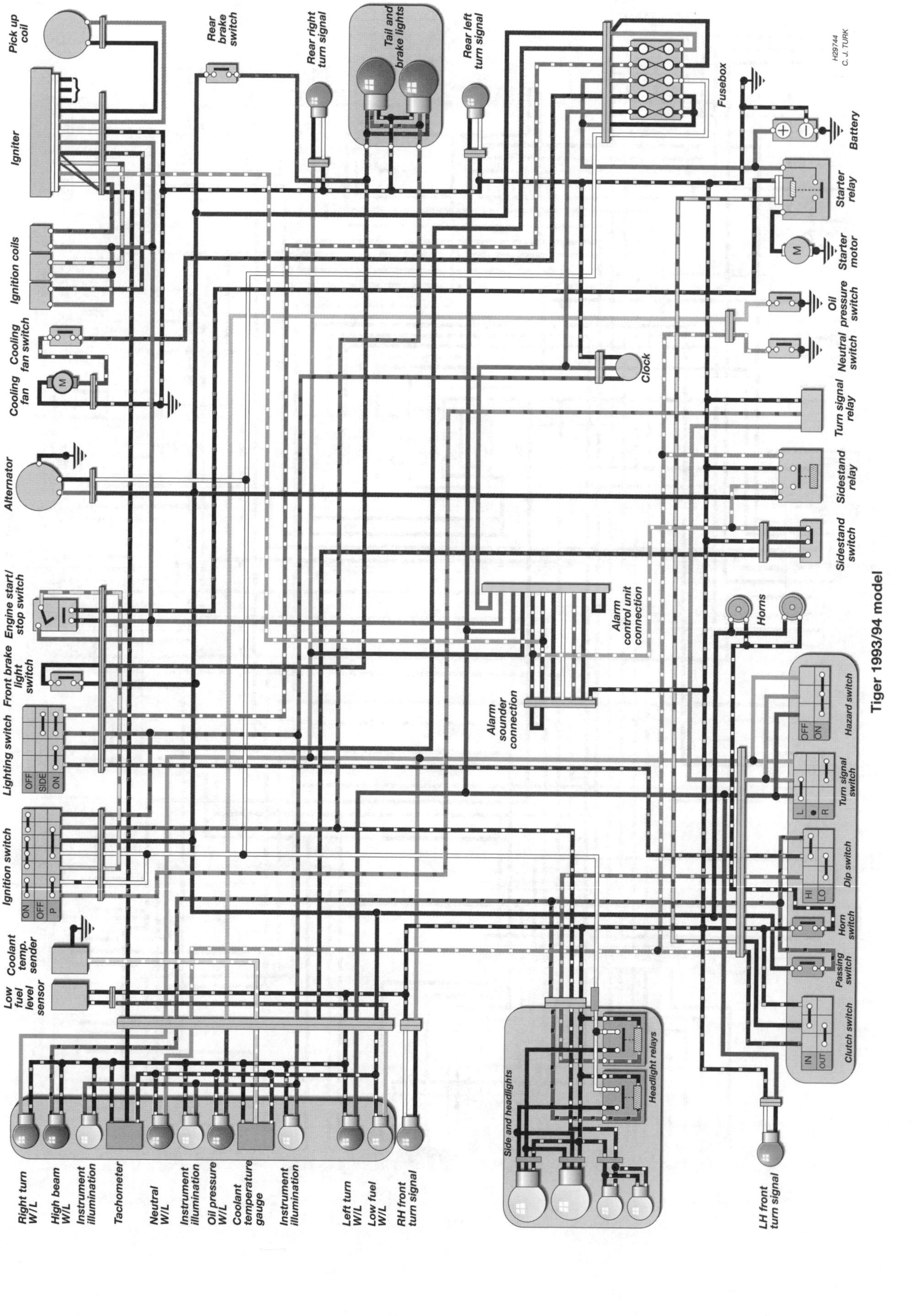
Pick up coil
Igniter
Ignition coils
Cooling fan switch
Cooling fan
Alternator
Engine start/stop switch
Front brake light switch
Lighting switch
OFF
SIDE
ON
Ignition switch
ON
OFF
P
Coolant temp. sender
Low fuel level sensor
Right turn W/L
High beam W/L
Instrument illumination
Tachometer
Neutral W/L
Instrument illumination
Oil pressure W/L
Coolant temperature gauge
Instrument illumination
Left turn W/L
Low fuel W/L
RH front turn signal
Rear brake switch
Rear right turn signal
Tail and brake lights
Rear left turn signal
Fusebox
Battery
Starter relay
Starter motor
Oil pressure switch
Neutral switch
Clock
Turn signal relay
Sidestand relay
Sidestand switch
Alarm control unit connection
Alarm sounder connection
Horns
Hazard switch
OFF
ON
Turn signal switch
L
R
Dip switch
HI
LO
Horn switch
Passing switch
Clutch switch
IN
OUT
Headlight relays
Side and headlights
LH front turn signal
H29744
C. J. TURK
Tiger 1993/94 model

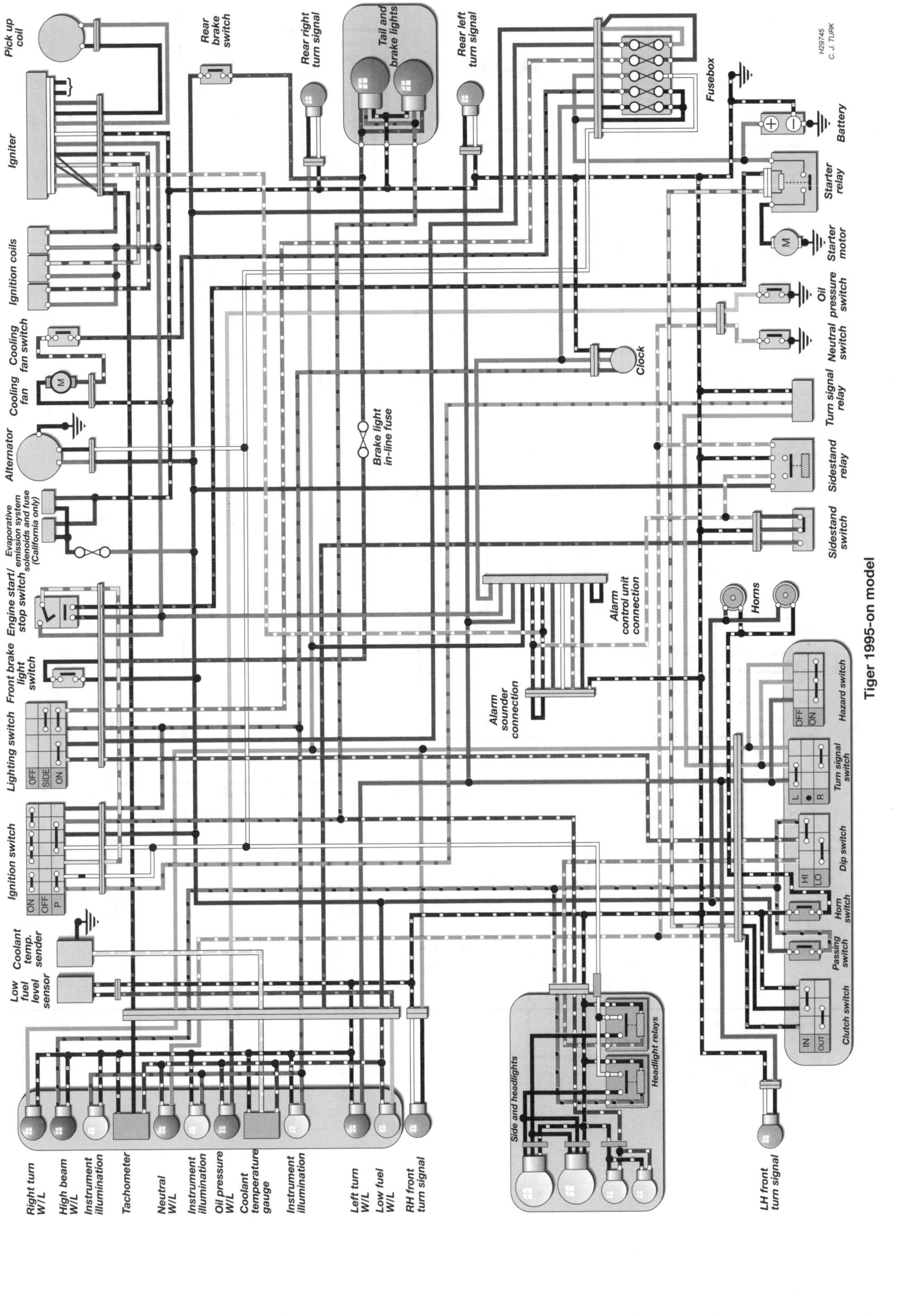

Tiger 1995-on model

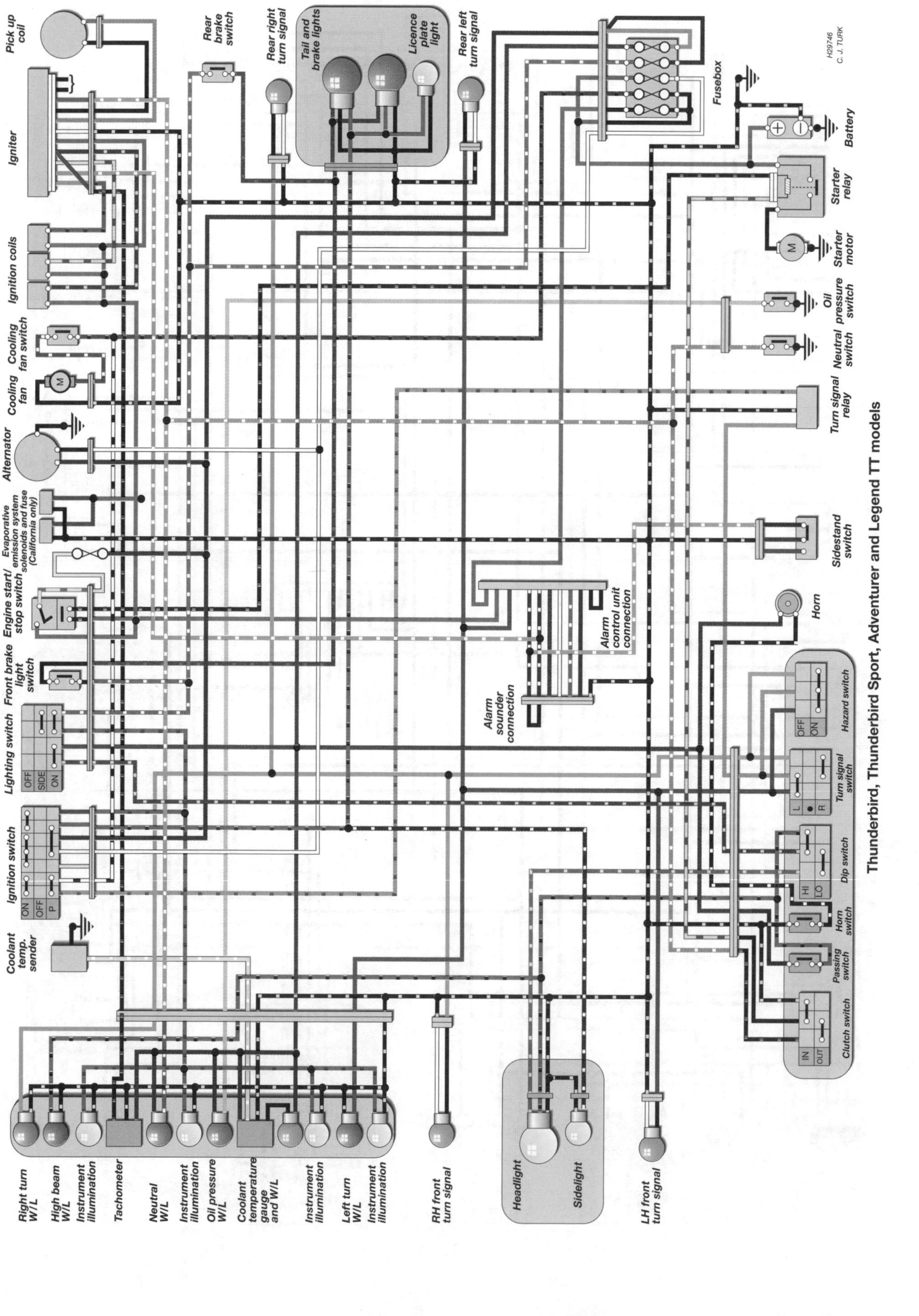

Thunderbird, Thunderbird Sport, Adventurer and Legend TT models

Dimensions and weights

Weight (dry)

900 Trophy up to VIN 29155 ....217 kg
900 Trophy from VIN 29156 ....220 kg
1200 Trophy up to VIN 29155 ....232 kg
1200 Trophy from VIN 29156 ....235 kg
900 Daytona ....213 kg
900 Daytona Super III ....211 kg
750 and 1000 Daytona ....not available
1200 Daytona ....225 kg
Trident ....212 kg
Sprint ....215 kg
Speed Triple ....209 kg
Thunderbird ....220 kg
Adventurer, Thunderbird Sport ....225 kg
Tiger ....209 kg

Wheelbase

750 and 1000 Daytona, 900 Trident ....1510 mm
Tiger and early Thunderbird ....1550 mm
Adventurer, Thunderbird Sport and later Thunderbird ......1580 mm
All other models ....1490 mm

Overall length

Trophy, 900 and 1200 Daytona, Speed Triple, Trident, Sprint ..2152 mm
750 and 1000 Daytona ....2160 mm
Thunderbird, Thunderbird Sport ....2250 mm
Adventurer ....2170 mm
Tiger ....2290 mm

Overall width

Trophy (up to VIN 29155), Daytona Super III, Speed Triple, Trident, Sprint ....760 mm
Trophy from VIN 29156 ....790 mm
All Daytona models except Super III ....690 mm
Thunderbird, Thunderbird Sport ....860 mm
Adventurer ....750 mm
Tiger ....920 mm

Overall height

Trophy (up to VIN 29155), 750 and 1000 Daytona ....1270 mm
Trophy from VIN 29156 ....1430 mm
900 and 1200 Daytona, Speed Triple ....1185 mm
Trident ....1090 mm
Sprint ....1265 mm
Thunderbird, Thunderbird Sport ....1150 mm
Adventurer ....1290 mm
Tiger ....1345 mm

Seat height

Trophy up to VIN 29155 ....780 mm
Trophy from VIN 29156 ....790 mm
750 and 1000 Daytona ....810 mm
900 and 1200 Daytona, Speed Triple ....790 mm
Trident, Sprint ....775 mm
Thunderbird, Thunderbird Sport, Adventurer ....750 mm
Tiger ....850 mm

Buying tools

A toolkit is a fundamental requirement for servicing and repairing a motorcycle. Although there will be an initial expense in building up enough tools for servicing, this will soon be offset by the savings made by doing the job yourself. As experience and confidence grow, additional tools can be added to enable the repair and overhaul of the motorcycle. Many of the specialist tools are expensive and not often used so it may be preferable to hire them, or for a group of friends or motorcycle club to join in the purchase.

As a rule, it is better to buy more expensive, good quality tools. Cheaper tools are likely to wear out faster and need to be renewed more often, nullifying the original saving.

Warning: To avoid the risk of a poor quality tool breaking in use, causing injury or damage to the component being worked on, always aim to purchase tools which meet the relevant national safety standards.

The following lists of tools do not represent the manufacturer's service tools, but serve as a guide to help the owner decide which tools are needed for this level of work. In addition, items such as an electric drill, hacksaw, files, soldering iron and a workbench equipped with a vice, may be needed. Although not classed as tools, a selection of bolts, screws, nuts, washers and pieces of tubing always come in useful.

For more information about tools, refer to the Haynes *Motorcycle Workshop Practice TechBook* (Bk. No. 3470).

Manufacturer's service tools

Inevitably certain tasks require the use of a service tool. Where possible an alternative tool or method of approach is recommended, but sometimes there is no option if personal injury or damage to the component is to be avoided. Where required, service tools are referred to in the relevant procedure.

Service tools can usually only be purchased from a motorcycle dealer and are identified by a part number. Some of the commonly-used tools, such as rotor pullers, are available in aftermarket form from mail-order motorcycle tool and accessory suppliers.

Maintenance and minor repair tools

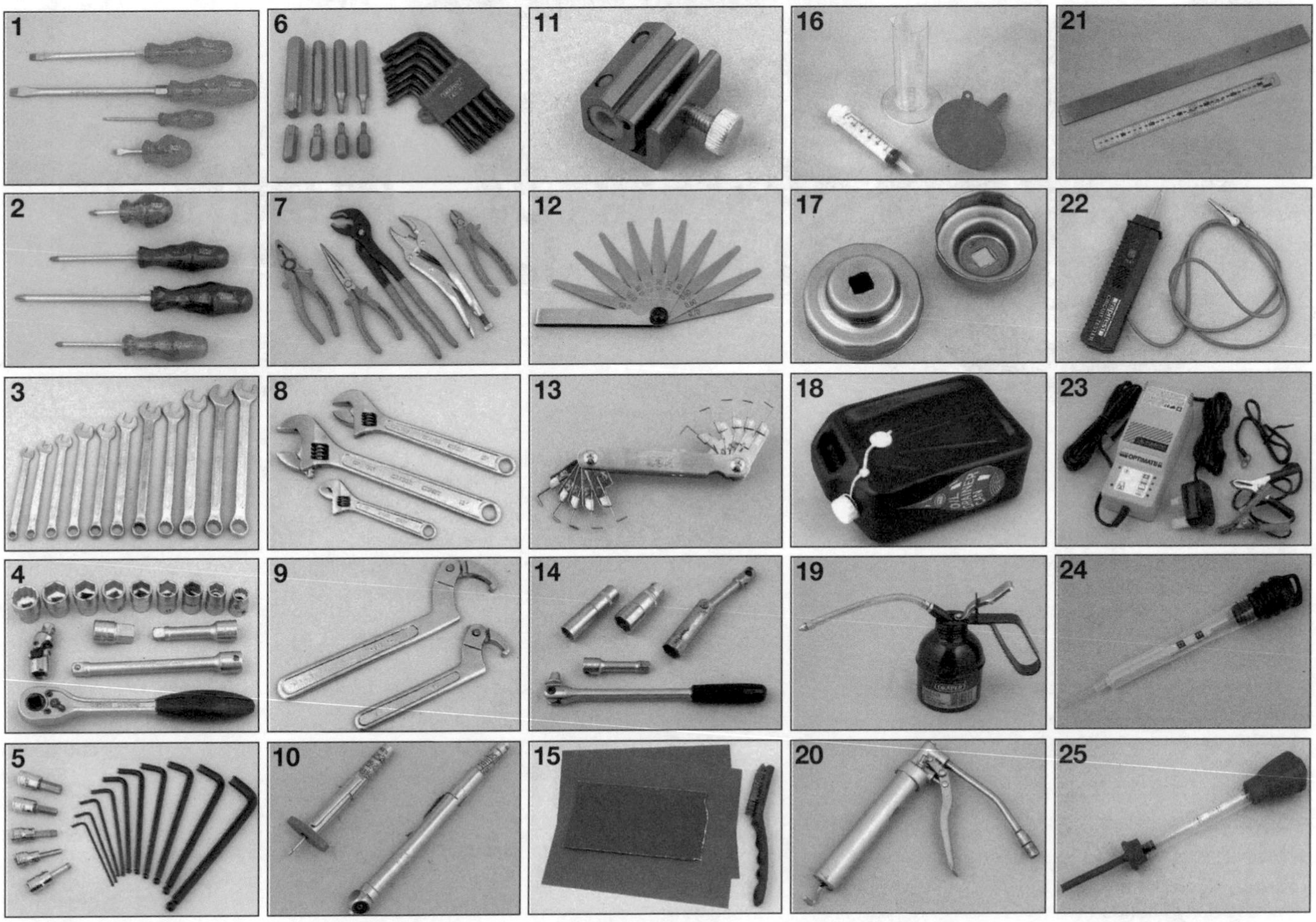

1 *Set of flat-bladed screwdrivers*
2 *Set of Phillips head screwdrivers*
3 *Combination open-end and ring spanners*
4 *Socket set (3/8 inch or 1/2 inch drive)*
5 *Set of Allen keys or bits*
6 *Set of Torx keys or bits*
7 *Pliers, cutters and self-locking grips (Mole grips)*
8 *Adjustable spanners*
9 *C-spanners*
10 *Tread depth gauge and tyre pressure gauge*
11 *Cable oiler clamp*
12 *Feeler gauges*
13 *Spark plug gap measuring tool*
14 *Spark plug spanner or deep plug sockets*
15 *Wire brush and emery paper*
16 *Calibrated syringe, measuring vessel and funnel*
17 *Oil filter adapters*
18 *Oil drainer can or tray*
19 *Pump type oil can*
20 *Grease gun*
21 *Straight-edge and steel rule*
22 *Continuity tester*
23 *Battery charger*
24 *Hydrometer (for battery specific gravity check)*
25 *Anti-freeze tester (for liquid-cooled engines)*

Repair and overhaul tools

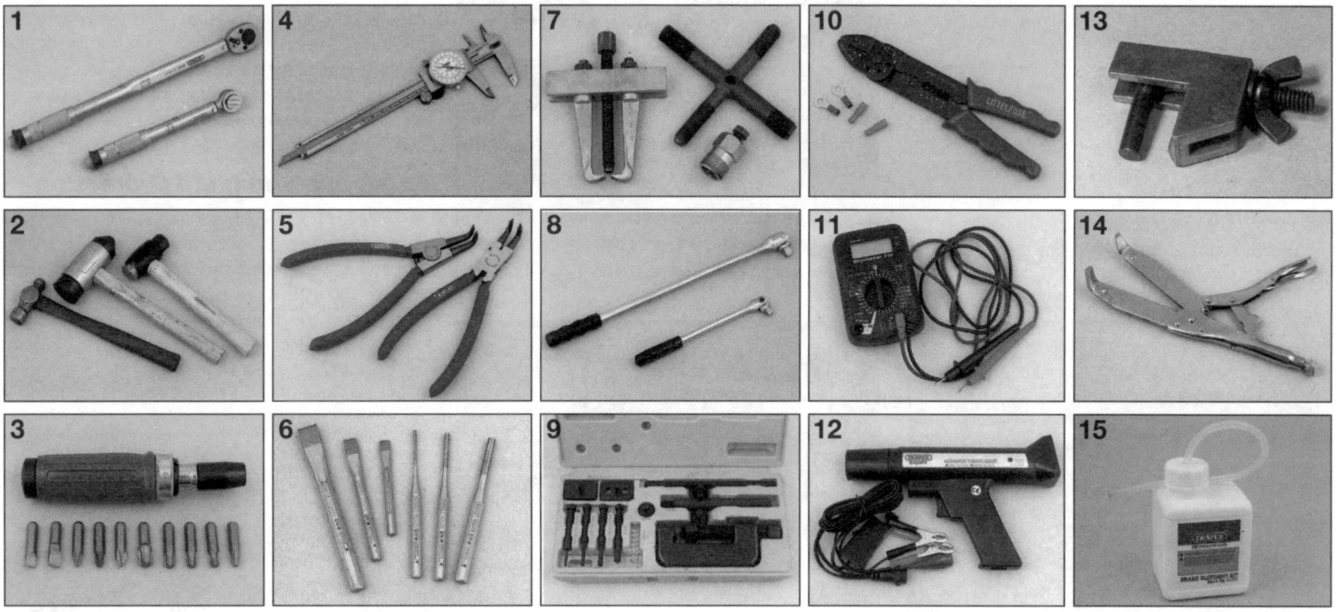

1 *Torque wrench (small and mid-ranges)*
2 *Conventional, plastic or soft-faced hammers*
3 *Impact driver set*
4 *Vernier gauge*
5 *Circlip pliers (internal and external, or combination)*
6 *Set of cold chisels and punches*
7 *Selection of pullers*
8 *Breaker bars*
9 *Chain breaking/ riveting tool set*
10 *Wire stripper and crimper tool*
11 *Multimeter (measures amps, volts and ohms)*
12 *Stroboscope (for dynamic timing checks)*
13 *Hose clamp (wingnut type shown)*
14 *Clutch holding tool*
15 *One-man brake/clutch bleeder kit*

Specialist tools

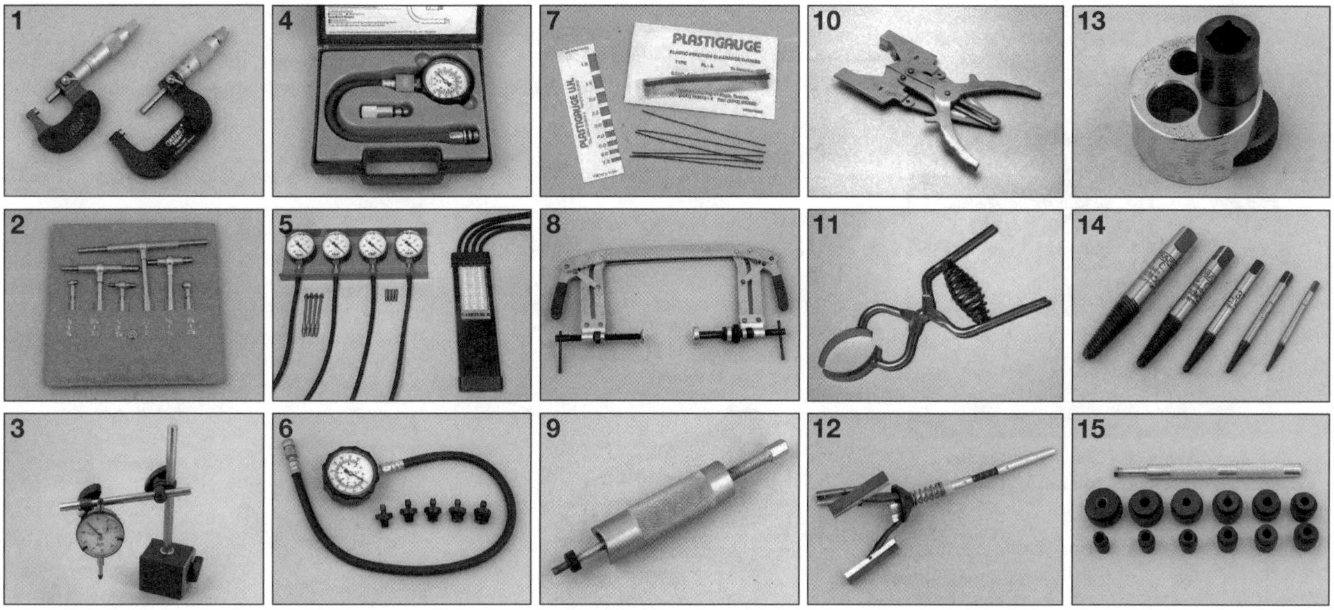

1 *Micrometers (external type)*
2 *Telescoping gauges*
3 *Dial gauge*
4 *Cylinder compression gauge*
5 *Vacuum gauges (left) or manometer (right)*
6 *Oil pressure gauge*
7 *Plastigauge kit*
8 *Valve spring compressor (4-stroke engines)*
9 *Piston pin drawbolt tool*
10 *Piston ring removal and installation tool*
11 *Piston ring clamp*
12 *Cylinder bore hone (stone type shown)*
13 *Stud extractor*
14 *Screw extractor set*
15 *Bearing driver set*

1 Workshop equipment and facilities

The workbench

- Work is made much easier by raising the bike up on a ramp - components are much more accessible if raised to waist level. The hydraulic or pneumatic types seen in the dealer's workshop are a sound investment if you undertake a lot of repairs or overhauls **(see illustration 1.1)**.

1.1 Hydraulic motorcycle ramp

- If raised off ground level, the bike must be supported on the ramp to avoid it falling. Most ramps incorporate a front wheel locating clamp which can be adjusted to suit different diameter wheels. When tightening the clamp, take care not to mark the wheel rim or damage the tyre - use wood blocks on each side to prevent this.
- Secure the bike to the ramp using tie-downs **(see illustration 1.2)**. If the bike has only a sidestand, and hence leans at a dangerous angle when raised, support the bike on an auxiliary stand.

1.2 Tie-downs are used around the passenger footrests to secure the bike

- Auxiliary (paddock) stands are widely available from mail order companies or motorcycle dealers and attach either to the wheel axle or swingarm pivot **(see illustration 1.3)**. If the motorcycle has a centrestand, you can support it under the crankcase to prevent it toppling whilst either wheel is removed **(see illustration 1.4)**.

1.3 This auxiliary stand attaches to the swingarm pivot

1.4 Always use a block of wood between the engine and jack head when supporting the engine in this way

Fumes and fire

- Refer to the Safety first! page at the beginning of the manual for full details. Make sure your workshop is equipped with a fire extinguisher suitable for fuel-related fires (Class B fire - flammable liquids) - it is not sufficient to have a water-filled extinguisher.
- Always ensure adequate ventilation is available. Unless an exhaust gas extraction system is available for use, ensure that the engine is run outside of the workshop.
- If working on the fuel system, make sure the workshop is ventilated to avoid a build-up of fumes. This applies equally to fume build-up when charging a battery. Do not smoke or allow anyone else to smoke in the workshop.

Fluids

- If you need to drain fuel from the tank, store it in an approved container marked as suitable for the storage of petrol (gasoline) **(see illustration 1.5)**. Do not store fuel in glass jars or bottles.

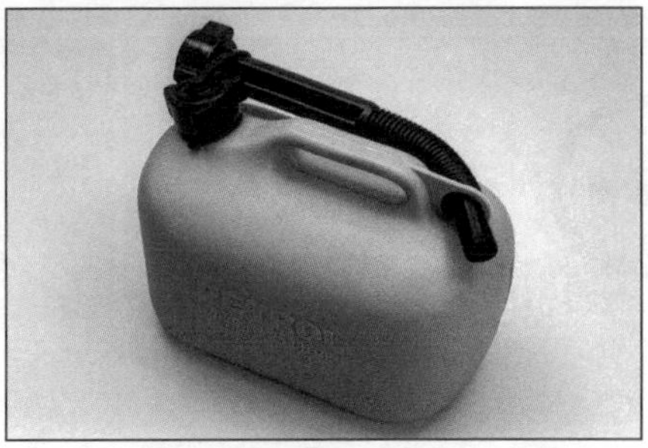

1.5 Use an approved can only for storing petrol (gasoline)

- Use proprietary engine degreasers or solvents which have a high flash-point, such as paraffin (kerosene), for cleaning off oil, grease and dirt - never use petrol (gasoline) for cleaning. Wear rubber gloves when handling solvent and engine degreaser. The fumes from certain solvents can be dangerous - always work in a well-ventilated area.

Dust, eye and hand protection

- Protect your lungs from inhalation of dust particles by wearing a filtering mask over the nose and mouth. Many frictional materials still contain asbestos which is dangerous to your health. Protect your eyes from spouts of liquid and sprung components by wearing a pair of protective goggles **(see illustration 1.6)**.

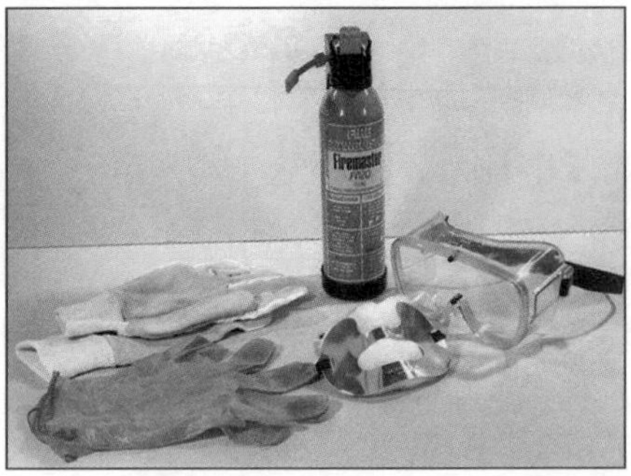

1.6 A fire extinguisher, goggles, mask and protective gloves should be at hand in the workshop

- Protect your hands from contact with solvents, fuel and oils by wearing rubber gloves. Alternatively apply a barrier cream to your hands before starting work. If handling hot components or fluids, wear suitable gloves to protect your hands from scalding and burns.

What to do with old fluids

- Old cleaning solvent, fuel, coolant and oils should not be poured down domestic drains or onto the ground. Package the fluid up in old oil containers, label it accordingly, and take it to a garage or disposal facility. Contact your local authority for location of such sites or ring the oil care hotline.

OIL CARE
FOLLOW THE CODE
OIL BANK LINE
0800 66 33 66

Note: It is antisocial and illegal to dump oil down the drain. To find the location of your local oil recycling bank, call this number free.

In the USA, note that any oil supplier must accept used oil for recycling.

2 Fasteners - screws, bolts and nuts

Fastener types and applications

Bolts and screws

● Fastener head types are either of hexagonal, Torx or splined design, with internal and external versions of each type **(see illustrations 2.1 and 2.2);** splined head fasteners are not in common use on motorcycles. The conventional slotted or Phillips head design is used for certain screws. Bolt or screw length is always measured from the underside of the head to the end of the item **(see illustration 2.11)**.

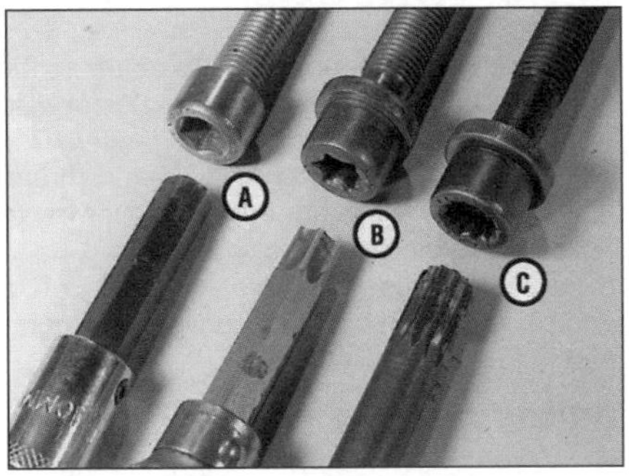

2.1 Internal hexagon/Allen (A), Torx (B) and splined (C) fasteners, with corresponding bits

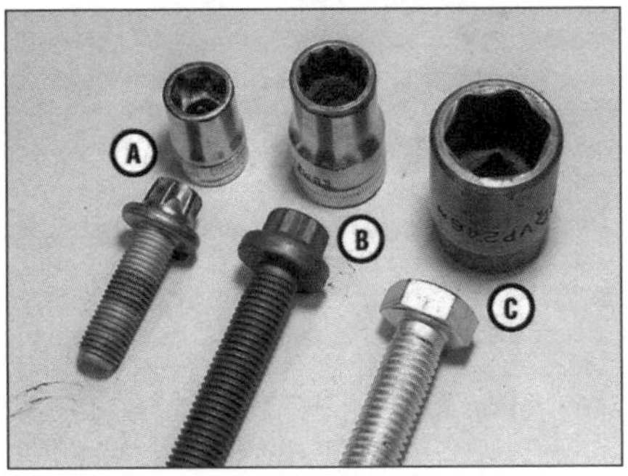

2.2 External Torx (A), splined (B) and hexagon (C) fasteners, with corresponding sockets

● Certain fasteners on the motorcycle have a tensile marking on their heads, the higher the marking the stronger the fastener. High tensile fasteners generally carry a 10 or higher marking. Never replace a high tensile fastener with one of a lower tensile strength.

Washers (see illustration 2.3)

● Plain washers are used between a fastener head and a component to prevent damage to the component or to spread the load when torque is applied. Plain washers can also be used as spacers or shims in certain assemblies. Copper or aluminium plain washers are often used as sealing washers on drain plugs.

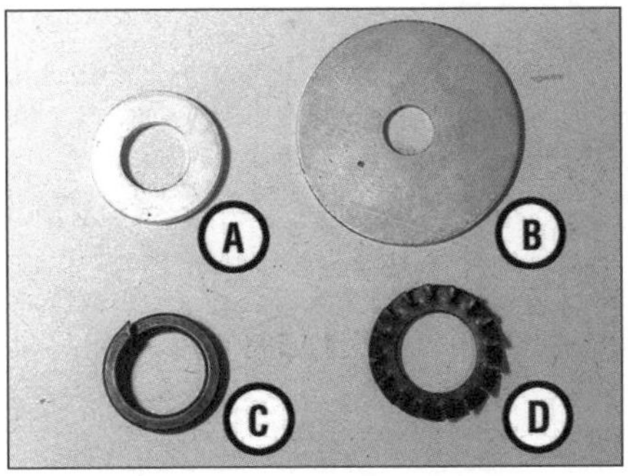

2.3 Plain washer (A), penny washer (B), spring washer (C) and serrated washer (D)

● The split-ring spring washer works by applying axial tension between the fastener head and component. If flattened, it is fatigued and must be renewed. If a plain (flat) washer is used on the fastener, position the spring washer between the fastener and the plain washer.

● Serrated star type washers dig into the fastener and component faces, preventing loosening. They are often used on electrical earth (ground) connections to the frame.

● Cone type washers (sometimes called Belleville) are conical and when tightened apply axial tension between the fastener head and component. They must be installed with the dished side against the component and often carry an OUTSIDE marking on their outer face. If flattened, they are fatigued and must be renewed.

● Tab washers are used to lock plain nuts or bolts on a shaft. A portion of the tab washer is bent up hard against one flat of the nut or bolt to prevent it loosening. Due to the tab washer being deformed in use, a new tab washer should be used every time it is disturbed.

● Wave washers are used to take up endfloat on a shaft. They provide light springing and prevent excessive side-to-side play of a component. Can be found on rocker arm shafts.

Nuts and split pins

● Conventional plain nuts are usually six-sided **(see illustration 2.4)**. They are sized by thread diameter and pitch. High tensile nuts carry a number on one end to denote their tensile strength.

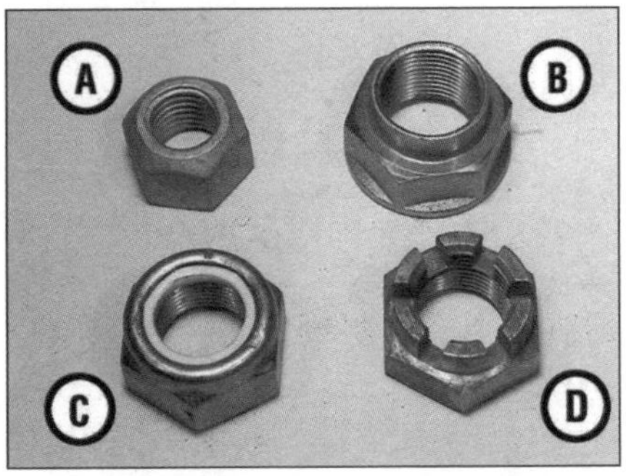

2.4 Plain nut (A), shouldered locknut (B), nylon insert nut (C) and castellated nut (D)

● Self-locking nuts either have a nylon insert, or two spring metal tabs, or a shoulder which is staked into a groove in the shaft - their advantage over conventional plain nuts is a resistance to loosening due to vibration. The nylon insert type can be used a number of times, but must be renewed when the friction of the nylon insert is reduced, ie when the nut spins freely on the shaft. The spring tab type can be reused unless the tabs are damaged. The shouldered type must be renewed every time it is disturbed.

● Split pins (cotter pins) are used to lock a castellated nut to a shaft or to prevent slackening of a plain nut. Common applications are wheel axles and brake torque arms. Because the split pin arms are deformed to lock around the nut a new split pin must always be used on installation - always fit the correct size split pin which will fit snugly in the shaft hole. Make sure the split pin arms are correctly located around the nut **(see illustrations 2.5 and 2.6)**.

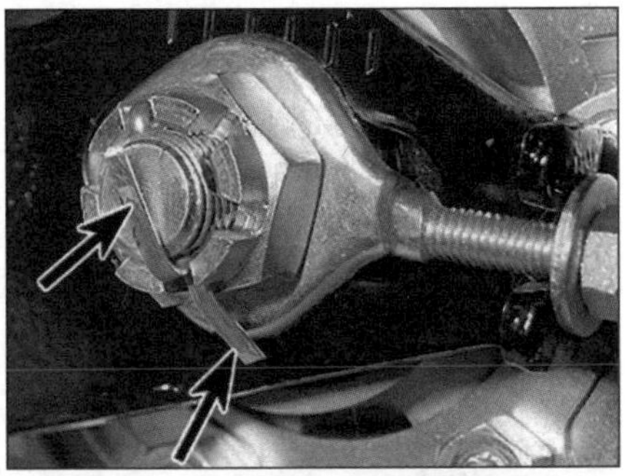

2.5 Bend split pin (cotter pin) arms as shown (arrows) to secure a castellated nut

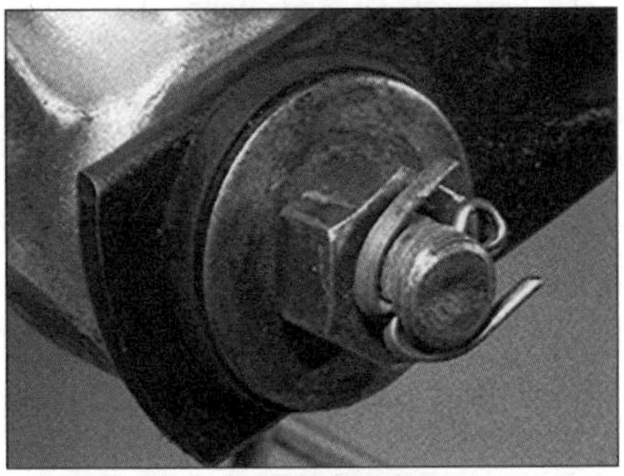

2.6 Bend split pin (cotter pin) arms as shown to secure a plain nut

> ***Caution: If the castellated nut slots do not align with the shaft hole after tightening to the torque setting, tighten the nut until the next slot aligns with the hole - never slacken the nut to align its slot.***

● R-pins (shaped like the letter R), or slip pins as they are sometimes called, are sprung and can be reused if they are otherwise in good condition. Always install R-pins with their closed end facing forwards **(see illustration 2.7)**.

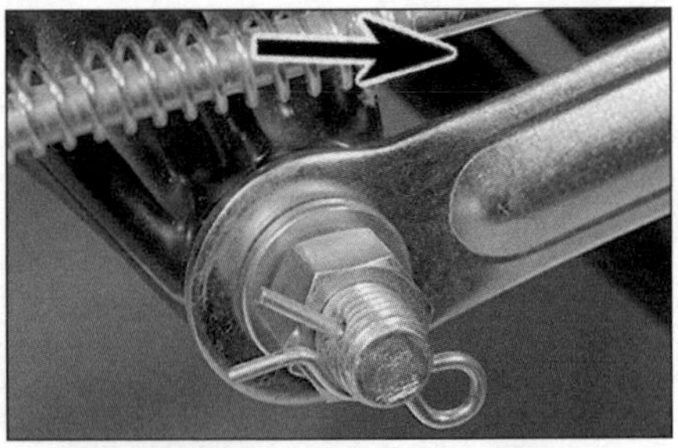

2.7 Correct fitting of R-pin. Arrow indicates forward direction

Circlips (see illustration 2.8)

- Circlips (sometimes called snap-rings) are used to retain components on a shaft or in a housing and have corresponding external or internal ears to permit removal. Parallel-sided (machined) circlips can be installed either way round in their groove, whereas stamped circlips (which have a chamfered edge on one face) must be installed with the chamfer facing away from the direction of thrust load **(see illustration 2.9)**.

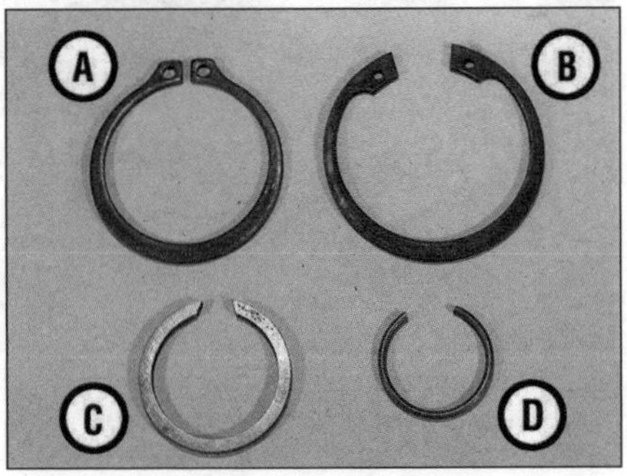

2.8 External stamped circlip (A), internal stamped circlip (B), machined circlip (C) and wire circlip (D)

- Always use circlip pliers to remove and install circlips; expand or compress them just enough to remove them. After installation, rotate the circlip in its groove to ensure it is securely seated. If installing a circlip on a splined shaft, always align its opening with a shaft channel to ensure the circlip ends are well supported and unlikely to catch **(see illustration 2.10)**.

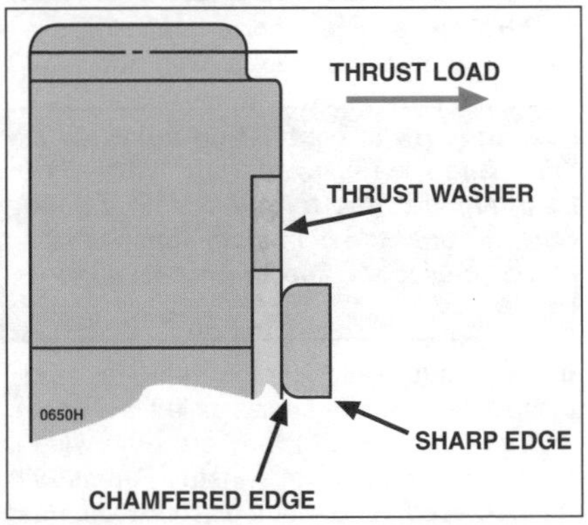

2.9 Correct fitting of a stamped circlip

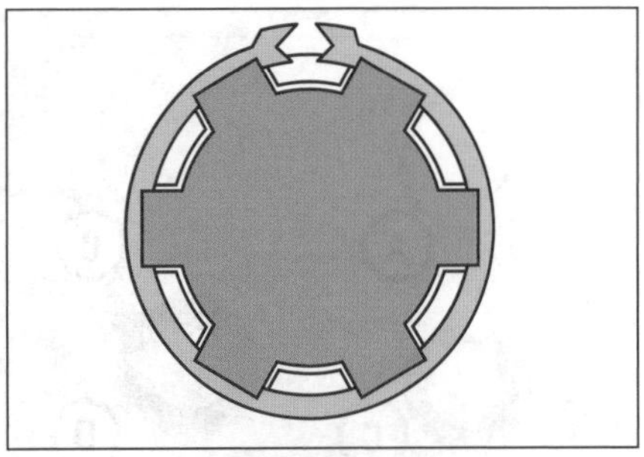

2.10 Align circlip opening with shaft channel

- Circlips can wear due to the thrust of components and become loose in their grooves, with the subsequent danger of becoming dislodged in operation. For this reason, renewal is advised every time a circlip is disturbed.
- Wire circlips are commonly used as piston pin retaining clips. If a removal tang is provided, long-nosed pliers can be used to dislodge them, otherwise careful use of a small flat-bladed screwdriver is necessary. Wire circlips should be renewed every time they are disturbed.

Thread diameter and pitch

- Diameter of a male thread (screw, bolt or stud) is the outside diameter of the threaded portion **(see illustration 2.11)**. Most motorcycle manufacturers use the ISO (International Standards Organisation) metric system expressed in millimetres, eg M6 refers to a 6 mm diameter thread. Sizing is the same for nuts, except that the thread diameter is measured across the valleys of the nut.
- Pitch is the distance between the peaks of the thread **(see illustration 2.11)**. It is expressed in millimetres, thus a common bolt size may be expressed as 6.0 x 1.0 mm (6 mm thread diameter and 1 mm pitch). Generally pitch increases in proportion to thread diameter, although there are always exceptions.
- Thread diameter and pitch are related for conventional fastener applications and the accompanying table can be used as a guide. Additionally, the AF (Across Flats), spanner or socket size dimension of the bolt or nut **(see illustration 2.11)** is linked to thread and pitch specification. Thread pitch can be measured with a thread gauge **(see illustration 2.12)**.

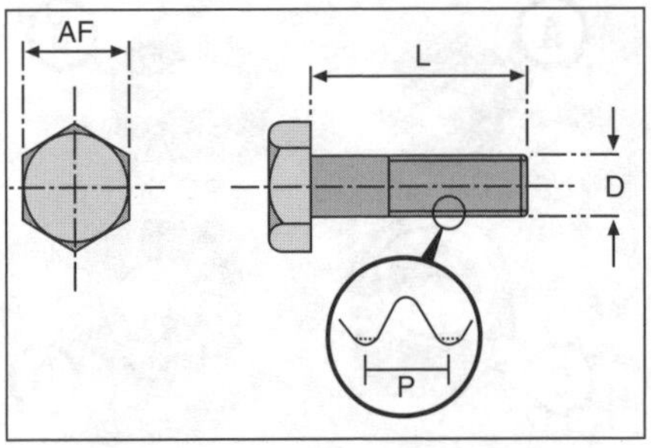

2.11 Fastener length (L), thread diameter (D), thread pitch (P) and head size (AF)

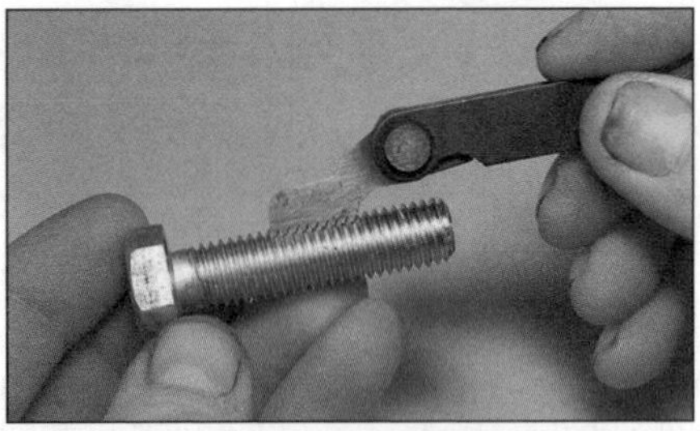

2.12 Using a thread gauge to measure pitch

AF size	Thread diameter x pitch (mm)
8 mm	M5 x 0.8
8 mm	M6 x 1.0
10 mm	M6 x 1.0
12 mm	M8 x 1.25
14 mm	M10 x 1.25
17 mm	M12 x 1.25

- The threads of most fasteners are of the right-hand type, ie they are turned clockwise to tighten and anti-clockwise to loosen. The reverse situation applies to left-hand thread fasteners, which are turned anti-clockwise to tighten and clockwise to loosen. Left-hand threads are used where rotation of a component might loosen a conventional right-hand thread fastener.

Seized fasteners

- Corrosion of external fasteners due to water or reaction between two dissimilar metals can occur over a period of time. It will build up sooner in wet conditions or in countries where salt is used on the roads during the winter. If a fastener is severely corroded it is likely that normal methods of removal will fail and result in its head being ruined. When you attempt removal, the fastener thread should be heard to crack free and unscrew easily - if it doesn't, stop there before damaging something.
- A smart tap on the head of the fastener will often succeed in breaking free corrosion which has occurred in the threads **(see illustration 2.13)**.
- An aerosol penetrating fluid (such as WD-40) applied the night beforehand may work its way down into the thread and ease removal. Depending on the location, you may be able to make up a Plasticine well around the fastener head and fill it with penetrating fluid.

2.13 A sharp tap on the head of a fastener will often break free a corroded thread

● If you are working on an engine internal component, corrosion will most likely not be a problem due to the well lubricated environment. However, components can be very tight and an impact driver is a useful tool in freeing them **(see illustration 2.14)**.

2.14 Using an impact driver to free a fastener

● Where corrosion has occurred between dissimilar metals (eg steel and aluminium alloy), the application of heat to the fastener head will create a disproportionate expansion rate between the two metals and break the seizure caused by the corrosion. Whether heat can be applied depends on the location of the fastener - any surrounding components likely to be damaged must first be removed **(see illustration 2.15)**. Heat can be applied using a paint stripper heat gun or clothes iron, or by immersing the component in boiling water - wear protective gloves to prevent scalding or burns to the hands.

2.15 Using heat to free a seized fastener

● As a last resort, it is possible to use a hammer and cold chisel to work the fastener head unscrewed **(see illustration 2.16)**. This will damage the fastener, but more importantly extreme care must be taken not to damage the surrounding component.

Caution: Remember that the component being secured is generally of more value than the bolt, nut or screw - when the fastener is freed, do not unscrew it with force, instead work the fastener back and forth when resistance is felt to prevent thread damage.

2.16 Using a hammer and chisel to free a seized fastener

Broken fasteners and damaged heads

● If the shank of a broken bolt or screw is accessible you can grip it with self-locking grips. The knurled wheel type stud extractor tool or self-gripping stud puller tool is particularly useful for removing the long studs which screw into the cylinder mouth surface of the crankcase or bolts and screws from which the head has broken off **(see illustration 2.17)**. Studs can also be removed by locking two nuts together on the threaded end of the stud and using a spanner on the lower nut **(see illustration 2.18)**.

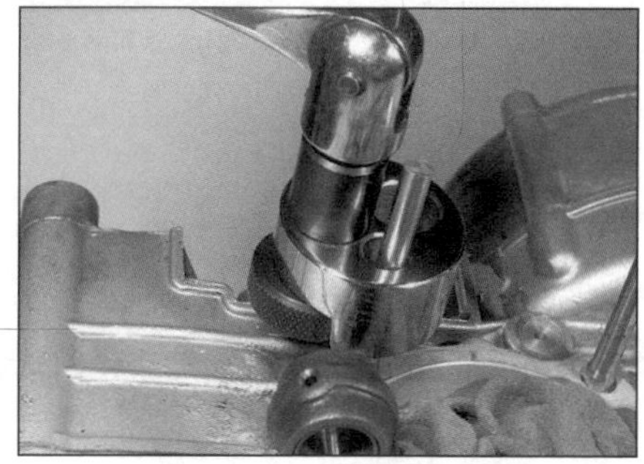

2.17 Using a stud extractor tool to remove a broken crankcase stud

2.18 Two nuts can be locked together to unscrew a stud from a component

● A bolt or screw which has broken off below or level with the casing must be extracted using a screw extractor set. Centre punch the fastener to centralise the drill bit, then drill a hole in the fastener **(see illustration 2.19)**. Select a drill bit which is approximately half to three-quarters the

2.19 When using a screw extractor, first drill a hole in the fastener . . .

diameter of the fastener and drill to a depth which will accommodate the extractor. Use the largest size extractor possible, but avoid leaving too small a wall thickness otherwise the extractor will merely force the fastener walls outwards wedging it in the casing thread.

● If a spiral type extractor is used, thread it anti-clockwise into the fastener. As it is screwed in, it will grip the fastener and unscrew it from the casing **(see illustration 2.20)**.

2.20 . . . then thread the extractor anti-clockwise into the fastener

● If a taper type extractor is used, tap it into the fastener so that it is firmly wedged in place. Unscrew the extractor (anti-clockwise) to draw the fastener out.

Warning: Stud extractors are very hard and may break off in the fastener if care is not taken - ask an engineer about spark erosion if this happens.

● Alternatively, the broken bolt/screw can be drilled out and the hole retapped for an oversize bolt/screw or a diamond-section thread insert. It is essential that the drilling is carried out squarely and to the correct depth, otherwise the casing may be ruined - if in doubt, entrust the work to an engineer.

● Bolts and nuts with rounded corners cause the correct size spanner or socket to slip when force is applied. Of the types of spanner/socket available always use a six-point type rather than an eight or twelve-point type - better grip

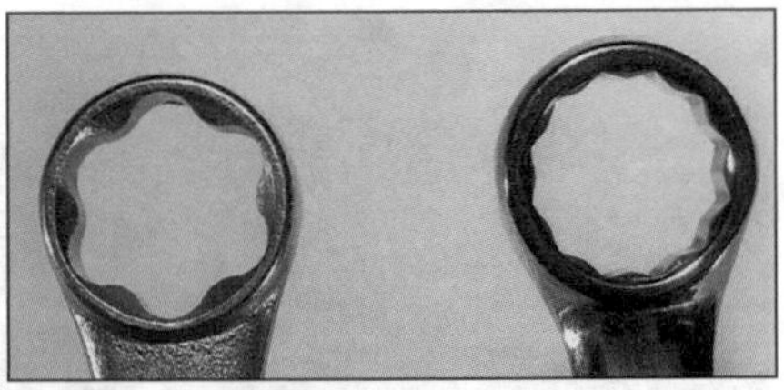

2.21 Comparison of surface drive ring spanner (left) with 12-point type (right)

is obtained. Surface drive spanners grip the middle of the hex flats, rather than the corners, and are thus good in cases of damaged heads **(see illustration 2.21)**.

- Slotted-head or Phillips-head screws are often damaged by the use of the wrong size screwdriver. Allen-head and Torx-head screws are much less likely to sustain damage. If enough of the screw head is exposed you can use a hacksaw to cut a slot in its head and then use a conventional flat-bladed screwdriver to remove it. Alternatively use a hammer and cold chisel to tap the head of the fastener around to slacken it. Always replace damaged fasteners with new ones, preferably Torx or Allen-head type.

HAYNES HiNT

A dab of valve grinding compound between the screw head and screw-driver tip will often give a good grip.

Thread repair

- Threads (particularly those in aluminium alloy components) can be damaged by overtightening, being assembled with dirt in the threads, or from a component working loose and vibrating. Eventually the thread will fail completely, and it will be impossible to tighten the fastener.
- If a thread is damaged or clogged with old locking compound it can be renovated with a thread repair tool (thread chaser) **(see illustrations 2.22 and 2.23)**; special thread chasers are available for spark plug hole threads. The tool will not cut a new thread, but clean and true the original thread. Make sure that you use the correct diameter and pitch tool. Similarly, external threads can be cleaned up with a die or a thread restorer file **(see illustration 2.24)**.

2.22 A thread repair tool being used to correct an internal thread

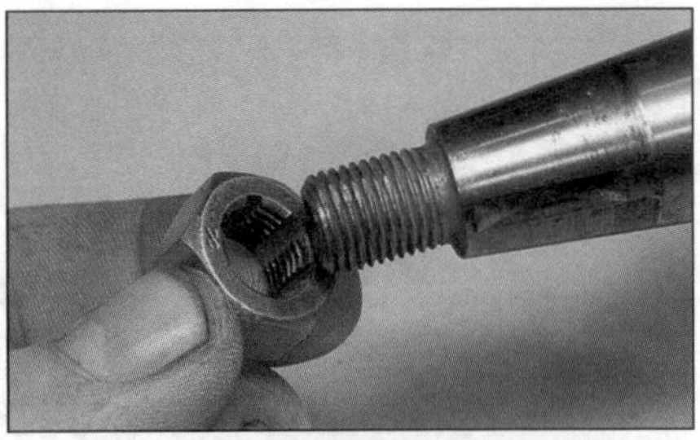

2.23 A thread repair tool being used to correct an external thread

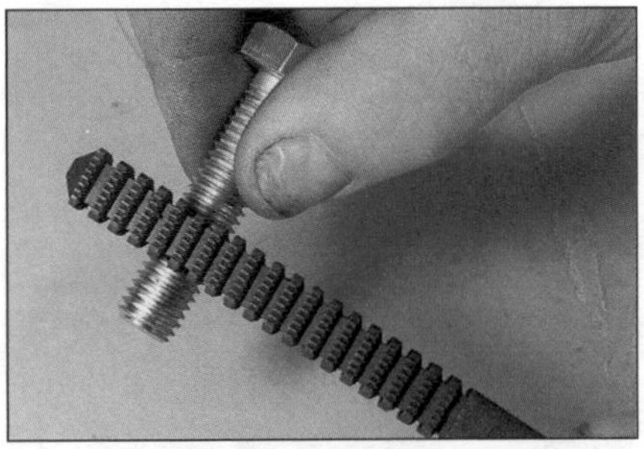

2.24 Using a thread restorer file

- It is possible to drill out the old thread and retap the component to the next thread size. This will work where there is enough surrounding material and a new bolt or screw can be obtained. Sometimes, however, this is not possible - such as where the bolt/screw passes through another component which must also be suitably modified, also in cases where a spark plug or oil drain plug cannot be obtained in a larger diameter thread size.
- The diamond-section thread insert (often known by its popular trade name of Heli-Coil) is a simple and effective method of renewing the thread and retaining the original size. A kit can be purchased which contains the tap, insert and installing tool **(see illustration 2.25)**. Drill out the damaged thread with the size drill specified **(see illustration 2.26)**. Carefully retap the thread **(see illustration 2.27)**. Install the insert on the installing tool and thread it slowly into place using a light downward pressure **(see illustrations 2.28 and 2.29)**. When positioned between a 1/4 and 1/2 turn below the surface withdraw the installing tool and use the break-off tool to press down on the tang, breaking it off **(see illustration 2.30)**.
- There are epoxy thread repair kits on the market which can rebuild stripped internal threads, although this repair should not be used on high load-bearing components.

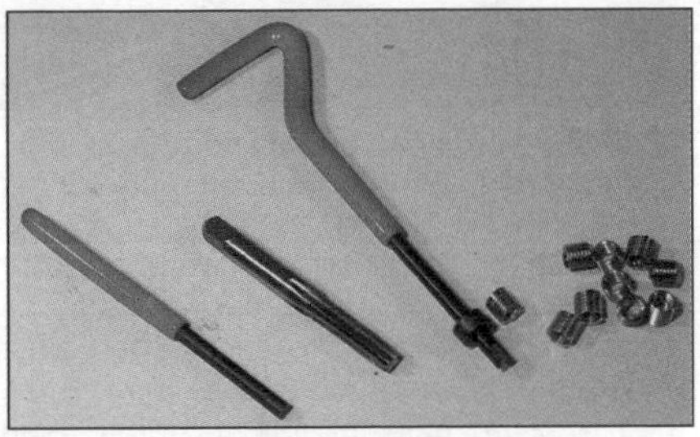

2.25 Obtain a thread insert kit to suit the thread diameter and pitch required

2.26 To install a thread insert, first drill out the original thread . . .

2.27 . . . tap a new thread . . .

2.28 . . . fit insert on the installing tool . . .

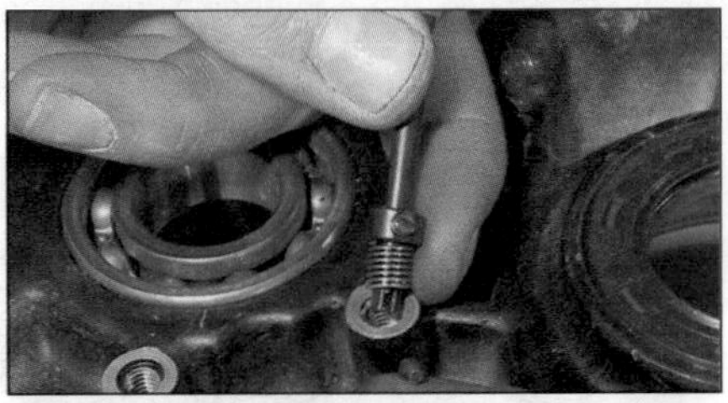

2.29 . . . and thread into the component . . .

2.30 . . . break off the tang when complete

Thread locking and sealing compounds

- Locking compounds are used in locations where the fastener is prone to loosening due to vibration or on important safety-related items which might cause loss of control of the motorcycle if they fail. It is also used where important fasteners cannot be secured by other means such as lockwashers or split pins.
- Before applying locking compound, make sure that the threads (internal and external) are clean and dry with all old compound removed. Select a compound to suit the component being secured - a non-permanent general locking and sealing type is suitable for most applications, but a high strength type is needed for permanent fixing of studs in castings. Apply a drop or two of the compound to the first few threads of the fastener, then thread it into place and tighten to the specified torque. Do not apply excessive thread locking compound otherwise the thread may be damaged on subsequent removal.
- Certain fasteners are impregnated with a dry film type coating of locking compound on their threads. Always renew this type of fastener if disturbed.
- Anti-seize compounds, such as copper-based greases, can be applied to protect threads from seizure due to extreme heat and corrosion. A common instance is spark plug threads and exhaust system fasteners.

3 Measuring tools and gauges

Feeler gauges

- Feeler gauges (or blades) are used for measuring small gaps and clearances **(see illustration 3.1)**. They can also be used to measure endfloat (sideplay) of a component on a shaft where access is not possible with a dial gauge.
- Feeler gauge sets should be treated with care and not bent or damaged. They are etched with their size on one face. Keep them clean and very lightly oiled to prevent corrosion build-up.

3.1 Feeler gauges are used for measuring small gaps and clearances - thickness is marked on one face of gauge

- When measuring a clearance, select a gauge which is a light sliding fit between the two components. You may need to use two gauges together to measure the clearance accurately.

Micrometers

- A micrometer is a precision tool capable of measuring to 0.01 or 0.001 of a millimetre. It should always be stored in its case and not in the general toolbox. It must be kept clean and never dropped, otherwise its frame or measuring anvils could be distorted resulting in inaccurate readings.
- External micrometers are used for measuring outside diameters of components and have many more applications than internal micrometers. Micrometers are available in different size ranges, eg 0 to 25 mm, 25 to 50 mm, and upwards in 25 mm steps; some large micrometers have interchangeable anvils to allow a range of measurements to be taken. Generally the largest precision measurement you are likely to take on a motorcycle is the piston diameter.
- Internal micrometers (or bore micrometers) are used for measuring inside diameters, such as valve guides and cylinder bores. Telescoping gauges and small hole gauges are used in conjunction with an external micrometer, whereas the more expensive internal micrometers have their own measuring device.

External micrometer

Note: *The conventional analogue type instrument is described. Although much easier to read, digital micrometers are considerably more expensive.*

- Always check the calibration of the micrometer before use. With the anvils closed (0 to 25 mm type) or set over a test gauge (for the larger types) the scale should read zero **(see illustration 3.2)**; make sure that the anvils (and test piece) are clean first. Any discrepancy can be adjusted by referring to the instructions supplied with the tool. Remember that the micrometer is a precision measuring tool - don't force the anvils closed, use the ratchet (4) on the end of the micrometer to close it. In this way, a measured force is always applied.

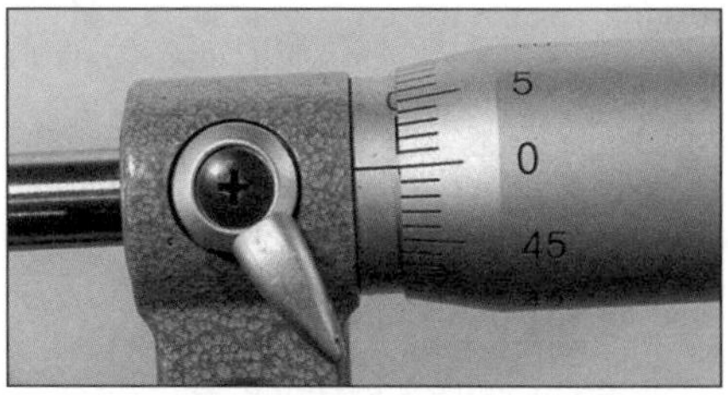

3.2 Check micrometer calibration before use

- To use, first make sure that the item being measured is clean. Place the anvil of the micrometer (1) against the item and use the thimble (2) to bring the spindle (3) lightly into contact with the other side of the item **(see illustration 3.3)**. Don't tighten the thimble down because this will damage the micrometer - instead use the ratchet (4) on the end of the micrometer. The ratchet mechanism applies a measured force preventing damage to the instrument.
- The micrometer is read by referring to the linear scale on the sleeve and the annular scale on the thimble. Read off the sleeve first to obtain the base measurement, then add the fine measurement from the thimble to obtain the overall reading. The linear scale on the sleeve represents the measuring range of the micrometer (eg 0 to 25 mm). The annular scale

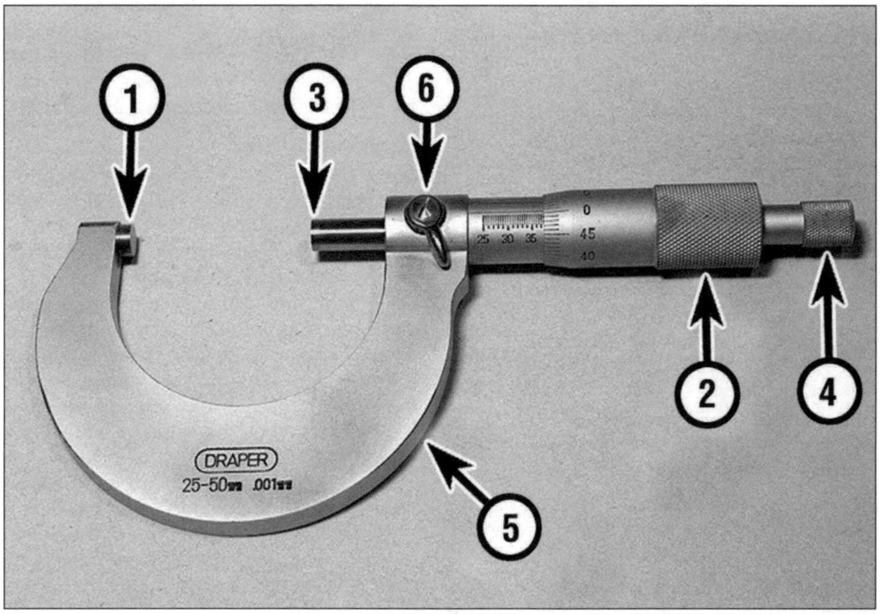

3.3 Micrometer component parts

1 Anvil
2 Thimble
3 Spindle
4 Ratchet
5 Frame
6 Locking lever

on the thimble will be in graduations of 0.01 mm (or as marked on the frame) - one full revolution of the thimble will move 0.5 mm on the linear scale. Take the reading where the datum line on the sleeve intersects the thimble's scale. Always position the eye directly above the scale otherwise an inaccurate reading will result.

In the example shown the item measures 2.95 mm **(see illustration 3.4)**:

Linear scale	2.00 mm
Linear scale	0.50 mm
Annular scale	0.45 mm
Total figure	**2.95 mm**

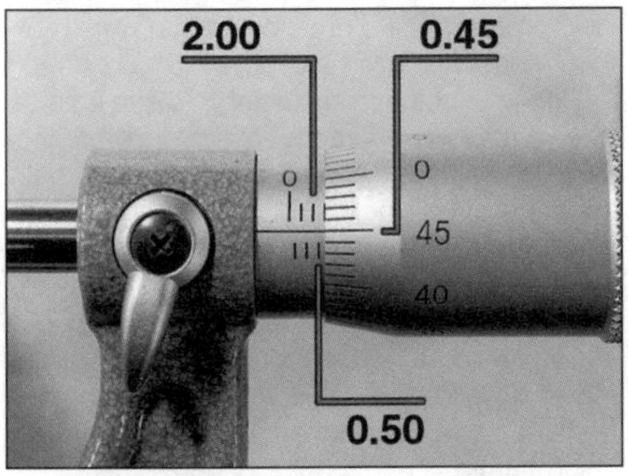

3.4 Micrometer reading of 2.95 mm

Most micrometers have a locking lever (6) on the frame to hold the setting in place, allowing the item to be removed from the micrometer.

- Some micrometers have a vernier scale on their sleeve, providing an even finer measurement to be taken, in 0.001 increments of a millimetre. Take the sleeve and thimble measurement as described above, then check which graduation on the vernier scale aligns with that of the annular scale on the thimble **Note:** *The eye must be perpendicular to the scale when taking the vernier reading - if necessary rotate the body of the micrometer to ensure this.* Multiply the vernier scale figure by 0.001 and add it to the base and fine measurement figures.

In the example shown the item measures 46.994 mm **(see illustrations 3.5 and 3.6)**:

Linear scale (base)	46.000 mm
Linear scale (base)	00.500 mm
Annular scale (fine)	00.490 mm
Vernier scale	00.004 mm
Total figure	**46.994 mm**

Internal micrometer

- Internal micrometers are available for measuring bore diameters, but are expensive and unlikely to be available for home use. It is suggested that a set of telescoping gauges and small hole gauges, both of which must be used with an external micrometer, will suffice for taking internal measurements on a motorcycle.
- Telescoping gauges can be used to measure internal diameters of components. Select a gauge with the correct size range, make sure its ends are clean and insert it into the bore. Expand the gauge, then lock its position and withdraw it from the bore **(see illustration 3.7)**. Measure across the gauge ends with a micrometer **(see illustration 3.8)**.
- Very small diameter bores (such as valve guides) are measured with a small hole gauge. Once adjusted to a slip-fit inside the component, its position is locked and the gauge withdrawn for measurement with a micrometer **(see illustrations 3.9 and 3.10)**.

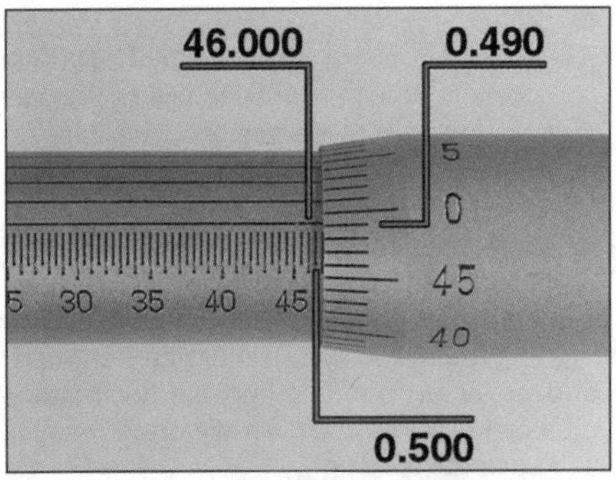

3.5 Micrometer reading of 46.99 mm on linear and annular scales . . .

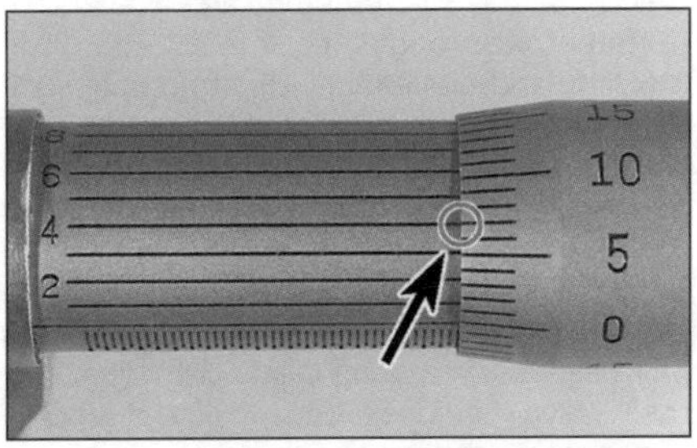

3.6 . . . and 0.004 mm on vernier scale

Vernier caliper

Note: *The conventional linear and dial gauge type instruments are described. Digital types are easier to read, but are far more expensive.*

- The vernier caliper does not provide the precision of a micrometer, but is versatile in being able to measure internal and external diameters. Some types also incorporate a depth gauge. It is ideal for measuring clutch plate friction material and spring free lengths.
- To use the conventional linear scale vernier, slacken off the vernier clamp screws (1) and set its jaws over (2), or inside (3), the item to be measured **(see illustration 3.11)**. Slide the jaw into contact, using the thumb-wheel (4) for fine movement of the sliding scale (5) then tighten the clamp screws (1). Read off the main scale (6) where the zero on the sliding scale (5) intersects it, taking the whole number to the left of the zero; this provides the base measurement. View along the sliding scale and select the division which lines up exactly with any of the divisions on the main scale, noting that the divisions usually represents 0.02 of a millimetre. Add this fine measurement to the base measurement to obtain the total reading.

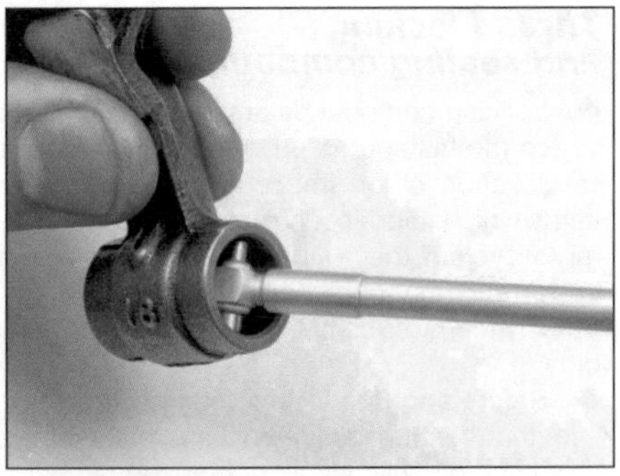

3.7 Expand the telescoping gauge in the bore, lock its position . . .

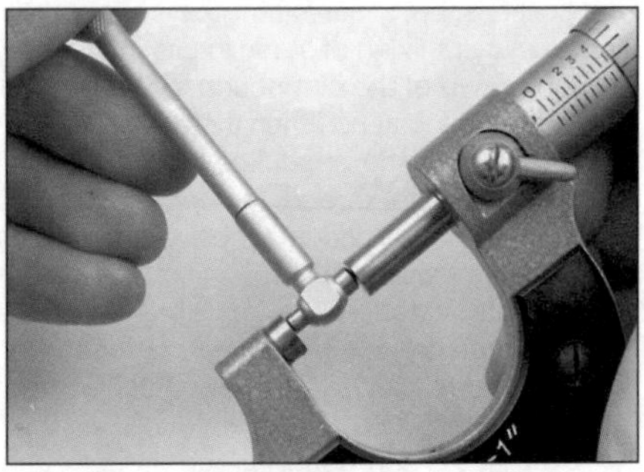

3.8 . . . then measure the gauge with a micrometer

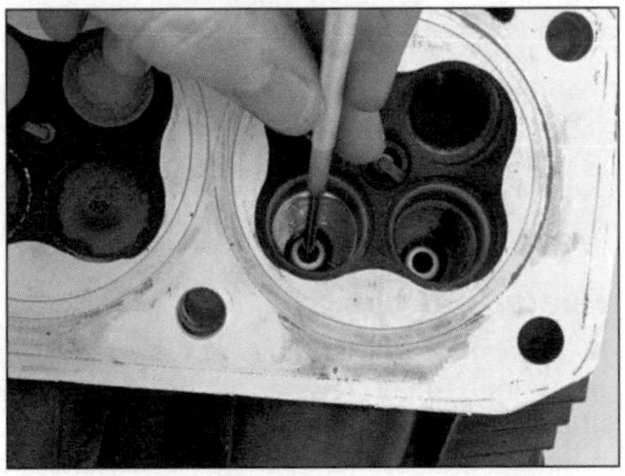

3.9 Expand the small hole gauge in the bore, lock its position . . .

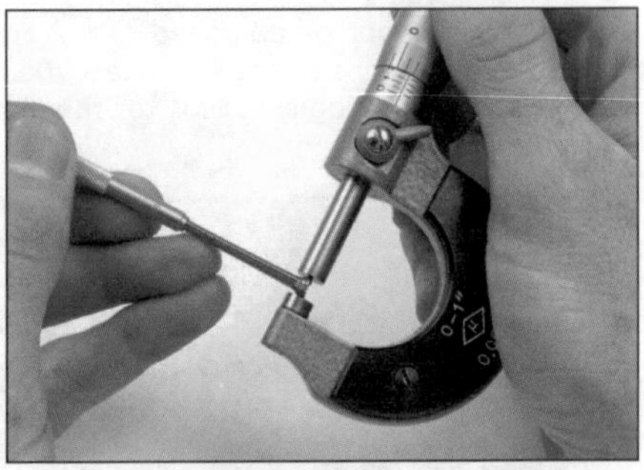

3.10 . . . then measure the gauge with a micrometer

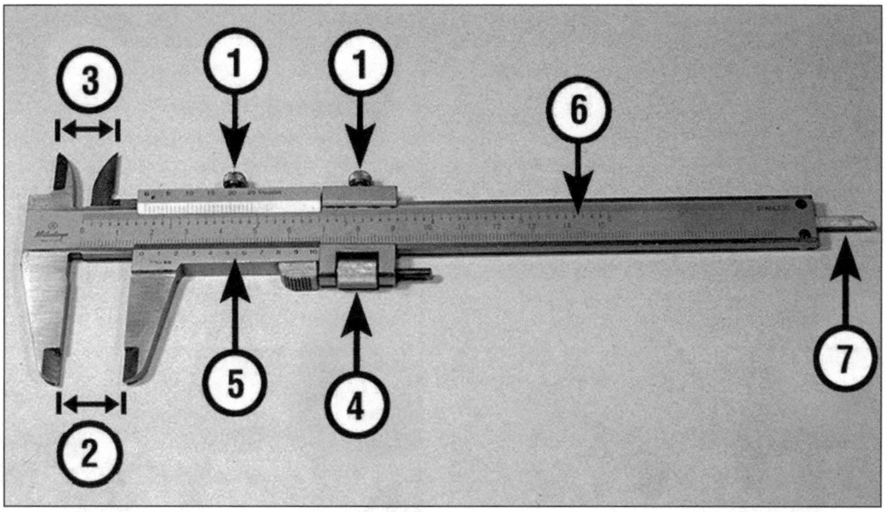

3.11 Vernier component parts (linear gauge)

1 Clamp screws
2 External jaws
3 Internal jaws
4 Thumbwheel
5 Sliding scale
6 Main scale
7 Depth gauge

In the example shown the item measures 55.92 mm **(see illustration 3.12)**:

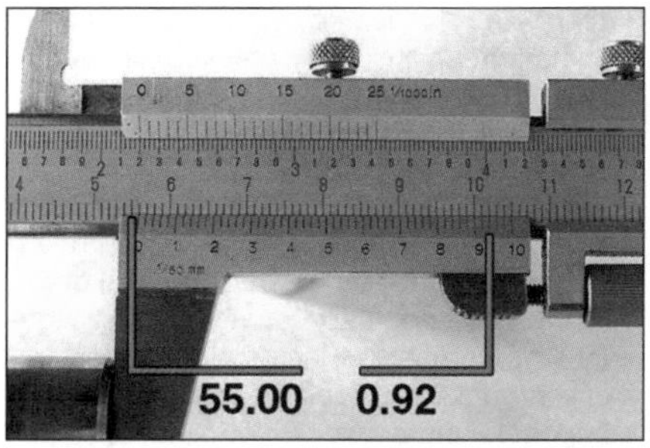

3.12 Vernier gauge reading of 55.92 mm

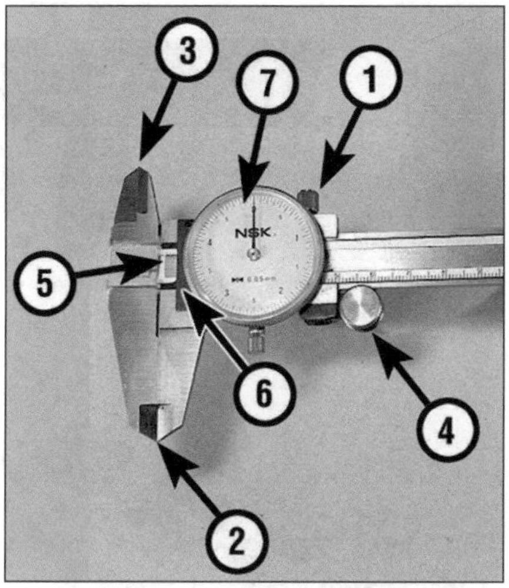

3.13 Vernier component parts (dial gauge)

1 Clamp screw
2 External jaws
3 Internal jaws
4 Thumbwheel
5 Main scale
6 Sliding scale
7 Dial gauge

Base measurement	55.00 mm
Fine measurement	00.92 mm
Total figure	**55.92 mm**

● Some vernier calipers are equipped with a dial gauge for fine measurement. Before use, check that the jaws are clean, then close them fully and check that the dial gauge reads zero. If necessary adjust the gauge ring accordingly. Slacken the vernier clamp screw (1) and set its jaws over (2), or inside (3), the item to be measured **(see illustration 3.13)**. Slide the jaws into contact, using the thumbwheel (4) for fine movement. Read off the main scale (5) where the edge of the sliding scale (6) intersects it, taking the whole number to the left of the zero; this provides the base measurement. Read off the needle position on the dial gauge (7) scale to provide the fine measurement; each division represents 0.05 of a millimetre. Add this fine measurement to the base measurement to obtain the total reading.

In the example shown the item measures 55.95 mm **(see illustration 3.14)**:

Base measurement	55.00 mm
Fine measurement	00.95 mm
Total figure	**55.95 mm**

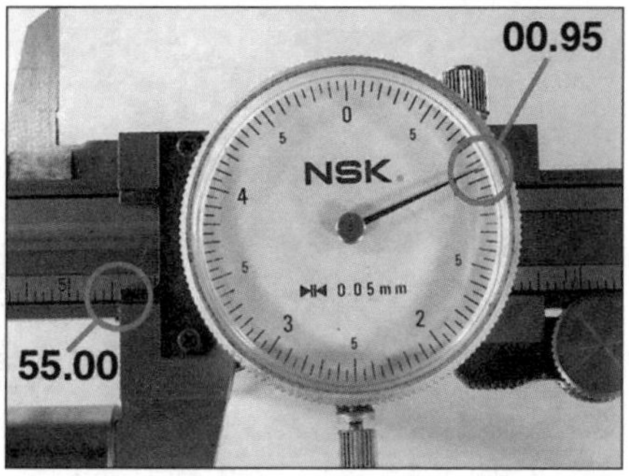

3.14 Vernier gauge reading of 55.95 mm

Plastigauge

● Plastigauge is a plastic material which can be compressed between two surfaces to measure the oil clearance between them. The width of the compressed Plastigauge is measured against a calibrated scale to determine the clearance.

● Common uses of Plastigauge are for measuring the clearance between crankshaft journal and main bearing inserts, between crankshaft journal and big-end bearing inserts, and between camshaft and bearing surfaces. The following example describes big-end oil clearance measurement.

● Handle the Plastigauge material carefully to prevent distortion. Using a sharp knife, cut a length which corresponds with the width of the bearing being measured and place it carefully across the journal so that it is parallel with the shaft **(see illustration 3.15)**. Carefully install both bearing shells and the connecting rod. Without rotating the rod on the journal tighten its bolts or nuts (as applicable) to the specified torque. The connecting rod and bearings are then disassembled and the crushed Plastigauge examined.

3.15 Plastigauge placed across shaft journal

● Using the scale provided in the Plastigauge kit, measure the width of the material to determine the oil clearance **(see illustration 3.16)**. Always remove all traces of Plastigauge after use using your fingernails.

Caution: Arriving at the correct clearance demands that the assembly is torqued correctly, according to the settings and sequence (where applicable) provided by the motorcycle manufacturer.

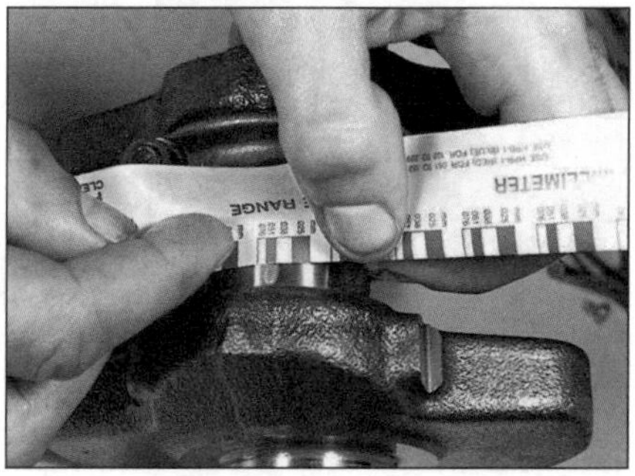

3.16 Measuring the width of the crushed Plastigauge

Dial gauge or DTI (Dial Test Indicator)

● A dial gauge can be used to accurately measure small amounts of movement. Typical uses are measuring shaft runout or shaft endfloat (sideplay) and setting piston position for ignition timing on two-strokes. A dial gauge set usually comes with a range of different probes and adapters and mounting equipment.

● The gauge needle must point to zero when at rest. Rotate the ring around its periphery to zero the gauge.

● Check that the gauge is capable of reading the extent of movement in the work. Most gauges have a small dial set in the face which records whole millimetres of movement as well as the fine scale around the face periphery which is calibrated in 0.01 mm divisions. Read off the small dial first to obtain the base measurement, then add the measurement from the fine scale to obtain the total reading.

In the example shown the gauge reads 1.48 mm **(see illustration 3.17)**:

Base measurement	1.00 mm
Fine measurement	0.48 mm
Total figure	**1.48 mm**

3.17 Dial gauge reading of 1.48 mm

● If measuring shaft runout, the shaft must be supported in vee-blocks and the gauge mounted on a stand perpendicular to the shaft. Rest the tip of the gauge against the centre of the shaft and rotate the shaft slowly whilst watching the gauge reading **(see illustration 3.18)**. Take several measurements along the length of the shaft and record the maximum gauge reading as the amount of runout in the shaft. **Note:** *The reading obtained will be total runout at that point - some manufacturers specify that the runout figure is halved to compare with their specified runout limit.*

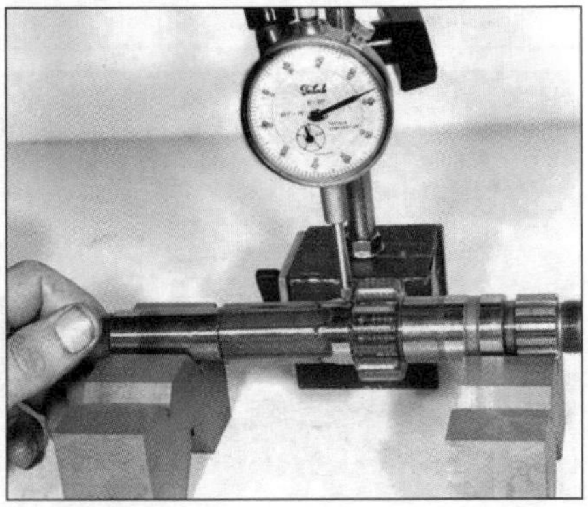

3.18 Using a dial gauge to measure shaft runout

● Endfloat (sideplay) measurement requires that the gauge is mounted securely to the surrounding component with its probe touching the end of the shaft. Using hand pressure, push and pull on the shaft noting the maximum endfloat recorded on the gauge **(see illustration 3.19)**.

3.19 Using a dial gauge to measure shaft endfloat

● A dial gauge with suitable adapters can be used to determine piston position BTDC on two-stroke engines for the purposes of ignition timing. The gauge, adapter and suitable length probe are installed in the place of the spark plug and the gauge zeroed at TDC. If the piston position is specified as 1.14 mm BTDC, rotate the engine back to 2.00 mm BTDC, then slowly forwards to 1.14 mm BTDC.

Cylinder compression gauges

● A compression gauge is used for measuring cylinder compression. Either the rubber-cone type or the threaded adapter type can be used. The latter is preferred to ensure a perfect seal against the cylinder head. A 0 to 300 psi (0 to 20 Bar) type gauge (for petrol/gasoline engines) will be suitable for motorcycles.

● The spark plug is removed and the gauge either held hard against the cylinder head (cone type) or the gauge adapter screwed into the cylinder head (threaded type) **(see illustration 3.20)**. Cylinder compression is measured with the engine turning over, but not running - carry out the compression test as described in *Fault Finding Equipment*. The gauge will hold the reading until manually released.

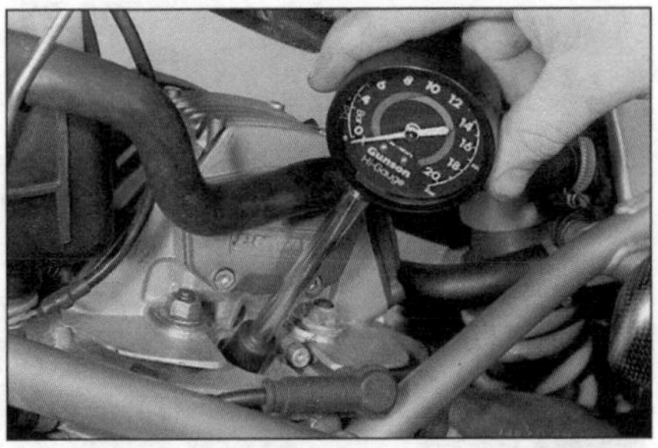

3.20 Using a rubber-cone type cylinder compression gauge

Oil pressure gauge

● An oil pressure gauge is used for measuring engine oil pressure. Most gauges come with a set of adapters to fit the thread of the take-off point **(see illustration 3.21)**. If the take-off point specified by the motorcycle manufacturer is an external oil pipe union, make sure that the specified replacement union is used to prevent oil starvation.

3.21 Oil pressure gauge and take-off point adapter (arrow)

● Oil pressure is measured with the engine running (at a specific rpm) and often the manufacturer will specify pressure limits for a cold and hot engine.

Straight-edge and surface plate

● If checking the gasket face of a component for warpage, place a steel rule or precision straight-edge across the gasket face and measure any gap between the straight-edge and component with feeler gauges **(see illustration 3.22)**. Check diagonally across the component and between mounting holes **(see illustration 3.23)**.

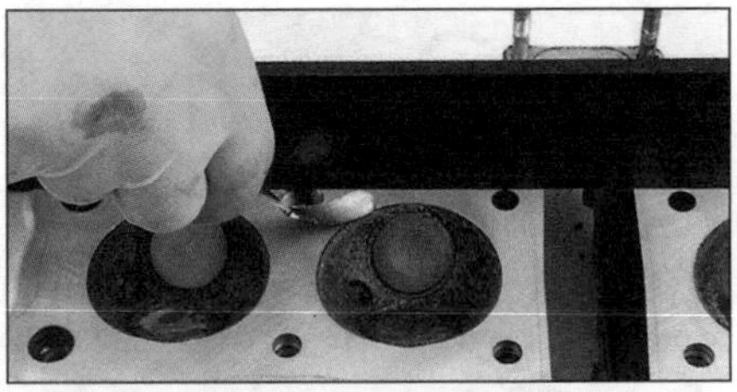

3.22 Use a straight-edge and feeler gauges to check for warpage

3.23 Check for warpage in these directions

● Checking individual components for warpage, such as clutch plain (metal) plates, requires a perfectly flat plate or piece or plate glass and feeler gauges.

4 Torque and leverage

What is torque?

● Torque describes the twisting force about a shaft. The amount of torque applied is determined by the distance from the centre of the shaft to the end of the lever and the amount of force being applied to the end of the lever; distance multiplied by force equals torque.

● The manufacturer applies a measured torque to a bolt or nut to ensure that it will not slacken in use and to hold two components securely together without movement in the joint. The actual torque setting depends on the thread size, bolt or nut material and the composition of the components being held.

● Too little torque may cause the fastener to loosen due to vibration, whereas too much torque will distort the joint faces of the component or cause the fastener to shear off. Always stick to the specified torque setting.

Using a torque wrench

● Check the calibration of the torque wrench and make sure it has a suitable range for the job. Torque wrenches are available in Nm (Newton-metres), kgf m (kilograms-force metre), lbf ft (pounds-feet), lbf in (inch-pounds). Do not confuse lbf ft with lbf in.

● Adjust the tool to the desired torque on the scale **(see illustration 4.1)**. If your torque wrench is not calibrated in the units specified, carefully convert the figure (see *Conversion Factors*). A manufacturer sometimes gives a torque setting as a range (8 to 10 Nm) rather than a single figure - in this case set the tool midway between the two settings. The same torque may be expressed as 9 Nm ± 1 Nm. Some torque wrenches have a method of locking the setting so that it isn't inadvertently altered during use.

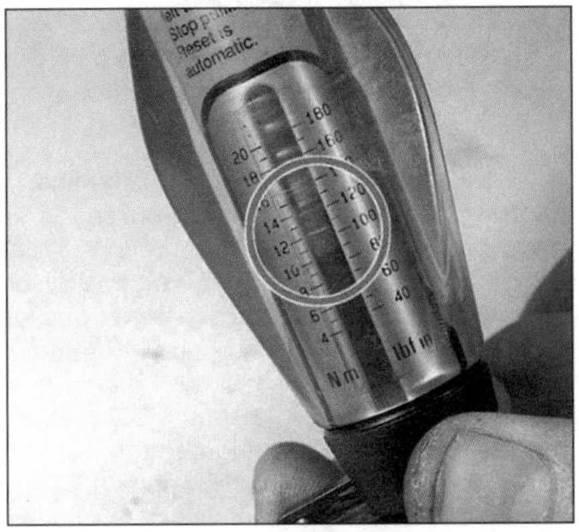

4.1 Set the torque wrench index mark to the setting required, in this case 12 Nm

● Install the bolts/nuts in their correct location and secure them lightly. Their threads must be clean and free of any old locking compound. Unless specified the threads and flange should be dry - oiled threads are necessary in certain circumstances and the manufacturer will take this into account in the specified torque figure. Similarly, the manufacturer may also specify the application of thread-locking compound.

● Tighten the fasteners in the specified sequence until the torque wrench clicks, indicating that the torque setting has been reached. Apply the torque again to double-check the setting. Where different thread diameter fasteners secure the component, as a rule tighten the larger diameter ones first.

● When the torque wrench has been finished with, release the lock (where applicable) and fully back off its setting to zero - do not leave the torque wrench tensioned. Also, do not use a torque wrench for slackening a fastener.

Angle-tightening

● Manufacturers often specify a figure in degrees for final tightening of a fastener. This usually follows tightening to a specific torque setting.

● A degree disc can be set and attached to the socket **(see illustration 4.2)** or a protractor can be used to mark the angle of movement on the bolt/nut head and the surrounding casting **(see illustration 4.3)**.

4.2 Angle tightening can be accomplished with a torque-angle gauge . . .

4.3 . . . or by marking the angle on the surrounding component

Loosening sequences

● Where more than one bolt/nut secures a component, loosen each fastener evenly a little at a time. In this way, not all the stress of the joint is held by one fastener and the components are not likely to distort.

● If a tightening sequence is provided, work in the REVERSE of this, but if not, work from the outside in, in a criss-cross sequence **(see illustration 4.4)**.

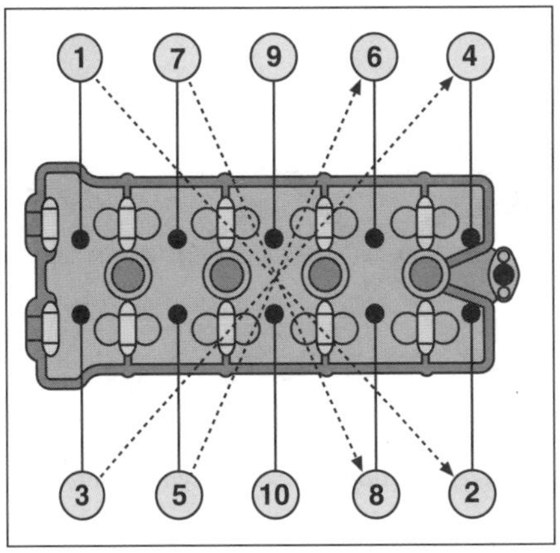

4.4 When slackening, work from the outside inwards

Tightening sequences

● If a component is held by more than one fastener it is important that the retaining bolts/nuts are tightened evenly to prevent uneven stress build-up and distortion of sealing faces. This is especially important on high-compression joints such as the cylinder head.

● A sequence is usually provided by the manufacturer, either in a diagram or actually marked in the casting. If not, always start in the centre and work outwards in a criss-cross pattern **(see illustration 4.5)**. Start off by securing all bolts/nuts finger-tight, then set the torque wrench and tighten each fastener by a small amount in sequence until the final torque is reached. By following this practice,

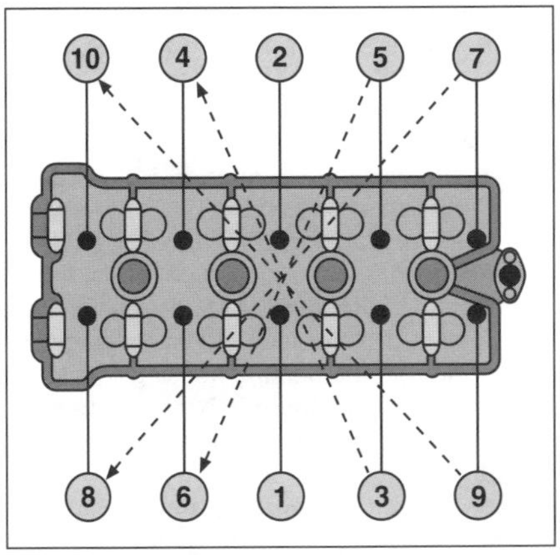

4.5 When tightening, work from the inside outwards

the joint will be held evenly and will not be distorted. Important joints, such as the cylinder head and big-end fasteners often have two- or three-stage torque settings.

Applying leverage

● Use tools at the correct angle. Position a socket wrench or spanner on the bolt/nut so that you pull it towards you when loosening. If this can't be done, push the spanner without curling your fingers around it **(see illustration 4.6)** - the spanner may slip or the fastener loosen suddenly, resulting in your fingers being crushed against a component.

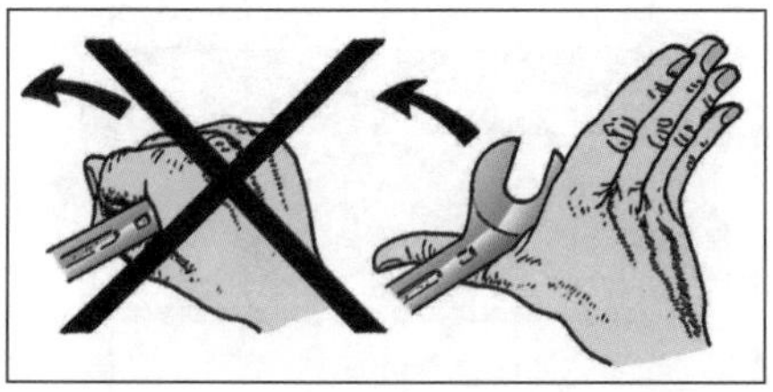

4.6 If you can't pull on the spanner to loosen a fastener, push with your hand open

● Additional leverage is gained by extending the length of the lever. The best way to do this is to use a breaker bar instead of the regular length tool, or to slip a length of tubing over the end of the spanner or socket wrench.

● If additional leverage will not work, the fastener head is either damaged or firmly corroded in place (see *Fasteners*).

5 Bearings

Bearing removal and installation

Drivers and sockets

● Before removing a bearing, always inspect the casing to see which way it must be driven out - some casings will have retaining plates or a cast step. Also check for any identifying markings on the bearing and if installed to a certain depth, measure this at this stage. Some roller bearings are sealed on one side - take note of the original fitted position.

● Bearings can be driven out of a casing using a bearing driver tool (with the correct size head) or a socket of the correct diameter. Select the driver head or socket so that it contacts the outer race of the bearing, not the balls/rollers or inner race. Always support the casing around the bearing housing with wood blocks, otherwise there is a risk of fracture. The bearing is driven out with a few blows on the driver or socket from a heavy mallet. Unless access is severely restricted (as with wheel bearings), a pin-punch is not recommended unless it is moved around the bearing to keep it square in its housing.

● The same equipment can be used to install bearings. Make sure the bearing housing is supported on wood blocks and line up the bearing in its housing. Fit the bearing as noted on removal - generally they are installed with their marked side facing outwards. Tap the bearing squarely into its housing using a driver or socket which bears only on the bearing's outer race - contact with the bearing balls/rollers or inner race will destroy it **(see illustrations 5.1 and 5.2)**.

● Check that the bearing inner race and balls/rollers rotate freely.

5.1 Using a bearing driver against the bearing's outer race

5.2 Using a large socket against the bearing's outer race

Pullers and slide-hammers

● Where a bearing is pressed on a shaft a puller will be required to extract it **(see illustration 5.3)**. Make sure that the puller clamp or legs fit securely behind the bearing and are unlikely to slip out. If pulling a bearing off a gear shaft for example, you may have to locate the puller behind a gear pinion if there is no access to the race and draw the gear pinion off the shaft as well **(see illustration 5.4)**.

5.3 This bearing puller clamps behind the bearing and pressure is applied to the shaft end to draw the bearing off

Caution: Ensure that the puller's centre bolt locates securely against the end of the shaft and will not slip when pressure is applied. Also ensure that puller does not damage the shaft end.

5.4 Where no access is available to the rear of the bearing, it is sometimes possible to draw off the adjacent component

● Operate the puller so that its centre bolt exerts pressure on the shaft end and draws the bearing off the shaft.

● When installing the bearing on the shaft, tap only on the bearing's inner race - contact with the balls/rollers or outer race with destroy the bearing. Use a socket or length of tubing as a drift which fits over the shaft end **(see illustration 5.5)**.

5.5 When installing a bearing on a shaft use a piece of tubing which bears only on the bearing's inner race

● Where a bearing locates in a blind hole in a casing, it cannot be driven or pulled out as described above. A slide-hammer with knife-edged bearing puller attachment will be required. The puller attachment passes through the bearing and when tightened expands to fit firmly behind the bearing **(see illustration 5.6)**. By operating the slide-hammer part of the tool the bearing is jarred out of its housing **(see illustration 5.7)**.

● It is possible, if the bearing is of reasonable weight, for it to drop out of its housing if the casing is heated as described opposite. If this

5.6 Expand the bearing puller so that it locks behind the bearing . . .

5.7 . . . attach the slide hammer to the bearing puller

method is attempted, first prepare a work surface which will enable the casing to be tapped face down to help dislodge the bearing - a wood surface is ideal since it will not damage the casing's gasket surface. Wearing protective gloves, tap the heated casing several times against the work surface to dislodge the bearing under its own weight **(see illustration 5.8)**.

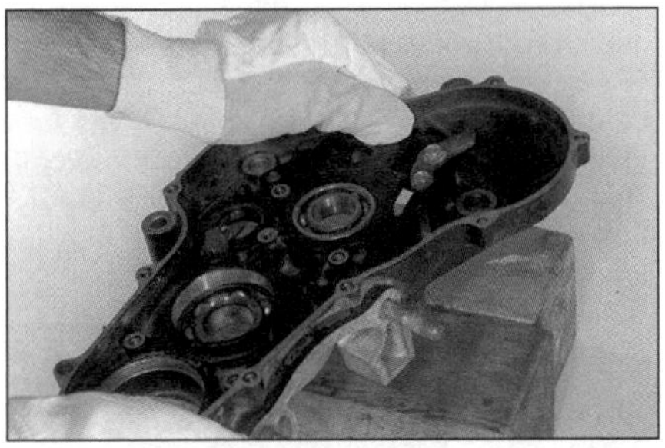

5.8 Tapping a casing face down on wood blocks can often dislodge a bearing

- Bearings can be installed in blind holes using the driver or socket method described above.

Drawbolts

- Where a bearing or bush is set in the eye of a component, such as a suspension linkage arm or connecting rod small-end, removal by drift may damage the component. Furthermore, a rubber bushing in a shock absorber eye cannot successfully be driven out of position. If access is available to a engineering press, the task is straightforward. If not, a drawbolt can be fabricated to extract the bearing or bush.

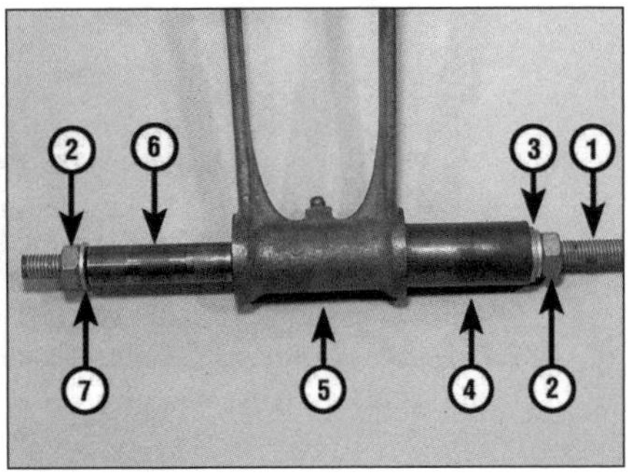

5.9 Drawbolt component parts assembled on a suspension arm

1 Bolt or length of threaded bar
2 Nuts
3 Washer (external diameter greater than tubing internal diameter)
4 Tubing (internal diameter sufficient to accommodate bearing)
5 Suspension arm with bearing
6 Tubing (external diameter slightly smaller than bearing)
7 Washer (external diameter slightly smaller than bearing)

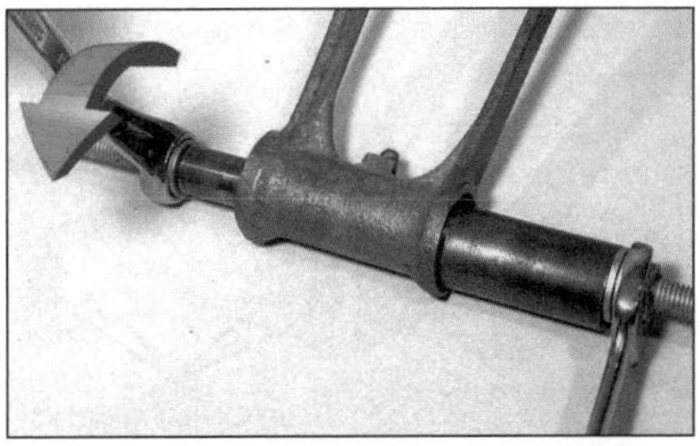

5.10 Drawing the bearing out of the suspension arm

- To extract the bearing/bush you will need a long bolt with nut (or piece of threaded bar with two nuts), a piece of tubing which has an internal diameter larger than the bearing/bush, another piece of tubing which has an external diameter slightly smaller than the bearing/ bush, and a selection of washers **(see illustrations 5.9 and 5.10)**. Note that the pieces of tubing must be of the same length, or longer, than the bearing/bush.
- The same kit (without the pieces of tubing) can be used to draw the new bearing/bush back into place **(see illustration 5.11)**.

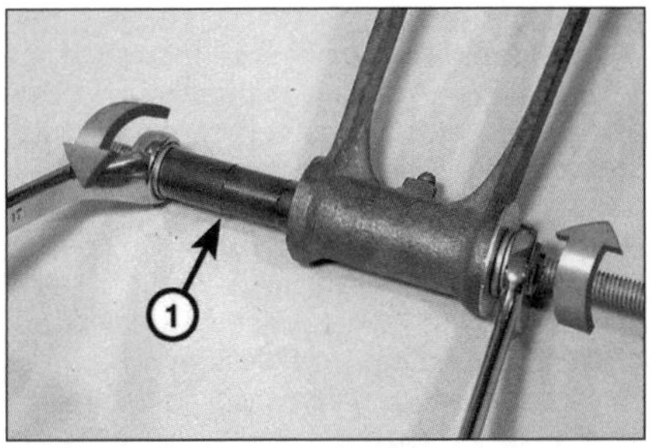

5.11 Installing a new bearing (1) in the suspension arm

Temperature change

- If the bearing's outer race is a tight fit in the casing, the aluminium casing can be heated to release its grip on the bearing. Aluminium will expand at a greater rate than the steel bearing outer race. There are several ways to do this, but avoid any localised extreme heat (such as a blow torch) - aluminium alloy has a low melting point.
- Approved methods of heating a casing are using a domestic oven (heated to 100°C) or immersing the casing in boiling water **(see illustration 5.12)**. Low temperature range localised heat sources such as a paint stripper heat gun or clothes iron can also be used **(see illustration 5.13)**. Alternatively, soak a rag in boiling water, wring it out and wrap it around the bearing housing.

> ***Warning: All of these methods require care in use to prevent scalding and burns to the hands. Wear protective gloves when handling hot components.***

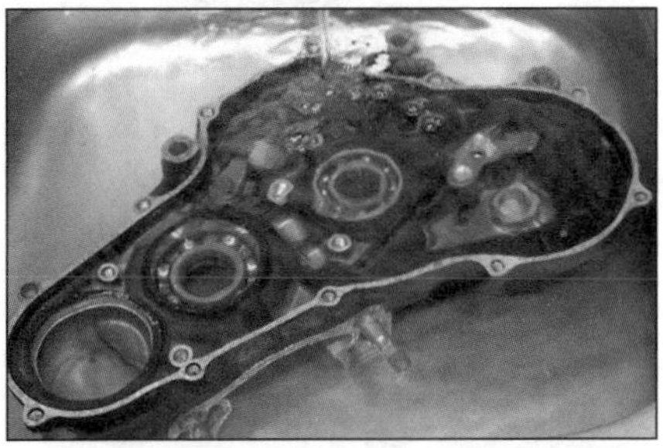

5.12 A casing can be immersed in a sink of boiling water to aid bearing removal

5.13 Using a localised heat source to aid bearing removal

- If heating the whole casing note that plastic components, such as the neutral switch, may suffer - remove them beforehand.
- After heating, remove the bearing as described above. You may find that the expansion is sufficient for the bearing to fall out of the casing under its own weight or with a light tap on the driver or socket.
- If necessary, the casing can be heated to aid bearing installation, and this is sometimes the recommended procedure if the motorcycle manufacturer has designed the housing and bearing fit with this intention.

● Installation of bearings can be eased by placing them in a freezer the night before installation. The steel bearing will contract slightly, allowing easy insertion in its housing. This is often useful when installing steering head outer races in the frame.

Bearing types and markings

● Plain shell bearings, ball bearings, needle roller bearings and tapered roller bearings will all be found on motorcycles **(see illustrations 5.14 and 5.15)**. The ball and roller types are usually caged between an inner and outer race, but uncaged variations may be found.

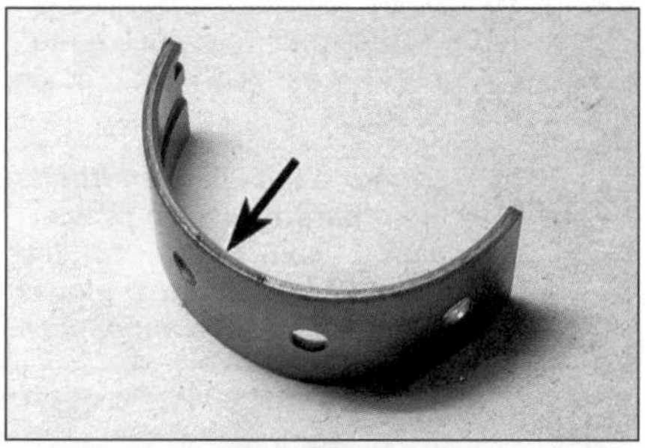

5.14 Shell bearings are either plain or grooved. They are usually identified by colour code (arrow)

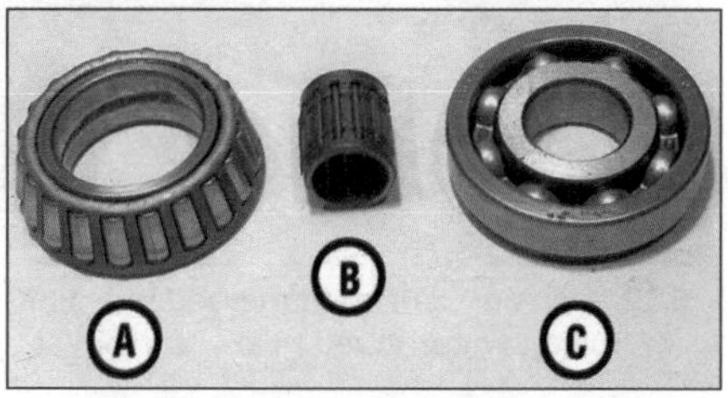

5.15 Tapered roller bearing (A), needle roller bearing (B) and ball journal bearing (C)

● Shell bearings (often called inserts) are usually found at the crankshaft main and connecting rod big-end where they are good at coping with high loads. They are made of a phosphor-bronze material and are impregnated with self-lubricating properties.

● Ball bearings and needle roller bearings consist of a steel inner and outer race with the balls or rollers between the races. They require constant lubrication by oil or grease and are good at coping with axial loads. Taper roller bearings consist of rollers set in a tapered cage set on the inner race; the outer race is separate. They are good at coping with axial loads and prevent movement along the shaft - a typical application is in the steering head.

● Bearing manufacturers produce bearings to ISO size standards and stamp one face of the bearing to indicate its internal and external diameter, load capacity and type **(see illustration 5.16)**.

● Metal bushes are usually of phosphor-bronze material. Rubber bushes are used in suspension mounting eyes. Fibre bushes have also been used in suspension pivots.

5.16 Typical bearing marking

Bearing fault finding

● If a bearing outer race has spun in its housing, the housing material will be damaged. You can use a bearing locking compound to bond the outer race in place if damage is not too severe.

● Shell bearings will fail due to damage of their working surface, as a result of lack of lubrication, corrosion or abrasive particles in the oil **(see illustration 5.17)**. Small particles of dirt in the oil may embed in the bearing material whereas larger particles will score the bearing and shaft journal. If a number of short journeys are made, insufficient heat will be generated to drive off condensation which has built up on the bearings.

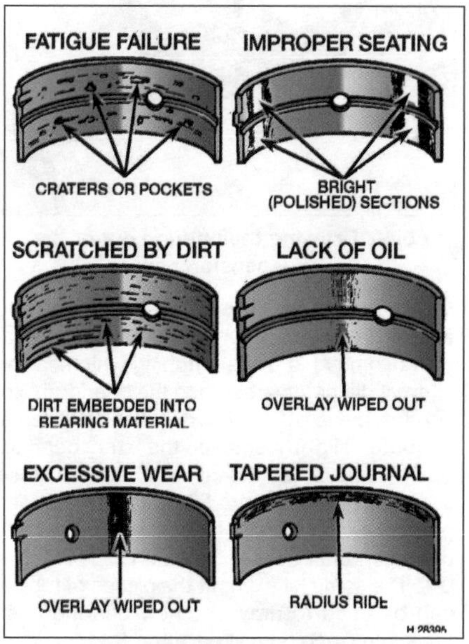

5.17 Typical bearing failures

● Ball and roller bearings will fail due to lack of lubrication or damage to the balls or rollers. Tapered-roller bearings can be damaged by overloading them. Unless the bearing is sealed on both sides, wash it in paraffin (kerosene) to remove all old grease then allow it to dry. Make a visual inspection looking to dented balls or rollers, damaged cages and worn or pitted races **(see illustration 5.18)**.

● A ball bearing can be checked for wear by listening to it when spun. Apply a film of light oil to the bearing and hold it close to the ear - hold the outer race with one hand and spin the inner race with the other hand **(see illustration 5.19)**. The bearing should be almost silent when spun; if it grates or rattles it is worn.

5.18 Example of ball journal bearing with damaged balls and cages

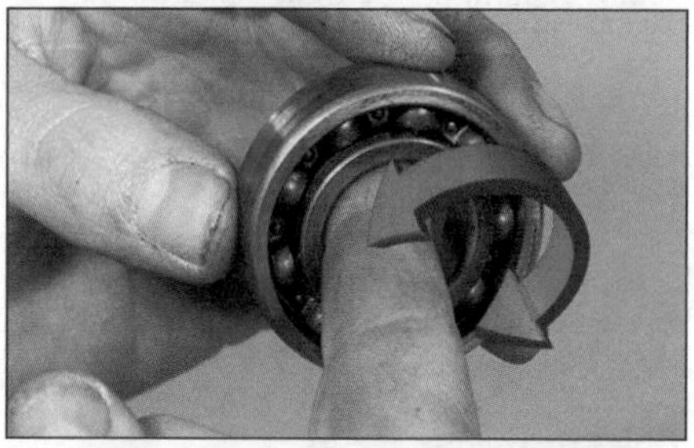

5.19 Hold outer race and listen to inner race when spun

6 Oil seals

Oil seal removal and installation

● Oil seals should be renewed every time a component is dismantled. This is because the seal lips will become set to the sealing surface and will not necessarily reseal.

● Oil seals can be prised out of position using a large flat-bladed screwdriver **(see illustration 6.1)**. In the case of crankcase seals, check first that the seal is not lipped on the inside, preventing its removal with the crankcases joined.

6.1 Prise out oil seals with a large flat-bladed screwdriver

● New seals are usually installed with their marked face (containing the seal reference code) outwards and the spring side towards the fluid being retained. In certain cases, such as a two-stroke engine crankshaft seal, a double lipped seal may be used due to there being fluid or gas on each side of the joint.

● Use a bearing driver or socket which bears only on the outer hard edge of the seal to install it in the casing - tapping on the inner edge will damage the sealing lip.

Oil seal types and markings

● Oil seals are usually of the single-lipped type. Double-lipped seals are found where a liquid or gas is on both sides of the joint.

● Oil seals can harden and lose their sealing ability if the motorcycle has been in storage for a long period - renewal is the only solution.

● Oil seal manufacturers also conform to the ISO markings for seal size - these are moulded into the outer face of the seal **(see illustration 6.2)**.

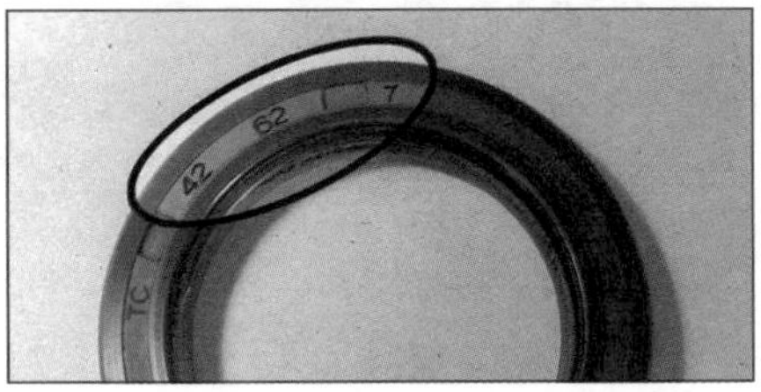

6.2 These oil seal markings indicate inside diameter, outside diameter and seal thickness

7 Gaskets and sealants

Types of gasket and sealant

● Gaskets are used to seal the mating surfaces between components and keep lubricants, fluids, vacuum or pressure contained within the assembly. Aluminium gaskets are sometimes found at the cylinder joints, but most gaskets are paper-based. If the mating surfaces of the components being joined are undamaged the gasket can be installed dry, although a dab of sealant or grease will be useful to hold it in place during assembly.

● RTV (Room Temperature Vulcanising) silicone rubber sealants cure when exposed to moisture in the atmosphere. These sealants are good at filling pits or irregular gasket faces, but will tend to be forced out of the joint under very high torque. They can be used to replace a paper gasket, but first make sure that the width of the paper gasket is not essential to the shimming of internal components. RTV sealants should not be used on components containing petrol (gasoline).

● Non-hardening, semi-hardening and hard setting liquid gasket compounds can be used with a gasket or between a metal-to-metal joint. Select the sealant to suit the application: universal non-hardening sealant can be used on virtually all joints; semi-hardening on joint faces which are rough or damaged; hard setting sealant on joints which require a permanent bond and are subjected to high temperature and pressure. **Note:** *Check first if the paper gasket has a bead of sealant impregnated in its surface before applying additional sealant.*

● When choosing a sealant, make sure it is suitable for the application, particularly if being applied in a high-temperature area or in the vicinity of fuel. Certain manufacturers produce sealants in either clear, silver or black colours to match the finish of the engine. This has a particular application on motorcycles where much of the engine is exposed.

● Do not over-apply sealant. That which is squeezed out on the outside of the joint can be wiped off, whereas an excess of sealant on the inside can break off and clog oilways.

Breaking a sealed joint

● Age, heat, pressure and the use of hard setting sealant can cause two components to stick together so tightly that they are difficult to separate using finger pressure alone. Do not resort to using levers unless there is a pry point provided for this purpose **(see illustration 7.1)** or else the gasket surfaces will be damaged.

● Use a soft-faced hammer **(see illustration 7.2)** or a wood block and conventional hammer to strike the component near the mating surface. Avoid hammering against cast extremities since they may break off. If this method fails, try using a wood wedge between the two components.

Caution: If the joint will not separate, double-check that you have removed all the fasteners.

7.1 If a pry point is provided, apply gently pressure with a flat-bladed screwdriver

7.2 Tap around the joint with a soft-faced mallet if necessary - don't strike cooling fins

Removal of old gasket and sealant

● Paper gaskets will most likely come away complete, leaving only a few traces stuck on

Most components have one or two hollow locating dowels between the two gasket faces. If a dowel cannot be removed, do not resort to gripping it with pliers - it will almost certainly be distorted. Install a close-fitting socket or Phillips screwdriver into the dowel and then grip the outer edge of the dowel to free it.

the sealing faces of the components. It is imperative that all traces are removed to ensure correct sealing of the new gasket.

● Very carefully scrape all traces of gasket away making sure that the sealing surfaces are not gouged or scored by the scraper **(see illustrations 7.3, 7.4 and 7.5)**. Stubborn deposits can be removed by spraying with an aerosol gasket remover. Final preparation of

7.3 Paper gaskets can be scraped off with a gasket scraper tool . . .

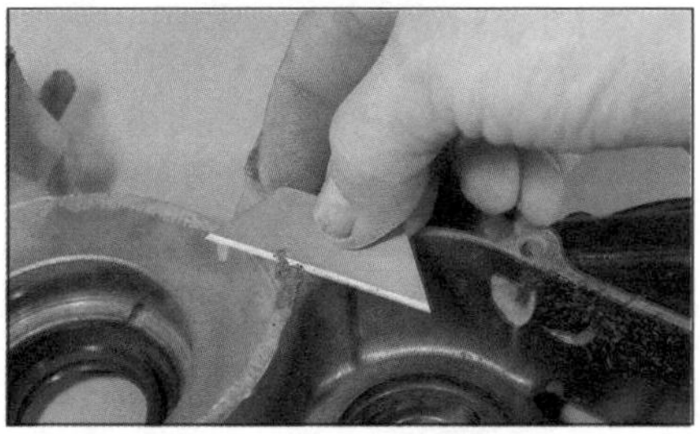

7.4 . . . a knife blade . . .

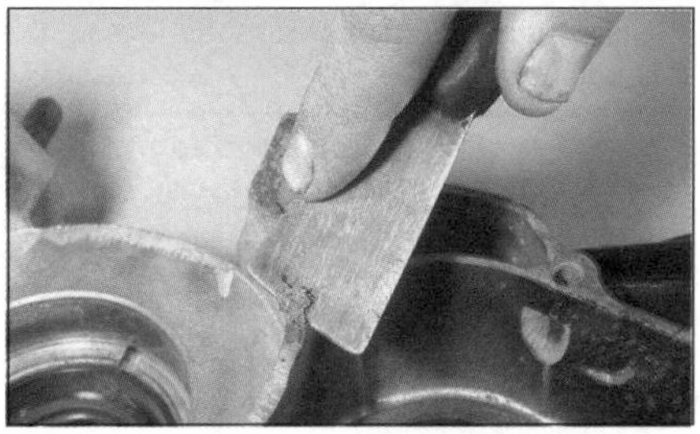

7.5 . . . or a household scraper

7.6 Fine abrasive paper is wrapped around a flat file to clean up the gasket face

7.7 A kitchen scourer can be used on stubborn deposits

the gasket surface can be made with very fine abrasive paper or a plastic kitchen scourer **(see illustrations 7.6 and 7.7)**.

- Old sealant can be scraped or peeled off components, depending on the type originally used. Note that gasket removal compounds are available to avoid scraping the components clean; make sure the gasket remover suits the type of sealant used.

8 Chains

Breaking and joining final drive chains

- Drive chains for all but small bikes are continuous and do not have a clip-type connecting link. The chain must be broken using a chain breaker tool and the new chain securely riveted together using a new soft rivet-type link. Never use a clip-type connecting link instead of a rivet-type link, except in an emergency. Various chain breaking and riveting tools are available, either as separate tools or combined as illustrated in the accompanying photographs - read the instructions supplied with the tool carefully.

Warning: The need to rivet the new link pins correctly cannot be overstressed - loss of control of the motorcycle is very likely to result if the chain breaks in use.

- Rotate the chain and look for the soft link. The soft link pins look like they have been deeply centre-punched instead of peened over like all the other pins **(see illustration 8.9)** and its sideplate may be a different colour. Position the soft link midway between the sprockets and assemble the chain breaker tool over one of the soft link pins **(see illustration 8.1)**. Operate the tool to push the pin out through the chain **(see illustration 8.2)**. On an O-ring chain, remove the O-rings **(see illustration 8.3)**. Carry out the same procedure on the other soft link pin.

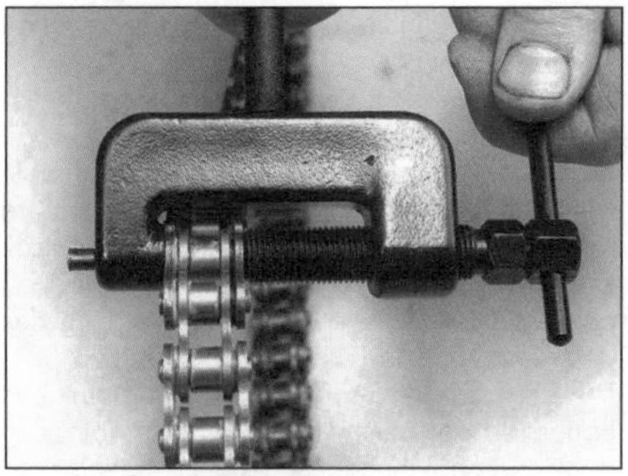

8.1 Tighten the chain breaker to push the pin out of the link . . .

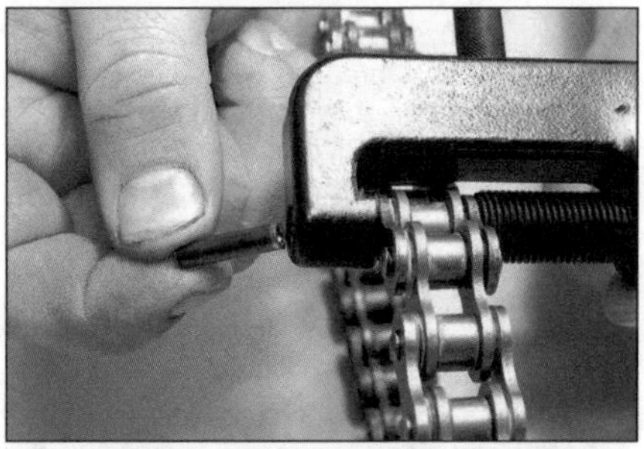

8.2 . . . withdraw the pin, remove the tool . . .

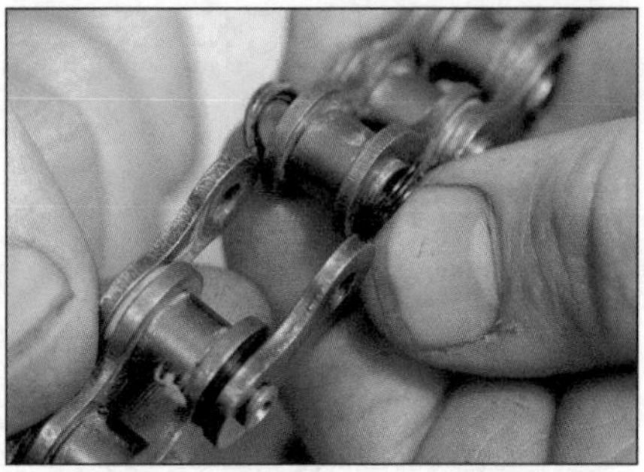

8.3 . . . and separate the chain link

Caution: Certain soft link pins (particularly on the larger chains) may require their ends to be filed or ground off before they can be pressed out using the tool.

- Check that you have the correct size and strength (standard or heavy duty) new soft link - do not reuse the old link. Look for the size marking on the chain sideplates **(see illustration 8.10)**.
- Position the chain ends so that they are engaged over the rear sprocket. On an O-ring chain, install a new O-ring over each pin of the link and insert the link through the two chain ends **(see illustration 8.4)**. Install a new O-ring over the end of each pin, followed by the sideplate (with the chain manufacturer's marking facing outwards) **(see illustrations 8.5 and 8.6)**. On an unsealed chain, insert the link through the two chain ends, then install the sideplate with the chain manufacturer's marking facing outwards.

8.4 Insert the new soft link, with O-rings, through the chain ends . . .

8.5 . . . install the O-rings over the pin ends . . .

8.6 . . . followed by the sideplate

- Note that it may not be possible to install the sideplate using finger pressure alone. If using a joining tool, assemble it so that the plates of the tool clamp the link and press the sideplate over the pins **(see illustration 8.7)**. Otherwise, use two small sockets placed over

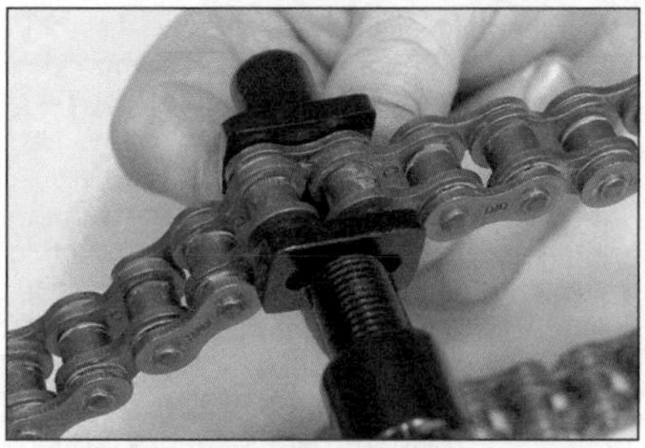

8.7 Push the sideplate into position using a clamp

8.8 Assemble the chain riveting tool over one pin at a time and tighten it fully

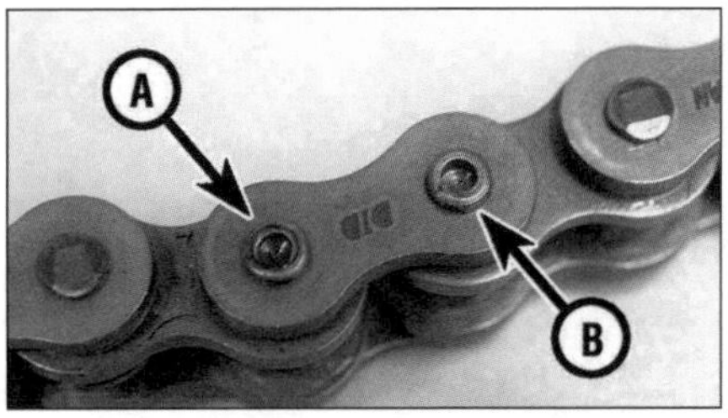

8.9 Pin end correctly riveted (A), pin end unriveted (B)

the rivet ends and two pieces of the wood between a G-clamp. Operate the clamp to press the sideplate over the pins.

- Assemble the joining tool over one pin (following the maker's instructions) and tighten the tool down to spread the pin end securely **(see illustrations 8.8 and 8.9)**. Do the same on the other pin.

> ***Warning: Check that the pin ends are secure and that there is no danger of the sideplate coming loose. If the pin ends are cracked the soft link must be renewed.***

Final drive chain sizing

- Chains are sized using a three digit number, followed by a suffix to denote the chain type **(see illustration 8.10)**. Chain type is either standard or heavy duty (thicker sideplates), and also unsealed or O-ring/X-ring type.
- The first digit of the number relates to the pitch of the chain, ie the distance from the centre of one pin to the centre of the next pin **(see illustration 8.11)**. Pitch is expressed in eighths of an inch, as follows:

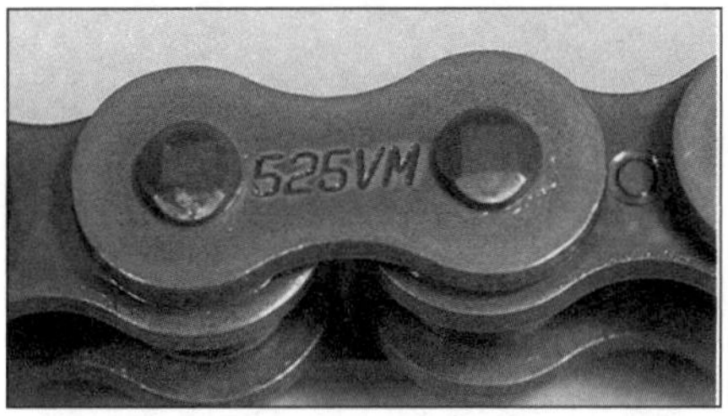

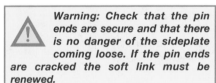

8.10 Typical chain size and type marking

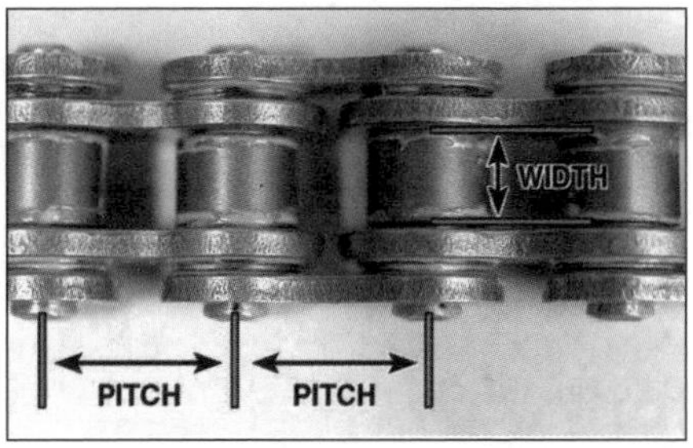

8.11 Chain dimensions

Sizes commencing with a 4 (eg 428) have a pitch of 1/2 inch (12.7 mm)

Sizes commencing with a 5 (eg 520) have a pitch of 5/8 inch (15.9 mm)

Sizes commencing with a 6 (eg 630) have a pitch of 3/4 inch (19.1 mm)

- The second and third digits of the chain size relate to the width of the rollers, again in imperial units, eg the 525 shown has 5/16 inch (7.94 mm) rollers **(see illustration 8.11)**.

9 Hoses

Clamping to prevent flow

- Small-bore flexible hoses can be clamped to prevent fluid flow whilst a component is worked on. Whichever method is used, ensure that the hose material is not permanently distorted or damaged by the clamp.

*a) A brake hose clamp available from auto accessory shops **(see illustration 9.1)**.*
*b) A wingnut type hose clamp **(see illustration 9.2)**.*

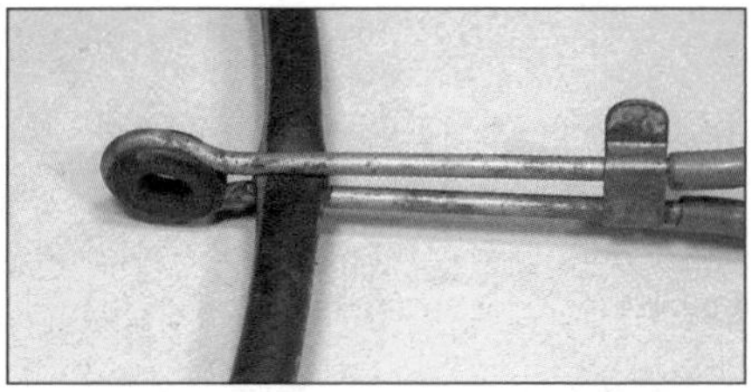

9.1 Hoses can be clamped with an automotive brake hose clamp . . .

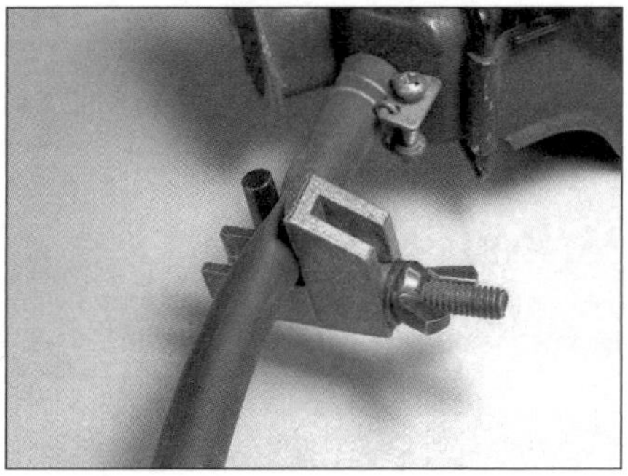

9.2 . . . a wingnut type hose clamp . . .

*c) Two sockets placed each side of the hose and held with straight-jawed self-locking grips **(see illustration 9.3)**.*
*d) Thick card each side of the hose held between straight-jawed self-locking grips **(see illustration 9.4)**.*

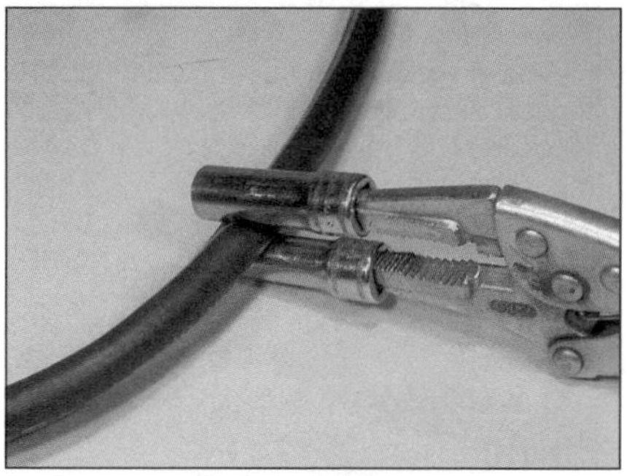

9.3 . . . two sockets and a pair of self-locking grips . . .

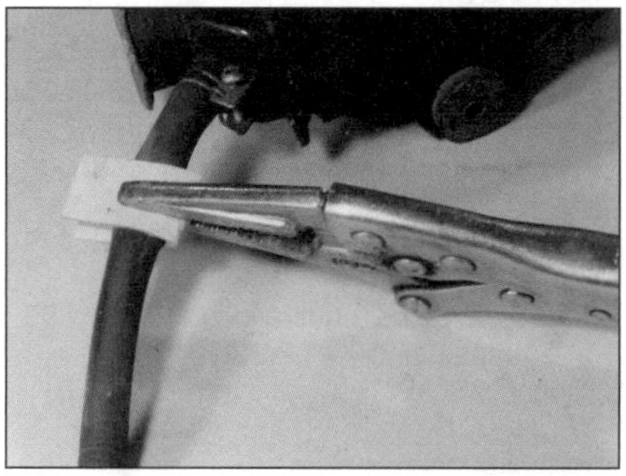

9.4 . . . or thick card and self-locking grips

Freeing and fitting hoses

- Always make sure the hose clamp is moved well clear of the hose end. Grip the hose with your hand and rotate it whilst pulling it off the union. If the hose has hardened due to age and will not move, slit it with a sharp knife and peel its ends off the union **(see illustration 9.5)**.
- Resist the temptation to use grease or soap on the unions to aid installation; although it helps the hose slip over the union it will equally aid the escape of fluid from the joint. It is preferable to soften the hose ends in hot water and wet the inside surface of the hose with water or a fluid which will evaporate.

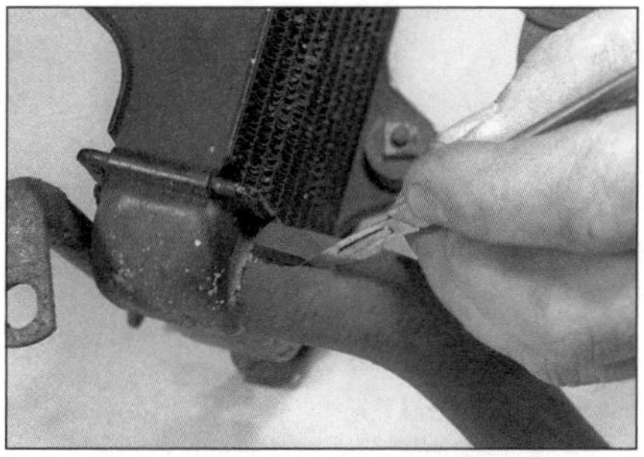

9.5 Cutting a coolant hose free with a sharp knife

Conversion Factors

Length (distance)

Inches (in)	x 25.4	= Millimetres (mm)	x 0.0394	= Inches (in)
Feet (ft)	x 0.305	= Metres (m)	x 3.281	= Feet (ft)
Miles	x 1.609	= Kilometres (km)	x 0.621	= Miles

Volume (capacity)

Cubic inches (cu in; in³)	x 16.387	= Cubic centimetres (cc; cm³)	x 0.061	= Cubic inches (cu in; in³)
Imperial pints (Imp pt)	x 0.568	= Litres (l)	x 1.76	= Imperial pints (Imp pt)
Imperial quarts (Imp qt)	x 1.137	= Litres (l)	x 0.88	= Imperial quarts (Imp qt)
Imperial quarts (Imp qt)	x 1.201	= US quarts (US qt)	x 0.833	= Imperial quarts (Imp qt)
US quarts (US qt)	x 0.946	= Litres (l)	x 1.057	= US quarts (US qt)
Imperial gallons (Imp gal)	x 4.546	= Litres (l)	x 0.22	= Imperial gallons (Imp gal)
Imperial gallons (Imp gal)	x 1.201	= US gallons (US gal)	x 0.833	= Imperial gallons (Imp gal)
US gallons (US gal)	x 3.785	= Litres (l)	x 0.264	= US gallons (US gal)

Mass (weight)

Ounces (oz)	x 28.35	= Grams (g)	x 0.035	= Ounces (oz)
Pounds (lb)	x 0.454	= Kilograms (kg)	x 2.205	= Pounds (lb)

Force

Ounces-force (ozf; oz)	x 0.278	= Newtons (N)	x 3.6	= Ounces-force (ozf; oz)
Pounds-force (lbf; lb)	x 4.448	= Newtons (N)	x 0.225	= Pounds-force (lbf; lb)
Newtons (N)	x 0.1	= Kilograms-force (kgf; kg)	x 9.81	= Newtons (N)

Pressure

Pounds-force per square inch (psi; lbf/in²; lb/in²)	x 0.070	= Kilograms-force per square centimetre (kgf/cm²; kg/cm²)	x 14.223	= Pounds-force per square inch (psi; lbf/in²; lb/in²)
Pounds-force per square inch (psi; lbf/in²; lb/in²)	x 0.068	= Atmospheres (atm)	x 14.696	= Pounds-force per square inch (psi; lbf/in²; lb/in²)
Pounds-force per square inch (psi; lbf/in²; lb/in²)	x 0.069	= Bars	x 14.5	= Pounds-force per square inch (psi; lbf/in²; lb/in²)
Pounds-force per square inch (psi; lbf/in²; lb/in²)	x 6.895	= Kilopascals (kPa)	x 0.145	= Pounds-force per square inch (psi; lbf/in²; lb/in²)
Kilopascals (kPa)	x 0.01	= Kilograms-force per square centimetre (kgf/cm²; kg/cm²)	x 98.1	= Kilopascals (kPa)
Millibar (mbar)	x 100	= Pascals (Pa)	x 0.01	= Millibar (mbar)
Millibar (mbar)	x 0.0145	= Pounds-force per square inch (psi; lbf/in²; lb/in²)	x 68.947	= Millibar (mbar)
Millibar (mbar)	x 0.75	= Millimetres of mercury (mmHg)	x 1.333	= Millibar (mbar)
Millibar (mbar)	x 0.401	= Inches of water (inH_2O)	x 2.491	= Millibar (mbar)
Millimetres of mercury (mmHg)	x 0.535	= Inches of water (inH_2O)	x 1.868	= Millimetres of mercury (mmHg)
Inches of water (inH_2O)	x 0.036	= Pounds-force per square inch (psi; lbf/in²; lb/in²)	x 27.68	= Inches of water (inH_2O)

Torque (moment of force)

Pounds-force inches (lbf in; lb in)	x 1.152	= Kilograms-force centimetre (kgf cm; kg cm)	x 0.868	= Pounds-force inches (lbf in; lb in)
Pounds-force inches (lbf in; lb in)	x 0.113	= Newton metres (Nm)	x 8.85	= Pounds-force inches (lbf in; lb in)
Pounds-force inches (lbf in; lb in)	x 0.083	= Pounds-force feet (lbf ft; lb ft)	x 12	= Pounds-force inches (lbf in; lb in)
Pounds-force feet (lbf ft; lb ft)	x 0.138	= Kilograms-force metres (kgf m; kg m)	x 7.233	= Pounds-force feet (lbf ft; lb ft)
Pounds-force feet (lbf ft; lb ft)	x 1.356	= Newton metres (Nm)	x 0.738	= Pounds-force feet (lbf ft; lb ft)
Newton metres (Nm)	x 0.102	= Kilograms-force metres (kgf m; kg m)	x 9.804	= Newton metres (Nm)

Power

Horsepower (hp)	x 745.7	= Watts (W)	x 0.0013	= Horsepower (hp)

Velocity (speed)

Miles per hour (miles/hr; mph)	x 1.609	= Kilometres per hour (km/hr; kph)	x 0.621	= Miles per hour (miles/hr; mph)

Fuel consumption*

Miles per gallon (mpg)	x 0.354	= Kilometres per litre (km/l)	x 2.825	= Miles per gallon (mpg)

Temperature

Degrees Fahrenheit = (°C x 1.8) + 32   Degrees Celsius (Degrees Centigrade; °C) = (°F - 32) x 0.56

** It is common practice to convert from miles per gallon (mpg) to litres/100 kilometres (l/100km), where mpg x l/100 km = 282*

Motorcycle Chemicals and Lubricants

A number of chemicals and lubricants are available for use in motorcycle maintenance and repair. They include a wide variety of products ranging from cleaning solvents and degreasers to lubricants and protective sprays for rubber, plastic and vinyl.

- **Contact point/spark plug cleaner** is a solvent used to clean oily film and dirt from points, grime from electrical connectors and oil deposits from spark plugs. It is oil free and leaves no residue. It can also be used to remove gum and varnish from carburettor jets and other orifices.
- **Carburettor cleaner** is similar to contact point/spark plug cleaner but it usually has a stronger solvent and may leave a slight oily reside. It is not recommended for cleaning electrical components or connections.
- **Brake system cleaner** is used to remove grease or brake fluid from brake system components (where clean surfaces are absolutely necessary and petroleum-based solvents cannot be used); it also leaves no residue.
- **Silicone-based lubricants** are used to protect rubber parts such as hoses and grommets, and are used as lubricants for hinges and locks.
- **Multi-purpose grease** is an all purpose lubricant used wherever grease is more practical than a liquid lubricant such as oil. Some multi-purpose grease is coloured white and specially formulated to be more resistant to water than ordinary grease.
- **Gear oil** (sometimes called gear lube) is a specially designed oil used in transmissions and final drive units, as well as other areas where high friction, high temperature lubrication is required. It is available in a number of viscosities (weights) for various applications.
- **Motor oil**, of course, is the lubricant specially formulated for use in the engine. It normally contains a wide variety of additives to prevent corrosion and reduce foaming and wear. Motor oil comes in various weights (viscosity ratings) of from 5 to 80. The recommended weight of the oil depends on the seasonal temperature and the demands on the engine. Light oil is used in cold climates and under light load conditions; heavy oil is used in hot climates and where high loads are encountered. Multi-viscosity oils are designed to have characteristics of both light and heavy oils and are available in a number of weights from 5W-20 to 20W-50.
- **Petrol additives** perform several functions, depending on their chemical makeup. They usually contain solvents that help dissolve gum and varnish that build up on carburettor and inlet parts. They also serve to break down carbon deposits that form on the inside surfaces of the combustion chambers. Some additives contain upper cylinder lubricants for valves and piston rings.
- **Brake and clutch fluid** is a specially formulated hydraulic fluid that can withstand the heat and pressure encountered in brake/clutch systems. Care must be taken that this fluid does not come in contact with painted surfaces or plastics. An opened container should always be resealed to prevent contamination by water or dirt.
- **Chain lubricants** are formulated especially for use on motorcycle final drive chains. A good chain lube should adhere well and have good penetrating qualities to be effective as a lubricant inside the chain and on the side plates, pins and rollers. Most chain lubes are either the foaming type or quick drying type and are usually marketed as sprays. Take care to use a lubricant marked as being suitable for O-ring chains.
- **Degreasers** are heavy duty solvents used to remove grease and grime that may accumulate on engine and frame components. They can be sprayed or brushed on and, depending on the type, are rinsed with either water or solvent.
- **Solvents** are used alone or in combination with degreasers to clean parts and assemblies during repair and overhaul. The home mechanic should use only solvents that are non-flammable and that do not produce irritating fumes.
- **Gasket sealing compounds** may be used in conjunction with gaskets, to improve their sealing capabilities, or alone, to seal metal-to-metal joints. Many gasket sealers can withstand extreme heat, some are impervious to petrol and lubricants, while others are capable of filling and sealing large cavities. Depending on the intended use, gasket sealers either dry hard or stay relatively soft and pliable. They are usually applied by hand, with a brush, or are sprayed on the gasket sealing surfaces.
- **Thread locking compound** is an adhesive locking compound that prevents threaded fasteners from loosening because of vibration. It is available in a variety of types for different applications.
- **Moisture dispersants** are usually sprays that can be used to dry out electrical components such as the fuse block and wiring connectors. Some types can also be used as treatment for rubber and as a lubricant for hinges, cables and locks.
- **Waxes and polishes** are used to help protect painted and plated surfaces from the weather. Different types of paint may require the use of different types of wax polish. Some polishes utilise a chemical or abrasive cleaner to help remove the top layer of oxidised (dull) paint on older vehicles. In recent years, many non-wax polishes (that contain a wide variety of chemicals such as polymers and silicones) have been introduced. These non-wax polishes are usually easier to apply and last longer than conventional waxes and polishes.

About the MOT Test

In the UK, all vehicles more than three years old are subject to an annual test to ensure that they meet minimum safety requirements. A current test certificate must be issued before a machine can be used on public roads, and is required before a road fund licence can be issued. Riding without a current test certificate will also invalidate your insurance.

For most owners, the MOT test is an annual cause for anxiety, and this is largely due to owners not being sure what needs to be checked prior to submitting the motorcycle for testing. The simple answer is that a fully roadworthy motorcycle will have no difficulty in passing the test.

This is a guide to getting your motorcycle through the MOT test. Obviously it will not be possible to examine the motorcycle to the same standard as the professional MOT tester, particularly in view of the equipment required for some of the checks. However, working through the following procedures will enable you to identify any problem areas before submitting the motorcycle for the test.

It has only been possible to summarise the test requirements here, based on the regulations in force at the time of printing. Test standards are becoming increasingly stringent, although there are some exemptions for older vehicles. More information about the MOT test can be obtained from the TSO publications, *How Safe is your Motorcycle* and *The MOT Inspection Manual for Motorcycle Testing*.

Many of the checks require that one of the wheels is raised off the ground. If the motorcycle doesn't have a centre stand, note that an auxiliary stand will be required. Additionally, the help of an assistant may prove useful.

Certain exceptions apply to machines under 50 cc, machines without a lighting system, and Classic bikes - if in doubt about any of the requirements listed below seek confirmation from an MOT tester prior to submitting the motorcycle for the test.

Check that the frame number is clearly visible.

HAYNES HiNT ***If a component is in borderline condition, the tester has discretion in deciding whether to pass or fail it. If the motorcycle presented is clean and evidently well cared for, the tester may be more inclined to pass a borderline component than if the motorcycle is scruffy and apparently neglected.***

Electrical System

Lights, turn signals, horn and reflector

✔ With the ignition on, check the operation of the following electrical components. **Note:** *The electrical components on certain small-capacity machines are powered by the generator, requiring that the engine is run for this check.*

a) Headlight and tail light. Check that both illuminate in the low and high beam switch positions.

b) Position lights. Check that the front position (or sidelight) and tail light illuminate in this switch position.

c) Turn signals. Check that all flash at the correct rate, and that the warning light(s) function correctly. Check that the turn signal switch works correctly.

c) Hazard warning system (where fitted). Check that all four turn signals flash in this switch position.

d) Brake stop light. Check that the light comes on when the front and rear brakes are independently applied. Models first used on or after 1st April 1986 must have a brake light switch on each brake.

e) Horn. Check that the sound is continuous and of reasonable volume.

✔ Check that there is a red reflector on the rear of the machine, either mounted separately or as part of the tail light lens.

✔ Check the condition of the headlight, tail light and turn signal lenses.

Headlight beam height

✔ The MOT tester will perform a headlight beam height check using specialised beam setting equipment **(see illustration 1)**. This equipment will not be available to the home mechanic, but if you suspect that the headlight is incorrectly set or may have been maladjusted in the past, you can perform a rough test as follows.

✔ Position the bike in a straight line facing a brick wall. The bike must be off its stand, upright and with a rider seated. Measure the height from the ground to the centre of the headlight and mark a horizontal line on the wall at this height. Position the motorcycle 3.8 metres from the wall and draw a vertical line up the wall central to the centreline of the motorcycle. Switch to dipped beam and check that the beam pattern falls slightly lower than the horizontal line and to the left of the vertical line **(see illustration 2)**.

1

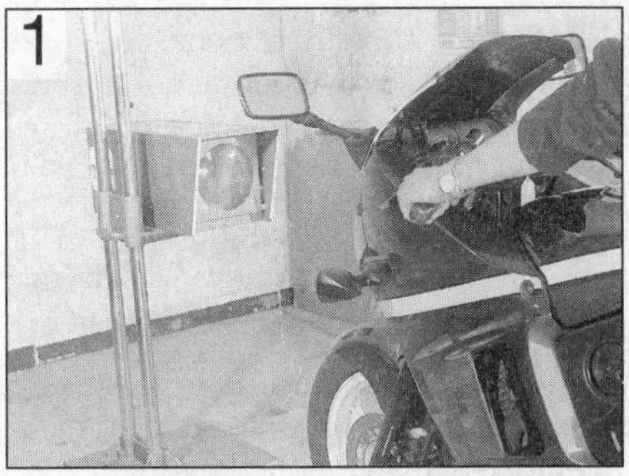

Headlight beam height checking equipment

2

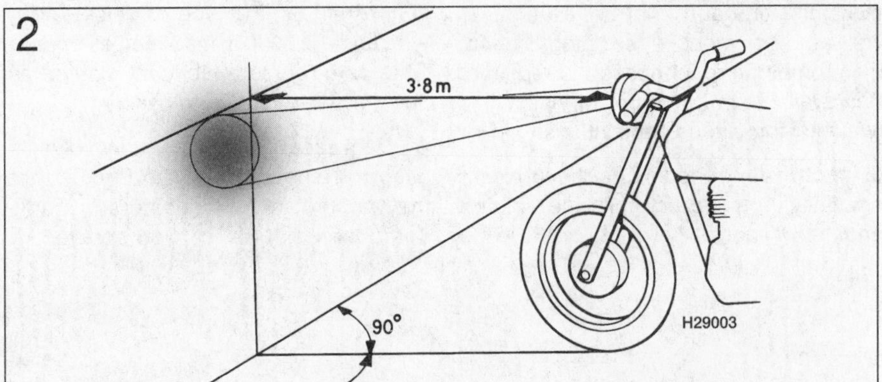

Home workshop beam alignment check

Exhaust System and Final Drive

Exhaust

✔ Check that the exhaust mountings are secure and that the system does not foul any of the rear suspension components.

✔ Start the motorcycle. When the revs are increased, check that the exhaust is neither holed nor leaking from any of its joints. On a linked system, check that the collector box is not leaking due to corrosion.

✔ Note that the exhaust decibel level ("loudness" of the exhaust) is assessed at the discretion of the tester. If the motorcycle was first used on or after 1st January 1985 the silencer must carry the BSAU 193 stamp, or a marking relating to its make and model, or be of OE (original equipment) manufacture. If the silencer is marked NOT FOR ROAD USE, RACING USE ONLY or similar, it will fail the MOT.

Final drive

✔ On chain or belt drive machines, check that the chain/belt is in good condition and does not have excessive slack. Also check that the sprocket is securely mounted on the rear wheel hub. Check that the chain/belt guard is in place.

✔ On shaft drive bikes, check for oil leaking from the drive unit and fouling the rear tyre.

Steering and Suspension

Steering

✔ With the front wheel raised off the ground, rotate the steering from lock to lock. The handlebar or switches must not contact the fuel tank or be close enough to trap the rider's hand. Problems can be caused by damaged lock stops on the lower yoke and frame, or by the fitting of non-standard handlebars.

✔ When performing the lock to lock check, also ensure that the steering moves freely without drag or notchiness. Steering movement can be impaired by poorly routed cables, or by overtight head bearings or worn bearings. The tester will perform a check of the steering head bearing lower race by mounting the front wheel on a surface plate, then performing a lock to lock check with the weight of the machine on the lower bearing **(see illustration 3)**.

✔ Grasp the fork sliders (lower legs) and attempt to push and pull on the forks **(see illustration 4)**. Any play in the steering head bearings will be felt. Note that in extreme cases, wear of the front fork bushes can be misinterpreted for head bearing play.

Front wheel mounted on a surface plate for steering head bearing lower race check

✔ Check that the handlebars are securely mounted.

✔ Check that the handlebar grip rubbers are secure. They should by bonded to the bar left end and to the throttle cable pulley on the right end.

Front suspension

✔ With the motorcycle off the stand, hold the front brake on and pump the front forks up and down **(see illustration 5)**. Check that they are adequately damped.

Checking the steering head bearings for freeplay

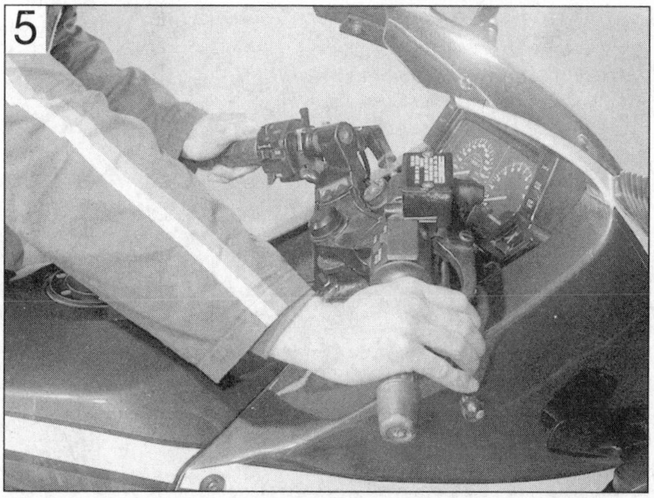

Hold the front brake on and pump the front forks up and down to check operation

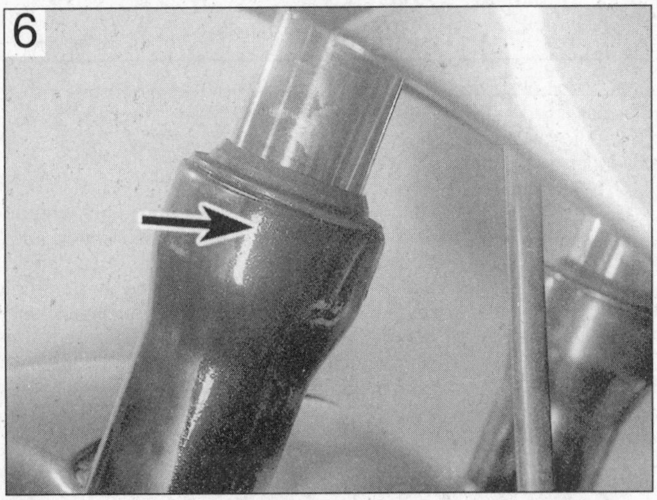

Inspect the area around the fork dust seal for oil leakage (arrow)

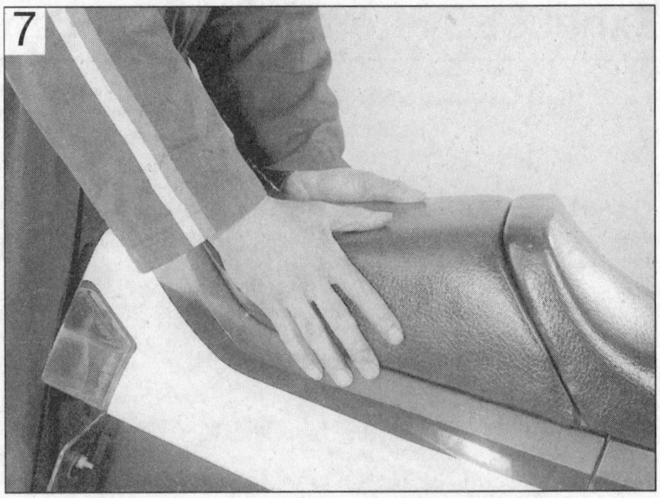

Bounce the rear of the motorcycle to check rear suspension operation

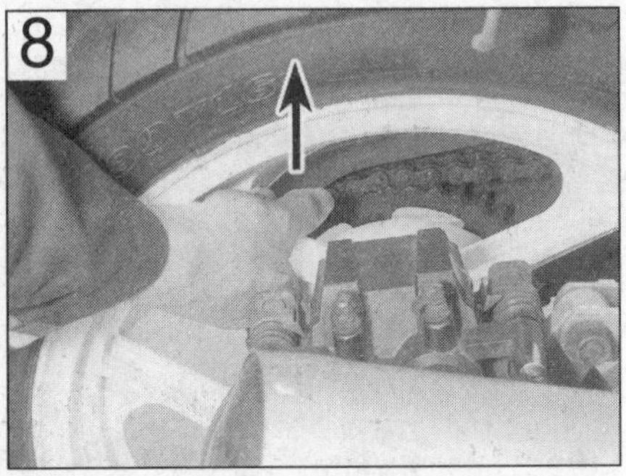

Checking for rear suspension linkage play

✔ Inspect the area above and around the front fork oil seals **(see illustration 6)**. There should be no sign of oil on the fork tube (stanchion) nor leaking down the slider (lower leg). On models so equipped, check that there is no oil leaking from the anti-dive units.

✔ On models with swingarm front suspension, check that there is no freeplay in the linkage when moved from side to side.

Rear suspension

✔ With the motorcycle off the stand and an assistant supporting the motorcycle by its handlebars, bounce the rear suspension **(see illustration 7)**. Check that the suspension components do not foul on any of the cycle parts and check that the shock absorber(s) provide adequate damping.

✔ Visually inspect the shock absorber(s) and check that there is no sign of oil leakage from its damper. This is somewhat restricted on certain single shock models due to the location of the shock absorber.

✔ With the rear wheel raised off the ground, grasp the wheel at the highest point and attempt to pull it up **(see illustration 8)**. Any play in the swingarm pivot or suspension linkage bearings will be felt as movement. **Note:** *Do not confuse play with actual suspension movement.* Failure to lubricate suspension linkage bearings can lead to bearing failure **(see illustration 9)**.

✔ With the rear wheel raised off the ground, grasp the swingarm ends and attempt to move the swingarm from side to side and forwards and backwards - any play indicates wear of the swingarm pivot bearings **(see illustration 10)**.

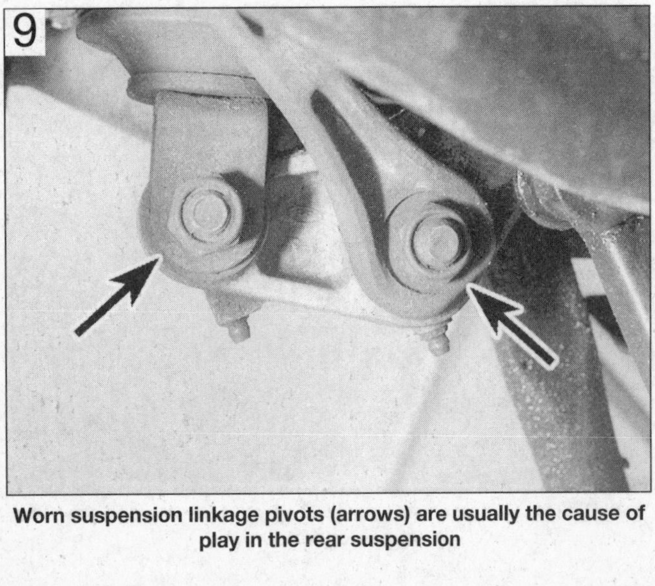

Worn suspension linkage pivots (arrows) are usually the cause of play in the rear suspension

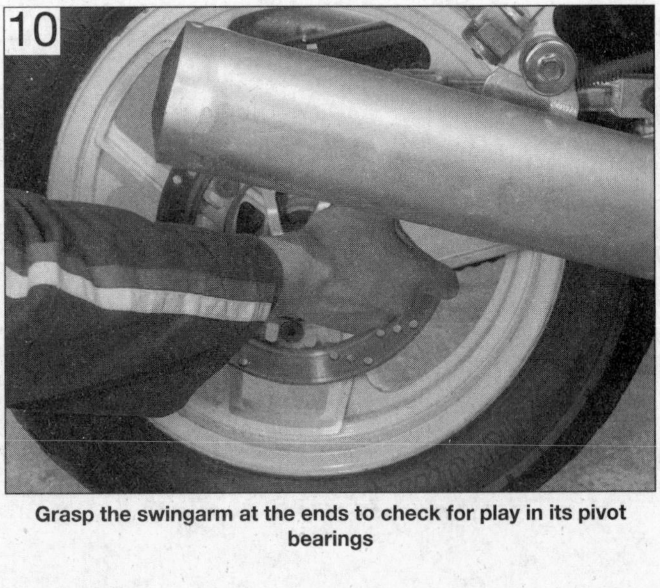

Grasp the swingarm at the ends to check for play in its pivot bearings

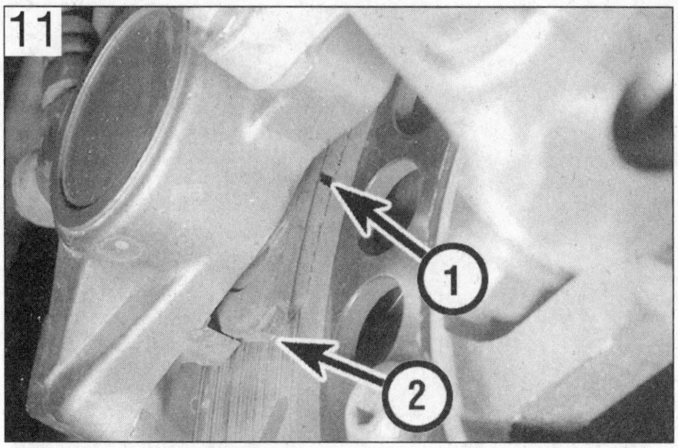

Brake pad wear can usually be viewed without removing the caliper. Most pads have wear indicator grooves (1) and some also have indicator tangs (2)

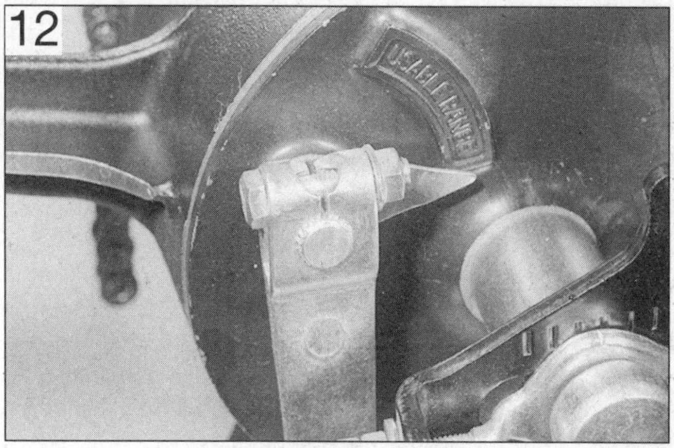

On drum brakes, check the angle of the operating lever with the brake fully applied. Most drum brakes have a wear indicator pointer and scale.

Brakes, Wheels and Tyres

Brakes

✔ With the wheel raised off the ground, apply the brake then free it off, and check that the wheel is about to revolve freely without brake drag.

✔ On disc brakes, examine the disc itself. Check that it is securely mounted and not cracked.

✔ On disc brakes, view the pad material through the caliper mouth and check that the pads are not worn down beyond the limit **(see illustration 11)**.

✔ On drum brakes, check that when the brake is applied the angle between the operating lever and cable or rod is not too great **(see illustration 12)**. Check also that the operating lever doesn't foul any other components.

✔ On disc brakes, examine the flexible hoses from top to bottom. Have an assistant hold the brake on so that the fluid in the hose is under pressure, and check that there is no sign of fluid leakage, bulges or cracking. If there are any metal brake pipes or unions, check that these are free from corrosion and damage. Where a brake-linked anti-dive system is fitted, check the hoses to the anti-dive in a similar manner.

✔ Check that the rear brake torque arm is secure and that its fasteners are secured by self-locking nuts or castellated nuts with split-pins or R-pins **(see illustration 13)**.

✔ On models with ABS, check that the self-check warning light in the instrument panel works.

✔ The MOT tester will perform a test of the motorcycle's braking efficiency based on a calculation of rider and motorcycle weight. Although this cannot be carried out at home, you can at least ensure that the braking systems are properly maintained. For hydraulic disc brakes, check the fluid level, lever/pedal feel (bleed of air if its spongy) and pad material. For drum brakes, check adjustment, cable or rod operation and shoe lining thickness.

Wheels and tyres

✔ Check the wheel condition. Cast wheels should be free from cracks and if of the built-up design, all fasteners should be secure. Spoked wheels should be checked for broken, corroded, loose or bent spokes.

✔ With the wheel raised off the ground, spin the wheel and visually check that the tyre and wheel run true. Check that the tyre does not foul the suspension or mudguards.

✔ With the wheel raised off the ground, grasp the wheel and attempt to move it about the axle (spindle) **(see illustration 14)**. Any play felt here indicates wheel bearing failure.

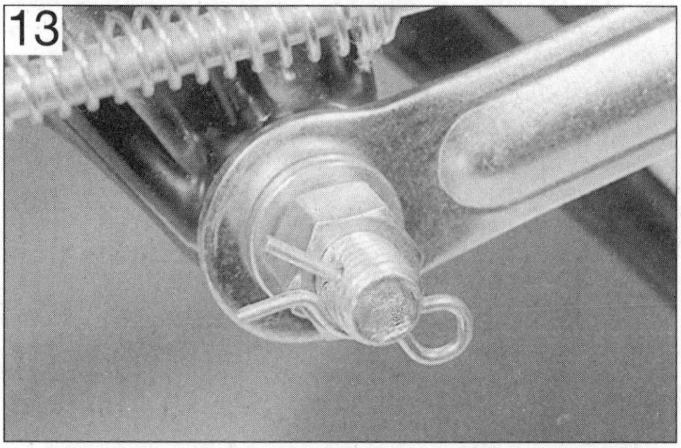

Brake torque arm must be properly secured at both ends

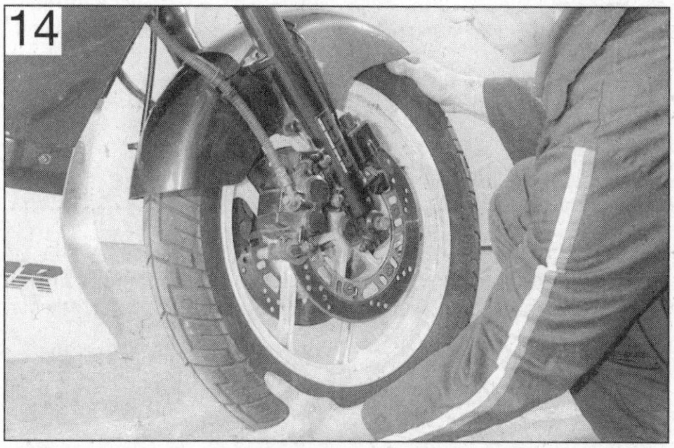

Check for wheel bearing play by trying to move the wheel about the axle (spindle)

Checking the tyre tread depth

Tyre direction of rotation arrow can be found on tyre sidewall

Castellated type wheel axle (spindle) nut must be secured by a split pin or R-pin

Two straightedges are used to check wheel alignment

✔ Check the tyre tread depth, tread condition and sidewall condition **(see illustration 15)**.

✔ Check the tyre type. Front and rear tyre types must be compatible and be suitable for road use. Tyres marked NOT FOR ROAD USE, COMPETITION USE ONLY or similar, will fail the MOT.

✔ If the tyre sidewall carries a direction of rotation arrow, this must be pointing in the direction of normal wheel rotation **(see illustration 16)**.

✔ Check that the wheel axle (spindle) nuts (where applicable) are properly secured. A self-locking nut or castellated nut with a split-pin or R-pin can be used **(see illustration 17)**.

✔ Wheel alignment is checked with the motorcycle off the stand and a rider seated. With the front wheel pointing straight ahead, two perfectly straight lengths of metal or wood and placed against the sidewalls of both tyres **(see illustration 18)**. The gap each side of the front tyre must be equidistant on both sides. Incorrect wheel alignment may be due to a cocked rear wheel (often as the result of poor chain adjustment) or in extreme cases, a bent frame.

General checks and condition

✔ Check the security of all major fasteners, bodypanels, seat, fairings (where fitted) and mudguards.

✔ Check that the rider and pillion footrests, handlebar levers and brake pedal are securely mounted.

✔ Check for corrosion on the frame or any load-bearing components. If severe, this may affect the structure, particularly under stress.

Sidecars

A motorcycle fitted with a sidecar requires additional checks relating to the stability of the machine and security of attachment and swivel joints, plus specific wheel alignment (toe-in) requirements. Additionally, tyre and lighting requirements differ from conventional motorcycle use. Owners are advised to check MOT test requirements with an official test centre.

Preparing for storage

Before you start

If repairs or an overhaul is needed, see that this is carried out now rather than left until you want to ride the bike again.

Give the bike a good wash and scrub all dirt from its underside. Make sure the bike dries completely before preparing for storage.

Engine

● Remove the spark plug(s) and lubricate the cylinder bores with approximately a teaspoon of motor oil using a spout-type oil can **(see illustration 1)**. Reinstall the spark plug(s). Crank the engine over a couple of times to coat the piston rings and bores with oil. If the bike has a kickstart, use this to turn the engine over. If not, flick the kill switch to the OFF position and crank the engine over on the starter **(see illustration 2)**. If the nature on the ignition system prevents the starter operating with the kill switch in the OFF position, remove the spark plugs and fit them back in their caps; ensure that the plugs are earthed (grounded) against the cylinder head when the starter is operated **(see illustration 3)**.

Warning: It is important that the plugs are earthed (grounded) away from the spark plug holes otherwise there is a risk of atomised fuel from the cylinders igniting.

HAYNES HiNT

On a single cylinder four-stroke engine, you can seal the combustion chamber completely by positioning the piston at TDC on the compression stroke.

● Drain the carburettor(s) otherwise there is a risk of jets becoming blocked by gum deposits from the fuel **(see illustration 4)**.

● If the bike is going into long-term storage, consider adding a fuel stabiliser to the fuel in the tank. If the tank is drained completely, corrosion of its internal surfaces may occur if left unprotected for a long period. The tank can be treated with a rust preventative especially for this purpose. Alternatively, remove the tank and pour half a litre of motor oil into it, install the filler cap and shake the tank to coat its internals with oil before draining off the excess. The same effect can also be achieved by spraying WD40 or a similar water-dispersant around the inside of the tank via its flexible nozzle.

● Make sure the cooling system contains the correct mix of antifreeze. Antifreeze also contains important corrosion inhibitors.

● The air intakes and exhaust can be sealed off by covering or plugging the openings. Ensure that you do not seal in any condensation; run the engine until it is hot,

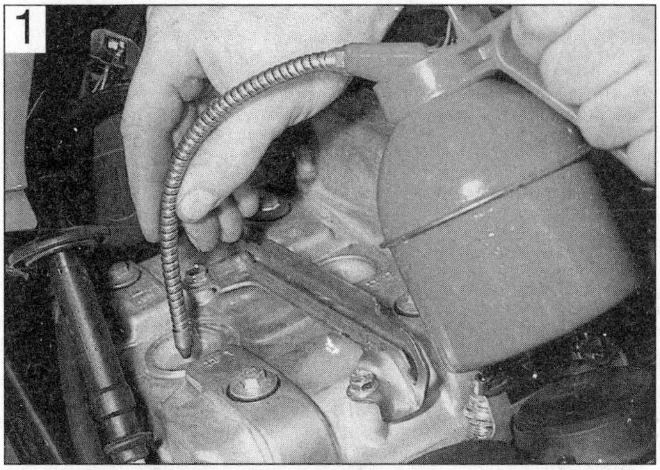

Squirt a drop of motor oil into each cylinder

Flick the kill switch to OFF . . .

. . . and ensure that the metal bodies of the plugs (arrows) are earthed against the cylinder head

Connect a hose to the carburettor float chamber drain stub (arrow) and unscrew the drain screw

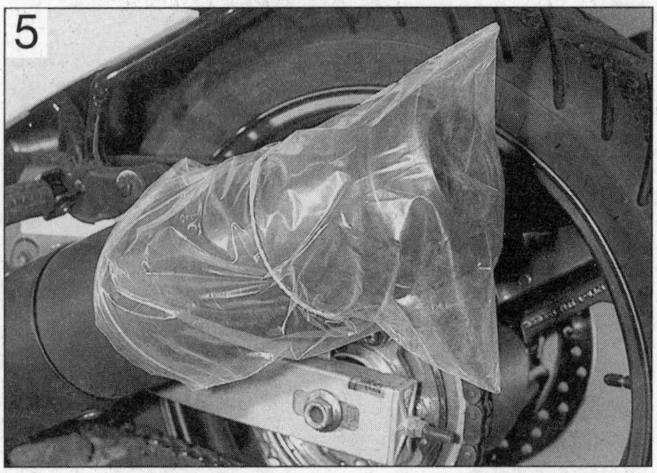

Exhausts can be sealed off with a plastic bag

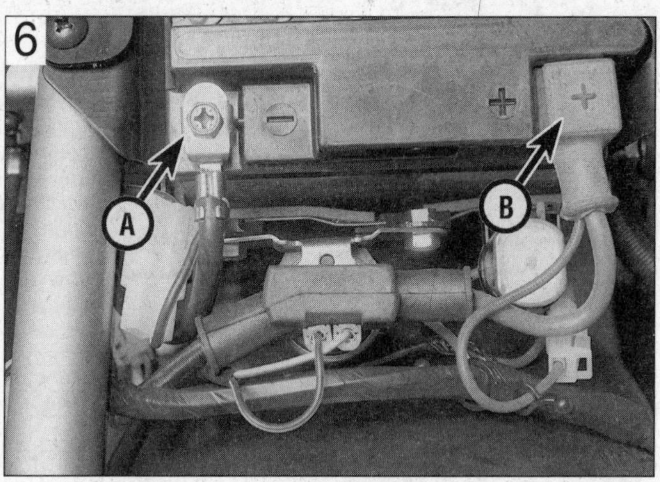

Disconnect the negative lead (A) first, followed by the positive lead (B)

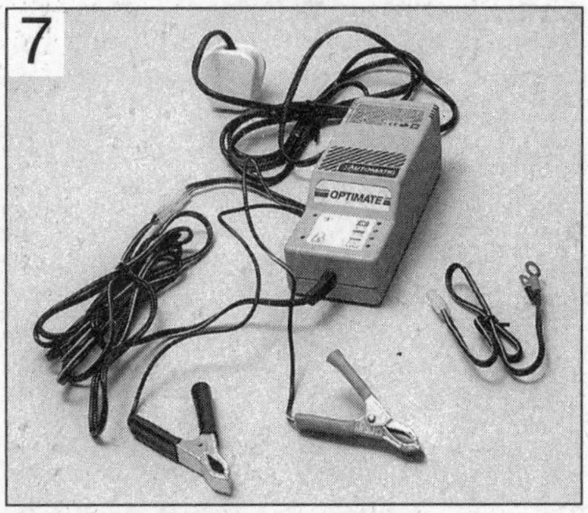

Use a suitable battery charger - this kit also assess battery condition

then switch off and allow to cool. Tape a piece of thick plastic over the silencer end(s) **(see illustration 5)**. Note that some advocate pouring a tablespoon of motor oil into the silencer(s) before sealing them off.

Battery

- Remove it from the bike - in extreme cases of cold the battery may freeze and crack its case **(see illustration 6)**.
- Check the electrolyte level and top up if necessary (conventional refillable batteries). Clean the terminals.
- Store the battery off the motorcycle and away from any sources of fire. Position a wooden block under the battery if it is to sit on the ground.
- Give the battery a trickle charge for a few hours every month **(see illustration 7)**.

Tyres

- Place the bike on its centrestand or an auxiliary stand which will support the motorcycle in an upright position. Position wood blocks under the tyres to keep them off the ground and to provide insulation from damp. If the bike is being put into long-term storage, ideally both tyres should be off the ground; not only will this protect the tyres, but will also ensure that no load is placed on the steering head or wheel bearings.
- Deflate each tyre by 5 to 10 psi, no more or the beads may unseat from the rim, making subsequent inflation difficult on tubeless tyres.

Pivots and controls

- Lubricate all lever, pedal, stand and footrest pivot points. If grease nipples are fitted to the rear suspension components, apply lubricant to the pivots.
- Lubricate all control cables.

Cycle components

- Apply a wax protectant to all painted and plastic components. Wipe off any excess, but don't polish to a shine. Where fitted, clean the screen with soap and water.
- Coat metal parts with Vaseline (petroleum jelly). When applying this to the fork tubes, do not compress the forks otherwise the seals will rot from contact with the Vaseline.
- Apply a vinyl cleaner to the seat.

Storage conditions

- Aim to store the bike in a shed or garage which does not leak and is free from damp.
- Drape an old blanket or bedspread over the bike to protect it from dust and direct contact with sunlight (which will fade paint). This also hides the bike from prying eyes. Beware of tight-fitting plastic covers which may allow condensation to form and settle on the bike.

Getting back on the road

Engine and transmission

- Change the oil and replace the oil filter. If this was done prior to storage, check that the oil hasn't emulsified - a thick whitish substance which occurs through condensation.
- Remove the spark plugs. Using a spout-type oil can, squirt a few drops of oil into the cylinder(s). This will provide initial lubrication as the piston rings and bores comes back into contact. Service the spark plugs, or fit new ones, and install them in the engine.
- Check that the clutch isn't stuck on. The plates can stick together if left standing for some time, preventing clutch operation. Engage a gear and try rocking the bike back and forth with the clutch lever held against the handlebar. If this doesn't work on cable-operated clutches, hold the clutch lever back against the handlebar with a strong elastic band or cable tie for a couple of hours **(see illustration 8)**.
- If the air intakes or silencer end(s) were blocked off, remove the bung or cover used.
- If the fuel tank was coated with a rust

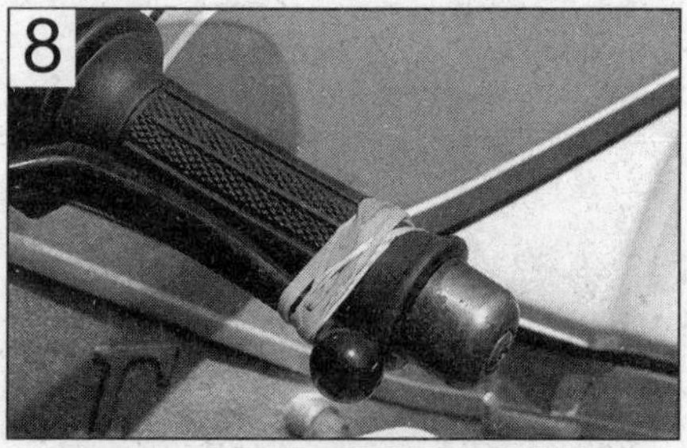

Hold clutch lever back against the handlebar with elastic bands or a cable tie

preventative, oil or a stabiliser added to the fuel, drain and flush the tank and dispose of the fuel sensibly. If no action was taken with the fuel tank prior to storage, it is advised that the old fuel is disposed of since it will go off over a period of time. Refill the fuel tank with fresh fuel.

Frame and running gear

- Oil all pivot points and cables.
- Check the tyre pressures. They will definitely need inflating if pressures were reduced for storage.
- Lubricate the final drive chain (where applicable).
- Remove any protective coating applied to the fork tubes (stanchions) since this may well destroy the fork seals. If the fork tubes weren't protected and have picked up rust spots, remove them with very fine abrasive paper and refinish with metal polish.
- Check that both brakes operate correctly. Apply each brake hard and check that it's not possible to move the motorcycle forwards, then check that the brake frees off again once released. Brake caliper pistons can stick due to corrosion around the piston head, or on the sliding caliper types, due to corrosion of the slider pins. If the brake doesn't free after repeated operation, take the caliper off for examination. Similarly drum brakes can stick due to a seized operating cam, cable or rod linkage.
- If the motorcycle has been in long-term storage, renew the brake fluid and clutch fluid (where applicable).
- Depending on where the bike has been stored, the wiring, cables and hoses may have been nibbled by rodents. Make a visual check and investigate disturbed wiring loom tape.

Battery

- If the battery has been previously removal and given top up charges it can simply be reconnected. Remember to connect the positive cable first and the negative cable last.
- On conventional refillable batteries, if the battery has not received any attention, remove it from the motorcycle and check its electrolyte level. Top up if necessary then charge the battery. If the battery fails to hold a charge and a visual checks show heavy white sulphation of the plates, the battery is probably defective and must be renewed. This is particularly likely if the battery is old. Confirm battery condition with a specific gravity check.
- On sealed (MF) batteries, if the battery has not received any attention, remove it from the motorcycle and charge it according to the information on the battery case - if the battery fails to hold a charge it must be renewed.

Starting procedure

- If a kickstart is fitted, turn the engine over a couple of times with the ignition OFF to distribute oil around the engine. If no kickstart is fitted, flick the engine kill switch OFF and the ignition ON and crank the engine over a couple of times to work oil around the upper cylinder components. If the nature of the ignition system is such that the starter won't work with the kill switch OFF, remove the spark plugs, fit them back into their caps and earth (ground) their bodies on the cylinder head. Reinstall the spark plugs afterwards.
- Switch the kill switch to RUN, operate the choke and start the engine. If the engine won't start don't continue cranking the engine - not only will this flatten the battery, but the starter motor will overheat. Switch the ignition off and try again later. If the engine refuses to start, go through the fault finding procedures in this manual. **Note:** *If the bike has been in storage for a long time, old fuel or a carburettor blockage may be the problem. Gum deposits in carburettors can block jets - if a carburettor cleaner doesn't prove successful the carburettors must be dismantled for cleaning.*
- Once the engine has started, check that the lights, turn signals and horn work properly.
- Treat the bike gently for the first ride and check all fluid levels on completion. Settle the bike back into the maintenance schedule.

This Section provides an easy reference-guide to the more common faults that are likely to afflict your machine. Obviously, the opportunities are almost limitless for faults to occur as a result of obscure failures, and to try and cover all eventualities would require a book. Indeed, a number have been written on the subject.

Successful troubleshooting is not a mysterious 'black art' but the application of a bit of knowledge combined with a systematic and logical approach to the problem. Approach any troubleshooting by first accurately identifying the symptom and then checking through the list of possible causes, starting with the simplest or most obvious and progressing in stages to the most complex.

Take nothing for granted, but above all apply liberal quantities of common sense.

The main symptom of a fault is given in the text as a major heading below which are listed the various systems or areas which may contain the fault. Details of each possible cause for a fault and the remedial action to be taken are given, in brief, in the paragraphs below each heading. Further information should be sought in the relevant Chapter.

1 Engine doesn't start or is difficult to start

Starter motor doesn't rotate

- ☐ Engine kill switch OFF.
- ☐ Fuse blown. Check main fuse (Chapter 9).
- ☐ Battery voltage low. Check and recharge battery (Chapter 9).
- ☐ Starter motor defective. Make sure the wiring to the starter is secure. Make sure the starter relay clicks when the start button is pushed. If the relay clicks, then the fault is in the wiring or motor.
- ☐ Starter relay faulty. Check it according to the procedure in Chapter 9.
- ☐ Starter switch not contacting. The contacts could be wet, corroded or dirty. Disassemble and clean the switch (Chapter 9).
- ☐ Wiring open or shorted. Check all wiring connections and harnesses to make sure that they are dry, tight and not corroded. Also check for broken or frayed wires that can cause a short to ground (earth) (see wiring diagram, Chapter 9).
- ☐ Ignition (main) switch defective. Check the switch according to the procedure in Chapter 9. Renew the switch if it is defective.
- ☐ Engine kill switch defective. Check for wet, dirty or corroded contacts. Clean or renew the switch as necessary (Chapter 9).
- ☐ Faulty neutral, or clutch switch. Check the wiring to each switch and the switch itself according to the procedures in Chapter 9.

Starter motor rotates but engine does not turn over

- ☐ Starter motor clutch defective. Inspect and repair or renew (Chapter 2).
- ☐ Damaged idler or starter gears. Inspect and renew the damaged parts (Chapter 2).

Starter works but engine won't turn over (seized)

- ☐ Seized engine caused by one or more internally damaged components. Failure due to wear, abuse or lack of lubrication. Damage can include seized valves, tappets, camshafts, pistons, crankshaft, connecting rod bearings. Refer to Chapter 2 for engine disassembly.
- ☐ Fault in starter drive from alternator driveshaft gear, to auxiliary gear, clutch outer drum teeth and primary drive gear on crankshaft.

No fuel flow

- ☐ No fuel in tank.
- ☐ Fuel filter blockage or blocked/pinch fuel hose(s) (see Chapter 1).
- ☐ Fuel tank breather hose obstructed (fault in evaporative loss system on California models).
- ☐ Float needle valve clogged. For all of the valves to be clogged, either a very bad batch of fuel with an unusual additive has been used, or some other foreign material has entered the tank. Many times after a machine has been stored for many months without running, the fuel turns to a varnish-like liquid and forms deposits on the inlet needle valves and jets. The carburettors should be removed and overhauled if draining the float chambers doesn't solve the problem.

Engine flooded

- ☐ Float height too high. Check as described in Chapter 4.
- ☐ Float needle valve worn or stuck open. A piece of dirt, rust or other debris can cause the valve to seat improperly, causing excess fuel to be admitted to the float chamber. In this case, the float chamber should be cleaned and the needle valve and seat inspected. If the needle and seat are worn, then the leaking will persist and the parts should be renewed (Chapter 4).
- ☐ Starting technique incorrect. Under normal circumstances (ie, if all the carburettor functions are sound) the machine should start with little or no throttle. When the engine is cold, the choke should be operated and the engine started without opening the throttle. When the engine is at operating temperature, only a very slight amount of throttle should be necessary.

No spark or weak spark

- ☐ Ignition switch OFF.
- ☐ Engine kill switch turned to the OFF position.
- ☐ Battery voltage low. Check and recharge the battery as necessary (Chapter 9).
- ☐ Spark plugs dirty, defective or worn out. Locate reason for fouled plugs using spark plug condition chart and follow the plug maintenance procedures (Chapter 1).
- ☐ Spark plug caps or secondary (HT) wiring faulty. Check condition. Renew either or both components if cracks or deterioration are evident (Chapter 5).
- ☐ Spark plug caps not making good contact. Make sure that the plug caps fit snugly over the plug ends.
- ☐ Igniter defective. Check the igniter, referring to Chapter 5 for details.
- ☐ Pick-up coil defective. Check the coil, referring to Chapter 5 for details.
- ☐ Ignition HT coils defective. Check the coils, referring to Chapter 5.
- ☐ Ignition or kill switch shorted. This is usually caused by water, corrosion, damage or excessive wear. The switches can be disassembled and cleaned with electrical contact cleaner. If cleaning does not help, renew the switches (Chapter 9).
- ☐ Wiring shorted or broken between:
  - *a) Ignition (main) switch and engine kill switch (or blown fuse)*
  - *b) Igniter and engine kill switch*
  - *c) Igniter and ignition HT coils*
  - *d) Ignition HT coils and spark plugs*
  - *e) Igniter and pick-up coil*
- ☐ Make sure that all wiring connections are clean, dry and tight. Look for chafed and broken wires (Chapters 5 and 9).

Compression low

- ☐ Spark plugs loose. Remove the plugs and inspect their threads. Reinstall and tighten to the specified torque (Chapter 1).
- ☐ Cylinder head not sufficiently tightened down. If the cylinder head is suspected of being loose, then there's a chance that the gasket or head is damaged if the problem has persisted for any length of time. The head bolts should be tightened to the proper torque in the correct sequence (Chapter 2).
- ☐ Improper valve clearance. This means that the valve is not closing completely and compression pressure is leaking past the valve. Check and adjust the valve clearances (Chapter 1).
- ☐ Cylinder and/or piston worn. Excessive wear will cause compression pressure to leak past the rings. This is usually accompanied by worn rings as well. A top-end overhaul is necessary (Chapter 2).
- ☐ Piston rings worn, weak, broken, or sticking. Broken or sticking piston rings usually indicate a lubrication or carburation problem that causes excess carbon deposits or seizures to form on the pistons and rings. Top-end overhaul is necessary (Chapter 2).
- ☐ Piston ring-to-groove clearance excessive. This is caused by excessive wear of the piston ring lands. Piston renewal is necessary (Chapter 2).
- ☐ Cylinder head gasket damaged. If the head is allowed to become loose, or if excessive carbon build-up on the piston crown and combustion chamber causes extremely high compression, the head gasket may leak. Retorquing the head is not always sufficient to restore the seal, so gasket renewal is necessary (Chapter 2).
- ☐ Valve spring broken or weak. Caused by component failure or wear; the springs must be renewed (Chapter 2).
- ☐ Valve not seating properly. This is caused by a bent valve (from over-revving or improper valve adjustment), burned valve or seat (improper carburation) or an accumulation of carbon deposits on the seat (from carburation or lubrication problems). The valves must be cleaned and/or renewed and the seats serviced if possible (Chapter 2).

1 Engine doesn't start or is difficult to start (continued)

Stalls after starting

- ☐ Improper choke action. Make sure the choke linkage shaft is getting a full stroke and staying in the out position (Chapter 4).
- ☐ Ignition malfunction. See Chapter 5.
- ☐ Carburettor malfunction. See Chapter 4.
- ☐ Fuel contaminated. The fuel can be contaminated with either dirt or water, or can change chemically if the machine is allowed to sit for several months or more. Drain the tank and float chambers (Chapter 4).
- ☐ Inlet air leak. Check for loose carburettor-to-inlet manifold connections, missing vacuum take-off caps or hoses, or loose carburettor tops (Chapter 4).
- ☐ Engine idle speed incorrect. Turn idle adjusting screw until the engine idles at the specified rpm (Chapter 1).

Rough idle

- ☐ Ignition malfunction. See Chapter 5.
- ☐ Idle speed incorrect. See Chapter 1.
- ☐ Carburettors not synchronised. Adjust carburettors with vacuum gauge or manometer set as described in Chapter 1.
- ☐ Carburettor malfunction. See Chapter 4.
- ☐ Fuel contaminated. The fuel can be contaminated with either dirt or water, or can change chemically if the machine is allowed to sit for several months or more. Drain the tank and float chambers (Chapter 4).
- ☐ Inlet air leak. Check for loose carburettor-to-inlet manifold connections, missing vacuum take-off caps, or damaged evaporative loss system hoses on California models (Chapter 4).
- ☐ Airbox requires draining (Chapter 1). In extreme cases, the element or air inlets may be blocked (Chapter 4).

2 Poor running at low speed

Spark weak

- ☐ Battery voltage low. Check and recharge battery (Chapter 9).
- ☐ Spark plugs fouled, defective or worn out. Refer to Chapter 1 for spark plug maintenance.
- ☐ Spark plug cap or HT wiring defective. Refer to Chapters 1 and 5 for details on the ignition system.
- ☐ Spark plug caps not making contact.
- ☐ Incorrect spark plugs. Wrong type, heat range or cap configuration. Check and install correct plugs listed in Chapter 1.
- ☐ Igniter defective. See Chapter 5.
- ☐ Pick-up coil defective. See Chapter 5.
- ☐ Ignition HT coils defective. See Chapter 5.

Fuel/air mixture incorrect

- ☐ Pilot screws out of adjustment (Chapter 4).
- ☐ Pilot jet or air passage clogged. Remove and overhaul the carburettors (Chapter 4).
- ☐ Air bleed holes clogged. Remove carburettor and blow out all passages (Chapter 4).
- ☐ Airbox poorly sealed. Look for cracks, holes or loose clamps and renew or repair defective parts.
- ☐ Fuel level too high or too low. Check the float height (Chapter 4).
- ☐ Fuel tank breather hose obstructed (not California models).
- ☐ Carburettor inlet manifolds loose. Check for cracks, breaks, tears or loose clamps. Renew the rubber inlet manifold joints if split or perished.

Compression low

- ☐ Spark plugs loose. Remove the plugs and inspect their threads. Reinstall and tighten to the specified torque (Chapter 1).
- ☐ Cylinder head not sufficiently tightened down. If the cylinder head is suspected of being loose, then there's a chance that the gasket and head are damaged if the problem has persisted for any length of time. The head bolts should be tightened to the proper torque in the correct sequence (Chapter 2).
- ☐ Improper valve clearance. This means that the valve is not closing completely and compression pressure is leaking past the valve. Check and adjust the valve clearances (Chapter 1).
- ☐ Cylinder and/or piston worn. Excessive wear will cause compression pressure to leak past the rings. This is usually accompanied by worn rings as well. A top-end overhaul is necessary (Chapter 2).
- ☐ Piston rings worn, weak, broken, or sticking. Broken or sticking piston rings usually indicate a lubrication or carburation problem that causes excess carbon deposits or seizures to form on the pistons and rings. Top-end overhaul is necessary (Chapter 2).
- ☐ Piston ring-to-groove clearance excessive. This is caused by excessive wear of the piston ring lands. Piston renewal is necessary (Chapter 2).
- ☐ Cylinder head gasket damaged. If the head is allowed to become loose, or if excessive carbon build-up on the piston crown and combustion chamber causes extremely high compression, the head gasket may leak. Retorquing the head is not always sufficient to restore the seal, so gasket renewal is necessary (Chapter 2).
- ☐ Valve spring broken or weak. Caused by component failure or wear; the springs must be renewed (Chapter 2).
- ☐ Valve not seating properly. This is caused by a bent valve (from over-revving or improper valve adjustment), burned valve or seat (improper carburation) or an accumulation of carbon deposits on the seat (from carburation, lubrication problems). The valves must be cleaned and/or renewed and the seats serviced if possible (Chapter 2).

Poor acceleration

- ☐ Carburettors leaking or dirty. Overhaul the carburettors (Chapter 4).
- ☐ Timing not advancing. The pick-up coil or the igniter may be defective. If so, they must be renewed, as they can't be repaired. Timing check can be performed to confirm (Chapter 5).
- ☐ Carburettors not synchronised. Adjust them with a vacuum gauge set or manometer (Chapter 1).
- ☐ Engine oil viscosity too high. Using a heavier oil than that recommended in Chapter 1 can damage the oil pump or lubrication system and cause drag on the engine.
- ☐ Brakes dragging. Usually caused by debris which has entered the brake piston seals, or from a warped disc or bent axle. Repair as necessary (Chapter 7).

3 Poor running or no power at high speed

Firing incorrect

- ☐ Airbox element restricted or air inlets blocked. Drain the airbox (Chapter 1) and if necessary renew it (Chapter 4).
- ☐ Spark plugs fouled, defective or worn out. See Chapter 1 for spark plug maintenance.
- ☐ Spark plug caps or HT wiring defective. See Chapters 1 and 5 for details of the ignition system.
- ☐ Spark plug caps not in good contact. See Chapter 5.
- ☐ Incorrect spark plugs. Wrong type, heat range or cap configuration. Check and install correct plugs listed in Chapter 1.
- ☐ Igniter defective. See Chapter 5.
- ☐ Ignition HT coils defective. See Chapter 5.

Fuel/air mixture incorrect

- ☐ Main jet clogged. Dirt, water or other contaminants can clog the main jets. Clean the fuel filter(s), the float chamber area, and the jets and carburettor orifices (Chapter 4).
- ☐ Main jet wrong size. The standard jetting is for sea level atmospheric pressure and oxygen content.
- ☐ Air bleed holes clogged. Remove and overhaul carburettors (Chapter 4).
- ☐ Airbox requires draining (Chapter 1). Airbox element clogged (Chapter 4).
- ☐ Airbox housing poorly sealed. Look for cracks, holes or loose clamps, and renew or repair defective parts.
- ☐ Fuel level too high or too low. Check the float height (Chapter 4).
- ☐ Fuel tank breather hose obstructed (not California models).
- ☐ Carburettor inlet manifolds loose. Check for cracks, breaks, tears or loose clamps. Renew the rubber inlet manifolds if they are split or perished (Chapter 4).

Compression low

- ☐ Spark plugs loose. Remove the plugs and inspect their threads. Reinstall and tighten to the specified torque (Chapter 1).
- ☐ Cylinder head not sufficiently tightened down. If the cylinder head is suspected of being loose, then there's a chance that the gasket and head are damaged if the problem has persisted for any length of time. The head bolts should be tightened to the proper torque in the correct sequence (Chapter 2).
- ☐ Improper valve clearance. This means that the valve is not closing completely and compression pressure is leaking past the valve. Check and adjust the valve clearances (Chapter 1).
- ☐ Cylinder and/or piston worn. Excessive wear will cause compression pressure to leak past the rings. This is usually accompanied by worn rings as well. A top-end overhaul is necessary (Chapter 2).
- ☐ Piston rings worn, weak, broken, or sticking. Broken or sticking piston rings usually indicate a lubrication or carburation problem that causes excess carbon deposits or seizures to form on the pistons and rings. Top-end overhaul is necessary (Chapter 2).
- ☐ Piston ring-to-groove clearance excessive. This is caused by excessive wear of the piston ring lands. Piston renewal is necessary (Chapter 2).
- ☐ Cylinder head gasket damaged. If the head is allowed to become loose, or if excessive carbon build-up on the piston crown and combustion chamber causes extremely high compression, the head gasket may leak. Retorquing the head is not always sufficient to restore the seal, so gasket renewal is necessary (Chapter 2).
- ☐ Valve spring broken or weak. Caused by component failure or wear; the springs must be renewed (Chapter 2).
- ☐ Valve not seating properly. This is caused by a bent valve (from over-revving or improper valve adjustment), burned valve or seat (improper carburation) or an accumulation of carbon deposits on the seat (from carburation or lubrication problems). The valves must be cleaned and/or renewed and the seats serviced if possible (Chapter 2).

Knocking or pinking

- ☐ Carbon build-up in combustion chamber. Use of a fuel additive that will dissolve the adhesive bonding the carbon particles to the crown and chamber is the easiest way to remove the build-up. Otherwise, the cylinder head will have to be removed and decarbonised (Chapter 2).
- ☐ Incorrect or poor quality fuel. Old or improper grades of fuel can cause detonation. This causes the piston to rattle, thus the knocking or pinging sound. Drain old fuel and always use the recommended fuel grade.
- ☐ Spark plug heat range incorrect. Uncontrolled detonation indicates the plug heat range is too hot. The plug in effect becomes a glow plug. Install the proper heat range plug (Chapter 1).
- ☐ Improper air/fuel mixture. This will cause the cylinder to run hot, which leads to detonation. Clogged jets or an air leak can cause this imbalance. See Chapter 4.

Miscellaneous causes

- ☐ Throttle valve doesn't open fully. Adjust the throttle grip freeplay (Chapter 1).
- ☐ Clutch slipping. May be caused by loose or worn clutch components. Refer to Chapter 2 for clutch overhaul procedures.
- ☐ Timing not advancing. Check as described in Chapter 5.
- ☐ Engine oil viscosity too high. Using a heavier oil than the one recommended in Chapter 1 can damage the oil pump or lubrication system and cause drag on the engine.
- ☐ Brakes dragging. Usually caused by debris which has entered the brake piston seals, or from a warped disc or bent axle. Repair as necessary.

4 Overheating

Engine overheats

- ☐ Coolant level low. Check and add coolant (Chapter 1).
- ☐ Leak in cooling system. Check cooling system hoses and radiator for leaks and other damage. Repair or renew parts as necessary (Chapter 3).
- ☐ Thermostat sticking open or closed. Check and renew as described in Chapter 3.
- ☐ Faulty radiator cap. Remove the cap and have it pressure tested.
- ☐ Coolant passages clogged. Have the entire system drained and flushed, then refill with fresh coolant.
- ☐ Water pump defective. Remove the pump and check the components (Chapter 3).
- ☐ Clogged radiator fins. Clean them by blowing compressed air through the fins from the rear of the radiator.
- ☐ Cooling fan or fan switch fault (Chapter 3).

Firing incorrect

- ☐ Spark plugs fouled, defective or worn out. See Chapter 1 for spark plug maintenance.
- ☐ Incorrect spark plugs.
- ☐ Faulty ignition HT coils (Chapter 5).

Fuel/air mixture incorrect

- ☐ Main jet clogged. Dirt, water and other contaminants can clog the main jets. Clean the fuel filter(s), the float chamber area and the jets and carburettor orifices (Chapter 4).
- ☐ Main jet wrong size. The standard jetting is for sea level atmospheric pressure and oxygen content.
- ☐ Airbox requires draining (Chapter 1).
- ☐ Airbox element or air inlets clogged (Chapter 4).
- ☐ Airbox poorly sealed. Look for cracks, holes or loose clamps and renew or repair.
- ☐ Fuel level too low. Check float height (Chapter 4).
- ☐ Fuel tank breather hose obstructed (not California models).
- ☐ Carburettor inlet manifolds loose. Check for cracks, breaks, tears or loose clamps. Renew the rubber inlet manifold joints if split or perished.

Compression too high

- ☐ Carbon build-up in combustion chamber. Use of a fuel additive that will dissolve the adhesive bonding the carbon particles to the piston crown and chamber is the easiest way to remove the build-up. Otherwise, the cylinder head will have to be removed and decarbonised (Chapter 2).

Engine load excessive

- ☐ Clutch slipping. Can be caused by damaged, loose or worn clutch components. Refer to Chapter 2 for overhaul procedures.
- ☐ Engine oil level too high. The addition of too much oil will cause pressurisation of the crankcase and inefficient engine operation. Check Specifications and drain to proper level (Chapter 1).
- ☐ Engine oil viscosity too high. Using a heavier oil than the one recommended in Chapter 1 can damage the oil pump or lubrication system as well as cause drag on the engine.
- ☐ Brakes dragging. Usually caused by debris which has entered the brake piston seals, or from a warped disc or bent axle. Repair as necessary.

Lubrication inadequate

- ☐ Engine oil level too low. Friction caused by intermittent lack of lubrication or from oil that is overworked can cause overheating. The oil provides a definite cooling function in the engine. Check the oil level (Chapter 1).
- ☐ Poor quality engine oil or incorrect viscosity or type. Oil is rated not only according to viscosity but also according to type. Some oils are not rated high enough for use in this engine. Check the Specifications section and change to the correct oil (Chapter 1).

Miscellaneous causes

- ☐ Modification to exhaust system. Most aftermarket exhaust systems cause the engine to run leaner, which make them run hotter. When installing an accessory exhaust system, always rejet the carburettors.

5 Clutch problems

Clutch slipping

- ☐ Clutch master cylinder reservoir fluid level too high (Chapter 1).
- ☐ Friction plates worn or warped. Overhaul the clutch assembly (Chapter 2).
- ☐ Plain plates warped (Chapter 2).
- ☐ Clutch springs broken or weak. Old or heat-damaged (from slipping clutch) springs should be renewed (Chapter 2).
- ☐ Clutch centre or outer drum unevenly worn. This causes improper engagement of the plates. Renew the damaged or worn parts (Chapter 2).

Clutch not disengaging completely

- ☐ Clutch master cylinder fluid level too low (Chapter 1).
- ☐ Clutch plates warped or damaged. This will cause clutch drag, which in turn will cause the machine to creep. Overhaul the clutch assembly (Chapter 2).
- ☐ Clutch spring tension uneven. Usually caused by a sagged or broken spring. Check and renew the springs as a set (Chapter 2).
- ☐ Engine oil deteriorated. Old, thin, worn out oil will not provide proper lubrication for the plates, causing the clutch to drag. Renew the oil and filter (Chapter 1).
- ☐ Engine oil viscosity too high. Using a heavier oil than recommended in Chapter 1 can cause the plates to stick together, putting a drag on the engine. Change to the correct weight oil (Chapter 1).
- ☐ Clutch outer drum guide seized on mainshaft. Lack of lubrication, severe wear or damage can cause the bush to seize on the shaft. Overhaul of the clutch, and perhaps transmission, may be necessary to repair the damage (Chapter 2).
- ☐ Clutch pushrod bent. Check and if necessary renew (Chapter 2).
- ☐ Loose clutch centre nut. Causes drum and centre misalignment putting a drag on the engine. Engagement adjustment continually varies. Overhaul the clutch assembly (Chapter 2).

6 Gearshifting problems

Doesn't go into gear or pedal doesn't return

- ☐ Clutch not disengaging. See Section 5.
- ☐ Selector fork(s) bent or seized. Overhaul the transmission (Chapter 2).
- ☐ Gear(s) stuck on shaft. Most often caused by a lack of lubrication or excessive wear in transmission bearings and bushes. Overhaul the transmission (Chapter 2).
- ☐ Gearchange drum binding. Caused by lubrication failure or excessive wear. Renew the drum and bearing (Chapter 2).
- ☐ Gearchange shaft quadrant teeth or carrier pawls faulty. Overhaul gearchange mechanism (Chapter 2).
- ☐ Gearchange shaft return spring weak or broken (Chapter 2).
- ☐ Gearchange shaft splines stripped out of lever/pedal or shaft, caused by allowing the lever to get loose or from dropping the machine. Renew necessary parts (Chapter 2).
- ☐ Detent arm broken or worn. Full engagement and rotary movement of selector drum results. Renew the arm (Chapter 2).

Jumps out of gear

- ☐ Selector fork(s) worn. Overhaul the mechanism (Chapter 2).
- ☐ Gear groove(s) worn. Overhaul the mechanism (Chapter 2).
- ☐ Gear dogs or dog slots worn or damaged. The gears should be inspected and renewed. No attempt should be made to service the worn parts. Disassembly the gearshafts and renew the damaged gears (Chapter 2).

Overshifts

- ☐ Gear detent arm spring weak or broken (Chapter 2).
- ☐ Gearchange shaft quadrant teeth or carrier pawls faulty. Overhaul mechanism (Chapter 2).

7 Abnormal engine noise

Knocking or pinking

- ☐ Carbon build-up in combustion chamber. Use of a fuel additive that will dissolve the adhesive bonding the carbon particles to the piston crown and chamber is the easiest way to remove the build-up. Otherwise, the cylinder head will have to be removed and decarbonised (Chapter 2).
- ☐ Incorrect or poor quality fuel. Old or improper fuel can cause detonation. This causes the pistons to rattle, thus the knocking or pinging sound. Drain the old fuel and always use the recommended grade fuel (Chapter 4).
- ☐ Spark plug heat range incorrect. Uncontrolled detonation indicates that the plug heat range is too hot. The plug in effect becomes a glow plug, raising cylinder temperatures. Install the proper heat range plug (Chapter 1).
- ☐ Improper air/fuel mixture. This will cause the cylinders to run hot and lead to detonation. Clogged jets or an air leak can cause this imbalance. See Chapter 4.

Piston slap or rattling

- ☐ Cylinder-to-piston clearance excessive. Inspect and overhaul top-end parts (Chapter 2).
- ☐ Connecting rod bent. Caused by over-revving, trying to start a badly flooded engine or from ingesting a foreign object into the combustion chamber. Renew the damaged parts (Chapter 2).
- ☐ Piston pin or piston pin bore worn or seized from wear or lack of lubrication. Inspect and damaged parts (Chapter 2).
- ☐ Piston ring(s) worn, broken or sticking. Overhaul the top-end (Chapter 2).
- ☐ Piston seizure damage. Usually from lack of lubrication or overheating. Renew the pistons and liners, as necessary (Chapter 2).
- ☐ Connecting rod upper or lower end clearance excessive. Caused by excessive wear or lack of lubrication. Renew worn parts.

Valve noise

- ☐ Incorrect valve clearances. Adjust the clearances by referring to Chapter 1.
- ☐ Valve spring broken or weak. Check and renew weak valve springs (Chapter 2).
- ☐ Camshaft or cylinder head worn or damaged. Lack of lubrication at high rpm is usually the cause of damage. Insufficient oil or failure to change the oil at the recommended intervals are the chief causes. Since there are no replaceable bearings in the head, the head itself will have to be renewed if there is excessive wear or damage (Chapter 2).

Other noise

- ☐ Cylinder head gasket leaking.
- ☐ Exhaust pipe leaking at cylinder head connection. Caused by improper fit of pipe(s) or loose exhaust flange. All exhaust fasteners should be tightened evenly and carefully. Failure to do this will lead to a leak.
- ☐ Crankshaft runout excessive. Caused by a bent crankshaft (from over-revving) or damage from an upper cylinder component failure. Can also be attributed to dropping the machine on either of the crankshaft ends.
- ☐ Engine mounting bolts loose. Tighten all engine mount bolts (Chapter 2).
- ☐ Crankshaft bearings worn (Chapter 2).
- ☐ Cam chain tensioner defective. Renew according to the procedure in Chapter 2.
- ☐ Cam chain, sprockets or blades worn (Chapter 2).
- ☐ Whine or rattling from balancers on 4 cylinder engine. Adjust (Chapter 2).

8 Abnormal transmission and final drive noise

Clutch noise

- ☐ Clutch outer drum/friction plate clearance excessive (Chapter 2).
- ☐ Loose or damaged clutch pressure plate and/or bolts (Chapter 2).

Transmission noise

- ☐ Bearings worn. Also includes the possibility that the shafts are worn. Overhaul the transmission (Chapter 2).
- ☐ Gears worn or chipped (Chapter 2).
- ☐ Metal chips jammed in gear teeth. Probably pieces from a broken clutch, gear or gearshift mechanism that were picked up by the gears. This will cause early bearing failure (Chapter 2).
- ☐ Engine oil level too low. Causes a howl from transmission. Also affects engine power and clutch operation (Chapter 1).

Final drive noise

- ☐ Chain not adjusted properly (Chapter 1).
- ☐ Engine sprocket or rear sprocket loose. Tighten fasteners (Chapter 6).
- ☐ Sprocket(s) worn. Renew both sprockets and the chain (Chapter 6).
- ☐ Rear sprocket warped. Renew both sprockets and the chain (Chapter 6).
- ☐ Wheel coupling damper worn. Renew the damper (Chapter 6).

9 Abnormal frame and suspension noise

Front end noise

- ☐ Low fluid level or improper viscosity oil in forks. This can sound like spurting and is usually accompanied by irregular fork action (Chapter 6).
- ☐ Spring weak or broken. Makes a clicking or scraping sound. Fork oil, when drained, will have a lot of metal particles in it (Chapter 6).
- ☐ Steering head bearings loose or damaged. Clicks when braking. Check and adjust or renew as necessary (Chapters 1 and 6).
- ☐ Fork yoke clamps loose. Make sure all clamp pinch bolts are tight (Chapter 6).
- ☐ Fork tube bent. Good possibility if machine has been dropped. Renew the tube (Chapter 6).
- ☐ Front axle or axle clamp bolt loose. Tighten them to the specified torque (Chapter 6).

Shock absorber noise

- ☐ Fluid level incorrect. Indicates a leak caused by defective seal. Shock will be covered with oil. Renew the shock (Chapter 6).
- ☐ Defective shock absorber with internal damage. This is in the body of the shock and can't be remedied. The shock must be renewed (Chapter 6).
- ☐ Bent or damaged shock body. Renew the shock (Chapter 6).

Brake noise

- ☐ Squeal caused by dust on brake pads. Usually found in combination with glazed pads. Clean using brake cleaning solvent (Chapter 7).
- ☐ Contamination of brake pads. Oil, brake fluid or dirt causing brake to chatter or squeal. Clean or renew the pads (Chapter 7).
- ☐ Pads glazed. Caused by excessive heat from prolonged use or from contamination. Do not use sandpaper, emery cloth, carborundum cloth or any other abrasive to roughen the pad surfaces as abrasives will stay in the pad material and damage the disc. A very fine flat file can be used, but pad renewal is suggested as a cure (Chapter 7).
- ☐ Disc warped. Can cause a chattering, clicking or intermittent squeal. Usually accompanied by a pulsating lever and uneven braking. Renew the disc (Chapter 7).
- ☐ Loose or worn wheel bearings. Check and renew as needed (Chapter 7).

10 Oil pressure warning light comes on

Engine lubrication system

- ☐ Engine oil pump defective, blocked oil strainer gauze, blocked oil filter or failed relief valve. Carry out oil pressure check (Chapter 2).
- ☐ Engine oil level low. Inspect for leak or other problem causing low oil level and add recommended oil (Chapter 1).
- ☐ Engine oil viscosity too low. Very old, thin oil or an improper weight of oil used in the engine. Change to correct oil (Chapter 1).
- ☐ Camshaft or journals worn. Excessive wear causing drop in oil pressure. Renew cam and/or/cylinder head. Abnormal wear could be caused by oil starvation at high rpm from low oil level or improper weight or type of oil (Chapter 1).
- ☐ Crankshaft and/or bearings worn. Same problems as *'Camshaft or journals worn'* above. Check and renew the crankshaft and/or bearings (Chapter 2).

Electrical system

- ☐ Oil pressure switch defective. Check the switch according to the procedure in Chapter 9. Renew it if it is defective.
- ☐ Oil pressure indicator light circuit defective. Check for pinched, shorted, disconnected or damaged wiring (Chapter 9).

11 Excessive exhaust smoke

White smoke

- ☐ Piston oil ring worn. The ring may be broken or damaged, causing oil from the crankcase to be pulled past the piston into the combustion chamber. Renew the rings (Chapter 2).
- ☐ Cylinder liners worn, cracked, or scored. Caused by overheating or oil starvation. Install new liners (Chapter 2).
- ☐ Valve oil seal damaged or worn. Renew the oil seals (Chapter 2).
- ☐ Valve guide worn. Measure the valve guide inside diameter (Chapter 2).
- ☐ Engine oil level too high, which causes the oil to be forced past the rings. Drain oil to the proper level (Chapter 1).
- ☐ Abnormal crankcase pressurisation, which forces oil past the rings. Clogged breather hose is usually the cause.

Black smoke

- ☐ Airbox element or air inlets clogged (Chapter 4).
- ☐ Main jet too large or loose. Compare the jet size to the Specifications (Chapter 4).
- ☐ Choke cable or linkage shaft stuck, causing fuel to be pulled through choke circuit (Chapter 4).
- ☐ No choke cable freeplay (Chapter 1).
- ☐ Fuel level too high. Check and adjust the float height(s) as necessary (Chapter 4).
- ☐ Float needle valve held off needle seat. Clean the float chambers and renew the needles and seats if necessary (Chapter 4).

Brown smoke

- ☐ Main jet too small or clogged. Lean condition caused by wrong size main jet or by a restricted orifice. Clean float chambers and jets and compare jet size to Specifications (Chapter 4).
- ☐ Fuel flow insufficient. Float needle valve stuck closed. Float height incorrect. Restricted fuel hose(s) or filter(s). Clean hose/filter and float chamber and adjust float heights if necessary.
- ☐ Carburettor inlet manifold clamps loose (Chapter 4).
- ☐ Airbox poorly sealed (Chapter 1).

12 Poor handling or stability

Handlebar hard to turn

- ☐ Steering head bearing freeplay incorrect. Check adjustment as described in Chapter 1.
- ☐ Bearings damaged. Roughness can be felt as the bars are turned from side-to-side. Renew the bearings (Chapter 6).
- ☐ Races dented or worn. Denting results from wear in only one position (eg, straightahead), from a collision, hitting a pothole or dropping the machine. Renew the bearings (Chapter 6).
- ☐ Steering stem lubrication inadequate. Causes are grease getting hard from age or being washed out by high pressure jet washes. Disassemble steering head and repack bearings (Chapter 6).
- ☐ Steering stem bent. Caused by a collision, hitting a pothole or by dropping the machine. Renew the damaged part. Don't try to straighten the steering stem (Chapter 6).
- ☐ Front tyre air pressure too low (Chapter 1).

Handlebar shakes or vibrates excessively

- ☐ Tyres worn or out of balance (Chapter 7).
- ☐ Swingarm bearings worn. Renew worn bearings by referring to Chapter 6.
- ☐ Rim(s) warped or damaged. Inspect wheels for runout (Chapter 7).
- ☐ Wheel bearings worn. Worn front or rear wheel bearings can cause poor tracking. Worn front bearings will cause wobble (Chapter 7).
- ☐ Handlebar clamp bolts loose (Chapter 6).
- ☐ Fork yoke clamp bolts loose. Tighten them to the specified torque (Chapter 6).
- ☐ Engine mounting bolts loose. Will cause excessive vibration with increased engine rpm (Chapter 2).

Handlebar pulls to one side

- ☐ Frame bent. Definitely suspect this if the machine has been dropped. May or may not be accompanied by cracking near the bend. Renew the frame (Chapter 6).
- ☐ Wheels out of alignment. May be caused by incorrect alignment of rear wheel in swingarm, or more seriously, from bent steering stem or frame (Chapter 6).
- ☐ Swingarm bent or twisted. Renew the swingarm (Chapter 6).
- ☐ Steering stem bent. Caused by impact damage or by dropping the motorcycle. Renew the steering stem (Chapter 6).
- ☐ Fork tube bent. Disassemble the forks and renew the damaged parts (Chapter 6).
- ☐ Fork oil level uneven. Check and add or drain as necessary (Chapter 6).

Poor shock absorbing qualities

- ☐ Too hard:
  - *a) Fork oil level excessive (Chapter 6).*
  - *b) Fork oil viscosity too high. Use a lighter oil (see the Specifications in Chapter 6).*
  - *c) Fork tube bent. Causes a harsh, sticking feeling (Chapter 6).*
  - *d) Fork internal damage (Chapter 6).*
  - *e) Shock shaft or body bent or damaged (Chapter 6).*
  - *f) Shock internal damage.*
  - *g) Tyre pressure too high (Chapter 1).*
  - *h) Incorrect suspension adjustment (Chapter 6).*
- ☐ Too soft:
  - *a) Fork or shock oil insufficient and/or leaking (Chapter 6).*
  - *b) Fork oil level too low (Chapter 6).*
  - *c) Fork oil viscosity too light (Chapter 6).*
  - *d) Fork springs weak or broken (Chapter 6).*
  - *e) Shock internal damage or leakage (Chapter 6).*
  - *f) Incorrect suspension adjustment (Chapter 6).*

13 Braking problems

Brakes are spongy, don't hold

- ☐ Air in brake line. Caused by inattention to master cylinder fluid level or by leakage. Locate problem and bleed brakes (Chapter 7).
- ☐ Pad or disc worn (Chapters 1 and 7).
- ☐ Brake fluid leak. Inspect system carefully and rectify leak.
- ☐ Contaminated pads. Caused by contamination with oil, grease, brake fluid, etc. Clean or renew the pads. Clean disc thoroughly with brake cleaner (Chapter 7).
- ☐ Brake fluid deteriorated. Fluid is old or contaminated. Drain system, replenish with new fluid and bleed the system (Chapter 7).
- ☐ Master cylinder internal parts worn or damaged causing fluid to bypass (Chapter 7).
- ☐ Master cylinder bore scratched by foreign material or broken spring. Repair or renew the master cylinder (Chapter 7).
- ☐ Disc warped. Renew the disc (Chapter 7).

Brake lever or pedal pulsates

- ☐ Disc warped. Renew the disc (Chapter 7).
- ☐ Axle bent. Renew the axle (Chapter 7).
- ☐ Brake caliper bolts loose (Chapter 7).
- ☐ Brake caliper slider bracket pins (sliding caliper), causing caliper to bind. Lubricate the pins or renew them if they are corroded or bent (Chapter 7).
- ☐ Wheel bearings damaged or worn (Chapter 7).

Brakes drag

- ☐ Master cylinder piston seized. Caused by wear or damage to piston or cylinder bore (Chapter 7).
- ☐ Lever balky or stuck. Check pivot and lubricate (Chapter 7).
- ☐ Brake caliper binds. Caused by inadequate lubrication or damage to caliper slider bracket pins (sliding caliper) (Chapter 7).
- ☐ Brake caliper piston seized in bore. Caused by wear or ingestion of dirt past deteriorated seal (Chapter 7).
- ☐ Brake pad damaged. Pad material separated from backing plate. Usually caused by faulty manufacturing process or from contact with chemicals. Renew the pads (Chapter 7).
- ☐ Pads improperly installed (Chapter 7).

14 Electrical problems

Battery dead or weak

- ☐ Battery faulty. Caused by sulphated plates which are shorted through sedimentation. Also, broken battery terminal making only occasional contact (Chapter 9).
- ☐ Battery cables making poor contact (Chapter 9).
- ☐ Load excessive. Caused by addition of high wattage lights or other electrical accessories.
- ☐ Ignition (main) switch defective. Switch either earths internally or fails to shut off system. Renew the switch (Chapter 9).
- ☐ Rectifier defective (Chapter 9).
- ☐ Alternator stator coil open or shorted (Chapter 9).
- ☐ Wiring faulty. Wiring earthed or connections loose (Chapter 9).

Battery overcharged

- ☐ Regulator defective. Overcharging is noticed when battery gets excessively warm (Chapter 9).
- ☐ Battery defective. Renew the battery (Chapter 9).
- ☐ Battery amperage too low, wrong type or size. Install manufacturer's specified amp-hour battery to handle charging load (Chapter 9)

Checking engine compression

- Low compression will result in exhaust smoke, heavy oil consumption, poor starting and poor performance. A compression test will provide useful information about an engine's condition and if performed regularly, can give warning of trouble before any other symptoms become apparent.
- A compression gauge will be required, along with an adapter to suit the spark plug hole thread size. Note that the screw-in type gauge/adapter set up is preferable to the rubber cone type.
- Before carrying out the test, first check the valve clearances as described in Chapter 1.

1 Run the engine until it reaches normal operating temperature, then stop it and remove the spark plug(s), taking care not to scald your hands on the hot components.

2 Install the gauge adapter and compression gauge in No. 1 cylinder spark plug hole **(see illustration 1)**.

Screw the compression gauge adapter into the spark plug hole, then screw the gauge into the adapter

3 On kickstart-equipped motorcycles, make sure the ignition switch is OFF, then open the throttle fully and kick the engine over a couple of times until the gauge reading stabilises.

4 On motorcycles with electric start only, the procedure will differ depending on the nature of the ignition system. Flick the engine kill switch (engine stop switch) to OFF and turn the ignition switch ON; open the throttle fully and crank the engine over on the starter motor for a couple of revolutions until the gauge reading stabilises. If the starter will not operate with the kill switch OFF, turn the ignition switch OFF and refer to the next paragraph.

5 Install the spark plugs back into their suppressor caps and arrange the plug electrodes so that their metal bodies are earthed (grounded) against the cylinder head; this is essential to prevent damage to the ignition system as the engine is spun over **(see illustration 2)**. Position the plugs well away from the plug holes otherwise there is a risk of atomised fuel escaping from the combustion chambers and igniting. As a safety precaution, cover the top of the valve cover with rag. Now turn the ignition switch ON and kill switch ON, open the throttle fully and crank the engine over on the starter motor for a couple of revolutions until the gauge reading stabilises.

All spark plugs must be earthed (grounded) against the cylinder head

6 After one or two revolutions the pressure should build up to a maximum figure and then stabilise. Take a note of this reading and on multi-cylinder engines repeat the test on the remaining cylinders.

7 The correct pressures are given in Chapter 2 Specifications. If the results fall within the specified range and on multi-cylinder engines all are relatively equal, the engine is in good condition. If there is a marked difference between the readings, or if the readings are lower than specified, inspection of the top-end components will be required.

8 Low compression pressure may be due to worn cylinder bores, pistons or rings, failure of the cylinder head gasket, worn valve seals, or poor valve seating.

9 To distinguish between cylinder/piston wear and valve leakage, pour a small quantity of oil into the bore to temporarily seal the piston rings, then repeat the compression tests **(see illustration 3)**. If the readings show a noticeable increase in pressure this confirms that the cylinder bore, piston, or rings are worn. If, however, no change is indicated, the cylinder head gasket or valves should be examined.

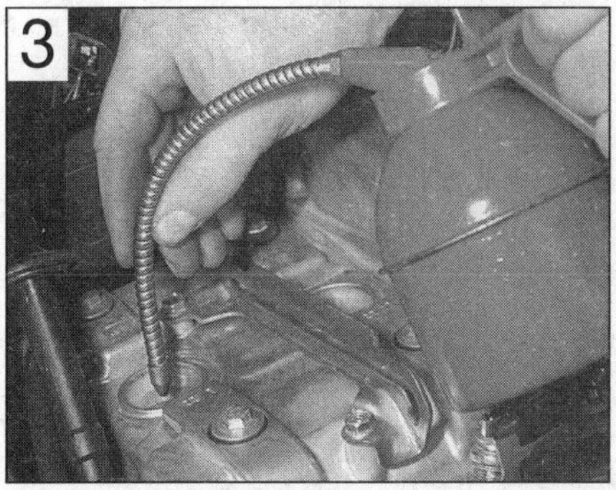

Bores can be temporarily sealed with a squirt of motor oil

10 High compression pressure indicates excessive carbon build-up in the combustion chamber and on the piston crown. If this is the case the cylinder head should be removed and the deposits removed. Note that excessive carbon build-up is less likely with the used on modern fuels.

Checking battery open-circuit voltage

Warning: The gases produced by the battery are explosive - never smoke or create any sparks in the vicinity of the battery. Never allow the electrolyte to contact your skin or clothing - if it does, wash it off and seek immediate medical attention.

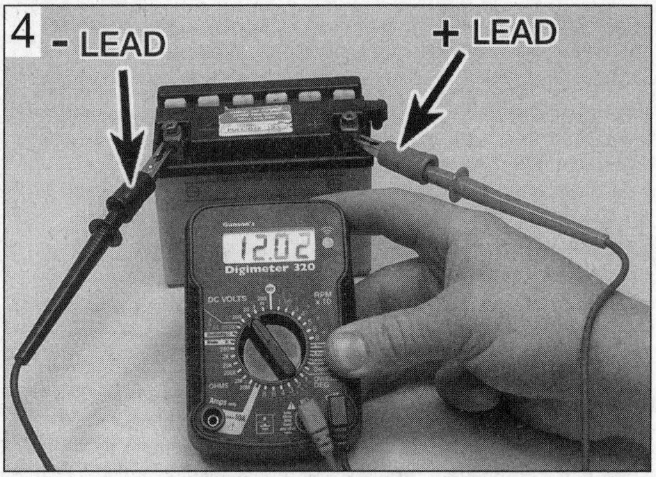

Measuring open-circuit battery voltage

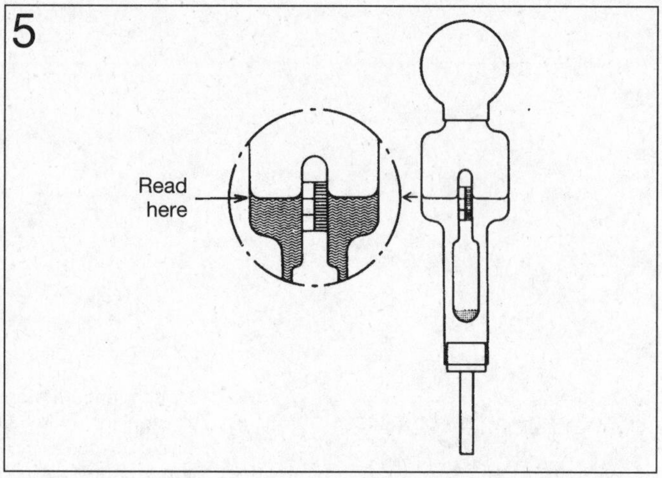

Float-type hydrometer for measuring battery specific gravity

- Before any electrical fault is investigated the battery should be checked.
- You'll need a dc voltmeter or multimeter to check battery voltage. Check that the leads are inserted in the correct terminals on the meter, red lead to positive (+ve), black lead to negative (-ve). Incorrect connections can damage the meter.
- A sound fully-charged 12 volt battery should produce between 12.3 and 12.6 volts across its terminals (12.8 volts for a maintenance-free battery). On machines with a 6 volt battery, voltage should be between 6.1 and 6.3 volts.

1 Set a multimeter to the 0 to 20 volts dc range and connect its probes across the battery terminals. Connect the meter's positive (+ve) probe, usually red, to the battery positive (+ve) terminal, followed by the meter's negative (-ve) probe, usually black, to the battery negative terminal (-ve) **(see illustration 4)**.

2 If battery voltage is low (below 10 volts on a 12 volt battery or below 4 volts on a six volt battery), charge the battery and test the voltage again. If the battery repeatedly goes flat, investigate the motorcycle's charging system.

Checking battery specific gravity (SG)

Warning: The gases produced by the battery are explosive - never smoke or create any sparks in the vicinity of the battery. Never allow the electrolyte to contact your skin or clothing - if it does, wash it off and seek immediate medical attention.

- The specific gravity check gives an indication of a battery's state of charge.
- A hydrometer is used for measuring specific gravity. Make sure you purchase one which has a small enough hose to insert in the aperture of a motorcycle battery.
- Specific gravity is simply a measure of the electrolyte's density compared with that of water. Water has an SG of 1.000 and fully-charged battery electrolyte is about 26% heavier, at 1.260.
- Specific gravity checks are not possible on maintenance-free batteries. Testing the open-circuit voltage is the only means of determining their state of charge.

1 To measure SG, remove the battery from the motorcycle and remove the first cell cap. Draw some electrolyte into the hydrometer and note the reading **(see illustration 5)**. Return the electrolyte to the cell and install the cap.

2 The reading should be in the region of 1.260 to 1.280. If SG is below 1.200 the battery needs charging. Note that SG will vary with temperature; it should be measured at 20°C (68°F). Add 0.007 to the reading for every 10°C above 20°C, and subtract 0.007 from the reading for every 10°C below 20°C. Add 0.004 to the reading for every 10°F above 68°F, and subtract 0.004 from the reading for every 10°F below 68°F.

3 When the check is complete, rinse the hydrometer thoroughly with clean water.

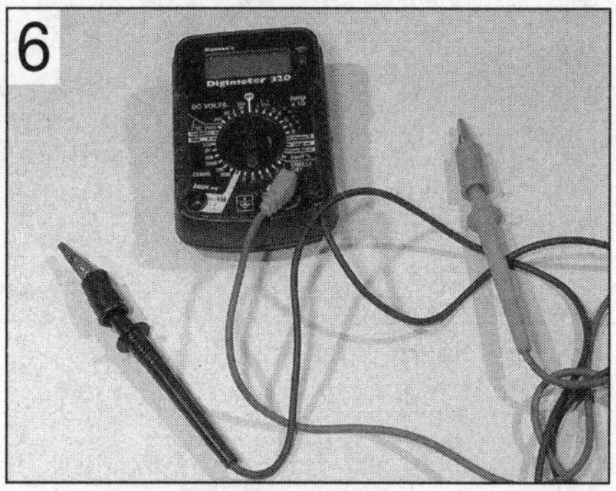

Digital multimeter can be used for all electrical tests

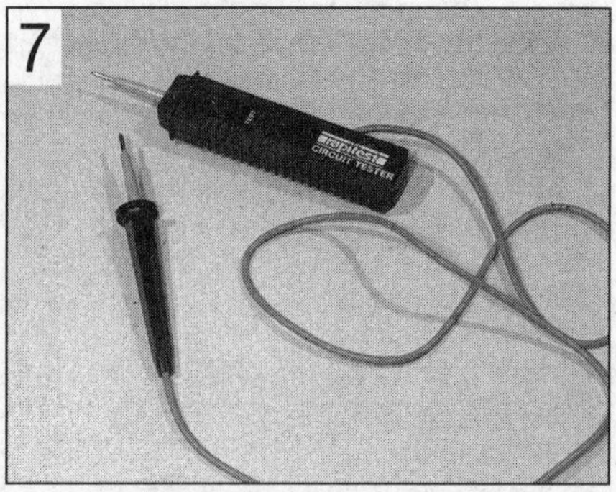

Battery-powered continuity tester

Checking for continuity

- The term continuity describes the uninterrupted flow of electricity through an electrical circuit. A continuity check will determine whether an **open-circuit** situation exists.
- Continuity can be checked with an ohmmeter, multimeter, continuity tester or battery and bulb test circuit **(see illustrations 6, 7 and 8)**.

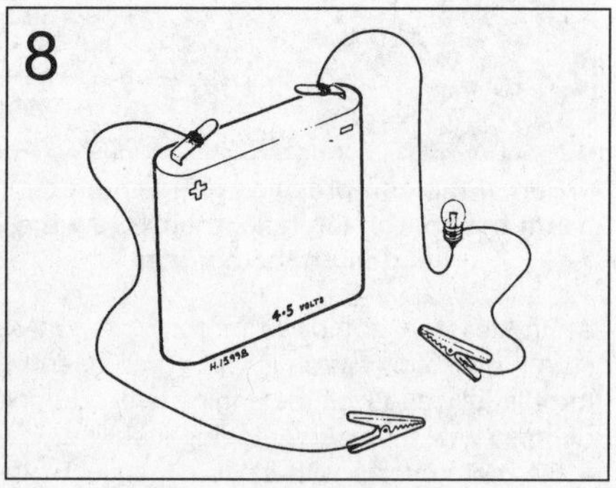

Battery and bulb test circuit

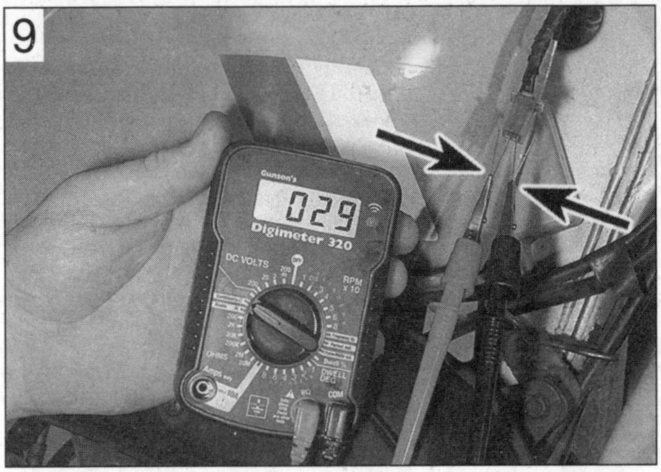

Continuity check of front brake light switch using a meter - note split pins used to access connector terminals

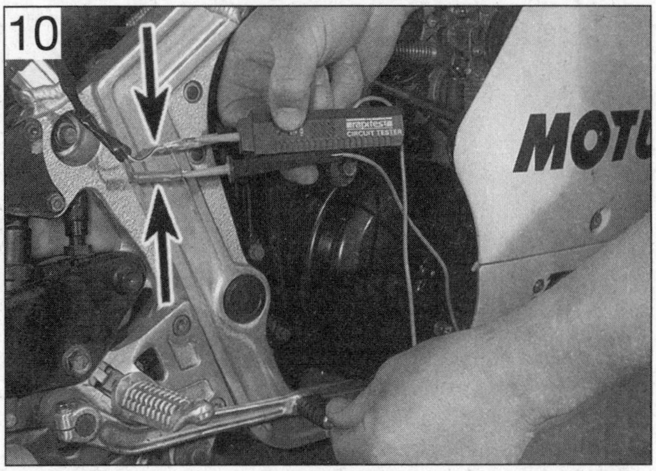

Continuity check of rear brake light switch using a continuity tester

- All of these instruments are self-powered by a battery, therefore the checks are made with the ignition OFF.
- As a safety precaution, always disconnect the battery negative (-ve) lead before making checks, particularly if ignition switch checks are being made.
- If using a meter, select the appropriate ohms scale and check that the meter reads infinity (∞). Touch the meter probes together and check that meter reads zero; where necessary adjust the meter so that it reads zero.
- After using a meter, always switch it OFF to conserve its battery.

Switch checks

1 If a switch is at fault, trace its wiring up to the wiring connectors. Separate the wire connectors and inspect them for security and condition. A build-up of dirt or corrosion here will most likely be the cause of the problem - clean up and apply a water dispersant such as WD40.

2 If using a test meter, set the meter to the ohms x 10 scale and connect its probes across the wires from the switch **(see illustration 9)**. Simple ON/OFF type switches, such as brake light switches, only have two wires whereas combination switches, like the ignition switch, have many internal links. Study the wiring diagram to ensure that you are connecting across the correct pair of wires. Continuity (low or no measurable resistance - 0 ohms) should be indicated with the switch ON and no continuity (high resistance) with it OFF.

3 Note that the polarity of the test probes doesn't matter for continuity checks, although care should be taken to follow specific test procedures if a diode or solid-state component is being checked.

4 A continuity tester or battery and bulb circuit can be used in the same way. Connect its probes as described above **(see illustration 10)**. The light should come on to indicate continuity in the ON switch position, but should extinguish in the OFF position.

Wiring checks

- Many electrical faults are caused by damaged wiring, often due to incorrect routing or chaffing on frame components.
- Loose, wet or corroded wire connectors can also be the cause of electrical problems, especially in exposed locations.

1 A continuity check can be made on a single length of wire by disconnecting it at each end and connecting a meter or continuity tester across both ends of the wire **(see illustration 11)**.

2 Continuity (low or no resistance - 0 ohms) should be indicated if the wire is good. If no continuity (high resistance) is shown, suspect a broken wire.

Checking for voltage

- A voltage check can determine whether current is reaching a component.
- Voltage can be checked with a dc voltmeter, multimeter set on the dc volts scale, test light or buzzer **(see illustrations 12 and 13)**. A meter has the advantage of being able to measure actual voltage.
- When using a meter, check that its leads are inserted in the correct terminals on the meter, red to positive (+ve), black to negative (-ve). Incorrect connections can damage the meter.
- A voltmeter (or multimeter set to the dc volts scale) should always be connected in parallel (across the load). Connecting it in series will destroy the meter.
- Voltage checks are made with the ignition ON.

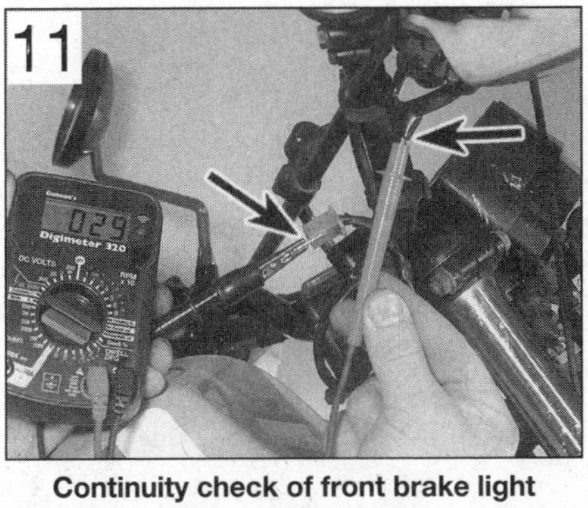

Continuity check of front brake light switch sub-harness

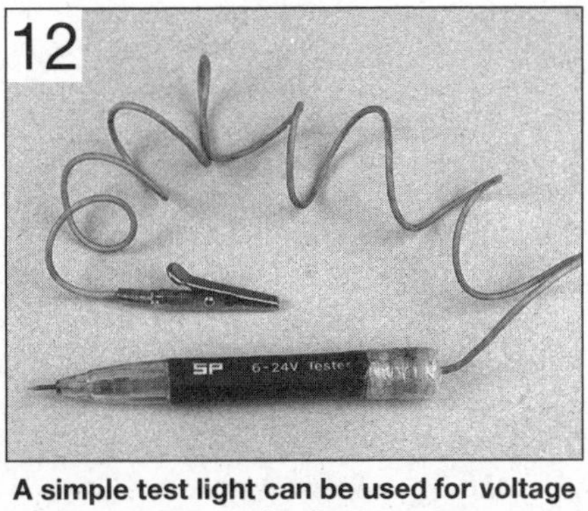

A simple test light can be used for voltage checks

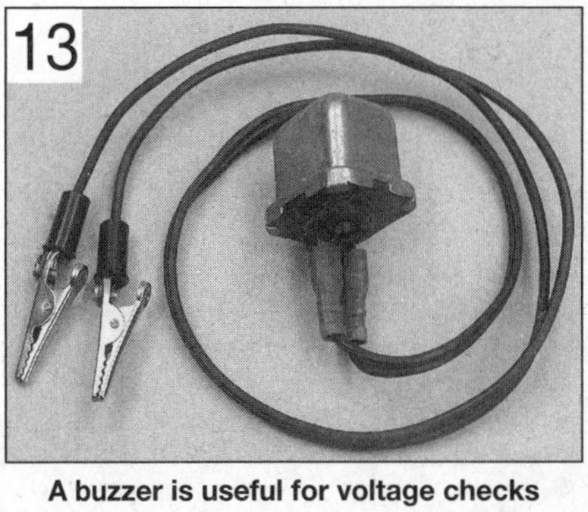

A buzzer is useful for voltage checks

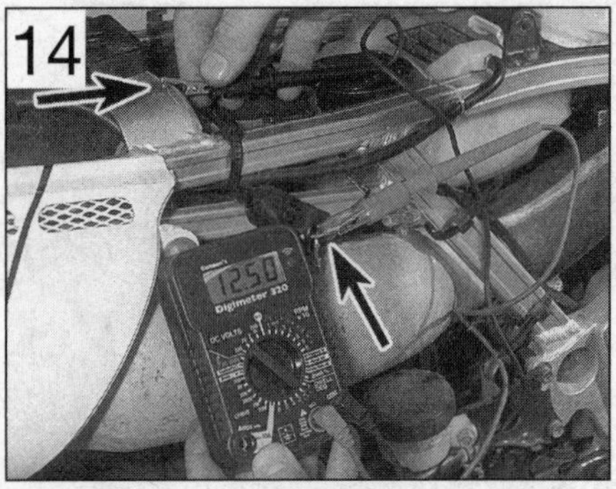

Checking for voltage at the rear brake light power supply wire using a meter . . .

1 First identify the relevant wiring circuit by referring to the wiring diagram at the end of this manual. If other electrical components share the same power supply (ie are fed from the same fuse), take note whether they are working correctly - this is useful information in deciding where to start checking the circuit.

2 If using a meter, check first that the meter leads are plugged into the correct terminals on the meter (see above). Set the meter to the dc volts function, at a range suitable for the battery voltage. Connect the meter red probe (+ve) to the power supply wire and the black probe to a good metal earth (ground) on the motorcycle's frame or directly to the battery negative (-ve) terminal **(see illustration 14)**. Battery voltage should be shown on the meter

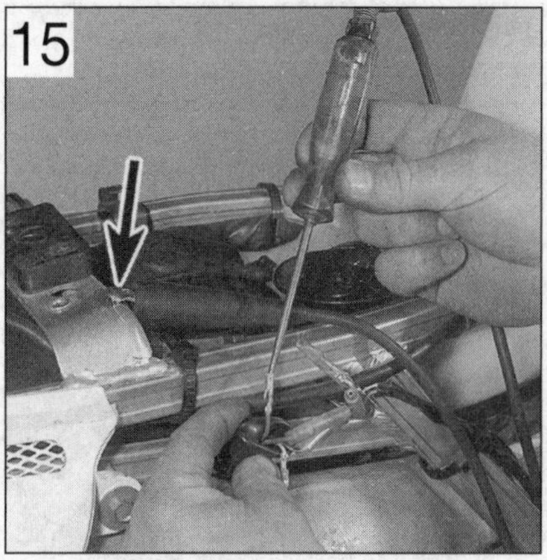

. . . or a test light - note the earth connection to the frame (arrow)

with the ignition switched ON.

3 If using a test light or buzzer, connect its positive (+ve) probe to the power supply terminal and its negative (-ve) probe to a good earth (ground) on the motorcycle's frame or directly to the battery negative (-ve) terminal **(see illustration 15)**. With the ignition ON, the test light should illuminate or the buzzer sound.

4 If no voltage is indicated, work back towards the fuse continuing to check for voltage. When you reach a point where there is voltage, you know the problem lies between that point and your last check point.

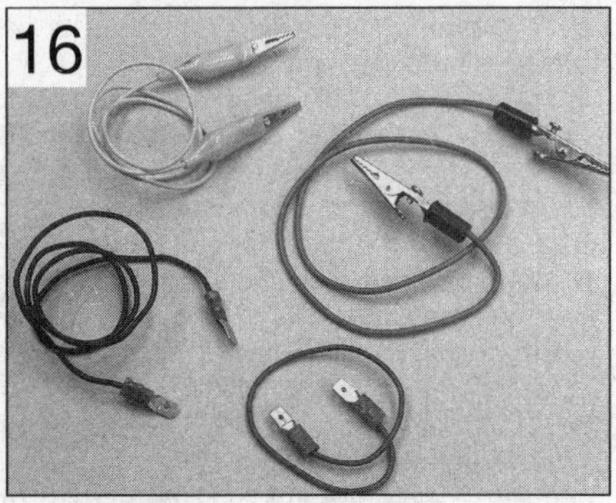

A selection of jumper wires for making earth (ground) checks

Checking the earth (ground)

- Earth connections are made either directly to the engine or frame (such as sensors, neutral switch etc. which only have a positive feed) or by a separate wire into the earth circuit of the wiring harness. Alternatively a short earth wire is sometimes run directly from the component to the motorcycle's frame.
- Corrosion is often the cause of a poor earth connection.
- If total failure is experienced, check the security of the main earth lead from the negative (-ve) terminal of the battery and also the main earth (ground) point on the wiring harness. If corroded, dismantle the connection and clean all surfaces back to bare metal.

1 To check the earth on a component, use an insulated jumper wire to temporarily bypass its earth connection **(see illustration 16)**. Connect one end of the jumper wire between the earth terminal or metal body of the component and the other end to the motorcycle's frame.

2 If the circuit works with the jumper wire installed, the original earth circuit is faulty. Check the wiring for open-circuits or poor connections. Clean up direct earth connections, removing all traces of corrosion and remake the joint. Apply petroleum jelly to the joint to prevent future corrosion.

Tracing a short-circuit

- A short-circuit occurs where current shorts to earth (ground) bypassing the circuit components. This usually results in a blown fuse.
- A short-circuit is most likely to occur where the insulation has worn through due to wiring chafing on a component, allowing a direct path to earth (ground) on the frame.

1 Remove any bodypanels necessary to access the circuit wiring.

2 Check that all electrical switches in the circuit are OFF, then remove the circuit fuse and connect a test light, buzzer or voltmeter (set to the dc scale) across the fuse terminals. No voltage should be shown.

3 Move the wiring from side to side whilst observing the test light or meter. When the test light comes on, buzzer sounds or meter shows voltage, you have found the cause of the short. It will usually shown up as damaged or burned insulation.

4 Note that the same test can be performed on each component in the circuit, even the switch.

A

ABS (Anti-lock braking system) A system, usually electronically controlled, that senses incipient wheel lockup during braking and relieves hydraulic pressure at wheel which is about to skid.
Aftermarket Components suitable for the motorcycle, but not produced by the motorcycle manufacturer.
Allen key A hexagonal wrench which fits into a recessed hexagonal hole.
Alternating current (ac) Current produced by an alternator. Requires converting to direct current by a rectifier for charging purposes.
Alternator Converts mechanical energy from the engine into electrical energy to charge the battery and power the electrical system.
Ampere (amp) A unit of measurement for the flow of electrical current. Current = Volts ÷ Ohms.
Ampere-hour (Ah) Measure of battery capacity.
Angle-tightening A torque expressed in degrees. Often follows a conventional tightening torque for cylinder head or main bearing fasteners **(see illustration)**.

Angle-tightening cylinder head bolts

Antifreeze A substance (usually ethylene glycol) mixed with water, and added to the cooling system, to prevent freezing of the coolant in winter. Antifreeze also contains chemicals to inhibit corrosion and the formation of rust and other deposits that would tend to clog the radiator and coolant passages and reduce cooling efficiency.
Anti-dive System attached to the fork lower leg (slider) to prevent fork dive when braking hard.
Anti-seize compound A coating that reduces the risk of seizing on fasteners that are subjected to high temperatures, such as exhaust clamp bolts and nuts.
API American Petroleum Institute. A quality standard for 4-stroke motor oils.
Asbestos A natural fibrous mineral with great heat resistance, commonly used in the composition of brake friction materials. Asbestos is a health hazard and the dust created by brake systems should never be inhaled or ingested.
ATF Automatic Transmission Fluid. Often used in front forks.
ATU Automatic Timing Unit. Mechanical device for advancing the ignition timing on early engines.
ATV All Terrain Vehicle. Often called a Quad.
Axial play Side-to-side movement.
Axle A shaft on which a wheel revolves. Also known as a spindle.

B

Backlash The amount of movement between meshed components when one component is held still. Usually applies to gear teeth.
Ball bearing A bearing consisting of a hardened inner and outer race with hardened steel balls between the two races.
Bearings Used between two working surfaces to prevent wear of the components and a build-up of heat. Four types of bearing are commonly used on motorcycles: plain shell bearings, ball bearings, tapered roller bearings and needle roller bearings.
Bevel gears Used to turn the drive through 90°. Typical applications are shaft final drive and camshaft drive **(see illustration)**.

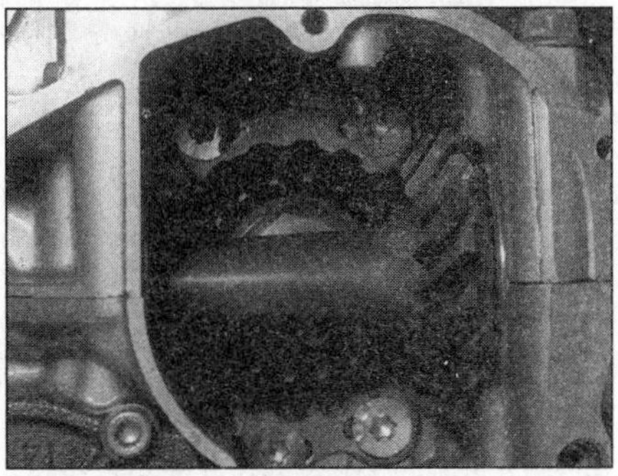

Bevel gears are used to turn the drive through 90°

BHP Brake Horsepower. The British measurement for engine power output. Power output is now usually expressed in kilowatts (kW).
Bias-belted tyre Similar construction to radial tyre, but with outer belt running at an angle to the wheel rim.
Big-end bearing The bearing in the end of the connecting rod that's attached to the crankshaft.
Bleeding The process of removing air from an hydraulic system via a bleed nipple or bleed screw.
Bottom-end A description of an engine's crankcase components and all components contained there-in.
BTDC Before Top Dead Centre in terms of piston position. Ignition timing is often expressed in terms of degrees or millimetres BTDC.
Bush A cylindrical metal or rubber component used between two moving parts.
Burr Rough edge left on a component after machining or as a result of excessive wear.

C

Cam chain The chain which takes drive from the crankshaft to the camshaft(s).
Canister The main component in an evaporative emission control system (California market only); contains activated charcoal granules to trap vapours from the fuel system rather than allowing them to vent to the atmosphere.
Castellated Resembling the parapets along the top of a castle wall. For example, a castellated wheel axle or spindle nut.
Catalytic converter A device in the exhaust system of some machines which converts certain pollutants in the exhaust gases into less harmful substances.
Charging system Description of the components which charge the battery, ie the alternator, rectifer and regulator.
Circlip A ring-shaped clip used to prevent endwise movement of cylindrical parts and shafts. An internal circlip is installed in a groove in a housing; an external circlip fits into a groove on the outside of a cylindrical piece such as a shaft. Also known as a snap-ring.
Clearance The amount of space between two parts. For example, between a piston and a cylinder, between a bearing and a journal, etc.
Coil spring A spiral of elastic steel found in various sizes throughout a vehicle, for example as a springing medium in the suspension and in the valve train.
Compression Reduction in volume, and increase in pressure and temperature, of a gas, caused by squeezing it into a smaller space.
Compression damping Controls the speed the suspension compresses when hitting a bump.
Compression ratio The relationship between cylinder volume when the piston is at top dead centre and cylinder volume when the piston is at bottom dead centre.
Continuity The uninterrupted path in the flow of electricity. Little or no measurable resistance.
Continuity tester Self-powered bleeper or test light which indicates continuity.
Cp Candlepower. Bulb rating commonly found on US motorcycles.
Crossply tyre Tyre plies arranged in a criss-cross pattern. Usually four or six plies used, hence 4PR or 6PR in tyre size codes.
Cush drive Rubber damper segments fitted between the rear wheel and final drive sprocket to absorb transmission shocks **(see illustration)**.

Cush drive rubbers dampen out transmission shocks

D

Degree disc Calibrated disc for measuring piston position. Expressed in degrees.
Dial gauge Clock-type gauge with adapters for measuring runout and piston position. Expressed in mm or inches.
Diaphragm The rubber membrane in a master cylinder or carburettor which seals the upper chamber.
Diaphragm spring A single sprung plate often used in clutches.
Direct current (dc) Current produced by a dc generator.

Decarbonisation The process of removing carbon deposits - typically from the combustion chamber, valves and exhaust port/system.
Detonation Destructive and damaging explosion of fuel/air mixture in combustion chamber instead of controlled burning.
Diode An electrical valve which only allows current to flow in one direction. Commonly used in rectifiers and starter interlock systems.
Disc valve (or rotary valve) A induction system used on some two-stroke engines.
Double-overhead camshaft (DOHC) An engine that uses two overhead camshafts, one for the intake valves and one for the exhaust valves.
Drivebelt A toothed belt used to transmit drive to the rear wheel on some motorcycles. A drivebelt has also been used to drive the camshafts. Drivebelts are usually made of Kevlar.
Driveshaft Any shaft used to transmit motion. Commonly used when referring to the final driveshaft on shaft drive motorcycles.

E

Earth return The return path of an electrical circuit, utilising the motorcycle's frame.
ECU (Electronic Control Unit) A computer which controls (for instance) an ignition system, or an anti-lock braking system.
EGO Exhaust Gas Oxygen sensor. Sometimes called a Lambda sensor.
Electrolyte The fluid in a lead-acid battery.
EMS (Engine Management System) A computer controlled system which manages the fuel injection and the ignition systems in an integrated fashion.
Endfloat The amount of lengthways movement between two parts. As applied to a crankshaft, the distance that the crankshaft can move side-to-side in the crankcase.
Endless chain A chain having no joining link. Common use for cam chains and final drive chains.
EP (Extreme Pressure) Oil type used in locations where high loads are applied, such as between gear teeth.
Evaporative emission control system Describes a charcoal filled canister which stores fuel vapours from the tank rather than allowing them to vent to the atmosphere. Usually only fitted to California models and referred to as an EVAP system.
Expansion chamber Section of two-stroke engine exhaust system so designed to improve engine efficiency and boost power.

F

Feeler blade or gauge A thin strip or blade of hardened steel, ground to an exact thickness, used to check or measure clearances between parts.
Final drive Description of the drive from the transmission to the rear wheel. Usually by chain or shaft, but sometimes by belt.
Firing order The order in which the engine cylinders fire, or deliver their power strokes, beginning with the number one cylinder.
Flooding Term used to describe a high fuel level in the carburettor float chambers, leading to fuel overflow. Also refers to excess fuel in the combustion chamber due to incorrect starting technique.
Free length The no-load state of a component when measured. Clutch, valve and fork spring lengths are measured at rest, without any preload.
Freeplay The amount of travel before any action takes place. The looseness in a linkage, or an assembly of parts, between the initial application of force and actual movement. For example, the distance the rear brake pedal moves before the rear brake is actuated.
Fuel injection The fuel/air mixture is metered electronically and directed into the engine intake ports (indirect injection) or into the cylinders (direct injection). Sensors supply information on engine speed and conditions.
Fuel/air mixture The charge of fuel and air going into the engine. See **Stoichiometric ratio**.
Fuse An electrical device which protects a circuit against accidental overload. The typical fuse contains a soft piece of metal which is calibrated to melt at a predetermined current flow (expressed as amps) and break the circuit.

G

Gap The distance the spark must travel in jumping from the centre electrode to the side electrode in a spark plug. Also refers to the distance between the ignition rotor and the pickup coil in an electronic ignition system.
Gasket Any thin, soft material - usually cork, cardboard, asbestos or soft metal - installed between two metal surfaces to ensure a good seal. For instance, the cylinder head gasket seals the joint between the block and the cylinder head.
Gauge An instrument panel display used to monitor engine conditions. A gauge with a movable pointer on a dial or a fixed scale is an analogue gauge. A gauge with a numerical readout is called a digital gauge.
Gear ratios The drive ratio of a pair of gears in a gearbox, calculated on their number of teeth.
Glaze-busting see **Honing**
Grinding Process for renovating the valve face and valve seat contact area in the cylinder head.
Gudgeon pin The shaft which connects the connecting rod small-end with the piston. Often called a piston pin or wrist pin.

H

Helical gears Gear teeth are slightly curved and produce less gear noise that straight-cut gears. Often used for primary drives.

Installing a Helicoil thread insert in a cylinder head

Helicoil A thread insert repair system. Commonly used as a repair for stripped spark plug threads **(see illustration)**.
Honing A process used to break down the glaze on a cylinder bore (also called glaze-busting). Can also be carried out to roughen a rebored cylinder to aid ring bedding-in.
HT (High Tension) Description of the electrical circuit from the secondary winding of the ignition coil to the spark plug.
Hydraulic A liquid filled system used to transmit pressure from one component to another. Common uses on motorcycles are brakes and clutches.
Hydrometer An instrument for measuring the specific gravity of a lead-acid battery.
Hygroscopic Water absorbing. In motorcycle applications, braking efficiency will be reduced if DOT 3 or 4 hydraulic fluid absorbs water from the air - care must be taken to keep new brake fluid in tightly sealed containers.

I

Ibf ft Pounds-force feet. An imperial unit of torque. Sometimes written as ft-lbs.
Ibf in Pound-force inch. An imperial unit of torque, applied to components where a very low torque is required. Sometimes written as in-lbs.
IC Abbreviation for Integrated Circuit.
Ignition advance Means of increasing the timing of the spark at higher engine speeds. Done by mechanical means (ATU) on early engines or electronically by the ignition control unit on later engines.
Ignition timing The moment at which the spark plug fires, expressed in the number of crankshaft degrees before the piston reaches the top of its stroke, or in the number of millimetres before the piston reaches the top of its stroke.
Infinity (∞) Description of an open-circuit electrical state, where no continuity exists.
Inverted forks (upside down forks) The sliders or lower legs are held in the yokes and the fork tubes or stanchions are connected to the wheel axle (spindle). Less unsprung weight and stiffer construction than conventional forks.

J

JASO Quality standard for 2-stroke oils.
Joule The unit of electrical energy.
Journal The bearing surface of a shaft.

K

Kickstart Mechanical means of turning the engine over for starting purposes. Only usually fitted to mopeds, small capacity motorcycles and off-road motorcycles.
Kill switch Handebar-mounted switch for emergency ignition cut-out. Cuts the ignition circuit on all models, and additionally prevent starter motor operation on others.
km Symbol for kilometre.
kmh Abbreviation for kilometres per hour.

L

Lambda (λ) sensor A sensor fitted in the exhaust system to measure the exhaust gas oxygen content (excess air factor).

Lapping see **Grinding**.
LCD Abbreviation for Liquid Crystal Display.
LED Abbreviation for Light Emitting Diode.
Liner A steel cylinder liner inserted in a aluminium alloy cylinder block.
Locknut A nut used to lock an adjustment nut, or other threaded component, in place.
Lockstops The lugs on the lower triple clamp (yoke) which abut those on the frame, preventing handlebar-to-fuel tank contact.
Lockwasher A form of washer designed to prevent an attaching nut from working loose.
LT Low Tension Description of the electrical circuit from the power supply to the primary winding of the ignition coil.

M

Main bearings The bearings between the crankshaft and crankcase.
Maintenance-free (MF) battery A sealed battery which cannot be topped up.
Manometer Mercury-filled calibrated tubes used to measure intake tract vacuum. Used to synchronise carburettors on multi-cylinder engines.
Micrometer A precision measuring instrument that measures component outside diameters **(see illustration)**.

Tappet shims are measured with a micrometer

MON (Motor Octane Number) A measure of a fuel's resistance to knock.
Monograde oil An oil with a single viscosity, eg SAE80W.
Monoshock A single suspension unit linking the swingarm or suspension linkage to the frame.
mph Abbreviation for miles per hour.
Multigrade oil Having a wide viscosity range (eg 10W40). The W stands for Winter, thus the viscosity ranges from SAE10 when cold to SAE40 when hot.
Multimeter An electrical test instrument with the capability to measure voltage, current and resistance. Some meters also incorporate a continuity tester and buzzer.

N

Needle roller bearing Inner race of caged needle rollers and hardened outer race. Examples of uncaged needle rollers can be found on some engines. Commonly used in rear suspension applications and in two-stroke engines.
Nm Newton metres.
NOx Oxides of Nitrogen. A common toxic pollutant emitted by petrol engines at higher temperatures.

O

Octane The measure of a fuel's resistance to knock.
OE (Original Equipment) Relates to components fitted to a motorcycle as standard or replacement parts supplied by the motorcycle manufacturer.
Ohm The unit of electrical resistance. Ohms = Volts ÷ Current.
Ohmmeter An instrument for measuring electrical resistance.
Oil cooler System for diverting engine oil outside of the engine to a radiator for cooling purposes.
Oil injection A system of two-stroke engine lubrication where oil is pump-fed to the engine in accordance with throttle position.
Open-circuit An electrical condition where there is a break in the flow of electricity - no continuity (high resistance).
O-ring A type of sealing ring made of a special rubber-like material; in use, the O-ring is compressed into a groove to provide the sealing action.
Oversize (OS) Term used for piston and ring size options fitted to a rebored cylinder.
Overhead cam (sohc) engine An engine with single camshaft located on top of the cylinder head.
Overhead valve (ohv) engine An engine with the valves located in the cylinder head, but with the camshaft located in the engine block or crankcase.
Oxygen sensor A device installed in the exhaust system which senses the oxygen content in the exhaust and converts this information into an electric current. Also called a Lambda sensor.

P

Plastigauge A thin strip of plastic thread, available in different sizes, used for measuring clearances. For example, a strip of Plastigauge is laid across a bearing journal. The parts are assembled and dismantled; the width of the crushed strip indicates the clearance between journal and bearing.
Polarity Either negative or positive earth (ground), determined by which battery lead is connected to the frame (earth return). Modern motorcycles are usually negative earth.
Pre-ignition A situation where the fuel/air mixture ignites before the spark plug fires. Often due to a hot spot in the combustion chamber caused by carbon build-up. Engine has a tendency to 'run-on'.
Pre-load (suspension) The amount a spring is compressed when in the unloaded state. Preload can be applied by gas, spacer or mechanical adjuster.
Premix The method of engine lubrication on older two-stroke engines. Engine oil is mixed with the petrol in the fuel tank in a specific ratio. The fuel/oil mix is sometimes referred to as "petroil".
Primary drive Description of the drive from the crankshaft to the clutch. Usually by gear or chain.
PS Pfedestärke - a German interpretation of BHP.
PSI Pounds-force per square inch. Imperial measurement of tyre pressure and cylinder pressure measurement.
PTFE Polytetrafluroethylene. A low friction substance.
Pulse secondary air injection system A process of promoting the burning of excess fuel present in the exhaust gases by routing fresh air into the exhaust ports.

Q

Quartz halogen bulb Tungsten filament surrounded by a halogen gas. Typically used for the headlight **(see illustration)**.

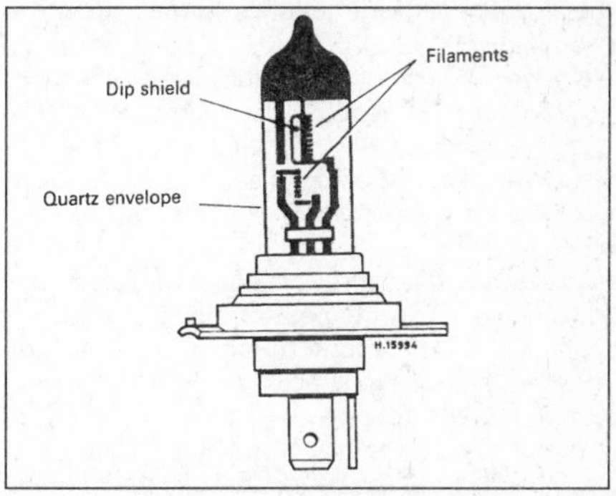

Quartz halogen headlight bulb construction

R

Rack-and-pinion A pinion gear on the end of a shaft that mates with a rack (think of a geared wheel opened up and laid flat). Sometimes used in clutch operating systems.
Radial play Up and down movement about a shaft.
Radial ply tyres Tyre plies run across the tyre (from bead to bead) and around the circumference of the tyre. Less resistant to tread distortion than other tyre types.
Radiator A liquid-to-air heat transfer device designed to reduce the temperature of the coolant in a liquid cooled engine.
Rake A feature of steering geometry - the angle of the steering head in relation to the vertical **(see illustration)**.

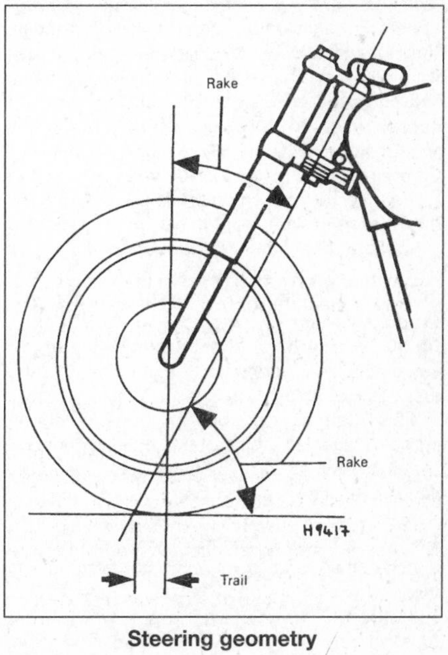

Steering geometry

Rebore Providing a new working surface to the cylinder bore by boring out the old surface. Necessitates the use of oversize piston and rings.
Rebound damping A means of controlling the oscillation of a suspension unit spring after it has been compressed. Resists the spring's natural tendency to bounce back after being compressed.
Rectifier Device for converting the ac output of an alternator into dc for battery charging.
Reed valve An induction system commonly used on two-stroke engines.
Regulator Device for maintaining the charging voltage from the generator or alternator within a specified range.
Relay A electrical device used to switch heavy current on and off by using a low current auxiliary circuit.
Resistance Measured in ohms. An electrical component's ability to pass electrical current.
RON (Research Octane Number) A measure of a fuel's resistance to knock.
rpm revolutions per minute.
Runout The amount of wobble (in-and-out movement) of a wheel or shaft as it's rotated. The amount a shaft rotates `out-of-true'. The out-of-round condition of a rotating part.

S

SAE (Society of Automotive Engineers) A standard for the viscosity of a fluid.
Sealant A liquid or paste used to prevent leakage at a joint. Sometimes used in conjunction with a gasket.
Service limit Term for the point where a component is no longer useable and must be renewed.
Shaft drive A method of transmitting drive from the transmission to the rear wheel.
Shell bearings Plain bearings consisting of two shell halves. Most often used as big-end and main bearings in a four-stroke engine. Often called bearing inserts.
Shim Thin spacer, commonly used to adjust the clearance or relative positions between two parts. For example, shims inserted into or under tappets or followers to control valve clearances. Clearance is adjusted by changing the thickness of the shim.
Short-circuit An electrical condition where current shorts to earth (ground) bypassing the circuit components.
Skimming Process to correct warpage or repair a damaged surface, eg on brake discs or drums.
Slide-hammer A special puller that screws into or hooks onto a component such as a shaft or bearing; a heavy sliding handle on the shaft bottoms against the end of the shaft to knock the component free.
Small-end bearing The bearing in the upper end of the connecting rod at its joint with the gudgeon pin.
Spalling Damage to camshaft lobes or bearing journals shown as pitting of the working surface.
Specific gravity (SG) The state of charge of the electrolyte in a lead-acid battery. A measure of the electrolyte's density compared with water.
Straight-cut gears Common type gear used on gearbox shafts and for oil pump and water pump drives.
Stanchion The inner sliding part of the front forks, held by the yokes. Often called a fork tube.
Stoichiometric ratio The optimum chemical air/fuel ratio for a petrol engine, said to be 14.7 parts of air to 1 part of fuel.
Sulphuric acid The liquid (electrolyte) used in a lead-acid battery. Poisonous and extremely corrosive.
Surface grinding (lapping) Process to correct a warped gasket face, commonly used on cylinder heads.

T

Tapered-roller bearing Tapered inner race of caged needle rollers and separate tapered outer race. Examples of taper roller bearings can be found on steering heads.
Tappet A cylindrical component which transmits motion from the cam to the valve stem, either directly or via a pushrod and rocker arm. Also called a cam follower.
TCS Traction Control System. An electronically-controlled system which senses wheel spin and reduces engine speed accordingly.
TDC Top Dead Centre denotes that the piston is at its highest point in the cylinder.
Thread-locking compound Solution applied to fastener threads to prevent slackening. Select type to suit application.
Thrust washer A washer positioned between two moving components on a shaft. For example, between gear pinions on gearshaft.
Timing chain See **Cam Chain.**
Timing light Stroboscopic lamp for carrying out ignition timing checks with the engine running.
Top-end A description of an engine's cylinder block, head and valve gear components.
Torque Turning or twisting force about a shaft.
Torque setting A prescribed tightness specified by the motorcycle manufacturer to ensure that the bolt or nut is secured correctly. Undertightening can result in the bolt or nut coming loose or a surface not being sealed. Overtightening can result in stripped threads, distortion or damage to the component being retained.
Torx key A six-point wrench.
Tracer A stripe of a second colour applied to a wire insulator to distinguish that wire from another one with the same colour insulator. For example, Br/W is often used to denote a brown insulator with a white tracer.
Trail A feature of steering geometry. Distance from the steering head axis to the tyre's central contact point.
Triple clamps The cast components which extend from the steering head and support the fork stanchions or tubes. Often called fork yokes.
Turbocharger A centrifugal device, driven by exhaust gases, that pressurises the intake air. Normally used to increase the power output from a given engine displacement.
TWI Abbreviation for Tyre Wear Indicator. Indicates the location of the tread depth indicator bars on tyres.

U

Universal joint or U-joint (UJ) A double-pivoted connection for transmitting power from a driving to a driven shaft through an angle. Typically found in shaft drive assemblies.
Unsprung weight Anything not supported by the bike's suspension (ie the wheel, tyres, brakes, final drive and bottom (moving) part of the suspension).

V

Vacuum gauges Clock-type gauges for measuring intake tract vacuum. Used for carburettor synchronisation on multi-cylinder engines.
Valve A device through which the flow of liquid, gas or vacuum may be stopped, started or regulated by a moveable part that opens, shuts or partially obstructs one or more ports or passageways. The intake and exhaust valves in the cylinder head are of the poppet type.
Valve clearance The clearance between the valve tip (the end of the valve stem) and the rocker arm or tappet/follower. The valve clearance is measured when the valve is closed. The correct clearance is important - if too small the valve won't close fully and will burn out, whereas if too large noisy operation will result.
Valve lift The amount a valve is lifted off its seat by the camshaft lobe.
Valve timing The exact setting for the opening and closing of the valves in relation to piston position.
Vernier caliper A precision measuring instrument that measures inside and outside dimensions. Not quite as accurate as a micrometer, but more convenient.
VIN Vehicle Identification Number. Term for the bike's engine and frame numbers.
Viscosity The thickness of a liquid or its resistance to flow.
Volt A unit for expressing electrical "pressure" in a circuit. Volts = current x ohms.

W

Water pump A mechanically-driven device for moving coolant around the engine.
Watt A unit for expressing electrical power. Watts = volts x current.
Wear limit see **Service limit**
Wet liner A liquid-cooled engine design where the pistons run in liners which are directly surrounded by coolant **(see illustration)**.

Wet liner arrangement

Wheelbase Distance from the centre of the front wheel to the centre of the rear wheel.
Wiring harness or loom Describes the electrical wires running the length of the motorcycle and enclosed in tape or plastic sheathing. Wiring coming off the main harness is usually referred to as a sub harness.
Woodruff key A key of semi-circular or square section used to locate a gear to a shaft. Often used to locate the alternator rotor on the crankshaft.
Wrist pin Another name for gudgeon or piston pin.

Note: *References throughout this index are in the form – "Chapter number" • "page number"*

D

E

F

G

H

I

L

M

N

O

P

R